Sociology with Representative Research

Contributors

Labor Union
Gouldner, Alvin
Greer, Scott
Lipset, Seymour M.,
  Martin Trow, and
  James Coleman
Rose, Arnold
Strauss, George
  and Leonard R. Sayles
Whyte, William F.
Wilensky, Harold L.

University
Caplow, Theodore E.,
  and Reece J. McGee
Corson, John J.
Wilson, Logan

Shipyard
Archibald, Katherine

Factory
Abegglen, James
Dalton, Melville
Ellsworth, John S.
Guest, Robert H.
Jacques, Eliot
Lafitte, Paul
Sayles, Leonard R.
Touraine, Alain
Walker, Charles R.,
  and Robert H. Guest
Warner, W. Lloyd, and
  J. O. Low

Welfare Agency
Seeley, John R.
Wilensky, Harold L., and
  Charles R. Lebeaux

Government Agency
Blau, Peter M.
Crozier, Michel
Selznick, Philip
Francis, Roy G., and
  Robert C. Stone
Weiss, Robert S.

Prison
Clemmer, Donald
Cressey, Donald R., *et al.*

Library
Garceau, Oliver

Power Plant
Mann, Floyd, and
  Richard L. Hoffman

Office
Mills, C. Wright
Morse, Nancy C.

Hospital
Argyris, Chris
Caudill, William A.
Coser, Rose Lamb
Stanton, Alfred H., and
  Morris S. Schwartz

Dock
Liverpool University
  Industrial Research Staff

HD6961.M55   93370

LIBRARY
EMORY & HENRY
COLLEGE

EMORY, VIRGINIA

Industrial
Sociology

HARPER & ROW, PUBLISHERS

New York, Evanston, and London

Industrial Sociology

The Sociology of Work Organizations

Second Edition

DELBERT C. MILLER

Professor of Sociology and Business Administration
Indiana University

WILLIAM H. FORM

Professor of Sociology
Associate, School of Labor and Industrial Relations
Michigan State University

INDUSTRIAL SOCIOLOGY: An Introduction to the Sociology of
Work Relations. Copyright, 1951, by Harper & Brothers.

INDUSTRIAL SOCIOLOGY: The Sociology of Work Organizations, Second Edition. Copyright © 1964 by Delbert C.
Miller and William H. Form.

Printed in the United States of America. All rights reserved. No part of this book may be used or reproduced in
any manner whatsoever without written permission except
in the case of brief quotations embodied in critical articles
and reviews. For information address
Harper & Row, Publishers, Incorporated, 49 East 33rd
Street, New York 16, N.Y.

C–O

LIBRARY OF CONGRESS CATALOG CARD NUMBER: 64-10221

HD
6961
.M55

Contents

v

93370

EMORY AND HENRY LIBRARY

PART III. THE INDIVIDUAL IN THE WORLD OF WORK

PART IV. MAJOR PROBLEMS OF APPLIED INDUSTRIAL AND ORGANIZATIONAL SOCIOLOGY

PART V. INDUSTRY, COMMUNITY, AND SOCIETY

APPENDIXES

INDEX

Preface

to

First Edition

THIS IS A BOOK about work with especial attention to the people who work and the social relations existing among them. The sociology of work relations is a study of people in jobs everywhere —in the factory, home, store, office, field, hospital, mine and government.

Work has always been the major preoccupation of man. Most of his waking hours have revolved around the struggle to produce and sustain himself. This struggle has been the source of much of his happiness and despair. It is a theme of this book that both personal satisfaction and efficient production are mutually interdependent in work activity. Neither of these ends is possible without recognizing the total social situation in which people find themselves. The sociology of work relations becomes a study of the interrelations between work and the social milieu in which the worker moves.

In many ways it is unfortunate that most of the research in industrial sociology has been done on the factory. This has led to a semantic confusion—one of identifying research on the factory with industrial sociology. Already many of us are prone to look at the factory as the main locus of work. The fact is that not more than one-quarter of the workers in the United States are employed in factories. The workers in trade, transportation, government, and other services constitute significant proportions of the labor force.

We prefer to use the word "industrial" in its broader meaning:

as referring to *all* forms of economic activity, including financial, commercial, productive, and professional enterprises generally. Industrial sociology includes the study of occupations, and all the social groups that affect work behavior. The field, so conceived, investigates the interrelationships between the work behavior of the individual and the other aspects of his social behavior. No hard and fast boundary lines can be drawn between work, play, worship, and family living. What the worker encounters in the social environment of his work has significance for him not only on the job but also in his participation within the local community. His family, his church, and his club all feel the repercussions of habits and attitudes acquired at work.

In modern times the relationship between work and other social activity has been obscured. The removal of work from the home or the neighborhood to the wide reaches of the industrial city has tended to block it off as a separate, distinct, and almost isolated social activity. In the past, work was not segregated as abruptly from other aspects of living as in the contemporary urban community. Then, work was geared more into a *way of life*. It was differentiated only in part from resting, eating, worshiping, and playing. Medieval guilds recognized that occupations and industries draw people together because of similarity of interests. Guilds were the organizational reflections of the need for association, for learning of skills, for protection of position, for social participation in and out of work. It was only after the industrial revolution, accompanied by urbanization and specialization of occupations, that work began to differentiate itself from leisure and social life.

The focus of attention shifted away from the worker and his social relationships. Production, money, and profit became the ends of economic activity; not satisfaction, self-direction, and a sense of achievement. The worker became increasingly a commodity, another cost of production. He himself began to consider his income as the only purpose of his work.

Chapter I describes how this very emphasis on production, profit, and income finally led to a rediscovery that working cannot be divorced from living. It is now known that production, profit, and industrial peace depend in large measure on the recognition that industry is a complex of interacting groups and individuals. Technological progress alone does not solve the major problems in our work plants. These problems will be solved only by increasing knowledge and understanding of human relations in industry. Industrial sociology is a relatively new discipline dedicated to this end.

The field of industrial sociology has a steadily growing body of research studies and theory. This book seeks to introduce new research, integrate available materials, and provide a frame of reference for the study of work relations. Teachers, students, executives, personnel, and labor leaders will find reports of new developments as well as different perspectives regarding industrial relations. A glossary of terms is provided in the back of the book for those uninitiated in the field of industrial sociology.

The authors have tested this book in the classroom several semesters and have found that the book may be used for either a two-semester course in industrial occupational sociology, or for two separate courses. The instructor will, of course, decide how the book may be used for one or more courses. The writers have found that for a semester course in Industrial Sociology, Parts I, II, and III offer a suitable survey of the field. A course in Occupational Sociology or the Social Adjustment of the Worker will find Parts IV and V particularly fruitful. Much of the material in the second half of the book may also be valuable for a course in Industry and the Community.

ACKNOWLEDGMENTS

It would be impossible to acknowledge here all of the indebtedness the authors owe to colleagues, students, union and business leaders for their help and suggestions in making this book possible. Wherever possible we have indicated in the text specific contributions of these people. We want to mention specifically several people who have helped us especially. Professor F. Stuart Chapin has critically read the manuscript and has given us many valuable suggestions. Professor C. P. Loomis provided us material aid for typing some of the manuscript, and has stimulated many ideas. We are indebted particularly to our wives: Rosemary

Parisa Miller for assistance in drafting the illustrations and Mildred M. Form for typing many of the drafts. Both assisted us in the laborious task of editing the manuscript.

DELBERT C. MILLER
WILLIAM H. FORM

December, 1950

Preface
to
Second Edition

THIS TEXT is the product of almost two decades of writing and classroom testing. The two authors began the original writing for this book in 1945 when they were members of the Kent State University faculty. Miller then served successively at the University of Washington, Pennsylvania State University, and Indiana University, while Form served at Michigan State University in Sociology, and at the School of Labor and Industrial Relations. During the last twenty years the authors have participated extensively in management and labor training. The present volume is a sum of their classroom and research experiences.

The first edition of this book appeared in English in 1951 and was translated into German and published by Westdeutscher Verlag at Cologne, Germany in 1957. From teachers and students who used this original text we have secured advice and recommendations. Most of the teachers have indicated their need for a treatment which bridges the wide range of student academic majors. They have emphasized the necessity to provide an international view of industrialization portraying the industrial and work problems in other cultures at their different stages of development. They have also said that since they commonly have the student for only one course in industrial sociology, an introductory text should extend over all areas of the field. They have therefore suggested the following subjects as essential.

1. Cultural patterns of industrialization and their relations to the total society.
2. Behavior of work and labor union organizations.
3. Career and adjustment problems of employees and union members.
4. Occupational and industrial changes in the labor force.
5. Industry, labor, and community relations.
6. Applied organizational sociology with the new research on decision making, leadership, morale, and productivity.

We have included these areas of study (and some others), and have tried to knit them together by distinctive sociological approaches. Our theoretical orientation is broad. Historical sociology is widely used in presenting the cultural patterns of industrialization. The cultural approach is used in introducing the student to organizational behavior and to selected field projects which implement this approach. Structural-functional analysis is extensively utilized in the treatment of organization in its part-whole relations. Social psychology is the source for much data on the social adjustment of the employee. The quantitative approach is stressed particularly in the applied research area where relationships between leadership, morale, and productivity have been sought. Among the variety of approaches, an underlying position always dominates: analysis must begin with organizational structure before proceeding to explanations of personal behavior.

Whatever his future occupation may be, we want the student to acquire new ways of thinking about work behavior. We have tried to incorporate concepts and theories which are guiding the professional sociologist and to place these in a setting which reflects the scientific strivings of the field of sociology. Above all, we have tried to make the study of industrial and organizational behavior a liberal experience—to demonstrate that work behavior is social behavior and, as such, may be one of the most fulfilling and enriching experiences of life. We urge the practical student to reflect upon the fact that *he may very likely assume the work direction of others* in a few years. He will probably be a salaried worker and will probably be employed in a large organization. His insights and performance will depend in part upon how well he has assimilated the social knowledge accumulated in this book. The woman student should also remember that she will probably work for an organization a large part of her life. We know that nine out of ten girls will be working an average of 25 years between the late teens and age 65. If she is a housewife, her husband will be struggling with problems of organizational behavior, and her ability to understand his problems and offer him insights will enrich their general relationship. In these senses, industrial and organizational sociology is a preparation for marriage and life adjustment.

We are indebted to many persons for their contributions to this book. The growing body of researchers, now too numerous to mention, have provided the accumulated base of knowledge which has compelled a new edition.

We owe much to our undergraduate and graduate students for their analyses of work organizations. Their term projects have revealed social processes of work in such diverse organizations as fishing boats, lumber camps, military bases, fraternities and sororities, Chinese restaurants, summer camps, and road construction crews. Dr. Karl Scheussler of Indiana University and Dr. Jack Stieber of Michigan State University have made available typing and mimeograph services, and have constantly encouraged us. We appreciate the many supplementary services our wives have given to this book. We are also grateful to Jane Wellman, Jane Sunderland, Rita Hosler, Katherine Lehman, and Jacqueline Greene, for their enthusiastic help in preparing the manuscript.

Delbert C. Miller
William H. Form

September, 1963

Bibliography of Representative Research Contributors to Industrial and Organizational Sociology Exhibiting Scope of the Field

Department Store
  Donovan, Francis, *The Saleslady*, University of Chicago Press, 1929.
  Lombard, George F. F., *Behavior in a Selling Group*, Graduate School of Business Administration, Harvard University, 1955.

Hotel
  Hayne, Norman S., *Hotel Life*, University of North Carolina Press, 1936.
  Lentz, Edith, "The Tremont Hotel Study," Committee on Human Relations in Industry, University of Chicago (hectographed), 1945.

Restaurant
  Whyte, William F., *Human Relations in the Restaurant Industry*, McGraw-Hill, 1948.

Railroad
  Cottrell, W. F., *The Railroader*, Stanford, 1940.
  Katz, D., *et al.*, *Productivity, Supervision and Morale Among Railroad Workers*, University of Michigan Survey Research Center, 1951.

Insurance
  Katz, D., *et al.*, *Productivity, Supervision, and Morale in an Office Situation*, University of Michigan Institute for Social Research, 1950.
  Likert, R., and J. M. Willits, *Morale and Agency Management*, Life Insurance Sales Research Bureau, 1940.

Bank
  Argyris, Chris, *Organization of a Bank*, Yale, Labor and Management Center, 1954.
  Lockwood, David, *The Black Coated Worker: A Study in Class Consciousness*, G. Allen, 1958.

Farm

Eaton, Joseph, *Exploring Tomorrow's Agriculture,* Harper & Row, 1953.

Gross, Edward, *Work and Society,* Crowell, 1958.

Arensberg, Conrad M., *The Irish Countryman,* Macmillan, 1937.

Woofter, W. J., Jr., *Landlord and Tenant on the Cotton Plantation,* Research Monograph No. 5, Works Progress Administration, 1936.

Power Plant

Mann, Floyd C., and Richard L. Hoffman, *Automation and the Worker, A Study of Social Change in Power Plants,* Holt, Rinehart and Winston, 1960.

Courtroom

Snyder, Eloise C., "The Supreme Court as a Small Group," *Social Forces,* 1958, Vol. 36, pp. 232–238.

Strodtbeck, Fred L., Rita M. James, and C. Hawkins, "Social Status in Jury Deliberations," *American Sociological Review,* December, 1957, pp. 713–719.

Air Base

Bowers, Raymond V., *et al., Studies in Organizational Effectiveness,* Contributions to Military Sociology, United States Air Force, Office of Scientific Research, 1962.

Gross, Edward, "Some Functional Consequences of Primary Controls in Formal Work Organizations," *American Sociological Review,* August, 1953, pp. 368–371.

Hunter, Floyd, *Host Community and Air Force Base,* University of North Carolina Press, November, 1952.

Mack, Raymond W., "The Prestige System of an Air Base: Squadron Ranking and Morale," *American Sociological Review,* June, 1954, pp. 281–287.

Miller, Delbert C., and Nahum Z. Medalia, "Efficiency, Leadership and Morale in Small Military Organizations (Radar Bases)," *Sociological Review,* July, 1955, pp. 93–108.

Thompson, James D., "Authority and Power in Identical Organizations," *American Journal of Sociology,* November, 1956, pp. 290–301.

Naval Ships and Installations

Homans, George C., "The Small Warship," *American Sociological Review,* June, 1946, pp. 294–300.

Richardson, Stephen A., "Organizational Contrasts on English and American Ships," *Administrative Science Quarterly,* September, 1956.

Public Utility
   Bakke, E. W., *Bonds of Organization*, Yale, 1950.

Army Bases and Field Sites
   Janowitz, Morris, *Sociology and the Military Establishment*, Russell Sage, 1959.
   Rose, Arnold, *et al.*, "Human Behavior in Military Society," *American Journal of Sociology*, March, 1946, pp. 359–508 (entire issue).
   Stouffer, Samuel A., and others, *The American Soldier*, Princeton, 1949, Vols. 1 and 2.

Research Laboratory
   Brown, Paula, "Bureaucracy in a Government Laboratory," *Social Forces*, 1954, Vol. 32, pp. 259–268.
   Marcson, Simon, *The Scientist in American Industry*, Industrial Relations Section, Department of Economics, Princeton University, 1960.
   Pelz, Donald C., "Some Social Factors Related to Performance in a Research Organization," *Administrative Science Quarterly*, 1956, Vol. 1, pp. 310–325.
   Weschler, Irving R., Murray Kahane, and Robert Tannenbaum, "Job Satisfaction, Productivity, and Morale: A Case Study," *Occupational Psychology*, January, 1952.

Voluntary Organization
   Sills, David L., *The Volunteers*, Free Press, 1955.
   Tannenbaum, A. S., *A Study of the League of Women Voters of the United States: Factors in League Effectiveness*, University of Michigan Institute for Social Research, 1958. (Reprinted in R. Likert, *New Patterns of Management*, McGraw-Hill, 1961.)

Law Firm
   Smigel, Erwin O., "The Impact of Recruitment on the Organization of the Law Firm," *American Sociological Review*, 1960, Vol. 25, pp. 55–60.

Mine
   Zweig, Ferdinand, *Men in the Pits*, Gollancz, 1948.

Labor Union
   Gouldner, Alvin, *Wildcat Strike*, Antioch Press, 1954.
   Greer, Scott, *Last Man Out*, Free Press, 1959.
   Lipset, Seymour M., Martin Trow, and James Coleman, *Union Democracy: The Inside Politics of the International Typographical Union*, Free Press, 1956.
   Rose, Arnold, *Union Solidarity*, University of Minnesota Press, 1962.

Strauss, George, and Leonard R. Sayles, *The Local Union*, Harper & Row, 1953.

Whyte, William F., *Pattern for Industrial Peace*, Harper & Row, 1951.

Wilensky, Harold L., *Intellectuals in Labor Unions*, Free Press, 1956.

University

Caplow, Theodore, and Reece J. McGee, *The Academic Marketplace*, Basic Books, 1958.

Corson, John J., *Governance of Colleges and Universities*, McGraw-Hill, 1960.

Wilson, Logan, *The Academic Man*, Oxford, 1942.

Shipyard

Archibald, Katherine, *Wartime Shipyard*, University of California Press, 1947.

Factory

Abegglen, James, *The Japanese Factory*, Free Press, 1958.

Dalton, Melville, *Men Who Manage*, Wiley, 1959.

Ellsworth, John S., Jr., *Factory Folkways*, Yale, 1952.

Guest, Robert H., *Organizational Change: The Effect of Successful Leadership*, Dorsey, 1962.

Jacques, Eliot, *The Changing Culture of the Factory*, Dryden, 1952.

Lafitte, Paul, *Social Structure and Personality in the Factory*, Macmillan, 1958.

Sayles, Leonard R., *Behavior of Industrial Work Groups*, Wiley, 1958.

Touraine, Alain, *L'Evolution du Travail Ouvrier aux Usines Renault*, Centre National de la Recherche Scientifique, 1955.

Walker, Charles R., and Robert H. Guest, *The Man on the Assembly Line*, Harvard, 1952.

Warner, W. Lloyd, and J. O. Low, *The Social System of the Modern Factory*, Yale, 1947.

Welfare Agency

Seeley, John R., *et al.*, *Community Chest, A Case Study in Philanthropy*, University of Toronto Press, 1957.

Wilensky, Harold L., and Charles N. Lebeaux, *Industrial Society and Social Welfare*, Russell Sage, 1958.

Government Agency

Blau, Peter M., *The Dynamics of Bureaucracy*, University of Chicago Press, 1955.

Crozier, Michel, *The French Bureaucratic System,* Stanford, 1962.
Francis, Roy G., and Robert C. Stone, *Service and Procedure in Bureaucracy,* University of Minnesota Press, 1956.
Selznick, Philip, *TVA and the Grass Roots,* University of Chicago Press, 1949.
Weiss, Robert S., *Processes of Organization,* University of Michigan, Survey Research Center, 1956.

Prison
    Clemmer, Donald, *The Prison Community,* Christopher, 1940.
    Cressey, Donald R., *The Prison: Studies in Institutional Organization and Change,* Holt, Rinehart and Winston, 1961.

Library
    Garceau, Oliver, *The Public Library in the Political Process,* Columbia, 1949.

School
    Gordon, C. Wayne, *The Social System of the High School,* Free Press, 1957.
    Gross, Neal, Ward S. Mason, and Alexander W. McEachern, *Explorations in Role Analysis, Studies of the School Superintendency Role,* Wiley, 1958.

Office
    Mills, C. Wright, *White Collar Worker,* Oxford, 1951.
    Morse, Nancy C., *Satisfactions in the White-Collar Job,* University of Michigan, Institute for Social Research, 1953.

Hospital
    Argyris, Chris, *Diagnosing Human Relations in Organizations: The Case Study of a Hospital,* Yale, Labor and Management Center, 1956.
    Caudill, William A., *The Psychiatric Hospital in a Small Society,* Harvard, 1958.
    Coser, Rose Lamb, "Authority and Decision Making in a Hospital," *American Sociological Review,* 1961, Vol. 26, pp. 28–39.
    Stanton, Alfred H., and Morris S. Schwartz, *The Mental Hospital,* Basic Books, 1954.

Dock
    Liverpool University Industrial Research Staff, *The Dock Worker,* Liverpool University, 1954.

Bibliography of Representative Contributors to Organizational Theory, from the Social Science Disciplines and Applied Fields

Industrial Sociology

Bakke, E. W., "Concept of the Social Organization," in Mason Haire (Ed.), *Modern Organization Theory*, Wiley, 1959.

Bendix, Reinhard, *Work and Authority in Industry*, Wiley, 1956.

Blau, Peter M., *Bureaucracy in Modern Society*, Random House, 1962.

Dubin, Robert, "Stability of Human Organizations," in Mason Haire (Ed.), *Modern Organization Theory*, Wiley, 1959.

Durkheim, Emile, *The Division of Labor in Society*, trans., George Simpson, Macmillan, 1933.

Etzioni, Amitai (Ed.), *Complex Organizations: A Sociological Reader*, Holt, Rinehart and Winston, 1961.

Etzioni, Amitai, *A Comparative Analysis of Complex Organizations*, Free Press, 1961.

Friedmann, Georges, *Industrial Society: The Emergence of Human Problems of Automation*, Free Press, 1955.

Gouldner, Alvin W., *Patterns of Industrial Bureaucracy*, Free Press, 1954.

Hickman, C. Addison, and Kuhn, Manford H., *Individuals, Groups, and Economic Behavior*, Holt, Rinehart and Winston, 1956.

Homans, George, *The Human Group*, Harcourt, Brace & World, 1950.

Homans, George, *Social Behavior: Its Elementary Forms*, Harcourt, Brace & World, 1961.

Meadows, Paul, *The Culture of Industrial Man*, University of Nebraska Press, 1950.

Merton, Robert, *et al.*, *Reader in Bureaucracy*, Free Press, 1952.

Moore Wilbert E., *The Conduct of the Corporation,* Random House, 1962.

Parsons, Talcott, and Neil J. Smelser, *Economy and Society,* Free Press, 1956.

Selznick, Philip, *Leadership in Administration,* Harper & Row, 1957.

Thompson, James D., *et al., Comparative Studies in Administration,* University of Pittsburgh Press, 1959.

Weber, Max, *The Theory of Social and Economic Organization* trans., A. M. Henderson and Talcott Parsons, Oxford, 1947.

Whyte, William F., *et al., Money and Motivation: An Analysis of Incentives in Industry,* Harper & Row, 1955.

Industrial Social Psychology

Argyris, Chris, *Personality and Organization,* Harper & Row, 1957.

Argyris, Chris, *Understanding Organizational Behavior,* Dorsey, 1960.

Bass, Bernard M., *Leadership, Psychology, and Organizational Behavior,* Harper & Row, 1960.

Likert, Rensis, *New Patterns of Management,* McGraw-Hill, 1961.

Mayo, Elton, *The Social Problems of an Industrial Civilization,* Harvard, 1945.

McGregor, Douglas, *The Human Side of Enterprise,* McGraw-Hill, 1960.

Schutz, William C., *FIRO, A Three Dimensional Theory of Interpersonal Behavior,* Holt, Rinehart and Winston, 1960.

Shartle, Carroll L., *Effective Performance and Leadership,* Prentice-Hall, 1956.

Stagner, Ross, *The Psychology of Industrial Conflict,* Wiley, 1956.

Stogdill, Ralph M., *Individual Behavior and Group Achievement,* Oxford, 1959.

Tannenbaum, Robert, Irving R. Weschler, and Fred Massarik, *Leadership and Organization,* McGraw-Hill, 1961.

Thibaut, John W., and Harold H. Kelley, *The Social Psychology of Groups,* Wiley, 1959.

Industrial and Personnel Management

Barnard, Chester, *The Function of an Executive,* Harvard, 1938.

Haire, Mason (Ed.), *Organizational Theory in Industrial Practice*, Wiley, 1962. (See especially Glenn Gilman, "An Inquiry into the Nature and Use of Authority.")

Mason, Ward S. (Ed.), *The Corporation in Modern Society*, Harvard, 1960.

Rubenstein, Albert H., and Chadwick J. Haberstroh, *Some Theories of Organization*, Irwin, 1960.

Roethlisberger, Fritz J., and William J. Dickson, *Management and the Worker*, Harvard, 1939.

Economics

Boulding, Kenneth, *The Organizational Revolution*, Harper & Row, 1953.

Katona, George, *Psychological Analysis and Economic Behavior*, McGraw-Hill, 1951.

Kerr, Clark, John T. Dunlop, Frederick H. Harbison, and Charles M. Myers, *Industrialism and Industrial Man*, Harvard, 1960.

Siegel, Sidney, and Lawrence E. Fouraker, *Bargaining and Group Decision Making*, McGraw-Hill, 1960.

Veblen, Thorstein, *The Theory of Business Enterprise*, Mentor Books, 1958.

Political Science and Public Administration

Drucker, Peter, *The New Society*, Harper & Row, 1950.

Golembiewski, Robert T., *Behavior and Organization*, Rand Mc-Nally, 1962.

March, James G., and Herbert A. Simon, *Organizations*, Wiley, 1958.

Presthus, Robert, *The Organizational Society*, Knopf, 1962.

Simon, Herbert A., *Administrative Behavior*, Macmillan, 1958.

Thompson, Victor A., *Modern Organization, A General Theory*, Knopf, 1961.

Applied Anthropology

Chapple, Eliot D., and Conrad M. Arensberg, *Measuring Human Relations: An Introduction to the Study of the Interaction of Individuals*, Genetic Psychology Monograph No. 22, The Journal Press, 1940.

Herskovits, Melville J., *Economic Anthropolgy*, Knopf, 1960.

Leighton, Alexander, *The Governing of Men*, Princeton, 1945.

PART I · The Universal Impact of Industrialization

PART I describes industrialization as a world-wide process which is sweeping all societies into rapid organizational changes. The first chapter establishes this theme and shows how industrial and organizational sociology has come to cope with some of the problems presented. The convergence within sociology and the social sciences generally is traced so that the growing research and theoretical base may be carefully observed. Chapter 2 is a historical analysis of industrialization and its impact on societies. Special attention is given to the mature industrial society. The aim is to understand the process by which other world states may evolve and to predict social changes which are likely to occur as industrialization proceeds. The United States has a mature industrial economy and thus it may be used as one model to predict changes in less developed countries. The industrial and occupational changes in the United States are introduced to provide a base for such comparisons. Finally, the impact of industrialization on the local community is described.

It is a prime task of sociology to show the interrelatedness of social forces as they penetrate into society and community. In this part, industrialization is described as a massive force altering the organizations and values of the total society. On this background, the operations of all work organizations are shaped and forged.

CHAPTER 1

Industrial Society
and
Industrial Sociology

INDUSTRIALISM

Probably the outstanding characteristic of contemporary Western societies is that they have been forced into a situation where change is a constant phenomenon. So dynamic is this pattern of change that it is irresistibly spreading to the entire world. Usually the change is conceived as emanating from persistent technological innovations which come to constitute a cultural pattern. While such an explanation is grossly correct, it is an oversimplification, for technological innovations are accompanied, if not preceded, by changes in values and social organization. It is not an exaggeration to suggest that the so-called industrial revolution was accompanied from the very beginning by an organizational revolution, and that both accompanied a change in value systems. Today the revolutions in technology, organization, and values are constantly altering both traditional and industrial societies.

It is often overlooked that the revolution in manufacturing which gained impetus in eighteenth-century western Europe was preceded by changes in the values of the societies that composed it. While many different values became modified, the underlying change was the invasion of rational thought into many areas previously considered sacred. The area which felt the greatest application of rational systems of thought was economics, particularly in manufacturing. In an interdependent society all other social institutions had to make corresponding adjustments. In this particular sense, we can think of the industrial revolution as creating an industrial society. The general purpose of industrial sociology is to study this broad process of industrialization and its impact on various segments of the society by the application of general sociological principles.

It is strange that industrial sociology emerged in the United States at a time when the number of people engaged in manufacturing was surpassed by the number employed in nonmanufacturing or service industries. Although less than a quarter of its population is currently occupied in manufacturing, the United States, like several western European countries, is a mature industrial society. Apparently the structures of industrializing societies exhibit a predictable pattern; the number of people engaged in manufacturing increases until it surpasses the number engaged in agriculture. At a further stage, the proportion of workers employed in the so-called service (nonmanufacturing) industries exceeds that of workers in manufacturing while the proportion engaged in agriculture continues to decline. Obviously this condition would be impossible without an increasingly efficient system of manufacturing which can support a growing number of workers in "nonproduction" industries. Thus, although a minority of workers may be employed in manufacturing industries, it is possible to have an industrialized economy. Moreover, the economy may be characterized as "industrial" in the sense that nonmanufacturing work organizations increasingly model their values and structures after manufacturing organizations. Marketing, wholesaling, retailing, transportation, communication, education, health care, banking, and other services are becoming "factories" in marketing, wholesaling, retailing, transportation, communication, education, and so on.

The impact of the industrial complex manifests itself also in the nonindustrial or noneconomic realm. That is to say, other institutions of the society respond to the demands and needs of the economic institutions, and this seems to be the case irrespective of the pattern of property ownership found in the society. To be sure, although other institutions do have an impact on the functioning of the economy, the reverse process, as Polanyi suggests, tends to be general in industrial societies.[1] Thus one of the main functions of government is to control the economy; one

[1] Karl Polanyi, *The Great Transformation,* Holt, 1944, p. 75.

of the main problems of education is to train people for technical and other roles in the economy; one of the main functions of the family is to socialize individuals for living in this type of economy; one of the main problems of religion is to reinterpret life meanings to people who are exposed to the economic instabilities; and the main task of welfare is to provide for those cast adrift by the malfunctions of the economy.

EVOLUTION OF INDUSTRIAL SOCIOLOGY

Industrial sociology not only is concerned broadly with the study of industrial society but also is concerned with the analysis of the social organization of work. Although the greatest number of researches tend to cover industrial enterprises, any type of work organization may be studied. As organizational sociology has joined with industrial sociology, enormous advances have been made in building up comparative knowledge of formal organizations. When Mayo and his associates completed their work in 1944, they had reported on a textile mill and three manufacturing plants producing telephone equipment, metal parts, and aircraft.[2] Since that time research has been extended to department stores, hotels, restaurants, railroads, insurance companies, banks, air bases, naval ships and installations, army bases, public utilities, scientific research laboratories, hospitals, labor unions, universities, shipyard, a great variety of factories, government agencies, prisons, public libraries, schools, power plants, offices, welfare agencies, voluntary organizations, farms, mines, courtrooms, and law firms. The outline, "Scope of Industrial and Organizational Sociology" (pp. xiv–xv, preceding Chapter 1), depicts the enlarging scope of industrial and organizational sociology. A selected bibliography of research is appended to it.

Convergence of Industrial and Organizational Sociology

Organizational sociology has developed on the base stimulated by industrial sociologists but it is growing at a rapid pace because of the desire to apply sociological knowledge to special organizational sites. Since 1950 several "new" fields of sociology

[2] The best short survey of Elton Mayo's work is his summary volume, *The Social Problems of an Industrial Civilization*, Harvard, 1945.

have arisen, such as medical sociology, educational sociology, military sociology, human relations in government, and others. The present scene is one of a vast convergence both within sociology itself and between sociology and other disciplines interested in problems of work. The American Sociological Society has a section on the Sociology of Complex Organizations as well as one on Industrial Sociology. It is difficult to draw a line between these interests except that organizational sociologists may more commonly be reporting on a hospital, prison, or welfare agency, while industrial sociologists may be describing a bank, a public utility, or a factory.

Community sociologists are being joined by industrial sociologists who share their research on industry-labor-community relations. Until recently, occupational and industrial sociologists were almost the same people. However, there are signs that the two areas must divide, for the knowledge and skill associated with each are overburdening the researchers.

Political sociologists are finding many industrial sociologists at their side in the study of community power. Interdisciplinary interest in organizational problems has never been higher, and no Ford Foundation grant could have done what intellectual and cultural forces have accomplished in drawing social scientists and applied disciplines together. Name a problem such as morale or work efficiency in an organization, and you may find working on it a social psychologist, a political scientist, an applied anthropologist, a sociologist, a personnel management researcher, an industrial management researcher, an educational researcher, a social work researcher, a home economist, and many others. Inside the corporation the staff men assigned to work on such a problem may have the most widely varying training, as indeed will be true of the management consultants hired to alleviate the problem.

Cornell University sponsors an *Administrative Science Quarterly* whose purpose epitomizes the entire interdisciplinary trend. The journal seeks to encourage a common endeavor among all disciplines to enrich the theory and research of administration in any organization which is oriented to the attainment of a relatively specific type of goal. Industrial psychology, which once stood alone studying the human problems of work, has been joined by a mighty gathering. Large research centers are now staffed with interdisciplinary experts who secure funds from foundations, business firms, and professional associations. The Bureau of Applied Social Research at Columbia and the Survey Research Centers at Michigan and California are three of the largest university institutes devoted to seeking principles of social organization. In 1947 the Michigan Survey Research Center set forth a ten-year program of research. The planning statement reads:

> Since the research is being planned so as to discover principles of social organization which have the widest possible application and validity, it will be necessary to study the structure and operation of a wide variety of groups. Groups engaged in widely different kinds of activities will be studied and they will be of different sizes and degrees of complexity. Thus, the social organization of various kinds of industries will be studied: Production, distribution and office management will each be studied and at different levels of organization. It will be desirable to study specific offices and plants as well as the over-all organization of some of our largest industries. Similarly, studies will be made in all kinds of governmental agencies—Federal, State, and local—military and civilian—and at different levels of organization. Various kinds of group organizations, such as professional, occupational, and special interest will be studied also.[3]

The Survey Research Center has moved rapidly toward this objective. A similar objective is shared in the United States by a wide array of workers and universities. And a host of research institutes have been adding to the growing flow of research reports. Besides the Michigan, Columbia, and California centers other institutes with like objectives include the Personnel Research Board at Ohio State University; the Social Science Institute of North Carolina, of Washington University (St. Louis), Colorado, Harvard, Wisconsin, and Florida; the Industrial Relations Centers at the Universities of Chicago, Minnesota, California, Yale, Illinois, and Michigan State; the Sociological Research Laboratory at Washington and Washington State; the Administrative Research Center at Pittsburgh; the Harvard Business Research Center; the National Opinion Research Center at Chicago; and many others.

The convergence of the various fields has enriched theory as

---

[3] *A Program of Research on the Fundamental Problems of Organizing Human Behavior,* Survey Research Center, University of Michigan Press, March, 1947, p. 3.

well as research. "Representative Contributors to Organizational Theory" (pp. xxii–xxiii) lists some major theorists who have contributed to industrial and organizational sociology. Most of the boundaries which were once neatly labeled Industrial Sociology, Industrial Psychology, Human Relations in Business, Public Administrations, and so on have now been obscured. The disciplines are pulled together like research teams in a large corporate laboratory. Research workers are agreed that type of work organization is not a meaningful boundary for a discipline because the social and administrative processes occur in substantially the same general form in manufacturing, commercial, civil, educational, military, and hospital organizations.[4]

COMPARATIVE ORGANIZATIONAL ANALYSIS

Fruitful efforts have been directed toward finding ways of conceptualizing similarities and dissimilarities in various types of work organizations. For example, Gross has suggested that organizations in several institutional sectors may be classified by the way unity is achieved by their participants. He suggests two extreme poles—a unity based on consensus and a unity based on symbiosis.[5] A consensual tie is one in which people subscribe to the same set of values, or are united by agreement. A symbiotic tie is one in which people are united because each has something to give which the other needs. Consensual relations tend to be governed by emotions, sentiments, mores, and implicit understandings. Symbiotic relations tend to be governed by reason, self-interest, and formally agreed-upon rules. Figure 1.1 shows both economic and noneconomic types of organizations arrayed along a continuum from consensus to symbiosis. As one moves from left to right on the continuum, work organizations tend to increase in size and complexity. As the size of the organization increases it becomes difficult to maintain unity on a primary consensual level, and symbiotic elements become more and more important. This classification is useful in understanding how social processes in an organization may be affected. Leadership, for example, must be altered to fit a highly symbiotic organiza-

[4] Edward H. Litchfield, "Note on a General Theory of Administration," *Administration Science Quarterly*, June, 1956, p. 28.

[5] Edward Gross, *Work and Society*, Crowell, 1958, p. 268.

tion. It may be necessary to train leaders in "human relations" to overcome the lack of unity achieved by consensual organizations.

Consensus					Symbiosis
NONECONOMIC					
Welfare Agency	Doctor's Clinic	Church	College	Government Department	Army
ECONOMIC					
Farm	Corner Grocery	Small Restaurant	Small Factory	Large Factory	Giant Corporation with Branch Plants

FIG. 1.1. Organizations Distinguished by Nature of Unity That Binds Participants to the Organization. (Suggested by Edward Gross, Work and Society, Crowell, 1958, p. 269.)

Etzioni has proposed another dimension which may be more useful in classifying work organizations.[6] This is the increasing degree of commitment required from lower participants for the effective operation of the organization. Figure 1.2 shows an array of work organizations on a commitment continuum. This dimension of commitment focuses on efforts to build morale sufficient to secure performance appropriate to the goals of the organization.

Low Commitment of Lower Participants					High Commitments of Lower Participants	
NONECONOMIC						
Prison Inmates	Enlisted Men in Peacetime Army	Welfare Recipients	Contributors to Community Chest	Students	Mental Patients in Hospital	Religious Members
ECONOMIC						
Migrant Workers	Day Laborers	Assembly Line Worker	Trade Union Member	Cooperative Society Member	Patrons of Beauty Parlor	Family Business Owners

FIG. 1.2. Organizations Distinguished by Degree of Commitment Required from "Lower" Participants of the Organization. (Suggested by Amitai Etzioni, Complex Organization, A Sociological Reader, Holt, 1961, p. 187.)

[6] Amitai Etzioni (ed.), Complex Organizations: A Sociological Reader, Holt, 1961, p. 187. Cf. Etzioni, A Comparative Study of Complex Organization, Free Press, 1961, pp. 8–22.

Bureaucratic organizations are sweeping into all institutional sectors of society—economic, religious, welfare, government, and education. Max Weber, Toennies, Burnham, and others have been aware of the effect of increasing size and complexity of organizations. They have indicated that organizations may be arrayed from nonbureaucratic to highly bureaucratic types according to the number of characteristics they possess as shown in Table 1.1. This table summarizes the dimensions used by various writers who have described bureaucratic models of organizations.[7]

TABLE 1.1. Attributes of Bureaucracy

Dimensions of Bureaucracy	Authors							
	1	2	3	4	5	6	7	8
Hierarchy of Authority	*	*	*	*	*	*	*	*
Divisions of Labor	*	*	*	*	*	*	*	
Technically Competent Participants	*	*	*	*	*		*	*
Procedural Devices for Work Situations	*	*	*	*		*		*
Rules Governing Behavior of Positional Incumbents	*		*	*				*
Limited Authority of Office	*	*		*		*	*	
Differential Rewards by Office	*				*			
Impersonality of Personal Contact				*	*			
Administration Separate from Ownership	*	*						
Emphasis on Written Communication	*							
Rational Discipline	*							

Key to authors: (1) Weber; (2) Litwak; (3) Friedrich; (4) Merton; (5) Udy; (6) Heady; (7) Parsons; (8) Berger.

SOURCE: Richard H. Hall, "Intra-Organizational Structure Variation: An Application of the Bureaucratic Model," *Administrative Science Quarterly*, December, 1962, p. 298.

Organizations grouped by bureaucratic attributes are given in Fig. 1.3. It shows that the Catholic Church and the Army tend to be close to the classic case of bureaucracy. As organizations increase in size and complexity they seem to be adding more bureaucratic attributes.

[7] Richard H. Hall, "Intra-Organizational Structural Variation: An Application of the Bureaucratic Model," *Administrative Science Quarterly*, December, 1962, pp. 295–308.

Nonbureaucratic   Highly Bureaucratic

Voluntary Organizations	Small Colleges and Public Schools	Large University	Large Public School System	Large Corporation	Large Governmental Organizations	Military Organizations
Small Business						Catholic Church
	Political Parties				Large Hospital	
	Small Churches					

FIG. 1.3. Organizations Distinguished by Attributes of Bureaucracy.

Comparative analyses of organizations may be expected to multiply, for they promise to reveal new insights into various functional problems of organizations and how they may be met.[8] Cross-cultural studies are increasingly testing the effects of cultural variables on organizational behavior as societies are arrayed on a continuum from low to high technological development.

SOCIOLOGY OF WORK ORGANIZATIONS

Industrial sociology is a substantive area of general sociology which might more accurately be termed the sociology of work organizations or the sociology of the economy. It is mainly concerned with the application of sociological principles to the study of economic structures, changes in these structures, and values and ideologies related to them. These principles may be applied on the societal, community, and work levels. Industrial sociology is not primarily an applied discipline, although its modern popularity has been associated with studies of such problems as morale, productivity, absenteeism, and turnover done by the Harvard Business School during the Great Depression and World War II. This accidental historical concern with management problems

[8] James D. Thompson et al., Comparative Studies in Administration, University of Pittsburgh Press, 1959; Peter M. Blau and W. Richard Scott, Formal Organizations, Chandler, 1962, pp. 27–58; Talcott Parsons, Structure and Process in Modern Societies, Free Press, 1953, pp. 16–96.

led many to assume that industrial sociology was in fact a sociology to help management solve its problems. Of course, as a science, the discipline should have neither a pro-management nor a pro-union bias. The eagerness on the part of some sociologists to avoid identification as handmaidens of management led them to identify with the problems of organized labor. This was an error similar to the pro-management bias of earlier students. Industrial sociologists need not be concerned with the applications of their findings, or who will apply them. If their work has scientific merit, it will be used by many groups including labor or management. Part IV on applied problems shows how sociological principles may be used by both sides to resolve separate and common problems.

Basic Concepts and Orientations

The sociological perspective

There is a current tendency for sociology to lose its traditional concern for social organization by making role and individual behavior the focus of attention. This has been primarily the result of the increasing influence and popularity of social psychology. Moreover, there has also been a tendency since World War II to pursue descriptive studies of work organizations as ends in themselves. These have resulted in catalogues of local work customs, dictionaries of work argot, and endless descriptions of specific problems at work. Such an unsophisticated application of ethnography to contemporary society is contrary to the point of view taken here, namely, that all disciplines should be primarily concerned with general principles. Furthermore, the specification of general organizational patterns is logically prior to the analysis by social roles. The fundamental premise is that social structure conditions the concrete behavior of individuals and groups. The purpose of industrial sociology is to build a body of principles, the application of which transcends particular work organizations. While descriptions of various work organizations are necessary to analyze concrete behavior in specific organizations, the descriptions themselves do not constitute an adequate scientific objective. The position here assumed is that we move from the abstract to the concrete; from the analysis of social organization on its own level (social structure), to an analysis of interpersonal relations (social systems), to the analysis of concrete individual behavior. Whenever possible, such factors as the historical, societal, cultural, ecological, and demographic are used first to account for organizational behavior in nonpersonal terms. Societal, community, and institutional arrangements are considered as conditioning concrete organizations, suborganizations, and positions in those organizations. Thus we shall usually move from the study of larger social structures to the study of smaller ones, from organizational analysis to the analysis of interpersonal interaction patterns. This position may be described by setting forth the key elements in the structural-functional and social system approaches.

A. The structural-functional approach

This approach focuses attention on the way structures guide the functioning of any participant who is assigned to a given office or status. The key elements in the approach include *history, values, technological change, organizational goals,* and the *organizational complex.*

History. Economic organizations, like all social organizations, represent patterns of relations which men have worked out in the past. These arrangements obviously persist because they have survival value. That is, they have functions for groups who have power, authority, or legitimacy; and they give social organization a predictive character. Therefore history is always important in explaining the presence and persistence of work organizations. Unfortunately many sociologists act as if only the present can account for the present. In the analysis of industrial society, work organizations, and social processes we shall give history the position of primacy that it deserves. The reader will find a historical treatment of leadership and management concepts, the research history of industrial sociology, the history of labor organization, and many other historical descriptions to provide appropriate background.

Values. Social change occurs within the context of ends, goals, and norms held by organizations and actors within those organizations. The concept "value" is used to designate various projective phenomena and it is a necessary concept for organizational analysis because much activity does not make sense in terms of the immediate situation, but does make sense in terms of long-range goals, ends, and objectives. Industrial society is characterized by a multiplicity of goals, ends, norms, and values. However, one basic value which seems to underlie much activity is the application of rationalism to maximize the attainment of economic or other rewards. Bureaucracies are large-scale organizations rationally created to maximize the attainment of material and other ends of various groups and persons.

Technological change. As already suggested, the application of rational thought to production has resulted in important structural changes in industrial society primarily through technological change and change in the material environment. Technological change has been almost invariably accompanied by continuing changes in the *division of labor,* which is also a feature of all industrial societies. Perhaps division of labor is a misnomer for a phenomenon which refers to the rational reallocation of functions among men *and* machines. Such reallocation processes are strong anti-traditional forces which stimulate social conflict so continuously that social conflict may also be considered a normal condition in industrial society. The basic position taken in this work is that technological organization and social organization should be thought of as aspects of the same phenomenon, that changes in one bring changes in the other, and that these changes stimulate social unrest and conflict.

Organizational goals. Industrial sociology and organizational sociology necessarily focus much attention on the behavior of large-scale organizations. Organizations may be studied (1) by examining individual interactions, with the objective of seeking patterns which are consensual (organizational), or (2) by studying organizational patterns first and then relating individual behavior to these patterns. The sociological orientation examined here assumes the primacy of organizational over personal goals. Especially in large-scale organization, personal ends must be articulated to organizational ones if the organization is to function effectively. When the articulation is carried to the extreme, the "organizational man" emerges.

Organizational complex. The components of a social structure are the offices, statuses, authority designations, responsibilities, and rules which define the expected behavior. A formal organizational chart, for example, is simply a map of official expectations. The patterns of expected behavior have an impersonal identity for they prescribe behavior for any incumbent who may fill an office. An organization complex refers to a given *configuration* or arrangement of offices or statuses which bear functional relationships to each other. It is not enough to find the prescribed behavior expected of one office; one must comprehend the appropriate relationships of the complex of offices.

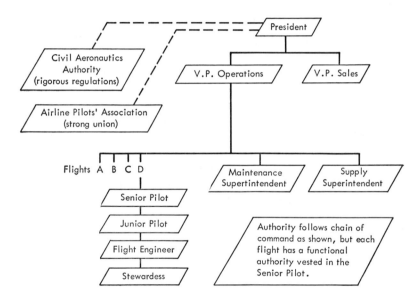

FIG. 1.4. A Partial Outline of an Airline Organization.

The first step in careful sociological analysis is to probe all the latent relationships. The skilled student will find that he may begin to make some tentative predictions about how incumbents will function from a sketchy organizational chart. Thus, Fig. 1.4 represents a partial picture of the organization of an airline. This is the only information available about the organization. An unusual feature is that functional authority is vested in the Senior Pilot. Like the surgeon in a hospital who is responsible for his operation, the pilot is held fully responsible for the airplane as regards the operation, safety of passengers and equipment, time schedule, and observance of all flight regulations. What tentative predictions can now be made? The following are suggested:

1. Operations will dominate in power and authority over sales. No matter how inconvenient disrupted schedules may be for sales, the sales division must always accommodate itself to operations. Considerable conflict may be expected, since sales will bear almost the whole burden of customer pressure which results from disruptions in operations.

2. The Senior Pilot will carry great authority in any operation of the airline which he defines as an essential responsibility for the safety of his airplane. The status of the Senior Pilot will be greater than that of the Maintenance Superintendent or the Supply Superintendent. Each superintendent will find himself in a staff (service) relationship, although the organization chart assigns them line responsibility for the maintenance and supply of the airplanes. In any contest between the pilot and the Vice-President for Operations, the pilot will exercise unusual authority. He can legitimatize his claims by draining authority from the Civil Aeronautics Authority or from the collective authority exercised by the strong pilots' union.

3. The Vice-President for Operations should ideally be a former pilot who has skills of mediation because the structure indicates that conflicts may arise between:

   a. Pilots and Maintenance (overlapping responsibility).
   b. Pilots and Supply (overlapping responsibility).
   c. V.P. for Operations and V.P. for Sales (radically different functional demands).
   d. V.P. for Operations and Civil Aeronautics Authority (observance of regulations).
   e. V.P. for Operations and Airline Pilots' Association (bargaining with strong union).

4. The President must be able to mediate these conflicts if they come to his desk. He should have qualities similar to those of the V.P. for Operations. He must be sympathetic to the pilots' point of view. He must redress the power imbalance between sales and operations.

These are tentative predictions. They were made without any more information than that given in Fig. 1.4. Of course, some predictions rest upon inductions based on analogous thinking. For example, the private doctors in a hospital have functional authority although hospital administrators have general authority for supply and maintenance. Hospital structure suggests the airline structure. Knowledge of one structure may be transferred to another. Thus a skill develops out of sociological training which enables one to combine knowledge and imagination to predict organizational behavior. The reliability and validity of such predictions are increased as more knowledge about the structure is accumulated. For this increased knowledge, the history of the organization is vital. Still richer insights may be gained by a "system view" of the organization.

B. The social system orientation

"Social system" is used here to refer to patterns of interpersonal relations found in concrete organizations. These patterns are the consequence of individual actors' playing out their social roles. Unlike the analysis on the social structure level, analysis of the social system takes into account the motivational attributes of the person who is responding to the specific other persons in concrete situations. Ideally, system analysis is used after the completion of the structural analysis.

Using the above case of the airline, we have the following material to help us in system analysis:

President. He is a new man just brought in to get the airline out of the red. He must succeed or he will be replaced by the Board. The President believes that greater efficiency in maintenance operations is necessary and has told the V.P. for Operations to tighten up.

V.P. for Operations. He is an old-timer who came up through maintenance and has been with the company for ten years, the last three years in his present position. The company has gone into the red during the time he has occupied his present position. He feels on the defensive.

V.P. for Sales. He has been with the company for five years in the position he now holds. He was brought in from the outside because of his success in sales operations in another airline company. He sees eye to eye with the President and believes a strong hand has been long overdue.

Maintenance Superintendent. He is a young aeronautical engineer with two years of experience in the company. He feels insecure because of a limited practical background and limited contact with the repair crews. The V.P. for Operations has told him to tighten up on the efficiency of his work because planes are to meet flight schedules. The only exception will be a hold for extremely hazardous weather as specified by the Civil Aeronautics Authority.

Pilot and Flight Crew. The pilot and flight crews have been stable employees of the airline and have excellent safety records. When told to take off in weather they regard as dangerous they have on numerous occasions refused to do so.

The President on hearing of these refusals of pilots to follow his order has put renewed pressure on the V.P. for Operations. The latter has talked with all of the pilots, who have told him they do not trust the quality of the maintenance work. They refuse to be responsible for the planes, charging that maintenance is slow and inefficient. The Pilots' Association has lodged a formal grievance with the President charging that safety standards are being violated. The President confers with the V.P. for Operations and suggests that he resume his earlier position as Maintenance Superintendent, which he refuses to do. The V.P. for Operations becomes increasingly hostile to the pilots and puts more and more pressure on all flight crews. As a result some pilots and crew members resign. The President holds the V.P. for Operations responsible, so the latter quits.

This example illustrates analysis of a social system in operation. Note how it supplements and amplifies the predicted tensions of the structural analysis. Concrete knowledge of the local situation is needed in system analysis. In this instance the financial position of the company explains why unusual organizational tensions have arisen. Moreover, the conflict between the Vice-President for Operations and other segments of the airline is better understood when we know about his mobility into his job and his fear of downward mobility. The heightened hostility between him and the pilots is clarified when we know that he had not had experience as a member of a pilot crew.

It is to be noted from this example that the sociological perspective is usually one step removed from the study of the idiosyncratic behavior of individuals, for it seeks to locate relations and functions of which individuals may be unaware. The fundamental principle is that the way people behave in an organization is influenced primarily by its social structure and secondarily by their personal situations.

Relations to Other Disciplines

Structural perspective in the study of industrial society is not limited to sociology. It is also found in history and economics. In the latter, John R. Commons, Thorstein Veblen, and Selig Perlman represent the "institutional school," which attempts to understand economic organizations within a broader social context. The labor economists in particular have increased our understanding of labor unions as social institutions. The works of Polanyi, Pirenne, Marx, Weber, and others analyze the forces in the historical development of modern capitalism, industrialism, and urbanism. It is difficult to classify these thinkers as belonging to any particular discipline because they studied socioeconomic phenomena in the broader context of history, which subject they approach from different directions.

Within general sociology, industrial sociology has been stimulated by the substantive and methodological contributions of related fields. Studies in social stratification and social mobility have provided insight into the social consequences of the distributive functions of the economy.[9] Urban sociologists have studied how economic changes have altered the pattern of the city and its institutions.[10] A related area has grown so rapidly that it now is a recognized field, called "industry and commu-

---

[9] Seymour Martin Lipset and Reinhard Bendix, *Social Mobility in Industrial Society,* University of California Press, 1959; W. Lloyd Warner and James C. Abegglen, *Occupational Mobility,* University of Minnesota Press, 1955.

[10] William H. Form, Joel Smith, Gregory P. Stone, and James Cowhig, "The Compatibility of Alternative Approaches to the Determination of Urban Sub-Areas," *American Sociological Review,* August, 1954, pp. 434–440; Jack P. Gibbs (ed.), *Urban Research Methods,* Van Nostrand, 1962.

nity."[11] This field attempts to study the relations of business and labor in all of the institutions of the city and their roles in local decision-making.

From the study of large-scale organization there has developed a theory of bureaucracy which is very useful in analyzing the internal organization and operation of business, labor, governmental, and other structures.[12] The sociology of occupations has furnished industrial sociology with profiles of important occupations in industry such as those of the manager, the foreman, the union officer, the professional, the auto worker, and others.[13] From studies in social movements and collective behavior industrial sociology finds material dealing with the development and spread of the labor union movement, the social processes of conflict found in strikes and related phenomena, and the emergence of new structures to handle social conflict.[14] Social psychology has contributed knowledge of interpersonal relations and social climates found within the social systems of labor, management, and government and other institutions.[15]

THE EMERGENCE OF MAJOR SOCIOLOGICAL PROBLEMS

Certain major sociological problems now dominate industrial and organizational sociology. The study of the following problems might well constitute the definition of the field:

1. The impact of industrialization on a society including its communities and work organizations. Interest in this problem

[11] William H. Form and Delbert C. Miller, *Industry, Labor, and Community*, Harper, 1960.

[12] Max Weber, *From Max Weber: Essays in Sociology*, trans. by H. H. Gerth and C. W. Mills, Oxford University Press, 1946; *The Theory of Social and Economic Organization*, trans. by A. M. Henderson and Talcott Parsons, Oxford University Press, 1947.

[13] Sigmund Nosow and William H. Form (eds.), *Man, Work, and Society*, Basic Books, 1962; Everett C. Hughes, *Men and Their Work*, Free Press, 1958.

[14] Delbert C. Miller, "The Application of Social System Analysis to a Labor-Management Conflict," *Journal of Conflict Resolution*, June, 1959, 3:146–152.

[15] Bernard M. Bass, *Leadership, Psychology, and Organizational Behavior*, Harper, 1960; Robert Tannenbaum, Irving R. Weschler, and Fred Massarik, *Leadership and Organization, A Behavioral Science Approach*, McGraw-Hill, 1961.

encompasses different stages of industrialization in societies with widely varying institutional and value structures.

2. The adaptation of formal organization with its rational definitions of responsibilities and goals to the informal organization of employees with their individual and group needs. Subproblems include:

   a. The allocation processes of power, status, and income rewards through formal and informal organizations.

   b. The accommodation of work organizations that must adapt to competitive environmental demands and employee collective bargaining associations that stress employee wants for power, status, and income.

3. The adaptive processes arising as employees seek to accommodate their personal needs and aspirations to the requirements of work positions in a given organization.

   The adjustments demanded by career or occupational mobility which characterize employees as they move in or through work organizations.

4. The organizational processes that foster morale, teamwork, and productivity.

   The functioning of leadership philosophies and practices which attempt to coordinate human activities rationally and at the same time motivate and commit employees to participate in organizational goals.

5. The governing relationships in work organizations that seek to balance formal with informal organizations in order to achieve more productive workers and more responsible citizens.

ORGANIZATION OF THIS BOOK

Part I of this book is concerned with the development of industrial society and the historical forces responsible for it. It seeks to develop a theory of how industrialism affects not only the general society but also its communities and work plants. This section also studies how trade associations, labor unions, and governmental organizations emerge to meet the problems of industrialism, and how technological change in the local plant affects the structure of the community and the broader society.

Part II analyzes the social organization of the work plant and its related management and union structures. Through the study of complex organizations we shall learn how management is organized, how its suborganizations are created, and how particular managerial positions handle recurrent problems. Special attention will be devoted to the emergence of communication systems between parts of a larger organization. Local labor union organizations will also be studied in this section. Particular attention will be devoted to their internal structure, the roles they develop, and how they articulate with local management in the resolution of grievances and other problems. The emergence of labor-management structures on both formal and informal levels will also be considered.

Three chapters are concerned with the processes allocating income, status, and power in industry. Collective bargaining is the formal master process which governs this allocation between labor and management on both local and national levels. A study of this process is concerned with the resolution of conflicts in the power structure, in which government plays an increasing regulative role.

The struggle for status or honor within and between labor and management is also studied on the national, community, and local levels. Quite often in traditional societies the prestige of various groups is commensurate with their social and economic power. This is not necessarily the case in industrial societies for various ethnic, racial, and other groups change conditions by organizing to increase their income, status, and power. We shall study these important and dynamic processes.

The income and the life chances of workers are determined not only by their abilities and economic functions but by their positions in the general society. An attempt is made to understand how local wage markets operate for various racial, ethnic, social class, and other groups in the community. Similarly an analysis will be made of how jobs are found and rewards distributed among various groups of both labor and management in the community.

Part III focuses on the individual in the world of work. The adjustment of employee to a work organization engages him in a net of cooperative and conflict relations as he seeks to satisfy his basic needs. A product of the twin forces of individual adjustment and organizational adaptation is found in the occupational mobility and career patterns in modern industry. Attention is given the changing meanings of work and leisure in Western society. An attempt is made to outline systematically by stratification levels the types of experiences which workers encounter in the socialization processes revolving around work. There is a description of the preparation for work, the early job histories, and experiences at the stable period of work life.

Part IV is concerned with the applied problems which face industry and labor unions in the work plant. It deals with the discovery and application of sociological principles in the building of morale and teamwork through individual and group methods in labor and management. There is an analysis of decision-making problems faced by the administrator as he seeks to govern the work organization.

Part V describes the relations between industry and labor in their contacts with other institutions in the local community. Industry and labor often become the two most powerful groups politically in the community. The industrialization of a community becomes not only a technological fact but also an organizational form as government, education, church, welfare, and mass communication are influenced by economic values and associations.

NOTE TO TEACHERS AND STUDENTS

A distinctive feature of this book is its attempt to make industrial society and the world of work an intimate part of the student's life. There is always the danger that "book learning" will remain an intellectual exercise and will not be made a part of the student's life. The world of work is too important and too ubiquitous for a course in industrial sociology to fail to have personal application. The ideal, of course, is to provide the class with access to a work organization as a laboratory, as part of the experience of taking a course in industrial and organizational sociology. Unfortunately this type of laboratory-teaching arrangement is not everywhere available. The use of case studies of work organizations, while undoubtedly worthwhile, is still too far removed from student life to provide a truly rich experience of fusing knowledge about and knowledge of work organization and work life. The best solution is to get the student to make a study either of a work organization which he knows something about or of one he can participate in directly or observe directly.

Many students are currently working, others have worked, and still others are seeking work experience. The authors have for a number of years made it a necessary requirement of their courses for students to make a sociological analysis of a work organization. To expedite this they have created a systematic outline which guides the student's work step by step, so that the chapters are translated into research steps which will insure the internalization of knowledge by applying it in an independent analysis. This wedding of book knowledge and firsthand research and observation is far superior to the field trip and the case study. It becomes an absorbing experience for the student to find that systematic application of social science knowledge deepens his understanding of work experience he has already had or vitalizes an experience he is now undergoing.

None should be bothered by the fact that access to a work plant may be difficult. The university cafeteria, the sorority house, the grocery store, the bank, the nearby airport, the barber shop, the union hall, the library, the city hall are all close by and available for sociological inspection.

The outline for the systematic observation of the work plant and instructions for its application are presented in Appendix A. The student is urged to make his analysis of his work plant on a schedule which parallels the reading of each chapter. Ideally a report on each chapter should be presented to the instructor every week or two so that the cumulative analysis will be over by the end of the semester.

Begin to work at once by doing the first tasks of the outline.

SELECTED BIBLIOGRAPHY

(Listing of U.S. and foreign publications)

Blau, Peter M., and W. Richard Scott, *Formal Organizations,* Chandler, 1962.

Brown, J. A. C., *The Social Psychology of Industry,* Penguin Books, Middlesex, England, 1954.

Caplow, Theodore, *The Sociology of Work*, University of Minnesota Press, 1954.

Davis, Keith, *Human Relations in Business*, McGraw-Hill, 1957.

Dubin, Robert, *The World of Work, Industrial Society and Human Relations*, Prentice-Hall, 1958.

Fogarty, Michael P., *Personality and Group Relations in Industry*, Longmans, 1956.

Form, William H., and Delbert C. Miller, *Industry, Labor, and Community*, Harper, 1960.

Friedmann, Georges, *Industrial Society: The Emergence of the Human Problems of Automation*, Free Press, 1955.

Gardner, Burleigh B., and David G. Moore, *Human Relations in Industry*, Irwin, 1955.

Gross, Edward, *Work and Society*, Crowell, 1958.

Knox, John B., *The Sociology of Industrial Relations*, Random House, 1956.

Miller, Delbert C., and William H. Form, *Industrial Sociology, An Introduction to the Sociology of Work Relations*, Harper, 1951.

Miller, Delbert C., and William H. Form, *Unternehmung, Betrieb und Umwelt*, Westdeutscher Verlag, Köln, 1957.

Moore, Wilbert E., *Industrial Relations and the Social Order*, Macmillan, 1951.

Neuloh, Otto, *Die Deutsche Betriebs verfassung*, J. C. B. Mohr, Tubingen, 1956.

Pagani, Angelo, and Antonio Carbonaro, *Sociologia Industriale*, Feltrinelli, Bologna, 1963.

Ramos, Guerreiro, *A Sociologica Industrial*, Rio de Janeiro, 1952.

Schneider, Eugene V., *Industrial Sociology, The Social Relations of Industry and the Community*, McGraw-Hill, 1957.

Scott, Jerome F., and R. P. Lynton, *The Community Factor in Modern Technology*, UNESCO, 1952.

Scott, William G., *Human Relations in Management, A Behavioral Science Approach: Philosophy, Analysis, and Issues*, Irwin, 1962.

Spaulding, Charles B., *An Introduction to Industrial Sociology*, Chandler, 1961.

Tredgold, R. F., *Human Relations in Modern Industry*, Duckworth, 1963.

Vincent, Melvin J., and Jackson Mayers, *New Foundations for Industrial Sociology*, Van Nostrand, 1959.

Whyte, William F., *Men at Work*, Irwin, 1961.

CHAPTER 2

Industrialization
and
Industrial Society

INTRODUCTION

A basic axiom of industrial sociology is that the work plant, community, and society, as social organizations, cannot be understood without reference to each other, for changes in one area facilitate changes in another. It is sometimes difficult to see how these changes operate in the contemporary scene, and for this reason a historical and comparative analysis is pursued to illuminate the entire process. It is not the purpose of this section to trace in detail the emergence of the industrial plant, community, and society. Rather, its purpose is to present a history without dates, a pattern of changes in which necessary accommodations must be made simultaneously in plant, community, and society. As Kerr and others have suggested, there is a "logic of industrialism," a predictable pattern of consequences attending industrialization which can be seen in the history of Western societies and in contemporary societies undergoing industrialization.[1] This pattern, of course, is not invariable in detail everywhere.

The characteristic features of the work plant, community, and society will be described in three historical epochs in Western society: the pre-industrial, the early industrial, and the mature industrial. A comparison between the first two eras clearly reveals the character of the technological, social, and cultural revolutions which upset the traditional society. It is more difficult to see the

[1] Clark Kerr, John T. Dunlop, Frederick H. Harbison, and Charles A. Myers, *Industrialism and Industrial Man,* Harvard, 1960, pp. 33–46.

26

current revolutions which are undermining the structure of the second era. Yet changes which have been gathering momentum since the turn of the twentieth century promise to usher in changes as great and as dramatic as those imposed on traditional societies of the late medieval period by the earlier industrialism.

For each of the three historical epochs, five different areas will be analyzed. The first deals with the structure of the economy; which includes the nature of technology, the social organization of production and other economic functions, the character of the occupational structure, and the type of labor and commodity markets. The second area of analysis is concerned with the traditional values which support the economic system and that larger society of which it is a part. The third area focuses on the social forces changing the economy and the larger society. Since social change usually does not occur without resistance and accommodations, the fourth area analyzes the responses to change, the emergent organizations, the reformulations of values which occur within the economic system, the community, and the broader society to meet the changes. Lastly, the analysis is concerned with the value contradictions and the organizational conflicts which emerge in dynamic changing situations.

SEARCH FOR A THEORY OF CHANGE

History is studied in order to learn how society changes and for the illumination it throws on the types of relationships existing among segments of the social organizations studied. Unfortunately, we have not yet arrived at a general and adequate theory of change. It is a temptation when studying industrial society to explain its evolution largely in terms of technological change or in the broader framework of economic determinism.

We go along with Moore in rejecting economic determinism as an oversimplification.[2] Clearly, economic motives are not biologically more important than other motives and are too intertwined with others to have an independent effect. Secondly, history and the comparative study of cultures reveal that non-economic elements of the society are capable of independent change. Third, industrial technology does not by itself "cause" a

[2] Wilbert E. Moore, *Economy and Society*, Doubleday, 1955, p. 34.

particular pattern of change; otherwise the same evolutionary patterns would be found wherever similar technologies are found, and this has not been the case. Last, the innovating role of the entrepreneur is usually restricted by social legislation or custom.[3]

The position here taken is that it is impossible to locate a universal single "cause" for industrial change in Western or any society. However, it appears reasonable to assume that basic to industrial development is a belief on the part of persons in functionally dominant positions in the goodness, necessity, and inevitableness of change in the form of economic "progress."[4] An accompanying belief is that the application of rational values is required to achieve economic "gain and progress." We do not need to trace how these two basic belief systems emerged in the West, but it appears that once present, they caused an unending concatenation of changes in the economic organization and in other parts of the society. Many of these consequent changes were unanticipated, and changes in ideologies and value systems were necessary to legitimate new forms of social organization. Thus we may support the conclusion expressed in the first chapter that technological, organizational, and ideological revolutions have occurred simultaneously in Western society and must be considered a unitary historical process. The pre-industrial society will be described briefly so that an understanding may be gained of the revolutionary changes which undermined it.

THE MEDIEVAL VILLAGE

During the Middle Ages, trading centers and villages slowly grew, attracting merchants, artisans, serfs, and others, many of whom sought refuge from the rigorous and sometimes oppressive life of the manors. Scholars have often idealized the stable social system of the manors, but Coulton has documented the severe economic and social conditions which stimulated revolts among the serfs. These revolts were also directed against the sometimes oppressive clergy and the monasteries.[5] Many fled and sought

[3] *Ibid.*, pp. 34–36.
[4] See Reinhard Bendix, *Work and Authority in Industry*, Wiley, 1956.
[5] G. G. Coulton, *Medieval Village, Manor and Monastery*, Harper, 1925, pp. 345–383.

refuge in the city. This escape to freedom has led some people to paint life in the city as stable and almost idyllic. Yet, as in the case of the manor, a closer study reveals that it, too, was marked by continuing dislocations and radical social changes. However, during the thirteenth to fifteenth centuries the social organization of the village did arrive at a temporary equilibrium, which will be described below. Three centuries of economic, social, and cultural changes followed, along with the Reformation, the Renaissance, and the industrial revolution, which wrecked the village social structure and ushered in industrial society.

The medieval village centered around four major institutions: church, guild, family, and market place.[6] As in previous eras, the economic system was still embedded in the other social institutions of the family, church, and guild through multiple bonds. Something approximating a folk-urban community had emerged. The guild was the main economic organization. It can be best conceived as an extended family of artisans engaged in handicraft production in the shop of the master. The guilds regulated the level of income received by all workers, and they controlled the technology of production, the quantity of production, the distribution of the products, the establishment of the price, the profit, and other economic affairs. Together they sought to regulate the entire economy. Equally important, they regulated the work relationships of the artisans through a graded system of apprentices, journeymen, and masters. These occupational levels had not only different functions but different responsibilities both toward each other and toward those in the larger community. As Durkheim so graphically describes it, the guild was at the same time a welfare, philanthropic, and religious organization which regulated both the work life and the nonwork life of its members.[7] In certain areas the guilds even assumed the primary function of governing the town.[8]

Perhaps it is not inaccurate to suggest that the objective of the guilds was to produce in the village a stable social organization similar to that which existed in the manor and monastery. The

[6] See Lewis Mumford, *The Culture of Cities,* Harcourt, Brace, 1939, pp. 13–72.

[7] Emile Durkheim, *The Division of Labor in Society,* trans. by George Simpson, Free Press, 1947, Preface to the Second Edition.

[8] Henri Pirenne, *Medieval Cities,* Doubleday, 1956, pp. 133–134.

guilds sought to bring stability, order, and responsibility within a new economic, social, and political context, and they succeeded to a remarkable degree. The social character of the medieval workman probably reflected this social organization.[9] He was deeply identified with his family, guild, church, and village, and his character structure was stable, secure, integrated, and predictable. At no period since that time has such stability been achieved in Western civilization.

Four centuries of revolutionary social changes so completely destroyed the medieval city that it left no surviving identifiable institutions. Concurrent economic, social, and cultural changes began at first slowly, and by the seventeenth and eighteenth centuries had completely altered the life and institutions of European villages and cities.[10] Although largely unrecognized today, gradual improvement occurred in technology during these centuries, especially in the cloth industry. Changes also occurred in the technology of military operations, navigation, and printing. More important, trade gradually increased until true markets appeared which could not be regulated by local and traditional mechanisms. As Polanyi clearly documents, the market phenomenon brought so many social and cultural changes with it that it eventually altered the entire society in its image.[11]

As the market emerged and destroyed the guilds, production, in England at least, moved out of the master's shop and into the home. A putting-out domestic system gradually evolved in which the merchant provided the worker with materials and later collected the finished goods and sold them to outside markets.[12] Thus, the important changes occurred in the organization of production and in the expansion of markets beyond the local community, which brought the merchant to a position of functional dominance in the economy. Gradually he seized the initiative and began to make all the important decisions such as the price of labor, the quantity of goods produced, and the price of

---

[9] Hans Gerth and C. Wright Mills, *Character and Social Structure,* Harcourt, Brace, 1953.

[10] J. Huizinga, *The Waning of the Middle Ages,* Doubleday, 1954.

[11] Karl Polanyi, *The Great Transformation,* Beacon Press, 1957, "Evolution of the Market Pattern," pp. 56–67.

[12] Wilbert E. Moore, *Industrial Relations and the Social Order,* Macmillan, 1951, pp. 17–24.

the product. Seeking to obtain more money to increase production and trade he began to organize a money market and create something resembling the contemporary corporation. In some cases he even organized production in such a way as to create a structure similar to that of the modern factory.[13] Parallel with these developments was the creation of capital pools, a money market, and a banking system.

The total impact of these seemingly small changes was basic. The guild system collapsed, unable to control forces beyond the village. Artisans were no longer able to determine their behavior or that of others, and their social world became at the same time less predictable and less secure. Their loss of social solidarity was just one indication of a society's losing its traditional cohesiveness in all other areas. The Catholic Church, so long a center of strength and stability, was being attacked within and without by new sects. The clergy was losing its special privileges to the prince, the state, and other groups. Even city and country relations began to become antagonistic, a situation which has lasted until today.

However, new structures appeared, and they attempted to handle some of the problems which transcended the local communities. Among the most important of these were nation-states, dynasties, and commercial organizations. These arose not only in response to the threat of non-Western powers, such as the Turks, but also in response to the need for social controls over wider areas of life. The idea of corporativeness embodied in the guilds was not entirely lost, for the corporation principle became the organizational model for larger social entities, such as the city, state, and nation.[14] The concern during this dynamic era was to establish control over the ever widening influences of the market and society.

As the patterns of change which developed from the thirteenth to the seventeenth century are examined, one may conclude that social forms, values, and ideologies changed much more rapidly than technology and the economy. Indeed, these nontechnological

[13] Henri Pirenne, "The Stages in the Social History of Capitalism," *American Historical Review*, April, 1914, pp. 494–515.

[14] John H. Mundy, and Peter Riesenberg, *The Medieval Town*, Van Nostrand, 1958, pp. 76–77.

changes, in institutions, values, and ideologies, made the subsequent impact of the industrial revolution, once it occurred, all the more significant. The most conspicuous changes in values occurred during the Renaissance and the Reformation. The former not only unleashed a free spirit of learning unknown in earlier centuries but accompanied an economic expansion of the Mediterranean world which permitted economic life to blossom and broaden. Not only was trade opened with the East, but its technology was also borrowed. This surge in commerce and trade stimulated learning and rationalism to a degree unknown before.

As Max Weber has so clearly shown, the religious individualism and freedom from traditional religious bonds stimulated by the Protestant Reformation made possible the development of an economic mentality in which the accumulation of economic goods was a legitimate and even sanctified end.[15] The Reformation also had the effect of breaking up the economic and spiritual dominance of the clergy and laid the groundwork for a later secular development. During this exciting era, scientific discoveries were being made which fostered new views of the physical and biological world as well as new perspectives on man's relations to nature. With rationalism, naturalism, and individualism, an irresistible anti-traditional movement began in which the characteristic belief was that change in itself was a desired value. These value alterations constituted a revolution of the mind without which industrialism and industrialization could not occur.[16] This was the groundwork which made the factory system possible.

THE INDUSTRIAL ERA

The plan of the following section is to describe the impact of the factory system on the organization of the work plant, community, and society from the middle of the eighteenth century to the close of the nineteenth century. More than anything else the factory system has been responsible for the fashioning of contem-

[15] *The Protestant Ethic and the Spirit of Capitalism,* trans. by Talcott Parsons, G. Allen, 1948.
[16] John Herman Randall, Jr., *The Making of the Modern Mind,* Houghton Mifflin, 1940, Book II.

porary Western societies. It is by its very nature dynamic, efficient, and tradition smashing. No other system of production can contend with it and survive. Certainly the remnants of the guild system and the putting-out system could not resist its attack for several obvious reasons. In particular, the putting-out system, which was dominant in early eighteenth-century England, was inherently unstable and unsuited to the market demands made upon it. The quality of work produced by rural and urban dwellers in their homes was uneven. Furthermore, it was difficult to train workers to conform to uniform standards of production, and the merchant had to spend too much time traveling to individual homes to provide materials and to collect the finished product. A system which gathered a number of workers under one roof, provided them with tools and materials, supervised and trained them, and paid cash wages was certainly a more efficient form of production.

The Factory System

Although earlier eras had developed the factory system in outward appearances, it took its characteristic form only in the latter part of the eighteenth century. Max Weber insists that the factory is limited to "organized workshops where non-human means of production are fully appropriated by an owner but workers are not; where there is internal specialization of functions and where mechanical power and machines which must be 'tended' are used."[17] This definition is so important that it must be amplified. The important thing to stress is that all of the conditions must be met simultaneously in order for the factory system to emerge, because most of the conditions occurred separately at earlier periods without the appearance of the factory system.

As indicated earlier, the rise of the factory system is impossible without the presence of a rational mentality which is applied to manufacturing.[18] By itself a rational mode of production is insufficient to create a factory system because mechanical power is also needed; otherwise production can be carried on in the home.

[17] Max Weber, *Theory of Social and Economic Organization,* trans. by A. M. Henderson and Talcott Parsons, Free Press and Falcon's Wing Press, 1947, p. 245.
[18] John Lawrence Hammond, "Factory Systems," *Encyclopedia of the Social Sciences,* Macmillan, 1930, Vol. 6, pp. 51–54.

Historically, the emergence of the factory system was accompanied by a revolution in technology and energy systems. Fred Cottrell has documented the point that steam power was a necessary characteristic of the factory system.[19] Steam freed plant location from riverside sites and water power and allowed a more concentrated and versatile application of power to a wide range of productive processes. As steam power was applied to many different machines, a continuous and conscious inventing process began which became an essential feature of the factory system. Cottrell also demonstrates that the use of high-energy machines forces an increasing amount of division of labor, for machines, at least at first, are created for a specific rather than general function. Moreover, the creation of a machine creates a specific occupation for an operator to run it, an occupation to repair it, and so on. This burgeoning of division of labor in production is in addition to increased division of labor in administration, research, sales, accounting, and other nonproduction activities.

It is difficult to overestimate the critical importance of a true market system for the functioning of the factory system. Not only does the latter need the market as a precondition for its existence, but once the factory system emerges it further stimulates the growth of the market. Ideally the market exists when money is exchangeable for goods and labor. Usually workers are paid in cash and they in turn must buy goods for subsistence in the market. Workers are also usually free to find jobs or change their jobs because the owner has no responsibility for them except to pay wages for work done. Building production and distribution facilities often requires accumulated capital, which may be borrowed in a money market. Thus we see that several types of markets operate with the factory system: a consumer market, a labor market, and a money market.[20]

Consequences for the local plant level

The factory usually contains a larger number of workers than were found in earlier types of production organizations. These workers are brought together in close physical contact because the machines they use are also close together, since they obtain their power from a restricted source of energy (e.g., the steam generat-

[19] W. Fred Cottrell, *Energy and Society,* McGraw-Hill, 1955, pp. 79–92.
[20] Weber, *op. cit.,* p. 223.

ing plant). Work at early stages of industrialization is usually heavier and dirtier than at later stages. The use of steam, the crowding of men and machines, and the still great reliance on muscle power create the characteristic factory atmosphere. As indicated above, the workers also become increasingly specialized and the impact of continuing division of labor is to move them from one job to another. These processes of bringing large numbers of workers together, specializing their labor, and forcing them to become more occupationally and geographically mobile inevitably take on increasing momentum.

As a matter of fact, a dialectical process occurs: on the one hand, forces are exerted which tend to make the worker's environment uniform; on the other hand, forces for heterogeneity manifest themselves. At lower occupational levels there is a tendency for unskilled and skilled workers to become semiskilled as their labor becomes mechanized. Semiskilled workers are exposed increasingly to similar conditions of work, similar supervision, similar work standards, and they receive similar pay. These conditions promote not only self-consciousness but common economic and political interests. Marx believed that this was the process by which class consciousness and ideologies arose among workers who bore the same relationships to production facilities.[21] His observation was grossly correct at the time he made it, but it was incomplete.

While tendencies toward uniformity exist, revolutions in technology and work organization call for more specialized skills and for more highly educated workers. As the factory system expands, more complex skills are needed, more research is needed, more coordination is needed, and more financial controls become necessary. To be sure, the overall trend is for new skills to arise and later become routinized under the ubiquitous pressures of rationalization. Probably the more mature the stage of industrialization, the greater the tendency for the factory environment to become more heterogeneous. The increasing problem of directing and controlling diversified structures fosters the growth of bureaucratic organization, which is an invariable accompaniment of the dynamic factory system.

[21] See Reinhard Bendix and Seymour Martin Lipset, "Karl Marx's Theory of Social Classes," in Bendix and Lipset (eds.), *Class, Status and Power,* Free Press, 1953, pp. 26–35.

Human consequences

It is apparent that the emergence of large-scale, internally differentiated bureaucratic structures tends to reduce feelings of plant-wide solidarity. Workers and managers with different occupations, educational backgrounds, incomes, and interests find it difficult to arrive at a consensus on any point. Durkheim very clearly foresaw that continued division of labor without the conscious creation of integrating structures would result in a state of normlessness which he called "anomie."[22] The absence or multiplicity of norms makes it difficult for workers to identify with the plant, the product, the manager, the owner, the customers, and others. In short, they lose a sense of plant community.

At the same time those workers with common interests in every part of the plant become aware of their mutual problems, which they feel are different from those of other workers. For them the plant becomes a place for their specific groups to bargain with management for wages or other privileges. The manipulative character of management is assimilated by the self-conscious groups as they begin to bargain, at first informally, for whatever advantages they may secure. This process later becomes formalized in labor union organization and it first occurs where rationalization has proceeded fastest, among the manual workers.[23]

The Manufacturing City

The city described in this section is the manufacturing city which existed in the United States and western Europe between 1800 and 1880, and cities in a similar stage of industrial development elsewhere. Factories in these cities specialized in the production of particular commodities, such as furniture, cloth, stoves, or steel, and this specialization gave the cities a characteristic appearance.[24] The factories were generally located close together and near the center of the city and the commercial area. Workers

[22] Durkheim, *op. cit.*

[23] See W. Lloyd Warner and J. O. Low, *The Social System of the Modern Factory*, Yale, 1947; Elliot Dunlap Smith and Richard Carter Nyman, *Technology and Labor*, Yale, 1959.

[24] See Ralph E. Turner, "The Industrial City; Center of Cultural Change," in Carolyn F. Ware (ed.), *The Cultural Approach to History*, Columbia, 1940, pp. 228–242.

typically lived close to the factories and walked to work or used mass transportation to get to work.[25] A consequence of this pattern of industrial concentration was that urban areas were distinctly separated from rural areas. Most of the city workers were recent migrants from the farm and lived in the transplanted rural neighborhoods, which retained some features of the rural society; they raised vegetable gardens and chickens, purchased from peddlers, etc. Slowly the folk-urban character of these neighborhoods disappeared as the people became socialized to the urban way of life.

As Mumford has pointed out, the early manufacturing city represented an ecological jumble with little or no land-use planning. The best land was appropriated by the industries, which pumped wastes into the river and poured soot onto the surrounding areas.[26] Housing was generally poor, and large numbers of people were crowded into tenement-like apartments. Health standards were low, communicable disease rates high. Reforms were necessary if only to prevent the collapse of the system.

The early industrial cities of the West typically had a rather rigid but simple stratification system, with the manufacturers and merchants having the greatest amount of income, status, and power. The few white-collar workers and professionals occupied a position below the merchants. Next came the skilled workers, who had an envied lot among the other manual workers. The bulk of the latter were semiskilled and unskilled laborers who sought to improve their economic and social status. Thus the class structure was rather highly crystallized, and the urban masses, the so-called proletariat, had at this stage a relatively high degree of class consciousness not found in earlier or later periods. This was the class situation which Marx and others described in the mid-nineteenth century and which spawned ideologically oriented class movements.[27] Usually the captains of industry and the merchants occupied the elected governmental offices and controlled the political and institutional life of the city directly or through

[25] Harlan W. Gilmore, *Transportation and the Growth of Cities,* Free Press, 1953, pp. 108–112.

[26] Mumford, *op. cit.,* Chap. 3, "The Insensate Industrial Town," pp. 143–222.

[27] Karl Marx and Friedrich Engels, "The Communist Manifesto," in V. F. Calverton (ed.), *The Making of Society,* Modern Library, 1937, pp. 339–375.

their representatives.[28] As will be demonstrated later, the position which these people take in government reflects the degree of urban industrial development.

The social problems confronting the manufacturing city were understandably numerous because a new type of urban social structure and a new type of urban personality structure were in process of formation. Crime, delinquency, and scandals in government were commonplace. Professionals, intellectuals, philanthropists, and social workers attempted to overcome the social pathology of the city through a series of drives, investigations, and reform movements. In general these were unsuccessful because what was needed was not honesty and compassion but new types of organizations suited to the urban milieu.[29] Slowly the almost overwhelming problems caused by unplanned industrialization and urbanization stimulated a large number of organizations to meet specific crises in health, crime, welfare, recreation, government, and education. These organizations were both governmental and private. Most spectacular and most important was the rise of mass education to train youth for jobs in industry and to impart to them an urban way of life which the family was unable to do.

Despite the disorganized aspects of the industrial city it developed a distinctive character of its own which probably was a response to its particular economic base. Despite its normlessness and almost anomic character the population tended to develop a pride in its city, and a rather high degree of identification with it.[30] It is difficult to account for the appearance of this urban loyalty. Perhaps it represented the survival of a pattern of locality identification which residents had had in their communities of birth, but more probably it was a genuine response to living in the most important type of locality then in existence. As will be shown below, community distinctiveness tends to diminish in more advance stages of industrialization.

---

[28] Robert O. Schulze, "Economic Dominants in Community Power Structure," *American Sociological Review*, February, 1958, pp. 3–9.

[29] See *The Autobiography of Lincoln Steffens*, Harcourt, Brace, 1931.

[30] Bert F. Hoselitz, "The City, the Factory and Economic Growth," *American Economic Review*, May, 1955, pp. 166–184.

Industrial Society

The city was the basic structural unit of the society during the period when manufacturing employed a majority of the urban labor force. To be sure, national markets had already developed and national organizations had been fashioned. As might be expected, the latter appeared first in the economic realm and then spread to cover the total range of other institutions. Thus business and labor organizations were formed on a national basis, and soon educational, recreational, professional, welfare, and other organizations followed suit. There were many signs that individual cities could not handle their internal problems by themselves, and that the national government had to take a more important role, especially in the area of social welfare. However, the industrial city dominated the life of the nation and of national associations until the turn of the century. Contemporary Americans find it hard to realize that the portrait of the city described above has already passed from the scene.

THE MATURE INDUSTRIAL ERA

How does the organization of plant, community, and society change as a more mature industrial base develops? The mature industrial economy may be arbitrarily defined as one in which a third or less of the labor force is engaged in agriculture and over half of the urban labor force is engaged in nonmanufacturing pursuits. When manufacturing employs a minority of the labor force to supply a majority with all of its material needs it must be extremely efficient and well developed. In mature industrial economies the majority of the urban population have typically been born in the cities and have learned to live in them. Indeed, the urban way of life and tradition have evolved to such an extent that we may speak of an urban-industrial society.[31] Some scholars prefer to call this type of society a mass society because institutions have been developed which transcend localities. They claim that the distinction between the city and the society becomes less

[31] Louis Wirth, "Urbanism as a Way of Life," *American Journal of Sociology*, July, 1938, pp. 1–24.

clear as industrialism forces a more and more uniform pattern of development throughout the entire society.

The Work Plant Level

Whereas in the earlier industrial era the image of the work plant we described was the factory, in the mature industrial era both manufacturing and nonmanufacturing work plants must be described. However, the distinction between the two is not as important as it first appears because they both develop similar structures. Plants in the mature industrial society are larger, cleaner, and more spread out. They are located in almost any part of the city—in the core, along highways, in the suburbs, and even in the open country. The primary reason why locations are more dispersed than in the earlier industrial era is that the different forms of energy converters used (from oil, gas, and electricity) can transport energy more efficiently than steam over greater distances. These fuels are also cleaner, with the result that the factories are cleaner and workers dress in street clothes, giving the plant an office appearance. The workers are not crowded close together in multi-story factories because the single-story building is generally a more efficient layout. The increased space occupied by machines tends to disperse workers more. Factories are less noisy and dirty, and the muscle required to operate modern machines is less than that required with the earlier semiautomatic machines. Thus plants in the same industry tend to look more alike, plants in different industries look increasingly similar, and schools tend to look more like plants and vice versa.

The markets which develop in the mature industrial economy are larger in scope, covering the nation and even large areas abroad. With the development of mass markets, private ownership becomes increasingly nonlocal, or absentee in character. A managerial elite therefore develops which seems to grow in number and importance with time. This latter trend holds for economies which are based on either private or public ownership.[32] The relative amount of space dedicated to office work increases in the mature economy as a greater proportion of workers fall in the white-collar categories and as more machines are used to help process the paper work just as machines are used to process mate-

[32] Kerr *et al., op. cit.,* and Bendix, *op. cit.*

rial goods in the factory. Larger laboratories also appear and these begin to look more like factories. As more women find employment in the factories, more men find employment in the offices. And, as offices demand a greater proportion of the labor force, a new class of worker appears which has many of the characteristics of the factory worker. Mills has dubbed the former the "salariat."[33] In conclusion, it has been observed that in the mature industrial economy offices look more like factories and factories begin to look more like offices.

One might expect the number of employees in particular establishments to increase indefinitely in the mature economy but this is not the case because industrial decentralization begins to set in. It is no longer necessary to have all the manufacturing operations concentrated in one place or in one community. As a matter of fact, the assembly of parts which are manufactured in many plants in many different communities becomes increasingly a pattern. Also, as markets expand, manufacturing and assembly operations are decentralized whenever a sufficiently large market develops in any geographic sector of the economy.

One of the myths concerning the mature economy is that mass markets enforce a growing uniformity on the number and quality of goods produced. Just the opposite is the case because technology becomes so versatile that the quality, quantity, and variety of goods manufactured are greater than ever before. Indeed, one of the things that the mass markets make possible is the creation of markets for specialized goods which did not appear at earlier periods.

Bureaucratization

One of the most striking features of the industrial era is the bureaucratization and formalization of almost every aspect of work plant organization. Elaborate wage and salary scales are designed, so as to diminish individual bargaining between workers and managers.[34] The personnel functions of owners and managers are transferred to personnel offices, which routinize and standard-

---

[33] C. Wright Mills, *White Collar*, Oxford University Press, 1951, chap. 9, "The Enormous File," pp. 189–214.

[34] See, for example, Jack Stieber, *Steel Industry Wage Structure*, Harvard, 1959.

ize hiring, promotion, transfer of workers, and other functions. Large offices are also developed to handle research, sales accounting, public relations, industrial relations, consumer relations, and so on. Internally, grievance and collective bargaining procedures with unions become increasingly institutionalized. And, as the work plant becomes more complex in its internal organization, labor unions develop similar complex and parallel structures. Bureaucratization and institutionalization tendencies are found in all types of industries and in all types of societies irrespective of the property systems which exist.

The social-psychological consequences of this kind of work organization on the character structure of employees may be deduced from theory. In general, employees lose a sense of personal identification with the product, the company, and even the union. Increasingly they place their fate in the hands of specialists and experts both in union and in management. Bureaucracies tend to make people more and more aware of their position in reference to others and promote a manipulative mentality. The tendency, therefore, is for employees to develop a low and temporary identification with as many segments of organization and separate organizations as might affect their destinies.[35] Their fate, indeed, is in the hands of an impersonal corporation and an impersonal union, which between them determine their careers. Drucker has suggested that this is the case in all types of employee societies,[36] and Nelson Foote has shown how it operates for union members.[37] In conclusion, we may say that the work plant in the mature industrial economy grows in size, extent, and internal complexity while exerting increasing controls over all employees in the process of directed social change.

The Metropolitan Complex

Changes parallel to those cited for the work plant occur on the community level. As we might expect, the ecology of the metropolis in the mature industrial era is not as dense as in the earlier

[35] See William H. Whyte, Jr., *The Organization Man*, Simon and Schuster, 1956.

[36] Peter F. Drucker, "The Employee Society," *American Journal of Sociology*, January, 1953, pp. 358–363.

[37] Nelson Foote, "The Professionalization of Unionism in Detroit," *American Journal of Sociology*, January, 1953, pp. 371–380.

industrial community. As a matter of fact, the spread of the urban industrial system creates vast urban regions which contain a series of central cities, satellite cities, suburbs, industrial developments, real estate developments and other types of localities. The development of the metropolis becomes so widespread that the entire society may be thought of as falling within the influence of identifiable metropolitan regions.[38] Understandably, the distinction between rural and urban communities, both physically and socially, diminishes as continuous urban regions or urban belts develop.[39] In some Western societies, as in Germany, England, and the United States, cities run into one another over stretches of hundreds of miles. Since work plants are found in the central city, the periphery, the suburbs, and even beyond, the commuting range of workers of all occupational levels tends to increase.[40]

Cities in the mature industrial era become less distinctive physically and socially for one important reason. They become less identified with a single manufactured product. As they grow in size they tend to diversify their manufacturing because their larger hinterland populations can support a wider variety of manufacturing. Further, there is a tendency for an increasingly heterogeneous population to demand greater variety of goods and services. Cities also tend to become cleaner and healthier places to live, primarily because the industries themselves are cleaner. Moreover, public health agencies strive to improve the health habits of the population and discipline industries to be concerned with their health problems. Municipal and larger branches of government also assume zoning and planning functions and so act to make the city more orderly. Not least in importance is the tendency for urban dwellers to learn to live in the city and make the necessary health adjustments for their survival.

[38] R. D. McKenzie, "The Rise of Metropolitan Communities," in President's Research Committee on Social Trends, *Recent Social Trends,* McGraw-Hill, 1933, pp. 443–496.

[39] Walter Firey, Charles P. Loomis, and J. Allan Beegle, "The Fusion of Urban and Rural," in Wheaton J. Lane (ed.), *Highways in Our National Life,* Princeton, 1951, pp. 154–164.

[40] Leo F. Schnore, "The Separation of Home and Work, a Problem for Human Ecology," *Social Forces,* May, 1954, pp. 336–343.

Stratification Systems

The stratification system of the metropolis becomes more complex and less clear than in the smaller manufacturing cities of the past. Since economic, prestige, and power positions no longer vary together, stratification anomalies result. Shifting industrial and occupational structures create socially and geographically mobile populations which may develop wealth incommensurate with their past status and grant power advantages to groups previously denied them.[41] The manipulation of the community power structures by owners and managers of industry is less evident in the larger metropolis because they participate less directly in the governmental process. Rarely do the captains of industry and labor union leaders occupy offices in city government. The latter increasingly is run by a body of professional civil servants and experts, who develop a bureaucracy not unlike that within industry.

It would be naïve to suggest that managers of industry and labor have no interest or no power in local government. To be sure, issues arise in which they have great interest, and they exert their power, which is very substantial. However, decisions on the state and national levels become more important than local decisions. Irrespective of the level of governmental concerns, the coalition which develops among interest groups is not frozen but tends to realign itself as issues change.[42] Moreover, there is a tendency for localities to develop large bureaucratic systems in education, welfare, communication, recreation, and other areas and to reduce issues in this routinization process. Changes in the operation of the organizations of these institutions are primarily instigated through the development of special interest associations. Understandably, the city spawns associations in a never ending process of fission and fusion.[43]

[41] See Gregory P. Stone and William H. Form, "Instabilities in Status: The Problem of Hierarchy in the Community Study of Status Arrangements," *American Sociological Review*, April, 1953, pp. 149–162; Gerhard Lenski, "Status Crystallization: a Non-Vertical Dimension of Social Status," *American Sociological Review*, August, 1954, pp. 405–513.

[42] Robert A. Dahl, "Business and Politics: A Critical Appraisal of Political Science," *American Political Science Review*, March, 1959, pp. 1–34; Morris Janowitz (ed.), *Community Political Systems*, Free Press, 1961.

[43] Herbert Goldhamer, "Voluntary Associations in the United States," *Third Year Course in the Study of Contemporary Society*, Vol. 1, 10th ed., September, 1942.

The social-psychological consequences of this type of urban structure on the character development of the urban dweller are parallel to those found in the work plant. He tends to experience a loss of community identity which parallels the diminution of community distinctiveness. At the same time he builds allegiances to larger social units and to more special units. To be sure, while some community identification survives,[44] the urban dweller finds it increasingly easy to move from one city to another and adjust to its social patterns.

Mass Society

The mass society emerges as the most important link between the work plant and individual communities. The network of communications is now so efficient that economic and social changes may be rapidly introduced and spread throughout the entire society. The mature industrial society also speeds the growth of national interest groups and associations which parallel product markets, money markets, occupational, and other markets. Thus education, welfare, and government develop national policies and agencies parallel to those built by national economic associations and interest groups.

Such a society has an increasing need for coordination and articulation of its separate parts. To a large extent government is able to facilitate a great many of the coordinating and regulative functions. This is more or less the case irrespective of the type of property system which exists. Thus, governments enact complex legal systems to regulate trade, supervise and contain the collective bargaining process, and assume responsibility for problems which the economic system produces, such as mass unemployment.

The dynamics of politics on the societal level are even greater than those on the local community level. The "politics of strange bedfellows" emerges as different groups temporarily join forces over temporary common interests against foes which also represent temporary alliances. According to Bell and Riesman, it is no longer correct to assume that permanent ideological conflict exists among opposing interest groups to form national economic and

---

[44] R. Richard Wohl and Anselm L. Strauss, "Symbolic Representation in the Urban Milieu," *American Journal of Sociology*, March, 1958, pp. 523–532; Anselm Strauss, *Urban Panorama*, University of California Press, 1961.

social policies.[45] Although this may be the trend for issues which specifically affect the welfare of specific groups, Mills and Hunter insist that there is considerable cooperation among interest groups and that they influence national policies more than appears to be the case at first blush. Hunter documented this tendency for a particular industry while Mills proposed that American economic elites are forming a permanent alliance with governmental and military leaders to control national policies.[46] The authors are inclined to support the positions of Hunter and Mills. To be sure, the policies of mass society are so complex that it is extremely difficult for any group or combination of groups to manipulate all parties engaged in the contest for power. Consequently the pluralistic society tends to develop a "mushy" social structure in which the many competing groups fail to arrive at consensus on national purposes. This condition permits extreme social and political movements to emerge, especially during periods of economic insecurity. Persistence of insecurity stimulates the development of totalitarian structures, which vigorously combat the rise of new political and economic movements.[47]

It is unnecessary to amplify the type of character structure which is stimulated to appear in this type of society. The market personality, the organization man, the other-directed character develops as society loses its internal cohesion.

CONCLUSIONS

This chapter sought to describe the patterns of relationships which exist between work plant, community, and society in three historical eras in western Europe and the United States. It was not directly concerned with tracing historical changes as such but with emphasizing the consequences which rational thoughtways and dynamic technology have for societies at different developmental stages. Although the details of the patterns described vary from one society to another, the basic pattern seems to be everywhere the same.

[45] David Riesman *et al., The Lonely Crowd,* Yale, 1951, pp. 242–255; Daniel Bell, *The End of Ideology,* Free Press, 1960, pp. 43–67.

[46] Floyd Hunter, *Top Leadership, U.S.A.,* University of North Carolina Press, 1959, pp. 160–191; C. Wright Mills, *The Power Elite,* Oxford University Press, 1956, pp. 269–297.

[47] William Kornhauser, *The Politics of Mass Society,* Free Press, 1959.

One concern which contemporary Western societies have today is whether technologically underdeveloped societies will experience the same changes and problems which Western societies went through in their own histories. Apparently the answer is in the negative because it is now possible for advanced societies to export much of their technology and social organization almost full-blown to other parts of the world which have receptive social structures. Recipient societies can learn much by borrowing, rather than experiencing directly all of the evolutionary steps of the Western societies. Although industrialization, urbanism, and bureaucratization may be hastened in technologically underdeveloped societies, the problems experienced by the West cannot be evaded altogether. Indeed, the problems which the new societies experience may be explosive because the "natural" accommodations evident in the slower evolutionary situation may not be permitted to develop. Undoubtedly the government of new nations will be much more directly and greatly involved in social change than was the case even in the most extreme instances in Western society.[48]

Yet clearly even the most technologically advanced societies will not escape the persistent difficulties brought on by changing technology and the insistent applications of rational thought. An advanced social science is needed to help the advanced society solve its problems because social science knowledge is not automatically applied.

SELECTED BIBLIOGRAPHY

Bendix, Reinhard, *Work and Authority in Industry,* Wiley, 1956.
Cottrell, W. Fred, *Energy and Society,* McGraw-Hill, 1955.
Gerth, H. H., and C. W. Mills, *Character and Social Structure,* Harcourt, Brace, 1953.
Hoselitz, Bert F., *Sociological Aspects of Economic Growth,* Free Press, 1960.
Kerr, Clark, J. T. Dunlop, F. H. Harbison, and C. A. Myers, *Industrialism and Industrial Man,* Harvard, 1960.
Moore, Wilbert E., *Industrial Relations and the Social Order,* Macmillan, 1951.

[48] Hoselitz, *op. cit.;* Kerr *et al., op. cit.;* Lyle W. Shannon, *Underdeveloped Areas: A Book of Readings and Research,* Harper, 1957, pp. 273 ff.

Mumford, Lewis, *The Culture of Cities,* Harcourt, Brace, 1938.
Pirenne, Henri, *Medieval Cities,* Princeton, 1925.
Polanyi, Karl, *The Great Transformation,* Holt, 1944.
Riesman, David, *et al., The Lonely Crowd,* Yale, 1951.
Sjoberg, Gideon, *The Pre-Industrial City,* Free Press, 1961.
Weber, Max, *Theory of Social and Economic Organization,* trans. by Talcott Parsons, Free Press and Falcon's Wing Press, 1947.

CHAPTER 3

The Forging
of Industrial
and Occupational Structures

We have just examined how industrialization alters the social organization of the work plant, the community, and the broader society. We shall now endeavor to demonstrate how industrialization and accompanying technological changes shape the industrial and occupational composition of the working population. There is enough evidence available to show that uniformities in such composition emerge in societies as they move from one stage of industrialization to another. The best concise information concerning the stage of industrialization may be obtained by analyzing labor force data found in the census reports. Unfortunately these data have not been sufficiently exploited by sociologists.[1] The data provide an abbreviated picture of the state of industrial development of a nation, the probable level of living, the amount of geographic mobility, the degree of productivity, the rate of economic development, and many other conditions. Moreover, other phenomena such as family composition, social mobility, social stratification, social solidarity, and organizational growth vary with the changing composition of the labor force. The reliability of these correlations will be increased as data from many societies are gathered and compared. There is considerable guesswork in the present state of knowledge.[2]

The data analyzed below refer primarily to the United States

[1] See Philip M. Hauser, "The Labor Force as a Field of Interest for the Sociologist," *American Sociological Review*, August, 1951, pp. 530–538.

[2] Wilbert E. Moore, "The Exportability of the 'Labor Force' Concept," *American Sociological Review*, February, 1953, pp. 68–72.

because fair information is available. However, an attempt is made to generalize the findings to nations in various states of industrialization. The historical data on changes in the American labor force should be thought of as illustrating changes accompanying industrialization generally and not as unique phenomena.

INDUSTRIAL TRENDS

It is difficult to obtain reliable historical statistics on industrial trends in the United States and elsewhere because the agencies collecting these data change classification systems continuously, so that data over the years are not comparable. Even if this were not the case, special care would be needed to interpret data because the categories used in different historical periods have different significance. Thus, Froomkin and Jaffe have shown in comparing the occupational structures of the United States and the Soviet Union in two different periods that a worker who operates a simple machine at an early stage of industrialization tends to be classified as a skilled worker, while he (or his operation) is classified as semiskilled in a more mature industrial economy.[3] The meaning of an industry classification changes with time. For example, manufacturing in a highly automated factory of today is quite different from manufacturing in the plants of a century ago. Despite these difficulties, gross statistics are useful to portray a picture of changing industrial structures.

Figure 3.1 portrays the changes in industrial composition in the United States for almost a century. For purposes of simplicity, the industries may be combined into productive and supportive categories. Agriculture, manufacturing, mining, forestry, fishing, and construction may be put into the productive category and the rest in service. The most dramatic change has been the decrease in the proportion of the labor force engaged in production from over three-quarters in 1870 to less than half in 1960. Most of the drop was due to the shrinking percentage of workers in agriculture. This shrinkage accompanies industrialization everywhere because agriculture is the main area from which workers can be recruited.

[3] Joseph Froomkin and A. J. Jaffe, "Occupational Skill and Socioeconomic Structure," *American Journal of Sociology*, July, 1953, pp. 42–48.

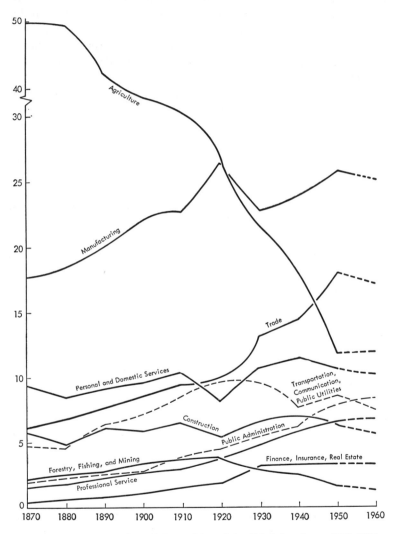

FIG. 3.1. Changes in Industrial Composition of the U.S. Labor Force, 1870–1960.

Thus, whereas in 1870 over a half of the labor force was engaged in agricultural pursuits, in 1960 only about one-tenth was so occupied. Since workers can be recruited from agriculture only if agricultural production is efficient enough to feed them without having their labor, it is apparent that mechanization of agriculture must simultaneously accompany the mechanization of manufacturing.

In general, manufacturing absorbs only a part of the labor force released from agriculture. American manufacturing in 1870 employed slightly less than one-fifth of the gainful workers, claimed one-quarter in 1920, and has fluctuated around that proportion ever since. The other production industries combined have always employed less than one-tenth of the total labor force. Obviously the greatest increases attending industrialization are found in the "supportive industries" of trade, transportation, the services, and public administration. The next chapter will analyze in detail the relationship between manufacturing and service employment found in various type cities.

The question may arise why a larger proportion of the labor force is not employed in manufacturing with the advent of large-scale manufacturing. The increasing proportion of workers in the supportive industries is needed not only to keep manufacturing going but to supply urban dwellers the special services which they can no longer supply for themselves. As large cities are built around manufacturing centers more people are needed in government, education, trade, finance, and so on. Table 3.1 shows that in France, the United States, Great Britain, Japan, and India, more workers are employed in trade and the services than in manufacturing. Even in Yugoslavia, where agriculture commands more than three-fourths the labor force, the proportion in service industries is close to that in industrial production. It is important to stress that this trend occurs in all types of economies: capitalist, socialistic, and mixed.[4]

Industrial trends have many social consequences. One of the most important is an increase of the population living in cities. The rising rate of urbanization in the United States is portrayed

[4] See Seymour Martin Lipset and Reinhard Bendix, *Social Mobility in Industrial Society,* University of California Press, 1959, pp. 11–75.

TABLE 3.1. Labor Force Distribution in Selected Countries by Broad Industrial Divisions and Metropolitan Populations

Countries and Dates	Agriculture, Forestry, Etc.	Industrial Production	Commerce, Services, Etc.	Population in Cities over 100,000
Great Britain (1931)	6.0%	46.1%	47.9%	45.2%
U.S.A. (1940)	18.5	31.8	49.7	28.8
France (1946)	36.5	29.8	33.7	16.3
Japan (1947)	52.5	23.3	24.2	—
India (1931)	67.1	10.5	22.4	4.1
Yugoslavia (1931)	78.7	11.1	10.2	6.3

SOURCE: W. S. Woytinsky and E. S. Woytinsky, *World Population and Production,* Twentieth Century Fund, 1953, pp. 425 and 117.

in Fig. 3.2. While only about 5 percent of the population lived in urban areas in 1790, almost 70 percent did so in 1960. The non-farm people living in rural areas greatly exceeded the farmers in 1960. As indicated in Chapter 2, nonfarm areas tend to be in the hinterland of a metropolis and are dominated by the urban economy. Increasingly, rural dwellers and even full-time farmers find urban employment in the city.[5] One-fifth of rural farm males reported holding more than one job in 1955, and almost seven-tenths of these were employed in nonagricultural industries.

Industrialism and urbanism are accompanied by growth in the size of plant, in terms of number of employees hired. In 1955 manufacturing plants hiring over 1000 employees constituted less than 1 percent of all plants; yet they hired about one-third of all employed in manufacturing.[6] This trend toward large-scale bureaucracies is also present in nonmanufacturing industries, such as communication, utilities, government, education, trade, and other services. Giant corporations arise which employ as many as half a million workers, and giant unions are formed in these in-dustries. The trend toward large-scale work organizations is found in all types of economies with different types of property

[5] J. Allan Beegle, "Some Aspects of the Social Significance of Recent Changes in the Farm Labor Force," Conference on Labor Mobility, 1961; *Current Population Reports,* "Job Mobility of Workers in 1955," Series P-50, No. 70, February, 1957.

[6] *Statistical Abstract of the United States,* 1959, p. 794.

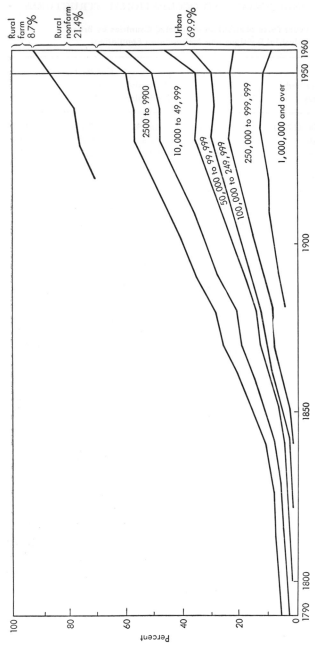

Rural farm 8.7%

Rural nonfarm 21.4%

Urban 69.9%

2500 to 9900

10,000 to 49,999

50,000 to 99,999

100,000 to 249,999

250,000 to 999,999

1,000,000 and over

Percent

FIG. 3.2. Population of the United States by Size of Place of Habitation, 1790–1950. (After Donald J. Bogue, "Urbanism in the United States, 1950," *American Journal of Sociology*, March, 1955, 472.)

systems. Indeed, it is probably facilitated by political centralization in noncapitalistic economies in process of rapid and conscious industrialization.

ACTIVITY GROUPS

Industrialization has an impact not only on the labor force but on the activities of the entire population. It changes the activities of men, women, and children of all ages. In the pre-industrial economy all family members are directly engaged in food production or supporting functions. Activities are differentiated primarily in terms of sex and age roles. Table 3.2 shows how the activities of different parts of the American population have changed since 1870. Children under five years usually have few prescribed activities. During urbanization and industrialization their proportion in the population tends to decline owing to the lower birth rate and the survival of larger proportions of people to maturity. A second trend typically found during industrialization is a rapid drop in the proportion of children between five and fifteen years not attending school. In the United States this group declined from one-tenth of the population in 1870 to a negligible part today. Understandably this trend is accompanied by a general increase in the proportion of persons attending school. It is not as large as might be anticipated, primarily because the increasing age of the population reduces the proportion of those below twenty years of age. However the growth in school population is significant, and it results mainly from the need of industrial societies to have a literate, trained, and disciplined labor force.

Table 3.2 shows that housewives not gainfully employed have formed an almost constant part of the total population. This fact needs interpretation because there is a tendency for married and single women to participate increasingly in the labor force with industrialization. The situation in Table 3.2 is explained by an increase in the older age groups and an accompanying tendency for a larger proportion of people to be married, so that the proportion of married women not working remains relatively constant.

Table 3.2 also reveals that the proportion of persons gainfully

TABLE 3.2. Primary Activities of the Total Population of the United States: 1870–1960
(Percentages)

Activity Group	1870	1880	1890	1900	1910	1920	1930	1940	1950	1960
Children under 5 years	14.3	13.8	12.4	12.1	11.5	10.9	9.3	8.0	10.7	11.3
Children 5 to 15 years not at school or gainfully occupied	10.7	6.8	6.8	6.7	3.8	3.7	2.9	1.7[a]	2.9	2.6
Persons attending school	16.6	19.8	18.6	17.7	19.6	20.6	22.7	20.3	19.2	25.7
Housewives not gainfully employed	21.3	21.9	21.7	21.6	21.2	21.5	21.3	22.0	21.4	19.2
Persons gainfully employed	32.4	34.7	37.2	38.3	40.6	39.6	39.8	40.1	39.9	38.1
Adults in institutions	.3	.4	.4	.5	.5	.6	.6	.9	.9[a]	1.1
Not accounted for	4.4	2.6	2.9	3.1	2.8	3.1	3.4	7.0[b]	5.0[b]	2.0[c]
Totals	100.0	100.0	100.0	100.0	100.0	100.0	100.0	100.0	100.0	100.0

[a] Estimated.

[b] Includes those unable to work. In earlier censuses these were partially included in the labor force.

[c] Includes 1.4 percent in the armed forces.

employed increased moderately over the years from about one-third in 1870 to about two-fifths today. One of the most striking characteristics of an industrial society is this growth in the labor force. As already suggested, it is due to declining infant mortality rates, an increase in the age of the surviving population, the tendency of more married and single women to work, and a declining death rate. When more and more people enter the labor force at a time when mechanization is decreasing labor needs, the economy may be hard pressed to provide sufficient jobs.

AGE AND SEX COMPOSITION
OF THE LABOR FORCE

Educational requirements, changing birth and death rates, and other factors should affect the age and sex structure of the labor force. Such changes over the past half-century are shown in Table 3.3. Almost two-thirds of the gainfully employed workers today fall in the age range of 16 to 44 years and the remaining third are 45 years or older. During the past sixty years those under 15 have declined to the vanishing point. The group aged 16 through 44 years, on the other hand, has remained fairly constant, although it has shown a recent tendency to decline. The age range from 45 to 64 has shown a slow and steady increase for both sexes, but more for the female than the male. This reflects the fact that women are more and more remaining in the labor force.

Older Workers

Table 3.2 does not reveal the growing proportion of aged persons who retire from the labor market. This universal trend is stimulated by expanding governmental social security provisions. Since World War II American industry has shown an increasing reluctance to hire older people. In the future it must do so or face the problem of supporting a growing proportion of non-producers. Social science evidence shows that withdrawal of the aged from the labor force has many negative psychological and social consequences.[7] The problem of the aged is not simply eco-

[7] See, for example, Harold J. Sheppard, Louis Ferman, and Seymour Faber, "Too Old to Work—Too Young to Retire," Special Committee on Unemployment Problems, U.S. Senate, December 21, 1959, GPO, 1960, pp. 49–53.

TABLE 3.3. Percent Distribution of Gainful Workers by Age and Sex for the United States: 1900–1960[a]

Age Ranges	1900	1910	1920	1930	1940[b]	1950[c]	1960[d]
			Male				
10–15	5.3	4.0	3.1	1.2	.5	.7	2.6
16–44	68.4	69.6	66.9	66.0	65.2	61.8	59.9
45–64	21.5	22.0	25.3	27.6	29.6	31.8	32.8
65 and over	4.5	4.2	4.5	5.1	4.6	5.6	4.7
Unknown	0.3	0.2	0.2	0.1	—	—	—
Totals	100.0	100.0	100.0	100.0	99.9	99.9	100.0
			Female				
10–15	9.1	5.8	4.2	1.9	.4	.6	4.2
16–44	74.9	78.1	77.6	77.7	77.9	69.4	56.9
45–64	13.1	13.6	15.7	17.8	19.6	27.0	35.0
65 and over	2.6	2.3	2.3	2.5	2.1	3.0	3.8
Unknown	0.3	0.2	0.2	0.1	—	—	—
Totals	100.0	100.0	100.0	100.0	100.0	100.0	100.0
		Total, Male and Female					
10–15	6.0	4.3	3.3	1.4	.5	.7	3.2
16–44	69.6	71.2	69.1	68.6	68.2	64.0	58.9
45–64	20.0	20.4	23.4	25.4	27.2	30.5	33.5
65 and over	4.1	3.9	4.0	4.5	4.0	4.9	4.4
Unknown	0.3	0.2	0.2	0.1	—	—	—
Totals	100.0	100.0	100.0	100.0	99.9	100.1	100.0

[a] Adapted from *Sixteenth Census of the United States. Comparative Occupation Statistics for the United States, 1870 to 1940*, GPO, 1943, Table XVII, p. 95.

[b] Adapted from *Sixteenth Census of the United States. Population.* Vol. III, *The Labor Force*, Part I, U.S. Summary, Table 5, p. 19. Only ages 14 and 15 are represented in the age range of 10 to 15 years.

[c] *Seventeenth Census of the United States. Population:* Bulletin PC 1. *Detailed Characteristics*, U.S. Summary, Table 127. Only ages 14 and 15 are represented in age range of 10 to 15 years for 1950 and 1960.

[d] Department of Labor, Bureau of Labor Statistics, *Employment and Earnings*, 1960.

nomic. If industry retains a larger share of older workers, it must make adjustments such as redesigning technical operations for workers with less energy, reconsidering the problem of inducting older workers into lower-status jobs, and related problems.

Women in the Labor Force

The failure to consider the nongainfully employed housewife as part of the labor force is, in a sense, unrealistic. Women probably contribute more than their share of labor to any society, including contemporary industrial society. It has been estimated that they contribute more than $160 billion worth of labor to the American economy. They also constitute a great reservoir of labor which can be tapped during periods of national emergency and prosperity. In all industrial societies women increasingly are entering the labor force earlier and remaining in it longer.[8] Not only do more of them work for pay, but the length of time they withdraw from the labor force to rear children is being reduced, with the result that their working life is being lengthened.[9] These trends are stimulated not only by lessening resistance to the employment of women but also by their increasing educational and vocational qualifications and their decreasing family responsibilities.[10] During and since World War II the proportion of women gainfully occupied in the United States increased as part of a long-term trend. Since 1870 it has been estimated that the number of working women has increased more than tenfold whereas their numerical increase has been about fourfold. In 1870 women comprised 15 percent of the total labor force; today more than one-third of the labor force is composed of women.

The increase of women workers in the labor force has been for all age groups above sixteen years for both married and single. As might be expected, the proportion of married women in the labor force has grown faster than the proportion of single women. In 1840, for example, married women constituted slightly more than a tenth of all working women, and this proportion steadily increased until in 1960 they comprised over half.[11] This rise was due not only to the general aging of the population but to the growing proportion of married women, and their younger age of marriage. More importantly, it reflected a changing cultural defi-

[8] National Manpower Council, *Womanpower*, Columbia, 1957.

[9] Gertrude Bancroft, *The American Labor Force, Its Growth and Changing Composition*, Wiley, 1958, p. 60.

[10] *Ibid.*, p. 35.

[11] Thomas C. Fichandler, "The Labor Force," in J. Frederic Dewhurst and associates, *America's Needs and Resources*, Twentieth Century Fund, 1955, chap. 20, p. 726. In 1961, the U.S. Census reported 60.4 percent.

nition of the role of the married woman in the economy and society.

The social consequences of having women work both for a work organization and for the home are enormous. The engineer has to take into account their unique physical and psychological characteristics in planning the technology of operations; supervisors must change their command techniques; labor unions must reorient their organizing techniques; and so on. Such adjustments will increase rather than decrease in the future.

OCCUPATIONAL TRENDS

Occupational statistics are the basic data for answering the question of what people do in a particular society. Clearly, the occupational composition of the economy is the direct reflection of its industrial composition. When industrial processes change, occupations must change. As the proportions of workers needed in a particular industry change, the proportions in the various occupations also change.[12] As in the case of industrial classifications, the basis of classifying occupations has shifted from one census to another, making comparisons difficult. Similarly, the meaning of occupational categories changes over time. Some efforts have been made by Alba Edwards and others to make the occupational categories used in the United States Census roughly comparable over the years. Edwards designed a crude socioeconomic scale, with income and education varying more or less systematically along a scale from professional to unskilled work.[13]

The labor force may be roughly divided into three categories—white-collar workers, manual workers, and farm workers. In turn, these may be divided into higher- and lower-skill occupational groupings as shown in Table 3.4. The main trends since the turn of the century are clear: a dramatic decrease in the proportion of farm workers, a slight increase in manual and service workers, and a spectacular increase in white-collar workers at all levels.

The reduced numbers in agriculture were explained above.

[12] See Sigmund Nosow and William H. Form (eds.), *Man, Work, and Society*, Basic Books, 1962, chap. 6, "Economic, Industrial, and Occupational Systems."

[13] See *Comparative Occupation Statistics for the United States, 1870 to 1940*, GPO, 1943, Tables 24, 25, p. 181.

Here we must note that there was only a small increase in the manual and service workers since 1910 despite the rapid urbanization and industrialization. Moreover, most of this increase is in the service sector. The advance in mechanization was reflected in the decrease of laborers and the increase of semiskilled machine operatives. In the service sector private domestic and household workers declined rapidly. The disappearance of the servant is characteristic of all industrializing societies, for industry generally pays higher cash wages than families can afford to pay to domestics.[14]

White-collar workers now exceed manual workers, exclusive of those in the service category. As late as 1900 white-collar workers comprised slightly less than one-fifth of the total whereas today they are about two-fifths. Within this broad classification the percentage of professional and managerial workers roughly doubled after 1900, as did the sales workers, while the proportion of office workers increased over four times. These trends dramatize the revolution in the office, the growth of large-scale white-collar bureaucracies, and the rise of skilled, semiskilled, and unskilled white-collar hierarchies.

Many of the above changes have been accompanied by a changing sex composition of occupational categories. Since the turn of the century the proportion of women engaged in farming has declined more rapidly than the proportion of men. While the proportion of women semiskilled operatives has remained almost constant, that of men in this category has doubled and that of unskilled workers has decreased 50 percent. The proportion of skilled workers among the men has risen slowly and steadily but the percentage of male professionals has almost doubled, and the clerical workers have increased even more.

Still more dramatic changes have occurred among the employed women. As is the case with the men, the percentage of women engaged in farm and domestic work has declined precipitously. Most of them did not spill over into manual work. The most spectacular increases, of course, have been in white-collar occupations, in which the number of women has almost tripled in

---

[14] C. Arnold Anderson and Mary Jean Bowman, "The Vanishing Servant and the Contemporary Status System of the American South," *American Journal of Sociology*, November, 1953, pp. 215–230.

TABLE 3.4. Percent Distribution by Major Occupation Group for the Economically Active Civilian Population by Sex, for the United States: 1900–1960

Major Occupation Group and Sex	1960	1950	1940	1930	1920	1910	1900
Both Sexes							
Total	100.0	100.0	100.0	100.0	100.0	100.0	100.0
White-collar workers	43.9	36.6	31.1	29.4	24.9	21.3	17.6
Professional, technical, and kindred workers	11.8	8.6	7.5	6.8	5.4	4.7	4.3
Managers, officials, and proprietors, exc. farm	10.8	8.7	7.3	7.4	6.6	6.6	5.8
Clerical and kindred workers	14.8	12.3	9.6	8.9	8.0	5.3	3.0
Sales workers	6.5	7.0	6.7	6.3	4.9	4.7	4.5
Manual and service workers	49.5	51.6	51.5	49.4	48.1	47.7	44.9
Manual workers	36.7	41.1	39.8	39.6	40.2	38.2	35.8
Craftsmen, foremen, and kindred workers	13.0	14.1	12.0	12.8	13.0	11.6	10.5
Operatives and kindred workers	18.8	20.4	18.4	15.8	15.6	14.6	12.8
Laborers, except farm and mine	4.9	6.6	9.4	11.0	11.6	12.0	12.5
Service workers	12.8	10.5	11.7	9.8	7.8	9.6	9.0
Private household workers	3.3	2.6	4.7	4.1	3.3	5.0	5.4
Service workers, except private household	9.5	7.9	7.1	5.7	4.5	4.6	3.6
Farm workers	6.6	11.8	17.4	21.2	27.0	30.9	37.5
Farmers and farm managers	4.2	7.4	10.4	12.4	15.3	16.5	19.9
Farm laborers and foremen	2.4	4.4	7.0	8.8	11.7	14.4	17.7
Male							
Total	100.0	100.0	100.0	100.0	100.0	100.0	100.0
White-collar workers	38.4	30.5	26.6	25.2	21.4	20.2	17.6
Professional, technical, and kindred workers	11.2	7.2	5.8	4.8	3.8	3.5	3.4
Managers, officials, and proprietors, exc. farm	13.9	10.5	8.6	8.8	7.8	7.7	6.8
Clerical and kindred workers	7.2	6.4	5.8	5.5	5.3	4.4	2.8
Sales workers	6.1	6.4	6.4	6.1	4.5	4.6	4.6

Occupation group							
Manual and service workers	40.8	45.1	48.2	50.0	51.7	54.6	52.9
Manual workers	37.6	41.3	44.5	45.2	45.6	48.4	46.2
Craftsmen, foremen, and kindred workers	12.6	14.1	16.0	16.2	15.5	19.0	18.9
Operatives and kindred workers	10.4	12.5	14.4	15.3	18.0	20.5	20.1
Laborers, except farm and mine	14.7	14.6	14.0	13.6	12.1	8.8	7.2
Service workers	3.1	3.8	3.7	4.8	6.1	6.2	6.7
Private household workers	0.2	0.2	0.2	0.2	0.3	0.2	.1
Service workers, except private household	2.9	3.6	3.6	4.6	5.7	6.0	6.6
Farm workers	41.7	34.7	30.4	24.8	21.7	14.9	8.7
Farmers and farm managers	23.0	19.7	18.4	15.2	13.3	10.0	6.1
Farm laborers and foremen	18.7	15.0	12.1	9.6	8.4	4.9	2.6
Female							
Total	100.0	100.0	100.0	100.0	100.0	100.0	100.0
White-collar workers	17.8	26.1	38.8	44.2	44.9	52.5	55.3
Professional, technical, and kindred workers	8.2	9.8	11.7	13.8	12.8	12.2	13.1
Managers, officials, and proprietors, exc. farm	1.4	2.0	2.2	2.7	3.3	4.3	4.7
Clerical and kindred workers	4.0	9.2	18.7	20.9	21.5	27.4	30.3
Sales workers	4.3	5.1	6.3	6.8	7.4	8.6	7.2
Manual and service workers	63.2	58.1	47.6	47.3	51.0	43.9	42.3
Manual workers	27.8	25.7	23.7	19.8	21.6	22.4	17.2
Craftsmen, foremen, and kindred workers	1.4	1.4	1.2	1.0	1.1	1.5	.9
Operatives and kindred workers	23.8	22.9	20.2	17.4	19.5	20.0	16.0
Laborers, except farm and mine	2.6	1.4	2.3	1.5	1.1	0.8	.3
Service workers	35.4	32.4	23.9	27.5	29.4	21.5	25.1
Private household workers	28.7	24.0	15.8	17.8	18.1	8.9	9.8
Service workers, except private household	6.8	8.5	8.1	9.7	11.3	12.6	15.3
Farm workers	18.9	15.8	13.5	8.4	4.0	3.7	2.4
Farmers and farm managers	5.9	3.8	3.2	2.4	1.2	0.7	.4
Farm laborers and foremen	13.1	12.0	10.3	6.0	2.8	2.9	2.0

SOURCES: David L. Kaplan and M. Claire Casey, *Occupational Trends in the United States, 1900 to 1950*, Bureau of the Census, Working Paper #5, U.S. Department of Commerce, 1958, pp. 6, 7. The 1960 data do not appear in this source.

fifty years. While the professional category has increased 50 percent during this time, office workers have gone up almost sevenfold. Only 4 percent of the women were clerical workers in 1900 and about three-tenths are so employed today. All of these trends are based on the entire labor force. Were we to analyze the urban labor force separately, they would stand out more sharply.

In general, increasing industrialization tends to raise the standard of living and the amount of leisure while lowering the number of hours worked.[15] This is the consequence of increasing utilization of mechanical and other forms of energy. Changes in occupational structure also alter the distribution of income, status, and power. Contrary to common belief, industrialization calls for a general raising of the educational levels and an increasing proportion of skilled workers (broadly defined as highly trained) to perform increasingly complex technical and coordinating functions. As Kerr and others have ably pointed out, countries at low levels of industrialization pay little or no attention to building an efficient labor force. With increasing industrialization management and the state invest more heavily in vocational and technical schools, until in advanced nations the entire labor force achieves a high level of education.[16] Yet differences in education are everywhere necessarily rewarded.[17] This tendency is confirmed for the United States in Table 3.5, which reveals that white-collar occupations typically call for higher education and provide higher incomes than the manual occupations, and that income and education vary with the amount of skill within the manual and white-collar hierarchies. There is only one notable exception in the relationship. Male craftsmen, foremen, and kindred workers earn higher incomes than clerical and sales workers, especially the latter, despite the fact that the craftsmen have less formal education.

[15] See Robert Dubin, *The World of Work,* Prentice-Hall, 1958, pp. 135–136; A. J. Jaffe and C. D. Steward, *Manpower Resources and Utilization,* Wiley, 1951, pp. 408–409.
[16] Clark Kerr, John T. Dunlop, Frederick H. Harbison, and Charles A. Myers, *Industrialism and Industrial Man,* Harvard, 1960, pp. 176–177.
[17] Kingsley Davis and Wilbert E. Moore, "A Conceptual Analysis of Stratification," *American Sociological Review,* June, 1942, pp. 309–321; Alex Inkeles, "Social Stratification and Mobility in the Soviet Union," *American Sociological Review,* August, 1950, pp. 465–479.

TABLE 3.5. Education (1957) and Income of Occupational Groups (1959)

Occupational Group	Adults with Some College Education[a]	Median Income[b]	
		Male	Female
Professional, technical, and kindred workers	78.7%	$6,725	$3,603
Farmers and farm managers	14.6	1,901	—
Nonfarm managers, officials, and proprietors	40.6	6,315	3,114
Clerical and kindred workers	30.2	4,904	3,061
Sales workers	41.7	4,802	1,606
Craftsmen, foremen, and kindred workers	14.7	5,355	—
Operatives and kindred workers	9.0	4,281	2,358
Private household workers	—	—	643
Service workers, except private households	13.9	3,391	1,431
Farm laborers: unpaid family workers	4.3	1,204	—
Laborers, except farm and mine	8.5	3,150	—
Total	25.7	4,658	2,288

[a] Current Population Reports, "Population Estimates," Bureau of the Census, Series P-20, No. 83, August, 1958, p. 18.

[b] Civilian labor force 14 years and over reporting some occupation in March, 1960. Current Population Reports, "Consumer Income," Bureau of the Census, Series P-60, No. 35, January, pp. 41, 42. Sample 26,000 representative households.

Mobility

Changes in industrial and occupational composition of the labor force reflect a dynamic economy in which new industries are established and old industries collapse, in which new occupations rise and old ones are discarded. Industrial societies also tend to increase the geographic mobility of the labor force and the rate of job changes.

In traditional societies residential moves from one community to another and from one occupation to another are rare. With industrialization both types of mobility become commonplace. For example, in the United States in 1950, one-third of the adults in nonfarm communities were reared on farms.[18] This situation reflects not only a great amount of residential change but a substantial amount of occupational change. Moreover, in any given

[18] Ronald and Deborah Freedman, "Farm Reared Elements in the Non-farm Population," *Rural Sociology*, March, 1956, pp. 50–51.

year a considerable proportion of the working population changes residence and occupation. Thus in 1950, one-sixth of the employed males changed their residence; 11 percent moved within the county and 6 percent moved to another county. Probably most of the latter changed their jobs.

Mobility varies by occupation.[19] As might be expected, occupations associated with holding or managing property and skilled occupations exhibit the least geographical mobility. Thus, as Table 3.6 shows, farm owners, managers, proprietors, officials,

TABLE 3.6. Mobility Experience of Occupational Groups for the United States: 1950
(Percentages)

Major Occupation Group, Male, Employed	Non-movers	Movers	
		Same County	Different County
Professional, technical, and kindred workers	77.4	11.5	9.3+
Farmers and farm managers	88.2	7.6	3.1
Managers, officials, and proprietors	84.5	9.6	4.6
Clerical and kindred workers	82.2	11.9	4.5
Sales workers	80.0	12.1	6.4+
Craftsmen, foremen, and kindred workers	82.1	11.9	4.8
Operatives and kindred workers	80.1	13.7	4.6
Service workers	81.6	12.0	4.5
Farm laborers	71.2	15.6	9.8+
Laborers, except farm and mine	79.4	13.4	5.3
Total (labor force)	80.0	11.1	5.9

SOURCE: *United States Census of Population, Special Report* P-E, No. 4B, Bureau of the Census, 1956, p. 15. Figures do not total 100 percent because no information is available on the movement of some workers.

and craftsmen have the lowest amount of mobility, along with clerical workers. Sales workers, operatives, and service workers are moderately mobile while both rural and urban unskilled laborers are very mobile. Surprisingly, professionals also exhibit a high degree of mobility, but not because of job insecurity as is the

[19] For regional and rural-urban differences see Donald J. Bogue, "Residential Mobility and Migration of Workers," in William Haber *et al.* (eds.), *Manpower in the United States,* Harper, 1954, pp. 143–153.

case for unskilled workers. In fact, mobility may enhance the position of professionals in their market. In terms of distance mobility, farm laborers, professionals, and sales persons tend to make more long-distance moves, while other occupations tend to move shorter distances.

As suggested above, although all residential moves do not accompany job changes, probably a majority of them do. Census data show that the unemployed are forced to move more often than the employed. Over one-quarter of the unemployed in 1950 moved, compared to less than one-fifth of the employed; and almost one-tenth of the unemployed moved to a different county, as compared to only 5 percent of the employed. Some direct evidence is available on the causes of these job moves. Data for 1955 suggest that almost two-fifths of the job changes were motivated by hopes of improving job status—to secure more pay, more interesting work, and to escape unpleasant aspects of the job. Almost one-fourth of the moves were forced by economic factors such as layoffs and business failures, and almost one-fifth were cases of giving up "temporary jobs." Thus, almost half of the moves were caused by economic conditions beyond the control of the workers.[20]

As Table 3.7 shows, about 15 percent of the workers in American industry changed jobs in 1955. This enormous amount of movement stimulated by industrial and economic changes represents a minimum of ten and a half million job moves. Of course, the extent of mobility varies by industry. The greatest amount was found in construction, where 27 percent of all employees changed jobs. Agriculture, wholesale trade, and retail trade also by their nature induce an above-average amount of job movement. The amount of movement among manufacturing workers is actually somewhat below that of nonagricultural workers. The most stable "industries" are the self-employed, public administration, transportation and communication, and utilities.

It is instructive to note the shifts in occupational and industrial affiliation which accompanied these job changes. The Census Bureau reported in 1955 that almost half of the workers who moved entered both a different occupation and a different indus-

[20] See source of Table 3.7.

TABLE 3.7. Percentages of Workers in the United States in Occupational and Industrial Categories Having Worked at Two or More Jobs in 1955

Occupational Groups		Industrial Groups	
Professional, technical, and kindred workers	13.4	Nonagriculture	15.5
Farmers and farm managers	18.8	Agriculture	18.8
Managers, officials, and proprietors	9.2	Forestry, fishing, and mining	16.5
Clerical and kindred workers	11.8	Construction	27.3
Sales workers	16.1	Manufacturing	13.7
Craftsmen, foremen, and kindred workers	16.1	Transportation, communication, and utilities	12.4
Operatives and kindred workers	16.1	Wholesale and retail trade	18.3
Private household workers	9.7	Service workers	14.4
Service workers	14.7	Public administration	11.0
Farm laborers and foremen	18.6	Self-employed	8.3
Laborers, except farm and mine	26.2		

SOURCE: *Current Population Reports,* "Labor Force," Bureau of the Census, Series P-50, No. 70, Tables 2 and 3, pp. 15–16.

try while three-tenths remained within the same occupation and the same industry. Twenty percent of the movers remained in the same occupation but went into a different industry and only 8 percent remained in the same industry but changed their occupation.[21]

As might be expected, those who experienced no change in occupation *or* industry when they moved tended to be highly skilled and qualified. Thus about two-thirds of the professionals stayed in the same industry and occupation compared to half of the craftsmen, clerical workers, and operatives and a small proportion of the sales clerks, laborers, and service workers. Occupational differences in the proportions changing jobs reveal similar patterns. Managers, officials, proprietors, and professional workers exhibited slight job changes. Office workers, skilled workers, and operatives showed an average amount of job change while laborers, both farm and nonfarm, experienced the greatest amount of job change.

[21] *United States Census of Population,* Report P-E, No. 4B, Bureau of the Census, 1956, Table D, p. 7.

As Reynolds and others have indicated, factors such as age and sex are related to the amount of job mobility.[22] Older workers and those with more job tenure are less mobile than younger, low-tenure workers. For example, in the United States in 1955 almost 30 percent of the workers 18–19 years old changed jobs as compared to only 10 percent of the workers over 55. Women were less mobile than men; only one-tenth of the women held two or more jobs in 1950 in contrast to almost two-tenths of the men.[23]

Unemployment

Almost all job changes are accompanied by some unemployment. Although economic insecurity is examined in more detail in a later chapter, certain preliminary observations may be made here. In all advanced industrial societies some unemployment is inevitable even when there is a high demand for labor. A minimum of 2 or 3 percent of unemployment is normal because this percentage of the labor force is in process of finding new jobs or exchanging jobs. It is difficult to maintain this minimum amount of unemployment.

The nature and duration of unemployment has economic causes and sociological consequences. Certain industries decay, and the skills of many workers become obsolete. Older workers not only find it difficult to learn new skills but experience a deterioration of old skills. After a time they may be forced to retire prematurely from the labor market. Technological changes in the steel, automobile, furniture, railroad, and other industries have recently created large pools of unemployment which are not being rapidly absorbed by new industries. Not only has this situation caused severe economic privation for many workers, but many communities are dying as a result of it.[24] Labor economists refer to it as "structural unemployment," a long-term inability of the market to readjust and absorb unemployed workers.

---

[22] Lloyd G. Reynolds, *The Structure of Labor Markets,* Harper & Row, 1951, pp. 113–155; Charles A. Myers and George P. Schultz, *The Dynamics of a Labor Market,* Prentice-Hall, 1951, pp. 21–44.

[23] *Current Population Reports,* Series P-50, No. 70, p. 14.

[24] See W. Fred Cottrell, "Death by Dieselization: A Case Study in the Reaction to Technological Change," *American Sociological Review,* June, 1951, pp. 358–365.

However, unemployment may be due to changes in plant organization as well as to technological changes. Centralization, decentralization, or reorganization of production often reduces manpower requirements and produces results similar to those emanating from rapid technological change.[25]

In a free economy, whatever the causes of unemployment, the consequences seem to be everywhere the same. Those who are economically most insecure—the youngest workers, those with the lowest wages, the least educated, and those who are socially and economically marginal—are unemployed first and for the longest periods. Table 3.8 shows that the professionals, proprietors, managers, and technical and skilled workers experience the least amount of unemployment, while the semiskilled and unskilled workers endure the greatest amount. The so-called secondary income earners, the young workers, and the oldest workers have the most part-time employment and unemployment. Moreover, socially marginal workers such as Negroes, foreign born, and rural migrants also experience great amounts of unemployment. Occasionally marginal workers are employed in marginal industries even during the most adverse economic circumstances, but in general, economic deprivation selectively hits socially marginal groups.

The very young and the older workers are disproportionately affected by dislocations of the market.[26] If 1956 is taken as an illustrative year, almost one-fifth of the workers between 18 and 19 years old experienced unemployment compared to less than one-tenth of workers of 25 and older. Again, less than two-fifths of the workers between the ages of 20 and 24 who were unemployed had two or more spells of unemployment during that year compared to one-half of the workers 45 years old and older.

Statistics for marital status tend to reflect similar forces at work. Thus, single men have more unemployment than married men. Apparently men from broken families suffer more unemployment, for the widowed, divorced, and men not living with their wives experienced more unemployment in 1956 than did stable mar-

[25] Leonard P. Adams and Robert L. Aronson, *Workers and Industrial Change,* Cornell, 1957, pp. 26–46; William H. Form and Henry Bloch, "Social Consequences of a Departmental Shutdown," unpublished manuscript, 1961.
[26] *Current Population Reports,* "Labor Force," Series P-50, No. 77, p. 18.

TABLE 3.8. Occupational and Industrial Attachment of Workers Experiencing Unemployment in the United States: 1956.

Occupational Group	Percent Experiencing Unemployment	Percent of Unemployed with Two or More Spells of Unemployment
Professional, technical, and kindred workers	3.2	31.6
Farmers and farm managers	1.5	—
Managers, officials, and proprietors	3.1	38.7
Clerical and kindred workers	6.9	29.6
Sales workers	6.5	29.0
Craftsmen, foremen, and kindred workers	13.6	48.5
Operatives and kindred workers	18.1	40.8
Private household workers	8.4	53.3
Service workers	11.0	38.4
Farm laborers and foremen	8.2	63.2
Laborers, except farm and mine	24.7	53.3
Total	10.4	43.2

Industry Group	Percent Experiencing Unemployment	Percent of Unemployed with Two or More Spells of Unemployment
Agriculture	5.6	61.8
Nonagriculture	11.0	42.1
Forestry, fishing, and mining	15.7	—
Construction	30.2	59.3
Manufacturing	14.7	37.9
Transportation, communication, and utilities	8.1	40.6
Wholesale and retail trade	10.8	36.1
Service workers	7.5	41.6
Public administration	4.5	—
Self-employed workers	4.1	55.3
Total	10.4	43.2

SOURCE: Current Population Reports, "Labor Force," Bureau of the Census, Series P-50, No. 77, p. 20, Tables 16, 17.

ried men. These and other factors related to unemployment will be systematically analyzed in a later chapter.

CONCLUSION

This brief survey of the labor force dramatizes the impact which industrialization has on the entire society. We have demonstrated how the activities of the entire population are affected: how people are forced increasingly into the cities; how children are drawn increasingly into schools to be trained; how women, married and single, become paid workers; how the productive working force expands; how the age structure of the population is changed; and so on. It was also shown that industrialization assumes a predictable pattern, that workers are distributed differently in various industries and occupations as the economy matures. Moreover, the trends indicated that workers experience an increasing amount of geographic and social mobility, and that the free economy causes periods of unemployment to which major adjustments must be made. Throughout the following chapters an analysis of the social implications of these changes will be examined in detail in the plant, community, and general society. We shall turn first to the community.

SELECTED BIBLIOGRAPHY

Anderson, H. D., and P. E. Davidson, *Recent Occupational Trends in American Labor,* Stanford, 1945.

Bancroft, Gertrude, *The American Labor Force, Its Growth and Changing Composition,* Columbia, 1957.

Dewhurst, J. Frederic, and associates, *America's Needs and Resources,* Twentieth Century Fund, 1955.

Haber, William, *et al.* (eds.), *Manpower in the United States,* Harper, 1954.

Jaffe, A. J., and C. D. Steward, *Manpower Resources and Utilization,* Wiley, 1951.

National Manpower Council, *Woman Power,* Columbia, 1958.

United States Census of the Population, Decennial Census 1900–1960 and *Current Population Reports,* Department of Commerce, Bureau of the Census.

Woytinsky, W. S., and E. S. Woytinsky, *World Population and Production, Trends and Outlook,* Twentieth Century Fund, 1933.

CHAPTER 4

Industry Shapes the Community

Industrial societies are by definition characterized by situations wherein economic agencies are more powerful than others, where industry initiates changes in the community, and where local institutions tend to be adaptive. The study of industry-community relations is a central concern of industrial sociology. It is a large area of study, and the authors have written a separate book on the subject, from which this chapter has been adapted.[1] The first premise of this field of study is that industry and community are highly interrelated and interdependent. While the economic institution and its agencies influence the spatial organization, the institutional life, and the decision-making process in the community, economic organizations are, in turn, affected by institutional and cultural forces in the community. These interdependencies are not simple, direct, and uniform. In some situations, as in a company town, the community may be considered part of the industry. In other communities industry must accommodate to particular and unique local features—religious, ethnic, social class, familial, governmental, and so on.

In industrial societies where private ownership exists and free institutions are permitted, business and labor union organizations are centrally involved in shaping the destiny of the local community and the wider society. Their power arouses the concern of other organizations, which, in turn, attempt to control or modify the industrial environment in which they live. For purposes of convenience, then, industry-community study may be divided into two areas: (1) how industry shapes or affects the

[1] William H. Form and Delbert C. Miller, *Industry, Labor, and Community*, Harper, 1960.

community and (2) how the community and its institutions affect the behavior of industry and its agencies.

THE COMMUNITY AS AN ECONOMIC MECHANISM

The distinctive characteristic of the industrial community is that a constellation of institutional organizations has grown up around a particular center of specialized function. This specialized function is the economic institution which provides the means of livelihood for the residents, lays down the physical structure of the community, and, indeed, fashions the patterns of social life and thought. Karl Marx, Max Weber, Emile Durkheim, and Thorstein Veblen are among those who described most forcefully the tremendous impact of economic organization upon the other social institutions, including the political, familial, religious, and recreational phases of social life.[2] Veblen said: "Any community may be viewed as an industrial or economic mechanism, the structure of which is made up of what is called its economic institutions. These institutions are habitual methods of carrying on the life process of the community in contact with the material environment in which it lives. When given methods of unfolding human activity in this given environment have been elaborated in this way, the life of the community will express itself with some facility in these habitual directions."[3]

A picture of community revolving about economic institutions is only a partial picture of reality, because the life of a community is a composite of many institutional forces. However, acceptance of community as an industrial or economic mechanism enables the student to see more clearly the pervasive influence of economic institutions. In such a frame of reference the community may be viewed as containing many dependent variables, each of which is influenced by factors initiated by industry. This direct chain of causation becomes the guiding framework for the analysis of this chapter. It will show how the economic structure of a

[2] Karl Marx, *Capital: A Critique of Political Economy*, Modern Library, 1936, pp. 11–13; Max Weber, *The Theory of Social and Economic Organization*, trans. T. Parsons and A. M. Henderson, Hodge, 1947; Emile Durkheim, *On the Division of Labor in Society*, trans. G. Simpson, Macmillan, 1933; Thorstein Veblen, *The Theory of the Leisure Class*, Macmillan, 1912.

[3] Veblen, *op. cit.*, p. 193.

community conditions its broad social and ecological organization. Although the following description is based on the operation of a "free enterprise" economy, some generalizations apply to any type of economy.

INDUSTRIAL IMPACTS ON COMMUNITY STRUCTURE

The term "industry" will refer to technology, economic enterprises, and their personnel and associated people. The purpose of this section is to deal successively with the impact of economic institutions on

1. Location of communities.
2. Size of the community.
3. Growth patterns of the community.
4. Functional type and occupational composition.
5. Total land-use pattern.
6. Power and social class structure.
7. Community character.

Industry and Technology Influence Community Location

A historic view of industrial location reveals that the location of plants follows the requirements of four rather distinct stages of technology: the modern craft age, the machine age, the power age, and the atomic age.

Importance of water power to the emergence of the modern craft age

The modern craft age was based on muscle and water power. The use of water wheels was a significant first step in the transition from animate to inanimate energy. The early growth of textile manufacturing occurred along the streams of New England, the largest developments of which were established at Lowell, Manchester, Lawrence, Holyoke, and Lewiston before the Civil War.[4] Water power was not transportable, and the

[4] T. R. Smith, *The Cotton Textile Industry of Fall River, Massachusetts— A Study of Industrial Localization,* King's Crown, 1944, Table 8, p. 42; W. Fred Cottrell, *Energy and Society,* McGraw-Hill, 1955.

plants were forced to concentrate at the site itself. Thus industry became centralized about good water-power sites. Flour milling cities, such as Minneapolis and Buffalo, testify to the early importance of water power.

Importance of coal and iron to the emergence of the machine age

Modern industrialization awaited the utilization of steam. The steam engine provided a means for converting fuel into mechanical energy and could be set up wherever fuel was obtainable. Coal was the cheapest of the most effective fuels for the steam engine. Since the fuel could be transported, it was possible to locate industry more widely. Still, transportation costs could not be ignored. The locational effect was to concentrate industry on navigable water where it was cheap to transport coal or in the coal fields themselves. The application of steam power to the textile industry led to the rapid growth in the Fall River-New Bedford area after the middle of the nineteenth century. In the same period a rapid growth occurred in the Pennsylvania coal fields. As the processes of steelmaking became established an area of heavy industry arose. It was cheaper to bring the iron over the Great Lakes water route to the coal than to attempt the reverse. In addition, the large consuming market was already established in the East. With the coming of the steam locomotive and an elaborate rail system, a vast industrial area was soon in existence. It stretched along the Atlantic seaboard between Portland, Maine, and Baltimore, Maryland, extended westward across the Appalachians as far as the west side of Lake Michigan, and reached from a line on the north through the lake ports of Toronto, Detroit, and Milwaukee to the Potomac and Ohio rivers on the south. Outlying districts may be identified particularly around Montreal and St. Louis. A separate region is found in the South Atlantic Piedmont. On the Pacific coast, manufacturing is now increasing, but until recently it has been of relatively minor importance compared with lumbering, agriculture, and commercial activites.

Iron and coal exert a dominant influence on the location of manufacturing because extremely large amounts are required by many industries. The amount of iron consumed is greater than that of all other metals combined. The equipment of modern industrial civilization is largely made of iron and steel; machines, tools, commercial and manufacturing buildings, and transportation facilities are all made primarily of steel. Most power and heat for industry as well as for rail transportation is still obtained from coal, although oil and gas are being increasingly used.

The location of heavy industry identifies the heart of an industrialized nation. The industrial heart of America lies within a triangular area including the Pittsburgh coal field and the south shores of Lake Erie and of Lake Michigan. In this relatively small area are found most of the iron and steel industries of the continent and the great variety of other heavy and light industries associated with them. The development of this strategic district is based primarily on its accessibility to iron, coal, and consuming markets. In addition, the coincidence of a rich agricultural area and nearness to sea routes is especially helpful to its sustained growth.[5]

Manufacturing stimulates commerce. The great commercial centers rise on the ocean ports of the North Atlantic and North Pacific, on the Great Lakes, and on rail centers. Since most industries collect raw material from different areas and distribute their products to different regions, proximity to the major trade routes is of great importance. The exchange route between North America and western Europe is the greatest trade route in the world.

Importance of electricity to the emergence of the power age

The power age is identified with the widespread use of electricity. The steam engine remains important because it becomes a prime agent for the generation of electricity and for other reasons, too. Hydroelectric power has been increasingly employed, but steam plants generate the largest quantity of electric power. Electric power has also had important locational effects on industry but far less revolutionary than those of steam. The ability to transmit electric energy as much as 1000 miles gives added flexibility to location.

It has been thought that the availability of electric power would

[5] Richard Hartshorne, in Emerson P. Schmidt (ed.), *Man and Society,* Prentice-Hall, 1937, pp. 359–372.

produce a general scattering of industry to small rural plants or even back into workers' homes, but no major shift has occurred. To be sure, plants no longer need to huddle around giant steam engines close to rail lines. The large modern factory using electric motors is a long, one-story, shedlike structure which increasingly appears in suburban locations. The rapid growth of satellite towns and cities is evidence of the pattern. The motor transport of products and workers and the transport of electrical energy make the new pattern possible.

Importance of atomic energy to the emergence of the atomic age

The atomic age provides a new fuel for steam-power stations. Heat can be developed and converted into electricity. The light weight of the fuel opens many new possibilities for airplane and marine engines. Use of atomic energy in submarine and merchant ships demonstrates an applicability of this superior fuel. The Atomic Energy Commission has announced successful "breeder" experiments which may eventually make possible release of great energy at lower costs. Certainly, the development of economical atomic fuels and reactors which could be transported cheaply in an airplane to any point in the world suggests revolutionary possibilities.

Perhaps another locational effect of the atomic age should be pointed out. The threat of the atomic bomb is encouraging dispersion of industry where feasible. In general, widespread dispersion of existing plants is considered so expensive as to be prohibitive, but the location of new plants may be more and more influenced by the threat of atomic bombing. Many large corporations are placing new plants in or near small cities, away from heavily industrialized areas.

The industrial heart of the United States remains where it has been for decades.[6] Nearly two-thirds of the nation's manufacturing is concentrated in New England, the Middle Atlantic area, and states of the East North Central region. The area is a little

[6] Cf. Frederic B. Garver, Francis M. Boddy, and Alvan J. Nixon, *The Location of Manufactures in the United States, 1899–1929,* University of Minnesota Press, 1934.

more than a seventh of the country's area. But in the years since 1939 industry has expanded all across the United States. Table 4.1 indicates the share of manufacturing in each of nine regional blocks of states in the United States for 1939 and 1953. Significant developments underlie these statistics. The most noteworthy trends and effects of location of manufacturing in the United States have been in the direction of equalization of the interre-

TABLE 4.1. **Share of All Manufacturing Employment in the Nine Regional Blocks of States**

Region	1939 Percentage	1953 Percentage
New England	11.6	9.2
Middle Atlantic	28.9	26.0
East North Central	27.6	29.7
West North Central	5.2	6.2
South Atlantic	11.9	10.9
East South Central	4.4	4.6
West South Central	3.7	4.5
Mountain	0.9	1.1
Pacific	5.8	7.8
	100.0	100.0

SOURCE: Bureau of the Census, Department of Commerce, 1952 *Annual Survey of Manufacture*, Series MAS-52-5, November 18, 1953, pp. 1–6.

gional distribution of industry and population, equalization in the degree of "industrialization" of various regions, greater concentration of population in urban areas, and suburbanization of both population and manufacturing.[7] Per capita income of the United States shows a marked trend toward regional equality.[8]

Vigorous efforts are being made by local and state organizations to attract industry to their communities. Merchants and manufacturers have been in the forefront of these efforts. Sometimes the chamber of commerce takes the lead; sometimes the city gov-

[7] Edgar M. Hoover, *The Location of Economic Activity*, McGraw-Hill, 1948, p. 165.

[8] Editors of *Fortune*, *The Changing American Market*, Hanover House, 1955.

ernment sets up an industrial development organization. Industrial land development is the order of the day through continuous advertising and promotion.[9]

Local inducements are often reinforced by state support. Pennsylvania has established an Industrial Development Authority which offers special assistance to community industrial programs through provisions of 25-year, 2 percent interest second mortgage loans to assure low-cost financing of new plant building in Pennsylvania.[10] North Carolina has established a 5000-acre Research Triangle Park to attract industry by offering the nearby research facilities of its three major universities.[11] The independent effect of these planned efforts is undetermined, but there is no doubt that they encourage the location of new industry in particular communities. Industry is being wooed with competitive vigor as the geographical scope of profitable locations is enlarged by the improved technology of the atomic age. One urban geographer has shown that even amenities such as climate and cultural inducements may be decisive factors in winning industry to a state or local community.[12]

Industry Influences the Size of the Community

The multiplication factor

The size of a community depends mainly on the size of the industrial base which undergirds it. The industrial base is composed of two parts: the basic activities and the service activities. Basic activities are those producing goods and services for sale outside the community; service activites are those carried on for internal consumption only. Thus, the basic activities support the service activities. The proportion is commonly measured by the number of basic employees (those working for an export activity) and the number of service employees (those working for internal consumption). Economists, in analyzing the growth of an area, often speak of the "multiplication factor." They refer to the fact that any development that provides new jobs in basic activities

[9] "Lincoln Industrial Park," *New York Times*, October 13, 1957, sec. 10.
[10] *New York Times*, November 8, 1957, sec. 10.
[11] *Ibid.*, November 17, 1957, sec. 10.
[12] Edward L. Ullman, "Amenities as a Factor in Urban Growth," *Geographical Review*, January, 1954, pp. 119–132.

also creates jobs in service activities. Table 4.2 shows the re-
productive process which is set in motion by the expansion of
manufacturing. It shows some of the many supporting jobs that
are required as new jobs are created in manufacturing. However,
the ratio of basic to service activity varies according to city size
and function and also according to the classification of basic
activities and service activities. Indeed, there may be a great deal
of variation within a given city over time. All one can say as a

TABLE 4.2. Every 100 Jobs in Industry Create These Additional Jobs

Jobs	Percentage	Jobs	Percentage
Bus drivers	.42	Architects	.06
Department store clerks	2.5	Electricians	.22
Lawyers and judges	.44	Miners	2.2
Waitresses	1.6	Real estate agents	.16
Plumbers	.13	Nurses	1.0
Doctors	.57	Shoe repairmen	.16
Painters	1.0	Teachers	.50
Firemen	.30	Pharmacists	.25
Dressmakers	.44	Editors and reporters	.25
Bank clerks	.66	Florists	.13
Stenos, typists	2.2	Plasterers	.13
Cleaners, laundrymen	1.6	Mechanics, machinists	2.2
Carpenters	2.6	Postmen	.50
Musicians	.44	Bookkeepers	2.0
Truck and tractor drivers	4.0	Dentists	.20
Gas station attendants	.40	Telephone operators	1.0
Printers	.22	Technical engineers	.14
Beauticians, barbers	1.0	Shoe clerks	.20
Policemen	.57	Photographers	.14
Highway workers	.10	Entertainers	.13
Librarians	.14	Bakers	.33
Food clerks	1.3	Farmers	28.5
Cooks	.66	Tailors, furriers	.40
Newsboys	.09	Hardware clerks	.44

This table is based on a ratio of civilian jobs in manufacturing to the number not
in manufacturing. In the table that ratio is assumed to be 1 to 2.6. This is higher than
the multiplication factors which are described because of the classification of all
jobs *not in manufacturing* as supportive. Many nonmanufacturing jobs which produce
goods and services for export are basic activities. See *Better Living,* Employee's Magazine of E. I. DuPont Co., May–June, 1954, p. 14.

generalization is that the multiplication factor arises because basic activities require service activities in a specialized industrial economy and that basic activities generally originate and support the service activities. Therefore the multiplication factor is not accidental; it is a product of the economy in a local area and has a definite range of values.

The search for values of the multiplication factor has led to an examination of the ratio between basic and service activities in many cities. The ratio for cities over 10,000 population appears fairly certain to be between 1 to .5 and 1 to 2. The larger the city, all other things being equal, the larger the service component should be, because a larger range of specialties will be supported by the larger market.[13] In small cities from 10,000 to 120,000 the ratios range between 1 to .6 and 1 to .9.[14] As larger cities are examined, the ratio of service employees to basic is seen to increase. Wichita, Kansas, with about 200,000 population, has averaged about 1 basic to 1.4 service workers from 1940 to 1950. Cincinnati, with 787,000, had a 1 to 1.7 ratio. New York City comes to about 1 to 2.[15] The ratio of basic to service employment can vary rather widely in the same city depending on the business activities. In Wichita, Kansas, the ratio varied from 1 to 2.5 in 1939, to 1 to .6 in 1944. This variation is a large one and was brought about largely by fluctuation in airplane production.

The multiplication factor can be very serious in the augmented impact of basic activities in a community where one basic industry provides the bulk of employment in manufacturing. In Seattle, Washington, the Boeing Aircraft Company is the largest employer

[13] Edward R. Ullman, "The Basic-Service Ratio and the Areal Support of Cities," in David A. Revzan and Ernest A. Engelbert (eds.), *Proceedings, Western Committee on Regional Economic Analysis, Social Science Research Council,* University of California, June 25–27, 1953, pp. 110–123.

[14] Medford, Oregon (20,000 population), basic to service ratio, 1 to .8; Oshkosh, Wisconsin (42,000), basic to service ration, 1 to .6; Albuquerque, New Mexico (100,000), basic to service ratio, 1 to .9; Madison, Wisconsin (110,000), basic to service ratio, 1 to .8; Brockton area, Massachusetts (120,000), basic to service ratio, 1 to .8.

[15] Ullman, "The Basic-Service Ratio . . . ," p. 120. Cf. the newly developed "minimum expectation method" as shown in Ullman's *Major Characteristics of the San Francisco Economic Base,* Discussion Paper No. 8, University of Washington, June 24, 1958.

of labor. Its principal product (Boeing bombers and missiles) fluctuates with war and defense needs of the nation, and the fluctuations have repercussions throughout the entire community. The president of the Seattle Chamber of Commerce, Mr. Thomas N. Pelly, in 1951 voiced feelings that have been repeatedly emphasized:

> Seattle furnishes one of the nation's prime examples as to what might and could occur if a single industry became the basis for our entire living. I am speaking of the Boeing Airplane Company, one of the city's really great businesses. Eleven short years ago Boeing employed a little more than 5,000 persons; seven years ago employment at Boeing jumped to in excess of 45,733 but in the following year, 1945, more than 35,000 workers suddenly found themselves without a job. In 1947, employment went up again to almost 17,000 but dropped within five months to 6,740. These are violent fluctuations causing great instability, not only in the lives of the individuals and their families, but in the activities of hundreds of related businesses and their employees.[16]

It may be concluded not only that industry determines size of the community but also that the industrial base may greatly affect the stability of the community. Furthermore, industry plays a dominant role in the growth patterns of various communities.

Industry Shapes the Growth Patterns of the Community

The life cycle of a community

Many communities seem destined to live and to die. Some may have rebirths like Athens and Rome, but all cities are constantly expanding or contracting with the vicissitudes of economic, geographic, and social change. Some communities have short cycles of life and growth; others have very long lives. A mining town, for example, appears with the discovery and demand for the resources its area possesses. When the resources vanish, only the ghost of its former prosperity remains. The collapse may happen in a decade or two. A community built on a sole resource which is exhausted very slowly or on a trade and industrial complex might well have a life cycle spanning centuries.

Paul Landis studied the three iron-mining towns of Virginia, Hibbing, and Eveleth, Minnesota, over a period extending from

[16] *Seattle Times*, August 19, 1951.

1895 to 1930.[17] He found that these towns characteristically experienced three phases of a relatively short life cycle: (1) a rapid growth to maturity, (2) a period of relatively stable population, and then (3) a rapid decline. The towns exhibited four kinds of synchronous cycles which he called physicosocial, cultural, biosocial, and psychosocial. The physicosocial cycle includes an early period of quest and discovery of ore; the subsequent period of exploitation, which soon put shipments above discoveries and hastened the depletion of high-grade ore; and finally a period of conservation of a rapidly diminishing resource.

The rhythm in cultural cycles is exhibited in three stages of material culture of the community mores. The simple material culture gave way to a lavish material culture, which faded into decay with the decline of the community. The mores developed around a tolerance of prostitution, gambling, fighting, and drinking, later succeeded by a reform of vice but an establishment of patronage and extravagance. As ore reserves declined, economy mores emerged.

The biosocial cycle refers to the growth of population. In the beginning the mining town was composed of adults, probably consisting chiefly of single young men, between the ages of twenty and forty, venturesome in temperament and full of vitality and courage. The second period was characterized by an abnormally large child population. And finally, declining opportunity caused youth to leave for fields of opportunity elsewhere. The old, with vested interests in the community, remained.

The psychosocial cycle has to do with the group attitudes as these changed from an early period of community integration when people worked together in the face of common dangers. This was followed by the ascendancy of the large mining company, when conflict developed between the community and the mining company. High taxes were levied against the mining companies, and the towns began a regime of spending that led the companies to institute lawsuits and various restraining actions against town building and recreation programs. This situation continued until the companies became more powerful and made the communities bow to tax policies more advantageous to them.

[17] Paul H. Landis, *Three Iron Mining Communities,* Edwards, 1938.

The cycles are shown in Fig. 4.1 with the appropriate data for each stage.

Four Patterns of Growth

These three iron-mining towns demonstrate a life cycle that can be observed in one generation. Thus, time is telescoped and it is possible to study the full cycle. This is not ordinarily the case because cities outlive the observer. But cities may be observed in various stages of their growth pattern to see how industry affects them. Over a given time period, "growth" patterns of communities will be of four major types: *rapid growth, continuous growth, relatively stable growth,* and *decline.* These patterns correspond to the phases of a cycle, and any community might exhibit any of the phases in any sequence. A cross section of American communities at any given time will exhibit all of these patterns of growth.

RAPID GROWTH

The rapid growth pattern in the United States is occurring largely in the cities located along the Gulf coast, in the Southwest, and in the West. Here industry is booming because of increased discovery and use of oil and gas, the increase in such war industry production as shipbuilding and airplane manufacturing, and the growth of many new civilian industries. Available labor and space facilities have encouraged growth, and amenities such as climate are attracting the sick and the healthy, the young and the old.

Intensive studies have been made of the boom pattern in some cities. Havighurst and Morgan report on Seneca, Illinois, a small town of 1235 in 1942 but with a population of 6600 two years later. The boom was due to the location of a shipyard next to the village. In a little less than three years $82 million were paid in wages to the shipyard workers. To care for the inrush of workers, public housing projects were built; business, churches, and schools expanded; and the whole institutional complex of the village was transformed.[18] Carr and Stermer describe a similar process of

[18] Robert Havighurst and H. Gerthon Morgan, *The Social History of a War Boom Community,* Longmans, 1951.

Phase Of Cycle

Maximum

Minimum

	Pioneer Period (Growth)	Conflict Period (Maturity)	Period of Decay
Physicosocial Cycles			
Geographical Resource Cycle	Extent of ore unknown	Abundant supply located	Supply rapidly diminished
Social Policy Cycle	Discovery and development	Exploitation	Conservation
Cultural Cycles			
Life Evaluation Cycle	Life held cheap	Well-developed protective community	Protective culture
Moral Standards Cycle	Tolerance of vice	Tolerance of paternalism and graft	Economic mores in government
Material Culture Cycle	Simple material culture	Lavish material culture	Decay of material culture
Biosocial Cycles			
Birth Rate Cycle	Few married couples and few births	High birth rate	Low birth rate
Age Group Cycle	Young adult males	Disproportionately large number of children	Disproportionately large number of old people
Population Growth Cycle	Boom growth	Stable population	Decline
Sex Ratio Cycle	Males predominant	Males predominant	Balanced sex ratio
Psychosocial Cycles			
Group Relations Cycle	Integration	Conflict	Conflict
Dominance and Submission Cycle	Public ascendancy	Mining company ascendancy	Mining company ascendancy
Industrial Groups Cycle	Individual capitalists	Predatory corporations	Predatory corporations

FIG. 4.1. Life Cycle of the Mining Town Civilization. (From Paul H. Landis, *Three Iron Mining Communities,* Edwards, 1938, pp. 130–131.)

boom in Willow Run, a village transformed by the entry of air-plane manufacture.[19]

CONTINUOUS GROWTH

This pattern is appearing in cities that are developing new industries and expanding established industries. New industries especially stimulate rapid growth. The DuPont Company has adopted a policy of decentralizing its operations in relatively small cities over the United States, placing plants in twenty-five sites in fourteen states. At Montague, Michigan, the new neoprene plant is pumping a $2,000,000 annual pay roll into nearby com-munities. Carefully planned training programs, a month of tune-up operations, and dummy process runs have helped 200 new employees step from local farms, shops, and schoolrooms into a twentieth-century chemical plant. These employees are engaged in the basic activity which sets the multiplication factor operating to increase service employment and population. New industry is one source of rapid growth; expansion of established industry is another. In an interdependent economy the demand of one ex-panding industry often sends repercussions through a large part of the entire economy. The supply requirements of the Boeing Aircraft Company draw on every state in the nation for raw materials and parts.

Diversified cities with a broad base of industries create an es-pecially stable economic base for the community. If these indus-tries support systematic research and introduce new products, industry maintains its vitality and strengthens its position.

STABLE GROWTH

The slow or constant growth pattern may be found where a city has developed an established economy which remains in a relatively stable position. A consumer goods industry like flour milling and food processing has a rather steady demand for its products. If the community is an agricultural service center it may continue for years with a slow growth pattern, since its hinterland is probably making a fairly steady demand for serv-ices. The community with a stable growth pattern may be facing

[19] Lowell J. Carr and James E. Stermer, *Willow Run, A Study in Indus-trialization and Cultural Inadequacy*, Harper, 1952.

a real decline. A shift in technology or in service may have placed it in a disadvantaged position.

DECLINE

The diminished or declining growth pattern is often associated with exhaustion of resources or a shift in technology. The cities with gross declines are in coal- and iron-mining areas where mechanization of production and decline in the richer or less expensively produced ores have brought reductions in populations. Some cities die slowly, some rapidly. The standard metropolitan area of Scranton, Pennsylvania, demonstrates a declining growth pattern of long duration. The city may be considered as having been in decline since 1910, when its growth was less than the average population growth in the United States. It may continue to decline, stabilize at a lower level, or attract new industry and experience a stable growth pattern. With its large population, its immediate life is not threatened with extinction.

Technological change is another factor constantly threatening the growth pattern of the community. Charles R. Walker in *Steeltown* describes the impact of such a change on Ellwood City, Pennsylvania, when the National Tube Company announced that operations of its plant there would be moved to Gary, Indiana.[20] The change was brought about in part by new technical requirements of continuous seamless tube mills. The company employed 4000 workers, two-thirds of the city's industrial workers, in a city of 14,000. The announcement brought first shock and resentment. Then a struggle to keep the plant followed. Finally, efforts were turned to acquiring new industry for the community.

Caliente, Nevada, a small railroad town, was also faced with technical change. Cottrell describes how the introduction of the Diesel locomotive brought new maintenance requirements. As the distance between servicing points was lengthened, Caliente was bypassed; and for Caliente this was death—death bv Dieselization: "Those who have raised children see friendships broken and neighborhoods disintegrated. The childless more freely shake the dust of Caliente from their feet. Those who built their per-

[20] Charles R. Walker, *Steeltown*, Harper, 1950.

sonalities into the structure of the community watch their work destroyed."[21]

Four growth patterns have been described, each with its implications for the life of the community. These patterns result from many different causes. All the growth patterns are becoming more and more dependent on events and actions of people far removed from the immediate community. Yet it is the local community which must adjust to the economic forces conditioning its growth or decline.

Industry Differentiates Communities by Functional Type and Occupational Composition

Functional types

The most widely accepted functional classification of cities was made by Chauncy D. Harris.[22] Nine principal types of cities are recognized: (1) manufacturing, (2) manufacturing—mixed, (3) retail, (4) diversified, (5) wholesale, (6) transportation, (7) mining, (8) university, and (9) resort and retirement. One-fourth of the cities over 10,000 population in the United States are manufacturing cities; a little more than one-fifth are either industrial cities or diversified cities in which manufacturing predominates; one-eighth are diversified cities in which retailing predominates; one-sixth are residential cities; and the remaining cities have single functions, for example, mining, transportation, education, resort, or government.

Manufacturing, wholesale and retail trade, and transportation are the fundamental economic functions to keep in mind, for even the state capitals and educational, recreational, cultural, and religious centers are largely dependent upon these basic economic activities to furnish employment for the bulk of the labor

[21] W. F. Cottrell, "Death by Dieselization: A Case Study in the Reaction to Technological Change," *American Sociological Review,* June, 1951.

[22] Chauncy D. Harris, "A Functional Classification of Cities in the United States," *Geographical Review,* January, 1943, pp. 86–99. Cf. Grace Kneedler Ohlson, "Economic Classification of Cities," *Municipal Yearbook,* 1949, pp. 31–39; Victor Jones, "Economic Classification of Cities and Metropolitan Areas," *Municipal Yearbook,* 1953, pp. 49–54, 69; Howard J. Nelson, "A Service Classification of American Cities," *Economic Geography,* July, 1955, pp. 189–210.

force.[23] If cities were classified by the proportion of manufacturing, Gary, Indiana, would emerge as the manufacturing city par excellence. It has 68.9 percent of its workers engaged in industrial activities. Since Gary is one of Chicago's satellites, a great many of the latter city's services and attractions are rather readily available to the people of Gary. Were it not for this fact it would probably not be possible for so large a proportion of the labor force to be engaged in manufacturing. Miami, Florida, Washington, D.C., and Sacramento, California, each with manufacturing supplying employment to less than 11 percent, are cities which supply many services to their own population, to visitors, and to persons outside the city.

Occupational composition

Cities which differ in their industrial composition may be expected to have different occupational structures. Wide variations in occupational profiles of four cities are clearly portrayed in Fig. 4.2: Irvington, New Jersey; Rochester, Minnesota; Reading, Pennsylvania; and Youngstown, Ohio. Obviously variations in income, education, and style of life accompany different occupational structures. Gillen believes that these are the chief factors which make for the differences between cities. His research led him to view the occupational distribution of the city as the single best indicator of income and education.[24] This discovery makes possible an estimate of community character, as will be demonstrated in a later section.

Industry Affects the Total Land-Use Pattern

Common patterns

Different types of industries and economic functions have different spatial requirements. To a large extent these requirements fix the ecological patterns of cities. For example, the central business district is the predominent center of retail and wholesale activities and ancillary establishments serving the needs of

[23] T. Lynn Smith, "The Functions of American Cities," in T. Lynn Smith and C. A. McMahan (eds.), *Urban Life,* Dryden, 1951, p. 102.
[24] Paul Bates Gillen, *The Distribution of Occupations as a City Yardstick,* King's Crown, 1951.

DETERMINING THE OCCUPATIONAL PROFILE

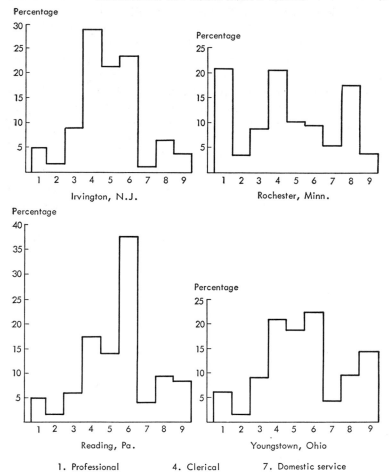

1. Professional
2. Semiprofessional
3. Proprietors
4. Clerical
5. Crafts
6. Operatives
7. Domestic service
8. Service
9. Laborers

FIG. 4.2. The Occupational Profiles of Four Cities. (From Paul Bates Gillen, *The Distribution of Occupations as a City Yardstick,* King's Crown, 1951, p. 24.)

workers, shoppers, and others who frequent the area. The large department stores are here, as well as specialized retail shops, hotels, publishing firms, theaters and movie houses, concert halls, travel bureaus, and other concerns providing goods and services to the entire city and its tributary region. The warehouses are usually located close by. To be sure, retail areas do appear in other parts of the city. In the United States the proportion of retail service units outside central business districts tends to increase with size of city. In the larger cities there are areas or districts devoted exclusively to certain types of stores.

Manufacturing may be divided into heavy industry, which requires a great deal of space and turns out bulky products, and light industry, which includes products of small size and weight and generally requires a small ground area per worker. Products of heavy industry include automobiles, airplanes, petroleum products, farm machinery, flour, sugar, lumber, steel, cement, meat products, railroad cars, and locomotives. Until the late nineteenth century, heavy industry in Europe and the United States tended to locate in the central portions of the cities, near wharves, docks, and railroad sidings and close to the center of supply.

During the twentieth century heavy industry has developed along railroad lines, river valleys, and ocean or lake fronts, commonly on the outskirts of the city or even well beyond the city's boundaries. River valley developments have occurred in the Youngstown, Pittsburgh, and Kansas City areas, while the tendency to locate on water fronts may be noted in the Chicago and Philadelphia districts.

Light industry is commonly at the edge of the central business district near the center of the city. Sometimes wholesaling and light manufacturing establishments are located in the same general area.

Decentralization

Both heavy and light industries may seek locations farther away from the central business district toward the outskirts of the city or across a city's boundaries into peripheral areas. Among the reasons for such decentralization may be a need for more space, access to ground water, lower rentals, lower labor costs, lower tax rates, and freedom from zoning restrictions. Developments in transportation, particularly motor transport trucks and belt railroad lines linked with the regular railway systems, have helped to free industry of its direct dependence on central freight terminals. A survey by Woodbury and his associates presents considerable evidence of decentralization in the United States.[25] The yardstick used by Woodbury is the percentage change in production workers in central cities, satellite cities, and industrial peripheries (outside of the central city). From 1899 to 1947 there was a long-run decline from 39.5 percent to 32.2 percent of manufacturing workers found in the central city, with an increase of 14.6 percent to 19.8 percent in the periphery.

Residential areas

Residential areas are settled in accordance with the location of the industrial and commercial functions. While zoning restrictions may effectively bar the invasion of stores and factories, the prevalence of spot zoning and ribbon developments of business dispersion along streets, highways, and rail lines opens the residential district to invasion or the threat of invasion. Homeowners, in a dynamic American city, are always on the move, seeking quiet and clean districts where residential property may be protected from the growth of business and industry.

Industry Influences the Power and Social Class Structure of the Community

Power structure

Formal power relations in industry are clearly specified by the supervisory ladder. Since the community is not as unilaterally organized as industry, its power relations are not easily seen, but they range from the almost complete dominance by industry as found in a company town to a minor power position for industry as, for example, in a government-dominated town. Although great variations in relative power exist, a historical trend may nonetheless be noted.

The power ladder in the industrial communities of the nineteenth century (and in many smaller industrial communities today) duplicated the supervisory hierarchy completely. No important organization could function contrary to the wishes of business. The officers of local organizations were either business

[25] Coleman Woodbury (ed.), *The Future of Cities and Urban Redevelopment*, University of Chicago Press, 1953, pp. 253–255.

managers or their approved substitutes. This situation was considered normal. Businessmen believed that they were natural leaders, that they knew what was good for the community, and that what was good for business was also good for the community. Most people today still believe this, and in most communities businessmen continue to dominate community organizations. In smaller communities, where both managers and workers participate in the same organizations, there can be no opposition to industry on any major issue; the power of the plant supervisors carries over into town affairs. Resistance to management can be easily located, and those who resist may be dismissed.

Warner and his associates have documented this type of business class control as it exists today in a town of 6000 people. The leading industry in "Jonesville" is an appliance manufacturing concern. Seven hundred of the city's 2000 urban employees work there.

> The economic and social force of The Mill affects every part of the life of the community. Everyone recognizes its power. Politicians, hat in hand, wait upon Mr. Waddell, manager of The Mill, to find out what he thinks. Civic leaders seek out the manager of The Mill for the answers to such important questions as "Shall the tax rate be increased to improve the education our young people are getting?"—"Shall the new minister be Mr. Jones or Mr. Smith?"—"Should the city support various civic and moral enterprises?"—"Should new industries enter the town and possibly compete with The Mill for the town's available labor supply?" They want to know what Mr. Waddell thinks. Mr. Waddell usually lets them know.[26]

Such a pattern is more difficult to maintain in large cities, as may be accounted for historically. As communities grew, common participation of all members in the same organizations tended to decrease. Consequently the number of organizations that employers could control diminished, with the result that they partially withdrew from active community participation and "responsibility." With expanding urbanization and the spread of the impersonal labor market, insecurity grew among the workers. They tried to meet this problem partly by organizing labor unions and by challenging industry's leadership in the community. Their

[26] W. Lloyd Warner and associates, *Democracy in Jonesville,* Harper, 1949, p. 101.

power has grown, and businessmen have shown a growing concern lest they lose out in the struggle to retain community power.

Whitehead has made a sophisticated but conservative case for businessmen to reassert their leadership and assume major responsibility in community affairs.[27] He suggests that they use their "tremendous advantages" of natural dominance, organizational backing, legal knowledge, business skills, and physical resources to get sympathetic understanding of business problems by the local people.

No longer able to control local cliques and the multitude of new organizations, industry has launched a double-barreled program. One part consists of adding a public relations department to its own structure; the other part encompasses a broad community program including such things as student scholarships, athletic teams, youth organizations, community services, and many philanthropies. Both the public relations department and the community services are aimed largely at the manual and white-collar workers. Increasingly, labor groups are supporting a parallel development in order to obtain acceptance and representation in community decision-making.

Social class structure

Sociologists long ago observed that the social class structure of the community was closely related to its economic base.[28] Early Marxists insisted that the main class cleavage in the community was between the industrial workers and the owners of productive facilities. Subsequent studies have refined this simplistic analysis, so that we are now aware that other economic and social forces influence social class stratification. It is also apparent that several social classes may exist in a community, and that the number and relative size of these classes depend on locality characteristics.

Warner and his associates devised an Index of Status Characteristics to identify classes, using occupation, source of income, house type, and dwelling area. All of these factors have been

[27] T. N. Whitehead, *Leadership in a Free Society*, Harvard, 1936, p. 172.
[28] In later chapters, the concept "status group" is used in place of "social class," so that there will be less confusion with the economic category of stratification, viz., "class."

shown to be important in measuring social class differences.[29] However, most students of social class behavior agree that if one desires a single measure of the overall complex of class behavior, the basis of all the variables, a scale of occupations is clearly the most efficient instrument to use.[30]

Since industry contributes a large part of the occupational composition and differentiation to a community, its influence in shaping social classes is very great. Donald Wray has demonstrated how the occupational structure of a medium-sized Illinois city is translated into the social structure of the city. Figure 4.3

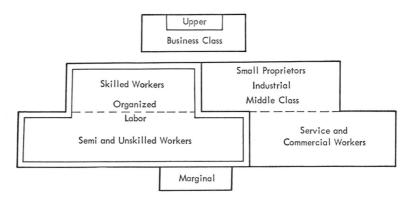

FIG. 4.3. Illini City Social Structure. (Redrawn from Donald E. Wray, *The Community and Labor-Management Relations,* Institute of Labor and Industrial Relations, University of Illinois, 1953, p. 47.)

shows the social stratification of "Illini City," population 66,269 (in 1950). The top business class includes the owners and executives of the larger enterprises and most of the professional men. A small clique within this dominant class consists of the old-line families, which are a subgroup rather than a distinct social stratum. The business class as a whole represents the locus of economic, social, and organizational control over the life of the city.

A fairly wide gap separated the business class from the rest of

[29] W. L. Warner, M. Meeker, and K. Eells, *Social Class in America,* Science Research, 1949.

[30] Joseph A. Kahl and James A. Davis, "A Comparison of Indexes of Socio-Economic Status," *American Sociological Review,* June, 1955, pp. 317–325.

the common people. A middle-class segment was composed of skilled workers and small proprietors, white-collar workers, and minor professionals. A significant split within the middle class arose from the fact that the skilled workers were affiliated with unions, and were "wage earners" in contrast to the "salaried" middle class. The skilled workers were oriented toward organized labor, while the salaried white-collar workers identified their interests with the top business class. The line between a "middle" class and a "lower" class was indistinct and difficult to define and was likewise split into an employer-employee division of primary identification. The "lower" class (lower-paid wage earners) was therefore divided in terms of union affiliation, though the problem of membership was primarily a matter of place of employment.

Of course, communities with different industrial-occupational structures would be expected to exhibit different class profiles and cleavages. As Fig. 4.2 suggests, Youngstown, Ohio, might be expected to exhibit a pattern closer to the Marxist ideal, for example, than Rochester, Minnesota. Although classes might have different meaning in the Soviet orbit, differences among cities would also be found there that might have consequences for the local patterns of stratification.

Industry Influences Community Character

The physical appearance of a community to a large extent reflects its industrial composition. The drab, smoky mill towns along the Monongahela River of Pennsylvania derive their appearance from the steel industry. In contrast, Washington, D.C., with its concentration of white-collar government workers, presents the face of a city that is freer of industrial grime and smoke. And in the largest metropolitan centers, the pace and variety of community life itself reflect the myriad behavior patterns which a complex of industry may endow.

It may appear at first blush that qualitative characteristics of a community, such as "goodness" would not be a function of its industrial and economic base. However, E. L. Thorndike made a comprehensive attempt to measure city goodness by assembling 37 characteristics for 310 American cities. Goodness was defined in terms of degree of health, presence of social and cultural activities, amounts spent on recreational activities, and so on. The data for each city were cumulated into a score, which Thorndike termed the Goodness or G score. The base line for city comparison was derived by adopting the lowest score in each of the thirty-seven items. For the operating administrator he prepared a ten-item city yardstick which calls for data that may be fairly easily obtained.[31]

Thorndike ascribed 60 percent of the variation among cities to "personal qualities" of the population, such as their education, customs, and ideals; 25 percent to differences in income; and the remaining 15 percent to all other factors. In summary, the principal factors that affect a city are the quality and financial ability of its people. These characteristics tend to move together, although the possession of money does not automatically and invariably produce individuals of high "quality."[32] The distribution of occupations includes both education and income of people and therefore is highly related to the relative quality of a city.[33] Thus, the pattern of occupation may be used as the basis for deriving an index of the relative worth of cities.

This high relationship between occupational distribution and goodness of a city suggests that the industrial composition of the city is an economic base conditioning its social character. The occupational distribution influences many characteristics of community life, including income, health, education, and the like. All that a city does by way of government or through the encouragement of the work of voluntary agencies is based on the people and, most importantly, on how they earn their living. Gillen contends, "No consideration of any kind about a city can get very far away from the occupational distribution."[34]

These findings suggest that there is a chain of causation which originates with the industrial composition of the community.

[31] E. L. Thorndike, *Your City*, Harcourt, Brace, 1939, pp. 153–156.

[32] Robert C. Angell reports in his study of the moral integration of cities that the correlation of moral integration with income was zero. See "The Moral Integration of American Cities," *American Journal of Sociology*, July, 1951, p. 16.

[33] Gillen reports coefficients of correlation between his occupational indices, and Thorndike's G scores in three groups of cities as .82, .89, and .35. See Gillen, *op. cit.*, p. 44.

[34] *Ibid.*, p. 108.

Industrial composition shapes the occupational structure of the community. The occupational structure influences the income and educational levels of the community. When these levels are set, many other community variables are affected, including health, education, housing, and cultural attainments. This chain might be diagramed as follows:

Industrial Composition of the Community	→	Occupational Composition of the Community	→	Income and Educational Levels of the Community	→	Health, Housing, Education, Cultural Institutions

INFLUENCE OF TECHNOLOGICAL CHANGE ON ORGANIZATIONAL CHANGE IN THE COMMUNITY

The Relation of Technological Change to Community Life

Industry-community relations may be viewed as a continuum of relationships running from the production line to family and community adjustment.[35] Work plant organization is human organization. In the factory, hospital, and department store, workers are arranged in such a way as to encourage the greatest amount of cooperative effort. The positions that men occupy in work organization to a large extent fix their social position at work *and* in the community. A change in a worker's status in his work plant tends to be quickly reflected in the community groups to which he belongs. Thus changes in work organization affect community organizations as well.

Before the industrial revolution, technical organization remained relatively stable. A balanced adjustment between work and community life was the rule. With the advent of industrialism, the chief characteristic of technical organization became change. Profit was derived not only by improving machinery but also by improving work organization. Indeed, technical and mechanical alterations in production forced changes in the organization of workers in the plant, and this rearrangement in turn disturbed social patterns in the community.

The general social effects of invention and technological change

[35] Conrad Arensberg, "Industry and Community," *American Journal of Sociology,* July, 1942, p. 8.

93370

EMORY AND HENRY LIBRARY

have been catalogued by Ogburn, the Rosens, and others.[36] For example, the automobile has made possible an increased growth of many established industries like steel as well as the rise of many new industries—refineries, filling stations, garages, auto parts stores, and hot-dog stands. The whole pattern of rural life has been revolutionized by the tractor and the automobile. The line between rural and urban life grows less sharp with each passing year. Horace Miner has been exploring the specific effects of inventions on rural life to determine more precisely the manner in which rural organization has been influenced by technological change.[37]

Technological Change and Community Solidarity

Warner and Low have presented a historical account of how changes in the technology of the shoe industry altered social relations both in and outside the factory.[38] They have shown that during the early factory period the skill hierarchy dominated workers' lives and largely fixed their status positions in the community. The hierarchy of crafts was at the same time an age-grade system through which young men expected to pass. The factories themselves were under the informal control of community traditions. Shoe manufacturers, who were accepted by all classes as leaders, felt a responsibility toward the community.

The mechanization of shoe production largely destroyed the skill hierarchy *and* the age-grade system that accompanied it. Skilled workers became semiskilled, and semiskilled workers remained on that level. Since young men could no longer anticipate an ascent into jobs requiring greater skills, they lost hope and security. The older people also lost security, status, as well as confidence in local leaders. Along with changes in production went a change in the structure of business ownership. Big city financiers assumed financial and directional control of local factories. Thus

[36] William F. Ogburn and S. C. Gilfillan, *Recent Social Trends*, McGraw-Hill, 1938, chap. III; S. McKee Rosen and Laura Rosen, *Technology and Society*, Macmillan, 1941.

[37] Horace Miner, *Agriculture and Culture*, University of Michigan Press, 1949.

[38] W. Lloyd Warner and J. O. Low, *The Social System of the Modern Factory*, Yale, 1947. Cf. Warner and associates, *op. cit.*, pp. 101–114.

the changes in occupational structure and financial control shattered the network of personal relations, loyalties, and obligations.

This fact was not appreciated until a strike was called by the workers in a town that absentee managers considered union-proof and strike-proof. The managers were surprised at the amount of support the strikers received from small businessmen, churchmen, the police, and others. The reason was that the captains of industry were no longer the community leaders. They could not count on the support of local influentials. Consequently, the workers won the strike, and an industrial union became a part of the social fabric of Yankee City. Equally important, leadership in the factory, as far as the workers were concerned, passed from management to the union.

Technological Change and Social Class

Ordinarily the composition of social classes does not change rapidly. When changes do occur they usually arise from changes in social relations brought about by industrial change. Smith reports how shifts in the class system of a New England town were produced by the introduction of the stretch-out in a textile mill.[39] In this case the technical process of cloth making was gradually altered, while the actual process of weaving remained essentially the same. Important changes were also introduced in the organization of workers, particularly by breaking down their jobs in the weaving process. In the early days a weaver had complete charge of the loom—cleaning it, loading shuttle bobbins in the creel, tying the ends of yarn together, picking out the flaws in the cloth, repairing the "smashes," and so on. With mechanical, material, and process improvements, the weaver attended more and more looms and spent less time on skilled work. The time he spent on *unskilled* work, however, grew so great that mills began to hire unskilled workers to take over the weavers' routine operations. Consequently weavers were expected to attend even more looms. Fewer weavers were needed, with the result that many had to become unskilled hands.[40]

[39] Elliott Dunlap Smith with Richmond Carter Nyman, *Technology and Labor*, Yale, 1939.
[40] *Ibid.*, pp. 1–4.

Further, as mechanical improvements and labor rationalization expanded, the demand for technical college-trained specialists and supervisors also grew. Top managers were recruited increasingly from these college-trained technicians and decreasingly from mill operatives. The college-trained men had little or no contact with the workers, either in the plant or in the community. The net result of all these changes was an emphasis on the difference between labor and management. There was a decrease in common goals and common participation in the community. Formal education replaced work experience as the main avenue into management. In this case, then, *class distinctions in the community were almost entirely a product of changes in industrial organization.* Political and social issues in the town were directly related to the organizational structure and changes in the industry.

Other studies are needed to assess the effect of speedup, transfer and promotion, seasonal layoffs, mechanization, rationalization, quality controls, and other industrial changes on family and community relations. No doubt such studies will further document the fact that modern industry has a tendency to shatter social relations both within itself and in the community. Each change creates more instability and insecurity, and the fractures spread throughout the entire society. This trend has not gone completely unchallenged. There have developed within the community and in the work plant formal and informal structures to resist innovations.[41]

Resisting Effects of Technological Change

The rise of labor unions is often attributed to the unsettling effects of technological and organizational changes. Unions are fighting some industrial changes directly, attempting to soften the effects of others, and encouraging those which increase the security of the workers.

In such industries as building construction, which are by nature dynamic and unsettling, particularly strong unions have arisen. They have sought to minimize the effects of insecurity by controlling the recruitment of workers, setting the pace of work, resisting technological improvements, and establishing benefit

[41] See Benjamin M. Selekman, *Labor Relations and Human Relations,* McGraw-Hill, 1947, Chap. VI.

funds.[42] These measures have fallen short of stabilizing the industry, because the industry is only part of a larger society which lacks integration. Increasingly, therefore, unions have been driven to participate in local and national affairs to widen their influence.

The social changes that technology brings to the community are not the result of purposeful and intentional behavior on the part of industrialists. However, the desire to introduce technological innovations springs largely from an attempt to cut costs and operate more efficiently. Businessmen say competition in a free enterprise system demands that more efficient methods be adopted and that social disruptions are a necessary cost of progress. Any interference with the right to introduce technological improvements is strongly resisted by managements as a challenge to a sacred prerogative.

CONCLUSION

Industry has many wide and pervasive effects in molding the form and function of the community. The influence of economic institutions in a mass production society is more than a mere local phenomenon. Karl Polanyi traces out implications of this fact:

Ultimately that is why the control of the economic system by the market is of overwhelming consequence to the whole organization of society, it means no less than the running of society as an adjunct to the market. Instead of the economy being embedded in social relations, social relations are embedded in the economic system. The vital importance of the economic factor to the existence of society precludes any other result. For once the economic system is organized in separate institutions, based on specific motives and conferring a special status, society must be shaped in such a manner as to allow that system to function according to its own laws. This is the meaning of the familiar assertion that a market economy can function only in a market society.[43]

Society and local community are parts of common social processes. The values by which and for which people live appear in any representative sample of their society. The community is a segment of the society differentiated only by its local individu-

---

[42] Whitehead, *op. cit.*, p. 161.
[43] Karl Polanyi, *The Great Transformation*, Holt, 1944, p. 57.

ality. A society in which economic institutions dominate produces communities which function as "economic mechanisms," and through them the life of a people unfolds.

SELECTED BIBLIOGRAPHY

Allen, F., W. Ogburn, H. Hart, M. Nimkoff, and D. C. Miller, *Technology and Social Change,* Appleton-Century-Crofts, 1957.

Cottrell, W. F., "Death by Dieselization: A Case Study in the Reaction to Technological Change," *American Sociological Review,* June, 1951, pp. 358–365.

Cottrell, W. F., *Energy and Society,* McGraw-Hill, 1955.

Form, William H., "The Place of Social Structure in the Determination of Land Use: Some Implications for a Theory of Urban Ecology," *Social Forces,* May, 1954, pp. 317–323.

Gilmore, Harlan W., *Transportation and the Growth of Cities,* Free Press, 1953.

Hawley, Amos H., *Human Ecology,* Ronald, 1950.

Hoover, Edgar M., *The Location of Economic Activity,* McGraw-Hill, 1948.

Landis, Paul H., *Three Iron Mining Communities,* Edwards, 1938.

Ullman, Edward L., "The Basic-Service Ratio and the Areal Support of Cities," *Proceedings,* Western Committee on Regional Economic Analysis of the Social Science Research Council, University of California, June 25–27, 1953, pp. 110–123.

Walker, Charles R., *Steeltown,* Harper, 1950.

Warner, W. Lloyd, and J. O. Low, *The Social System of the Modern Factory,* Yale, 1947.

PART II · The Structure and Function of Work Organizations

Purposive work organizations arise wherever men seek to earn a living or to achieve specified goals. Such organizations include factories, offices, stores, government agencies, fraternities, military bases, hospitals, churches, homes, and all of the other types of organizations shown on the charts preceding Part I. They have one characteristic in common. Each must have a structure. They cannot function by letting each member do whatever he thinks needs to be done; rather, they must first organize. As duties are divided, responsibilities assigned, and procedures adopted, formal structure begins to take shape. This formal organization serves as a guide and tends to give the organization an identity of its own independent of the people who form it. The organization may grow, and as it hires people to operate part of it, management appears. Management is an authority system which requires subordinate employees.

This part of the book deals with the structure and functions of work organizations. It begins by observing the work tasks which must be organized into formal structures of work and management. Then the behavior of work groups is shown to be a network of interrelated informal activities which constantly influence formal organization. Union organization is described as a structure of employee representation to act as a countervailing power in relations with management. The final chapters describe how the enduring social patterns of power, economic class, and status cut through the formal and informal organizations. Max Weber's insights and concepts are used to describe both formal and informal patterns of stratification as people seek to control others, secure economic security, and gain status or prestige.

CHAPTER 5

Formal Organization

WHAT IS ORGANIZATION?

The question of organization brings up a variety of images to different people. To some it means a kind of group—a union, lodge, or church. To others it calls to mind a number of offices in an association or society. Still others think of it as the means of introducing system or order into a group.

To the labor leader or business executive, organization is a much more specific concept. It refers to a method of arranging men and materials. It represents an effective way of getting things done most efficiently. Organization is needed as the efforts of more and more people must be coordinated. It means, therefore, allocating authority to some individuals, delegating it to others, dispersing functions to still others, and keeping records of all activities.

No one will quarrel with these concepts of organization as far as they go. The scientist, however, is not content to use the specific definitions of particular groups. He is interested in the general phenomenon of organization and its manifestations everywhere. From a sociological point of view, social organization arises whenever people interact on a continuous basis in pursuit of common goals. Organization consists of the routines which group members display in their behavior toward each other. More exactly, organization consists of the behavior expectations that the people have toward one another as group members. The actual behavior of the members may not conform to these ideal expectations because many factors may intrude. The latter may include unusual events, individual differences, and interaction with other groups.

The sociological concept of organization is, then, simple and concrete. It consists of records of "observing the behavior of individuals in groups." All the uniform, routine, or conventional ways of group action constitute social organization. When these expected patterns of behavior are not observed, disequilibrium, disorganization, or social change ensues.

THE ORGANIZATION OF WORK

Purposive organizations of all kinds form when there are tasks to be performed. In the study of formal organization, work tasks must be the starting point. Formal organization of management arises as a response to the problems posed in the organizing of work tasks. Modern manufacturing provides a good illustration because there is sufficient specialization of tasks to demonstrate the origins of management structure in work.

Often a person from another culture can see things which the inhabitants fail to observe in their very midst. To get such an outsider's view let us try to imagine a skilled craftsman from the eighteenth century as he would observe our industrial culture. He is not totally ignorant of our culture, for he is familiar with our language and some of the elements of modern technology.

Material Culture and Technical Organization

Probably the first thing to impress him would be the abundant material culture of industry. He would be amazed at the amount and variability of such artifacts as giant boring mills, cash registers, and assembly lines. He would soon notice that some people are making things, others are carrying things, and others are exchanging things. He would be most intrigued, perhaps, by the places in which things are made.

Let us take him to a typical factory in America in the 1960s. His first perceptions will be of material objects. As he approaches the factory, he observes that it is a low one- or two-story building covering a relatively large area. He notices that it is a large building which houses many different kinds of objects. Figure 5.1 shows what he sees. We shall try to describe some of his reactions.

As he enters he sees a honeycomb of rather small cells or rooms in which are found tables, storage boxes, contraptions that make

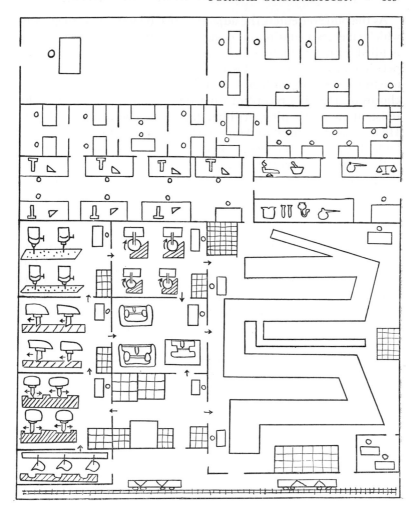

FIG. 5.1. The Material Culture of a Modern Factory. Can you identify the artifacts and basic social divisions?

marks on paper, black horns into which people speak, and innumerable large and small sheets of paper with some strange and some familiar markings. The rooms appear light and clean, and there is an underlying murmur of voices mixed with an incessant clatter from the marking and other contraptions.

As the observer enters the adjacent area, he sees a vast shed from which emerges a continuous clang and clatter of metal. The room is filled with large and small machines, each of which emits its peculiar cacophony. On closer observation he notes that similar machines are grouped together in different parts of the shed. The chorus of noise is a record of what the machines are doing to the resistant metal—shaping, drilling, stamping, grinding, and milling. He is amazed at the abundance of steel and iron. In a nearby area he finds the source of these materials. He sees caldrons brimming with shimmering, molten metal. Huge ladles and pans filled with the liquid travel around the shed spilling their contents in designated places.

He wanders off to another section of the factory and enters another vast room. It appears more quiet, somewhat lighter, and more airy. There are many more people here. They are lined up rather close together. Some of them are running machines, but most of them are working with hand tools. Some of the workers have huge shallow trays before them. Inside the trays are many small pockets or compartments filled with different-shaped pieces of metal from which workers are picking out pieces at a rapid rate.

Other people are seen lined up alongside a moving counter. All kinds of metal pieces are found on the counter. The workers pick off the pieces they need, then occasionally place the assembled pieces back on the counter. The pieces on the counter become larger and larger until they get to the end of the line. The product is now completed or "manufactured." It is put into boxes by other machines and loaded into contrivances by still other machines.

Social Organization

As our observer continues to study the plant, its physical layout and machines hold less interest for him. He wants to know more about the people in the factory. He begins to study their behavior, as shown in Fig. 5.2. This figure describes the social organization of the factory. He watches the workers come to the plant in the morning, noticing that they all live away from the plant. Some of them live close by, others farther away. Those that live closer enter one side of the sheds. As soon as they are inside, they change

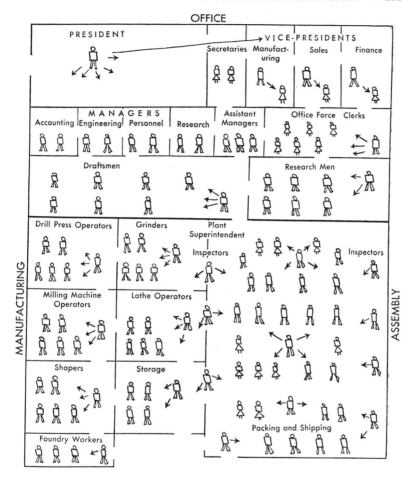

FIG. 5.2. The Social Organization of a Modern Factory.

their clothes and put on darker garments. A few workers arrive already dressed in darker garments, and they do not change their clothes. Those who live farther away come to the plant later. They enter it by a different door. Although their clothes are light in color they do not change them.

Our observer notices that these two classes of workers, the early and late arrivals, have little to do with each other. The early arrivals work with the machines and other large objects; the others work with paper. He is told that the clean group works in the "office" and the dirtier group works in the "shop." This distinction, he discovers, is very important.

As he scrutinizes the workers in the shop, he notices that those who are near one another do much the same thing. Most of the workers stay at the same place all day long tending machines. A few, however, wander around from place to place, talking to other workers who are doing similar things. These men are called "foremen." The areas they cover or their routes are referred to as "departments." Only men are allowed to work in the metal-working departments in this society. There is the foundry department, which prepares and casts the metal. The metal is then cut up and processed by other departments. It is shaped in one department, milled in another, drilled in another, ground in another, and finished in another. These departments are more closely related to one another than to any other department. One man, the "superintendent" walks around all of these departments, talking mostly to the foremen as they walk around in their smaller areas. Sometimes the foremen leave their areas and go to the superintendent for a talk.

In a nearby area are the moving counters. Here the workers, including women, put together the pieces made in the other part of the factory. They are sometimes called "assemblers." The assemblers stay in one place all day long. But here again there are a few men who walk around in designated areas. Some of them only look at the products and put marks on them. They are the "inspectors." Foremen are also walking about talking here and there to the workers. At the end of the counters, the products are boxed, put into trucks or freight cars, and taken away. Pieces of paper are sent to the "office" periodically to inform the people "up" there of these movements.

As the observer looks at the office, he notices that it, too, is subdivided into sections or departments. Here it is more difficult to tell who the foremen are because many people are moving around. Everybody seems to be doing the same thing because they all are making marks on paper and talking. However, he notices that there are more women working here than in other parts of the plant. The women have smaller places on which to put their papers than the men. The men generally tell the women what to do. None of the workers seem to be making anything—all they do is write and talk. Despite this it appears that they regard themselves as better than the people in the shop.

The functions of the office slowly become clear. The office, it seems, is closely related to activities in the shop. Some of the workers order the materials for the shop; others sell the products made. Some of the men are constantly planning to improve the machines in the shop. Others are concerned with coordinating the work of the departments. Then there are "specialists" who keep track of green pieces of paper and put them into envelopes. Everything done must be recorded, and this is the job of the younger women in the offices.

Power Groupings

The longer the observer stays in the office the more he realizes that it is the place where decisions are made which change things in the plant. Much of the activity of the "walkers" in the shop is in obedience to orders from the large-desk men in the office. The observer notes that the large-desk men in the large empty rooms have more authority over other workers. The smaller-desk men in small rooms have less authority. The largest-desk men have jurisdiction in general over the entire work plant. They delegate specific power over smaller groups to smaller-desk men. On the plant floor, the smaller the area of the walkers, the more specific and smaller is their authority. Finally, all the way down the "line," there are persons who obey everybody and give orders to nobody. The observer is not surprised when he learns that these are the "workers." The walking men he identifies as the "bosses." Everywhere he sees the bosses busily observing the behavior of others and reporting it to people with the bigger desks. The big-desk workers then give commands. When they are carried out, reports are given to them and the process is repeated over and over.

Much of the activity in the plant is concerned with giving orders, carrying them out, and reporting on them. Occasionally the workers in the shed object to the commands of the large-desk men. Then they meet together in small groups on the plant floor. Sometimes all the plant workers are called together outside the plant. Their representatives from these meetings, called stewards and union officials, meet with the desk men and tell them what the workers want. Only by these means do the workers have any influence on the large-desk men. Working, obeying, reporting, and holding meetings seem to be the main activities of the workers. These things are related to the accumulation of green pieces of paper in envelopes at the end of the week.

Our observer has now seen how the material culture and its technical organization has given rise to management, an authority system with the responsibility of getting the work done. The growth of management over the century which our observer was asked to leap is still another remarkable history.[1]

THE ORGANIZATION OF MANAGEMENT

Growth of Management

Very few occupational groups are as self-conscious as modern executives and managers. This narcissism has not always existed; it is the product of particular historical changes occurring in the economic system. The evolution of modern management organization has accompanied the growth and expansion of business and industry, a growth which probably could not have occurred without two accompanying social movements. The first of these was the development of the natural sciences. The second was the growth of a vigorous capitalistic economy which employed the discoveries of science for private profit. Under the twin stimulations of applied science (technology) and capitalistic enterprise the size of businesses grew. The advantage of large-scale production for both technological and financial reasons was soon apparent. The ability to expand production on the basis of technical improvements grew faster than the ability of private individuals to finance plant expansion. Under these conditions, the corporate form of business enterprise was invented and diffused.

The growth of the corporation had two important consequences. One was the dispersion of owners (or stockholders), who had little or no contact with the actual operation of business. The

---

[1] A. A. Berle, Jr., *The Twentieth Century Capitalist Revolution*, Harcourt, Brace, 1954; Charles A. Beard and Mary R. Beard, *The Rise of American Civilization*, Macmillan, Vol. II, 1928.

extent of the separation of owners from workers was documented in a study by Berle and Means. They discovered that, as early as 1929, 94 percent of all manufactured products were made by corporations.[2] The second consequence of corporate growth was the impetus it gave to the occupational division of labor. As financing was made available to introduce new machines and new operations, the growth of specialized occupations increased enormously. Data from the census and the *Dictionary of Occupational Titles* present graphic evidence of the proliferation of occupations in America today. Admitting an incomplete enumeration, the latter publication in 1949 located 22,028 different occupational jobs which were known by an additional 17,995 titles, making a total of 40,023 defined titles. In a 1955 supplement, 2260 new and revised definitions were added.[3]

Functions of Management

With owners dispersed and unable to attend to the direction of business, and with industry growing in size and complexity, there was a pressing need to *coordinate effectively the activities of many people*. This is the management or executive function. As industry grew larger and more complex the executive process became more crucial. Barnard, who has made an important study of the management process, indicates that its three main functions are (1) to provide a system of communication, (2) to promote the securing of essential efforts, and (3) to formulate and define purpose for the organization.[4]

Although Barnard has substituted a vocabulary of cooperation for a vocabulary of command in his analysis of executive functions, he is nonetheless correct in suggesting that management's duties are essentially devoted toward coordination of human, not technical, activity. It is difficult to overstress the role of management as one which is directed toward people and the integration of their efforts.

Figure 5.3 depicts how the functions of management grow as a response to large-scale organization. As the number of persons

[2] See Adolf A. Berle, Jr., and Gardiner C. Means, *The Modern Corporation and Private Property*, Macmillan, 1933, p. 39.

[3] *Dictionary of Occupational Titles*, United States Employment Service, GPO, 1949, p. xi; Supplement I, 1955, p. v.

[4] C. I. Barnard, *The Functions of the Executive*, Harvard, 1947, p. 217.

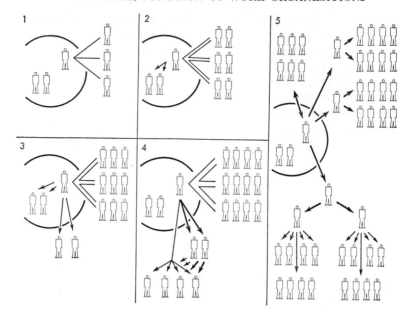

FIG. 5.3. Expansion of a Work Plant and the Rise and Change of Management Function. (1) The craftsman sells to a few customers. (2) As the volume of his business increases, his sons begin to work under his direction. (3) With further increase in sales, he employs apprentices outside the family, and a factory hierarchy develops with foremen supervising the workers under his direction while he continues to sell directly to his customers. (4) With a larger volume of business, all the manufacturing is done outside the family, and a factory hierarchy develops with foremen supervising the workers under his direction while he continues to sell directly to his customers. (5) With further expansion he invites others to buy shares of his business. He delegates his sales duties to others, delegates his supervision over manufacturing to another, and spends most of his time integrating the activities of everyone. (Adapted from Eliot D. Chapple and Carleton S. Coon, *Principles of Anthropology*, Holt, 1942, p. 369.)

in an organization increases, their relationships expand geometrically. Since it is management's task to coordinate people, management activities increase tremendously with expanding size of organization. The functions of management are of course performed in the smallest enterprises; even if the business consists of two individuals, coordination must take place. As a small business grows, the duties of the manager become more pressing until all his energy must be devoted to them. With further expansion of business, the management functions must be subdivided, for they become too burdensome for one person. Thus management becomes a specialized occupation with many sub-classifications.

Formal Organization

This approach to organization is not commonly utilized by all social scientists. When the economist speaks of the organization of business, or when the political scientist describes the organization of government, each is referring to only one aspect of social organization, namely, *formal organization*. Urwick's definition is typical of business administrators. He says organization is "dividing up all of the activities which are necessary to any purpose and arranging them in groups which are assigned to individuals."[5] Although this idea is drawn with an eye on practical problems of administration, it contains the essential elements included in formal organization. Among the things included would be all written specifications of individual relationships in the group, all rights, duties, and privileges that are formally assigned to personal and group roles, and all rituals and regulations that are created as models of personal and group activity. C. I. Barnard in his book *The Functions of the Executive* summarizes the characteristics of formal organization in a pithy definition: "The central hypothesis of this book is that the most useful concept for the analysis of cooperative systems is embodied in the definition of formal organization as a *system of consciously coordinated activities of two or more persons*."[6]

Barnard specifically emphasizes that his definition of formal organization *excludes* the physical environment (e.g., a plant) the particular social situations, and the specific members of the organization.[7] Formal organizations are (1) impersonal or non-personal in nature, (2) composed of members who bear ideal *relationships* with each other, and (3) usually parts of larger cooperative systems.[8]

The reader may think it contradictory that people are necessary to organization and yet specific individuals and social situations are excluded in the definition of organization. The distinctions

[5] L. Urwick, *Management of Tomorrow*, Nisbet, 1933, p. 53.
[6] Barnard, *op. cit.*, p. 73.
[7] *Ibid.*, p. 64.
[8] *Ibid., passim*, pp. 74–80.

between "office" and person may clarify the point. The judge, the teacher, the priest may be thought of as offices or statuses that particular individuals hold. The judge must act toward the violator of the law in accord with formally constituted specifications. His relationship with the violator is impersonal. In the capacity of a judge, a husband may have to pronounce sentence on a traffic violator, who may happen to be his wife. In the formal organization of the court, *the persons are incidental to their defined relationships.* So it is with formal organization generally.

The specific social situation is not included in formal organization for similar reasons. To elaborate our illustration: On a particular morning our judge may have a hangover; his wife may have just told him she must have an operation. Certainly these unusual circumstances will alter the operation of the court, yet such situations are too fluid to be considered as part of a system of relations that typically govern the behavior of the court.

When we describe the formal organization of business or union, we are concerned with the relations as specified in the organizational charts. Some of these relations are (1) the authority relations, or what offices have authority over other offices, (2) what offices or groups are responsible to what other offices, (3) what groups have what specific functions (auditing, cleaning, managing), and (4) who reports what to whom (the communication system).

These relations are found in formal organizations everywhere. They are present in labor, business, political, educational, religious, and other organizations. The specific relations may be structured differently in different organizations, but the types of relations themselves are universal, and therefore noncultural.

This view of formal organization is valuable, but, as the reader is already aware, it is not concerned with the person *in the act of fulfilling his role.* When one begins to examine formal organization in actual operation, one notes that people do not altogether live up to the specific definitions of their offices. And this is to be expected because formal organization cannot take into account the individual attributes of the person in an office and in changing situations. In fact, it may be stated as a principle that "whenever persons are placed in continued formal contact, in whatever circumstances, their relationships become characterized by actions and reactions over and above formal expectations."[9] To assume that the big boss's secretary, especially if she's pretty, has no influence on his job is naïve. It is also naïve to assume that such personal relations as might develop are totally unpatterned or inconsequential. In fact, the sociologist believes that the personal relations existing among members of an organization which are not represented by the "blueprint" constitute another aspect of organization: informal organization. Informal organization plays as important a part in the functioning of social organization as formal organization.

Informal Organization

Informal organization consists of a number of things. It is composed of the animosities and friendships among the people who work together. It contains the primary groups, cliques, and congeniality groups that develop in shop or office. It further consists of the folkways, mores, norms, and values which guide the behavior of workers, sometimes in the fulfillment of the goals of formal organization and sometimes in the blockage of those goals. Informal organization is a source of much social control. In it a prestige and power structure evolves which may be at variance with similar structures in the formal organization. In fact, the relation of the informal organization to the formal organization determines how effectively the latter will function.

The Constituent Segments of the Work Plant

The distinction between formal and informal organization is made only for analytic purposes. The functioning of informal organization may be meaningless without knowledge of the formal structure to which it is associated. The reverse may be equally true. The study of the "invisible" informal aspect of organization is a primary contribution of sociology to the field of organization and administration, as is the study of the interrelations of informal and formal organization.

Figure 5.4 portrays the constituent parts of the social organization of a work plant. In the diagram the basic vertical line divides management from the union. In the management section the

9 Wilbert E. Moore, *Industrial Relations and the Social Order*, Macmillan, rev. ed., 1951, p. 274.

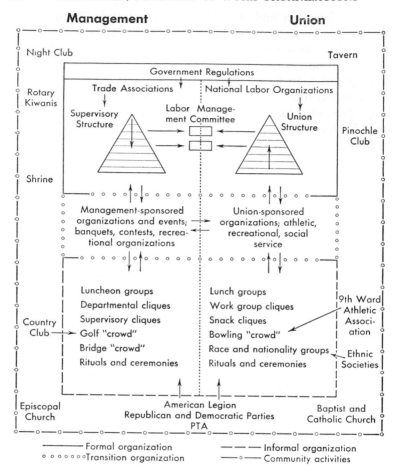

FIG. 5.4. Simplified Diagram of the Social Organization of Work Plants in Their Community and Society Setting. Only the major social segments are presented so that their interactive relations may be emphasized.

supervisory structure comprises most of the formal organization. The union structure represents the formal aspect of organization in the employees' section. Management and union are divided internally into formal, informal, and "transition" organizations. While a union may not be present in many work organizations, sometimes employees have associations to represent them. When no formal organization of the employees exists, the informal activities of employees may serve as adaptive substitutes for the accommodation of employees to management. The model used for analysis in Part II will contain a union.

This diagram illustrates a number of things: first, that a work organization has a much more complex organization than is evident at first glance; second, that the organizational divisions into management and union, formal and informal, although useful, are somewhat arbitrary. Social organization is a functioning, interacting whole. For example, as we shall demonstrate later, the operation of management's supervisory structure cannot be understood without an analysis of management's informal organization and the formal and informal organization of employees with which it interacts. Nor may the operation of any other aspect of the organization be appreciated without knowledge of the rest of the interacting parts. The third fact indicated by the diagram is that the social organization of a work plant is part of a larger complex, namely, the community and the society. A complete analysis of work organization must consider how the community and the society, through their own formal and informal organizations, influence the operation of the work plant.

It is difficult if not impossible to describe the interaction of the main segments of the work organization without first analyzing its individual parts. Those parts of the structure which interact more frequently and intensively will be treated together.

Formal Organization: A Theory of Superordination

Figure 5.5 portrays the skeletal social organization of management. Perhaps the most important idea shown in the figure is that formal management organization is only a segment of an integrated work organization. For purposes of analysis we shall examine formal or "blueprint" organization separately. The upper portion of Fig. 5.5 depicts that structure in a factory. Although much variation may be found in the formal structures of factories, department stores, labor unions, governments, or other enterprises, the principles of organization are much the same almost irrespective of the function or the size of the organization.

The blueprint organization in Fig. 5.5 suggests that the typical factory organization is rather complex. If *all* the formal relations

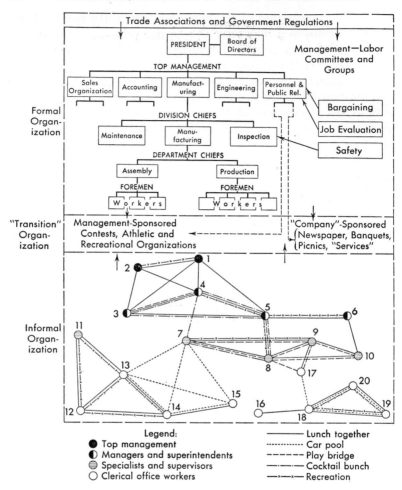

FIG. 5.5. The Social Organization of Management.

and divisions were shown, the diagram would appear even more complicated. The larger the organization, the more intricate this structure would probably become. The feeling that the structure is complex arises partly from the fact that observers usually try to see the *whole organization from the top down.*

It is more realistic to do exactly the reverse. Barnard emphasizes this point when he says, "All large formal organizations are constituted of numbers of small organizations. It is impossible to create large organizations except by combining small organizations."[10] *All organizations are made up of a number of small basic or unit organizations.* These range in size from two to twenty people, but average about ten people. The size of the basic or unit organizations must be small because adequate communication, which is a requisite for cooperative behavior, is best achieved in small groups. Complex organizations are *not*, therefore, mass organizations which have been subdivided into smaller ones. On the contrary, they are structures which result from the historical process of increasing the number of unit organizations. Most organizations grow by social fission. Each unit organization is divided in two, and individuals are added to each group. Since communication and cooperation between the units are necessary for the total structure to function effectively, an executive organization develops.

In each unit organization there is an executive function to be performed. This may be discharged by one or several people. In the lower levels of complex structures the executive function in the unit organizations is usually handled by one individual, commonly called the foreman or supervisor. "The executives of several unit organizations as a group, usually with at least one other person as a superior, form an executive organization. Accordingly, persons specializing in the executive functions in most cases are members of, or contributors to, two units of organization in one complex organization—first, the so-called 'working' unit, and second, the executive unit."[11]

Thus the foreman is regarded sometimes as a supervisor and other times as a member of a work crew. So it is with other executives. "This simultaneous contribution to two organizations by a single act appears to be the critical fact in all complex organizations; that is, the complex is made an organic whole by it."[12]

The work plant, and especially its formal organization, is like an organism composed of many cells and coordinated by a nervous system which reaches every cell. This nervous system is the

[10] Barnard, *op. cit.*, pp. 104–105.
[11] *Ibid.*, p. 111.
[12] *Ibid.*, p. 112.

executive organization, which is sketched out in the organization chart.

Another attribute of complex structures is that they grow *from the bottom to the top by the process of superordination;* or, *looked at in reverse, organization grows by waves of subordination.* Both processes are needed if the rights, duties, and limitations of the unit organizations are to be properly circumscribed. By their very nature unit organizations perform only part of the work. Therefore, their activities must be controlled by other organizations if teamwork is to be achieved. We shall now proceed to detail the ways in which the basic units are related to each other in the formal organization.

HOW THE COMPONENTS OF FORMAL ORGANIZATION ARE SUPPOSED TO OPERATE

Bureaucracy: A Society of Unequals

Bureaucracy may be defined as the pyramiding of unit organizations. As such, it is the typical form of large-scale organizations. The term "bureaucracy" has been unfortunately abused by businessmen and others when they want to refer to governmental inefficiency. But as one businessman said after serving in government, "We in business have bureaucracy just like the government. Only we call it 'system.'" Of course, he was correct, for bureaucracies grow when any enterprise begins to expand, whether it is a factory, department store, government, hospital, university, labor union, or cooperative.

A manager in a nation-wide grocery chain relates his firsthand experiences with the growth of bureaucracy:

When I first came to work for this organization about ten years ago, my boss handed me a guide, which was about a half-inch thick. He told me, "You'll find the answers to some of your questions in this guide. Half of the instructions in it are useless. But if you get stuck, just give me a ring, and we'll talk your problem over." Mind you, today every manager is given a thirteen-volume library to guide him in his work. And furthermore, there is a guide index for the guide.

As suggested, bureaucracy is simply a hierarchical arrangement of unit organizations. It is, or should be, an orderly arrangement of units based on division of function and authority. This means that a bureaucracy is an organization or a society of unequals.

The basic inequalities are exemplified in the *supervisory hierarchy,* which forms a pyramid of authority. The hierarchy may be visualized as several layers of authority. At the top is the president, who has greatest power. His subordinates are the managers, division chiefs, department chiefs, foremen, and workers, in that order. Although variations exist in the names given to offices in the layers, everywhere the structure is coordinated by a series of superior-subordinate or man-boss relations.[13] Figure 5.6 shows that

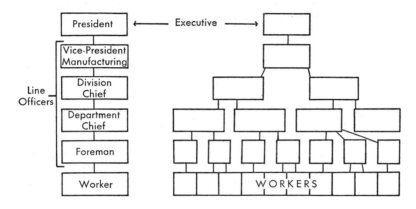

FIG. 5.6. Line Organization Shown as a Straight Line and as a Pyramid.

in such a structure the man on the top presumably directs and controls the entire organization. Excepting him and the workers in the lowest layer, everybody in between reports to a boss and is in turn a boss over several other people. Thus the big boss *looks down* the supervisory structure, the workers fret about the bosses *above* them, and division chiefs, department heads, superintendents, and managers worry *both* about their bosses and about those whom they boss. Each rank is responsible for doing a specific job and is accountable to someone who wants it done.

The Line Organization

The part of the structure which is dedicated to getting the work out is called the *line organization.* Theoretically, there is a direct line from the man at the top of the hierarchy to the worker

[13] Burleigh B. Gardner and David G. Moore, *Human Relations in Industry,* Irwin, rev. ed., 1950, p. 15.

who actually makes the product or provides the service. Obviously the top officer or the big boss cannot oversee everyone's work in the plant. Hence he issues some orders to the vice-president, who is then responsible for their execution. To facilitate this the president presumably delegates some of his authority to the vice-president. The vice-president in turn issues orders to the division chief and subdelegates enough authority to enable him to carry out orders. This process is continued down the line to the actual workers. Obviously, the larger the organization, the longer is the line of authority and the greater the social distance between the worker and the big boss. All the intermediaries from the big boss to the workers are necessary because the number of persons a boss can properly supervise must remain relatively small.[14]

The greater the number of layers in a structure, the less do the people in each layer know of the activities of people in other parts of the work plant. Higher executives do not have a complete or reliable picture of what is happening on the plant floor. Indeed, they do not need complete information. Their job is to formulate general objectives and policies. Each intermediary translates these objectives into more concrete and specific commands to the level below, until the worker is given specific instructions to punch a half-inch hole into this piece of metal.

Of course, other things must be done besides punching holes. The fantastic amount of division of labor and specialization in the modern factory points to the multitude of tasks that are done. The greater the number of tasks, the more complex the line organization becomes. A proliferation of offices occurs. The president is now assisted by more than one vice-president. Each vice-president is assigned special tasks and is given a *different* area of authority. Each vice-president has under him *several* division chiefs, each of whom has specific duties. As seen in Fig. 5.6, this process of subdivision is repeated down the line, with the end result that the organizational chart looks like a pyramid.

Functional Organization

The second basic division in the work structure is the functional organization. Each vertical segment in Fig. 5.6 represents a group which has a distinct function to perform. In an automobile plant,

[14] Moore, *op. cit.*, p. 75.

for example, a different department manufactures the ignition system, and so on. A plant may be functionally divided in various ways. The division may correspond to items, as in the auto plant. Divisions may be based on a process rather than a product. For example, one department may do all the wiring for any product manufactured, another may do all the printing, drilling, or packing for all other departments. Functional divisions or departments may be based on other principles—the use of similar materials, the need for similar skills in different processes, or the most efficient handling of bulk or materials. Efficiency is *supposed* to determine how the departments are to be organized. However, this is not always the case, and how work is divided may reflect the tastes of those who have power.

Since specialization has proceeded so far in our industrial organizations, functional charts of large organizations are extremely complicated. In fact, it is almost impossible to picture clearly all of the functional divisions, departments, subdepartments, and units in such an organization as the Ford Motor Company. Some segments are too minute; others overlap in several directions at once. Since functional divisions are not as clear as authority divisions, squabbles tend to develop over them. We shall treat these problems in another section.

Staff Organization

We have indicated that authority not only may be delegated but may be divided into spheres of specialization. Since policy-forming executives in larger organizations do not always have the technical competence to translate general policies into specific orders, they must integrate into their organization people who do have the technical competence. In addition to these advisers, other specialists who have little to do with production are needed. For example, research, hiring, training, keeping financial records, and selling are all specialist services that are not involved directly in the main purpose of the organization. The technical advisers and people who provide specialist services are considered to be part of the *staff* organization. Strictly speaking, although staff members have no authority over line organization, they must be integrated into that organization. The staff may be integrated into the line organization in four ways: (1) A line official may have staff assistants who advise him on policy. This means a staff man is placed in a "horizontal" relationship at any level where his skill is needed. (2) A high staff official may direct a staff organization, such as Finance, Engineering, or Personnel. Staff organizations are charged with serving any line official or other staff organization who may need their services. Figure 5.7 shows the first alternative on the left and the second alternative on the right. Actually these alternatives rarely exist in separate forms;

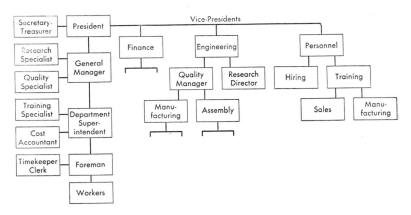

FIG. 5.7. Ideal Typical Integrations of Staff.

usually both techniques of incorporating staff services are used simultaneously. (3) Specialists may occupy positions as line managers. They may direct research, labor relations, or engineering and at the same time supervise a production department. (4) Still another method of employing staff is to give it authority under certain conditions to insert orders directly into the line organization.

All of these techniques of integrating staff may be used in the same organization. Thus in actual cases line-staff distinctions may be somewhat hazy. The fact that there is no agreement on the best way to integrate the staff into the line organization means that many conflicts arise. These conflicts are sometimes heightened because staff people not only consider themselves part of management but also feel a status superiority over some line officials. Often their expertise gives them an informal authority no organization chart can restrict.

Three Fundamental Relationships of Formal Organization

Urwick holds that there are three fundamental relationships in formal organization.[15] These are *line* relationships, *specialized* relationships, and *general staff* relationships. The differences among them can be defined very simply by indicating the kinds of authority and responsibility involved in each. These three vital relationships are shown in Fig. 5.8.

RELATION	AUTHORITY	RESPONSIBILITY
Line	Direct	General
Specialist	Indirect	Specialized
General	Representative	Auxiliary

FIG. 5.8. The Line, Specialist, and General Staff Relationships of Formal Organization. (After Urwick.)

1. *Line relations*

Line relations are easily understood. They are the normal relations between superior and direct subordinate, and they persist whatever the function may be. The subordinate may be a line subordinate, a specialist of some kind, or a general staff officer ("assistant to" an executive). Broadly, the superior is responsible to the undertaking for the subordinate. The subordinate has to do whatever his superior directs him to do. Thus in the line relationship between a superior and a subordinate authority is direct and responsibility is general.

2. *Specialist relations*

The specialist relationship arises whenever a person is charged with a functional responsibility for a particular subject because

---

[15] Lyndall Urwick, *Notes on the Theory of Organization,* American Management Association. New York, 1952, pp. 71–75.

of specialized knowledge or experience. He derives his responsibility from his specialized ability, but he is held directly responsible to someone else. The specialist staff man is always engaged directly or indirectly in a job for the line organization. The authority he derives is necessarily indirect. Theoretically it is always exercised through his own superior. In practice, once the superior is satisfied that the specialist staff subordinate is competent and has established a good working relationship with the officials he advises, the specialist can do most of his work without further formal authority. "The real work of the world is always done by individuals who trust each other and whose good relations are informal."[16] However, the specialist who goes outside the limits of his specialized responsibility is "asking for trouble."

3. General staff relations

The general staff officer has no authority of his own. He is merely an extension of his chief's personality, and his authority is only as a representative of the chief. His responsibility is limited to tasks directly assigned to him as an extension of instructions given to him by his superior. He cannot give orders to anyone unless authorized to do so. He is usually instructed not to give information or advice unless it is requested. The principal function of the general staff officer is to relieve the superior of a large burden of office work and daily details. He may undertake special assignments to gather information or to clear up trouble spots.

Each of these relationships establishes roles and boundaries of action and constitutes a matrix of expectations. Violations of the expectations by the incumbent will evoke suspicion, resentment, conflict, and hostility. The expectations are important mores of work life and sanctions are applied to secure their conformance. In some cases the organization approximates the ideal type while in other cases it represents mixtures of these fundamental relationships. Line, specialist, and general staff distinctions are often blurred. Functions overlap and responsibility is ambiguous. But

[16] *Ibid.*, p. 72.

whatever the particular situation, there will always be underlying expectations based on formal or informal authority distinctions.

The Communication Organization

A generally recognized sociological maxim is that the larger and more complex the social organization, the greater the need for coordinating it. The modern factory, with its extensive specialization, is subject to this principle. Ideally speaking, a properly functioning organization should be self-coordinating. If the supervisory structure, functional divisions, and staff organizations dovetailed perfectly, little coordination would be needed. Orders would go down the line, functions would be parceled out, advice would be given where needed, and jobs would be completed.

But this is rarely the case because social organization is not a machine. Human elements insert themselves. Goals may be impossible of fulfillment; orders may not be clearly expressed; new problems arise which require special attention; financial emergencies must be solved; certain managers may be incompetent. Executives feel that whenever possible they should reduce these problems, and one way of doing so is to make sure that communication flows freely. To minimize the possibility of misinterpretation orders are issued down the line in *written* form whenever possible. Written orders issued by top management are quite general. They become more detailed as they go down the line.

In order to know what is going on, top management expects daily, weekly, monthly, semiannual, and annual reports from subordinates. Daily reports flow up the line, usually in written form. They contain information on the general problems encountered as well as the achievements. The lower the supervisory level, the more detailed are the reports. As they flow up the line, they become more general and less technical. On the bases of these reports managers on all levels issue new orders to meet both the new and the older problems.

All kinds of commands and reports flow up and down the line. They may be classified into four categories: technical, financial, inspectional, and attitudinal. The first three are formally recognized by management. The last, although not so recognized, is nonetheless present. The ideas, feelings, sentiments, and gossip of all groups travel up and down the line.

Although communication between departments on the same level occurs, theoretically it is not supposed to be direct. Reports, desires for service, or criticisms that one department has of another are supposed to be sent up the line until they reach an executive who heads the organizations involved. They are then held, revised, or sent directly down the line to the appropriate officials and departments. The reason for this circuitous route is to inform higher officials of things occurring below them.

An illustration demonstrates the degree to which the channels of communication can become formalized. In a nation-wide wholesale grocery business each executive has a printed list of the kinds of things he may discuss with executives in different divisions of the organization. If a matter arises which has not been anticipated in the printed list, the individual must seek permission from his superior two levels up the line to discuss it with the appropriate official in another division. If the request is approved, a high official in the appropriate division is contacted, from whom permission to communicate is sought. This request is passed down the line and acted upon. If approved, it must go back up the line, over to the original division, and down the line to the initiating person. Then direct communication is authorized. This process is called observing the channels, and it consumes a lot of time. It is especially frustrating when the communicants are located just across the hall. In such cases direct contacts are resorted to and formal requests for communication are initiated to be on the safe side. Frequently, however, the individual does not know whom he should contact. All he knows is that he must seek permission from his immediate boss and wait. Going directly to the person or office up or down the line without attention to procedure is called *short-circuiting* the line. This is usually frowned upon, for everyone wants to know all the important information. To be caught without knowledge by a superior is a source of embarrassment.

In summary, the *theory* of formal organization is in itself quite simple. It holds that throughout the organization there is a strict definition of authority and responsibility. Similarly, there is an equally precise definition of the functions of every department.

Free and accurate communication flows from every part of the organization to every other part. Every action is guided by the principle of what is best for the organization as a whole.

Implicit Assumptions of Formal Organization

In addition to the described attributes of formal organization there are several implied assumptions. The first of these is that formal organization is necessary to achieve organizational goals. It is necessary because it is by nature impersonal, logical, and efficient. An organization can function best when individual idiosyncrasies, sentiments, and prejudices do not interfere with official activities. Thus, if offices and roles are defined as a series of rights and duties, the individual element in social interaction is reduced.

The second assumption of formal organization is that it is the only organization. In the literal sense many managers believe the only organization that exists is that portrayed on the blueprints. To them, good organization is simply that which duplicates the blueprint structure.

A third assumption is that formal organization is flexible and that it can meet problems readily. If, for example, a factory department needs more men, it may borrow them from another department which has a temporary excess. The men and departments involved will agree to such an expediency for it is to everyone's benefit. Underlying the thinking here is the idea that the chief aim of organization and personnel is to achieve organizational goals. When the enterprise achieves this end, the employees automatically achieve their individual aims. In other words, efficient workers make an effective organization, and vice versa. What is best for the organization in the immediate and distant future is best for the individual workers.

THE FUNCTIONING OF FORMAL ORGANIZATION

Formal Organization as Human Organization

We have briefly described the theory of formal organization and some of the assumptions underlying it. Although formal organization is designed to subject production to logical planning, things never seem to go "according to plan." This is evidenced by the many "problems" managers encounter. They find that no matter how carefully they organize, how much concerned they are with anticipating problems, unanticipated ones always arise: (1) Some parts of the organization function better than others. (2) The line does not follow suggestions of staff. (3) New recruits are difficult to secure. (4) Central management is in conflict with divisional management. (5) Community relations are disturbing. (6) Disagreements arise in the interpretation of orders.

For these kinds of eventualities formal organization offers little guidance because it is created as a guidepost for the routine, the typical, and the foreseeable. Although it provides the framework for dealing with new problems, they are foreseen as capable of routine treatment. This does not mean that formal organization is sterile and useless. On the contrary, it is both necessary and inevitable, to realize sustained cooperation of many people and groups. But even though an organization cannot be understood without knowledge of its formal structure, it is equally true that the most complete knowledge of formal organization does not tell us how the enterprise actually functions.

The reason is quickly identified. The most important variable in the organization chart has been absent, namely, people. Formal organization looks on the people that inhabit the different offices or positions as constants. It assumes that all of the workers in a plant are unrelated individuals, or that their relations are only those which are specified on the chart; that as individuals, they think and act logically in a manner calculated to promote their economic self-interest; that the motive of this individualistic, rational, and selfish behavior is to promote the economic well-being of themselves and the enterprise.[17]

The Perspectives of the Sociologists

Sociologists not only deny the reality of these assumptions but suggest alternative ones. Whenever they examine organizations—economic, political, religious, educational, or others—they do so with a special set of tools, concepts, or ideas. One of the most fundamental ideas is that people can be understood only in their social relations with one another. *Social relations, not individuals,*

---

[17] Elton Mayo has referred to these assumptions as "the rabble hypothesis." See his *The Social Problems of an Industrial Civilization,* Harvard, 1945, p. 40.

are the basic units of observation. Since social relations constitute the essence of groups, sociologists begin looking for social relations or groups whenever they examine human activity. This is what we shall do as we study the social organization that develops around the formal organization of management.

The sociological point of view does not demand an examination of the relations of specific individuals and situations. Rather, it seeks to find the kinds of social relations that may be expected to develop under certain stable conditions. It proceeds by applying what is already known about human relations in general to typical and recurrent situations—in this case, work situations.

The major generalizations that the sociologist applies to the study of work organization may be stated as follows:

1. Individuals who are in physical and social contact almost invariably form groups which have structure and permanence.

2. Specific relations tend to become social relations. Thus, economic, political, or educational relations between people tend to become more widely defined as general social relations.

3. Social relations may be examined in their static and dynamic aspects. In the static sense the sum total of a worker's specified relations to others in the structure is called his *work position.* It is composed of a number of rights, duties, functions, and obligations. In the dynamic sense, the carrying out of these rights, duties, and responsibilities is the *work role.* All people in every stable group have positions and roles, and all groups may be analyzed as coordinated series of positions and roles.

4. Interaction between people always *involves communication* of meanings through symbols. To understand group structure one studies the amount, direction, frequency, intensity, and content of communication.

5. Every group shares a number of ideas, beliefs, customs, values, and sentiments. Sometimes these are integrated into a system or an ideology. Individual and group behavior cannot be fully comprehended without knowledge of the prevailing ideologies.

6. Whenever people in a group have different social characteristics or functions, social stratification invariably ensues. In our society stratification is based, among other things, on money,

prestige, and authority. In turn, class, status, and power organizations arise in society which reflect these bases of stratification.

7. All groups tend to regard themselves as somewhat separate and superior to all other groups. Ethnocentrism, social distance, and segmentation develop between groups.

8. Formal structure never describes completely the relations among people. Friendships, cliques, and small informal groups develop which often function contrary to the expectations of formal structures.

9. All groups may be thought of as representing an equilibrium of integrative and disintegrative forces. The group always is in a dynamic process of being built up or torn down.

Communication and Segmentation Problems

Work organizations also exhibit these principles. In work plants the same two contradictory pressures or tendencies may be found. One is to coordinate small groups so that their individual identity is reduced; the other is to preserve as much individual identity in the small group as possible. The tendency of a larger group to divide into smaller ones is called *the segmentation tendency*. When these small groups subordinate their purposes to the larger organization, effective coordination is attained and there are no organizational problems. When different parts struggle to dominate each other or retain independence, segmentation tendencies are greater than the coordination or integration tendencies. Sociologists speak of this state as a disequilibrium of forces. The theory of formal organization seems to ignore segmentation and integration forces.

This attitude is unfortunate because the division of a large organization into many smaller parts introduces problems of communication. People in one segment fail to understand what people in another segment are doing or trying to do.

Thus an entirely new problem of communication is created. Elton Mayo has emphasized the importance of communication in strong terms. He says, "I believe that social study should begin with careful observation of what may be described as communication: that is, the capacity of an individual to communicate his feelings and ideas to another, the capacity of groups to communicate effectively and intimately with each other. This problem is, beyond all reasonable doubt, the outstanding defect that civilization is facing today."[18]

The relation of communication and segmentation

Communication is basic to the understanding of human relations in a work plant whether it is large or small. In a large plant the many segmented parts tend to multiply the difficulties of securing clear and accurate communication.

Theoretically the line is supposed to carry all communication, orders going down and reports going up. Orders are never supposed to flow up the line, and reports about the "big boys" are not supposed to go down the line. Apart from orders and reports, a third type of communication, though acknowledged, is often neglected. It may be called "peer" communication because it is horizontal in nature. When equals or peers consult and advise with each other, there are no orders or reports in the strict sense. Peer communication is important because it provides an excellent index to the processes of segmentation and integration. For example, the fact that foremen of two departments frequently consult each other and are friendly, whereas they rarely consult or have social contacts with other foremen, provides a clue to the relative integration or segmentation of the departments of the work plant.

Segmentation of groups does not occur accidentally. It develops naturally in the manner that communication travels up and down the line. The very nature of the man-boss linkage affects the accuracy, speed, and content of communication.[19] Obviously, the more levels communication must travel through, the less complete and accurate it will be. A superior is only kidding himself if he thinks he has comprehensive knowledge of what is going on as close as two levels below him. He is largely dependent for what knowledge he does have on what the intervening supervisors want to tell him. Supervisors presumably report all the information which their bosses need to make decisions. This ideal is seldom achieved, however. More frequently bosses do not get the important information; indeed, irrelevant details often clutter their desks, making efficient administration an impossibility.

[18] *Ibid.*, p. 22.
[19] See Gardner and Moore, *op. cit.*, Chap. 3, "The Line of Authority and Communication," for an excellent discussion of this problem.

DISTORTION UP THE LINE

Gardner points out that each supervisor wants to have a good record for himself and for his department. In his efforts to make a good impression the communication he sends up the line is distorted. There is the tendency to give the boss what he wants to hear, namely, that "operations are going according to plan." Also, subordinates are likely to "cover up" when things do not so move,[20] in the hope that the job will soon be straightened out and the boss won't find out what the situation really is.

Thus, each responsible person up and down the line acts as a *sieve* or *filter*. Orders going down the line should be concise, accurate, and complete. In the process of interpretation, and of making orders increasingly specific, errors or omissions sometimes intrude themselves. Orders may be issued too late; they may be incomplete, inaccurate, or ambiguous. Sometimes information which should not be released is accidentally circulated. Thus communication going down the line can become as distorted and filtered as information traveling in the reverse direction.

From these observations it is apparent that formal communication does not travel evenly, freely, and accurately from each section to all other sections of the work plant. There may be little or no interchange of information between some departments of the organization. This isolation may be the result of previous friction, physical segregation, or other factors.

On the other hand, there may be frequent, rapid, and accurate communication between two or more sections of the organization. Or communication may travel rapidly, but it may be inaccurate or antagonistic in content. The communication flow among the segments of an organization can be accurately charted. It should be recorded in terms of its source, frequency, duration, direction, intensity, and content. Such a diagram for a particular plant would be of invaluable aid in examining its problems.

Even with such a diagram, however, all problems would not be solved. Some writers have asserted that if there is free and open communication in a work plant people will understand each other and problems will be automatically solved. Although many problems may be reduced by good communication, all of them

[20] *Ibid.*, pp. 39–41.

cannot be erased, for several reasons. First, it is impossible for any group to anticipate all the information another wants. Even if supplying all the information were possible, some would not regard it as desirable. To withhold information is sometimes as vital as to release it. Yet withholding communication may arouse resentment in other groups. Even when there is no restraint on releasing facts, people will interpret them differently and act upon them differently. This issue is especially important when different segments of an organization do not share the same values. Further, when groups do not want to cooperate, free communication between them does not necessarily reduce the friction. In fact, *it may increase it*. In the following sections we shall demonstrate how organizations develop internal ruptures which increase rather than decrease the friction within them.

Time segmentation

Sometimes segmentation develops within organizations because of the difficulty in synchronizing activities. Strains develop particularly in an industry which has two or more shifts.[21] In the first place, the "regular shift" regards itself as the most important shift. Most of the staff is present during the day. Problems of the regular shift are met and solved, with the expectation that the following shift will merely follow precedent. The regular shift is frequently regarded as the big moneymaker; the others as secondary. They keep the plant going and, by doing so, keep costs down. The members of the second and third shift, however, do not regard themselves as secondary. They are quick to feel slights and insults.

All too often, there is little or no face-to-face communication up and down the line between the people in the various shifts. The sum total of communication is often no more than hastily scribbled "memos" pointing out the difficulties of the last shift and setting the quotas for the next shift. Rarely is there social or recreational contact between shifts. Obviously, this incomplete and impersonal communication is the source of irritation.

On paper little distinction is made between the shifts. They

[21] Paul and Faith Pigors, "Human Aspects of Multiple Shift Operations," Publications in Social Science, Series 2, No. 13, Massachusetts Institute of Technology, 1944.

are all part of the organization. Theoretically each shift's performance should dovetail neatly into the others'. Since the interdependence of the shifts is real, anything that interferes with the fulfillment of expectations is a source of frustration. Problems between the shifts cannot be as adequately met as those arising within a shift, for the physical presence of people is often needed to meet problems on the spot.

Since no shift has complete dominance and advantage over the other, each shift can make the life of the next miserable. When poor relations develop between shifts, the irritations are cumulative. Each shift tries to outdo the other in inconveniences it can concoct for the other. The causes for intershift tensions may appear petty and unimportant to outsiders. To the workers themselves these irritations seem to mount to obsessive proportions. The ravings of a foreman in a tube-making department of a New York factory demonstrate this obsession:

> We're in a hell of a fix tonight. Everything's gone wrong from the first minute. But what can you expect from Krieger and his bunch? Krieger scribbled me a note to keep on making ⅜″ tubing. His men as usual stopped the machines with the whistle, leaving the stock inside of the machines. Naturally we thought they was making ⅜″. So for two hours we've been making half-inch. We're supposed to turn out thirty thousand feet of ⅜″ tonight, but we'll never make it. . . . I'll catch hell for not checking the dies first. So we looked for the dies in the cabinet. The cabinet was locked and Krieger had the keys. So while I send Charlie to get the keys I ask the men to clean up the machines and sweep up. I get the lip from them because they claim that Krieger's men always leave them the dirty work. 'Course my boys ain't angels exactly. Krieger blowed off the other night on account of my men put so much grease on the stock that it was almost impossible to handle. I tell you, half of this trouble wouldn't happen if the chief took an interest in this department and in this shift. I usually see him leaving as I come in, taking off like a bat out of hell, to play golf or something.

Similar problems of time segmentation occur within a shift, especially when work teams are dependent on other teams for supply of materials. When one group in an interrelated work flow organization fails to meet a time schedule, total production is affected. Antagonisms which arise out of a failure to integrate work teams and plans to improve work flow will be examined in one of the later sections of this chapter.

Space segmentation

The organization chart does not reveal a common occurrence, namely, the spatial segregation of parts of a division or department. During World War II, especially the pressing demand for space resulted in the physical separation of closely interdependent unit organizations. For example, the Sperry Gyroscope Company operated its main Brooklyn plant, rented large terminal buildings in Brooklyn, built a plant on Long Island, and maintained an office in Manhattan, New York. The work of numerous plants spread over a fifty-mile radius had to be organized. Problems of coordinating the different units of the factory naturally arose.

There are several ways in which units of an organization may be physically segregated. Sometimes the offices of executives, staff, and clerical workers are distant from the operational divisions. Such a split increases the segmentation of office and plant organizations. This is to be avoided if at all possible for even under normal conditions the relations between office and plant tend to be touchy. Another common device is to segregate the central plant from the subsidiary plants, which perform specialized services. Still another technique is to create as many self-sufficient organizations as possible, with the central organization exercising a minimum of control. This is the case in the headquarters-field arrangement.

Irrespective of the method of spatial segregation, each section tends to regard itself as more important than any other unit, or as having problems which are unique or more pressing than those in other parts of the organization. This attitude is understandable, because physical segregation reduces free, direct, and personal communication. As a principle, the greater the physical segregation of component units of an organization, the greater are the problems of coordinating activity. The greater the segregation in physical space, the greater the tendency to be divided by social space.

To lessen social distance, to increase communication, and to promote the feeling of interdependence single-story plants with few or no partitions between and within departments are being built instead of multi-story buildings.

An interesting illustration of spatial segmentation was evident in a banking firm in Lansing, Michigan. The job of processing checks was done by two groups of girls under the same supervisor. Half of the girls in this department worked on the main floor and the second half worked upstairs. To all intents and purposes their jobs were identical. When new girls were hired they went to work on the ground floor. When vacancies occurred upstairs, girls were taken from the downstairs group. An antagonism developed between these two groups, each regarding the other as aloof, unfriendly, and troublesome. By informal agreement each group ate lunch at a different time and even used the rest rooms at different times. When a girl from downstairs joined the upstairs crew, she was soon accepted, but the downstairs crew would have very little to do with her. Such social distance and ethnocentrism has been known to develop even between junior executives who occupied different sides of the same room. Of course, spatial segregation alone does not produce cleavages. Other factors are equally important.

Organizational strictures

The places where cleavages are most likely to develop in work plants are along the "natural" divisions of the structure. That is, wherever there are breaks, as between supervisory levels or between functional units, there is a greater likelihood of segmentation. This should be expected since it is usually more difficult to coordinate disparate units than similar ones. Within an organizational unit there usually is more communication, similarity of function, and commonness of purpose. Although it is true that organizational divisions increase the interdependence among the divisions, machinery to effect coordination does not grow automatically to meet the problem.

The organizational breaks where cleavage or segmentation is likely to be highest are (1) at the divisional, subdivisional, and department breaks; (2) between the supervisory levels; and (3) between the line and staff organizations.

DIVISIONAL AND RELATED CLEAVAGES

It is scarcely necessary to demonstrate that antagonisms exist between divisions, departments, sections, and other units. The mere creation of an organizational unit brings cleavage, but other factors operate. The coordination of segments is seldom perfect, and the defects add to the difficulties. Assembly, for example, is dependent on Manufacturing for its materials; Manufacturing is in turn dependent on the Purchasing division; the latter in turn has to operate within a budget, and so on.

Each section, division, or department wants a "good record." Each is trying to impress top management with its performance. *Yet its performance depends on the perfect cooperation of the other sections.* This is next to impossible. Assembly may be held up because Manufacturing is not supplying the needed items. When the supply is good, quality may be low. As a result, Assembly may be slowed up. The chief of Assembly then puts pressure on Manufacturing to keep up supplies *and* quality. His organization becomes aware of his impatience. The Assembly chief may use Manufacturing as a scapegoat for his own inadequacies or for his bad luck. On the other hand, he will take the credit when his section is performing better than the others.

Other less formal factors may augment distance between units of the structure. Some division heads are the "fair-haired boys" of the big boss. They get most of the breaks. In addition, one department may have more skilled, more highly educated, more experienced personnel than another; its members may flaunt their superiority feelings in their relations with people of other departments. Members of other departments may resent the advantageous position of their fellow workers and begin to look upon them as deadly rivals. Thus, in-groups are formed which develop insulation against communication with other divisions. A number of protective rituals are soon evolved which make group members more self-conscious and provincial. These tendencies are sometimes encouraged by supervisors. Loyalty toward the division is rewarded. But loyalty is a two-edged sword. Although it may increase *esprit de corps* within the department, it may also reduce cooperation with the entire organization. Whereas it may be pursued at first for the purpose of increasing output, it later may become an end in itself.

SUPERVISORY LEVELS

In the next chapter we shall explain in some detail the functions and problems in various supervisory levels. Here we shall deal with some of the general reasons that cleavages appear between the levels. Tensions arise between the supervisory levels because the different functions, identifications, authority, and responsibilities of each level inevitably come into conflict. Each level feels it could do a better job if the other levels would cooperate with it in its every problem.

It is the human tendency of every executive to see the total organization from the peculiar perspective of his level. Obviously, the image of each is a product of his unique experiences and problems. Since the perspectives of each level cannot be the same, the problem of communicating desires and achievements arises. On the basis of this kind of partial and incomplete communication segmentation tendencies increase. No supervisory level—indeed, no section of the organization—has a completely accurate view of the whole structure. Nor can the whole be seen accurately from a partisan point of view. Only the outside observer can gain such a perspective, even approximately.

The feeling of each level is very strong that its problems are unique and that no one can really understand them unless he is physically on the spot. Supervisors consider their problems not only unique but of greater magnitude. Listening to the "gripe session" of supervisors is a good way to observe the pervasive belief that each level has problems that are unusual and difficult. The participants of these sessions don't communicate or inform. They just release tensions in the hope that they will get sympathy.

In addition, each supervisory level is at the same time subordinate and superordinate to others. On each, there is a pressure from above to produce. Authority, with all its incipient threats, accompanies this pressure and promotes feelings of insecurity. The supervisor often feels that his chief has too much authority to expect so much of a man who has limited authority. Among supervisors the sentiment universally persists that one should have more authority to resist pressure and to enlist cooperation. Subordinates often complain that their chiefs "pass the buck" to them; that they get only the tough problems or the dirty menial tasks.

Supervisors make the same demands on their subordinates that their chiefs make on them. As chiefs they feel their performance depends on the cooperation of those below them. Their reaction to this kind of dependency results in pressure and demands. Overweighted with work, they pass down the menial and difficult jobs. They cannot understand why they do not get all that they expect. Thus, how a supervisor feels and acts depends upon whether he is looking down or looking up the structure. The different ways he acts do not strike him as contradictory or unreasonable. Yet this contradiction makes for segmentation in the structure.

STAFF AND LINE

The cleavages between supervisory levels are paralleled by those arising between line and staff organizations. The line organization is concerned with manufacturing the product or providing the service. Staff organization includes all the remaining functions, such as sales, engineering, personnel, and accounting. Theoretically, the staff organization is supposed to advise and assist the line organization on its problems and provide such services as hiring, training, and research.

Antagonisms between line and staff exist in almost every organization. This does not mean that the whole staff has antagonistic feelings toward line. As a matter of fact the watertight distinctions between staff and line are not always found in industry. Cleavages between these two parts of the organization generally occur over specific functions at specific times. Since we cannot survey all of the situations leading to cleavages, we shall examine the general cause of segmentation.

The line is a united organization with one supervisory hierarchy. It is well aware of its central position in the organization and of the subsidiary position of the staff. The staff, on the other hand, is often composed of several organizations, each having its own supervisory structure. The fact that the staff is not a united structure, plus the fact that its role is considered secondary, decreases the possibility of unrestrained cooperation with the line.

The staff finds it difficult to prove to the line that it is worth its salt. Line officers often comment that they make the money for the organization while the staff spends it in nonessential ways. Line men often feel that the plant can partly dispense with many staff functions. To them staff people often appear impractical and theoretical. Their services might be more useful if they were under the dominance of line officers. In difficult times, staff funds are cut and line people do take over some of their functions.

Thus the staff is often put on the defensive. It must prove *the need for and profitability of* large sales, research, personnel, and accounting organizations. It can do this largely at the expense of the lower parts of the line organization. For example, the cost accounting officials can "prove" to top management that a particular line division is losing money. The research division can "prove" that antiquated methods are responsible for this loss. Personnel can "prove" that it can repair the situation by introducing new training and selection methods. Thus all the staff groups can justify their existence by *criticizing the line*. Nobody loves a critic.

The frustations of the staff are increased by the fact that it has no power to enforce its recommendations. Since it cannot, except in unusual situations, insert commands into the line organization, it seeks more authority. The line resists because it does not want its routines broken by every new idea the staff concocts. Under these conditions the staff seeks to influence top management to insert its recommendations into the line. It is successful in this regard because its members are in continual physical and social contact with top management. Whereas the attention of the line is on the departments that produce the goods or provide the service, the focus of the staff is on top management.

On the other hand, only the upper levels of line officers come into close contact with top management. In general, staff people are more highly educated than line people. The specialist or professional training of staff members makes them feel superior to the less formally trained line officers. In addition, staff feels a sense of superiority because its members are and always have been white-collar people. Many line officers, on the other hand, have risen through the ranks. They have ambivalent feelings concerning their social origins and their present social position. Consequently they sometimes feel antagonistic toward staff people *per se*.

Although all major segments of work organizations suffer from the threat of invasion from other sections, the line organization is most exposed. It is therefore the division which is most aggressive in maintaining the sacredness of its boundaries. Yet boundary maintenance must be flexible in the face of offensive threats by other departments. Dynamic line organizations engage in two types of activities to maintain control. First, they create a "spy network" to discover what changes other sections—engineering, cost accounting, control—plan for the line. Second, they prepare defenses against these threats. The defenses may be of two varieties. The first and less effective is the preparation of a case against changes so well prepared in advance that it is difficult to refute. The second is the creation of informal parallel organizations within the line. For example, an informal engineering department is created to change production, an informal cost department is started, and so on. The purpose of the parallel organizations is to anticipate changes and to institute change *within the context of departmental tradition,* and to maintain control and boundaries against excessive demands of other sections.[22]

Social and cultural differences

The existence of social and cultural differences among various segments of work organizations is infrequently recognized. Although the formal structure is designed to minimize the influences that arise from differences in personality, social experiences, and cultural background, it cannot do away with them altogether. It is almost impossible to keep interhuman contacts within formally defined limits. The economic, political, and religious sentiments of people sooner or later are expressed. Cliques, friendships, enemies, and allies invariably arise on the basis of sentiment agreement or disagreement. The appeal made to the slogan "Business is business" points to the sociological reality that business is often mixed up with other sentiments.

The work plant is one of the major areas where the subcultures meet and interact. Foreign cultures and lower-class culture are expressed in the behavior of the workers on the plant floor. Some of the difficulties that arise between supervisory levels reflect the cultural differences between workers and managers. Managers are usually native Americans, imbued with the values of time, profit, success, and ambition. If their workers do not share these values, as is often the case, managers sometimes feel that the workers are

[22] Melville Dalton, *Men Who Manage,* Wiley, 1959, pp. 71–109.

stupid or even subhuman. Tardiness, absenteeism, and the observing of certain rituals may be anathema to supervisors, but it may be customary behavior to many workers. Such differences in cultural backgrounds tend to restrict the communication and understanding between groups. Indeed, cultural differences often promote antagonisms, for intolerance seems to be almost a universal trait.

Other areas of cultural conflict are exhibited in factory life. The antagonisms between office and factory reflect the middle-class-lower-class antipathy in our society. Sometimes conflicts occur because men and women compete over the same jobs. Departments which interact may have members representing different educational levels, different national origins, different religions, and so on. The cultural differences in the work plant should be known and plotted, to enable the analyst to assess some of the sources of segmentation there. What seems at first to be segmentation based on spatial, organizational, or functional divisions may in reality be due to cultural differences.

Ideological contradictions

In addition to the cleavages caused by cultural differences, cleavages may arise from contradictory traits within the culture. One contradiction, specially inherent in business thinking, is the conflict between teamwork and individualism. One primary ideal in business organization is the desire for a smooth-functioning team. Many of the ideals of sports pervade the idea system (ideology) of management. Among them are: Business is a competitive affair; to win out, teamwork is necessary. Each man not only should be an expert in his position but should be loyal to the team. Cooperation is essential to victory. The team is more important than the individual. No man should play for the grandstand.

A conflicting ideal is that every worker should be personally ambitious to make a good record. Rewards are distributed according to the achievements of the individual in the competitive struggle inside and outside the organization. The success of the worker is measured in his ability to outperform his fellow workers. This *individualistic, competitive, struggling* ideology sets individuals against individuals. Every worker is urged to do his best no matter whom he may hurt in the process. Everyone is encouraged to entertain the thought that he can do a better job than his boss. Indeed, he may even aspire to replace his boss if his performance is unusually good. If he can demonstrate that a person, group, or department is not doing a good job, and further, if he can point the way to doing a better job himself, he is rewarded. The other person, group, or department will be punished, reprimanded, or demoted, as the case may be.

Cooperation and competition, group consciousness and individualism, loyalty and mobility are not necessarily compatible. It is quite possible that such a contradictory atmosphere breeds insecurity feelings rather than high teamwork and morale. When a worker feels that at any time one of his subordinates or colleagues may threaten his position, he is filled with distrust and suspicion. Far from developing an atmosphere of uninhibited, spontaneous cooperation, this system breeds a structure of strange contradictions.

Managers of some concerns accept tensions as a normal, if not desirable, aspect of business life. One of them bluntly admitted that he was suspicious of subordinates who genuinely liked their superiors. When this is the case, he contended, the superior is not doing a good job. The job of the executive is to find something wrong with the work of subordinates. People who find things wrong should not be liked by subordinates. Thus it is necessary for him to be feared, so that he can constantly keep workers alive to the necessity of improving their work.

Two illustrations may demonstrate the unintended consequences of the contradictory elements in management ideology.[23] During World War II the Treasury Department in Washington, D.C., hired many girls to sort canceled checks. A bulletin board was erected which showed how many checks each girl had sorted during the month. The objective was to stimulate the girls to do more work. Promotion was to be based on the number of checks sorted. At first the girls were anxious to know where they stood. At the end of each month they would scan the bulletin board to find their positions. The girls at the lower end of the scale soon began to hate this system. They indicated that it did not take into

[23] Robert Merton, "Unanticipated Consequences of Purposive Social Action," *American Sociological Review*, December, 1936, pp. 894–904.

account absences and other eventualities. Far from stimulating them, it seemed to encouraged squabbling and absenteeism. Those at the top of the scale soon found that increases in salary were limited by the salary scale. After reaching the top rung of the scale they no longer tried to produce more. This case illustrates the fact that management ideology is not always accepted, and when accepted often has unanticipated consequences by causing cleavages.

A national grocery chain evolved a complex method of evaluating the managers of the individual stores. Each manager is constantly stimulated to improve his rating. He is told that promotions are based on his competitive position with other store managers. The company lets him know when he is not doing well, but it never tells him where he stands in reference to other store managers. A manager never knows how "good" he really is. A high executive justified this "keep-them-in-the-dark policy" by suggesting that it was a good incentive device. He said, "If a man knows that he is on top or close to the top, he will not continue to improve. If he doesn't know how he stands he will try to improve continually."

In this case top management operated under the assumption that all men have the same motives. It imputed to the store managers a restless ambition to operate in an ill-defined or undefined situation. As it happened, many local managers were discouraged by the lack of information. Some of them went to other organizations where they would know where they stood. Those who remained got together informally to compare their performances. Thus the inconsistent ideology of management promoted a conspiracy among the workers, motivated by the desire to lessen some of the pressure from the top.

We have seen in this section that the social organization of the work plant is an interactive system composed of many parts. The *formal* and *informal* organizations of labor and management constitute major divisions. These organizations split into many smaller segments. Management's main role in industry is to secure cooperative effort among its unit organizations. This is a difficult task because of the inherent and persistent tendency of large enterprises to become fragmented into smaller groups having a separate identity. *Such tendencies toward segmentation in the structure interfere with the free flow of communication between sections of the larger organization.* The main blocks to free communication flow tend to occur between all the different sections of the structure. Among these are *line and staff, office and plant, different supervisory levels,* and *functional divisions.* Cleavages between groups are emphasized by the *social* and *cultural differences* that exist among work groups in the plant. Contradictions in *management ideology* also punctuate the natural cleavages that arise.

WORK FLOW AND SEGMENTATION

Everyone in a work plant may be considered as either directly or indirectly concerned with making the work flow. Some workers are obviously directly concerned with processing the flow of goods. Others are indirectly concerned when they service people or machines that actually move the work or the services. There is a growing awareness that work flow is an index of both coordination and the state of human relations. When jams occur in work flow, production drops, tempers flare, and frantic efforts are made to smash the bottlenecks. What connections exist between the smooth and efficient flow of work and "good" or "bad" human relations, and why?

The Line of Pressure

When William Whyte studied the restaurant industry, he observed that the fluctuating flow of customers introduced some serious problems of work flow and human relations. The surge of hungry customers at the conventional mealtime hours set up pressures which affected almost every worker. The customer originates every action which sets into motion the complex organization of a large restaurant. With the placing of his order a *line of pressure* is initiated, and it lengthens as the worker is directed to produce food or accompanying service. Figure 5.9 portrays the line of pressure in a large restaurant. Here it can be seen how pressure is transmitted from customers to waitresses and then onward to pantry workers, runners, cooks, and food preparers. Meanwhile, the supervisors "breathe down the necks" of the various workers for whom they are responsible. The cry is

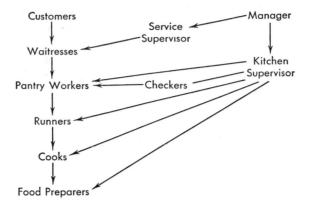

FIG. 5.9. Line of Pressure in a Large Restaurant.

hurry! hurry! hurry! The strain on human relationships grows as the pressure mounts. At times, the strain becomes too great and taut nerves can take no more. Crying and emotional upsets on the part of the waitresses are common problems. Antagonistic feelings tend to surge up among all workers. The supervisor needs social skills of a high order to meet these problems. Improvement in the work flow also helps morale and heads off human relations problems. Whyte has studied this work flow and has identified the points at which friction develops. One example will illustrate how important small details can be.

The point of contact between waitresses and pantry people also deserves supervisory attention. In Jessup's restaurant, when supplies did not come up, the waitresses felt frustrated not only because they were delayed but also because they could not understand what was going on. When they demanded the attention of the countermen, this only created friction. If the pantry supervisor had been able to step in between the two groups, explain the situation to the waitresses, and let them blow off steam to her, it seems likely that the flood of tears could have been avoided. It may be worth while to experiment in developing a go-between role for the pantry supervisor.

Before we leave the service pantry, we should look at the social role of the insignificant-looking spindle. It serves to fend off from pantry people a good deal (but not all) of the pressure exerted by waitresses. Where we have men (unaccustomed to taking orders from women) behind the counter, it seems likely that the spindle makes the difference between a workable system and one that would blow up. . . . The spindle is also of great importance where we have middle-aged counter-women and young waitresses. . . .

To sum it up, wherever the people on the receiving end of the orders are related to the order givers as males vs. females, or older vs. younger, then it is important for the pantry people to have some impersonal barrier to block the pressure from themselves. Even when such differences are eliminated, the use of spindles makes the job easier for the pantry people.[24]

This illustration, in which the lowly spindle plays such a major role, verifies the importance of small details in the flow of work.

The Sociography of Work Flow

The work flow in any work plant may be compared to a river. Initial actions at the headwaters of the main stream start the flow of goods or services. Unfinished parts flow downstream from worker to worker. Tributary services flow into the main stream, and the work nears completion at the river's end. This stream concept and image has several advantages. It enables an observer to visualize clearly and to plot graphically whatever a department or an individual contributes to the work flow at the physical spot where his contribution is made.[25]

Figure 5.10 is a sociographic map of work flow in an auto accessory department in a Sears, Roebuck and Company retail store. The elements of work flow consist of (a) the main stream, (b) tributaries (into main stream), and (c) points of origination of action. The sequence of actions represented in the map begins when

1. Customer purchases merchandise.
2. Clerk delivers merchandise, collects money, and returns change.
3. If merchandise is to be installed free, customer takes invoice to service station attendant (4).
4. Service station attendant receives invoice order, checks his stock, and, if he has the appliance, installs it in customer's automobile.

[24] From *Human Relations in the Restaurant Industry,* by William F. Whyte, 1948. Courtesy of McGraw-Hill Book Company.

[25] We are indebted to F. L. W. Richardson, Jr., and Charles R. Walker for this concept as described in *Human Relations in an Expanding Company,* Yale, 1948, pp. 54–85.

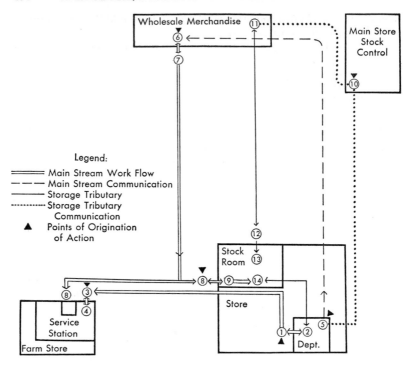

FIG. 5.10. Sociographic Map of Work Flow in an Auto Accessory Department.

5. Department manager keeps inventory control books. If stockroom merchandise is low, he telephones store warehouse clerk and orders merchandise sent to store stockroom.
6. Warehouse clerk obtains merchandise from stock and delivers to trucker at dock with orders to deliver to service station or store. (Overlap here since the station is close to store.)
7. Trucker picks up merchandise with his orders.
8. Trucker delivers merchandise to service station if needed immediately or to receiving clerk (9) to be stored.
9. Receiving clerk takes merchandise and places it in merchandise bins.
10. On this tributary, the department manager (5) orders merchandise from main store stock control by mail or phone when his books show need for supplies.

11. Shipping clerk takes orders and delivers at dock to trucker.
12. Trucker delivers merchandise to store.
13. Receiving clerk accepts goods and places it in bins.
14. When counter stock is low, clerk fills it from store stock-room.[26]

Smooth work flow is important in the operation of this depart-ment. For example, the type of relationship between the shipping clerk and the truckers can save or lose money for the company. The truckers, who are not Sears employees since the trucks are contracted from a trucking concern, may not be too cooperative in minimizing damage in transport or in creating good customer relations. The shipping clerk, by creating friendly relations with the truckers, can help this situation. A good shipping clerk "kids" the drivers, never demands a delivery, but secures their coopera-tion by including them in his work group and getting them to respect him as a man. The truckers are usually strong men physi-cally, and if the shipping clerk can "hold up" his end of a re-frigerator they learn to include him in their group. Similarly, it is necessary to bring the truckers into the store organization so that they will realize some of the clerks' problems and come to cooperate with them.

Work Flow in the Factory

Richardson and Walker have made a sociographic analysis of work flow in the factory of the International Business Machines Corporation at Endicott, New York. In 1940 the company was organized on a job shop system. This system had many advan-tages, but as the company expanded various jams occurred in assembly.

In 1947 a progressive assembly system was adopted. Parts and assemblies now flowed downstream without returning to a cen-tral storeroom, as they had in the previous system. As a result, the researchers report that not only was a more economical plan effected but also better human relations were developed in the smoother work flow. Figure 5.11 compares the upstream and downstream relations in 1940 and 1947. As the jams in flow of

[26] The data for this map were collected by Douglas M. Allan, 1950.

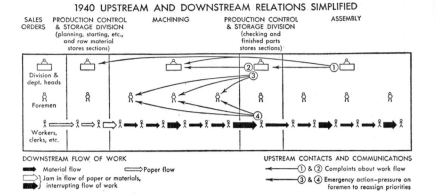

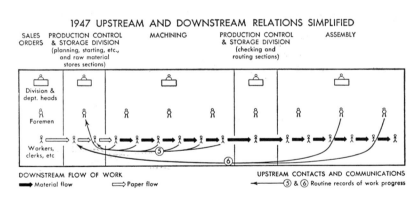

FIG. 5.11. Upstream and Downstream Relations at International Business Machines Corporation. (From F. L. W. Richardson, Jr., and Charles R. Walker, *Human Relations in an Expanding Company,* Yale, 1948, pp. 82–83.)

paper or material are removed the smoother flow of 1947 is produced.

Richardson and Walker have this to say about their study:

The introduction of new assembly operations are seldom analyzed strictly from the standpoint of human relations. This has been the sole object of this presentation. Matters of work flow, layout, assembly, and control are commonly considered the sole province of the engineer.

This study demonstrates that they are of equal concern to the student of human relations in the modern factory. . . . In a large factory, it is one thing to install a new layout and plan new schedules, but it is another to achieve and maintain a smooth functioning operation.[27]

In the IBM Corporation the Yale scientists examined both vertical and horizontal contacts. These include:

I. Vertical
  A. Downward communication.
  B. Upward communication.
II. Horizontal
  A. Work flow contacts.
  B. Contacts with staff and service departments.
  C. Contacts among friends and in informal cliques.[28]

Three changes occurred in the vertical contacts between 1940 and 1947:

1. A cessation of upstream contacts from assembly foremen to their division heads regarding work flow complaints.
2. Cessation of downstream contacts from machining foremen to their men: cessation of interrupting and reassigning jobs because of holdups.
3. Increased opportunity for worker-foreman contacts, arising out of availability of more time to foremen because of better work flow.

Changes in horizontal and oblique contacts also took place:

1. The downstream flow of work from employer to employee became far smoother.
2. In the paper flow sections (office) near the head of the work stream production planners now had better communication with employees downstream in the material flow sections.
3. Many upstream complaints and emergency contacts were greatly diminished.
4. Contacts between assembly foremen with contiguous positions along the work stream increased considerably.[29]

Such dramatic results promise a fruitful future for the study

[27] Richardson and Walker, *op. cit.*, p. 81.
[28] *Ibid.*, p. 4.
[29] *Ibid.*, pp. 84–85.

of work flow and segmentation problems. Large organizations do not have to stand by and watch communication lines become jammed and human relations made worse. The trend toward greater centralization, longer lines of communication, multiplication of staff functions, and greater segmentation reaches a point of diminishing returns. The scientific study of work flow and communication can lead the way to an intelligent countertrend with emphasis on better communication and integrated work teams.

REPERCUSSIONS OF ORGANIZATIONAL PROBLEMS IN LARGER SOCIAL SYSTEMS

It is an axiom of social systems that a change in one part will send repercussions throughout the entire system. A reorganization of management will often affect every member within the organization as well as many persons outside.[30] As was pointed out by Barnard earlier in this chapter, formal organizations are parts of larger social systems. This is especially well shown in an illustration which involved a flour-milling company, its trade association, its two unions, and an American Federation of Labor Regional Council and its international union officials. The case is described by an industrial sociologist who was called in by management of a large flour-milling company to act as a consultant at the time when the problem appeared ready to erupt into a strike. In the analysis which follows, note how the organizational complex conditions the role relationships and how the consultant must probe for anticipatory reactions. The consultant's role is revealed as a predictor who must help management weigh alternative actions.[31]

The Organizational Complex of Labor-Management Relations in Company X

When the labor contract was opened for negotiation in the spring of 1957, there was an established pattern of labor-manage-

[30] Conrad M. Arensberg and Douglas McGregor, "Determination of Morale in an Industrial Company," *Applied Anthropology*, 1942, vol. I, pp. 12–34. Also analyzed in George C. Homans, *The Human Group*, Harcourt, Brace, 1950, pp. 369–414.

[31] Delbert C. Miller, "The Application of Social System Analysis to Labor Management Conflict, A Consultant's Case Study," *Conflict Resolution*, June, 1959, pp. 146–152.

ment relations of ten years' standing. The company contained two unions with which it bargained. One was Local 68, an AFL union composed of 220 workers in the mill headed by leaders whom the company had found "easy to deal with"; the other was Local 3 of the International Longshore Workers' Union (ILWU) representing ninety workers in the warehouse and headed by aggressive leaders who had been "driving hard bargains" and had been trying constantly to increase their power. The company was a member of a Trade Association, which bargained for an area contract with the AFL Council representing Local 68. At the same time, the company bargained independently with Local 3 of the ILWU. A parity agreement covering general wage increases and working conditions had been signed with Local 3 each time a new agreement had been negotiated with Local 68. The established bargaining system is shown in Fig. 5.12.

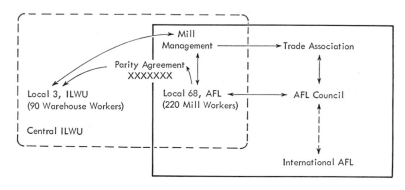

FIG. 5.12. The Established Bargaining System of the Labor-Management Parties of Company X.

A Labor-Management Problem and the Disruption of a Social System

The following account is described as it happened:

The established bargaining system became disrupted about eighteen months prior to the entry of the consultant. The disruption occurred when differences over expulsion of some international union officials arose between the AFL Council and its constituent member, Local 68. Since then, a feud has been going on between them and getting ever more bitter. The precipitating factors giving rise to the present labor-management problem are now these: Local 68 has withdrawn from the AFL Council and asks the company to bargain independently with it. The AFL Council refuses to recognize this right of secession and demands that Local 68 return immediately so that a new labor contract may be negotiated. The council has notified the company that it must bargain with the council in writing a new contract for Local 68.

The Trade Association is disturbed because company X is its largest member and it may no longer be needed if the company should recognize Local 68 as an independent union. Moreover, the association may face increasing difficulties in holding its other members, especially if new labor contracts in company X should put its remaining members at a competitive disadvantage. The association feels that its very survival may now be at stake. The company is equally disturbed lest it lose control of its position of maintaining similar contract provisions with its area competitors, and it is especially concerned about its future competitive position if the plant were to be struck. Under its Trade Association agreement members agree to deliver flour from their own supplies to fill orders for a struck plant. The company feels that it may lose these important advantages because of an interunion organization "squabble" for which it is not responsible in the slightest degree. This is why the general manager has been putting pressure on the industrial relations director and on the leaders of Local 68 to see that the local gets back into the AFL Council.

Local 68 is disturbed because of pressure coming from the company, the association, and the council to reassume its membership in the council. It feels that everyone is asking it to surrender its principles of justice and to humiliate itself. After all the bitter feeling, the leaders cannot see themselves "crawling back to those dirty four-flushers in the Council." They are determined to resist every pressure to get them back and to insist upon an independent bargaining role with the company. The time for reopening the contract is now. Every day that goes by means that they are working without a contract.

The general manager has told the industrial relations director to get a contract signed. His words are: "Tell 68 they are going back into the AFL Council. We are going to sign a contract with the Council and 68 can take it or lump it. We must act this week." The industrial relations director has said, "You'll have a strike on your hands!" The consultant has been asked, "What should the company do?"

An Analysis of Alternate Social Systems for the Parties

Up to this point the consultant had secured the patterned bargaining relationship of the parties and had a factual picture of the factors precipitating the problem. He took the view that an understanding of the interlocking character of the social system was of critical importance, since a resolution of the problem involved the possible necessity of establishing an alternate social system in place of the traditional bargaining social system. Figures 5.13 and 5.14 show two alternate social systems that might be

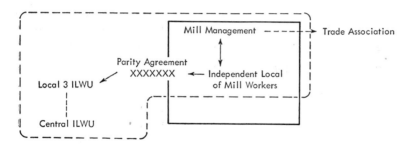

FIG. 5.13. Alternate Social System II.

instituted if the traditional system were permanently disrupted. An analysis of all three systems follows.

A. The established social system I

This is the social system (Fig. 5.12) which had included the management of company X, Local 68, Local 3, the AFL Council, Central ILWU, and the Trade Association. Each party had functioned within an established pattern for ten years and had derived mutual benefits. Now, even though disrupted by the feud of Local 68 with the AFL Council, the former economic advantages would be retained if harmony could be restored to the system.

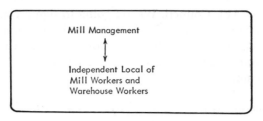

FIG. 5.14. Alternate Social System III.

B. Alternate social system II

This social system would include the management of company X, Local 68 (independent), Local 3 (ILWU), Central ILWU, and the Trade Association (see Fig. 5.13). It would involve recognition of the demand of Local 68 for independent status. It would involve a new arrangement with the Trade Association, since it would no longer function to negotiate the contract with the AFL Council. The Trade Association might be dropped entirely unless a new role could be developed for its services.

C. Alternate social system III

This system would include the management of company X and a single new independent union composed of former Local 68 and Local 3 (see Fig. 5.14). Such a new union might be created through a National Labor Relations Board election. The company would cut ties with the Trade Association, and the two unions would disaffiliate from their international union.

The problem of analysis now becomes one of weighing the possibility of creating a new social system or reestablishing the traditional pattern. The goals to be met include in each instance such objectives as long-run industrial peace and high levels of productive efficiency in plant operations. It is interesting to note that alternate systems II and III involve a loss of identification with central organizations. These are identifications which had been built up over the years for protection of the parties against adverse market conditions for goods or labor.

Appraising Alternate Action Patterns

Three alternate action patterns were presented by the industrial relations director. The consultant, working with the industrial relations director, analyzed each action pattern as to possible repercussions upon the *values of each participant, pattern of control,* and *social costs incurred.* The appraisal work sheet is shown.

APPRAISAL WORK SHEET

Alternate Action Patterns

1. *Reconstruct Established Bargaining Pattern.* Company will refuse to bargain outside the Trade Association and insist that Local 68 go back into the AFL Council.

   A. Values of Each Participant
   Local 68 is humiliated by being forced to return to the Council. Company is satisfied to establish tried and successful area of bargaining; fear of competitive disadvantage in future strikes is dispelled and the power of Local 3 is diminished. Association is satisfied as desire to maintain area bargaining is achieved.

   B. Pattern of Control
   Require Local 68 to return to Council by NLRB decision. Company will work with Council and Association to get Local 68 to go back to Council. Association puts pressure on Council to achieve reestablishment of traditional pattern.

   C. Social Costs
   Local plant relations which have been very good may be seriously weakened if Local 68 is coerced to return to the Council. A strike may result.

2. *Institute a New Bargaining Pattern with Recognition of the Mill Workers in an Independent Union.*

   A. Values of Each Participant
   Local 68 is highly pleased to achieve an independent social and bargaining position. Local 3 is pleased and believes that it may now have more influence over Local 68 and the company. Company wants to keep area bargaining conditions inside the new arrangement. Association wants to keep the company in the Association and maintain area bargaining rates and working conditions; however, Association is very displeased with the company and the unions for disrupting the established pattern.

   B. Pattern of Control
   Local 68 is weakened slightly but feels secure as long as Local 68 and Local 3 maintain parity agreement. Local 3 senses it will be stronger because of its aggressive leadership and it may capture Local 68 for its union. Company loses Association as bargaining agent. It will need to establish new controls over Local 68 lest Local 3 become real power. Association puts pressure on Council and on company to reestablish the traditional pattern.

C. Social Costs
Company is afraid of the growing potential power of Local 3 in bargaining. There is the danger to the company of their sales being pirated during a future strike if they should leave the Association. Association may lose Company X as member and thus lose strength. It faces future difficulty with Association members in the likelihood of inequities in agreements.

3. *Institute a New Bargaining Pattern with Recognition of a Single Independent Union of Mill and Warehouse Workers.*

A. Values of Each Participant
Local 68 wants independence and fears militant leadership of Local 3, especially when backed by Central ILWU. Local 3 is strongly opposed to a combined union and fears company is trying to weaken Local 3 by absorbing it in the larger mill-workers' union. Company would be able to bargain with only one union. Association would be satisfied if company continues to use Association as a bargaining agent.

B. Pattern of Control
Mill workers could be weakened by aggressive leadership power of warehouse workers; warehouse workers could be weakened by voting strength of mill workers. Company might find it harder to control a stronger single union, especially if mill and warehouse workers should get together for their mutual advantage; Association bargaining might be made difficult or impossible by demands from a single strong union.

C. Social Costs
Mill workers placed in weaker position with possible loss of independence from aggressive leaders among warehouse workers. Warehouse workers placed in a weaker position unless their leaders can compensate for loss of voting strength. Company may have serious in-plant labor trouble if the new, single, independent union is created under pressure from the company and from the government.

Conclusion Reached by Industrial Relations Director

At the termination of consultation, the industrial relations director reached a preliminary recommendation. The consultant made no recommendations because he took the view that a responsible official could do this best within the context of the situation. He knew that the industrial relations director would have to persuade the general manager on the wisdom of any course of action. It was the industrial relations director who feared that Local 68 could not be forced back into the AFL Council and, if such an attempt were made, would bring a strike action. His conclusions, based on the social analysis prepared by the consultant, were now as follows:

1. Recognize right of Local 68 to bargain independently. Do not put pressure upon the local to affiliate with the AFL Council against its will.

2. Seek to reconcile the AFL Council to the necessity of inducing Local 68 to return. Failing this, seek authorization of Local 68 as independent bargaining unit. NLRB would be petitioned to hold globe election in which Local 68 would vote in secret election for continued affiliation with council or independent status.

3. Secure a parity agreement clause that states no strike action will be taken without vote of both unions. This will put power of strike in hands of Local 68, a less-aggressive union.

4. Maintain associate membership in the Trade Association. Use it as clearing house for information and to secure bargaining help when needed.

Management Action

The industrial relations director reported his recommendations to the general manager. The manager maintained that everything must be done to restore the traditional bargaining pattern and get Local 68 back into the Council. Strategy was carefully discussed, and the two managers agreed now to put the *pressure on the AFL Council rather than on Local 68.* The general manager called the international vice-president of the AFL, located in a regional city center, and told him that the local council would have to "come off its high horse and get 68 back into the Council" or the AFL was going to lose one of its strongest unions. The international vice-president made a hurried trip to the big city. The vice-president convinced the AFL Council leaders that they must effect a reconciliation. The vice-president and the AFL Council president were quietly admitted by management upon the company grounds, and for some days they browsed about talking with Local 68 leaders and members. Finally, Local 68 voted to stay in—the Council had "eaten crow," and members of 68 were satisfied. (Local 68 leaders said "the big boys admitted their mistakes and practicaly got down on their knees and asked us to come back.")

A contract was later negotiated with high satisfaction to all parties. The result was a reestablishment of the traditional pattern. The established social system became reconstructed as it was of old, when Local 68 leaders became active in the Council, and all parties resumed their habitual roles. Here we have a validation of the principle that social systems tend toward equilibrium. The values of the established system were strong enough to maintain the "boundaries of the system" in the face of a strong threat to the survival of the system. Boundary maintenance resulted because the external economic and social environment remained relatively constant, and to regain equilibrium, the system needed only the redefinition of role expectations between Local 68 and the AFL Council.

The consultant's role may be seen as one of assisting in defining the alternate actions and their possible repercussions more sharply than they might otherwise have been defined and, perhaps, giving the industrial relations director more influence in resisting direct coercion of the local union. If this be true, then social diagnosis proved itself useful, because a wrong decision could easily have involved a large loss to the company and to the workers. In addition, labor relations might have been worsened for an indefinite period.

CONCLUSION

Formal organization has been shown to be an interrelated network of social relations. It has been pointed out that such networks have three qualities: they are stable, balanced, and delicate.[32] Stable, because structure conditions a functioning pattern that tends to follow the norms and sanctions inherent in it. Balanced, because each part is related to values which resist change and tend to hold the structure in equilibrium. Delicate, because the structure is flexible as well as stable, ever changing in minor details. A change in one part may send repercussions throughout all of the other parts of the structure.

To understand such networks, insight into the organization of work and the organization of management is a prerequisite. The view must be a total one embracing technical and social relations throughout the structure. This kind of overview is assisted by knowledge of management functions and values expressed in the

[32] Cf. F. S. Chapin, *Contemporary American Institutions*, Harper, 1935, p. 12.

various levels of management. This is the aim to be pursued in the next chapter.

SELECTED BIBLIOGRAPHY

Barnard, Chester I., *The Functions of an Executive*, Harvard, 1947.

Bendix, Reinhard, *Work and Authority in Industry*, Wiley, 1956.

Etzioni, Amitai (ed.), *Complex Organizations, A Sociological Reader*, Holt, 1961.

Gilman, Glen, "An Inquiry into the Nature and Use of Authority," in Mason Haire (ed.), *Organization Theory in Industrial Practice*, Wiley, 1962.

Haire, Mason (ed.), *Modern Organization Theory*, Wiley, 1959.

Haire, Mason (ed.), *Organization Theory in Industrial Practice*, Wiley, 1962.

March, James G., and Herbert A. Simon, *Organizations*, Wiley, 1958.

Simon, Herbert A., *Administrative Behavior*, Macmillan, 1958.

Thompson, Victor A., *Modern Organization*, Knopf, 1961.

CHAPTER 6

Top, Middle, and First-line Managerial Roles

WORK POSITIONS AS SOCIAL PATTERNS

The Gap Between Management Theory and Management Practice

In the last chapter we discussed the formal organization of management and described the theory of formal organization. It will be remembered that the theory of formal organization created a model which classical economists would be likely to call "pure" and "perfect" management. Inside the model managers would always get high production and the smoothest of human relations. These are the things managers *would like to achieve* through the formal structure. But problems are always arising and something is always going wrong. The problems of communication and segmentation already examined indicate that the gap between theory and practice grows fairly wide. And this breach tends to widen in spite of the best efforts which intelligent and experienced managers can give. Why? Let us explore in more detail the reasons for this breach.

To begin with, we have seen that human factors do intervene and affect the operation of formal management structure. Organizational cleavages which are unanticipated occur within the formal structure. Far from being a well-integrated organism, industry tends to be divided into a number of parts or groupings which have a quasi-independent existence. The process by which a larger organization separates into smaller segments is called, appropriately, segmentation. The forces facilitating segmentation arise from the nature of the structure and from the motives of its occupants, and so do the forces for organizational integration. Industry, like any human organization, contains an equilibrium of forces which simultaneously integrate and divide work groups. The processes of integration and segmentation are neither "good" nor "bad." They are natural processes which may be used to promote one end or another. The problem of administration requires that these processes be recognized and kept in balance.

In actual function, an organizational segment is composed of a number of people interacting according to expected patterns. It is unrealistic to ignore these specific behavior patterns. In order to get a more complete picture of the operation of management, we shall focus our attention on some of the more important managerial jobs and the problems that are tied to them. The technical duties connected with management's jobs are not the concern of the sociologist.

From a sociological point of view, a technical job description contains only a partial definition of the worker's behavior. The sociologist approaches the job with four major assumptions: (1) Every worker is a group member; (2) every group has a number of more or less well-defined patterns of behavior for each of its members; (3) the work plant is a conglomeration of work groups; and (4) a worker interacts and participates in these groups. Under these assumptions the job must be considered as a social element.

The Meaning of Work Position

When "job" is approached in this social sense, we call it a *work position*. The work position does not refer to an actual individual performing his job. Rather, it describes a series of typical functions and social relations which any person in the work position must observe. Irrespective of the occupant, the work position has three major aspects: (1) the technical operations of the job; (2) the physical locations of the worker on the job and all of the physical objects which compose and surround a given work position; (3) the social demands which must be fulfilled by anyone who is to perform adequately in the position. These demands include (a) The circumscribed round of activities, or the sequence of activities, demanded of the job; (b) the number and nature of the worker's contacts with other people or objects while on the job; and (c) the way in which the worker's activities fit into those of other workers and are viewed by other workers in their jobs.

If the observer gathers descriptions of all the main work positions in the organization and then relates them, he has a complete picture of the organization. It is not a picture of the operation, but a good structural or static view of organization. To know how the organization functions from day to day he would have to observe people acting in their work positions.

Work Role

When workers are actually engaged in fulfilling the expectations of their work positions, they are playing their *work roles.* The work role is the dynamic aspect of position. It is difficult to make concrete generalizations about roles because they are so dynamic. This work position and work role never coincide exactly. Role playing is affected by individual personalities acting in specific situations at designated times. However, much of the role may be understood and even predicted by studying the work position, because position defines the framework within which the role is played.

Work-Oriented Groups

Work position and work role are both group-oriented concepts. They differ from the usual concept of "job" because they consider the worker in *all* of his social relationships. Obviously the worker participates in formal and informal groups both inside and outside of the plant. The definition of his work position and work role demands an enumeration of all the work groups in which he participates and a description of the part he plays in each of them. We may classify the groups in which the worker is attached as nuclear, satellite, and societal work groups.

1. *Nuclear work groups*

The nuclear work group, containing people who interact daily on a face-to-face basis on the job, is usually composed of work positions that are physically adjacent and functionally interrelated. The contacts and interactions which are necessary to perform the job define the person's nuclear work group. Occasionally the contacts among members of a nuclear work group may be indirect—as reporting to the boss daily by telephone or by mail. Generally the group may be identified by observing the interaction of people on the job. Frequently, many workers belong to the same nuclear groups, as in the case of a telephone repair crew. Identifying such groups for other workers may be more difficult because some work positions do not dovetail neatly into each other.

2. Satellite work groups

There are other groups to which a worker belongs by virtue of his being an employee of a work plant. Contacts in these groups may be incidental to the job. For example, participation in the labor union, picnic committee, or safety committee is not part of the job. Although contacts in such groups may be occasional, the worker may be highly involved in them and derive considerable satisfaction and prestige from membership. Many satellite groups are informal in nature, e.g., the lunch group, the car pool, cliques on the job, the informal recreational groups, the company-sponsored teams, and clubs. Even though participation may occur outside of the plant, the fact that the members are employees of the same plant satisfies our definition of satellite work group. It is difficult to overstress the importance of these groups, for they may affect the worker's role and job performance.

3. Societal groups

Figure 6.1 portrays the group affiliation of an executive. His nuclear and satellite groups can be seen in the inner circles. The reader will note that the third concentric circle contains some groups which do not appear to be directly related to work or the work plant. Yet the church, neighborhood, and political party are included because they may bear significantly on work activity. Although the relation may not be obvious, many workers appreciate the importance of societal groups. Not infrequently, when an executive comes to a new community he "shops around" to find what organizations he is expected to join and what organizations it will be wise to join. He asks himself such questions as: What church do most of the executives attend? What neighborhoods do they live in? What service clubs do they join? What

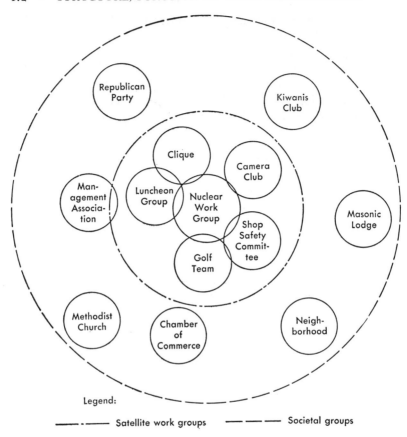

Legend:

——————— Satellite work groups   ————— Societal groups

FIG. 6.1. The Nuclear, Satellite, and Societal Group Affiliations of a Business Executive.

political party do they prefer? What lodges are considered "right"?

Some of these societal groups are apparently more related to work than others. The Management Association, the Chamber of Commerce, and Kiwanis are obviously work-oriented groups. In Fig. 6.1 they are placed closer to the center. Groups that are not so closely related to work are drawn farther away from the center. The relative relevance of the societal groups may be quite reversed in an actual situation. That is, purely "social" clubs may be more influential in business affairs than business organizations.

The worker accepts all these groups as an integral part of working and living. Although he may consider some of his contacts more important than others, his *group relations as a whole locate him in the social world of work*. Observing his behavior in these groups helps us come to a closer definition of his actual work role. In the following section we shall describe the typical work positions and work roles for several management jobs. Since space does not permit the analysis of all work positions, we shall describe three key positions: those of the president, the plant manager, and the foreman. The president is the chief of policy, the plant manager is head of operations, and the foreman is immediate overseer of production. As these three positions are analyzed we shall relate them to work positions commonly associated with them.

Although our analysis of work positions and work roles deals with managerial positions in industry, the same framework is useful in describing other work organizations. The three key positions are found in every type of organization. Table 6.1 compares the common titles of these positions in industry with those of some other large organizations.[1]

The major differences between any of the comparable positions in different work organizations are due mainly to differences in

TABLE 6.1. Comparison of Titles for Similar Positions in Industry, a Large Office (or Department Store), a University, a Large Public School System, a Hospital, a Government Agency, and a Church Hierarchy

Manage- ment Level	Industry	Large Office or Depart- ment Store	University	Large Public School System	Hospital	Govern- ment Agency	Church
Top	President	President	President	Superin- tendent	Adminis- trator	Adminis- trator	Bishop
Middle	Plant manager	General manager	Dean	Principal	Chief of medical staff	Division chief	Dean
First- line	Foreman	Supervisor or de- partment manager	Department head	Department head	Nursing super- visor	Section head	Rector

[1] Cf. material on universities with John J. Corson, *Governance of Colleges and Universities*, McGraw-Hill, 1960, pp. 72–96.

functional requirements of the organization and in the sanctioned exercise of authority. Decision-making authority is generally more sharply limited for university and hospital administrators than for those in industry or in government. There is no doubt that wide variations do exist in the role requirements of any of the three levels, yet similarities far outnumber differences. Although the following analysis has elected to focus on industrial positions, the student is urged to compare and to watch for similarities and differences in similar positions in other types of work organizations.

WORK POSITIONS AND WORK ROLES OF MANAGEMENT

The Big Boss

Formal functions

The work plant is generally directed by a chief executive officer—the big boss. His title may be president, chairman, director, commissar, secretary, or leader. Irrespective of title, he is the executive head of the organization. It is difficult to describe his position and role in detail because they differ somewhat with different sizes and types of enterprises. For our purposes we shall place the big boss in an organization large enough to need a layer of top managers, composed of vice-presidents or directors.

The duties of the big boss tend to be the same in all work plants. If he is not an honorary head, his primary job is to make the policy and see that "policy" is carried out. Several functions are ordinarily considered a part of his policy-making duties. He is primarily concerned with maintaining and improving the position of his enterprise. He must do everything possible to enable the organization to grow and survive. Even if he is head of a government department or bureau, he must be concerned with the survival and future growth of his organization. For in all large enterprises, departments are in a desperate struggle with each other to obtain funds, stay in favor with the super-chief and justify their existence. Survival activities may occupy most of the time of the big boss. In a monopolistic business, less attention needs to be paid to struggle for survival. However secure his organization, the big boss spends considerable time keeping abreast of financial reports, newsletters, market and business conditions. Central to the work position of the big boss, then, is the job of coordinating all parts of the enterprise, so that it will be able to survive foreseeable social, political, economic, and other changes.[2]

A closely related function of the chief executive is to maintain equilibrium within the organization so it functions smoothly. In well-balanced organizations this role will be minimal because the functions of the various segments dovetail nicely. But as we have noted, all organizations display segmentation tendencies, such as factional disputes between levels and departments, jealousies, and other problems. One major function of the big boss is to make and to keep the balance within the organization, by adjudicating these disputes.

On occasion, important problems of a technical nature require the attention of the chief executive. Or, as is more frequently the case, timid subordinates, afraid to make major decisions, push them up the line until they appear on the chief's desk. Many of the problems that reach the chief are exceptional and unusual ones. Most problems arising in a business should be anticipated and solved by the formal organization down the line. If this is the case, the job of the big boss is to deal with the unanticipated or the exceptional problems. Some bosses then conceive of their jobs as "governing by exception." Although others will not admit this as their primary function, it is nonetheless present in the jobs of all chief executives. Ideally, each exception which is ruled upon becomes a precedent, guiding behavior of subordinates in similar future cases. More frequently, however, the big boss insists upon handling certain kinds of problems whenever they arise.

Another function of the chief is to stimulate his organization to do more effective work. He tries to "keep tabs" on operations by reading reports on production costs, turnover, absenteeism, and other things. In addition, he attempts to stimulate each section to do better. On rare occasions, especially in the smaller plant, he may make a "tour of the plant," to see what is "really" going on. This usually is a pretense to show that he takes an interest in the plant. Since nobody likes the practice very much, the

[2] Burleigh B. Gardner and David G. Moore, *Human Relations in Industry,* Irwin, 1950, p. 62.

big boss usually retreats to his office and stays there. He feels his time is too valuable to spend on petty details.

The president's orientations, then, are off the floor and often outside of the plant itself. He considers it important to keep up his business and social contacts in the community. He may spend considerable time attending meetings of the Chamber of Commerce, Rotary Club, Red Cross, and the Management Association.

A typical day

Before the big boss arrives, his mail is sorted by his secretary. Reports from the managers and directors of the various departments are read, processed, and summarized by his staff assistants, with notations of the decisions that might be made. Around nine o'clock the big boss enters his office. He is usually above average in build, around fifty years old, and neatly dressed. He calls in his secretary and one of his staff assistants. He and his assistant discuss the important mail and the routine reports. The secretary makes a record of the letters to be sent out, of the orders to the assistant, and of decisions which must be carried out.

The chief then calls in the general manager or some other high line official. They review reports of the operating departments. The main problems arising in the departments are discussed, and whenever possible, decisions are made on how to proceed. But this session is for the most part an informative one for the big boss. Some routine decisions may be made, as well as some "exception" decisions. On the basis of this conference, if the boss really knows the business, he schedules meetings with operating chiefs, financial officers, personnel people, and others. The rest of the day is consumed with conferences that were arranged or scheduled for that day. In between the conferences are sandwiched short meetings with big customers, important visitors, and other influential people.

The day of the big boss is a day of conferences with small groups. At most four or five officials meet with him in his office or in one of the conference rooms. The men that participate in these conferences are officials on the next lower level—vice-presidents, directors, and managers. Each vice-president may bring to the conference three or four subofficials who do not participate in discussions unless they are asked to provide information. These assistant managers would not consider dropping in on the big boss unescorted by their superiors.

Occasionally the chief eats near one of the assistants at lunch time in the executive dining room. More often than not, however, he will be surrounded by vice-presidents. Lunch may be served in his office while a conference is being conducted. Probably once or twice a week he lunches uptown with high executive officials of other companies.

The afternoon is occupied with more conferences. Some time late in the afternoon there is a period of relaxation when no conferences are scheduled. At this time, staff assistants or the other high officials drop in for a chat. Problems arising during the day may be discussed, if it is not too inconvenient. If they involve getting more information, they are put on tomorrow's calendar. The big boss leaves the office exhausted, perhaps with the thought that conference work "takes more out of you than physical labor."

The big boss's range of social contact on the job is relatively small. He probably sees the same fifteen or twenty people every day. These people represent the upper two or three levels of management. The big boss's spatial mobility is also limited to his office and conference room. Although he may have a "feel" for his organization derived from inspecting its blueprints, his own job perspective is rather narrow. His world is an office world of appointments, official papers, and conferences.

The big boss and top managers

In a large organization there may be several vice-presidents, or managers, under the president. They represent, perhaps, manufacturing, engineering, sales, industrial relations, public relations, and finance. In smaller organizations two or three of these offices may be combined in one. On paper all of these officials appear equally important. They may even receive very similar salaries. *The problem of knowing the social situation at the top levels is one of arranging these officials in terms of their relations to the president, who is the big boss. It is also a problem of analyzing what kind of resources they have in their struggle with each other to gain the attention and confidence of the big boss.*

Each of these officials is a big boss over a section of the organization. His daily schedule and duties are not unlike those of the big boss. He, too, has subofficials under him. The larger the organization, the more the jobs of the top managers approach that of the president. Only their preoccupations are somewhat different. Each of them heads something like a political machine —a public relations machine, a sales machine, or a production machine, as the case may be. Each machine wants to protect or promote its security. Since each boss has some sovereignty over an area, he is jealous if someone interferes with his autonomy.

Generally speaking, the president does not want to interfere in the internal affairs of these suborganizations. He hesitates to order changes in their structure or functions unless he thinks it absolutely necessary. He likes to have harmony (often defined as lack of open conflict) between the sections of the enterprise. Therefore he gives the vice-presidents freedom to run their organizations as long as they are doing satisfactory jobs.

The president, however, shows greater interest in the operation of some departments than of others. Finance, production, and industrial relations attract his attention. Normally he spends much of his time with the secretary-treasurer of the organizaion. In fact, it is not unrealistic to think of the president as the chief financial officer, because the board of directors and stockholders hold him responsible for profit and loss. So the big boss must spend time with his chief financial officer, whether or not their interpersonal relations are pleasant.

The relations between president and head of production are also close. Since profits depend upon the performance of the line organization, it is to the president's interest to keep informed on production schedules, bottlenecks, and achievements of the production organization. Not infrequently the president has been chief of production, so he is in a position to give advice.

If the president is not himself the informal head of industrial relations, he spends a great deal of time with the manager of this division during periods of labor strife. Although he does not ordinarily concern himself with industrial relations, a strike or threat of strike means that the finances and profit will be affected. During a strike, then, he spends most of his day with his industrial relations manager.

Emergencies may appear in other sections of the organization, requiring the president to spend more of his time with the appropriate officials. Thus the work positions of the president and of top management are in part traditionally defined and in part situationally defined. It is important to know how close the relations of the boss and his satellites are "normally" to evaluate the social situation of the moment. Figure 6.2 shows an insider's chart of a given organization at a moment in time. Note how each formal relationship is influenced by the various role relations. Here is evidence of the importance of a social system analysis after a study of the formal structure has been made.

Irrespective of situations, however, the president has two roles which he constantly plays. One is that of *instigation,* to stimulate all parts of his organization to do a better job. He must never allow his interest and attention to flag to the point that one part of the structure lags behind others. His second role is that of the *veto.* Each vice-president or manager wants his organization to be tops. For example, the head of manufacturing demands new and expensive machinery, the personnel director wants to institute a training program, the sales manager desires to step up advertising, the financial officer wants to institute better cost analysis methods. The president must learn when, to whom, and how to say *yes* and *no.* Getting knowledge to back his *no* occupies much more time than saying yes.

The social relations of the big boss in an actual work situation are portrayed in Fig. 6.3. The three concentric rings around the president connote the varying degrees of interaction. In the first ring are the president's private secretary and his two staff assistants. They form a tight primary group because they are in daily contact with the boss. In the second ring are the secretary-treasurer and the vice-presidents of production and engineering. The big boss does not interact with these three as extensively or intensively as with those in ring 1. In this case some antagonism exists between the big boss and the vice-president of production, whereas free interaction characterizes relations with the secretary-treasurer and the vice-president of engineering. In the third ring are the vice-president of sales and the industrial relations manager. The big boss interacts with the sales executive only when necessary. Close interaction between the boss and the industrial relations manager depends upon the state of labor-management relations. Relations between the boss and the board of directors

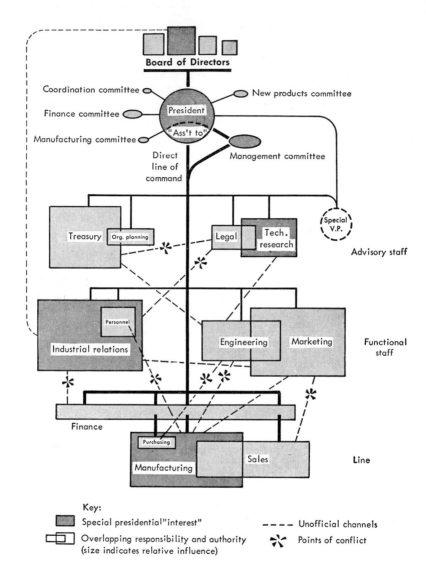

Board of Directors

Coordination committee

Finance committee

Manufacturing committee

President

"Ass't to"

New products committee

Direct
line of
command

Management committee

Treasury   Org. planning   Legal   Tech. research

Special V.P.

Advisory staff

Personnel

Industrial relations

Engineering   Marketing

Functional staff

Finance

Purchasing

Manufacturing   Sales

Line

Key:
- Special presidential "interest"
- Overlapping responsibility and authority (size indicates relative influence)
- – – – Unofficial channels
- Points of conflict

FIG. 6.2. An Insider's Organization Chart. This array of lines, squares, circles, lozenges, and rectangles shows some of the things that might happen to an orthodox organization chart if it were redrawn to reflect what actually goes on in a company. The company, the Turbid Corporation, is hypothetical, but most readers will recognize some familiar situations. Turbid's president is repeatedly asked to settle arguments among the manufacturing, purchasing, finance, and sales divisions, each of which

are formal and most distant. This kind of positional analysis should be made in reference to many positions before the social analysis of a work plant is completed.

Relations among top managers

In most large corporations it is possible to rank the vice-presidents in terms of (1) their influence on general policy, (2) their importance in running the enterprise, (3) their general status or prestige level, and (4) their economic power. The relative rank of top managers in each of these four categories is not stationary, and much of their time and energy is devoted to moving up these ladders. The relative rank of underlings in each suborganization is affected by the status rank of their boss. For example, in the case presented above, the assistant managers, secretaries, and other personnel in engineering have higher rank than do similar jobs in the sales division.

All kinds of political devices are used by the top managers to gain influence, prestige, and money. Two or three of them may form a clique to help each other against other cliques. Since the financial and production chiefs have natural "ins" with the president, cliques tend to form about them.

Not infrequently everyone in top management owns stocks in the corporation. The more stock they own or control, the greater their likelihood of gaining more influence. If they can control

---

wants its say on inventories. But the most frequent conflicts occur between these "line" functions and those so-called "staff" departments like engineering and marketing that exercise authority over the line through their specialized knowledge.

Turbid's aggressive managers, however, pay scant attention to jurisdictional distinctions. The industrial relations department's authority, for instance, completely overlaps the personnel department's because of (1) the president's enthusiasm for industrial relations, and (2) the emphasis on labor relations in the public utterances of Turbid's dominant board member. Similarly, Turbid's finance chief has so much drag with the president that his department cuts right across all decisions handed down the line of command. The dotted circle (upper right) symbolizes the post held by the fun-loving brother of Turbid's president, who is incapable of managerial functioning and dangles, the fruit of nepotism. The president is surrounded by committees, one so dominant it can give orders down the line as well as advice to him. His young "assistant to" in his confidential status colors much of what the boss hears from the twelve executives who jealously insist on reporting directly to the chief. (From Perrin Stryker, "Can Management Be Managed?" *Fortune*, July, 1953, p. 101.)

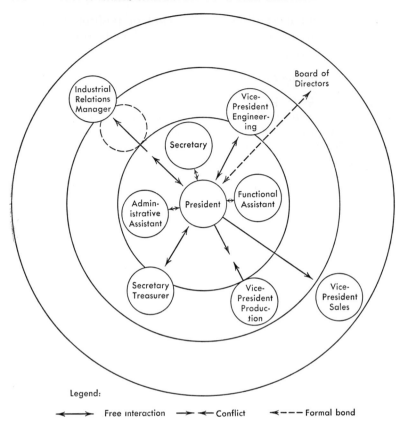

FIG. 6.3. The Social Atom of a Company President.

enough votes they can become executive vice-presidents and sit on the board of directors. Once on the board they may be in position to unseat managers and even the president. Therefore, many top executives spend much time making contacts among stockholders and gathering proxies so that they can become more influential.

"Nonofficial" aspects of the work role

The duties of the big boss are not over at the end of the day, because his work role dominates almost all of his living. His "extracurricular" contacts are in the factory associations, social clubs, business associations, and the community.

"DUTY" CONTACTS

There are certain "duty" contacts which the big boss must develop and sustain. Frequently, the lower executives of business organize occupational and recreational groups. The Supervisory Association is an example of the first, and the Bowling League illustrates the second. The president may be asked to preside over the association or to give a talk; he is also expected to make an occasional appearance at the social affairs of lower executives. On the average of once a week, he has one of these "duty" calls to perform. He rationalizes that "It is time well spent in personnel relations. It's a good idea to mix with the men and let them know you're a human being."

The vice-presidents and managers also have duty contacts, although they may not be as pressing as those of the president. Generally speaking, the farther down the line, the less time is spent on these duties and social functions. But even the foreman has to spend some time on them. Each department, such as engineering, materials, production planning, and manufacturing, may have an annual picnic, athletic teams, and clubs. The managers may be asked to encourage these organizations with their presence. They may also be requested to attend the company-wide picnic, the monthly dance, and other events, to impress on everyone that they take an interest in the whole organization.

SOCIAL CLUBS

Apart from internal duty contacts, high officials spend much of their time developing contacts. Some of these contacts are closely connected to their work positions. The president, for example, may endeavor to develop social contacts with members of the board of directors and important stockholders. Not infrequently high officials must maintain enough stock votes or strength to stay in office. Therefore time and energy must be consumed entertaining people who can help their positions. One way to meet these people is to join their clubs and organizations. The country club, boating club, university club, and fraternity are just a few sources of social contacts. The reader may review a few "social participation profiles" of businessmen in *Who's Who*. For example,

Seary, Harry Lauderdale, life ins.; *b.* Galatin, Tenn., Nov. 25, 1872; *s.* George Edward and Mary (Lauderdale) S.; student, Vanderbilt, 1890–1893; LL.B, Georgetown U., 1894; *m.* Margaret Ballentine, Dec. 17, 1902; 1 son, Harry L. In practice of law, Dallas, Tex., 1894–1915; pres. Southland Life Ins. Co. since 1915; res. Am. Rio Grande Land & Irrigation Co. since 1902; v. p. Dallas Power & Light Co.; dir. Tex. Power and Light Company. City Commissioner, Dallas, Tex., 1907–1911; mem. Nat. Council Defense, World War; Pres. Amer. Life Conv., 1917–1918; dir. Tex. State Fair Assoc.; member, Kappa Alpha. Democrat. Mem. Christian Church. Mason (32, Shriner). *Clubs:* Dallas Athletic Fincastle Lake, Little Sandy Lake (Dallas); Shary Yacht (Point Isabel, Texas). *Home:* 3707 Beverly Drive, Highland Park, Dallas. *Office:* Southland Life Bldg., Dallas, Tex.

BUSINESS ASSOCIATIONS

Business associations are also part of the extra-plant social life of the top executives. The Chamber of Commerce, Management Association, Society of Engineers, City Club are just a few of these. Business organizations shade off into semi-business groups such as Kiwanis, Rotary, and Lions. Participation in these clubs often constitutes the "community" activity of many business leaders.

COMMUNITY ACTIVITIES

However, some presidents urge their executives to get out into "genuine" community activities: to work for the Red Cross, political organizations, planning commission, community chest, and others. Indeed, many of these organizations have the same social members as the service clubs. Industrial and business leaders feel that this kind of work is a "contribution" of their organization to the community. Men are released from their official duties to participate in these "worthy" activities. It is a principle that the lower down the line one is, the less are his chances of being released from work routine to participate in community life.

Motives that impel community participation are mixed. There is a tradition that businessmen should serve their communities, and most executives follow this tradition. But participation may also be considered an unofficial part of public relations. Since the relations between industry and community are frequently intimate and important, it pays to have the good will of prominent people in the community. Not to be neglected is the fact that such participation is another channel for making business contacts. Apart from the fact that business people think and act alike, and therefore find their own company congenial, community organizations are a good place to develop business contacts.

Ideology of top management

Warner and Abegglen have found it necessary to distinguish between two types of big business leaders. The birth elite are those whose fathers were major executives or owners of large businesses. The mobile elite are all others whose fathers were in other occupational categories. It is interesting to note that these two types of leaders differ in their way of life, with the birth elite bringing a background of status expectations and community obligations established by the fathers' example. The mobile elite must acquire what the birth elite must maintain. However, the background differences do not place big business leaders far apart. Slightly over half are sons of owners or executives of business firms and 14 percent are the sons of professional men—doctors, engineers, ministers, lawyers, teachers, or men in other professional pursuits. In all, two of every three leaders of American business come from families whose economic and social positions are well above average for the nation. And what differences remain in background are easily dissolved by higher education and larger incomes.[3]

As a result of the similar backgrounds, experience, social participation, and frequent contacts, the big boss and his top executives think very much alike on social, political, and economic issues.

Top management is a *highly self-conscious* group, widely separated from the mass of people. The adulation that many people have for the captains of industry understandably affects their self-conception. Like those in other occupational groups, top executives are not only self-conscious but conscious of their *self-importance*. Their ethnocentrism leads them to believe that they have special gifts and attributes not generally shared by the popu-

[3] W. Lloyd Warner and James Abegglen, *Big Business Leaders in America,* Harper, 1955.

lation. The greatest of these is the ability to manage and organize people. They feel that good management is the biggest asset of any organization; without it, a business community or nation could not progress. Other virtues they honor, apart from occupational knowledge, are energy, dynamic ambition, initiative, leadership, and "personality."

During World War II, the esteem that management had for its own skills was sloganized as "know-how" and "can do." Technical knowledge and organizational skill are considered absolute requisites for executive success. The intense admiration for skills and achievements leads to the questions "What can he do?" "How good is he?"

A common question managers ask is "What kind of fellow is he?" They are preoccupied with the personal and social attributes of a man. Although they consider technical skill more important than all other factors, they are also concerned with "developing" personality and social "know-how." The veritable deluge of books and pamphlets in recent years on how to make friends and develop personality reflects the faith that "personality and social success" are learnable. A tightening of the channels of upward mobility may be no small factor in the sale of such "success" books.

Top management is an *authority-conscious* group. Men at the top of the supervisory structure are consumed with decision-making and commanding. Yet they do not like to believe that men obey them because they have power. This thought derives from a wish to be appreciated both as persons and as officials. In meetings of business executives one or two speeches are invariably devoted to the *importance of leadership,* the *development of leadership,* the *techniques of leadership,* and the *role of leadership* in industry.[4] Perhaps the American political ideal of democratic leadership is so powerful that executives want to realize it in business. Obviously they want to be and like to be thought of as leaders. They want to feel that they command because they are gifted to lead; that others obey because they recognize this ability. The cult of leadership may be an integral part of the larger American tradition of individual mobility in a free society.

Another facet in the ideology of management is *social respon-*

[4] See Schuyler Dean Hoslett, *Human Factors in Management,* Park College Press, 1946, Part I.

sibility. Chief executives do not like to believe that their only motive in business is profit. They like to feel that as leaders of industry they must assume the responsibility of directing the community. Since many workers and investors are dependent upon them for their livelihood, they feel obliged to do a good job.[5] Unions and other such organizations interfere with this responsibility. The business leader likes to look at himself as a man who has dedicated his life to the *service* of investors, employees, and customers. He feels that his salary includes a payment for a stewardship which he owes to the community. He derives much satisfaction from the knowledge that he is serving his stewardship well.

In exercising his calling, the business leader feels that the *good of the organization* is paramount. Unlike other people, he must be concerned with the entire enterprise. It is his duty to think of the requirements of the *whole* organization. Although he may hurt people in the process, he feels that this hardheartedness is really hardheadedness, for the entire organization would suffer if he did not play this role.

The good executive feels that a good business is one that is *making money.* Money is an indicator of efficiency, as well as a goal. It is simultaneously an incentive and a yardstick. Without it, business would founder in a sea of inefficiency. Another element in the thought system of managers is costs. The causes of inefficiency are thought to be almost invariably internal, and the cure of inefficiency must start from within. The first step in this cure is to *cut costs, by whatever means are available.* Cutting costs and keeping them down is one of the major jobs of executives, for costs and profits are very closely related. Any organization that doesn't keep costs down is not a good organization. That is why government is inefficient. It costs too much, and the way to make it efficient is to cut its budget. It will, like business, find ways to be more efficient.

The thinking continues: A good business cannot prosper without *good organization.* Any business can be better organized; and poor business can often be saved by reorganization. Many businessmen falsely believe that organization is a science and should be applied like a science. The executive feels that he cannot be

[5] J. David Houser, *What People Want from Business,* McGraw-Hill, 1938.

queasy about the application of his science. Personality and sentiment should not enter into the science of business administration. The more this happens, the more inefficient business will be.

Administrative roles and patterns of the president

Research has been demonstrating that one of the most significant variables is the pattern of organization which the president elects to build.[6] He can function with a man-to-man pattern or a group pattern, as shown in Figs. 6.4 and 6.5. These two patterns

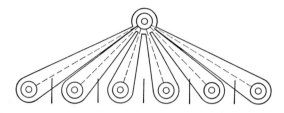

FIG. 6.4. Man-to-Man Pattern of Organization. (After R. Likert, *New Patterns of Management,* McGraw-Hill, 1961, p. 107.)

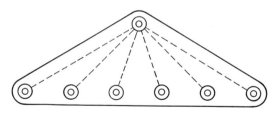

FIG. 6.5. Group Pattern of Organization. (After R. Likert, *New Patterns of Management,* McGraw-Hill, 1961, p. 107.)

involve widely different role behavior. A president who operates with the man-to-man pattern assumes sole responsibility for top-level decisions. He regularly holds meetings of the people who report to him for purposes of sharing information, but not for decision-making. This is what may happen under this pattern:

The vice-president in charge of sales, for example, goes to the president with a problem and a recommendation. Because it in-

[6] Rensis Likert, *New Patterns of Management,* McGraw-Hill, 1961, p. 107.

volves a production change, the vice-president in charge of manufacturing is called in. On the basis of the discussion with the two vice-presidents and the recommendations they make, the president arrives at a decision. However, the decision usually will affect other vice-presidents and subordinates whose interests were not represented. Under the circumstances, they are not likely to accept this decision wholeheartedly or strive hard to implement it. Instead, they usually begin to plan how they can get decisions from the president which are going to be beneficial to them but not necessarily to sales and manufacturing. Moreover, when the president holds informational meetings, each vice-president who has some important facts bearing on an action which he wants the president to approve carefully avoids communication. Each vice-president learns to share only trivial information in these meetings. Fear and distrust may grow as vice-presidents vie for power. Upward communications are likely to be highly filtered. A subordinate's future in an organization often is influenced appreciably by how well he senses and communicates to his boss information which fits the latter's orientation.

The group pattern is built on the conception of an organization in which members are knit into overlapping functional groups (see Fig. 6.5). A president can seek to offer leadership such that each member of the organization will view his experience as supportive and as building and maintaining his sense of personal worth and importance. The president will strive to build working groups. He may hold meetings of his top staff regularly to solve problems and make decisions.[7] Every member of his staff will be asked to propose problems for consideration, but each problem is looked at from a company-wide point of view. It is not possible for one department to force a decision beneficial to itself but detrimental to other departments if the group as a whole makes the decisions. The vice-presidents reporting to the president, such as manufacturing, sales, and research, contribute their technical knowledge in the decision-making process. Others contribute stimulating and original ideas. The general counsel may help the group do a more vigorous job of evaluating ideas. In this process vice-presidents learn of methods which they imitate in

[7] This topic is further discussed in the present text in Chapter 17, "The Governing of the Work Organization."

their leadership of subordinate groups. At its best, such top leadership creates a supportive climate throughout the organization; it becomes the model toward which others strive. Thus, the entire organization begins to function quite differently although the organization chart will show no difference from that of an organization operating on a man-to-man basis.

Obviously there are differences in the ways different executives think their businesses should be run. Some believe they should rule with an iron hand; others believe in more permissive methods. Some feel that money is the chief object; others think it is satisfaction from a job well done. We have tried to describe just a few traits in the idea system of men who generally play the roles of top management.

As far as production goes, top management thinks that this depends on a *good plant manager*. If things are not going right, the plant manager is probably blamed. Let us inspect the position and role of the plant manager.

The Plant Manager and His Satellites

There are many titles in vogue for the official who is head of operations. He may be called executive vice-president, plant manager, bureau head, dean, general superintendent, or chief of production. In larger industrial organizations he is usually vice-president in charge of production; in smaller plants he is usually called plant manager. Irrespective of his title, his position, functions, and duties are very similar. Although middle management in industry will be discussed here, similarities exist regardless of work organization.

Functions of the plant manager

The plant manager occupies an important and strategic position. Everyone, including his supervisors, recognizes that he is the head of the most important section of the plant. In a sense, all other departments are supposed to help his department function more effectively. On the success or failure of the line rests the financial position and the very survival of the entire plant. Therefore, hardly any decision of consequence can be made without at least consulting the head of operations.

Plant managers are top managers, and one of their functions is to participate in making plant policy. Since policy affects the operation of the line most directly, the role of the chief of operations in planning sessions is critical. If he is an unwilling party to major decisions, trouble may be expected. As a matter of fact, when the plant manager does not concur in general policy, the policy is usually altered in line with his wishes or he is fired.

To avoid continuous bickering with top management, the plant manager is often given a considerable amount of autonomy in planning. He spends a great deal of his time in planning production or services for the organization. Frequently he heads a large staff which does little but plan production. Thus the plant manager is engaged in planning at two levels: overall plant policy planning, and production or service planning.

Aside from planning, the chief responsibility of the plant manager is to oversee production or service. Of course, he is too far removed from the plant floor to supervise production directly. In fact, it is not unusual for him to stay out of the plant and work entirely with his office staff. However, he must keep close tabs on the production schedules of the various departments or sections. He and his staff are occupied with production goals or schedules, designing work flow, and *coordinating* the work of the departments. With the growth of organizational size, coordination becomes increasingly complex and difficult. It is dependent upon (1) carefully drawing up the large overall production plans, (2) scheduling the plan into definite time periods, (3) breaking down the overall plan and schedule into smaller component parts, (4) obtaining periodic reports of the progress of the smaller plans and the overall plan, and (5) readjusting plans and schedules of the whole and the parts in the face of restricting circumstances.

The daily behavior of the plant manager is not unlike that of the president. He begins his day by reading a series of *reports* from engineers, staff officers, and foremen. Unlike those which the president receives, the reports are much more specific and technical. They deal with the progress of plans and problems that arise on the plant floor. Besides going over written reports, the plant manager engages in a number of formal and informal conferences, the purpose of which is to gain additional information that he wants. On the basis of these reports and conferences, further meetings are held with key individuals—accountants, engineers, inspection supervisors, and others—to iron out problems and project further plans.

The plant manager, if he is going to be effective in conference work, not only must be a good coordinator but must have technical knowledge. Like top management he must be a good executive, but he must also have the knowledge to understand the problems that arise and suggest ways to solve them. For this reason he must be either (1) a professionally trained person—an engineer, scholar, doctor, chef (depending on the industry)—or (2) a person who has had wide practical experience by working up from the plant floor. The greater his capacity to *follow up reports* with detailed suggestions on what needs to be done, the better he is. Top management expects him to do a good job, irrespective of the kind of men he has under him.

Some of the functions that we have listed for the plant manager may be performed by two or three line officials in larger organizations. For example, participation in overall company policy may be the job of the executive vice-president, production planning may be the job of another vice-president, and technical supervision may be given to the plant superintendent. In this section we are *not* concerned with the general policy planner. He is oriented too much like the president to be considered on a genuinely different level. We are concerned with the manager who is oriented downward to the actual problems of the production organization.

Work position of the plant manager

The plant manager's work position may be analyzed by studying his relationship to (1) the top management of the plant, (2) the various staff departments and their members, and (3) his own organization. We shall consider each of these relations.

1. RELATION TO TOP MANAGEMENT

A strong cleavage exists between top management and the plant manager who is oriented downward. The latter feels that he heads the most important section of the organization and should be master of his own baliwick. His ever present thought is to *get out the production.* Top management may make demands that interfere with his production schedules and the rate of output. Since many of the top executives have entered the organization through such channels as sales, accounting, and personnel, they do not share the attitudes and background of the plant manager. Such contrasts are especially noticeable if the plant manager has risen through the ranks and has not had much formal education. He is likely to regard management's ideas as criticisms. Impulsively he tends to ward off interaction with the top by taking the attitude that he is boss of his organization. Gardner's illustration demonstrates the irritation of top management over this situation. A top executive said:

"For all the influence I have you would never know that the plant is part of the company. Why, if I go into the plant for anything, I hardly get to the door before the superintendent is standing by my side, and he stays with me until I leave. And I know that I only get to see the things he wants me to see. And trying to introduce any changes is a hopeless task; it's like pushing against a stone wall. Even when he seems to agree to something, it goes only slowly and half-heartedly, and there are dozens of things wrong with it."[8]

2. RELATIONS TO THE STAFFS

Many of the pressures that top management exerts on the plant chief are usually changes desired by the various staff departments. In theory, the staff departments are at the service of the line organization. Although the line should consult the staff on its problems, it frequently feels that it needs only minimal services. If the staff organizations acquiesce in this feeling, they are signing their own death warrants. Organizations which are to survive must justify their existence and their right to be useful in the scheme of things. Since the staff has representatives in top management, it can literally demand that the shop organization use its services. Many of the squabbles in industry may be understood with this situation in mind. We shall examine several sources of pressures on the shop manager and his staff.

a. Pressure from Finance. In the discussion of the work role of the president, the importance of the finance organization was emphasized. This organization parallels the entire work plant from top to bottom. It is concerned with company profits, but it

[8] Gardner and Moore, *op. cit.*, p. 60.

is equally concerned with costs in every nook and cranny. Special concern is shown in the financial status of the line department. To evaluate this status, finance organizations have evolved accounting systems which can theoretically measure the costs of every operation, in every section, in every department of the entire plant. At almost any time, the accounting division can give top management the prevailing cost-profit picture of the line and its departments. It can also compare this record with past performance.

The plant manager and his organization are bothered by the accounting staff in two ways. First, the accounting activities disrupt the relations among the departments in the line. Second, the accounting process naturally restricts the freedom of the line organization. In the first instance, the finance organization prepares cost reports for each department in the line. Since previous reports become standards for present performance, each foreman or division chief is concerned with his record. Instead of trying to improve his section irrespective of anything, he operates in terms of what will look good on the record. Every supervisor keeps an informal check on his cost picture, with the end result that the *line organization is running informally a parallel* finance organization. Thus, much of the time and energy of the supervisor is occupied in duplicating the functions of another organization.

The plant manager is affected by the financial preoccupation of his underlings in an indirect way. For example, a poor record in Assembly may be due to slipshod work in Manufacturing, failure of Supply to provide requisite materials, the fact that Maintenance fell down on its job of repairing machinery, high absenteeism rate, or other factors. Since the accounting reports do not reflect these extenuating circumstances, the head of Assembly is called on the carpet. He naturally feels a resentment against other department heads who may be responsible for his poor record. Recriminations against other departments are brought to the plant manager. The latter would not have to play a mediating and repressive role if he were not subject to pressure from the accounting organization.

The animosities that the plant manager builds against the finance organization are more direct in matters of general policy.

In order to keep up production schedules, he needs better materials, new machines, higher-skilled workers, and more space. All these may entail expenditure of money and reduction of profits. Usually the treasurer is a conservative individual who dislikes disbursing large funds. Plant managers see this as resistance to production, and they get angry, and relations between these two officials are not usually cordial.

b. Pressure from Inspection. Sometimes the inspection organization is separate from the line. Since it is the job of Inspection to pass on the quality of work, it plays a critical role. Aside from the fact that nobody loves a critic, overcritical inspection can affect the cost adversely. Wastes and rejects do not look good on a department's records. Consequently *the line organization sets up informally its own parallel inspection system* when the regular inspectors get too rigid. Bad parts do not reach inspection points.[9] If inspection discovers this ruse, the inspection head "beefs" about it to the plant manager, who berates his men while informally backing them up. The preoccupation of the plant manager is to get out production, even if quality must be lowered. The head of Inspection will fight this, especially if his relations to the plant manager are strained. Therefore, the plant manager must spend some time either fighting inspection or courting its good will. It is desirable to have the good will of Inspection because inspection standards are often flimsy and dependent on the personal judgment of the inspectors. "Rough" or "easy" inspection depends on the social relations between the heads of Inspection and line organization. One of the sources of irritation that the heads cannot overcome is the antagonism between inspectors and workers. The former are white-collar workers who feel superior to the manual workers. This attitude does not make for cordial relations.

Sometimes inspection is under the control of the plant manager. Inspection foremen then feel like a tool of the boss because they cannot perform honest functions. Their craving for independence does not make the manager's job easier.

c. Pressure from Engineering. If Inspection feels superior to the shop organization, the Engineering and Research people feel

[9] *Ibid.,* p. 108.

like Brahmin. Research people have generally had professional and technical training to find new ways of improving the product and its manufacture. Consequently, engineering or research organizations continually exert *pressure to change the prevailing methods of operation.*[10]

Presumably both line and Engineering are interested in improving the product or service. However, the plant manager and his assistants hate to disrupt production and delay work schedules. Further, if they have risen from the ranks, they have an almost religious belief in the traditional methods of operation. Untrained in theory, they can only visualize small changes that bring immediately visible results.

For these reasons the plant manager may not consult Engineering frequently. But Engineering justifies its existence by the number of "advances" it introduces in manufacturing. A research organization is expensive to support. If it does not "pay off," its funds may be curtailed, or it may even be liquidated. On the other hand, if Research is constantly finding something wrong or something to improve, the head of production begins to feel that his organization "is being shown up." He puts pressure on his men to anticipate changes which Engineering may find, thus getting credit from top management. In fact, the intimate acquaintance that the line has with production often enables it to find improvements which engineers overlook. If the shop does this too effectively, the research organization feels it is not earning its way and is being "shown up" by less-trained people. It seeks to offer more basic suggestions for improvement.

These are frequently resisted because they are too "theoretical," "harebrained," or "textbookish." Research cannot institute its ideas unless it gets management support. In the face of resistance from line officers, it seeks *more authority* from management to put its ideas into practice. To demonstrate this need, it criticizes and never praises the line. Backed up by the president, the "prima donnas" usually get what they want. Animosity arises and the line resists giving staff any more authority.

An executive vice-president of a clay products company in Ohio and Pennsylvania writes of his problems of inducing changes in tradition-bound plants dominated by old-line superintendents:

[10] *Ibid.*, p. 88.

I have at present the job of filling certain key spots such as that of chief engineer, sales manager of the pottery division, and unfortunately, the replacement of certain other key men as they have not been functioning for quite some time. I have finally gotten the production superintendent to cooperate with the sales department to produce what the market requires, and have gotten the sales department to start to plan by making market analysis, on a logical basis. Despite some resistance from an old line superintendent, I am installing material handling equipment in our plants and directing other purchases to reduce manual labor in quantity, and to make certain jobs easier to perform so that we can attract good workers. Most of our operations were of the hand labor type, as our base rate for common labor in 1933 was 37 cents per hour and in 1947 is $1.01 per hour. It would have taken perhaps ten years to pay for a new piece of labor saving machinery then, but the same piece of machinery or material handling equipment would now pay for itself in about six months or a year. Due to the low labor rate, *the incentive to modernize was not strong,* and . . . over the past ten years, little was done. Our company apparently recognized the trend as we started to build a plant about six years ago which I am just getting into operation. It is completely modern, and shows that our stuff can be manufactured as other things can be. Most of our other plants should be torn down in part, at least, and started over again. But our investment in each plant represents about $500,000 or more, or a total of four million in the eight plants and branch warehouses, which also should be modernized with material handling equipment. We do not have enough money to do all of this right now, although each step will pay for itself and give us a working set-up that will enable us to compete in the competitive market now here. We are as well off as anyone in our business. Our low production and the up-to-date aggressiveness of such companies as Johns-Manville Corporation, with transit pipe and others with concrete pipe and cement pipe manufacturers, fiber pipe, cast iron pipe, aluminum pipe, etc., have made heavy inroads on our market and will continue to do so if our price gets out of line or our merchandising policy lets the public forget about the superior quality of our products. We are trying to get younger men into our business and desperately trying to get a better caliber of employees in our plants. Unfortunately, due to our reputation for low pay and disagreeable work we can't get them, even though our rates are up and working conditions so much better.

d. Pressure from Industrial Relations and Personnel. Most plant managers and superintendents want an experienced and highly skilled labor force. They also want power to use this labor as they see fit. In the past, they hired, trained, transferred, promoted, and paid workers as they wished. With the advent of unions, personnel and industrial relations departments evolved which absorbed some of their functions. The attitude of plant supervisors toward this development has been mixed. On the one hand, they were glad to get rid of functions which occupied much of their time; on the other hand, they resented the new departments because they restricted their freedom in the treatment of workers.

For example, when the personnel department chooses workers according to job specifications, it limits the range of job transferability. Plant managers, on the other hand, like workers who can be easily shifted around. But shifting can be done only by consulting the personnel organization, which then changes pay rate, withholding tax, seniority provisions, and so on. The extra paper work and the delays involved hamper the plant manager, in fact, anything that slows down production schedules incurs his ire. Similarly, when unions cannot agree with management on wages and other provisions, shop heads get impatient. They are likely to agree to almost anything, as long as it does not interfere with production.

Top labor relations and personnel people are part of management and have an influence on policy formation which plant people must follow. When the plant manager dislikes a directive, he and his subordinates may sabotage it by various indirect means. The effect is to make the work of the staff appear ineffective and even ludicrous.

Top management of a New York precision instrument company decided to institute a supervisory training program. The industrial relations director, with the strong support of the president, inaugurated a series of training meetings for supervisors and foremen. The director asked for a half-million dollars to make the program work. Resistance arose from all sides. In the first place, the secretary-treasurer balked at the sum. He complained that the company could not afford such an extravagant program. His advice for a trial on a reduced scale received backing from other staff departments, which did not want to see Industrial Relations grow so powerful. Although the program was primarily designed to help the line, the plant manager gave it only silent approval. A limited program was finally installed.

Figure 6.6 shows what actually followed. The plant manager as head of the line let it be known to his subordinates that the

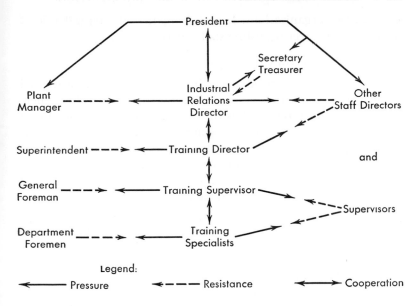

FIG. 6.6. Internal Pressures and Resistance Around a Supervisory Training Program.

training scheme was not to be taken too seriously. They should cooperate, but not spend too much time at the training sessions. In addition, the foremen were reminded that their presence at the training sessions was voluntary, and that their primary job was to get out production.

Thus, at every point along the supervisory hierarchy the training staff confronted resistance. Attendance at training sessions was good at first but then began to slacken in the face of pressing production schedules. Supervisors in other staff departments, who were also participating in training sessions, complained that the program was oriented to factory supervisors and had little application to office problems. The training supervisors and specialists encountered increased resistance. In desperation they prepared for the president an evaluation of their program, which described the resistances of the plant manager and his staff. A stormy session ensued between line and industrial relations officials which did not improve matters. This case illustrates the principle that relations between two offices must finally be analyzed as relations between two organizations. It also dramatizes the typical role of the factory manager regarding staff functions.

3. RELATION TO OWN ORGANIZATION

Contacts of the plant manager in his organization are limited to such supervisory personnel as division chief, general foremen, and department foremen. His contacts with individual workmen are negligible. Aside from the general relations between supervisory levels examined above, other specific relations between the levels of the line organization may be considered.

The chief of the shop organization wants good foremen and supervisors. He realizes that he cannot do a good job unless he has capable men with a high capacity for cooperation and loyalty. Like other managers, he wants his men to take up responsibilities voluntarily and not bother him with petty details. However, individual foremen are sometimes not in position to know what a petty detail is. Consequently, when they consult him, he becomes somewhat impatient. One reason for his impatience is that he is often unable to give help on problems with which he has little intimate acquaintance. He sees his organization as a number of integrated parts and not as a series of minute problems.

The superiority attitudes that plant managers display toward their foremen and supervisors derive from the fact that they are better educated and have had broader factory experience. From his vantage point, the manager can see the operation of his entire organization, so that he appears omniscient to those who can see only part of it. In addition, he is definitely marked as part of management by his spatial segregation from the plant floor, his office surroundings, his clerical staff, and other management paraphernalia.

Foremen and supervisors bring to the plant manager many of their problems. They complain that operation sheets are too technical and far removed from the practical conditions in the shop. Engineers are then called in to revise and simplify these sheets and schedules. Subordinates may also complain about men, materials, and machines. Although the plant manager may not have the power to remedy these problems, he does not want to admit it to his men. An example will clarify this situation.

Foremen frequently complain about their workers; they need

more help, some men should be dismissed, others should be transferred. The manager promises to rectify the situation. He goes to
the personnel department with these problems and gets promises
of action. Inevitably, delays occur and foremen get impatient.
The plant manager becomes irked by their impatience because
he has little control over hiring, firing, and transference of men.

Other problems are brought to the manager which he cannot
deal with directly. New machines! Better maintenance! Better
materials! More materials! Prompt delivery! More authority!—
are continual demands of the foremen. The chief has little responsibility or control over some of these demands. He can only
say that he will "see what he can do," and insist that the men do a
better job with what they have.

Social orientations of the plant manager

The social life of the plant manager depends to a large degree
on his job orientations and work history. If he is a professional
engineer, he probably has aspirations to belong to the top
echelons of management. In a large plant, he wants to become
executive vice-president or perhaps even president. Therefore,
he seeks to develop social contacts with the men who are now
filling these offices. Despite the fact that he may be having some
difficulties with the finance officer, head of industrial relations,
and others, he cannot afford to alienate himself from their good
graces. He will try to join their social clubs and participate in
their social activities.

Difficulties usually confront the plant manager who tries to
join in the social circle of top management. He is tied down to
his office and the plant to a far greater degree than are other managers. It is hard for him to take two or three hours out of the
middle of the day to attend a meeting of a business and social
club downtown. Problems within the plant demand his constant
attention and cannot be as easily postponed as can other staff
problems.

The plant manager who has risen from the ranks has a different
orientation. He has probably climbed as far as he can go. His limited formal education and the cultural attributes of his working-
class background make him feel insecure among business-class
people. His use of slang and factory argot especially tends to mark

him off somewhat from other executives. If he prefers not to climb to the top, he has a secure position in his own organization. Under him there are usually several well-trained men who cultivate his good graces. He can "lord it over" the college boys by showing them insights gained from practical experience.

The social life of the downward-oriented plant manager is spent with his assistants, the heads of divisions, and some old cronies in the shop. He also spends some time with staff people with whom he has contacts on the job. They tend to be those who are second-in-line in the accounting, industrial relations, engineering, and other departments. *They compose the social links between top management and operating heads in the line.*

The social life of the line organization is often quite elaborate. Since the organization is inclined to feel somewhat autonomous compared with the rest of the plant, it generally creates parallel social organizations. Because the line is the largest segment of the plant, its social program is likely to be impressive. A separate picnic is held, a separate bowling league is instituted, a separate paper is published. The plant manager who attends many of these events takes off his vest and is really "one of the boys" for a day.

The informal social contacts of the plant manager and his accociates are with white-collar people. However, they do not as a rule take as active a role in community and civic organizations as does top management. Although the plant manager may be encouraged to "get into the community," he cannot give it the requisite time and energy. Public relations are not as important in his job as with top management.

Ideology[11]

The prevailing social ideas of plant managers are not significantly different from those of top management. Both groups feel that they occupy high positions by virtue of their abilities; both believe in the importance of managerial responsibility; both have an ardent faith in free enterprise capitalism; both are highly conscious of costs and profits; both are highly self-conscious; and both support the dominant values in the community.

In one or two ways the values of the two groups differ. Plant

[11] See Thorstein Veblen, *Engineers and the Price System,* Viking, 1940.

managers agree that top management may be necessary, but they firmly believe plant people are more important. In some instances operating chiefs feel that they could run the organization better without the "help" of the big boys. Underlying this notion is the thought that technical knowledge is more important than organizational knowledge. All the community participation, planning, labor relations, cost accounting, research, and public relations are almost parasitical because they do not contribute income to the enterprise. Plant managers regard much of the activity of top management as political and wasteful. They feel that the public misplaces respect, because the people who *do things,* who actually plan and supervise production, should receive highest esteem. They feel that there wouldn't be labor, public relations, and other problems if the people who were supervising the actual work had more authority. Some deep-rooted ideas are that plant people are guided by science and reason, that they are accustomed to solving practical problems in a practical way, that there is no room for politics and sentiment among practical people. Therefore, they contend, everybody's economic and social welfare would be increased if plant people were given more power to exercise their practical knowledge and experience as they see fit.

Recruiting and training for middle management

Many companies (at least thirty-five large corporations) are now formally training their selected young college recruits in management practices and views. The indoctrination may last as long as two years and occasionally as long as seven, during which time classroom work and a succession of assignments are alternated. In the General Electric program human relations teaching pervades the whole program. The trainee learns human relations by doing as well as by precept. In Schenectady the trainee enjoys what is essentially a continuation of fraternity life. Getting along with one's peers is as important in class as in after-hours social life. A heavy premium is put on communication with one's superiors.

"First-name informality is encouraged on both sides, and the trainees quickly learn not to be inhibited in taking the initiative. If you're smart, as soon as you know your way around you start telephoning," says one trainee. "I or anybody else," another trainee points out, "can walk into a manager's office just as easily as we can each other's. By ten o'clock of the day I hit the New York office, I was calling everybody by his first name."[12]

THE CORPORATION WIFE

Wives are also being given a screening inspection. Increasingly, corporations are interviewing the wife before hiring an executive. Ordinarily, the screening is accomplished via "informal" social visits. If a prospective executive lives elsewhere, companies often suggest strongly that he bring his wife along for the interview, perhaps on the pretext that she may want to size up the community and the housing situation. The visit can be a harrowing experience for the wife. If the company is a close-knit one, she may be put through a group interview in depth by the combined cadre of executives and their wives. If the prospective executive and his wife both pass the tests, the corporation continues in one way or another to keep an eye on the wife. The promotability of a man includes the social promotability of the wife. With a remarkable consensus, corporation officials sketch the ideal wife as one who (1) is highly adaptable, (2) is highly gregarious, (3) realizes her husband belongs to the corporation.[13] Many management consultants are advising their clients to gather data on the wife in assembling the personnel record of an executive. They suggest such information as: Does she complement him? Is she a helpmate or a millstone? A nagger? Understanding? Does she resent his traveling? Does she criticize him publicly? Is she loud? Is she a lady?[14] When a promotion is pending for her husband, many companies have the wife seen individually at carefully arranged dinners or luncheons. The norms of acceptable behavior are many.

Too much drinking is taboo.

Complaining when her husband works late, fussing over a transfer, engaging in controversial activity are noted as negative liabilities.

Failure to adapt to upper movement of her husband by refusing to grow into new company and community status. The Pattern requires

---

[12] "The Crown Princes of Business," *Fortune*, October, 1953.

[13] William H. Whyte, Jr., and editors of *Fortune, Is Anybody Listening?* Simon and Schuster, 1952, p. 146.

[14] *Ibid.*, p. 182.

accession to appropriate friends, house, neighborhood, and community affiliations.

Don't talk shop with the girls, particularly those who have husbands in the same department.

Don't turn up at the office unless you absolutely have to.

Be attractive. There is a strong correlation between executive success and the wife's appearance.

Don't be too good. Keep up with your social peers but don't push ahead.[15]

No one has done the definitive study on the wife clique and its impact on the husband's career. It is well known that a wife can be an important communication channel gathering information of great importance to establishing the "right" interpersonal relations which can mean so much to the gamesmanship of success. Moreover, the wife who can win double approval—acceptance by company wives as a companion and by the husbands as an attractive conversationalist or a sexually exciting woman— is the corporation wife who can make her Sammy run. Without these assets his climb may be more difficult. As a minimum the wife must learn to accept the corporation and the way of life which it requires.

First-Line Supervisors

The first-line supervisor constitutes the third basic level in the supervisory hierarchy. He is the man who is supposed to do the actual job of supervising production or service. This involves daily face-to-face contact with the workers. Various titles are current for his office, including supervisor, foreman, chief, leader, and straw boss. The variety of nomenclature is somewhat disturbing because sometimes the designations are used synonymously and sometimes differently. The definition of first-line supervision varies from plant to plant and from industry to industry. Apart from this confusion, the distinctions within the ranks of first-line supervision are not always drawn.

In large-scale industry the designation of foreman, supervisor, and chief extends from superintendent to the leading hand in a small working group. For example, in the Hawthorne plant, the general foreman is five levels above the worker. Below him in the supervisory ladder are the foreman, assistant foreman, section

[15] *Ibid.*, p. 156.

chief, group chief, and finally the operator.[16] In smaller plants, the foreman may be the only official between the superintendent and the worker. In the office common titles for this level are supervisor and chief, never foreman.

The work position of a foreman or supervisor must be more clearly defined. For our purposes this position is an office that requires supervision of the actual production or service as a full-time job. The person filling this office must have official contacts with both supervisory officials and the operators or clerks on the job. He must spend most of his time on the plant floor supervising personally, or supervising people who are part-time supervisors and part-time workers. Paper work must not occupy so much of his time that he has to have a secretary. He does not spend more than one-third of his day on it. In fact, paper work irritates him and keeps him off the floor. Further, he does not participate in policy-making. In short, his orientation is downward toward the workers and their problems. He must have enough authority so that workers obey his technical commands. For purposes of convenience we shall use the term "supervisor" or "foreman" for the work position having these characteristics. In an actual plant two or three positions may together fulfill our requirements. They shall be treated as a single position here.

To the social scientist, the foreman's position is a significant index to the internal forces of organization which are becoming general to all supervisory positions. It is the position of foremen that has felt the brunt of both mass production technological advances and organizational changes emerging in larger-scale bureaucracies. These same forces now bearing upon the foreman are similarly coming to impinge on all supervisors in commercial, governmental, and educational institutions. The first-line supervisor can be considered a common type for which the foreman's position is in the cultural lead.

The supervisor's functions

Listing the supervisor's functions is precarious because there is no general agreement on what they are or ought to be. For no other work position is there as much controversy on role, position,

[16] F. J. Roethlisberger and W. J. Dickson, *Management and the Worker*, Harvard, 1947, p. 11.

and function as for the supervisor or foreman. In addition to the fact that his role, position, and functions vary with plants, the definition of his position is in a state of transition. Drucker points out that two generations ago "There were a few plants in this country where the foreman was a semi-independent contractor who had undertaken to supply a certain product or to do a certain process at a stipulated rate. If he could do the job more cheaply, the difference was his profit; . . . if he lost out on the transaction the loss was his. In other words, the foreman was close to being an independent businessman, except that he did not own his capital equipment."[17]

Obviously this is not the situation today. The supervisor is at the bottom of the management hierarchy. There are some who would even debate this. They feel that supervisors are mass production workers, whose occupation is to hound other workers to produce more. Without entering this debate directly, we can state that the main task of the supervisor is to oversee production. *His job is to insure that the production or service schedules set up by higher executives are actually fulfilled.* While performing this function he must handle any on-the-spot eventualities which may interfere with schedule fulfillment. This is a more difficult job than it sounds because many kinds of contingencies may arise which, because of his peculiar role, he may not be able to resolve.

F. J. Roethlisberger, in a penetrating article on the foreman's position, states that his job is much more difficult than it was a generation ago.[18] The foreman, he contends, must know more than his old-time counterpart. This fact is revealed in the foremanship training programs of modern industry. According to these he must know

. . . not only (1) the company's policies, rules, and regulations and (2) the company's cost system, payment system, manufacturing methods, and inspection regulations, in particular, but also frequently (3) control, and time and motion study in general. He also has to know (4) the labor laws of the United States, (5) the labor laws of the state in which the company operates, and (6) the specific labor contract which exists between his company and the local union. He has to know (7) how to

---

[17] Peter F. Drucker, *The Concept of the Corporation,* John Day, 1946, p. 163.
[18] Fritz J. Roethlisberger, "The Foreman: Master and Victim of Double Talk," in Hoslett, *op. cit.,* p. 56.

induct, instruct, and train new workers; (8) how to handle, and where possible, prevent grievances; (9) how to improve conditions of safety; (10) how to correct workers and maintain discipline; (11) how never to lose his temper and always be "fair"; (12) how to get and obtain cooperation from the wide assortment of people with the shop steward. And in some companies he is supposed to know (13) how to do the jobs he supervises better than the employees themselves. Indeed, as some forman training programs seem to conceive the foreman's job, he has to be a manager, a cost accountant, an engineer, a lawyer, a teacher, a leader, an inspector, a disciplinarian, a counselor, a friend, and above all, an example."[19]

The foreman's "little" helpers

One would imagine that a job requiring all this knowledge would make its holder the cock of the roost. It may be true that all the knowledge the foreman is supposed to have does him no harm. However, in view of his actual position, all these requisites turn out to be double-talk because the foreman cannot use his knowledge as he sees fit. On the contrary, he is ordered what to do, when to do it, and how to do it. If a problem arises in his department he cannot solve it with his knowledge. Someone else (usually on the staff) knows more about it than he does; someone else has had a role in formulating policy on that problem; someone else expects to be consulted about it.

Is there a question of changing machines around? "Call in Engineering." Should an operator be promoted, transferred, or fired? "Call in the boss, personnel office, and the union!" Is the product good enough to go through? "Call in Cost and Quality Control!" Is operator Y falling down on the job? "Call the steward!" The foreman is responsible for technical efficiency, personnel relations, quality of production, keeping costs down, labor relations, and other things. Yet he has little or no authority to fulfill his responsibility. All kinds of staff people are anxious to "help" him.

Relations to the staff

Possibly, modern industry could not function without staff participation in the problems of first-line operations. But this does not solve the foreman's dilemma, because staff men not only

---

[19] *Ibid.*, p. 54.

participate in the foreman's job but are the source of the stream of unending changes that bombard him and his workers. Engineers, technologists, and accountants are responsible for changes on the plant floor. Before one set of technical and financial codes becomes the *modus vivendi* of the shop, other codes are proposed and installed. The foreman cannot protest for he has no authority or specialized knowledge. And the staffs keep justifying their worth to the organization by the new techniques and financial checks that they introduce.

All eyes are on the plant floor, where the money is made. Almost all changes proposed by management and the staffs are aimed at the foreman and his workers. In a sense everybody is a threat to any security or status the foreman may have. What is more important, his performance and that of his workers is being made increasingly measurable. Production by nature is more measurable than are other types of labor. The number of workers, units produced, the cost of items, and scrap are all measurable. The work of the plant manager, president, engineer, and accountant is not measured, partly because it is more difficult to measure, but, more important, *because these people are in a better position to resist measurement of their performance*. The measurement of his performance increases the foreman's insecurity. The fact that his position may be short-circuited makes the position even more insecure. If the foreman just had to report to his boss, he could cover up and report only favorable things. After all, this is what everybody else does. However, many staff people can report the foreman's activities to his boss and higher management. The union can and does go over his head. So do Inspection, Cost Control, Engineering, and other organizations. Down to the foreman comes the question "Why didn't you inform us?" Down come commands to cooperate with the staff people. Down come new people and new studies of his workers' performance. A foreman's life is not a happy one.

The foreman and the union

To the foreman the union is like another staff organization which limits his functions and authority. The union does not, as Roethlisberger would have us believe, remove "the last vestiges of initiative, judgment, and what is more important, personal relations with his subordinates."[20] True, it does introduce a new set of rules which the foreman must observe in his conduct toward the workers. But the volume, mass, and complexity of these rules are not greater or more disturbing than those imposed by the staff organizations. On the contrary, union rules, being fixed by contract, define precedents and relationships that create order and stability on the plant floor. Management directives tend to introduce more changes in the foreman's activities. In fact, as Gardner points out, the foreman on occasion uses the union as a means of short-circuiting his line. When he feels that his department has needs which his boss has failed to attend to, he may resort to the artifice of urging the union to ask top management to do something about the situation.[21] However, this technique is not very commonly used.

The attitude of the foreman toward the union may be hostile or friendly, depending on his past experiences with it. If he has been a union man, he may not resent union restrictions on his activities. If he considers his job a step up the management ladder, he may resent the union's restrictions. In any case, it is another organization which limits his freedom of action.

Figure 6.7 summarizes the changes that have occurred in the foreman's role in the last generation or two. The diagram on the left portrays the functions he once had; the other diagram names the staff organizations that have absorbed each function. The sizes of the pieces of the pie are only crude approximations of the time spent on each function. In summary, the problems the plant manager has in his relations to staff organizations are but a part of his daily routine. The foreman, however, is deprived of the prestige which comes with social distance. "He is an ideal scapegoat for the expression of any disturbances in the social equilibrium."[22]

The foreman and his boss

Every worker in each level of the supervisory structure is preoccupied with what his boss thinks of him. The foreman is no

[20] *Ibid.*, p. 64.
[21] Gardner and Moore, *op. cit.*, pp. 126–127.
[22] Roethlisberger and Dickson, *op. cit.*, p. 368.

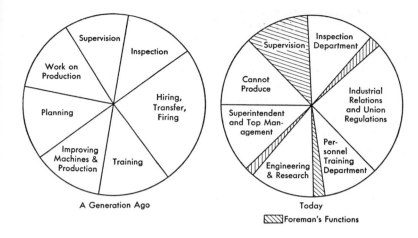

A Generation Ago

Today

Foreman's Functions

FIG. 6.7. The Foreman's Functions: A Generation Ago and Today.

exception. If superiors are displeased, they can make his life miserable. Indeed, they can take away his job. Just as the worker spends a great deal of time worrying about how his performance affects the attitudes of his foreman, the foreman, in turn, worries about his relations to his boss.

There is some evidence to support the idea that the foreman's position exposes him to the strongest kind of worker-boss cleavage. It is necessary to explain the tensions arising between the supervisor and his boss to understand the former's position. Although the foreman is at the bottom of the supervisory hierarchy, he has little or none of management's prerogatives. In the literal sense, if not in the organizational sense, *the management ladder ends with the foreman's boss.* Supervisors are left with the role of urging workers on so that production schedules materialize. Under this situation the pressure from top-level executives is on the lowest management official who has *authority as well as responsibility.* He, of course, is the supervisor's boss: the superintendent, division chief, or some such official. The pressure of all management levels focuses upon him because he, not the foreman, is the culmination of a series of management links. *The pressure that is applied on the foreman is to make him a salesman for management's ideas.*

The foreman's double exposure

The foreman's work position is the only one in the entire structure that daily deals with *both* management and labor first-hand. His difficulties arise *not so much out of lack of authority as out of the relative impossibility of reconciling two rather incompatible ideologies or systems of sentiment.* Such a sharp cleavage does not appear among the upper levels because there is essential ideological agreement *within* the management hierarchy. The supervisor in the office, for example, does not face the problems of the foreman because office workers are more amenable to management ideology.

Management and worker ideologies whipsaw the foreman. The foreman's boss and all levels above him are imbued with the "logic of cost and efficiency." That is, their concern is to make profit by applying rational economic principles to production. Consequently, they view the work plant as an impersonal economic machine which makes money. The workers are also units to be considered in this process of moneymaking. Although managers do not regard relations among themselves impersonally, they do think of problems on the plant floor as impersonal, financial ones.

The foreman's boss has assimilated this ideology of cost and efficiency[23] and tries to imbue it in his foremen. The latter, however, have to deal with workers who usually do not share management's conception of their role as cost items. Workers do not consider themselves machines to be moved about and used according to the best logic of efficiency.[24] They have emotional stakes in their work and want to be considered accordingly. Management is sometimes aware of this fact on its own level but does not seem to see it on the worker's level. The superintendent's view of the men below the foremen is impersonal.

The foreman, like any worker in the structure, does not want to incur the disapproval of his boss openly by violating norms of efficient economic behavior. Yet he must deal with the workers as people. He must meet situations which clear economic thinking cannot predict. He knows that he cannot disregard workers' sentiments about jobs, rates, profits, and procedures. He knows "it is

[23] See section on ideology of the plant manager above.
[24] See Chapter 8, "Power and Union Organization."

impossible to uphold strictly the logic of efficiency without sometimes demoralizing the group." If he informs the superintendent of all of the workers' resentments to management ideology, his boss will berate him for having so much dissension in his section. If he does not report these matters, his boss discovers them through other channels. Either path is dangerous.

The modern supervisory functions

Elton Mayo pointed out that all supervisors and managers share three major functions: technical, administrative, and human relations functions. The performance evaluation may have such questions as

1. How well does the supervisor know the technical side of his job—the operations and maintenance of the equipment for which he is responsible?
2. How well does the supervisor do the administrative side of his job—by this we mean planning and scheduling the work, indicating clearly when work is to be finished, assigning the right job to the right man, inspecting and following up on the work that is to be done, etc.?
3. How well does the supervisor do the *human relations* side of the job—getting people to work well together, getting individuals to do the best they can, giving recognition for good work done, letting people know where they stand, etc.?[25]

In the past five decades more attention has been directed toward the administrative and human relations functions. A higher educational level is being demanded in supervisory posts. Some plants insist on a college graduate for the foreman's position and pay salaries between $8000 and $12,000. It has been suggested that most supervisors when they can shift their attention from the pressure of immediate assignments hold the following human relations goals:

1. To raise the level of human motivation.
2. To increase the readiness of subordinates to accept change.
3. To improve the quality of all decisions.
4. To develop teamwork and morale.
5. To further the individual development of employees.[26]

[25] Floyd C. Mann and L. Richard Hoffman, *Automation and the Worker,* Holt, 1960, pp. 143–144.
[26] Robert Tannenbaum, Irving R. Weschler, and Fred Massarik, *Leadership and Organization,* McGraw-Hill, 1961, p. 78.

All supervisors are being "helped" today in the pursuit of their tasks—personnel departments help screen some of the applicants, training departments attempt to provide training on the administrative and human relations functions, staff experts help explain the new machines and equipment from computers to visual aids. Special functionaries worry about organizational effectiveness and the test specialists devise measurement techniques. Morale surveys, supervisory reviews, and exit interviewing are common techniques in large organizations. Everyone is compelled to agree that the scientific method should be used in evaluating procedures. The lines of command grow longer and supervisors find themselves ever further separated by communication and authority differentials between the top and the bottom rung of management. No one is quite sure whether the supervisor is doing the job he should be doing. His paper work is increasing but almost everyone is agreed that it should be reduced. His conference time is increasing but it is agreed that he should have more direct individual contact with members of his department. He is expected to get around more and find out what other departments are doing but he can't get away from his desk because of the pressure of reports. Top management can't understand why he is unable to report more quickly and his subordinates think he is spending too much time on desk work. It becomes his responsibility alone to balance the conflicting demands made upon him.

Orientations of the foreman

The supervisor under the modern order is expected to become a leader. He is expected to increase the employees' commitment to the organization, its management, and its objectives and regulations; to reduce complaints and strikes, absenteeism and turnover; to communicate the employees' complaints, feelings, and attitudes upward. In doing all this he comes closer to the employees and more involved in personal relations with them. But this puts strains on his loyalty to management and his ability to enforce unpopular orders when necessary. As we have shown, the potential significance of the supervisor's role has grown but the human relations approach makes the task more demanding and the supervisor's authority more difficult to maintain.[27]

Under the new demands, there seem to be four ways for the supervisor to work out his complicated role, each with its own stresses and strains:[28] (1) identification with department chief and management, (2) identification with the workers under him, (3) dual identification, (4) isolation, or identification with other foremen.

IDENTIFICATION WITH DEPARTMENT CHIEF

When the foreman identifies with his superior, he embraces management ideology. He tends to be critical of his workers, finds fault with their work, and presses them for ever greater output.[29] This situation often occurs when the foreman is brought in from the outside with the expectation that he will be moved up into an executive job. Even if this is not the case, the foreman who identifies upward develops social distance toward his workers. The latter will not confide in him or have much to do with him outside of work. On the contrary, they will withhold information, restrict their work, and use the union to make his life uncomfortable. Gardner has illustrated this situation in a diagram which is reproduced as Fig. 6.8. Drucker believes that this type of identification must exist if the present economic system is to survive in Ameria.[30] The following is a worker's view of a boss dominated by management ideology.

Before the war I was employed at the tipple of the Rice Brothers Coal Company, and it was there that I came in contact with this man whom I shall never forget.

Herbert Dias, better known as Herb, was a nervous, wizened, little man with coal black eyes that peered out from behind a pair of thick-lensed glasses; those same peering eyes seemed never to miss a thing that went on around him. Herb was the proud possessor of the title of tipple boss, and to know that meant he was lord and master over all his domain, the tipple. No king ruling from his throne was ever more domineering than Herb as he nervously paced the floor seeing that all

[27] Amitai Etzioni, "Human Relations and the Foreman," *Pacific Sociological Review,* Spring, 1958, pp. 33–38.

[28] F. J. Roethlisberger, *Management and Morale,* Harvard, 1943, p. 38.

[29] Gardner and Moore, *op. cit.,* pp. 48–49.

[30] Drucker, *op. cit.,* p. 174.

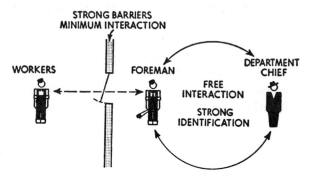

FIG. 6.8. Foreman Identified with Department Chief. (Adapted from Burleigh B. Gardner, *Human Relations in Industry,* Irwin, 1945, p. 44.)

work was functioning according to his directions. Whenever some minor mechanical breakdown caused the stoppage of production, Herb was always on hand explaining how to repair the damage and trying to hurry the mechanics in their work; about all he succeeded in doing, however, was getting in someone else's way.

The men in the tipple had very little respect for Herb when it came to a problem of fair treatment of the workers. Almost invariably on payday there was always an argument between Herb and the men as to how many hours of overtime pay was due them on that check. Herb never wrote down any overtime unless it was an hour or more but the men figured they should be reimbursed for the numerous fractional hours that they worked.

Herb did have one good quality, however; he took his job seriously. But the responsibility of seeing that the tipple ran smoothly made him hard to get along with at times.

IDENTIFICATION WITH THE WORKERS

When the foreman is sympathetic with his workers he tends to accept the ideology of labor. A foreman in this situation considers the sentiments of his men, is friendly toward them, and has social contacts with them on and off the job. Identifying with his men tends to increase social distance toward his chief. Free communication with his chief is reduced, for the foreman tries to cover up for his men, resist changes imposed from above, understand the union's demands, and modify his orders to fit the local situation.

This type of identification probably occurs more frequently when the foreman has risen from the ranks and has no aspirations to climb the management ladder. Since upward mobility from the plant floor to managerial positions seems to be diminishing, downward foreman identification may be increasing. The rewards the foreman obtains from this type of identification are those of leadership, for both management and workers regard him with respect.

A student describes how a boss identified with his workers behaves:

> His name was Sullivan, a plain, ordinary Irish name. His looks could have been any one of those of the several million Irishmen living in this country. But to me, he was more than any other boss for whom I have worked. These past few years in which I have not seen him have made me appreciate him more than ever before. There have been countless times when I have tried to analyze his being liked so much.
>
> There was no doubt in anyone's mind that he was capable. But how many hundreds of bosses have we encountered who have been capable but disliked very much? He had a cheery disposition, a good sense of humor, a straightforward way of speaking, and an ability to keep the employee interested in his job.
>
> But those qualities I have just mentioned sound more like platitudes copied out of a textbook. They seem old and rather worn and do not find the real character of my boss' personality.
>
> The thing I am going to say is something we have all heard thousands of times. It is a thing that must be said this way because I have not uncovered a better way of saying it. It is a word that has been battered back and forth from the mouths of laymen to those of the wealthy.
>
> That word is *respect*. Sullivan respected his employees. He respected their feeble excuses for coming in late to work. He respected their rights to ask for more pay and less hours. He respected their right to go home when not feeling well. He respected the fact that these men were human beings and not mere animals. And in that man I not only discovered the best boss for whom I have ever worked, but I have also discovered the core of happiness.

This pattern of relations is reported frequently. In one study of foremen, all of whom had come up from the ranks, 87 percent reported that in order to be effective they must strive hard (1) to keep everyone busy with work that (2) guarantees a fair take-home pay, (3) to distribute the easy and tough jobs fairly, and (4) to leave the employees alone as much as possible. "In short, a successful foreman, from the foreman's point of view, is neither directive nor is he the expert in human relations that some imply he ought to be." Argyris calls the ensuing relationship between foreman and workers a psychological work contract. The employees will maintain high production, low grievances, etc., if the foreman guarantees to respect the norms of the employees' informal culture, let the employees alone, and make certain they have adequate wages and secure jobs.[31]

DUAL IDENTIFICATION

The third type of identification refers to an attempt to straddle the line between management and labor and maintain a loyalty to both. Dual identification is most difficult, because very few people have the ability to satisfy both management and labor at the same time. However, such an identification can occur where foremen or managers have risen from the ranks and retain a certain sympathy for the worker's way of life. Climbing, however, has a way of eliminating most of these sympathies, and a foreman tends to accept his role as a part of management.

Dual identification is commonly observed among newly appointed foremen. Their recent and perhaps long experience as workers and union members has given them both friends among and sympathies for workingmen. Moreover, there is always the prospect that the road they have taken into foremanship may lead back, at the first drop in sales, to the machine and the worker status from whence they came. In such an eventuality the question is always whether the union will receive them and restore the seniority which they gave up when they became foremen. Meanwhile, as new foremen they are told that they now represent management. One plant manager described his method of inducting new foremen. He said,

> Well, I get the new foremen together in the conference room and I tell them that they are now part of management and that they must think and act like managers. I tell them that managers have four big responsibilities. I draw a small square. At the base I write PROFITS. This is the most important because none of us, I say, can be sure of our jobs unless business can make a profit. Then on one side of the square I place COSTS, on the other side, QUALITY, and on the top, SAFETY or SECURITY of your men. I give them about fifteen minutes of lecture on these responsibilities, ask them if they have any questions, and send them back to the floor.

[31] Chris Argyris, *Understanding Organization Behavior*, Dorsey, 1960, p. 96.

With these instructions ringing in their ears foremen must decide upon their future role. Those who attempt to ignore the conflict of sentiments between management and labor isolate themselves from both. By keeping their contacts minimal and formal, they may be able to operate like a "mugwump" as long as no issue arises which demands a showdown. In the case of a showdown the foremen are likely to side with management. From then on they are identified as management-oriented.

IDENTIFICATION WITH OTHER FOREMEN

Another and more unusual adjustment for the foreman is for him to attempt to become a third power in the struggle. By forming a labor union with other foremen he can refuse to be pushed around by either management or labor. Although foremen may form unions, the protection of the Taft-Hartley Act has been denied them. They must go it alone. Sometimes they act informally—that is, they get together with each other and decide to "get tough" with any who threaten their position. Under present conditions, however, this course would be based more on courage than on strength. It does reveal, however, a feeling on the part of foremen that although they are neither fish nor fowl they do not intend to remain the "men in the middle" very long. Any redefinition of their status will probably place them with organized labor. At least, the European experience reveals a tendency for foremen and technicians to become unionized.

Multiple-role behavior of a marginal man

The supervisor may find himself playing all of these different roles on different occasions. He is not cast in a stable role situation, yet all of the forces tend to pull him into the position where he must learn to acquire dual loyalty and appropriate behavior. Mann and Dent have shown that when supervisors are regarded by their employees as pulling for both the company and the employees they rate high in both the employees' regard and the management's regard. At least, that is the way it works out in the Accounting Division of the Detroit Edison Company.[32] In the

---

[32] Floyd C. Mann and James Dent, *Appraisals of Supervisors and Attitudes of Their Employees in an Electric Power Company,* University of Michigan, Institute for Social Research, 1954.

long run, all managerial leaders must accept the fact that they have to reconcile conflicting interests and needs regardless of the identification which they make. They must do this in a marginal position from which they are pulled back and forth continually between management demands and employee demands.

Authority of the supervisor

We have shown that the supervisor must make accommodations to historic changes in the general definition of his role and also to specific factors which may be present in his particular work environment. A central thread runs through all of these factors and that is the supervisor's authority. The difference between line and staff is disappearing.[33] The supervisor, whether a line officer or a staff officer, increasingly gains his authority by the use of influence and persuasion; his force comes from an expertise based on an understanding of the cooperative process which he is trying to direct. The erosion of line authority as the only authority system has occurred because of two changes. The first has been the democratization of the labor force buttressed by changing economic and social ideals and reinforced by labor organizations. The second has been the growth in importance of staff functions. Haire quotes an executive who said, "Such and such a department used to be staff, but it has become so important that it's now a line function."[34] In many organizations Marketing has been the first department to be officially recognized as coequal with Production, but in actual practice most staff functions have been accorded unofficial authority. If a staff is to accept responsibility for its behavior it must also have authority. It has steadily gained that authority by the necessity which gives rise to its functions. Sales, Labor Relations, Engineering, Finance, Personnel, and Public Relations have all won their place as sources of expertise basic to the functioning of the line and to the total enterprise. The line supervisor has become more and more like a staff supervisor because as internal differences in the importance of functions diminished the same sociocultural environment dominated. Collab-

---

[33] Mason Haire (ed.), *Organization Theory in Industrial Practice,* Wiley, 1962, pp. 4–6.
[34] *Ibid.,* p. 5.

orative effort now has a common denominator—all supervisors must become competent in the technical, administrative, and human relations responsibilities and play roles in close cooperative relations with those functionaries with whom their responsibilities intertwine.

Social life of the foreman

The informal associations of the foreman in and outside the work plant depend upon the type of identification he makes and the type of identification he makes depends on his social background and his primary reference group. A family background anchored in support of labor will predispose toward identification with employees. A conservative family background tends to push him toward an identification with management. What he actually does depends on his primary reference group. The question becomes: What does he want to be and with whom does he want to be associated?

If he identifies with management he seeks to lunch with, confide in, and associate with other foremen and people in the stratum above him. Unless he can climb the management ladder, however, it is unlikely that his "advances" will be entirely reciprocated. Even when the superintendent makes it his business to visit his foremen, he is usually too preoccupied with technical work and social contacts within his "set" to spend much time with them.

On occasion, foremen's "clubs" are organized by management to promote solidarity among foremen and to make them feel a part of management. The typical routine in these clubs is to have dinners periodically, listen to speeches by a high management official, be exposed to supervisory training, and be encouraged to be loyal to the business. Without such an organization, foremen will seek social contacts according to their individual inclinations.

We have examined the work positions and work roles of three levels of management. In the analysis of work roles especially, it was necessary to consider the social relations between two or more jobs. The formal theory of management which ignores these social relations omits an important segment of work organization.

To understand the dynamic life of an organization it is necessary to examine these relations as they fit together in informal organization.

SELECTED BIBLIOGRAPHY

Argyris, Chris, *Executive Leadership: An Appraisal of a Manager in Action,* Harper, 1953.

Chamberlain, Neil W., *Management in Motion,* Yale Labor and Management Center, 1950.

Copeland, Melvin T., *The Executive at Work,* Harvard, 1952.

Dalton, Melville, *Men Who Manage,* Wiley, 1959.

Dill, William R., Thomas L. Hilton, and Walter R. Reitman, *The New Managers,* Prentice-Hall, 1962.

Granick, David, *Management of the Industrial Firm in the U.S.S.R.,* Columbia, 1954.

Learned, Edmund P., David N. Ulrich, and Donald R. Booz, *Executive Action,* Harvard University Graduate School of Business Administration, 1951.

Lewis, Roy, and Rosemary Stewart, *The Managers: A New Evaluation of the English, German, and American Executive,* Mentor Books, 1958.

Mann, Floyd C., and L. Richard Hoffman, *Automation and the Worker,* Holt, 1960.

Mills, C. Wright, *White Collar,* Oxford University Press, 1951.

Moore, Wilbert E., *The Conduct of the Corporation,* Random House, 1962.

Ulrich, David N., Donald R. Booz, and Paul R. Laurence, *Management Behavior and Foreman Attitude,* Harvard, 1950.

Walker, Charles R., Robert H. Guest, and Arthur Turner, *The Foreman on the Assembly Line,* Harvard, 1956.

Warner, W. Lloyd, and James Abegglen, *Big Business Leaders in America,* Harper, 1955.

CHAPTER 7

The Behavior
of
Work Groups

INTRODUCTION

Managerial Myopia

Many American businessmen operate with a rather simple picture of work life. The objective of life is "success," that is, the maximization of production and profit. The ingredients of success (apart from individual ability) are improved technology, trained personnel, and good organization. If success is not forthcoming, one of these ingredients is lacking. The prescription in any case is simple and obvious. Get new machinery, get better-trained people, and undergo a thorough reorganization.

Administrators have clung to this simple view of their universe despite mounting contrary evidence. For example, many plants with antiquated machinery, untrained personnel, and haphazard organization seem to defy dire predictions of doom.[1] How can one explain the fact that plants with modern equipment, highly trained engineers, and model organizational schemes sometimes founder in the economic struggle? During World War II some of the new defense plants which had the best equipment, personnel, and administrative organization had poor production records. What is more remarkable, people often preferred to work in older, poorly lighted, poorly ventilated, and ill-kept plants.[2] The

---

[1] William J. Goode and Irving Fowler, "Incentive Factors in a Low Morale Plant," *American Sociological Review,* October, 1949, pp. 618–623.

[2] E. Mayo, *Social Problems of an Industrial Civilization,* Harvard, 1945, p. 96. Cf. Peter Drucker, "Why Men Strike," *Harper's Magazine,* November, 1946, p. 391.

literature is replete with instances of industrial strife in plants that were considered technical and organizational models.

To explain such occurrences executives have examined "intangibles" like morale, teamwork, and cooperation. Characteristically, they defined these intangibles largely in terms of production and profits. Thus, they conceived morale as a willingness to work hard and produce. However, what is morale in one organization is not morale in another. Workers may have high internal morale when they participate in a slowdown or strike. That many businessmen do not consider this morale testifies to their inability to deal with human and social problems.

To be sure, executives believe that they are attending to "human problems" when they study supervision, wage rates, and incentive schemes. In previous chapters we have signified that these are primarily human problems in formal organizations. Officials have devoted too much thought to this kind of organization and not enough to the sum total of social organization in the plant, including informal organization.

Informal organization constitutes that network of personal and social relations which are not defined or prescribed by formal organization.

In formal organization sanctions are instituted in an "office" while in informal organizations sanctions are applied by group members to codes of their own making. Moreover, informal organizations include *only* that behavior which has some relevance to role performance at work or in work-related organizations, e.g., management-, union-, or company-sponsored organizations and activities. There is much behavior in the work place that has no relevance to organizational behavior. For example, going to lunch and conversing about baseball may be an informal activity but it may not be part of informal work organization unless it can be shown that it has some consequence for a work-related activity—morale, production, voting for the union, and so on.

Segments of Informal Organization

Informal organization is a rather complex structure, made up of the following interrelated items:

1. Congeniality groups, such as gangs, friendships, and cliques.
2. An organization and structure which defines the relations be-

tween these groups, in terms of rights, obligations, prestige, and influence.

3. Codes of conduct for group members, including customs and norms. These may be arbitrarily divided into two sections:

   a. *Internal* codes, which regulate activities within the informal social organization.

   b. *External* codes, which regulate activities toward formal organization (management and union) and other formally or informally organized out-groups.

4. Scheme of ideas, beliefs, and values which underlie and support the code of conduct and group activities, such as "folk" knowledge, prejudices, stereotypes, myths, and ideologies which give meaning to occurrences.

5. Informal group activities, related to or independent of formal work behavior. Ceremonies, rites, gambling, recreation, swearing, and joking are examples.

6. Communication systems which inform members of ideas, sentiments, and occurrences vital to group solidarity and action.

Since organization is an interrelated functioning organism, the division of informal organization into these six sections is an arbitrary, but convenient, way to understand the subject. Each aspect of informal organization will be described below in detail.

Illustrations of Informal Organization in Operation

One apparent reason why informal social organization has been infrequently recognized is that it is often invisible to the untrained observer. When any organization is running smoothly, it is natural to assume that the formal structure is in control. However, unusual things do happen in organizations which cannot be explained by analysis of the formal organization alone. Some of these "unexplainable" events are the following:

A wildcat strike occurs without forewarning.

Union members will not respond to the discipline of their officers.

A union is "suddenly" organized without apparent aid from organizers, in a situation where "unrest" was unknown to managers.

Absenteeism rises suddenly without apparent cause.

There is a rash of stealing, destructiveness, and sabotage.

A brawl occurs during an executive conference between two groups which had shown no evidence of antagonism in previous meetings.

One department excels another comparable department in production, earnings, and performance without apparent cause.

A group inaugurates a number of social functions—dances, athletics, and picnics—whereas another group never engages in social affairs.

A rumor sweeps through the plant like wildfire: The plant is going to close down or move away, a big bonus is coming through, Negroes are going to be hired, and so on.

As long as events like these are regarded as irregularities, the observer is not fully aware of existent informal social organization. He is likely to explain such occurrences in terms of the personalities involved, their insidious motives, or unusual circumstances.

Importance of Informal Organization

Everyone has at one time or another recognized that his interpersonal relations are critical to his success or failure. Sometimes these relations take the form of "pull," "drag," "prejudice," and "favoritism." In America such things are regarded as unfortunate, undemocratic, and perhaps somewhat inevitable. They are considered private problems outside the realm of scientific investigation.

As a matter of fact, pull, favoritism, and prejudice are group phenomena capable of sociological investigation. They occur in work organizations as an extension of friendships, clique life, and personal antagonisms. Anyone who studies friendships, cliques, and hostilities of a group will find that they constitute an integrated system of relationships. As such, they are as much a part of the social organization as the supervisory and the union structures. Thus, informal relations are not accidental, incidental, or tangential. On the contrary, no organization can function effectively if it does not contain a parallel spontaneous network of interpersonal relations.

The study of informal organization is important if for no other reason than that it is needed to get the *entire* picture of organization. The student of social organization needs to know how *both* formal and informal organizations operate. The relationship between these two types of organization is not supplementary but interactive. In a very real sense, then, it is impossible to understand how the supervisory structure actually operates without systematic knowledge of the ongoing informal relations in it. It is equally true that knowledge of informal organization is made more meaningful when it is considered in relation to the formal structure with which it is interacting.

To understand informal organization it is helpful to use the social systems approach. Here we are concerned with people interpreting their social roles in the context of concrete situations. Thus, "local" knowledge is needed to understand the operation of both formal and informal organizations.

Although there is consensus on how formal structure should operate, there is no such normative conception for informal organization. Therefore, it is useful to study informal organization by case instances to see what forms it takes. Perhaps by outlining the technique of studying informal organizations we can show how it arises.

HOW TO STUDY INFORMAL ORGANIZATION

The Need for Group Focus

To study informal organization or any kind of organization one must study existing social relations. This simple and obvious fact is more often ignored than recognized. Even social scientists sometimes forget that their *unit of observation is the social relationship* and not the individual.

Roethlisberger and Dickson, who pioneered in the study of informal organization in industry, suffered from the common misconception of the nature of the group. They felt that it was necessary to study each individual to get a picture of the group. Finally, by examining every person's relations to others, they concluded that they were actually observing a group and not a number of individuals.[3] In other words, they ended where they should

[3] F. J. Roethlisberger and William J. Dickson, *Management and the Worker*, Harvard, 1947, chaps. 7 and 17.

have begun—with a hypothesis that individuals reflect the previous existence of a group.

The conception of the group as an additive phenomenon is difficult to erase. It is pictured thus:

$$\text{Individuals } A + B + C + D = \text{Group}$$

The sociologist begins with a different approach. He recognizes that the individual can be understood only in process of *interacting* with other people. He is less interested in persons than in their interrelations. *Interrelationship defines the group, not a mere collection of individuals.* Thus a number of women shoppers crowding the street on a Friday afternoon do not compose a group. A diagram showing the interactive and sociological conception of a group follows.

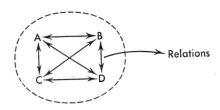

If a person wants to study informal social life in a work plant he must almost slavishly follow a few simple rules:

1. Keep your eye *primarily* on people, and secondarily on what they are producing or servicing.
2. Observe how they *react to each other.*
3. Listen to what they say and don't say; observe what they do and don't do in reference to each other.
4. Note the degree to which saying and doing jibe with each other.
5. Find the ideas, beliefs, and attitudes on which they generally agree or disagree.
6. Appraise how stable or unstable your findings are as situations change.
7. Do not become a factor in the situation you are observing. If

this is impossible, try to analyze your relations to the group as you would analyze any other person's.[4]

Moreover, as the observer moves into a specific work situation, he should have some questions which he wants answered, some hunches that he wants to test, and some ideas on how to get the best answers. Although questions, hypotheses, and methodology will vary with research interests, a few basic guides to research in informal organization will be helpful.

Technical, Sociotechnical, and Social Behavior

The first thing an observer should determine is which behavior is *essentially* technical, which is sociotechnical, and which is social. These three types of behavior should not be confused, and the relations between them should be ascertained.

Behavior which is essentially technical is usually referred to as "skill." The tailor cutting his cloth, the draftsman drawing his plans, the researcher conducting an experiment are largely engaged in technical behavior. Thus, a drill press operator can do his job whether he is an introvert or an extrovert, single or married, Negro or white, Protestant or Catholic, in the presence or absence of other people. Much of this behavior may be thought of as nonsocial. It is the chief interest of the engineer and the apprentice, not of the social scientist. The only social aspect to technical behavior is the social rank or meaning that others assign it. Thus the performance of the job may be affected by the worker's reaction to its social rank.[5] Not much work activity begins and ends on the technological level, for workers are also forced to interact by the nature of their work. Technical behavior which involves social interaction may be designated as *sociotechnical behavior*.

Let us examine the sociotechnical behavior of an "isolated" cloth cutter in a mill. In the morning he goes to the supply depot to get his cloth, or the buggyman delivers it to him. The cutter

---

[4] This difficult problem is discussed in an important article by Burleigh B. Gardner and William Foote Whyte, "Methods for the Study of Human Relations in Industry," *American Sociological Review,* October, 1946, pp. 506–512.

[5] See William Foote Whyte, *Human Relations in the Restaurant Industry,* McGraw-Hill, 1948, chap. 4, "Status in the Kitchen."

must give the supply clerk a check or receipt. A few times a day a foreman checks his work, complains about the wastages and bad cuttings. Occasionally he is handed company notices. At the end of the week someone gives him a pay check or his wages. Once in a while he is asked to teach his job to a new worker. Once a month he attends a union or company meeting. All these are social acts that are incumbent on him as a cloth cutter and worker. In short, some social behavior is a necessary component to technical behavior and cannot be totally separated from it. It is as much a part of the job as are the manual skills.[6]

Jobs vary in the amount of sociotechnical behavior they contain. Members of a repair crew or assembly team, foremen, salesmen have jobs with considerable sociotechnical behavior. The point where sociotechnical behavior may be distinguished from purely technical on the one hand and purely social on the other is difficult to make out. In some occupations the purely technical and sociotechnical behaviors overlap and coincide almost completely. This is especially the case for the personnel director, the interviewer, the industrial relations expert, and others. Human relations are their business. Their technical skills are skills in interpersonal relations.

The third level of work behavior is purely social. Whenever people interact in formal organization they tend to develop interests in each other as persons. Any behavior which is not a function of formal organization is social. Joking, razzing, eating lunch together, playing cards, cutting down on production are examples of social behavior. Of course, it is necessary to realize how each type of behavior affects the other. Razzing may arise out of the inability to practice the technical skills correctly, and interpersonal tensions may arise out of contacts which are sociotechnical in nature.

Technical organization and sociotechnical behavior must be analyzed in order to have a bench mark with which to compare social behavior. Technical organization throws some workers together, keeps others segregated, permits others to have contacts. The formation of many informal groupings may be largely explained in terms of the formal and technical organization of the

6 See F. L. W. Richardson, Jr., and Charles R. Walker, "Work Flow and Human Relations," *Harvard Business Review,* January, 1949, pp. 107–122.

work plant.[7] If it develops where one would *not* expect it (because of sociotechnical differences in occupational routines), the reason for such behavior should be quickly explored.

In addition to the effect of technical organization on social contacts, there are a number of *shop rules,* policies, and practices that affect social life in the plant. They may deal with the amount of talking permitted on the job, the routine to follow in case of an accident, how to contact the steward, whom to see about a suggestion, complaint, or assistance. These data must be known beforehand to enable the investigator to evaluate whether the behavior of workers happens to be formally or informally prescribed. When the total amount of interaction is compared with that made necessary by sociotechnical behavior and shop rules, we have an index of the degree to which informal organization has grown. In some cases it may even be useful as an index of union or company morale.

It is useful to look at informal social behavior by observing a new employee finding his place in the structure.

How an Employee Finds His Place

The new employee must learn many things about the social behavior in his work situation. He must learn *who's who* (the informal status pattern or pecking order), *what's what* (the "ropes" or how things are done), and *what's up* (the current situation in his work area). But most important of all he must learn how he fits in. He must learn to play an acceptable role and no formal organization chart or manual will help him very much. He must know how role boundaries are established by his associates. The definition of roles by work groups is a surprisingly complex matter, as the following will illustrate.

Group definition of role

The group definition of a given work role is made up of certain expectations. These must be fulfilled regardless of who the particular worker may be. A carpenter is supposed to wear a particular work costume including the proper kind of overalls, shirt, hat, and shoes. He is supposed to understand the use of certain tools. He joins the union and supports it by striking against his em-

[7] Leonard R. Sayles, *Behavior of Industrial Work Groups,* Wiley, 1958.

ployer if the majority of the members of his local union vote to
do so. He will not scab on his fellow workers. He will talk like
his fellow workers, which means that he will not use big words or
any words for that matter which the group does not understand.
He will probably bring his lunch in a pail. He will tend to eat as
they eat and he will not criticize them if they have different eating
habits. He will listen to dirty stories and tell some of his own. He
will probably vote the Democratic ticket and express political
views in conformance with those of his associates.

A carpenter placed in a work group with these expectations is
under great pressure to conform. Ideally his own definition of the
work role will coincide with the group definition. The deviations
from this ideal are the source of difficulty in placement. These
deviations seem to be of particular importance in the case of
supervisory and managerial appointments. The sad last words of
outgoing administrators have often been, "I didn't know that was
what they expected. If I had known . . ."

Two types of deviations may be analyzed as occurring in the
role definitions held by a worker and his work group. The worker
may be a subordinate or a supervisor. (1) In either instance he
may overevaluate and overplay the role which the group expects
him to play, causing the group to feel a pressure to which its
members will react in some way. Their reactions will depend
largely upon their approval of the worker's or supervisor's motives. (2) If the worker or supervisor underevaluates and under-
plays his role, he will eventually come to feel the pressure of the
group, which will demand changes to place the work role in conformance with their expectation. All of the social controls may
be utilized to secure that conformity—ridicule, complaint, soldiering, insubordination, and others. These types of deviations from
the ideal coincidence of individual definition of work role with
the group definition cannot explain the many specific problems
arising in this area of group assignment.

However, industrial sociologists have begun to identify the
more important social factors which locate the work role definitions as made by workers in the innumerable work groups. Although the interaction patterns of many groupings that actually
arise will not be subject to direct control, it is possible to improve the social placement of workers and to stimulate more

cohesive work groups. These possibilities become more certain as the determinants of successful social placement and group collaboration are identified. Successful social placement in a work position requires knowledge of the social factors operating to determine work role definition.

Social factors operating to establish role definitions

Among the various social factors influencing role definitions within different work groups are (1) ascribed status behavior of the work positions, (2) informal code of the work groups, (3) age, (4) sex, (5) marital status, (6) social background, (7) length of service, (8) race, and (9) ethnic identity.[8]

1. ASCRIBED STATUS BEHAVIOR OF THE WORK POSITION

Every work position has an ascribed status. Ralph Linton, the anthropologist, has defined an ascribed status as one which is assigned to individuals without reference to their innate differences or abilities. When it comes to ascription of occupational status, we find that each occupation has a ranking within some family of occupations and within the range of all occupations generally. Whyte has discovered the status rankings ascribed to workers in the restaurant industry. The following is the usual hierarchy of ascribed status:

Owner
Manager
Assistant manager
Cost control superintendent
Food production manager
Chef
General kitchen superintendent
Hostess
Head waitress—if in superintendent capacity
Checker
Superintendent of countermen
Superintendent of dishwashers
Waitresses
Countermen
Food preparers
1. those who cook
2. salad

[8] Refer also to Chapter 12, "Status and Prestige in the Work Organization."

3. chicken preparation
   a. white meat
   b. dark meat
4. meat
   a. beef
   b. pork
      roasts
      frying
5. chicken cooking
6. vegetables
   a. parsley
   b. chives
   c. celery
   d. beans—green
   e. spinach
   f. carrots
   g. potatoes
   h. onions
7. fish
Runners
Dishwashers
Charwomen[9]

This hierarchy determines in advance the kinds of status behavior which will be expected of each member who works within it. Any worker is expected to defer to those above him in status and to receive the respect of those below him in status. This deference expectation may display itself in many different ways. Whyte describes how a cook (high status) reacted to pressure from a runner (low status). The runner had tried to get the cook to prepare food faster. The cook made this comment,

That guy would try to come down in the kitchen and tell us what to do. But not me. No, sir. He came down here one day and tried to tell me what to do. He said to me, "We're going to be very busy today." I just looked at him, "Yeah?" I said. "Who are you? Go on upstairs. Go on. Mind your own business." Can you beat that! "We're going to be very busy today!" He never came down and told *me* anything again. "Who are you?" I asked him. That's all I had to say to him.[10]

2. INFORMAL CODE OF THE WORK GROUP

Most work groups hold certain definite ideas as to the way in which an individual should conduct himself within the group.

---

[9] Drawn from Whyte, *op. cit.*, pp. 33–46.
[10] From *Ibid*. Courtesy of McGraw-Hill.

These ideas are connected chiefly with occupation, output, and supervision.

In the bank wiring observation group at Hawthorne, Roethlisberger and Dickson report, the workers had a very definite idea of how much work should be turned out. A member who turned out too much was called a "rate buster"; one who turned out too little a "chiseler." Moreover, a worker who told a supervisor anything that would seem to act to the detriment of a fellow worker was a "squealer."

This behavior is in essence no different from that which takes place in a schoolroom, whether it is occupied by students eight or eighty years of age. The students come to consider themselves part of an in-group under pressure imposed by an out-group composed of teachers and administrators. If a student works extremely hard for a high grade he is called a "greasy grind" or a "Phi Bete." If he tries to get a passing record by playing upon the ego of his teacher with techniques of flattery, he is called a variety of names ranging from "apple polisher" to "quill shooter." If he wants to be a "regular guy" he will try to give the appearance of one who is not working very hard and who positively will do no "apple polishing."

E. Wight Bakke has set down the definition of a socially respected industrial worker as made by the workers themselves. He says that "the socially respected worker 'has money in his pocket,' 'has the cash to buy what he needs,' 'is thrifty and a man of foresight,' 'is prepared for a rainy day,' 'owns property,' 'is a good provider,' 'doesn't let his family down,' 'sees to it that his kids are educated,' and himself is a graduate of the school of hard knocks."[11]

Katherine Archibald confirms these observations through her own study of shipyard workers.

Though shipyard workers showed little interest in the broad issues of ethics, they respected definite commandments for the regulation of the familial system. A man was as good or bad as his practice of the family virtues; his acts possessed or lacked merit as they affected his family. The harshest words that one boss had for a member of his gang too often late to work were that he obviously had no regard for the security of his wife and children and was a poor provider. "His old lady sure ought to ride into him," the boss asserted, "losing money from his checks

[11] E. Wight Bakke, *The Unemployed Worker*, Yale, 1940, p. 15.

the way he does by being late about every morning—and him with four kids, too." . . . A discussion with a minister was reported at some length to me by a worker, out of pride in his own position. "A minister asked me," he said, "how I could hope to be a Christian if I didn't go to church every Sunday and say my prayers at night. Well, I told him that being good to my wife and paying my gas bills on time was Christianity enough for me, and I didn't need to pray because I thanked God every day by working hard for the sake of my wife and kid."[12]

These illustrations convey the importance of the informal code in depicting the socially acceptable role as defined by the work group. Such characteristics constitute behavior expectations which must be fulfilled if the worker is to acquire full social acceptance.

So far in this discussion the demand has been shown to be twofold. The worker must play the role designated by the status ascribed to the work position he fills. In addition, he must play the role designated by the informal code of the group. When a new worker is to be fitted into a work group these two demands will often loom larger in successful placement than the technical competence required for the work position. The need to get this social data and make them a part of the job description is obviously important. The social scientist must offer assistance in formulating the method and instruments necessary to systematize such data. Many factors need to be considered. Age is one that must not be ignored.

3. AGE

Age differentiates workers on the basis of status, interests, and physical energy. Each of these differences may be important in determining social participation the group.

Thus Whyte found that a waitress over thirty might be quite a different worker in orientation from a younger waitress. In one large restaurant he observed four waitresses over thirty who ate together and saw each other outside of work. One of them had this to say: "Most of these waitresses are younger than I am, and this kidding around that they do seems childish and boring to me. Of course, they are much younger, and you have to think you were young once yourself and just like that, although in my

---

[12] Katherine Archibald, *Wartime Shipyard,* University of California Press, 1947, pp. 224–225.

own case I don't think I ever was so flighty because I had lots of responsibility."[13]

4. SEX

Every anthropologist knows that sex differences have been common bases for differentiating the labor and the rights of members in social life. In contemporary society sex differences do not cut the occupational roles so sharply as they formerly did but they are nonetheless far-reaching in work life.

Katherine Archibald describes the role of sex in the wartime shipyard:

Sex attitudes made up the tangled background of the male worker's point of view. Sex was his great avocational interest; whether bounded by the proprieties of marriage or unconstrained in the reaches of bachelor fancy, it was the spice of his existence, the principal joy of his social life. The largest part of shipyard conversation, beyond the routine of the day's necessities, was occupied with some aspect of the pleasures or the problems of sex; and shipyard jokes were broad and racy in the extreme. Emphasized in this interest was the sexual role of women, which influenced every association between the sexes and surrounded with an atmosphere of obscure emotionality each area of unfamiliar and unusual cooperation. The emphasis upon sex, moreover, as it evoked the biological distinctions between men and women, also reinforced the lines of social demarcation. Traditions supposedly governing the proper division of labor between men and women were linked with even more profoundly rooted traditions concerning divisions in biological function, and change in the structure of the former might seem to imply a threat to the latter's sacrosanct stability. . . . Thus, on my first day of work in the yards I was warned by the superintendent of my craft that any flirting with the men in the yards would result in dire consequences for me. "Remember what I told you," he called after me as I left his office; "give a man an inch and he'll take a mile, and if there's any funny business on the job, it'll be you who goes out like a light."[14]

In this description of "the proper division of labor between men and women" is evidence that sexual differences must be considered as an important factor in social placement wherever such differences matter in organizing work teams.

5. AND 6. MARITAL STATUS AND SOCIAL BACKGROUND

The two factors of marital status and social background may be treated together for the significance of both in placement is that

---

[13] From Whyte, *op. cit.* Courtesy of McGraw-Hill.
[14] Archibald, *op. cit.*, pp. 18–20.

they may induce differentials in interest. Two waitresses indicate these differences. The first stresses the differences due to marital status; the second, those due to social background.

> They've asked me to go down there but I wouldn't do it. I'm the oldest girl on this floor, so I could go down anytime. The trouble is, the girls down there are older, and they're a different type from us up here. A lot of those girls are married. They talk about different things. I just wouldn't fit in. And you know some of them, even if they are married, they go out. Some of those girls have asked me to go with them on dates, and I've refused. But if I was working down there with them, I couldn't refuse, could I? I'd be going out with them, and I'd get like them myself. . . .
>
> There is one main division, I think. There are the girls who work here a long time, the professional waitress type. Then there are the other girls who aren't waiting on tables as a career. Those two groups talk differently, and I wouldn't feel at home in the first group at all. I feel uncomfortable when I am with those girls. You can even tell it down in the girls' rest room. Even when the girls are all mixed up, sitting on different sides of the room, you'll have two conversations going right across the room. The two groups will talk right across each other, and they just don't mix in.[15]

7. LENGTH OF SERVICE

The length of service which a worker has given to one employer is ordinarily regarded as the basis for certain rights and obligations. New workers are expected to wait their turn before being admitted to full status. Thus a work group made up of workers with considerable seniority will expect the new worker to earn the rights won by a long length of service. They will expect the newcomer to defer to their greater knowledge of the work plant and its characteristic patterns. He will be expected to restrain any hopes for advancement until the seniority rights of older workers are recognized. The newcomers who appear as strangers to their long association may find it difficult to secure a place of acceptance in a well-knit group of older workers.

E. C. Hughes observed the informal organization of women workers in the polishing room of a certain work plant:

> The cliques in this room are not mutually exclusive and sharply defined. There is a central group, the "Old Girls," made up of young women of from twenty-two to thirty-three years of age and of an average

[15] From Whyte, *op. cit.* Courtesy of McGraw-Hill.

length of service of about five years. The "Old Girls" eat in the cafeteria; each usually manages to eat with at least one or two of her clique fellows. Another group, also of long service, bring their lunches and eat in the lounge. But there is little association between them and the "Old Girls" clique. There are a number of smaller satellite cliques, each attached by at least one common member to the "Old Girls." It appears likely that a new girl may be sponsored into the organization through the satellite cliques. We observed one girl who was, when first interviewed, unfriendly toward other workers, a "lone wolf." Two months later she had been accepted. . . .[16]

8. RACE

The largest minority group in America is the American Negro group. If a Negro is to win a place in a white or mixed work group he must play the role which is expected. That role is most often prescribed as the part of an inferior who will willingly take the lowest-paid, most onerous jobs and will entertain no hopes of promotion to anything better. Katherine Archibald describes the relations of Negroes and whites at Moore Dry Dock, Oakland, California, which hired about 20 percent of Negro personnel in shipbuilding during the war years.

On the hulls and in the shops, Negroes and whites cooperated in countless tasks, white shoulders straining beside black, and to a casual observer the relationships of the two races seemed miraculously free from tension. The slightest touch, however, revealed the impermanence of the surface calm and the depth of the hatred beneath. In most of the whites the hatred was basic, a deep-seated and strong-flavored aversion that was evident in almost every gesture or remark which was not retarded by the Negro's presence and supposed readiness to take violent revenge for insults. The Negro was seldom even named in all-white talk except in appellations of implied derogation and antagonism, the most common being the timeworn "nigger" and the more recent "jigaboo" or "zigaboo" frequently shortened to "jig" and "zig."[17]

Attempts of a tolerant white person to establish normal friendly relations with Negroes in the shipyard brought derisive cries of "nigger lover" and other group pressures so strong that patterns of avoidance became the only acceptable conduct. No white woman could safely talk with a Negro man at length on any topic

---

[16] E. C. Hughes, "The Knitting of Racial Groups in Industry," *American Sociological Review*, October, 1946, p. 517.

[17] Archibald, *op. cit.*, p. 61.

without incurring the immediate and unequivocal reaction, "Well, when's the wedding going to be?"[18]

Such attitudes enforced social distance and created many solitaries. The solitary is a person who does not feel himself a part of any closely knit group. In the mixed group of white and Negro women workers which Hughes observed, "No Negro girl, no matter what her length of service, her production rate, or her personality, has found a place in the system of cliques of the white girls."[19]

Both Whyte in his observations of the Negro restaurant worker and Hughes in his study of the Negro factory worker report that attempts of Negroes to satisfy management's demands upon them often tend to further isolate them from the work group. The Negro's job security rests precariously with management satisfaction. Management demands may force the Negro worker to violate the informal group code as regards production and in giving information to management representatives.

All of these forces make the placement of the Negro difficult. However, it has been found that the manner in which Negroes are introduced into work groups is more significant in the success of Negro placement than are the generalized racial attitudes of the white workers concerned.[20] Mayo has reported that "we have indeed been surprised throughout this country during the war—East, Midwest, and California—by the ease with which colored people and others are absorbed into a working group if and when they have clearly 'made the team.' We are not prepared at this stage to make any generalizations upon a basis of so few instances; but as a tentative observation, the fact must give us pause."[21]

9. ETHNIC IDENTITY

Various work groups are marked by in-group attitudes tied to ethnic loyalties. When such in-group characteristics are determinants of social acceptance, the social placement of a new worker can proceed satisfactorily only in a clear recognition of the compulsive force of such attitudes. Orvis Collins spent six months

[18] *Ibid.*, p. 72.
[19] Hughes, *op. cit.*, p. 517.
[20] *Ibid.*
[21] Mayo, *op. cit.*, p. 110.

working and observing within a New England factory. He found an informal ethnic system of job occupancy and of expectation in promotion. Figure 7.1 is a representation of the ethnic job hierarchy in this factory.[22]

The figure shows that there are two sharply defined areas. The management area is dominated by Yankees and the supervisory

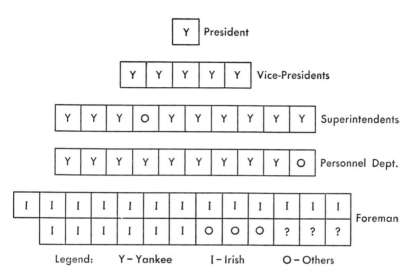

FIG. 7.1. Job-Ethnic Hierarchy in a New England Factory. The non-Yankee at the superintendent level is a testing engineer. The non-Yankee member of the personnel group is a young Italian who does safety cartoons and acts as a general errand boy. (Adapted from Orvis Collins, "Ethnic Behavior in Industry: Sponsorship and Rejection in a New England Factory," *American Journal of Sociology*, January, 1946, p. 294.)

area by the Irish. These tightly drawn ethnic groupings have led to the expectation that Yankees will be hired for management and that newly appointed foremen will be Irish. This does not mean that a foreman, for example, must be Irish, but it does mean that when management appoints a non-Irish foreman it will be with the blessing of the workers and the other foremen.

[22] Orvis Collins, "Ethnic Behavior in Industry: Sponsorship and Rejection in a New England Factory," *American Journal of Sociology*, January, 1946, p. 294.

When Peters, a Yankee, was promoted to be subforeman to replace Sullivan, who had been "old country" Irish, all hell broke loose. A walkout materialized. A formal grievance was lodged with management and the workers returned to work. Social pressure in the tightly integrated work group mounted. Several days later Peters the Yankee failed to come to work. It was announced that Peters was ill and that his job would be filled by a man named Murphy. Peters did not return to work!

THE ELEMENTARY FORMS OF INFORMAL BEHAVIOR

Shop Talk

Talking is an important part of social behavior. "People have ears but they hear not" applies to the world of work as well as to other areas. A complex theory is not needed to analyze the role of talk in informal organization. To assume that most shop talk is unimportant is to ignore an area of great social significance. Largely by listening to what people say one can learn their attitudes, values, sentiments, and idea systems. Once these things are known, it is possible to give meaning and interpretation to behavior and social events.

Amount of talking

Many executives who prohibit talking believe that it interferes with work. This may be true for some jobs but it is not for others. In fact, in many routine jobs conversation not only may improve performance but indicates a degree of adjustment to the job. In other circumstances the absence of talking may point to explosive situations in the making. Compatible workers with similar backgrounds and interests may be expected to be garrulous, and incompatible workers with different backgrounds may not communicate.

Content of talking

The content of conversation must be analyzed to understand informal organization of the group. If a group is organized it must share a minimum of common ideas, ideals, sentiments, and attitudes. A long interview or questionnaire is usually not needed to obtain the basic thoughts and feelings of a group. A content analysis of their conversations correlated to group behavior is a more naturalistic and realistic way to get a picture of group life.

From a content analysis of conversation we can obtain vital information on the group's interests. Does the worker talk mostly about production, baseball, sex, job climbing, or the union? What kinds of incidents that occur seem to be systematically avoided in the conversations? Do they concern the foreman, the size of the take-home pay, or the conduct of union leaders? Thus, basic data on informal group life would contain an analysis of interest and avoidance subjects ranked in order of the amount of talk. A ranking of interest-avoidance subjects such as the following provides a basis for understanding the context of informal organization. These subjects may be rearranged along different axes, such as the priorities of worry, the priorities of changes desired in the department, the priorities of job aspirations, and so on.

Interest Subjects	*Avoidance Subjects*
Golf and bridge	Managerial nepotism
Baseball and sex	New foreman
The change of the work rate	Foreman training program
The proposed medical plan	Union election
Stock and bond quotations	Company expense accounts

Talk and the sentiment-value system

From a content analysis of conversation, the basic sentiment and value system of the group under observation may be discerned. When the primary ideas, ideals, symbols, stereotypes, myths, folklore, and ideologies are uncovered, group activities and processes are capable of being fully understood.

It is particularly important to know the value system because it furnishes knowledge of the basis of group integration or lack of it. Although the group may be located in an economic organization, its cohesion may derive from noneconomic ties in ethnic, religious, political, or other associations. Of course the observer should be especially aware of the values which directly affect behavior in the plant. Sentiments about property, supervisors, taking orders, security and unemployment, savings and investment, politics and government, superior and inferior classes are some of the basic items to study.

In addition, it is vital to segregate which values, sentiments, and behavior patterns are held by the entire group, which are shared only partially, and which are divergent in nature. In a later section of this chapter we shall demonstrate how the value-sentiment system not only provides the basis for informal organization but also explains the "unpredictable occurrences" in work organizations.

Overt Behavior

Data on informal organization may also be gathered by direct observation of overt behavior. First it is desirable to locate people socially with respect to certain basic categories of occupation, sex, seniority, age, prestige, and authority. When groups are examined according to these and other factors, the social composition of the participants of each activity may be known.

At first, simple things may be observed, as who eats lunch with whom, who exchange jobs, who participate in horseplay, who are members of a car pool. Which people play together in and out of the plant? Who entertains whom? What groups form before, during, and after working hours? How persistent are they? What customs are developed for amusement, to display social solidarity or hostility? What folkways and rituals arise to express group attitudes toward "superiors" and "inferiors"? How is a new worker inducted into an informal group? How are informal groups tied together?

Other interesting things may be learned by posing simple questions. The stratification in informal groups may be obtained by observing who defers to whom in *any* kind of activity. Other patterns may be found by noticing who initiates action, who follows, and who assumes *what roles* in what activities. In a later section we shall suggest some answers to these questions.

INFORMAL ORGANIZATION OF MANAGEMENT

The tendency for informal groups to grow in formal structures is found everywhere, but literature on the informal organization of management is scanty.[23]

[23] Alexander Leighton, *The Governing of Men*, Princeton, 1945; Melville Dalton, *Men Who Manage*, Wiley, 1959; Edmund P. Learned, David N. Ulrich,

Why Ignored

The reasons why this subject has been ignored are not difficult to find. In the first place, managers have initiated most of the studies of work organization. They have followed the natural tendency to see their problems as caused by other groups. In the attempt to account for "resistance" to orders, "restriction" of production, absenteeism, and other problems, management-oriented students discovered that an informal organization exists among workers that sometimes runs contrary to management's plans. They imputed the rise of informal organization to the non-logical, emotional, and sentimental nature of the workers. On the other hand, they conceived management's behavior to be guided by the logic of cost and efficiency. They came to the conclusion that the conflict between sentiments and efficiency norms is responsible for many tensions in work relations. This thinking leads them to the thought that sentiment-bound informal organization does not exist in management, or if it does exist, it is negligible and unimportant.

Another reason for not seeing informal organization in management lies in the fact that office jobs are not as physically circumscribed as plant jobs are. If a machine operator is not working at a specific rate, this can be noted and measured. It is much more difficult to observe restrictions of output in office jobs, because moving about and talking to people may be part of the job. It is difficult to distinguish official and nonofficial behavior. If the machine operator talks at all, it is labeled unofficial behavior. Moreover, since workers are on hourly rates and office workers are on salary, a double standard is rationalized. Hourly workers are not expected to be off the job except at stated periods. Most managers may leave their desks at any time. The managers, particularly, regard themselves as on call. Since they give "extra" work to the company after regular hours, they can justify (to themselves) the length of almost any lunch hour or rest period they wish to take.

The more reserved behavior of middle-class people is also a good smoke screen for their nonofficial work activity. Their loaf-

and Donald R. Booz, *Executive Action*, Harvard University Graduate School of Business Administration, 1951; William H. Whyte, Jr., and editors of *Fortune, Is Anybody Listening?* Simon and Schuster, 1952.

ing is more restrained, whereas on the plant floor horseplay, joking, razzing, bottom slapping, and swearing are visible expressions of impulsive behavior. Middle-class researchers recognize more readily such overt conduct, which seems to be a departure from their work norms.

Management cliques

Anyone who has observed executives in action realizes that they are as clique-ridden as any group. Moore defines a clique as "an informal grouping of persons representing common interests which are at variance with their official capacities and relations, and which cut across formal patterns of contact and authority."[24] He suggests that management cliques tend to arise in organizations whenever there is a highly interactive competition for higher positions, and where the criteria for advancement are poorly defined.[25] Moore conceives a clique as a group whose main function is to protect incompetent workers in a competitive situation. Certainly this is one of the functions of a clique, but, as we shall show, it has other functions, the most important of which is providing patterns of conduct for the group. Managers accept these patterns so completely that they do not recognize their informal nature. "This is the way we do things in our company" is a recurrent phrase uttered on all supervisory levels. The more frequently it is heard, the more ingrained is informal organization.

Informal Organization and the Supervisory Structure

Almost every person in management structure is involved in social activities not prescribed by the job. Some participate in many activities of well-knit groups; others have less intensive and extensive social contacts. Some of the informal groups and cliques are concerned with promoting their common welfare and the position of the department. Others, based upon congeniality, are knit together by social and recreational activities.

Preliminary studies made by the authors seem to indicate that the informal organization of management closely parallels the

[24] Wilbert E. Moore, *Industrial Relations and the Social Order*, Macmillan, rev. ed., 1951, p. 140.
[25] *Ibid.*, p. 141.

supervisory structure to an amazing degree. In fact, with the exception of a few individuals who participate in the social life of different levels, the membership of informal groups is limited to people having similar jobs on the same supervisory level.

Figure 7.2 portrays part of the informal organization of management in a midwestern manufacturing concern. The social relations among all of the members are charted for five types of

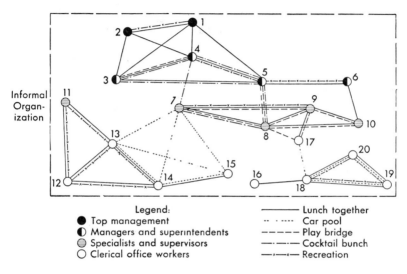

FIG. 7.2. Informal Organization of Management in a Midwestern Manufacturing Concern.

activities. The workers are also identified for their position in the supervisory hierarchy. A brief glance at the figure reveals a number of cliques that tend to parallel the supervisory structure. That is, clique members seem to come from the same level.

The president (1) and the executive vice-president (2) lunch and play golf together. Both of them lunch with managers and superintendents of the staff and production divisions. Neither of them has much more to do with other officials. Most of their contacts are with top executives in *other businesses* in the city. They are not very well integrated in the informal organization of the plant.

The manager and superintendents (3, 4, 5, and 6) are next highest in the supervisory hierarchy. Numbers 3, 4, and 5 (heads of Assembly, Engineering, and Industrial Relations respectively) form a close-knit clique. They lunch together, entertain one another, and play bridge. Number 6, who is the general foreman of Manufacturing, is not fully incorporated into this clique. He eats and bowls with the group occasionally but never entertains them at his home, nor is he ever invited to their homes. The general foreman is the only person in this level who is not college trained. The president never eats a meal with this Irish-born general foreman.

But the managerial clique is not absolutely closed. Number 7, who is a young, inexperienced engineer, entertains his boss at his home and is entertained in return. Sometimes he is invited by his boss's friends to a cocktail party. Number 7 has an unusually attractive young wife whom others consider an extremely "gracious" person. She will play an important role in her husband's career. Number 8 is the son-in-law of the industrial relations director. His father-in-law provides him contacts into the higher levels.

The young engineer (7) and his wife are in the center of a clique of supervisors and junior executives (7, 8, 9, and 10). The men not only eat together at work but with their wives form the nucleus of a bridge club. Note that the aggressive young engineer entertains only the son-in-law of the public relations director. In an effort to be popular with the office staff, he drives three of the female clerks to a bus line which is a mile from the factory. There is only one office girl who participates in the social life of the junior executives. She is a college-trained clerk (17) who is engaged to a supervisor in the accounting division (9). They are invited to play bridge with the clique.

The strongest clique (18, 19, 20) is composed of single girls who work in the office. These girls eat lunch together, are members of a car pool, and go to the movies together. Number 16 is a new girl who lives in another part of town. She is not yet fully inducted into the group. Although the clerical force is not a part of management, its physical proximity to management provides some of its members an opportunity to be tied into their informal organization. It is obvious from the diagram that this does not occur often. Neither the clerical clique nor the other clerks (12, 13, 14, 15) have much to do with management. The one exception is number 11. She is a divorced woman who heads a group of girls in the clerical pool. Although she lunches with her girls and participates in their recreation, she has nothing to do with the other supervisors and junior executives.

Social Induction

Fraternal organizations have typically developed ceremonies and rituals to initiate new members. On the factory floor the resemblance of social induction to formal initiation ceremonies is very apparent. Neophytes are razzed; they are "given a hard time"; they are asked to do absurd things. Although initiation to informal management groups is not so conspicuous, it is present nonetheless. The formal ceremony of induction is usually centered about the dinner or cocktail party at the home of the boss. The newcomer learns to keep careful account of the invitations he receives and compares them to the expected pattern of invitation. When the newcomer observes that the boss has had everyone over to dinner excepting himself, he is insecure. Until he is invited, he is not considered a fully accepted member of the group. Similar initiations and passage rituals (for promotion and transfer) among white-collar workers need to be studied. Of course, induction also occurs in the plant itself. It includes inviting the new man to lunch, exchanging gifts, placing him on "social" committees, and, above all else, testing his ability to "take it."

"Let's summer and winter with the guy," Kaiser men say as they look a candidate over. And " 'Mother,' Mrs. Kaiser, has a blackball too. The group of about twenty men has seen no new face for ten years."[26]

Climbing and Informal Organization

Many of the informal activities in management organization are understandable, if the observer is aware of the climbing mania existing among the supervisory staff. The strength, discontent, or

[26] "The Truth About Henry Kaiser," *Collier's,* August 3, 1946, p. 26.

esprit de corps of cliques depends in great measure on the ability of group members to fulfill their climbing aspirations.

American ideology insists that climbing depends upon ability and performance. An analysis of clique formation may begin with the questions: Who climbs? Who doesn't climb? Why do they climb or fail? What is the effect on clique formation of climbing? Or the failure to climb? The following case suggests what can happen when a clique struggle is instigated.

John M. was offered an appointment as head of a staff of thirty librarians. As a condition of acceptance he made the stipulation that the institution also hire two librarians who were his assistants in the library in which he was then employed. This was done. Upon accepting the job, M. appointed a third librarian who was recommended to him by a friend. These three new appointees were invited to M.'s home rather frequently; the rest of the staff was invited on one formal occasion. The new appointees came to be regarded as "M.'s group." The rest of the staff talked about themselves as the defeated "Old Guard." After certain promotions and merit raises went to members of "M.'s group," a basic social cleavage developed between the two cliques. M., who was personally accepted by the entire staff, had to spend much of his time soothing crying librarians and attempting to patch up "conflicts in personalities."

An analysis of the situation showed that the older workers on the staff had ambivalent feelings toward M. for three reasons. Although they liked him as a person, (1) he had violated the system of expectancies of promotion; (2) his new appointees violated line of authority by going to him directly with their problems; (3) he played favorites in the informal life of the library.

Other factors interfere with the operation of the climbing ideology. Not infrequently kinship relationships disturb the social equilibrium of the plant. Children and relatives of the executives violate the merit code by climbing ahead of people with greater ability, seniority, and experience. "Drag," "good looks," and "social background" are additional factors that violate the merit code. In Chapter 12, "Status and Prestige in the Work Organization," an analysis is made of the social factors responsible for informal cleavage along status or prestige lines. Other sentiments besides climbing and status are evident in management structure. Some of these powerful emotional forces deserve our further consideration.

Sentiments in Management Organization

In the discussion of work roles and positions, the ideology of managers was described. Other ideas and sentiments, however, are present in all management levels. One of the most important sentiments, pervading the entire informal social life of the supervisory structure, is *loyalty*. A person not only must be loyal to his department, division, or section; he must also be loyal to his chief. Irrespective of personal antagonisms within the plant, a good supervisor defends the enterprise to outsiders.

A plant worker may also share this sentiment, but he is not ostracized if he thinks and says, "This is a hell of a company." Since managers are part of the controlling agency, they are expected to endorse the organization all the time. They must act as if their "future" rests with the company.

Other sentiments revolve around the business of climbing. There are proper and improper methods of climbing. Although aggressiveness is an ideal attribute, "overaggressiveness" is not. The overly ambitious social climber is looked down upon by fellow managers. The number of times the boss and his family may be entertained is fairly well defined.

Overaggressiveness in other areas is also discouraged. An example illustrates this point. Lane and Briggs had charge of a section of insurance agents. Briggs complained about overaggressiveness in Lane. Previous to this charge, a higher executive had stimulated rivalry between these two men and between their organizations. Lane's section consistently sold more insurance than Briggs's. Despite the better performance of Lane's section he was not in rapport with the big boss. The latter had received many complaints to the effect that Lane and his boys were too aggressive. The friendly rivalry that existed between the two sections turned into bitter factionalism. The losing section complained that Lane, among other things, had advised his agents to invade the Briggs territory to revive lapsed cases. Although regulations were in effect which stated that all collecting and soliciting of new business should be pursued on an assigned area basis, no rule covered lapsed policies. In the past, lapsed cases had been left to the discretion of the collectors in the areas. If they cared to revive them they might. If not, they were neglected. This breach of a poorly defined procedure was defined as overaggressiveness, and Lane was asked to discontinue it.

The way in which work roles are played depends partly on the informal organization in the management structure. The dynamics of informal group life revolve around the ever pressing desire of its members to climb in the organization. Resistances toward this impulse create many personality problems and problems of group morale.

SOCIAL BASES OF INFORMAL NUCLEATIONS

The Total Picture

From an organizational point of view, informal organization may be perceived on five levels:

1. The general overall system of interlocking groups of all kinds.
2. Major publics, which may include interrelated cliques arising out of major local plant issues. These are often referred to as "crowds" or "bunches" or "gangs."
3. Cliques and congeniality groups formed more or less on the locality basis and engaging in common activities, as eating, joking, and work exchange.
4. Very intimate friends who may be part of larger cliques.
5. Isolated individuals who participate rarely in any kind of social life in the plant.

Figure 7.3 pictures the informal clique structure in a department of a small Ohio airplane headlight factory. Obviously this structure differs from the formal structure. The latter recognizes only occupational distinctions among the workers: foremen, inspectors, pressmen, assemblers. The informal organization, on the other hand, is much more complex. It is an unplanned structure that arises out of the spontaneous interaction of people. No doubt occupation and position in the supervisory structure play a role in the creation of informal groupings. However, other personal and social characteristics of workers play an equally important part. Together these formal, personal, and social factors provide the basis for group and clique formation.

Cliques

Figure 7.3 shows a number of overlapping groups. For arbitrary purposes these groups are labeled cliques, sub-cliques, and friendships. Informal groups are located by finding patterns of congeniality, social interaction, and consensus. For our purposes a

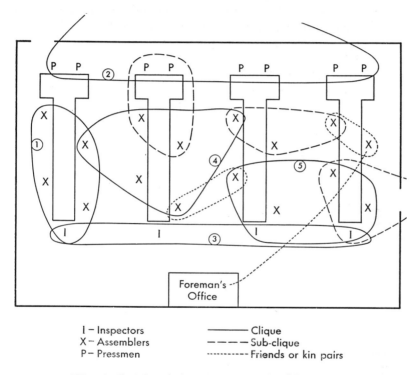

I – Inspectors
X – Assemblers
P – Pressmen

——— Clique
– – – – Sub-clique
·········· Friends or kin pairs

FIG. 7.3. The Informal Clique Structure in a Small Department.

clique includes several members who commonly associate, and a friendship group reflects *closer* association and compatibility of two or three work associates. The interlocking of these cliques, sub-cliques, and friendships throughout the entire work plant constitutes the plant's informal organization. Although informal ties connect management and labor groups, such connections are not as numerous as the ties within these groups. Two separate informal structures tend to develop, especially in the larger unionized work plants. We shall describe the informal relations existing among the workers.

Obviously these spontaneous, unplanned groups are very important to the worker. They are responsible for his social satisfactions on the job. From them he derives prestige and recognition of his personal qualities and problems. His ideas, ideals, and sentiments are forged within these groups. In short, he is a member of many groups, and his behavior is largely explained in terms of group pressures and customs.

The job of the sociologist is to explain how these spontaneous groups arise, what their social basis of membership is, what functions they serve, and what behavior typifies them. We shall first turn our attention to their social basis of membership.

Occupational bases

The formation of cliques in a work plant may often be explained in terms of occupational or technical distinctions among the workers. Those who have similar occupations tend to form status groups with informal membership rules. This is especially the case where workers have highly developed skills or craft. Cottrell's study of the railroader documents the importance of occupation in the informal groupings and work relationships on the job.[27] He describes how a regular status hierarchy, from firemen, engineers, and brakemen down to repairmen and section hands, controls group membership and customary behavior on the job. Although the clerks, station agents, and traffic department representatives have high white-collar status, they are not considered by others to be in the railroad craft. Pullman conductors, although in the craft, are not considered to be "regular" trainmen.

Sometimes very small job distinctions are singled out as the basis for group identification. Whyte's study of social groupings within the restaurant industry indicates that those who work with fish have lower rank than those who work with meat. Workers who specialize very slightly in the preparation of certain foods form cliques which are antagonistic toward cliques of other food "specialists."[28] The differences in function between professional

---

[27] W. Fred Cottrell, *The Railroader,* Stanford, 1940, especially chap. 3, "Technological and Social Groupings."

[28] Whyte, *op. cit.,* chap. 4, "Status in the Kitchen."

ranks in colleges are minimal, yet sufficiently large to furnish bases for group affiliation.

In addition to occupation, or in place of it, the social bases of informal group membership may be age, nationality, seniority, regional origin, or other factors. Solidarity arising from these ties may then be expressed through occupational pride, exchanging jobs, and mutual aid.

Let us examine the role of occupation in the formation of the informal groups portrayed in Fig. 7.3. There we have located five major cliques, three sub-cliques, and three friendship pairs. The inspectors, pressmen, and clique 4 (assemblers) form occupationally homogeneous groups, and so do one sub-clique and two friendship pairs (assemblers). However, cliques 1 and 5 and two sub-cliques cross job lines. Other factors besides technical distinctions on the job are responsible for social groupings because people in the same occupation often belong to different groups.

Spatial or ecological factors

Space may be an important factor in the formation of cliques. The first requisite of a group is communication, and the most rapid communication arises from face-to-face contact. Although daily face-to-face contacts need not occasion intimacy, they will lead to interaction over and above that required by sociotechnical relations. This is especially the case where physical mobility on the job is limited. If those who work next to each other perform similar jobs, interaction is facilitated, but it will usually occur regardless of occupational specialization.

Thus in Fig. 7.3 the inspectors regarded themselves as socially superior and expressed their solidarity by eating together, going to movies, riding to work together, and going to the washroom in pairs. However, they also participated in cliques 1 and 5 as well. These two cliques, clique 4, and the sub-cliques and friendship pairs appear to be based on proximity.

Since sociotechnical interaction was necessary between inspectors and assemblers, cliques containing both assemblers and inspectors developed. In these, inspectors tended to become the informal leaders for they initiated such activities as birthday parties, lunch trading, shopping sprees, and mutual aid.

It is difficult to ascertain what groups would form naturally on the basis of physical proximity alone. The arrangement

of walls, machines, and production technique is rarely so constituted as to force a particular nucleation. In Fig. 7.3, for example,
some of the members in the pressmen's clique and the sub-clique
of clique 5 belonged in other departments. The pressmen were
the only men in the department in question. They received higher
pay and had more status than the women. They ate lunch together
and engaged in recreation activities with men in other departments.

Where status and other social differences are not great, spatial
proximity plays a more important role in the process of group
making. Over a period of time, spatial recognition may be granted
to social cohesion. Thus, the older workers tend to locate near
each other, as do members of ethnic groups, races, neighborhood
cliques, and others. Once recognition is attached to a given location ("that's where the old-timers hang out"), space becomes an
important social item around which sentiments and attitudes are
formed.

Status or prestige elements[29]

It is characteristic of prestige to adhere to almost any personal
or social attribute in or out of the plant. As a consequence, informal groups tend to be ranked in terms of their prestige differences. The cliques in Fig. 7.3 were ranked in prestige in the
following order. From high to low:

> Pressmen—clique 2
> Inspectors—clique 3
> Old girls—clique 1
> Italian girls—clique 4
> Love-doves—north center sub-clique
> High school crowd—clique 5
> Old hens—northeast sub-clique

Extra-plant indices

The bases of status distinctions arise from both internal (plant)
differences and external (extra-plant) factors. In the headlight
factory occupational rank, an internal plant factor was the basis
of the prestige of the two highest cliques. Seniority was the basis
for solidarity in clique 1. Nationality, being in love, coming from

[29] This subject is treated in detail in Chapter 12, "Status and Prestige in
the Work Organization."

the same high school, and being old married women seem to be the ties in the remaining cliques. Although these social characteristics are not directly related to plant operation, they are important in determining status groups within the plant. The workers themselves do not distinguish between plant and extraplant personal and social attributes when they rank one another informally. This fact may be documented with an illustration:

General Motors has a large parts plant located in the outskirts of a middle-sized city in New York State. Its workers are recruited from the city and from the rural fringe. Residence seems to be fundamental in the formation of cliques in the plant. Those from the rural fringe associate with each other, discuss their farms, sell the produce they raise, vote Republican, and avoid criticism of management. They are regarded as "squares" by the urban cliques. The latter engage in recreational activities, sports talk, and drinking. There is no union in this plant, and questions of raises, promotions, and other squabbles are more closely related to the rural-urban origin of the participants than to other conditions.

Other "outside" factors may underlie nucleation or cleavages in the informal organization of industry. Some of these factors include membership in a car pool, personal compatibility, religious or organizational affiliation, political beliefs, social class origin, occupational aspiration, ethnic or racial background. Several studies have been made which demonstrate the force of special social factors in formation of informal groups.[30]

Multiple factors

More than one factor usually underlies group formation or cleavages. Nationality, seniority, technical skill, and attitude toward unions may operate simultaneously to form a group. Group members are rarely homogeneous in respect to all social indices. Thus, in Fig. 7.3 one girl in the Italian clique was of Scotch origin, a "new" girl was included in the "old bunch," and so on.

Common social background may be important in bringing people together, but the common experiences which mold a set of attitudes, sentiments, and customs on the job become increas-

[30] Hughes, *op. cit.;* Collins, *op. cit.,* Leslie D. Zeleny, "Selection of Compatible Flying Partners," *American Journal of Sociology,* March, 1947.

ingly important with time. After a group is formed, a person is admitted or expelled from it depending on his acceptance or rejectance of the group's sentiments and customs. The demographic characteristics of the group may change, but it is still the same group as long as the sentiments and customs persist in an atmosphere of personal and social compatibility. A group may remain intact despite the incompatibility of some of its members, but it is no longer a clique in the strict sense of the word.

Relating Cliques

If the above view of informal organization were abandoned at this point we would have a distorted and biased picture of it. Many students have tended to equate clique organizations with informal organization. They have been so engrossed with the importance of the small group that they have become small-group cultists. One almost suspects that they crave to rediscover the small sentiment-bound groups that may have been more extensive in a bygone era. Some "progressive" managers, when informed about the pervasiveness of clique organization, have considered reordering production to encourage small groups at the expense of large ones. Their thought is that it may be easier to manipulate smaller cliques than large formal groups, such as the union.

Both students and administrators should realize that a giant sociogram of the clique structure of a plant would still constitute an incomplete picture of the plant's informal organization. Although the diagram would show that groups and cliques were related, it would not show *how* they were related. The social bonds or lack of them among the cliques must be *qualitatively* studied to determine their significance.

In Fig. 7.3 several cliques were located. They might have been located quickly by merely asking people whom they preferred to work with, and then plotting all of their choices. But this would not have meant much without knowledge of the existing social situation. Cliques may reflect antagonistic relations between groups. They may, on the other hand, merely point to a haphazard distribution of congeniality groups. After all, there is a limit to the number of people that can go to lunch together, converse, or play cards.

When cliques do not reflect rivalry, antagonisms, or divisions of sociability, greater significance may reside in interclique relations. The important social fact is that cliques may be segments of larger groups which remain unrevealed by typical sociometric questions. Thus a sociogram of the clique structure of a plant may not reveal the presence of larger informally organized publics. The significances of cliques in a particular factory may be that they represent the cell structure of a nascent labor union. In this case clique integration is more important than the knowledge of independent cliques, for the cliques here represent a communication system and not internal group cleavages. The question must always be raised, Do cliques represent cleavages or integration? If no sentiments tie the cliques together, a plant does not have an informal organization in the full sense of the term. It has only a bunch of cliques incapable of uniting for or against management or labor on any issue. Administrations need not "worry" so much about the existence of cliques as they might about the integration of cliques.

Cliques and issues

The technique of locating cliques is based upon knowledge of association patterns such as eating, work trading, car pool participation, talking, friendship, and visiting. An intensive analysis of cliques may show that in some cases these indices are not sensitive to other social relations within the cliques. Many people who eat together, ride to work together, and trade jobs are not congenial or compatible. In fact, they may despise each other, argue incessantly, and fight over many issues. Such nucleations, then, are not congeniality groups but patterns of association.

An overintensive concentration on cliques may blind the investigator to issues which are broader than locality cliques. The important issues in the plant may be union organization, seniority systems, retirement plans, and recreational programs. Some cliques may be split internally on these issues, some may be internally united, some people from various cliques may unite on an issue. In the last case the workers are part of a *public* scattered all over the plant. They would not appear as a clique in a sociogram. Publics may be more important in some instances than congeniality groups or cliques. The activities of the public may explain what happens both within the plant and within the cliques.

This is especially the case when cliques are amorphous nuclei which break and re-form with changing issues and problems. Cliques form and shatter quickly when large numbers of people are being formally organized into a union or a pressure group. After a period the cliques may stabilize and become polarized. They then may exhibit social stratification, division of labor, "foreign" relations, and other attributes. Cliques should be analyzed also for their degree of integration and persistence. They may be tightly knit all-purpose cliques, tightly knit one-purpose cliques, or loosely knit all- or one-purpose cliques.

Five clique types

Dalton has identified five clique types which he calls the *vertical symbiotic clique, vertical parasitic clique, horizontal defensive clique, horizontal aggressive clique,* and the *random clique.*

1. The vertical symbiotic clique arises when a top officer is concerned to aid and protect some of his subordinates. He does this by concealing or minimizing their errors, occasional lapses, etc. He tries to build up their standing and interprets their behavior favorably to critical members of the department or in the organization generally. The subordinates respond by advising him of real or rumored threats to his position. They keep him informed of current work situations and discuss ways of dealing with "troublemakers" outside of the clique. Thus for all parties in the clique there is a satisfying exchange of services. Although dissimilar interests are at stake, each party comes to depend upon the other. Thus the name, "vertical symbiotic clique," refers to a vertically organized informal structure with the parties locked in mutual aid relationship.[31]

2. The vertical parasitic clique arises when a top officer is put in a position where lower-ranked persons receive more than they give and, indeed, may greatly damage the higher officer. This can occur when the lower-ranked persons are linked by kinship or some friendship ties to the top officer so that they are placed in a parasitic position. The top officer is obliged to make concessions because of his ties to the subordinates. The belief that these

[31] Dalton, *op. cit.,* p. 57.

"favorites" will get special advantages inspires fear in their associates. They hide things from the favored members so that the latter are unable to send favors up in the same degree as those which they receive. The higher official is not in a position to secure a fair return. And it may so work out that he will face a full-scale revolt among the less favored subordinates who decide to fight for equal advantages.

3. The horizontal defensive clique, arising in response to some crisis, cuts across departments to include officers of nearly the same rank. A threatened reorganization, introduction of a disliked top official, or the installation of some control mechanism are all typical conditions that bring on a crisis. Usually the clique is strong for only the limited time necessary to defeat or adjust to a threat.

4. The horizontal aggressive clique is brought into being by a cross-departmental drive to effect changes rather than resist them, to redefine responsibility or even directly shift it. The goal may be to get increased operating allowances, to check the expansion of some staff group, or to advance some member to a higher post so he can help the clique.

5. The random clique forms on the basis of friendship and social satisfaction. Its members usually cannot be classified in terms of formal rank, duties, or departmental origin. As a rule the members do not fit happily into their jobs or the informal activities about them. They would like to escape the confusion and boredom of their life. As a result they get away from their jobs when possible to indulge in unguarded talk about people and events. They learn few if any important secrets because of the barriers between them and the more important functional cliques. They do transmit small gossip providing points of leak from the functional groups as well as a source of information for them. In this way random cliques intensify informal activities in the organization.

The study of cliques within formal organizations is important because it is the operation of the formal structure that may give meaning to clique *functions*. Many cliques and publics would not be created were it not for the "need" for them inherent in the formal policies of union and management leaders. Poor formal organization often forces cliques to arise, so that the job may be done. In addition, cliques may communicate with each other through the channels provided by formal organization. The interaction of formal and informal organization is as critical an area of study as are the activities of either organization.

THE WORK CULTURE OF INFORMAL ORGANIZATIONS[32]

Every persistent group, including occupational and industrial groups, tends to develop a peculiar pattern of behavior. A newcomer to a work group is often made painfully aware of the fact that learning the job is only part of what he has to know to get along. The mature worker has assimilated the local culture so completely that he is often unaware that new workers are expected to conform to a rigid set of behavior patterns. Only the "greenhorn" and the individualist make him aware that he has learned something that others need to know.

The culture of informal work groups is varied, and may be learned only by studying local situations. However, an outline of the content and structure of work culture may be made for groups of similar social background. In this section we shall focus primarily on the work culture of manual employees. One thing that is a constant in work culture, irrespective of situation, is the culture and customs surrounding particular occupations.

Occupational Culture

Each new job does not require the employee to learn a new set of customs, traditions, rituals, and beliefs. Many of the customs practiced in particular work situations may be found existing elsewhere. An experienced railroader, carpenter, thief, or college professor has learned the folkways of his group. He knows how a "proper" railroader, thief, or carpenter should behave, and acts accordingly. His induction into a new work situation will be relatively rapid and easy, for "he knows the ropes and the score."

Apart from the fact that the experienced employee knows the occupational culture, he is also aware that no two work groups are exactly alike. On entering a new one, he is careful to find out

---

[32] All the material in this section applies equally well to management organization.

"the way things are done here." He does not act without thinking; he asks leading questions; he "feels out" the group until he finds out or is told what the local culture is. The neophyte, on the other hand, must learn not only the occupational culture but local culture as well.

Much of occupational culture concerns technical operations on the job. A novice may be noticed because he does his work exactly as he was taught. An experienced employee often violates the theoretical pattern of work routines. He has learned, or was taught on the job, certain short cuts, acceptable alternative routines, needless elaboration or refinement on some parts of the job, older manual processes now only rarely used, skills of closely related jobs, and other things.

Occupational Language

Part of the occupational culture is the development of jargon and a technical language and argot. Jargon is developed more extensively among highly skilled workers because "everyday language" does not contain words that refer to objects and occurrences at work. Listening to chemists, sociologists, toolmakers, or auto mechanics "talking shop" soon convinces the observer that he has to learn a new language to understand them.

The words that are substitutes for ordinary traditional words constitute an occupational argot.[33] Sometimes the argot has a semitechnical use—as an abbreviation for a longer phrase—but it also has a social function of identifying group members and creating social cohesion. The armed services have developed both a technical vocabulary and an argot. The words "floor," "ceiling," "walls," "toilet," "right and left hand" are common words with rather exact referents. But the navy insisted its argot be used: "deck," "overhead," "bulkheads," "head," "starboard" and "port." All cohesive groups tend to develop an argot, and work groups are no exceptions.[34]

Railroadmen have a colorful occupational language. Below is a sample. How much of it can you translate?

[33] Moore, *op. cit.*, p. 283.

[34] Teen-age "jive talk," student lingo, and talk of fraternal societies exemplify this fact. For collections of occupational argots see Cottrell, *op. cit.*, chap. 7, "Railroad Language," and Glossary; Edwin H. Sutherland (ed.), *The Professional Thief*, University of Chicago Press, 1937, especially Glossary.

At 3 P.M. Mott Haven Yard was a busy place. A crew of gandy dancers tamped methodically on a frog near the switching lead. L.S. 3 was all made up and ready to be doubled over. She had forty-six hog racks on the head end and sixty-five empty reefers on the hind end. Her crew were all new men on the run. Mike Madigan, the hog-head, had just been set up. Bill Blanchard, the fire-boy, was a boomer who had recently hired out. Jack Lewis, the brains of the outfit, had been a no bill since he was fired out of the Snakes for violating Rule "G." Brady Holms, the flagman, used to work the high iron in a monkey suit, and J. B. Wells was a "stu" brakeman, right off the street. Over on the hump lead, the yard rats were riding 'em in the clear and tying 'em down. The east side switcher was kicking loaded hoppers around, despite the violent washouts of the yardmixer who had discovered a hot box. Two Malleys were on the plug and three more were at the coal pocket. Our train, Number B.D. 5, was all ready to pull out. We were running light today with a few gondolas and twenty loaded westerns next to the buggy. Old Yellow Light gave us a highball and the tower gave us a ninety board on the high road. We slowly rolled out of Mott Haven.[35]

Some students have mistakenly included swearing or obscene language as part of the occupational language. Abundant blasphemy tends to be characteristic of male lower-class workers irrespective of occupation. Swearing is normal in their speech patterns both at work and outside of work. Although schools train students in the middle-class mode of nonswearing, swearing is consistent

[35] From a report from Fred A. McGlone. The translation runs as follows:

At 3 P.M. Mott Haven Yard was a busy place. A section crew worked methodically on a frog near the switching track. A frog is the point where the two rails come together on a crossover track. A westbound freight train, Number L.S. 3, was made up on two tracks and was getting ready to double over. It had forty-six hog cars next to the engine and the rest of the train consisted of sixty-five empty refrigerator cars. Its crew consisted of all new men on the run. Mike Madigan, the engineer, had recently been promoted from fireman to his present job. Bill Blanchard, the fireman, was a seasonal worker who had only three months' seniority. Jack Lewis, the conductor, had not belonged to the Brotherhood since he had been fired out of the Switchmen's Union for drinking. Brady Holms, the flagman, worked on the main line as a passenger brakeman at one time. J. B. Wells was a student brakeman and this was his first run. Over on the hill track, the yard brakemen were riding the cars and putting hand brakes on them. The east side switcher was shuffling loaded coal cars around, despite the stop motions of the yardmaster, who had discovered a smoking wheel. Two freight engines were on the water plug and three more were at the coal pocket. Our train, Number B.D. 5, was all ready to pull out. We had a small train today that consisted of twenty loaded cars next to the caboose, plus a few low-sided gondolas. The switchman gave us a "go ahead" motion, and the towerman gave us a clear signal for the main line. We slowly rolled out of Mott Haven.

behavior outside of school and at work. However, it soon loses much of its emotional context. It becomes a class mark, or a mark of social acceptance.[36] In the army, lumber camp, men's club, and in other all-male groups swearing is an intimate part of communication.

Each class tends to develop a characteristic vocabulary which it uses in many situations. It is easy to overestimate the meaningfulness or importance of this class vocabulary. In many instances swearing has no emotional connotations, just as polite language among middle-class working people may have little significance. "Thank you," "You're welcome," "please," "if you don't mind," "I beg your pardon" are hackneyed, well-worn middle-class phrases which serve as convenient bridges or terminations to conversation. Being courteous is part of middle-class culture, just as swearing tends to be characteristic of lower-class male culture. The meaning of politeness or swearing depends upon the situation. Being icily polite may convey as much aggression as swearing violently.

The hypothesis of Whiting Williams, that swearing on the part of lower-class people is a form of aggression against prescribed moral vocabulary of the community, needs to be tested. The same applies to the hypothesis that swearing is a response to conditions of tension and frustration.[37]

Technical language, argot, and class vocabulary are inextricably woven into a pattern of speaking. A worker who is fully integrated into the work group and its culture must literally know how to talk to be fully acculturated in the group.

There are other aspects of occupational acculturation, such as the development of a distinctive garb, sharing specific attitudes toward other occupational groups, engaging in unique initiation devices, sharing similar economic, political, and social sentiments. Wherever members of a particular occupation go, they carry this culture with them. Knowing the culture of a particular occupational group enables the scientist to predict large areas of informal behavior in many work situations.

[36] This is an explanation offered by Whiting Williams. See his *What's on the Workers' Mind*, Scribner, 1921.

[37] *Ibid*. See also Norman Mailer, *The Naked and the Dead*, Rinehart, 1948, for a realistic presentation of swearing in the army and the relation of swearing to conditions of tension.

Data on occupational cultures do not provide complete information on work culture for at least two important reasons. First, many work groups are composed of members of different occupations. When they interact, new behavior patterns arise. Occupational cultures seem to flourish best in relative isolation. Second, the occupational culture of semiskilled workers is not as unique or as clearly demarcated as are the cultures of the crafts and the professions. Both of these factors push the investigator into a study of specific work groups in specific social situations. Here the student should concentrate on the local culture, which contains the ceremonies, myths, rituals, and informal activities of the group.

Ceremonies and Rituals

Rituals and ceremonies are a form of prescribed and elaborated behavior which occur as culture traits and which are extraneous from the technological point of view.[38] Sometimes they are formal in nature, such as the presentation of awards at company banquets. However, many ceremonies and rituals arise informally in local work groups. They are important because they may reveal the basic ideas and beliefs of the group better than do other cultural traits.

Initiation rites are not restricted to primitive people and fraternal orders. The novice to a work group may be asked to get a left-handed monkey wrench, a glass saw, a diamond sharpener, or other nonexistent tools. This is done to impress him with his ignorance and "greenness" on the job. The new worker is often required to run errands and to do favors for the group members. At the same time he may be subjected to continual verbal abuse—"ribbing" and "razzing." Even the experienced worker is ridiculed and razzed sometimes. The object of this abuse is to test the individual's resourcefulness, his attitude toward the group, and his willingness to share group sentiments. It is part of the process of social induction which, if successful, marks the group acceptance of the individual. The induction process is complete when the individual practices with no self-consciousness the rituals of the group, when he believes in its myths and sentiments,

[38] Ruth Benedict, "Ritual," *Encyclopedia of the Social Sciences,* Macmillan. 1930.

and above all when he participates in the induction of other new-comers.

When workers change jobs (promotion, demotion, or firing) or when they retire, they often participate in a *rite of passage*. The rite may be nothing more than shaking hands with all members, receiving a gift, making a speech, or having a party. It may take the form of joking, giving advice, or backslapping. Nonetheless, there is a group compulsion to do something to indicate the termination of a relationship. The significance of the ritual varies somewhat with the situation. The function of the ritual may be to manifest group identification and loyalty, to ease the process of separation from the group, to emphasize the finality of the social rupture, or merely to indicate that all past animosities are forgiven and forgotten.

The rites of passage that occur in the community are often also observed in the office or factory. Engagement, marriage, birth of children, and death are observed with appropriate ceremony. Holidays and other events which occur periodically are the occasion for rites of intensification.[39] These rites are very important for they maintain, reinforce, and express feelings of solidarity in the group. They also symbolize the common values.

Rites of intensification are ceremonies which demonstrate the essential unity of the group. They may be quite simple, such as the custom of meeting before work in the locker room, exchanging greetings, pleasantries, and gossip. Other rites which are less frequently observed may provide greater emotional satisfaction. These may be the annual picnic, going to the opening night baseball game, stopping for a beer on the way home, celebrating Christmas or New Year's by holding a "spontaneous party" in the plant.

An inspector in an eastern radio factory, who was not fully accepted into his work group, inadvertently explained the function of such a rite when he said,

> You know, I cannot understand the fellows at the plant. All year long they argue and stab each other in the back. You can't imagine the swearing, fighting, and arguing that goes on all year long. Come the day before New Year's and everything is lovey-dovey. Today we didn't

[39] See Eliot D. Chapple and Carleton S. Coon, *Principles of Anthropology*, Holt, 1942, chap. 21, "Rites of Intensification."

do more than two hours' work. About ten o'clock the bottle was passed around. It was gone in no time. Then somebody sneaked out and got a couple of fifths. By noon everybody was happy. Where the food came from I don't know—but everybody spent the rest of the day eating and drinking, and having fun I suppose. . . . About an hour before quitting time everybody started to walk around and shout. Everybody was kissing everyone else. Old enemies were shaking hands and wishing each other Happy New Year. Come Monday everybody will feel pretty good toward the other fellow. Inside of a week they'll be cussing and stabbing each other in the back. I can't stand that kind of hypocrisy. Either a guy is your friend all the time or he isn't. The hell with this, "Happy New Year's, George" one day and "You s.o.b." the next.

The function of this ceremony was to restore the equilibrium of the group that had been disturbed by conflicts during the year. It was an expression of fundamental unity and belongingness. This and other rites reinforced the habitual relations within the group.

Conversation and Gossip

A great deal of the time of an integrated work group is spent in talking and gossiping. As suggested above, talk should be analyzed to know the interests and sentiments of the group. The content and variety of gossip depend upon the sociocultural background of the group and its own peculiar traditions.

All groups spend some time talking about work itself—quality of materials, technical problems, bottlenecks, production quotas, pay rates, qualities of the supervisors, union and company issues. The generalization may be made that the higher the skill, the more talk about technical problems of work. Skilled workers and professionals tend to talk more about their work than semiskilled and unskilled workers.

Although the manner in which it is discussed varies, sex is a common subject of conversation among all groups. Managers and executives often tell sex jokes of different degrees of sophistication. Personal sex experiences and relations are tabooed subjects for most middle-class people. Female white-collar workers also discuss sex problems and sexual irregularities, but crude sex jokes and personal experiences are kept at a minimum. Male manual workers discuss sex more freely and openly than other groups. They hold sex jokes at a premium, and often relate their own intimate sexual affairs with wives or paramours. Their sophistication about sex amazes some observers, but it is merely the extension of street-corner life and conversation into the plant. The hypothesis that "poverty of social experience" and general dissatisfaction with working conditions is responsible for this preoccupation with sex,[40] is untenable. Other subjects of conversation compete successfully with sex in all social levels of the plant.

For example, in management circles much of the talking concerns politics of promotion, household purchases, material acquisitions, and achievements of children. Women workers discuss clothing, family problems, dates, and the usual gossip. Manual workers, on the other hand, discuss politics, parties, drinking, and above all, recreation and sports. Interest in the latter arises naturally from the sports activities of the younger members outside the plant. But interest is also exhibited by nonplayers and by older members as well. "How did they do?" "How did they come out?" These questions can only refer to one thing—the performance of the home team in the last game.

All day long the discussion of sports continues—which is the best team in which league, the prospects of rookies, comparative scores, past glories of heroes and teams, the prospects of the coming season, and personal sports experiences. The amount of lore and knowledge about sports that many workers have is encyclopedic. Some employers have capitalized on this interest by providing sports and recreational facilities at the plant.

Myths and Beliefs

An analysis of the content of the conversations reveals that workers create myths, folklore, and fictions about their work situations. This is not surprising, since man is a myth maker wherever he is.[41] He mixes freely and unconsciously his factual knowledge, ideas, opinions, beliefs, and mythology into a system of thought (ideology) which guides his perception of all social situations. In order to understand and predict his behavior, then, the observer should be aware of this system of thought. An exploration of the

---

[40] Williams, *op. cit.*, pp. 303–305.
[41] Read Bain, "Man, the Myth Maker," *Scientific Monthly*, July, 1947, pp. 61–69.

content and function of folklore and mythology is especially useful because it discloses the basic ideals and sentiments which
motivate and make meaningful daily behavior.

An analysis of the thought system of people in all levels of the
supervisory structure reveals that all are about equally suggestible
to myth thinking and making. Nowhere is there more mythology
in management thinking than in the area of human relations.
Any serious student of industry is conversant with some of these
fictions of management. For example: workers are indolent, lazy,
and try to get away with everything; they respond only to economic motivations; they are emotional and animal-like; they will
follow any rabble-rousing leader. Workers in turn maintain fictions about bosses: they care only for profits; they are heartless;
they resort to subterfuge whenever possible. These fictions become
part of the tradition which guides behavior.

Since myths and folklore are elaborate and enduring, they must
have important functions to serve. One such function is the dramatic symbolization of group ideals and values. Tales about the
tremendous output or production of a mythical character persist
among many skilled groups. One young bricklayer perpetuated
such a myth when he mused,

> You know I'm not much good in the afternoons. None of us are, I
> guess. We're not as tough as the old folks. I can remember as a kid
> when old John Kiddy was building a house next door to us. One Satur-
> day morning him and his old lady decided to lay the north wall of the
> house. The old lady mixed the mud and John laid the bricks. You
> should of seen the old man work—he was seventy years old then. He was
> a demon—not a useless move—just laying row after row without a min-
> ute's rest. The old lady kept right up with him. By two o'clock they had
> her done. After cleaning up they went to a square dance. Yes sir, John
> Kiddy worked with my father's gang until he was eighty-five. Guess we
> ain't like the old folks. Just too soft.

Such a myth serves to fortify the important value of skill and
individual achievement. When other values threaten the place of
skill in determining status, the story is repeated, especially by
those who want to abide by the old order. Myths of this type may
even be fabricated to perpetuate a desired end.

The myth is an important factor in social adjustment. To know
what role it plays in the group one must know the values and
aspirations of the members, as well as their problems and frustra-

tions. For example, in an industrial structure where individual achievement is glorified but where promotion is rare, the myth may provide rationalizations for failure to climb. In such cases the myth may play a therapeutic role. Richard R. Myers has presented several illustrations in an important article.

In a Grand Rapids furniture concern, among the furniture craftsmen where the Dutch-Americans constitute a dominant group, the myth has it that one cannot become a supervisor without a good Dutch name. However, the records show supervisors with Jewish and South European names, some of long standing and some of more recent promotions. Similarly, interviews in a Detroit automotive parts manufacturing concern indicated a well developed belief among workers of Polish extraction that management regards "Hamtramck Poles" as trouble-makers and undesirable as supervisory types. Careful check, however, indicated that management proportionately employed more foremen of Polish background than of any other ethnic antecedents. *This myth is a reflection of the general self-consciousness and a sense of persecution which many Polish-Americans have in Detroit, and represents a device for easing personal frustration in a competitive situation.*[42]

All work groups have myths about themselves and about other groups with which they interact. Some myths function to preserve group values, some "explain" the social system, some maintain morale; others are fabricated consciously by leaders to achieve certain ends.[43]

Informal Activities

Much activity of an informal nature goes on in most work groups. Apparently technical behavior and union participation are rarely so arranged as to provide people with sufficient and satisfactory social relationships. They invariably devise social activities of all kinds to relieve the boredom of monotonous work, to obtain release from job tensions, to compensate for unsatisfactory social relationships, or to fulfill an endless variety of social demands.

The range of informal activities is enormous, for it varies with the cultural background of the workers. Much of it seems to be recreational in nature, such as gambling, horseplay, practical joking, smoking, and singing. However, conflict behavior is also

[42] "Myth and Status System in Industry," *Social Forces*, March, 1948, p. 335. Italics ours.
[43] *Ibid.*

evident, as fighting, politicking, and sabotage. Other behavior seems to be merely an expression of group living, such as lunching, trading jobs, loaning money, and forming a car pool. At first most of this activity may appear as random, haphazard responses of individuals to chance situations. Closer observation reveals that much of it is organized by the group to satisfy the recurrent demands in the work culture.

An illustration may be presented to elaborate this idea. A research committee in a college faculty group held weekly meetings to criticize the work being done and to develop plans for future research. Owing to the nature of the work, it was difficult for individuals to take full credit or blame for group achievements. Yet criticism and responsibility had to be placed somewhere if a good research report was to be issued. Although each member held all of the others in high respect, differences in opinion did develop. Incessant arguments occurred over the future direction of research, the interpretation of data, and the division of labor.

Two quasi-recreational activities arose as a response to the tension in these situations. The first occurred before the meetings. It took the form of verbal repartee, joking, razzing, humorous threats, boasting, and general hilarity. In the midst of this hilarity the chairman would suggest that the group get down to work. After a few jibes in his direction, work would actually begin in earnest.

At the end of the often exhausting and sometimes bitter sessions, the group would adjourn for an hour to a coffee shop across the street, where they would eat a snack, smoke a cigarette, and drink coffee. At the tables the antagonists would usually sit next to each other and continue their discussion. After a time attention turned to stories, daily incidents, and jokes. Invariably, by the time the group left the coffee shop differences were settled and agreements were made.

The functions of these quasi-recreational activities before and after the meetings were to maintain and restore group equilibrium. The joking had the effect of setting an atmosphere conducive to good will for the following period of tension. The coffee ritual had the effect of restoring mutual confidence and respect among the antagonists. As long as the group engaged in these activities it remained an effective research team.

Variations in this ritual are common. Among manual workers horseplay, work play, and practical joking are substitutes for verbal repartee. Giving the hotfoot, squirting water, and putting salt in coffee are examples of such work play. More techniques are developed to fit the situation. Machines are jammed, meters are decalibrated, tools are broken, and materials are hidden.

Although everyone, at one time or another, may be subjected to practical joking, some individuals are more frequently elected than others. The man who cannot "take" it, the member who gets "too big for his britches," and the low-status person often lead a miserable existence until they conform to group standards or leave. Occasionally standardized punishments are evolved for those who violate group customs. In the bank wiring room of Western Electric workers "binged" (struck a hard blow on the shoulder) each other for swearing, overproducing, and telling poor jokes.[44]

Many other informal activities occur in work groups. Gambling, card playing, horse betting, lotteries, football pools, and dice attract largest participation. Various explanations have been offered for widespread gambling. To be sure, gambling may relieve monotony on the job, but so do other activities. Since not much money is exchanged in card playing, the economic incentive in gambling is not great, as it is in the lottery and pools. Loyalty to the latter may be explained by their integration of workers in the racketeering and gambling interests in the community.[45] Gambling is not generally considered immoral among workers because it is a part of their tradition, like smoking, drinking, and joking. The campaigns of management to eliminate such activites thus face resistances of all kinds. Elaborate systems of secret signals are created to warn gamblers of approaching bosses. In many instances foremen make only a pretense of enforcing company rules. In fact, they may even collaborate with the men, for they realize that enforcement of rules may be more trouble than it's worth. In the following section we shall explore in greater detail how informal groups adjust to the rules and regulations of management and labor.

[44] Roethlisberger and Dickson, *op. cit.*, pp. 421–423.
[45] William F. Whyte, *Street Corner Society,* University of Chicago Press, 1943, Part II, "Racketeers and Politicians."

In summary, the culture of informal groups is made up of occupational culture and the culture of the local groups. Beliefs, myths, folklore, and rituals occupy a central place in the work culture, for they provide clues to the dominant sentiments and attitudes of the groups. Activities such as gambling, recreation, and ceremonies not only express group sentiments but also serve as social control devices.

FUNCTIONS OF INFORMAL ORGANIZATIONS

Social scientists have been intrigued with the question of why informal organization arises and persists. It is now known that the persistence of informal organizations can be accounted for by the functions they serve. Four of major importance are: perpetuating informal group culture, maintaining a communication system, exerting social control, and providing interest and fun in work life.

Perpetuation of Culture

Groups arise and persist because they satisfy the social needs of their members. These "needs," of course, are culturally defined by the group and are only indirectly related to biological and psychological mechanisms. Thus anything may be a need if it is so defined by the group. Needs may include accumulation of wealth, glorification of service, continuation of hostility, and sacrifice to maintain group traditions. In addition, all groups feel a need to perpetuate themselves. This is so fundamental that it is only very rarely questioned. It is "natural," essential, and almost inevitable that, once groups arise, they do everything they can to perpetuate themselves. All customs, folkways, mores, rituals, traditions, folklore, and mythology are assumed to be important and necessary for the survival of the group. Nobody questions why a custom should persist; and if they do, the answer usually is "Because we've always done it this way and there's no need to change."

Thus one of the main functions of informal work organization is to maintain whatever its members have found satisfying. This means that new members must be inculcated with the group's prevailing sentiments and traditions. Only an adequate system of communication can achieve this end.

Maintenance of a Communication System

Once a group is established within an organization it wants all the information that might affect its welfare either positively or negatively. Not infrequently informal groups suspect that managers will act in such a way as to harm their members. They want to know ahead of time what those acts will be so that plans may be made to counteract them. Thus informal groups that are not appraised of the policies, motives, and intentions behind specific orders are not only suspicious but anxious to get information. They try to tap the formal line of communication. Once this is done, information spreads like wildfire through the informal network of communication. If information is unavailable, the workers conjure up motives and discuss them. After this a pattern of action is planned to resist or encourage the anticipated policies of union or management administrators.

Since the informal communication system (the grapevine) is so intimately connected with formal organizations, it is easy to understand why it is virtually impossible to maintain secret plans or policies. Since chains of friendship span the entire work organization, the formal communication system is invariably tapped, after which it is impossible to stop the spread of news, unless another item is dropped purposely into the hopper to counteract previous leaks.

Four patterns of grapevine communication

The grapevine is more flexible than the formal organization channel. There are four different ways of visualizing it, as Fig. 7.4 indicates:

1. The single-strand chain—A tells B, who tells C, who tells D, and so on; this makes for a tenuous chain to a distant receiver. Such a chain is usually in mind when one speaks of how the grapevine distorts and filters information until the original item is not recognizable.
2. The gossip chain—A seeks and tells everyone else.
3. The probability chain—A communicates randomly, say to F and D, in accordance with the laws of probability; then F and D tell others in the same manner.
4. The cluster chain—A tells three selected others; perhaps one

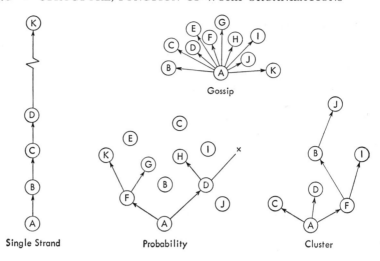

FIG. 7.4. Types of Communication Chains. (From Keith Davis, "Management Communication and the Grapevine," *Harvard Business Review*, September–October, 1953.)

of them tells two others; and then one of these two tells one other.[46]

Davis learned from each communication recipient how he first received a given piece of information and then traced it back to its source. His research, carried out in a factory for the manufacture of leather goods, revealed a predominance of the cluster chain. This means that only a few of the persons who knew a unit of information ever transmitted it. All others who received the information did not transmit it; they acted merely as passive receivers.

Secret sharing on the grapevine

Figure 7.5 illustrates how a secret traveled through the informal communication network of a radio station until almost everyone was informed.[47] The president and the general manager of the

---

[46] Keith Davis, "Management Communication and the Grapevine," *Harvard Business Review*, September–October, 1953. Cf. Delbert C. Miller, "Research Note on Mass Communication, How Our Community Heard about the Death of President Roosevelt," *American Sociological Review*, October, 1945, pp. 691–694.

[47] From a report by Robert M. Hallberg, University of Washington.

radio station planned to make a change that would affect all the personnel. This plan was supposed to be a secret until it was consummated. However, the program director was taken into their confidence. The president then told the studio engineer and the station attorney about the plan and pledged them to secrecy. While the general manager was confiding the secret to the secretary, the accountant dropped in and overheard it. He did not realize the full significance of the secret. In the meantime, the program director confided in the operations director, who told the secretary, who already knew. The studio engineer also told the secretary, who later reported it to the participant observer. The complete circuit of secret sharing may be traced in Fig. 7.5. Note how this secret sharing followed the cluster pattern.

It is just as important to know who doesn't participate in secret sharing and why. In the radio station, the general manager and the studio engineer did not like each other. For this reason the president did not tell the general manager that he had confided in the studio engineer. As a matter of fact, the president and the studio engineer always share secrets, as do the general manager and the secretary, as well as the program director and

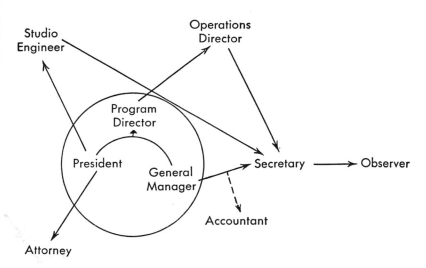

FIG. 7.5. How a Secret Traveled Through the Informal Communication Network of a Radio Station.

the operations director. The operations director only occasionally shares secrets with the secretary. The studio engineer shares secrets with the president. He rarely shares with anyone else, and on these rare occasions he tells the secretary. The latter usually shares secrets with the observer. The secret was, by the way, that a new general manager was being appointed.

A communication system, once it is established, functions to convey any information of interest to its members. Not only are official policies transmitted, but any news of interest. Baseball scores, results of horse races, news of sickness or death, political news, jokes, incidents, and just plain gossip circulate freely. It is the channel which functions to make and maintain public opinion in the plant. The "sudden resistance" that management often encounters when it makes "new" proposals on wages, hours, pensions, seniority, recreation, or other plans may be explained by the fact that these proposals have already leaked out and been thoroughly discussed. Thus it is often unnecessary for management or labor leaders to discuss things and "reason" with the workers. The latter have already discussed the matters and arrived at a consensus.

Informal communication—up or down?

The question as to which way most communication actually flows—up or down—has been given a surprising answer by research. The answer: generally up. The formal structure of an organization leads us to conceive of communication as a downward proposition. The focus of informal communication is directed upward. The concern is the standing of the worker with the "higher-ups." In one of the most original studies of this phenomenon, the University of Michigan Center for Group Dynamics used the device of planting rumors to trace the natural flow of communication. In an office of fifty people, seven "cooperators" agreed to note down every rumor they heard and the person who told it to them. Four or five rumors about the office were then planted. Nineteen rumor "transmissions" were picked up. Of these, thirteen were directed upward, four were directed to people on the same hierarchical levels, and only two went downward. It has been suggested that communication serves as a substitute for real upward mobility in the case of low-status persons.[48] All persons seem to secure a status satisfaction from an ability to be the first to communicate a prized bit of information to a higher-status person.

Informal communication roles

The communication functions of various persons may be divided into three relationships which appear to exist between individuals and the structure: (1) Some individuals have frequent, reciprocated, and important contacts with a limited number of other individuals, who in turn are closely interrelated and have few nonreciprocated and unimportant contacts outside of this group. (2) There are a few individuals who appear to be marginal to the organization in that their contacts in the organization are few in number, infrequent, and nonreciprocated. (3) Some individuals appear to function as "*liaison*" persons between groups and characteristically have many, frequent, reciprocated, and important contacts which cut across the contact group structure.[49] It has been said that he who is at the center of communication is at the center of power. One researcher has also found that he who is at the center of communication becomes a person of high status in the eyes of his group. Blau studied a government office and found that the relative number of contacts an agent received from his colleagues constituted the expression of their evaluation of his role in the group. Being approached often gave an agent a feeling of security in social situations which facilitated his interaction with outsiders as well as with members of his own group. Such an agent performed better by concentrating his energies upon the problems of his job.[50]

Social Control

One of the primary functions of informal social organization is social control. It is common knowledge that even the mere presence of other people influences or constrains behavior. Whenever informal organization exists (and only in very rare cases is

[48] Harold H. Kelley, "Communication in Experimentally Created Hierarchies," *Human Relations*, 1951, vol. 4, pp. 39–56; cf. Leon Festinger, "Informal Social Communication," *Psychological Review*, July, 1950, pp. 271–282.

[49] Eugene Jacobson and Stanley E. Seashore, "Communications Practice in Complex Organizations," *Journal of Social Issues*, Spring, 1951, p. 37.

[50] Peter Blau, "Patterns of Interaction Among a Group of Officials in a Government Agency," *Human Relations*, 1954, vol. 7, no. 3.

it absent), everyone feels some constraint on his freedom of action. Indeed, as Moore suggests, "The whole of informal organization seems to imply a substitution of group ends for competitive individual ends."[51] Since informal organization extends from the top to the bottom of the structure, it follows that everyone's behavior is somewhat informally controlled.

Informal organization is made up of many small though interconnected groups, operating within a formal structure. Therefore, from the point of view of the small individual groups social control is exerted (1) inwardly toward its own members and (2) outwardly toward other informal groups and toward the formal organizations.

Internal control

In general, social control is directed inward to make members conform to the culture of the group—its customs, ceremonies, rituals, and mythology. Conformity to the occupational and local work group culture is enforced by all the common techniques of ridicule, ostracism, and violence. Violation of even small rules may arouse a reaction against recalcitrant members.

An illustration will demonstrate this point. A straw boss of a gang of laborers wore an old cloth cap on the job. One day he appeared wearing a light-gray Stetson. The workers "razzed" him and asked him if he thought he was a big boss. He offered some excuse but reappeared the next day with the Stetson. Again the workers reacted, but more violently than on the previous day. On the third day the straw boss arrived on the job with his old hat. A similar negative reaction was directed against truck drivers who began to wear white shirts and ties on the job. In both cases, the workers accused the violators of going "high-hat." It is always possible for workers to impute motives to deviant behavior and find reasons why a custom should not be abandoned. It does not matter whether these motives are incorrect because group members feel that customs should be preserved.

Several rules of internal social control are found in almost all groups in industry. The most basic of these is the notion that each member should do his fair share of the work, especially where there is joint responsibility for output or service. In fact,

[51] Moore, *op. cit.*, p. 290.

where strong informal groups are present, there is no need for the foreman to enforce minimum standards of work. The group will do it for him, and much more effectively.[52] The instrument for enforcing conformity is often an elaborate set of expectations that have been called the indulgency pattern. This is a pattern of leniency in employee work activities practiced in the supervisor-employee work relationship. "Most workers expected that they were to 'do a job' and that there should be no constant check-up on you" and "When there is work to do they expect you to do it, but otherwise they leave you alone."[53]

They expected a "second chance"—that supervisors would warn workers before firing them and would listen to reasonable excuses for lateness. They expected opportunities to change their jobs within the plant, occasional use of company equipment and materials for home repairs, and special consideration in the event of injury while at work.

A broader interpretation of this concept of doing a fair share of work is found in the idea that no group member should profit at the expense of another member. Many specific informal rules demonstrate this principle. In seeking job advancements, for example, the group exerts pressure on its members to observe legitimate channels of promotion. Resort to favoritism, drag, or pull is regarded as disloyalty. In fact, any action is censured which operates to the detriment of the group.

It follows that reproach will be directed toward anyone who reduces a temporary or permanent advantage of the group, no matter how unfair that advantage may seem to be. Group loyalty is so highly valued that anyone who "squeals" is censured. This is particularly the case when someone gets away with violating a company policy. For example, the no-smoking rule is violated often by some groups, but not by others. Anyone, including the foreman, who reported this temporary or unfair advantage to higher management would be immediately censured, even by the nonsmokers.

This protection of the individual does not apply when the in-

[52] Roethlisberger and Dickson, *op. cit.;* Williams, *op. cit.*

[53] Alvin W. Gouldner, *Wildcat Strike*, Antioch Press, 1954, p. 19; Chris Argyris has called this the psychological work contract. See *Understanding Organizational Behavior*, Dorsey, 1960, p. 96, and described in Chapter 6, "Top, Middle, and First-Line Managerial Roles," of this text.

formal standards are violated. Vulnerable individuals and group advantages are protected only when the group interacts with the formal system. But the advantages that individuals or cliques have within the informal structure are generally disapproved.

External control

The control that informal groups exert over their members may be seen in their efforts to control the formal structures of management and labor. Management and union officer recognize that their plans, however carefully laid, are often violated or modified by the workers. Students have considered the problem of managing men, but they have neglected the problem of how the managed adjust to the efforts to manipulate them. It is inevitable that workers will try to adjust to or manage their managers.

Institutionalized evasion patterns have been carefully considered by a number of sociologists.[54] Merton has said that he believes such patterns arise when a cumulative stress situation appears in a social system. "You have to have the evasion as a kind of cushioning device; if you don't allow it something has to give and you're on the way to social change."[55]

One illustration of patterned evasion is found in the efforts of employees to restrict production. Although management's preoccupation with this subject is understandable, it displays their general ignorance of the total function of informal organization. That is, they see informal organization largely in the form of resistance and rarely in the form of assistance. Without the assistance of informal organization, formal organization would often be ineffective,[56] as is frequently the case when managers try to determine every detail in production. They are too far removed from production to envision many of the problems that arise. Yet frequently they give orders on the basis of presumed knowledge. If their orders were completely obeyed, confusion would result and production and morale would be lowered. In order to achieve

[54] For example, Robert Merton, Robin Williams, Talcott Parsons, Kingsley Davis, and others.

[55] Quoted from Charles P. Loomis and Zona K. Loomis, *Modern Social Theories,* Van Nostrand, 1961, p. 615.

[56] We are indebted to A. T. Hansen for the precise conceptualization of this problem.

the goals of the organization workers must often violate orders, resort to their own techniques of doing things, and disregard lines of authority. Without this kind of systematic sabotage much work could not be done. This unsolicited assistance in the form of disobedience and subterfuge is especially necessary to enable large bureaucracies to function effectively.

Restriction of production is commonly found at all levels irrespective of occupation.[57] It may be direct or indirect, sporadic or persistent, boss-ordered or spontaneous. In almost all cases it is related to the concept of a *fair day's work*. There is a group tendency to keep observable production within the capacity range of the average worker. Two important rules are, therefore, that the worker should not overproduce and be a "rate buster"; neither should he underproduce and be a "chiseler." Many illustrations may be found to demonstrate these group norms.

In a Michigan lumber yard the handling of lumber was standardized by the men. . . . The worker soon learned that he was expected to lift two pieces of a certain kind, one piece of another size, and so on. He felt that the standards specified about half what could have been handled comfortably. When pieces were small enough to handle alone he found that the other workers frowned on his picking a normal load. He was expected to handle about half the number of pieces which, when left to himself, he would have taken as a matter of course. This manner of handling was clearly a restrictive device worked out by the men themselves.[58]

Why restrictive productive practices persist even under almost perfect working conditions has puzzled many businessmen. Restriction in the face of good wages and adequate security provisions has led many researchers to conclude that workers are motivated by nonrational sentiments rather than logic. This position may appear reasonable to those unacquainted with the social and cultural life of workers.

In the first place, it is erroneous to feel that restriction is typical of manual workers alone. It is found among all workers. Secondly, workers restrict production because this is a part of their cultural tradition. Their collective experiences have taught them that it is

[57] See Stanley B. Mathewson, *Restriction of Output Among Unorganized Workers,* Viking, 1931; Donald Roy, "Quota Restriction and Goldbricking in a Machine Shop," *American Journal of Sociology,* March, 1952, pp. 427–442.
[58] Mathewson, *op. cit.,* p. 25.

not judicious to produce as much as they possibly can. Folk knowledge also provides reasons why they should restrict production.

The suspicion that workers have toward speedup schemes is a rational response to the tactics many employers have used in the past. The folklore of workers contains many stories of financial incentive plans that resulted in increased production with no increase in income. These stories are reinforced by the common notion that the employer profits from labor under any circumstances. Thus the worker feels that the more he puts out, the more the boss makes in proportion. Further, he believes that he always loses in the long run, because the boss's only motive is to have greater production for greater profit. Those ideas persist whether or not a labor union exists. Of course the presence of an organization functions to keep sentiments alive in a more systematic way.

To maintain his place in the group the worker must conform to these sentiments. The fear of being unemployed or under-employed further encourages restrictive practices. Even where there is plenty of work to do, the fear exists that this may not be the case in the future; so it is best to act in a uniform way. All efforts must be made to protect the job. The following illustrates a common occurrence in many factories:

In a tube-making plant in New Jersey it ordinarily took the machinists four days to set up a new job. One particular job was not completed after a full week's work. Scrap and other costs were running high. The night foreman casually asked McCarthy if he wanted to try his hand on the problem. Inside an hour and a half he had the machine set up. Although the day foreman was happy to hear that the problem was solved, he asked the night foreman not to allow McCarthy to do such work in the future. Although the plant was not unionized, the regular setup men threatened to quit as a group if a man with only a month and a half of experience in the plant was allowed to do their work. The fact that McCarthy had thirty years' experience on Brown and Sharpe automatic machines did not impress them.

Mathewson reports a similar case of slowdown to stretch out work. "The men in a stock room of another firm checked up every morning the available work. When it appeared slack, they passed the word around, 'Take it easy, not many orders on hand this morning.' This always gave the signal for slow work for the group of four men involved."[59]

Regulation of production takes many forms. It almost always appears whenever time setters are used. Sometimes it takes the form of sharing work when it is unevenly distributed. The pace of work may be regulated, so that most of the work is done in the morning and visiting takes place in the afternoon. Regulation may come at the behest of foremen, the union, or the men themselves.

Workers may also attempt to control the formal organization of the union through internal group pressures. If union officials and stewards displease workers, the same pressure devices are used on them that are used on managers and foremen. The life of the steward may be made very uncomfortable by too many requests for his services and by accusations of improper motives. Union officials may be embarrassed by a refusal of the employees to participate in union-management committees, by violations of contract stipulations, and by resort to a wildcat strike against union officials. Playing politics, building pressure groups and machines are activities that occur mainly in the informal groups of the work organization.

Patterned evasion occurs at all levels in the organization structure. Many managers routinely submit financial budgets and requests for personnel in excess of what they need because it is well known that higher officials customarily trim down all such budget and manpower requests. In political structures this is almost a requirement in order that the politician may strike the "economy posture" which is so endearing to a voting public. Such evasions distort the capability of an organization to present an honest picture, but the evasion is carried out nonetheless. Top management calls for absolute honesty in the budget requests made by subordinate managers, but everyone "topside" is happy when he is put in the position of being able to claim that he "trimmed the fat off" the budget requests he received. A good middle manager is one who can evade in such a way as to emerge from the budget battle with what he secretly sought originally.

[59] *Ibid.,* p. 26.

Interest and Fun in Work Life

Obviously informal social organization provides interest and fun in work life. Many jobs are so monotonous that they cannot occupy the attention and hold the interest of the workers. In addition to being humdrum they offer no bright future. Therefore, all of the satisfactions at work must derive from the interpersonal associations, and the activities that are spontaneously invented.

For example, the singing, gambling, playing, drinking, and smoking might conceivably be reduced if the job required the full attention of the worker and gave him satisfactions in return. When it does not, achievement is sought as the best storyteller, drinker, and practical jokester. It is difficult to overestimate the entertainment value provided by informal activities, just as it is easy to ignore the personal recognition and attention they supply for people who would otherwise be in anonymous surroundings.

In many instances the social life of informal groupings gives people their only social satisfactions. The amount of social participation for many urban people is so small that the work group functions to provide practically their only social outlet. This situation is exemplified in the pathetic case of an unemployed woolen mill worker who went to the factory every day at noon so she could have lunch with the girls.

CONCLUSION

Informal organization is observed when personalities and situations are considered apart from the formal operations of groups. Informal structures are more than a number of congeniality groups—they are composed of a network of spontaneous group relations that pervade the entire work organization. The morale or lack of morale in a plant is a result of the relation of informal group to managers and their policies.

Cliques and other informal groups have a culture of their own. It is made up in part of the occupational cultures of the members and the peculiar social heritage in the plant. Myths, ceremonies, rituals, and ideologies—all the components of culture—are found in informal groups. One of the main functions of informal groups is to perpetuate this culture. But equally important, informal group life gives the worker an additional channel to secure recognition and prestige from his fellow worker.

Many of the activities and ideas that find expression in informal organizations are set by the climate of union-management relations. As these two groups jockey for power and prestige, local work groups come to decisions that influence the ongoing struggle. These processes will be examined in detail in the following chapters.

SELECTED BIBLIOGRAPHY

Archibald, Katherine, *Wartime Shipyard,* University of California Press, 1947.

Blum, Fred H., *Toward a Democratic Work Process,* Harper, 1953.

Chinoy, Ely, *Automobile Workers and the American Dream,* Doubleday, 1955.

Cottrell, W. Fred, *The Railroader,* Stanford University Press, 1940.

Dalton, Melville, *Men Who Manage,* Wiley, 1959.

Firey, Walter, "Informal Organization and the Theory of Schism," *American Sociological Review,* February, 1948, pp. 15–24.

Hughes, Everett C., "The Knitting of Racial Groups in Industry," *American Sociological Review,* October, 1946, pp. 512–519.

Roethlisberger, F. J., and W. J. Dickson, *Management and the Worker,* Harvard, 1939.

Roy, Donald, "Quota Restriction and Goldbricking in a Machine Shop," *American Journal of Sociology,* March, 1952, pp. 427–442.

Sayles, Leonard R., *Behavior of Industrial Work Groups,* Wiley, 1958.

Whyte, William F., *Human Relations in the Restaurant Industry,* McGraw-Hill, 1948.

Williams, Whiting, *What's on the Worker's Mind?* Scribner, 1921.

Zweig, F., *The British Worker,* Penguin, 1952.

CHAPTER 8

Power
and
Union Organization

Up to this point, the work organization has been shown to be comprised of interdependent formal and informal structures which regulate and shape the role behavior of managers and workers alike. Although this analysis has described the hierarchical character of work organization, there are other dimensions of stratification operating within and between the suborganizations of industries. Complex social patterns emerge as people seek to control, gain prestige, or secure economic and monetary advantage over others. These patterns of control, prestige, and economic striving have been alluded to above, but they shall be described in great detail in the following five chapters.

The elaboration of the stratification concepts which underlie these chapters will be done in the introductions of chapters dedicated to each dimension of stratification. The power dimension will be analyzed first for two reasons. First, as Max Weber clearly explained, all stratification dimensions are established within a pattern of control, within a house of power. Changes in power relations among groups usually result in changes in their status and class relationships. Second, the labor union, which is primarily an agency to contest the power of management, may be most conveniently studied in the context of power. Three chapters are dedicated to the analysis of the labor union. Two of them examine the internal structure of unions as responses to management control and as having internal problems of control. The third will deal with the full range of social conflict patterns which exist between workers and management, from the informal devices of the slowdown and the wildcat strike to the more formal processes of grievance bargaining, collective bargaining, the strike, and governmental intervention.

As a result of the application of these power processes, economic forces, and management controls, a pattern of economic distribution (classes) emerges. The chapter "Income, Class, and Social Structure" shows how the distribution of power affects the life chances of groups as reflected in their income, type of available work, amount of employment and unemployment, and opportunities for economic security and upward mobility.

The final chapter on status organization emphasizes the manner in which prestige is distributed in work organizations and how this pattern is affected by the social, economic, and power positions of various groups. It also attacks the problem of status anxiety in our society and how it manifests itself in the world of work. Let us begin by examining the historical changes in the meaning of power and authority in work.

HISTORICAL CHANGES IN THE ORGANIZATION OF POWER

Two Cases: A Contrast in Authority Relations

I'm over seventy years old, do you know that? I don't look it, do I? It's not because I've had an easy life. You young Americans do not know what it is to work. Yes, I've worked all but the first ten years of my life. My father was a mule trader in the old country; he traded in mules and other animals. I was the oldest boy in the family, and my folks had plans for me to go to school, and then take care of my father's business. They were cautious people, so they took care of all eventualities. It was decided that first I should get an education, but also, to be on the safe side, I should learn a trade.

I went to school for four years, and I loved it. You know, in the old country you get a real education. I know more astronomy than most college graduates in America, do you know that? But to get back to my story. Father's business was going bad, and education was expensive, so I was taken out of school.

I can still remember the day when my father took me to the shop of the master cabinetmaker in the little town in which we were living. My father said to the old master, "Here he is. Make him learn and obey. Do not be afraid to apply the switch." These admonitions were not necessary. The master knew how to control the boys and to get most out of them. I soon learned that one must obey and honor the master just like your own father. He was always to be addressed "Teacher" or "Master."

Since I was the youngest boy, I did little but sweep and clean around the shop. Later I was asked to look at somebody working, to hold a piece of wood, and so on. If my attention lagged, Teacher flicked my ears; if I spoiled the stain he gave me a flogging; if I tarried on the way back from the apothecary (where we bought our dyes for the stains), he gave me a tongue lashing; if I complained of being tired, he might relent, but more often I received silent censure.

Day after day, I sanded wood, rubbed in finishes, polished and waxed until my arms ached. I despaired of ever learning anything. The days were long, for we worked from twelve to fourteen hours a day. And for all this backbreaking labor, we received fourteen cents a week, an occasional whipping, and continual remonstrations.

But it wasn't much better for the older boys and young men in the shop. They had to knuckle down to the Master, address him respectfully, and carry out his orders to the letter. Despite his severity, nobody disliked him. He was a kindly man underneath, perhaps better than most others. The important thing was that he turned out excellent craftsmen, who would never do a shoddy piece of work. We turned out real craftsmen in the old country. I know everything about cabinetmaking; from cutting down a log to putting on the final finish on a piece of furniture.

When I came to America I got a job in a furniture factory, and after a few years I became the foreman of the veneer department. Things were bad in the old country, and my master came to this country. I got him a job working in my department. Although I was his boss, I usually took his advice, and dutifully called him "Master" until the day he died. My children used to call him "Uncle Master" and his wife "Aunt Master," just like natural aunts and uncles, and obeyed them like they do me.

The following description was given by a nineteen-year-old boy.

Yeah, this is the first full-time job I ever had. A year ago June when I finished school, I got a job at Acme Radio Corporation. I polish up the radio cabinets when they come off the line. I don't like the job so much. It's not the kinda job I want, because you can't use your intelligence and initiative. It's kinda easy though. You put in your eight hours, and the pay is pretty good. The union's gonna try to get us a fifteen-cent increase. So I'll stick at it for a little while.

You know, that place would be a hell of a lot better if there wasn't so many guys tellin' you what to do. Bob, our foreman, is a nice kind of guy, but every once in a while he flies off the handle. I guess they have meetings about production or somethin', and after them meetin's, Bob starts to yell for more and better work. I suppose you can't blame him though. The superintendent gives the general foreman hell, the general foreman gives Bob hell, Bob gives us hell, and we raise hell among ourselves. Finally, Ralph (the steward) tells Bob off, and things are better for a little while.

It isn't so bad taking it from Bob, but then those inspectors think they're big cheeses. They ain't got any control over us, but every once in a while they tell us we ain't doing things right. They even get Bob worried. Then there's them rate setters and efficiency experts. They come snoopin' around and tell us how we are supposed to do our jobs. You should hear Ralph blow steam when they come around. I tell you if they would only leave Ralph and Bob work things out, everything would be all right. The company newspaper is always talkin' about loyalty. But how can you be loyal when everybody is on your neck all the time, and you don't have any chance for advancement?

These two cases exemplify two different systems of production and, more important, two types of power relationships. The first case illustrates a system with a clear authority structure, based on small production units having a graded skill hierarchy. All workers were directly and personally responsible to the master, and all neophytes were expected to follow the same steps to attain higher skill and status in the system. Custom defined authority, which was in turn supported by a system of generally approved norms and conventions. Authority was broad in scope; not only did the master craftsman have control over his workers and their labor, but he had the right to exert other kinds of discipline. He taught his apprentices to respect not only his authority but that of other older people as well. He shared with the parents the responsibility for rearing his wards. The master was expected to see that the apprentices went to church on religious days, that they did not become exposed to corrupting influences, and that their parents were informed of their progress. In short, he acted as a father surrogate.

The master himself was subject to indirect controls. Since he knew the parents of his apprentices, and since his apprentices were economic assets, he curbed his exploitative tendencies. The master's status in the community depended largely on how he ran his business. He had to be fair to his apprentices or they might go to another craftsman. He had to sell his goods at a fair price because he sold in a personal market. (The customer was always right when he knew the seller, and when customers knew one another.) Custom and tradition defined the authority relations by defining all social relations. Very few formal organizations were needed to enforce regulations, for custom defined behavior as well as the means of enforcing it.

This system worked well because it was not challenged by other systems. The family, the church, the school, the workshop, and the community all reinforced one another. A stable system is not necessarily an ideal system exemplified by harmony, reason, and balance, for general acceptance of a system does not imply that all members are satisfied with it. Tension, frustration, and dissatisfactions certainly existed in the traditional authority system. The certainty that sanctions would be applied to those who violated the norms assured its continued operation. Both cooperative and antagonistic relationships were intimate, personal, and institutionalized, and authority relations reflected this characteristic.

The contrast between this system and the authority structure of the modern work plant lies primarily in the formalization of relationships in the latter. Formalization is primarily a consequence of size; the larger the enterprise, the less the employer is able to oversee his workers. He necessarily becomes more preoccupied with his economic rather than his general relationships. Since the workers interact less with the big boss, they tend to regard him as an impersonal bargaining opponent. This desiccation of interpersonal relationships during industrialization is accompanied by the impersonalization of authority.

In the contemporary economy the bases of identification of the worker may be the plant, the industry, or the occupation, rather than the person. Since workers are stimulated to think in group terms they tend to associate problems of power with groups and not with individuals. The shift is from personal to impersonal power, from informal relations to contractual ones. For the worker the labor union is the vehicle which contests the power of the owners or manager. The union is first and foremost an agency for contest and control. We must explore some attributes of power.

NATURE OF POWER

The concept "power" has an unpalatable flavor to those who support democratic values. Power conveys the repugnant suggestion of "pushing people around," of social conflict. Aversion to conflict may obscure one's ability to perceive its positive functions. Yet it is true that the application of power is often so hidden that people are not aware that they are being manipulated to pursue the designs of others. Abramson and others believe that this secret component is the essence of power.[1] Exposure of resources and tactics in power situations gives opponents time to think, plan, and attack. Nevertheless, ordering and obedience are widespread realities. For this reason we have purposely selected the word "power" rather than more neutral designations such as "social control," "authority," and "influence."[2]

In some folk societies which have a well-integrated and stable social order the concept "social control" may be more adequate than "power" to describe subordinate-superordinate relationships. Custom and tradition operate as unconscious and informal authority. In contemporary, heterogeneous, and complex societies law, contract, and rules increasingly control activities. The tendency today is to create structures with rational and consciously derived sets of regulations to govern behavior. For connotative purposes, therefore, it is generally appropriate to employ the concept "power."

Max Weber's formulation of power is useful in this connection. He defined power in broadest terms as the probability of securing obedience.[3] A power situation exists whenever individuals or groups compete to control the behavior of others toward desired ends.[4] The power of groups may be measured in terms of the probability that others will obey them even if they don't want to. Power situations are social situations because interaction is a necessary ingredient of power.[5] Whenever groups interact in a power contest, politics exists; and the contending groups may be characterized as "parties." The exercise of power need

[1] E. Abramson, H. A. Cutter, R. W. Kautz, and M. Mendelson, "Social Power and Commitment, A Theoretical Statement," *American Sociological Review,* February, 1958, pp. 15–22.

[2] Of course, such distinctions are useful in some situations, which will be described later. For definitions see Robert Bierstedt, "An Analysis of Social Power," *American Sociological Review,* December, 1950, pp. 730–738.

[3] See H. H. Gerth and C. W. Mills (trans.), *From Max Weber: Essays in Sociology,* Oxford University Press, 1946, p. 180.

[4] See R. M. MacIver, *The Web of Government,* Macmillan, 1947, p. 82: "By social power we mean the capacity to command the service or the compliance of others."

[5] See Georg Simmel, *Conflict,* trans. by Kurt H. Wolff, Free Press, 1935, pp. 13–56.

not be always rational, purposeful, scheming, and autocratic, for people often get things done by using indirect, amorphous, and even benevolent methods. Irrespective of how power is exercised, its core characteristic is manipulation of people and groups toward desired ends.

Power in this sense includes many phenomena which are sometimes camouflaged by such terms as "influence," "leadership," "collaboration," "authority," "coordination," "mediation," and "arbitration." All of these concepts have technical meanings in sociology which point to the many different ways in which power may be organized. How power is used, disseminated, or concentrated is a basic and fundamental problem of industrial society. But the first task of the social scientist is to recognize the phenomenon wherever it exists, and to note its functional and dysfunctional consequences.

Unfortunately, power is popularly conceived on an all-or-none basis. Groups are assumed either to have or to not have power. This is erroneous, for groups vary not only in the amount of power they possess but also in the area where they apply it. Moreover, groups may share power in some situations and not in others. It follows that both power and cooperative relationships may exist simultaneously between parties. While parties may struggle for power in some areas, they may cooperate in others. Where a given system of control is accepted as legitimate by all participants, it is common to refer to power as "authority." Where the control problem is not settled we may speak of a power situation. Another misconception concerning the struggle for power is that it results in violence and has dysfunctional consequences for the parties involved. This is especially felt to be the case in labor-management relationships.

Positive Functions of Power

Power struggles and social conflict are necessary and inevitable in complex societies where groups are not coerced by totalitarian regimes.[6] For example, conflict tends to increase the morale of a group and overcomes its apathy. It tends to clarify group beliefs

---

[6] See Raymond W. Mack and Richard C. Snyder, "The Analysis of Social Conflict—Toward an Overview and Synthesis," *Conflict Resolution,* June, 1957, pp. 227–229; L. Coser, *The Functions of Social Conflict,* Free Press, 1956.

and objectives of action and, by so doing, makes organizational behavior more effective. Conflict also maintains interaction between parties and avoids isolated and separate developments. Creative conflict also prevents collusion by insisting on the pursuit of group ends. Of course, conflict also has its dysfunctional a pects. These are so well known that they merit no elaboration here.

As later evidence will demonstrate, in the United States the belief in collective bargaining necessarily implies an endorsement of some social conflict to settle differences between organized labor and organized management. Conflict is a necessary process both within and between groups in a democratically organized pluralistic society.[7] Thus we learned in the chapters on formal organization that the concept of legitimate authority had limited usefulness in management politics. With Dalton and Chamberlain we saw that the large industrial bureaucracy is characteristically concerned with the problem of the distribution of power.[8] The internal dynamics of contemporary bureaucracies was explained as a *struggle* among different segments of the organization, such as departments, supervisory levels, line and staff, and headquarters and field. As many have observed, this internal struggle is necessary to keep organizations efficient and effective to attain common ends; when it ceases, organizations become rigid and inefficient. When conflict becomes the end rather than a means of settling disputes, dysfunctional consequences occur. Therefore, conflict must be kept within definite limits if it is to contribute to efficient and effective organization.

Management Power and Responses to It

It will be recalled from Chapters 5–7 that except under extraordinary circumstances management controls the operation of the work organization. Historically the manager was the owner and had the right to determine operations. It was his prerogative to change the organization in any way he saw fit to maintain its efficiency and to increase his profits. This prerogative was later trans-

[7] See Harold L. Sheppard, "Approaches to Conflict in American Sociology," *British Journal of Sociology,* June, 1956, pp. 134–145.
[8] Melville Dalton, *Men Who Manage,* Wiley, 1959; Neil W. Chamberlain, *A General Theory of Economic Process,* Harper, 1955.

ferred to managers who were not owners. Thus a large amount of managerial authority in large-scale organization is functionally necessary, and it is found in both capitalist and noncapitalist societies.

Although organizations may experience long periods of stability, management must inevitably introduce changes in them. Technological and organizational innovations generally take the form of new machines, revised work organization, and new rules. These changes and rules must be analyzed for their impact on the fate of all workers, both managerial and nonmanagerial. Workers often interpret change as unnecessary or as threatening their traditional rights and social relationships. While their feelings are often justified, management decisions may also improve the situation for some. As salaries and wage levels are raised or lowered, people are made to feel more or less secure. Management also determines working conditions: hours of work, the spread of work, the kind of work done, and the atmosphere in which it is done.

Managerial decisions may also be interpreted as manipulating the social structure of the work plant and community. Organizational and technological changes may scatter the employees of a particular department and break long friendships. Occupational and wage changes also alter the economic and social status of employees in the plant and the community. This process has been carefully documented by Warner and Low, Smith and Nyman, and others,[9] whose studies reveal what might be anticipated: the employees are not idle bystanders watching the destruction of their economic and social investments in an ongoing order. *Their defensive actions result in the creation of an informal organization dedicated to protect their interest, or to the formation of labor unions, and often both.*

Managers have always realized that many of their acts have economic and social consequences for the lives of their employees. While managers have not questioned their moral right to manipulate their organizations, they have had different conceptions of what their responsibilities to their employees were. Bendix has

[9] W. Lloyd Warner and J. O. Low, *Social System of the Modern Factory,* Yale, 1947; Elliott Dunlap Smith and Richmond Carter Nyman, *Technology and Labor,* Yale, 1939.

dramatically documented the role of the nineteenth-century British and American managers who, under the influence of Malthusian doctrines, felt no responsibility for the fate of their workers.[10] This extreme attitude is not taken by typical managers all over the world. More often they assume some responsibility for the economic and social dislocations resulting from their behavior, especially in small communities which have one or a few industries.

Gilman has described the many paternalistic practices found in the "individualistic" villages in the southern Appalachian regions of the United States.[11] In traditional societies moving toward industrialism a greater amount of paternalism is practical for example, Abegglen has shown that some relations in the Japanese factory may be conceived as an extension of the family system with its filial and paternal obligations.[12] Even further extremes may be found among the Utopian villages where managers assumed complete responsibility for the social welfare of their workers. The most common pattern in the United States is for the manager to assume in theory that he has no obligations toward his workers but in practice to accept some responsibility.

THEORIES OF LABOR MOVEMENTS

This brief review of managerial and employee concerns with the consequences of managerial decisions demonstrates that it is the rule rather than the exception for employees to do something about the problems caused by internal organizational changes. Changes may be handled informally and spontaneously as they arise, or formal organization may be created, such as a labor union, to handle problems systematically. Sociologically, the functions of such organizations, whether formalized or not, are very similar. Thus a labor union may be thought of as one of a number of possible organizational responses to unstable situations generated in all large-scale organizations characterized by technological, economic, and social changes.

[10] Reinhard Bendix, *Work and Authority in Industry,* Wiley, 1956, pp. 86–98.

[11] Glenn Gilman, *Human Relations in the Industrial Southeast,* University of North Carolina Press, 1956, pp. 127–169.

[12] James C. Abegglen, *The Japanese Factory,* Free Press, 1958, pp. 11–25.

As noted in Chapters 5 and 6, management groups, parties, and cliques emerge in large bureaucracies because top management is unable to handle the special problems confronting specific managerial groups. As work organizations increase in size, heterogeneity, and complexity, the informal organizations on *both* the worker level and the managerial level are insufficient to handle the problems confronting them, and formal organizations are forged to meet these problems and to define new goals for the members.

The types of employee organizations which emerge (unions, professional societies, foremen clubs, worker committees, and others) differ because the economic, social, and political situations which confront various groups differ and because industries are located in communities of varying social and cultural characteristics. Sociologists should have a general theory which takes into account the common factors responsible for the appearance of all types of employee associations, as well as specific explanations which account for the appearance of special types of associations: the craft union, the industrial union, the professional association, management associations, foreman associations, trade associations, and others. Unfortunately, not much progress has been made toward such a general theory, although Moore and Dubin have made an auspicious start.[13] For the most part scholars have concentrated on the rise of labor unions among skilled and semiskilled manual workers.

Schneider has succinctly reviewed three theories of labor organization:[14]

Selig Perlman accounts for the rise of labor unions by emphasizing the tendency of workers to achieve job control and job ownership. By examining such work rules as hiring, firing, discipline, layoffs, apprenticeship training, sharing work, reallocating hours of work, and techniques to protect the job, Perlman concludes that a job scarcity consciousness underlies the American union movement. He asserts that the American worker is con-

---

[13] Wilbert E. Moore, "Notes for a General Theory of Labor Organization," *Industrial and Labor Relations Review,* April, 1960, pp. 389–397; Robert Dubin, *Working Union-Management Relations,* Prentice-Hall, 1958.

[14] Eugene V. Schneider, *Industrial Sociology,* McGraw-Hill, 1957, pp. 332–340.

cerned with the development of pragmatic goals and not with political action.[15]

Frank Tannenbaum attempts to account for the rise of the labor union by saying it is a drive on the part of the workers to create a collectivity similar to the medieval guilds.[16] He asserts that contemporary industrialism has alienated the worker from his job and from society. In order to minimize his loss of security he attempts to create a community (a labor union) in the work place. The eventual result of this activity is the creation of estates which carefully define the rights and duties of all participants. Tannenbaum considers the economic drives of the union secondary to its efforts to create a meaningful community.

The Webbs, as part of the mainstream of British socialism, evolved a theory of the labor movement which emphasizes labor's efforts to reduce the negative impact of economic competition.[17] One of their basic postulates is that the adverse effects of economic competition are concentrated on the workers. In defense the workers form a solidary organization with principles of common rule to regulate conditions of employment and restrict the number of workers in a given field. They achieve these goals by economic and political means.

Moore's Synthetic Theory

In seeking to arrive at a general theory of labor organization, Moore reviews these theories and concludes that each of them may be correct for different types of unions in different historical epochs.[18] He suggests that the basic question concerns the type of cohesion which binds workers together. In some cases it may be the plant, in other cases the industry, and in still others the craft, occupation, or general social rank. Thus Perlman's theory may be adequate to account for the rise of craft unions in a mature industrial society, while the Webbs may explain the development of class-conscious (social rank) unions in middle stages of industrial maturity.

[15] Selig Perlman, *A Theory of the Labor Movement,* Kelley, 1949.
[16] Frank Tannenbaum, *A Philosophy of Labor,* Knopf, 1951, p. 59.
[17] Sidney Webb and Beatrice Webb, *Industrial Democracy,* Longmans, 1926.
[18] *Ibid.,* p. 395.

The common factor in all of these theories is that self-conscious organizations are inevitably forged by particular market conditions. While groups differ in their economic, social, and political characteristics, they are all concerned with a single goal of attempting to control external conditions. Since their traditional rights have been challenged, they feel they can achieve their economic, political, and social goals only through formally organized structures.

One cause for the confusion in the theory of labor unions is that scholars confuse historical causes for the rise of unions with their present functions. Once organizations are created, they assume different functions in response to changing conditions. The degree to which a labor organization is formalized varies with the degree of control that it has over its environment. The cohesive informal work clique, an employee representation plan, a company union, a professional association, and an independent union may be thought of as different types of structures responding to similar needs in different situations. As a matter of fact, as formal labor organizations are instituted, earlier types of structures are not entirely abandoned, and they may continue to play some of the functions they performed previously.

Factors Which Distinguish Unions

It is difficult to generalize about labor union structure and behavior without referring to the factors which distinguish specific types of unions. Among these are the particular objectives of the unions, how they articulate to other segments of society, their distinctive internal structures, their sources of strength, and the types of tactics they use.

1. The objectives or goals of labor organizations vary in specificity, content, and priority. Some unions emphasize economic goals, others social, and still others political goals; and these may be arranged in different order of priority.

2. Labor organizations may articulate differently to other segments of society, depending in part on their legitimacy and status. In some situations unions are considered criminal conspiracies and have low status. The reverse situation also exists. Moreover, some labor organizations may be independent of government,

business, or the church, while others are in fact part of these larger structures.

3. The internal structure of labor organizations varies considerably. They may be organized on the basis of membership in a plant, an industry, an occupation, or a social class. They may be highly centralized or decentralized, highly bureaucratic or non-bureaucratic. Their control may be local and democratic or centralized and autocratic.

4. The sources of strengths vary. Some unions have considerable economic strength (large treasuries and property), while others have little economic strength but great internal social cohesion. Still others derive strength from sympathetic outsiders, such as the government, the church, or intellectuals.

5. The tactics which labor organizations employ vary from legalistic, orderly processes to violent clashing ones.

Obviously, these characteristics are related. For example, the amount and type of strength which a union possesses affects its tactics. How it articulates to other organizations affects its objectives as well as its internal structure and strength. Perhaps a typology of labor organizations may be created from the above observed elements. All too often, a simple dichotomy is suggested: business unions on the one hand and ideological or political unions on the other. This is an oversimplification because business unionism may have some revolutionary implications whereas political unionism is sometimes conservative and ineffective.

Types of Labor Unions

Dubin suggests that there are three main types of unions in the United States[19]. The so-called business unions are run by a staff whose primary function is to increase the economic well-being of the members. These wage-oriented unions are usually bureaucratic and controlled by officers who tend to have long tenure in office. Ordinarily, membership participation is minimal as long as the officers are successful in improving the economic positions of the members. Sometimes these unions become corrupt because there is too little membership control.

The second type of union in Dubin's classification is a welfare

[19] *Ibid.*, p. 72.

organization. Apart from seeking economic improvements, this type seeks to increase the welfare services both of the union and of the government. The ex-CIO unions tended to be of this character. They attempted to supplement the wages of the workers by obtaining insurance and "fringe benefits" from employers and getting government to broaden its social security provisions. In addition, they provided some services directly, such as clinics, hospitals, credit unions, and counseling.

The third type of union is "life embracing." That is, the union becomes a central institution in the life of the worker and seeks to help him in every realm. This type of organization is often found in a small one-industry community. Seidman and others have described the life-embracing character of the United Mine Workers in the United States.[20] Similar unions are found in industries that tend to be isolated from the mainstream of society, such as the longshoremen's union.

Ideological Unions

Ideological unions are primarily concerned with achieving social goals which are broader than the economic improvement of their members. As a matter of fact, ideological unions have a dream of what they want the entire society to become, and the union is seen as an instrument for realizing that dream. Ordinarily, the control of the government is seen as necessary to change the society, and in countries such as Germany, France, and Italy unions with diverse ideologies are the rule. Catholic trade unions embrace the principles of the Church and seek to put or keep the Catholic party in power. Likewise, the Communist trade unions support the program of their party first and consider the achievement of specific local economic objectives secondary. The so-called free, democratic trade unions also represent a particular ideology in this setting although they tend to be tied less directly to political parties. Ideological trade unions, by their nature, have different collective bargaining goals, different internal structures, and different economic policies.[21] Neufeld

[20] Joel Seidman, Jack London, Bernard Karsh, and Daisy L. Tagliacozzo, *The Worker Views His Union,* University of Chicago Press, 1958, chap. 2, "Coal Miners' Unionism as a Tradition," pp. 15–41.

[21] See Joseph LaPolombara, *The Italian Labor Movement: Problems and Prospects,* Cornell, 1957.

suggests that ideological trade unions arise and persist in countries which have low levels of technology; here government and not private enterprise must take the primary role in economic development. In such a setting union goals can be achieved only through great political involvement.[22]

Government-Dominated Unions

In some countries in both political right and left all labor is organized in unions which are part of the governmental administrative structure, part of the control apparatus of the state. Their functions are to insure a given rate of production, to reduce interruptions in the flow of goods and services, to acquire information about politically "unreliable" people, and to integrate employees to larger political and social movements. Manifestly, these are pseudo unions. Nonetheless, the fact that totalitarian governments consider it necessary to have organizations to represent the workers is in itself significant. Apparently even in such regimes a separate administrative device is necessary to deal with problems of worker discontent and to secure needed information. It appears to be generally undesirable and difficult to absorb all functions of the union in a traditional management structure.

Unions in Emerging Nations

Labor unions are found in many new nations which have only primitive industrial economies. In these cases the union ordinarily is not a phenomenon which emerges out of the local conditions but a transplanted organism which the new country feels is necessary for the development of a viable labor force. These unions are usually impotent in terms of the functions ordinarily associated with free labor unions in the West. Indeed, sometimes they represent nothing more than surviving expressions of political independence from colonial domination. Not uncommon in colonial situations, unions are developed by intellectuals as instruments of political protest. Obviously such unions must acquire different functions when economic and political independence is secured.

[22] Maurice F. Neufeld, "The Inevitability of Political Unionism in Underdeveloped Countries: Italy, the Exemplar," *Industrial and Labor Relations Review,* April, 1960, pp. 363–386.

American Trade Unions

American unions represent a particular response to the American scene. Although they have had periods when they were more ideologically oriented than at present, they have not been as ideologically disposed as the European unions. Yet American unions are generally stronger than European unions on several levels. They are economically more powerful; they have greater internal solidarity and are able to resist management at the local level more effectively. Although the goals of American unions have been pragmatic and short run, they have been successful in attaining them. Along with business, American unions have objected to governmental interference because they believe they can achieve their aims in a free enterprise society.

To be sure, some unions in the United States are similar to those in Europe in that they stress religious or ideological principles. For example, small but weak locals of the Labor Christian Association are found, primarily in Michigan and nearby states. These unions have members of the Dutch Reform Church and others who seek to insert religious values in union activity. Similarly, the American Catholic Trade Unions are independent voluntary associations organized within traditional unions, to see that the larger organizations abide by religious principles and combat the growth of communist influences.[23] Ideological unions are found among the longshoremen, the mine and mill workers, and the electric workers. They maintain a Marxist orientation despite the constant pressure exerted on them by the government and the larger union movement. The United States also has predatory unions which are organized as rackets—to "protect" employers against genuine labor unions. In addition, a few craft unions, such as the Typographical Workers of America, have been able to maintain an almost guildlike character even in the face of large-scale bureaucratic industrial growth.

LABOR AS A MOVEMENT AND AN INSTITUTION

Although unions historically have sought to control the local work situations, they have had to organize on a broader basis to

[23] See Philip Taft, "The Association of Catholic Trade Unions," *Industrial and Labor Relations Review,* January, 1949, pp. 210–218.

deal with forces as pervasive as the markets of which the plants are a part. Unions have had to spread and include members in related occupations in different plants in the community and in the wider society. This economic and social phenomenon was in fact a social movement. Kenneth Boulding captures the essence of labor's social movement:

. . . Behind the dirty union hall and even the shiftless or racketeering official there stands the Labor Movement, a stream of history which also has its saints and martyrs, its Mother Joneses and its Joe Hills, its songs and its stories and its traditions, giving a curious secret strength to its often commonplace embodiment. Alongside the job-conscious business-likeness there runs a stream of idealism, expressed in the concept of a "good union man." There have been many unsung sufferers for the cause—people who have suffered loss of jobs, black-listing, tarring-and-feathering, imprisonment, and even death because they have believed in the union, not as a means of personal advancement, but as a great movement in history for the betterment of the group.

It is this faith which ultimately gives the labor movement its strength, and which especially gives its strength to withstand the attacks of employers and of the state in periods when they have been hostile. Employers have a real competitive disadvantage in the struggle because they do not have so good a "mythology" as the labor movement, and because they do not have so vivid a sense of their purpose in history and their function in society. The myth of the self-regulating free market does not affect the springs of emotional life as deeply as the myth of a class struggle.[24]

The social movement of organized labor represented a common response to common situations faced by employees in different plants and communities. Successful techniques to control management were invented and then diffused to other unions to become part of a body of rules and traditions. A sense of identity was built up by dramatic events, by heroes, songs, and rituals. At a later stage the spontaneous social movement was supplemented by a process of conscious unionization and institutionalization. The ideal of the labor movement was and is to grow to the full extent of the market so that it may deal more effectively with all the forces impinging on it. Since product markets are interrelated, it is the ideal of the labor movement ultimately to organize the entire labor force. This has not been realized anywhere except

[24] Kenneth Boulding, *The Organizational Revolution*, Harper, 1953, pp. 97–98.

where governments have taken over the labor movement. In this eventuality unions lose their identity and power. However, a moderate amount of interindustry organization is necessary for unions to survive in an interdependent economy. For this reason they form federations and congresses on the local, state, national, and international levels.

The labor movement today is highly organized and institutionalized, just as business is. In fact, union locals are often *more* highly interrelated and institutionalized. To understand the behavior of labor unions one must know something about the institution and the social movement of which they are an intimate part.

Chapin has suggested that an institution has four attributes.[25] They are (1) dominant beliefs (attitudes) and behavior patterns, (2) symbolic culture elements, (3) utilitarian and material culture, and (4) written or oral codes that specify conduct.

1. Some of the dominant beliefs of unionism are solidarity in economic and social action, cooperative rather than individual economic action, loyalty to the traditions of unionism, suspicion toward employers' tactics, and the right of workers to organize for the advancement of their material and social goals. These beliefs are reflected in such behavior as attendance at union meetings, paying of dues, participation in strikes, and defending the unions' economic and social philosophies.

2. Collective symbolic representations are found in all union organizations from the smallest local to the largest federations and congresses. Over time, the unions have built up elaborate folklore and rituals not unlike those found among the Masons, Elks, and Knights of Columbus. In fact, many of the older craft unions were founded as fraternal orders. They developed a complex set of ceremonies—initiations, pledges, secret oaths, handclasps, uniforms, and burial and expulsion rites.

3. Unions also have accumulated a vast amount of property. Their investments in material goods is incalculable. Some of the material accumulations are union halls, labor lyceums, schools, international headquarters, camps, printing presses, amplifying equipment, books, movies, credit unions, health resorts, and even night clubs.

[25] F. Stuart Chapin, *Contemporary Social Institutions*, Harper, 1935, p. 6.

4. Unions have developed elaborate oral and written codes that systematically relate their dominant beliefs, rituals, and material culture. Complex sets of relationships are defined in the constitutions, bylaws, and contracts with the employers. In addition, there are written and unwritten charters of what constitutes good or bad unionism. Unions also establish a system of punishments and rewards to assure that codes and charters are kept alive and effective. Bakke grasped the institutional character of the union when he said,

> They develop an institutional life of their own beyond the lives of individual members. A basic objective of that development is strength and power and prestige as such. Internal conflicts must be ironed out. The membership must be bound together by a common philosophy and achievement. Power of many sorts has to be acquired. Protection against other unions must be sought. A strong internal government and leadership must be developed. . . . Every demand, every counter proposal, every compromise, must be measured against the need for survival and the growth of the union itself. Even the degree to which the clearly expressed wishes of the employees themselves can be followed by union leadership must face that test.[26]

THE FORMAL STRUCTURE OF AMERICAN UNIONS

It is important to know the characteristics of social structures for they have a direct bearing on organizational behavior. We shall first describe the organizations which labor unions as a totality have evolved on the national, state, and local levels and then the internal structures of the union local.

Most of the major national unions in the United States and Canada are autonomous bodies which, when taken together, make up the AFL–CIO. State and local bodies send delegates to the international convention which meets every two years. The convention is the broad policy-making body of the labor union movement. The executive officers and the executive board are elected by the delegates, who also pass laws or resolutions to guide the work of the officers and the boards. The executive officers, in turn, hire staffs to help them carry on the charges of the convention (see Fig. 8.1).

[26] E. Wight Bakke, *Mutual Survival: The Goal of Union and Management*, Harper, 1946, pp. 3, and 4.

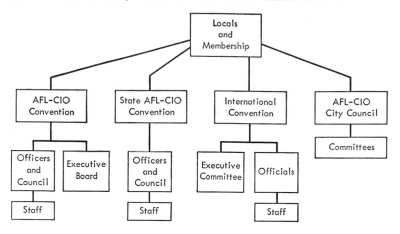

FIG. 8.1. Schematic Representation of American Labor Union Structure.

The primary function of the AFL–CIO is to control jurisdictions among the national and international unions. Its second major function is to "police" member organizations to assure that they are not dominated by Communists or racketeers. The third function is to organize the unorganized workers. The fourth function receives most attention from the press: shaping favorable legislative policies. Part of this function is the political education of the membership. Last, the AFL–CIO provides services for national and state bodies such as research, legal aid, educational materials, and public relations. Expulsion from the AFL–CIO is the main sanction which the labor movement has to control its members, and this is an important and powerful weapon.

Parallel state or provincial (for Canada) AFL–CIO bodies are found in most of the states, and these have structures with functions very similar to those of the parent organization. Delegates to the state convention are typically representatives of the union locals which are members of the AFL–CIO. State conventions are usually held every two years, at which time officials are elected and legislative policy is set. The state body's main function is to act as a pressure group in the field of state legislation. Like the national body, it is also concerned with organizing the unorganized, educating the public and union members on various local and national issues, engaging in research of importance to the member unions, and acting as a public relations arm for organized labor.[27]

All of the local unions in a particular community send representatives to the local AFL–CIO Council. The Council, or, as it is sometimes called, the City Central, is the community spokesman for organized labor. It has two primary functions: to give city-wide support (material and/or nonmaterial) to any local which is engaged in a strike and to represent organized labor on various social agencies in the community. The Council usually is represented in such community agencies as the Community Chest, Council of Social Agencies, and hospital boards.

The International Union

At the core of the American labor movement are the national unions, often called "international unions" because they contain Canadian locals. Some examples of these are the Communication Workers of America, the United Automobile Workers of America, the United Steel Workers of America, and the United Mine Workers. The structure of the international is very similar to that of the AFL–CIO. Theoretically, the internationals are controlled by the locals, which send delegates to an annual or biannual convention. The convention is the lawmaking body; it passes directives which the elected executive committee and officials are expected to carry out between conventions.[28] The executive committee, in turn, has a staff for various purposes such as research, education, legal aid, organization, and publicity.

The international is composed of various accredited locals in an industry, craft, or combination of both. Its main tasks are to assure the maintenance of a national pattern of bargaining among the locals and to coordinate the activities of the locals. The amount of power which the international body has varies from one union to another. Generally craft unions have greater local autonomy, whereas the so-called industrial unions are more highly centralized. The power which the international has over

[27] See "The State Body," film of the Labor Program Service of the School of Labor and Industrial Relations, Michigan State University, East Lansing, 1961.

[28] For one of the few empirical studies of the international convention see William A. Faunce, "Delegate Attitudes Toward the Convention in the UAW," *Industrial and Labor Relations Review,* July, 1962, pp. 463–473.

the locals usually is greater than that of the AFL–CIO over the internationals. The international can expel any local that does not live up to its standards, or take over their administration until problems have been satisfactorily solved. Where racketeers have gained control of the local or where financial problems have emerged, the international may impose a caretaker government. Another important function of the international is political action and the political education of its members. The international also has a fairly large staff of regional and local organizers to organize the unorganized. In addition, it often has a research, education, and legal staff to help locals solve their individual problems. The international also publishes a newspaper or a periodical.

Who Is Organized?

Every work organization with more than a score of workers has some kind of formal management organization. This is not the case with labor, for probably not more than 17,000,000 workers were unionized in the United States in 1962. About 40 percent of urban nonproprietary and nonprofessional employees are unionized. Although the proportion of enterprises which are unionized is unknown, some estimates exist of the proportion of employees covered by union agreements.

It is estimated that two-thirds of the wage earners in manufacturing are covered by union agreements.[29] However, in such industries as petroleum and coal products, rubber, transportation equipment, and primary metals, over 80 percent of the workers are covered. Equally high proportions are found in aluminum fabrication, automobile and air frame, men's clothing, nonferrous metal smelting and refining, shipbuilding, steel, coal mining, theatrical (professional actors and musicians), ship loading, and railroads.

Over 80 percent of the workers in the construction, maritime, local bus and street railway, trucking, and telegraph industries are union members; and about half of the workers in the baking, grains, leather, lumber, furniture, pottery, shoe, concrete, and woolen textiles industries are unionized.

[29] H. M. Doutz, "Collective Bargaining Coverage in Factory Employment, 1958," *Monthly Labor Review,* April, 1960, pp. 345–349.

Less than half of the workers belong to unions in the canning, chemicals, cotton textiles, paper, athletic goods, barbering, fishing, hotel, and laundering industries. Only one-quarter or less of the workers were organized, and the figure rose to 12 percent in the service trades (other than domestic), and in clerical, technical, and professional occupations of businesses classified under manufacturing, finance, and wholesale and retail trade. About 50,000 union contracts are currently in operation.

The proportion of the labor force which is unionized has varied considerably in the United States. In 1900 only 3 percent of the workers were organized, and the figure rose to 12 percent in 1920, a longtime peak. During the Great Depression (1930) the rate fell to less than 7 percent, but it rose steadily after the passage of the Wagner Labor Act in 1937. With the economic prosperity induced by World War II reached 23 percent in 1944. Since then the rate has stabilized at about one-quarter of the labor force.

Irving Bernstein has analyzed the causes of union growth in the United States.[30] He believes that long-run and short-run economic and social factors will make for a steady growth in union membership. Others feel that the era of union growth is terminated because the labor force is changing radically and because organized labor has been relatively unsuccessful in organizing employees in those industries which are growing most rapidly. Technological and other factors are decreasing the proportion of workers engaged in manufacturing and mining and increasing those in the services and professional and clerical occupations. However, Bernstein's analysis shows that unions are still growing despite changes in the industrial makeup of the nation.[31] Not only are they increasing the percentage of organized workers in manufacturing, but they are also increasing the unionization of the nonmanufacturing and white-collar sectors. In fact, the main areas of growth since 1956 have been in food, printing and publishing, paper, construction, air and truck transportation, trade, entertainment, building service, and government. Currently, 2.5

[30] Irving Bernstein, "Growth of American Unions," *American Economic Review*, June, 1954, pp. 308–317.

[31] Irving Bernstein, "The Growth of American Unions, 1945–60," *Labor History*, Spring, 1961, pp. 131–157.

million white-collar workers are organized, approximately 15 percent of the organizable in these occupations. Even smaller proportions of professional workers are unionized. Apparently unionism will continue to grow in the United States as it more than makes up its losses among the manual occupations by or-ganizing the broad spectrum of white-collar workers.

Only crude estimates can be made of the financial power and social importance of the unions. The money which unions handle from dues, initiation fees, special assessments, and retirement funds probably amounts to several billion dollars annually. Approximately a million persons are actively engaged in union affairs by virtue of being union officers or committee members. The money and energy spent in promoting and protecting the interests of employees are therefore considerable. Only churches among the private voluntary associations can boast of more members and greater resources than labor unions.

Unions exert more influence on economic and social events than their numbers warrant. Even in industries where their members are few they often set the pattern of wages, hours, and working conditions for nonunionized plants.[32] Employees who benefit from gains made by unions but who will not join the union are called "free riders." We shall ignore the "free riders" and non-unionized plants in this chapter, because employee associations which are not part of the labor movement are usually weak or management-oriented. Company unions, employee representation committees, and similar structures are not part of the labor movement and may be sometimes considered a part of management.

The Setting of Union Organization

The data on union strength reported above may not be translated directly into power terms, especially on the local level. Powerful as some locals may be, they usually do not have power comparable to that of management when it comes to determining the daily routines of the workers. Management has active jurisdiction over all workers during most of the working day. Since supervisors are continuously directing the activities of the workers, the latter are usually mostly preoccupied with *doing their*

[32] F. H. Harbison and R. Dubin, *Patterns of Union-Management Relations,* Science Research, 1947.

job and worrying about the boss. Probably workers are concerned with union affairs not more than 5 percent of the working day. At best, the average member attends a union meeting once a month, reads the union paper once a week, occasionally contacts his stewards, votes periodically for union officers, and pays his dues.

Of course, preoccupation with union affairs varies enormously from time to time. During organization campaigns, during wage disputes, strikes, or grievances, union matters may be of dominant interest for days. When crises are over, however, the involvement of the average worker is limited to an occasional (often compulsory) monthly or bimonthly meeting of the local. The apathy of the rank-and-file union member during noncritical periods is common knowledge.

As in all association, there are active leaders, enthusiastic and apathetic followers. The steward, the local officers, the representatives of the international, and committee members spend a great deal of energy on union affairs. Like their management counterparts, these labor executives live their union in their work as well as in their social life. It would be a mistake, then, to measure the strength of the union in terms of the amount of time and energy which the typical member or officer gives the organization.

The union is an institution and a social movement which springs into action when the need arises. We may think of it much as we think about the church. To gauge the influence of the church by counting the number of hours people spend in churches would be unrealistic. The rituals of baptisms, marriage, and burial are not unimportant because they are practiced infrequently. The influence of the clergy on legislation is much larger than might be anticipated from the amount of formal involvement of the membership in religious activities. So it is with the unions.

FUNCTIONS OF THE UNION LOCAL

By understanding the functions of an organization, one knows the social situations to which its members respond. Since the local is the basic unit of unionism, its functions do not differ substantially from those of unionism generally. Although singular circumstances may emphasize certain functions of particular locals, all locals generally meet similar social needs.

Economic Security

The basic function of the unions in the United States is to maintain or improve the economic position of workers. For a long time this was conceived to be their only function. Some labor economists evolved a theory that the union is primarily an association which sells labor to the employer. Dunlop advanced the most sophisticated view of this theory when he suggested that the union is primarily a wage-maximizing organization. So conceived, the union is much like a business enterprise which sells labor, and it behaves like a business.[33]

By itself this theory is too narrow, for even businesses usually are more than profit-maximizing enterprises. As we have seen, both businesses and labor unions have other social, political, and personal functions. Yet, narrow as the wage-maximizing theory is, it would be unrealistic to underestimate the economic role of the labor union. Since the discovery of the social importance of work, it has been fashionable for writers to claim that wages in themselves are not important to workers, but the *relations* among wages are. They suggest that the worker is really concerned with how his wages *compare* with those of others doing the same or similar jobs. When he feels an imbalance exists, a sense of unfairness drives him to urge the union to correct the situation. Thus conceived, the union is a mechanism to adjust wage inequities.[34]

While this may be an adequate explanation under some conditions, by itself the theory is as incomplete as the wage-maximizing theory. For one thing, it is a conservative interpretation which gives interpersonal feelings primacy over economic well-being. Obviously unions, like all institutions, have many purposes. Economic motives, like all others, operate in a system of interacting values. Describing single motives, like discussing separate institutional functions, is useful only for analytic purposes. In actuality, institutional functions and the personal motives which are related to them do not operate in isolation.

[33] John T. Dunlop, *Wage Determination Under Trade Unionism,* Macmillan, 1944, pp. 32–34, 119.

[34] Burleigh B. Gardner and David G. Moore, *Human Relations in Industry,* Irwin, 1955, pp. 124 ff.

Weighing the relative importance of institutional functions and the corresponding motives of members is always precarious. When done, it should be within the context of the value system of the larger society. In American society material values are fundamental, and the union cannot ignore this fact. As many union organizers can testify, the employee measures the effectiveness of his union in terms of the size of his pay envelope and his fringe benefits. He believes that union idealism has its place, but it does not buy the necessities and luxuries of life. Therefore, he constantly exerts pressure on the union to *raise wages* to the level of the most favored of his customary associates in the community.

The farsighted union leader tries to convince the rank and file that this single demand for high wage rates is shortsighted, and that their most important goal should be to gain control over those factors which make them economically *insecure*. He stresses the importance of a contract which controls (1) entrance into the trade, (2) hiring, (3) layoffs, (4) seniority, (5) amount of work, (6) effects of technological change, (7) wage and hours, and (8) unionized and nonunionized competitive situations.[35] The leader points out that the union succeeds best when it keeps all these control points in mind. He sometimes goes farther and insists that ultimately economic well-being rests on a favorable and facilitating political climate. He urges members to vote for favorable candidates and support them to achieve favorable legislation. The major task of a labor leader is to broaden the level of thinking of the members so that they appreciate the principle that their economic well-being is enhanced by broad planning on many fronts rather than achieving higher wage rates at the moment. The thoroughly assimilated union member embraces the broader goals of his leaders.

Resistance and Independence

The "logic" of management tends to regard employees as tools to be used according to the canons of efficiency. Managers move workers about, promote, demote, and release them according to the demands of the situation. However compassionate executives may be of the feelings of workers, in the ultimate sense these must

[35] See Sumner H. Slichter, *Union Policies and Industrial Management,* Brookings, 1941.

be considered secondary to the logic of efficiency. Workers are at the bottom of the structure and know they have limited power to convince management of the importance of their aspirations, feelings, and desires.

The union changes this situation. It considers employees first as persons with rights. It can communicate directly with higher management the personal hurts and grievances of employees and attempt to redress alleged wrongs. The individual worker feels he can stand up to his boss when he has the power of the union behind him. Thus a basic function of the union is to *resist* pressures from management. The local union is the instrument which informs bosses that they cannot push workers around. Even the least ardent union man appreciates this union function when it is effectively fulfilled.

Resistance to management aggression is supplemented by a positive function. The union takes advantage of a strong cultural compulsion among Americans to have a part in determining their destinies. Joining and supporting a union is a way of "doing something about working conditions." The employee can complain to his steward or committeeman. If the latter is ineffective, the employee can vote for another steward or officer in the next election. The union offers the worker other vehicles of action; he can vote on strike issues, be on committees, run for office, educate himself on union and economic problems, form a faction, and even fight against the union. All these give the worker a feeling that he can make his way in the world.

Golden and Ruttenberg report this reaction of workers in a Pennsylvania cork plant. During organization meetings for the proposed union, several people gave vent to their desires for independence from the company. Said a comely girl: "It's about time something like this happened. We have to stand on our own feet. They do everything for you but provide a husband, and I even know girls they got husbands for. And they what ain't got time to get pregnant, they get foster kids for." And a middle-aged man complained: "They lay out my work with so many instructions that there's nothing left for me to figure out for myself. The only reason they keep half of us is 'cause they ain't discovered a machine yet that would take our places."[36]

---

[36] Clinton S. Golden and Harold J. Ruttenberg, *The Dynamics of Industrial Democracy*, Harper, 1942, p. 15.

A radio wireman, in an interview with the authors, made this statement about independence fostered by the union:

> You ask me about the union. Several years ago, we finally got the CIO in here. All during the depression we had no union. The company increased our quotas up and up. Finally they broke down our jobs and brought the girls in the department. The union hasn't fixed the rates to where they used to be, but it has helped a lot. The best thing that happened is that the fellows don't feel they've got to play up to the foremen any more. If we got gripes, we take 'em up with the union. Sometimes something is done and sometimes it isn't. But at least we feel we're getting some place. . . . Of course, we get all kinds of fights in the union; but you get the feeling that we're all after the same things, and that's what really counts.[37]

In an authoritarian structure those who obey orders build up aggressions against those who give orders. This is especially the case in our culture, which highly values personal independence and equality.[38] The protection of the union allows the employee to voice his feelings against individual supervisors and against management. At union meetings and in the community he can decry the "injustice," "unfairness," "inhumanity," and "tyranny" of his bosses. He can even participate in direct action against his employer by resorting to the strike, slowdown, and even violence. In such situations unions have evolved specific institutionalized techniques of exerting pressures which not only are effective but give the member a sense of directing his destiny.

Personal Recognition

Many thinkers have considered the trade union as an instrument of class solidarity, an expression of the common values and ideals of the working class. They feel that the union must play a political role in national and international affairs to help the working class control the economy and the society. This socialist view of the union's function has not been generally accepted in the United States. In Europe and elsewhere, not only has the theory been accepted but many steps have been taken to realize it.

The dominant trade union philosophy in the United States is reflected in the thinking of Samuel Gompers, first president of the American Federation of Labor. He felt that American unions

---

[37] *Ibid.*

[38] See Chris Argyris, *Personality and Organization,* Harper, 1957, pp. 76–123.

should not support any society-saving or society-destroying scheme; they should concern themselves with immediate day-to-day improvements in the economic and social life of working people. The union had no ultimate ends as such, excepting the vague goal of "securing a better life for all."[39]

Such a position was calculated to appeal to the American wage earner. Traditionally, he did not conceive of himself as a member of a class, for he shared the prevailing ideal that his station in life was temporary. He or his children would become "successful" by achieving an independent professional or entrepreneurial status. Since a considerable number of workers rose in the occupational scale the appeals of unions for "class" loyalty had to be soft-pedaled. This situation still exists today even among automobile workers.[40] However, in other industries such as shipping, mining, and clothing, working-class appeals are still strong.

There is still uncertainty whether occupational mobility is increasing or decreasing in the United States.[41] Were it to decrease, working-class appeals of unions might have more attractions. Yet the development of a proletariat is not a necessary condition to developing a strong, if temporary, loyalty to the union and the working class. For example, as mechanization liquidates skills, employees may increasingly derive social status not so much from their occupation as from doing something about their present condition. The union provides a vehicle. For many workers, then, prestige is obtained not by getting out of the working class but by becoming an active part of it.

Bakke has enumerated some of the ways of achieving a socially respectable role through union participation.[42] The union, for example, provides a hierarchy of offices which ambitious people can climb. Prestige may be secured from playing a role of steward, committee member, and officer. Other roles are open which lead to recognition, such as standing up to the foreman, fighting for better working conditions for the gang, attending union meet-

[39] Samuel Gompers, *Labor and Common Welfare,* Dutton, 1919, pp. 7, 8, 20.

[40] Ely Chinoy, *Automobile Workers and the American Dream,* Doubleday, 1955.

[41] Seymour M. Lipset and Reinhard Bendix, *Social Mobility in Industrial Society,* University of California Press, 1959.

[42] E. Wight Bakke, "Why Workers Join Unions," *Personnel,* July, 1954, p. 4.

ings and conventions, *making real decisions and policy for* the union, exerting authority, and so on.

The stairways to recognition in the union should not be considered solely as an inferior alternative to blocked mobility at work. Although this may have been the case for many aspiring union leaders in the past, the labor movement has now developed a normal channel for mobility and recognition. Nelson Foote believes that as the union and the corporation together develop estate-like characteristics, all employees may become increasingly professionalized. As union members they will begin to build long-term job careers. Technological change will force them to prepare for new jobs and make them think in career terms just as many white-collar workers do today.[43]

Social Participation

For workers who are destined to stay on the same job level the rest of their lives, what function does the union serve? It defines an area of participation which is not only acceptable but respectable *in the eyes of the peer group*. To be considered a good union man, to be loyal, to represent the organization with dignity in the community are sources of gratification. Many employees join unions and remain loyal to them because membership is the way of obtaining and securing respect. "To be a regular guy," and "to show you're on the right side" have strong appeal as long as personal recognition is principally derived from one's peers.

But even to the middle-class public, the status of the union is undergoing a change. In the public eye the union has changed from a semicriminal conspiracy to a respectable social institution in the community. Some union officers are even members of Rotary and the Chamber of Commerce. The union has gained general respect as it has gained power and numbers. Its participation in community events like the Red Cross, bond drives, Civic Improvement Association, and Community Chest is now actively sought.[44] The union has given employees dignity and importance in the community by providing them organizational representation.

[43] Nelson Foote, "The Professionalization of Labor in Detroit," *American Journal of Sociology*, January, 1953, pp. 371–380.
[44] See Chapter 18.

As a social movement the union develops new organizations to meet the changing desires of the membership; it becomes an organization-building vehicle. Do the members want education? The union furnishes a school with all necessary paraphernalia. Do they need advice on personal and family problems? The union provides counselors and welfare workers. Do they want recreation? A program of athletics, picnics, singing, and hobbies is instituted. Is material help needed? The local becomes a welfare organization. Are community services being provided? The union becomes a pressure group in local politics. Is Congress looking out for the workers' interest? The union acts as a lobby. In short, the union moves toward the paternalistic welfare model described by Dubin.[45]

Unions promise to extend rather than curtail their functions in the future. Although other agencies (employers, the community, and the state) are competing to provide services, unions will continue to play a dominant role. For the union is closer to its members, controllable by them, and sensitive to their needs. More than any other organization, it acts in terms of experiences that workers understand. Whitehead believes that the past failure of American unionism was due to the fact that it ignored its primary function as an organ of social living. Indeed, he suggests that "the future of unions will depend on the degree to which social living is made a first concern to those who are in a position to lead."[46]

CONSEQUENCES OF UNION STRUCTURE

Despite the fact that unions perform several vital functions, like all large organizations they have problems of internal integration and cohesion. Just as management bureaucracies develop internal divisions, conflicts, factions, and segmentation tendencies, so do the unions on both the local and the national level. Just as we observed that informal organization and political problems emerge as structural responses to management's bureaucratic structure and values, so too do informal organization and political problems arise as structural responses to the union's democratic organization and ideology.

[45] *Ibid.*
[46] T. N. Whitehead, *Leadership in a Free Society*, Harvard, 1936, p. 146.

The tasks in this section and the following chapter will be to (1) present briefly the theory of formal union organization, (2) contrast this with management theory, (3) describe the formal union structure, and (4) analyze the social organizations which emerge as a response to union ideology and formal structure.

Theory of Formal Union Organization

The theory of union organization is essentially a democratic theory. If the reader knows the organizational principles of democracy he knows something about union structure. The central fact in a democratic organization is that the ultimate source of authority resides in the people—in this case the union members. The union exists for its members, not members for the union. Although responsibility is vested in the members, the exercise of that responsibility is a matter of individual discretion. Presumably the union citizen will take an interest in his organization, inform himself on its activities, and become a factor in its fate.

Since all union members theoretically have equal power by virtue of their ballot, the union is supposed to be concerned with the welfare of all its members, irrespective of their sex, color, creed, or occupation. Each group has the right to expect fair treatment within the union and in the union's dealings with the employers. If some do not get this treatment they must organize themselves as a pressure group to obtain it.

The security of officials in a democracy is often precarious. Union officers are elected for short terms and may be removed from office by vote of the electorate. A few staff offices are appointive but tenure in them is dependent upon the grace of elected officials. Since there is no inherent right to office, any office is available to any member in good standing. Presumably any elected member should be capable of handling the issues and problems of any office. The duties and responsibilities of offices are defined, not by a logic of efficiency, but by constitutional provisions. Thus, the functions of any union job may be changed at any time. Moreover, all major decisions (such as the calling of a strike) must be ultimately approved by the members, irrespective of their knowledge or the recommendations of their officers.

The techniques of settling issues in unions are those commonly used in democratic bodies. Anybody in the meeting may raise an issue; anyone may declare his feelings on the issue; and everyone may vote on it. The minority must, of course, abide by the decisions of the majority. By actively campaigning, however, the minority may influence enough members to reverse a given policy.

Thus, the union is theoretically an organization responsible to and run by amateurs who believe in democratic principles. This structure is pitted against an organized bureaucracy run by professionally trained managers who are appointed and responsible to the president, who is himself an appointed official. The contrast between management and union organization is important enough to merit separate attention.

Comparing Union and Management Organizations

Similarities

Arthur Ross, comparing similarities and dissimilarities between union and business organizations, indicates that both trade unions and business firms have formal purposes and official rationales, and both seek to maximize them.[47] For managers the aims are profit maximization; for union officials, the maximization of the economic welfare of union members. Actually, the means and ends of both groups are loosely defined. It is the job of management and union officials to define ends in the situational sense and manipulate conditions to realize diverse goals. Thus, managers must decide: How much profit is to be attempted? How immediately must profit be realized? Should profit come from expanded markets, decreased wages, or new products? Labor executives must decide what kind of "welfare" to pursue: higher immediate wages, vacations with wages, a good seniority system, or a closed shop. They also must decide which procedure to employ to attain a specific goal. What stratagem will work best— promises, threats, cajoling, a slowdown, or a strike?

Both labor and management officials are subject to pressures from those who want institutional ends to be defined so as to increase their welfare. The "lobbies" which try to influence corporate executives are the bankers, stockholders, the union, the trade association, employees, customers, and government agencies.[48] The pressures on union executives emanate from the rank

---

[47] Arthur Ross, *Trade Union Wage Policy,* University of California Press, 1948, chap. 2, "The Union as a Wage Fixing Institution."

[48] *Ibid.,* p. 25.

and file, the employers, international officials, other unions, the federations, and agencies of government.

One of the managerial functions of both sets of leaders is to reconcile their respective pressures. In viable structures the executives make decisions which are calculated to foster the growth and survival of the organization as a whole and not any one group. There is usually a close identification between the personal ambition of the leaders and organizational growth. A good "company man" fosters his organization, as does the good "union man."

Dissimilarities

The formal purpose of the union is vague. Business has a precise goal and a precise measure of its effectiveness, namely, profit and growth. For the union, "betterment" may mean almost anything, such as union recognition, higher wages, closed shop, shorter hours, improved working conditions, grievance procedure, or job security.[49] Some observers feel that both union and management are engaged in selling—the former, its goods; the latter, its labor. This is not strictly true, for the union only bargains for wages; it does not determine them.

The relation between the union and its members differs from that between stockholders and the corporation. Stockholders buy and sell their shares in the company, but this activity often has little effect on capital strength, whereas the acquisition or loss of union members greatly affects union strength. Stockholders are usually not concerned with the actual survival of the business, for they leave its operation in the hands of managers. Survival is a much more serious problem to union members and their leaders.[50]

While business needs capital and customers to survive, labor unions need not only economic strength but political tolerance as well. Although legislation can hamper business operations, it can actually destroy the unions. When hostility of powerful employers and their associations is added to legislative threats, the very survival of unions becomes problematic.

Both *apathy* and *participation* of the rank and file present problems of security and stability to unions and their leaders. Perlman

---

[49] *Ibid.*, p. 27.

[50] Benjamin A. Selekman, *Labor Relations and Human Relations*, McGraw-Hill, 1947, p. 176.

and Taft state, "The overshadowing problem of the American labor movement has always been the problem of staying organized. No other labor movement has ever had to contend with the fragility so characteristic of American labor organizations."[51] Union leaders are neurotic about participation. Unlike business managers, their tenure in office is dependent upon those below them, not those above them. As elected officials, their future depends upon voters who are often apathetic and uninformed. Since an aroused rank and file may throw a man out of office for a picayune matter, the union leader must be a politician as well as a manager to stay in power. When members are not aroused, leaders may stay in office indefinitely no matter what they do. Unions not only must guard against business and government; they must also guard against encroachment of rival unions.

A democracy, like any other organization, is supposed to get things done. But restrictions are placed on the means which may be used. If the members trust their leaders, they may give them almost autocratic powers. If untrusted, the leaders may be almost powerless. The tension in democratic organization arises from conflict between the two ideals of efficiency and responsibility. All types of compromises between these two ideals are found in various local and international unions.

The task remaining before us is to examine in greater depth the functioning of the union, especially on the local level. This is difficult because there is so much variation in types of union structures. In the next chapter we shall look at types of union structures, the role problems which confront union officials, and the organizational problems arising within the union.

SELECTED BIBLIOGRAPHY

Boulding, Kenneth, *The Organizational Revolution,* Harper, 1953.

Dubin, Robert, *Working Union-Management Relations,* Prentice-Hall, 1958.

Golden, Clinton S., and Harold J. Ruttenberg, *The Dynamics of Industrial Democracy,* Harper, 1942.

Moore, Wilbert E., "Notes for a General Theory of Labor Organiza-

[51]Selig Perlman and Philip Taft, *History of Labor in the United States, 1896–1932,* Macmillan, 1935, p. 7.

tion," *Industrial and Labor Relations Review*, April, 1960, pp. 389–397.

Perlman, Selig, *A Theory of the Labor Movement*, Kelley, 1949.

Ross, Arthur, *Trade Union Wage Policy*, University of California Press, 1948.

Selekman, Benjamin A., *Labor Relations and Human Relations*, McGraw-Hill, 1947.

Sheppard, Harold L., "Approaches to Conflict in American Sociology," *British Journal of Sociology*, June, 1956, pp. 134–145.

CHAPTER 9

Functions
and Roles
of Union Officials

TYPES OF UNION STRUCTURES

There are four main types of union structures in the United States.[1] In the first, unions are organized around an occupation, a craft, a group of crafts, or a profession. All members in any plant or enterprise in a particular community or region having these skills may be members of a union local. Secondly, unions may organize all employees in a given sector. That is, all employees in government, automobile factories, retail stores, restaurants, or clothing factories, irrespective of occupation, may belong to an "industrial type" union. A third type appears when a dynamic labor leader organizes employees in a region, irrespective of their occupation or industrial sector. The United Mine Workers' District 50 and the Teamsters union are cases in point.[2] Fourth, unions are organized on a plant basis. All employees in a particular plant or company may be in one local.

Union locals range in size from a half-dozen to over 100,000 members. The large majority have less than two or three hundred members, and only 10 percent have more than a thousand members.[3] The type of union local described below has about five hundred members and contains workers in several occupations who are employed in one or two plants in the locality. Figure 9.1 presents a typical structure for this kind of local. Cer-

---

[1] E. Wight Bakke and Clark Kerr, *Unions, Management, and the Public,* Harcourt, Brace, 1948, pp. 150–151.

[2] *Ibid.*

[3] Florence Peterson, *American Labor Unions,* Harper, 1945, p. 76.

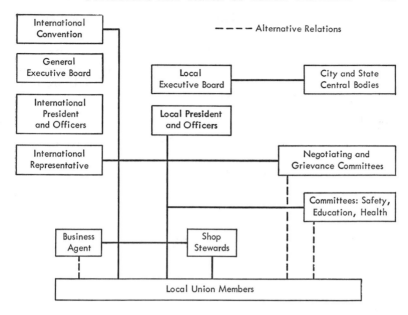

FIG. 9.1. The Formal Structure of a Union Local.

tain parts of the structure are omitted for purposes of clarity. The staff, organizers, and committees of the local and the international are not included. When Fig. 9.1 is compared to the typical management structure, two main differences are revealed. First, the local is intimately tied into its parent structures, the international union and the federation. Second, more lines emanate from the worker to substructures, which means that many officials are responsible to the members. We shall first examine the dynamics of union behavior by analyzing the role structures of local union officials and then proceed to intraorganizational problems.

FUNCTIONS AND ROLES OF LOCAL UNION OFFICIALS

The union local has about twenty elective offices. There are five to seven members on the executive board and about an equal number of executive officers. In addition, two important committees are sometimes elected, the negotiating and the grievance committees. The two most important officers, usually not elected, are the business agent and the international representative. Countless other committees—health, safety, sickness, picnic, education, flower, entertainment—are ordinarily appointed by the president. Whether elected or appointed, most officials are theoretically responsible to the members.[4]

President

The president is sometimes a full-time paid official in large locals. More frequently, he is a regular employee and is paid for each meeting over which he presides. His formal duties and functions are not very clearly defined. Like most chief executive officers, he is concerned with organizing and strengthening his charge. How he actually exerts his influence depends on his personal ambitions and the local political and social situation. In old and mature locals his role may be as perfunctory as the constitutional stipulations of his office. He presides over the bimonthly meetings, represents the local in interunion councils, attends sessions of the executive board, and participates in the bargaining process. But most of his time is preoccupied with the day-to-day administration of the contract agreement.

In newer, less stable locals, the president's role is more dynamic and difficult to play. If the union is insecure, the president must keep the membership girded for battle, by building morale and solidarity through anti-employer propaganda. At the same time he must secure discipline to stop impetuous groups from wrecking the inexperienced union. It is his business to (1) assess the employer's ability to pay, (2) gather data needed for bargaining, (3) predict employer tactics, (4) evolve countertactics, and (5) gauge the proclivity of the membership to strike. In addition, he must protect his position against those who seek it as a stepping stone to a career in the international.

When political or factional disputes infest the local, the president may play one of two roles. If he believes in business unions, he tries to suppress political ruptures in order to make the local effective in its struggle with employers. If he heads a faction, he tries to crush or neutralize the opposition by controlling ap-

[4] Leonard R. Sayles and George Strauss, *The Local Union: Its Place in the Industrial Plant,* Harper, 1953, pp. 7–13.

pointive positions and achieving a good record. In either case he attempts to pacify the articulate minorities, so that the organization is not imperiled. The president also is concerned with political problems in the international. If sympathetic with present conditions he interprets and justifies action of international officers. If unsympathetic he organizes members to form an opposition movement.

Executive Board

The executive board is an elective body which usually has a great deal of authority. The president, who sits with the board, presents all major matters to it for clearance before bringing them up before the membership. A union member or a group of members may ask the board to bring up particular problems at subsequent meetings of the local. Although the board cannot refuse to do this, it may present its recommendations along with the requests. However, the main function of the board is to prepare the next contract. In such a capacity it serves as a contract committee.

The board may discuss and recommend to the membership a wide range of matters. It may recommend a change in the dues, make reports on the operation of the seniority system, study grievances, consider relations with unions in the district or region, act as a jury on membership status, suggest the addition or removal of union services, urge political action, make investigations of expenditures, and so on. Membership on the board gives the employee an opportunity to exercise leadership. Board members (where permitted) often run for such offices as business agent or delegate to international conventions because they can exploit their contracts with union members to get elected or appointed.

Secretary-Treasurer

The secretary-treasurer, who is elected, performs the duties usually associated with the office. He is paid a few hundred dollars a year to keep the accounts, preserve minutes of meetings, and maintain membership rolls. In addition, he keeps records of the dues, local expenditures, and moneys sent to the international. Since he can draw on accounts, he is in a position to exert considerable influence. One source of his power flows from his right, under certain conditions, to refuse to sanction some expenditures. Some locals are beginning to hire bookkeepers or accountants to assume some of the duties of this office.[5] In middle-sized unions, the secretary-treasurer is often the only full-time paid official. When this is the case he has considerable influence because he can concentrate all of his energies on union affairs. His intimate knowledge of union operations places his services at a premium, and his reelection provides continuity to union operations.

Business Agent

The business agent is usually found in highly competitive and relatively small-scale industries rather than in such large enterprises as are commonly found in the steel, auto, and rubber industries.[6] He may be either an elected or an appointed official. Since he is often the only full-time paid official in smaller unions he is the most important. He has considerable power for several reasons.[7] First, he usually has been an employee for a long period of time and he has a thorough knowledge of the union's problems. Second, his functions cover the whole range of union activities. Third, he is constantly reelected and provides continuity to the local's activities.

The business agent is a jack-of-all-trades. His main job is to represent the union in the administration of the contract. He polices the activities of both employer and union: he checks working conditions in the shop; he scrutinizes the operation of the seniority system; he is on guard for nonunion employees working in the shop; he sees that other unions are not overstepping jurisdictional lines; and he sometimes acts as an employment agency.

In many unions the business agent is a grievance officer. He hears complaints from workers about unjust treatment, discrimination, and severe discipline.[8] When grievances cannot be settled at the lowest level, he accompanies the grievance chairman in sessions with higher management. At times the agent has some

[5] *Ibid.*, p. 79.

[6] Jack Barbash, *The Practice of Unionism*, Harper, 1956, pp. 101, 186–187, 191.

[7] Peterson, *op. cit.*, p. 29.

[8] Harry A. Millis and Royal E. Montgomery, *Organized Labor*, McGraw-Hill, 1945, p. 251.

of the responsibilities of the secretary-treasurer, for he may maintain the office, preserve records, and even collect dues. Sometimes he has charge of union publicity and the local's newspaper.

The business agent is usually an experienced and clever negotiator. Although unable to vote in contract sessions, he meets with the executive board and advises it how to act. During negotiations he gives advice to the bargaining and contract committees. As a professional union man with wide experience, he has influence out of proportion to his formally assigned duties.

International Representative

The international representative, or organizer, is a full-time paid official of the international organization. He is appointed to represent the international in the local's affairs. Sometimes he has a circuit of locals which he visits. Not uncommonly he is attached to a large local. His duties vary with his aggressiveness and the amount of control the international has over the local. His duties are growing because the international's functions, services, and influence over the locals are increasing.[9] Some of the controls commonly exerted by the international concern the conditions under which locals can be chartered, the amount of dues and initiation fees locals may charge, membership specifications, procedures for dealing with employers, and even work rules.[10]

The job of the international representative is to insure that these controls are enforced. Among other things, he examines the books of the local and sends reports to headquarters. He is more than a policeman, however, because he provides many services. As a seasoned union man who sees union problems in a broad perspective, he knows something about the economic state of the industry, wages, living costs, and profits in all localities in which the union is represented. This information is vital because internationals seek to maintain uniform working standards.

In negotiations with top management, the international representative carries the weight, influence, and prestige of the international. If occasion demands, he invites the international's lawyer, organizers, statisticians, economists, and strategists to negotiations. Especially in unions where industry-wide bargaining is the

[9] Jack Barbash, *Labor Unions in Action*, Harper, 1948, p. 57.
[10] Peterson, *op. cit.*, p. 58.

rule, inexperienced local officers need the advice of the representatives. Not infrequently, the latter have a stabilizing influence on the local. Neophytes may select an inopportune time to strike or make demands. The representative can discourage rash action by threatening to withdraw financial or other support of the international. If the local is still adamant, he tells it, in effect, "O.K. You're on your own. Don't come begging to us for help." This is usually enough to bring the local back in line with international policy.

Committees

Committees in the local may be classified according to their functions. The grievance, negotiation, and contract committees are concerned with *bargaining* relations with employers. Other committees *represent* the local in city, state, and regional union bodies. Health, safety, education, recreation, and other committees carry on many of the *internal social functions* of the union.

The grievance, negotiation, and contract committees are by far the most important, especially during bargaining sessions and other crises. Their members are either appointed or elected. Ordinarily, a committee post does not offer the member much opportunity for leadership. However, membership on these business committees may provide stepping stones to higher union jobs.

Members of the AFL–CIO councils (city centrals) and larger union bodies are usually local union officers. Many other thankless committee posts must be manned to keep the local functioning well. Unfortunately, performance in them is too often perfunctory and unimaginative. Yet officers realize that the committees are important if only to get a few members to increase their participation.

Stewards

Stewards or shop committeemen are usually elected by workers in a department of a plant. Strictly speaking, they are not union officers but departmental or occupational *representatives* of the workers. A union member who feels he has a grievance usually gets in touch with his steward. The problem may be one of seniority, promotion, favoritism, rate cutting, or job jurisdiction. If the steward feels the worker has a case he goes to the foreman and attempts to adjudicate the dispute on the spot. If they cannot come to an agreement, the case is turned over to the chief steward or the grievance committee, who go to higher management officials for settlement. Another function of the steward is to make sure that union agreements are lived up to in the shop. His only material reward for the often thankless job is seniority and his regular wages during the time spent on cases.

Members

Union members are an integral part of the union structure. Theoretically, they occupy the highest position because all union officials are directly or indirectly responsible to them. If the members are determined and organized, they can supposedly control the behavior of their officers and determine union policies. Moreover, they elect delegates to the international convention. As William A. Faunce has shown in the study of the delegates to the UAW international convention, almost half of them were first-time attenders at the convention.[11] Although a large proportion were ex-officers of locals, they did not necessarily represent present local officers. They could indeed take a position opposed by present officers because they were not legally bound to represent any position.

In conclusion, the formal structure of power is quite loose on the local union level. As in many democratic organizations, power, authority, and jurisdiction are often poorly defined. The mass of union members cannot exercise authority at all times because the union is often confronted with emergencies and officials must act quickly. Moreover, different officials are the focus of decision-making at different times. The grievance committee or executive board may be the center of activity at times and its members may have almost independent power. In another situation, the business agent or the international representative must

[11] W. A. Faunce, "Delegate Attitude Toward the Convention in the UAW," *Industrial and Labor Relations Review*, July, 1962, pp. 463–473.

have power. In management organization, on the other hand, power tends to reside among the same officers, almost irrespective of situations.

Three officials guide the daily routines of the local: the president, business agent, and international representative. Since the latter two are often appointive officials, they are not subject to direct pressure from the rank and file. Therefore, if they act in concert with the president, they can run the organization in the face of considerable opposition.

No attempt has been made in this section to portray how the union local actually functions. We have presented the formal structure of the union and its theory of formal organization. The gap between union theory and practice is as wide as that between the theoretical and actual operation of management organization. This does not mean that formal structure of unions is unimportant. It must be examined in the light of the typical situations it confronts and the common tensions that arise within it. This we shall do in the following section.

SEGMENTATION IN UNION STRUCTURES

In the chapter on management organization it was observed that bureaucracies have an innate tendency to segmentalize in predictable places: between functional divisions, supervisory levels, line and staff, and other juncture points. Cleavages among the subparts of the organization are emphasized when they coincide with social and cultural differences of the members of those parts. The result is the development of a managerial ideology that is contrary to the formal aims of the organization. "Pull," "cliques," and "management politics" were seen as structural responses to the characteristics of management organization. One of the primary tasks of management is to control these phenomena so that overall operations remain effective.

A parallel analysis may be made for union organization. It also is marked by cleavages which occur at predictable places: between officers and the rank and file, among the officers, among the social and occupational groups, between the local and the international, and between the union and the broader community. As with management organization, a redefinition of values is found in the union, as political machines arise in response to untenable positions. The task of the officers, as with managers in business, is to keep an effective organization functioning despite divisive tendencies.

Sociological analysis unfortunately tends to focus more on the disintegrative aspects of social structure than on its integrative aspects. This emphasis is understandable because integrative forces are not so easily observed. Common values, similar socialization, daily routines, functional interdependencies, and organizational operations bind people together in numerous ways of which they may be unaware. Although the following analysis will center on disjunctive aspects of union organization, we must bear in mind that unions do persist, that they are characterized by unarticulated loyalty and solidarity, and that many of the internal conflicts indeed have integrative consequences.

Characteristically, local unions do not need the continuous imperative coordination of subsystems so necessary in management organization. Constant manifestations of consensus and solidarity by the entire membership are not required for the daily functions of the union. Neither is mass participation and involvement a necessary condition of loyalty. What is necessary is a feeling of common destiny which can rouse the membership to collective action when necessary. Apparently most unions have this necessary substructure. Unlike the managers in a large bureaucracy, union members tend to be relatively homogeneous in economic level, social status, and power. The convergence of these stratification characteristics tends to produce a "social class" with a sense of common fate, temporary though that sense may be. Moreover, union members are bound, as we have seen, by a tradition of a conflict social movement. Last, and very important, is the integrative character of a democratic ideology, which places union officers in a service orientation toward the members rather than in a command posture. The examination of relations between officers and rank and file reveals both integrative and dissociative factors at work.

Union Leaders and the Rank and File

First let us examine how union members look at the local. The following impressions suggest that the first experiences which workers have are variable, but they all expect the union to behave democratically.

A rubber worker wrote:

I attended my first union meeting at the unusual hour of one o'clock in the morning. The committeemen went around to the third-shift workers and told us there was a meeting scheduled after work. We went to the local union hall, where the talks were going to be given. The hall wasn't very large, and smoke filled the room, for most of the men were smoking. There was quite a noise coming from the scraping of chairs and the murmur of everyone's voices.

The meeting was finally called to order; the president and secretary took their seats, and the meeting was started. The president of the union explained why we were called together. He was asking tire builders to drop one operation of their piecework rate, for they were running too high. He gave us data on the number of machines that were idle in the plant, and he said this was due to the high rate of production we were giving the company. The union had found that the company planned to move this idle machinery to a new plant they were building. This would remove a source of employment away from Akron, and the union planned to fight this action. The lowering of production was part of the plan to force the company to hire more men and fill the places on the empty machines. Another reason for dropping an operation was the amount of pay was exceeding the 10 percent over base rate; the union was afraid the company would cut the rate, thereby getting more production for less money. The increased production might lead to layoffs of some of the employees whose length of service was short. The president and older members gave examples and dates of the times they had seen this done.

The men in the audience agreed that this was the course to follow, but one argument came up. It was stated that we were but one shift and we wanted to now if the other shifts would also do the same. It was agreed, then, that each of the other shifts would hold separate meetings, and they would decide on the issue too. It was recorded that the third shift agreed with the issue and the meeting was adjourned.

A working girl inadvertently tells about her mystification of union functions:

I'd been working at Lamson and Sessions for about two weeks when a girl in my department comes around to me and says that it was necessary for a new employee to attend their first union meeting at the next one scheduled. I didn't care for the idea because I was only going to work three months.

It was on a Sunday and it took place above Wright's store. We were told to wait out in the hall while some kind of ceremony took place. About five minutes later they called us in and told us to repeat after the president of the union the oath. (There were about ten people in the whole room.)

Then we sat down in the back and the meeting got underway. There was one man who elected himself spokesman. He kept putting up new business which was turned down. He did, however, get a new typewriter for the secretary of the union. He was the most boring talker I had ever heard. He was the type that droned on and on while everybody slept.

He finally said something of interest and everybody started arguing. That lasted about half an hour. Then a man with one eye got up and said that he motioned the meeting be closed and some woman seconded the motion.

They put your clock number in a hat and had me (of all people) pick a number out of it. I picked out number five-eighty-two. That was my own number. Naturally everybody got a big kick out of that including myself, because I was made the proud owner of a five-dollar bill. The man with one eye comes around and slaps me on the back and says, "You're the second one that's done that."

Another worker relates how his attitude toward unionism changed:

I started on my first job with the idea in my mind that all unions were just racketeering organizations that innocent citizens like myself were forced to join. This thought had been carefully planted in my mind since the time when I was old enough to understand anything at all. Since that time, the idea had been cultivated and kept alive by the constant bombardment of propaganda by the newspapers, radio, and news magazines. For this reason, I was more than a little skeptical when told that I would have to join a union. However, I needed a job, so I thought it would pay me to join even if I did have to give part of my pay away to the union.

My first surprise came when I was asked for the initiation fee and the first month's dues. I found these to be reasonable and no more than one would pay to join any fraternal organization. I had imagined that all the officers would be the gangster type, especially the business agent. Therefore I was very much surprised to find that my immediate superior on my job was the president of the union and that the business agent was a mild, intelligent man who held down the same job that I had, only for a different company.

When I attended the first union meeting, which was well advertised, and to which all members were invited, I found that things were run in a very orderly fashion, by parliamentary rules. By this time my views on unions were beginning to change and I decided to find out more about the whole matter. I discovered that most of the people were just common ordinary citizens like myself. They spoke the same language, had the same ideas, and shared my likes and dislikes. When I asked what happened to the money that was collected as dues and initiation fees, I was told that, since I was now a member, I was free to inspect the books at any time I wanted to.

All the time I worked on that job, I found the union to be the protector of the worker. If the union member was in trouble, the union decided he had a just grievance, every member would stand behind him until the matter was taken care of. The union also sponsored a social life which included dances, outings, and other events which took some of the drudgery out of our everyday life.

At this time, my views concerning unions have changed completely from what they had been when I started working. I cannot speak for all unions, but if they are at all similar to the one I belonged to, I say "let there be more and stronger unions!"

Most people are not indignant when management does not adhere strictly to the formal requisites of bureaucratic theory, yet they become angry when unions do not behave democratically. There is no more reason to expect a democratic structure to operate according to its formal expectations than a bureaucratic one. Both types of organization inevitably develop internal strains and inconsistencies when confronted with changing problems and personnel. Formal organization represents an ideal mode of behavior and not the behavior itself.

The nature of union organization is such that the rank and file does not and cannot give detailed attention to union affairs. The union, like most democratic organizations, is neither a mobocracy nor a perpetual town meeting. Ordinarily, members attend occasional meetings but leave union operations in the hands of the officers. The union is strong and successful when officers effectively perform the functions of "delivering the goods" in terms of higher wages, shorter hours, and better working conditions.[12] Officer control and effectiveness may exist in both democratic and nondemocratic situations; by itself, it is not a negation of democratic principles. Usually unions idealize democracy and make provisions to realize it. As Ross says, "There are few institutions in the economic and social life of the nation with so many channels of communication between the rank and file and the leadership."[13] Most unionists recognize that considerable discretion

[12] Robert F. Hoxie, *Trade Unionism in the United States*, Appleton-Century-Crofts, 1923, p. 177.

[13] Arthur Ross, *Trade Union Wage Policy*, University of California Press, 1948, p. 38.

must be given to the officers if they are to have a permanent and effective organization.

In discussing trade union wage policy, Ross emphasizes the dependence of the rank and file on the officers: "The wage policy of a union, like the foreign policy of a nation, is poorly suited to the methods of primitive democracy."[14] The workers are dependent on the leadership for defining what is equitable, possible, and acceptable. It follows that when members reject a decision urged on them by their leaders, it is not vigorous democracy that is at work but rather internal demoralization. Revolts of the rank and file against the leaders tend to occur when the union is functioning poorly.

Even locals which have effective leadership and practice democratic procedures exhibit some cleavage between officers and the rank and file. Several forces operate to define the officers as "they" and the members as "we." Since most of the elected officials do not stand in hierarchical relationship with each other, they become conceived as a group. Once elected, they form a status group and a power elite which has certain jurisdiction over the membership. Working-class culture is characterized by a deep suspicion toward elites, irrespective of their social origins. Furthermore, the officers are thrown into continuous contact with one another and indeed become a self-conscious collectivity. They realize that their functions and responsibilities must alienate them from the rank and file, at least in part. The process of alienation will be described shortly.

When officers comprise a socially heterogeneous group representing a heterogeneous membership (e.g., heterogeneous in occupation, religion, social origin, and ethnicity), a divisive political dimension may be inserted within both the officer corps and the body politic. Such a situation tends to foster a patronage mentality in which the pursuit of offices may become more important than the pursuit of union goals. This is defined as "politics" by the members, and it magnifies cleavages, instability, or apathy.

Despite these tendencies, cleavages between union officers and members are usually not so sharp as those between management and the workers, for several reasons. First, the chains of man-boss relations that typify management organization are absent in the

14 *Ibid.*

union structure. Second, communication between members and officers is freer, more frequent, and more direct. Third, the thoughtways of both groups are very similar since union officers are almost universally recruited from the rank and file. Fourth, members tend to believe that they have ultimate control over major policy decisions in the union.[15]

Situational and Role Conflicts

Organizational effectiveness is highest when the role orientations of officers are harmonious with the situational demands of their position. Just as a different type of manager is needed when a company faces different market situations, a different type of union officer is needed when the union is just being organized, when it has achieved a *modus operandi* with management, when it faces a protracted strike, and so on. Unfortunately, the situational demands of the union do not wait upon the elegant matching of the role orientations of its officers. On the contrary, the same officials are often called upon to play considerably different roles simultaneously or serially. Obviously, most officials do not have the requisite versatility, a fact which reduces their effectiveness and creates dissatisfactions on the part of members and office aspirants.

Selekman points out that most union leaders perform four main roles:[16]

1. Commander of a fighting organization.
2. Administrative head of a fraternal society.
3. Business administrator of a labor marketing cooperative.
4. Democratic leader of a political association.

All of these roles concern policy determination and administration. Only in theory do the rank and file fix policy. If the members have confidence in the leaders, they will accept their recommendations on policies. The mass of union members do not have the time, capacity, or inclination to inform themselves on policy matters. Their acts tend to be in the nature of plebiscites; they vote "yes" or they veto.

---

[15] Sayles and Strauss, *op. cit.,* p. 236.
[16] Benjamin M. Selekman, *Labor Relations and Human Relations,* McGraw-Hill, 1947, p. 180.

The roles which union leaders are expected to play are not equally important at all times. The age of the local, the nature of its relation to the international, the kind of problems it currently faces, its degree of maturity, and the nature of its structure call for different types of role performance. Leaders are rare who play each part equally well. We shall examine how union leaders attempt to play and integrate each of these roles.

Fighting Leader

Union members evaluate the performance of their leaders by the kind of contract they secure. Even though bargaining may occur on an industry-wide basis, local leaders must take some responsibility for the kind of contract the union gets.[17] The worst accusation leveled against leaders is that they "sold out" to the employers, or that they were handed a "bill of goods." To avoid this charge officers try to convince members that they are *fighting hard* for them. They remind the members of the great strength of management and how hard it is to get concessions. They tell them that they cannot fight management alone; that all the members must stick and fight together.

Although the union leader is supposed to head a militant organization, many things conspire to make this role ineffective. Foremost is the fact that he has to fight management with a voluntary army over which he has no final authority. Indeed, as Muste suggested, the union leader is put in the anomalous position of being a democratic generalissimo. He is elected to office by his soldiers often on the eve of battle. His army votes on issues of war, peace, or armistice. The plan of attack is discussed in public debate by the soldiers! Secrecy, obedience, and loyalty, the heart of a military organization, are at low ebb.[18]

Other restrictions hamper the skillful execution of the role of the fighting leader. The international may send in negotiators (generals and diplomats) who do not know the local situation. The international may refuse permission to wage war, or to negotiate. It may insist on approving the terms of the armistice (con-

---

[17] In cases of industry-wide bargaining the international consults officers of locals, or the locals send representatives to the international negotiating committee. Locals then abide by the majority decision of this committee.

[18] A. J. Muste, "Functional Fights in Trade Unions," in J. B. S. Hardman (ed.), *American Labor Dynamics*, Harcourt, Brace, 1928, pp. 332–337.

tract). It may denounce the general to the soldiers and ask them
to throw him out.

The enemy, or employer, is rarely an "easy" opponent. His army
is an efficient bureaucracy run by professional generals. Moreover, for the union the purpose of battle is not to destroy the
enemy but to make him treat the soldiers better. In fact, if the
enemy perishes the soldiers may starve. Therefore, the opponent
must be treated with some consideration, for after the battle his
cooperation is needed. Furthermore, the armistice (contract) binds
the union and the enemy together. If the armistice is violated the
government may be called in.

Thus the union leader is confronted with difficult situations. He
tries to be a democratic general but finds he is accused of being
too timid or too autocratic. He worries about the kind of attack
he should make. If he decides to take the course of the diplomat,
he tries to collect all the economic data he can to negotiate. His
intelligence organization, however, may not be very effective and
the employers may have decided to fight. If so, he must revise his
plans and convince his men to gird for battle. Depending on their
mood, he is called courageous, alert, stupid, ineffective, or bun-
gling.

Union leaders must make many policy decisions in their dealings with employers. Although members may have instructed them
on such areas as the closed shop, jurisdiction, the training and
recruitment of workers, union recognition, higher wages, or
shorter hours, the officers may have to make new decisions prior
to getting member endorsement. They never are certain they will
get backing on these private decisions. Even though the military
role of the union leader may have been overdrawn, obviously
situational components make the role a difficult one to perform.

Fraternal Executive

Union officers are also supposed to be leaders of a fraternal
association. As such they are expected to build in the members
a feeling of loyalty and devotion toward one another and the
local. *Esprit de corps* is essential if the organization is to function
effectively during such crises as unemployment, strikes, and jurisdictional disputes. Leaders who want solidarity must know how
to make members aware of their common bonds and purposes.

They must imbue them with a willingness to endure hardships for the sake of the organization. Many officers find this assignment hard to carry out. If they are full-time officers, they cannot spend much time with workers on the plant floor. The longer they stay in office, the less they know the workers' problems and ideas. With high labor turnover they know fewer and fewer members personally. If they are not friendly they are called "stuck up" and lose popularity. If they play the fraternal role well, union leaders will not depart very far from the language, dress, ideas, and sentiments of the workers.

Yet the very nature of the job exposes the union leader to new experiences not shared by the members. As he comes in contact with management he may perceive management-labor relations in their totality for the first time. Unless he is ideologically rigid he changes and adjusts to his new perspective. Yet he must not depart too far from his earlier sentiments, for they are closer to those of the membership. If he changes too much he is considered a "sell-out" and no longer a brother who knows the problems of the working "stiff."

Still another problem that makes the fraternal role difficult is the task of welding a heterogeneous membership into a fraternal society. Union members represent many political groups, occupations, nationalities, races, religions, age groups, and interests. Many locals are made up of workers who have different social background, experience, and expectations. The Negro members may be concerned with equal treatment, women with equal pay, nationalities with the use of their native tongue, older men with security, younger men with high wages, politicians with votes, and so on.

To build the *esprit de corps* in such a mixed group by depending only on the energy, drive, and enthusiasm of the leader and his cohorts is no simple matter. Solidifying a heterogeneous group is made easier by creating meaningful rituals around initiation, suspension, reinstatement, promotion, and retirement. Shop codes, emblems, and songs may also help build a sense of identification, but men do not live by ritual alone. Solidarity grows as the union performs an increasing number of functions for its members. In their fraternal role, then, union officers must try to create a broad program. At their behest unions have assumed many functions which other institutions have failed to develop. Some of them deal with worker education (including union history), counseling, banking, credit facilities, medical care, insurance, cooperative housing, legal advice, recreation, vacation facilities, cooperative buying, and political action.[19] The more needs the unions meet, the closer they approach the objective of becoming a community for the members. This is one of the main reasons why union leaders fight employer welfare efforts. They argue that union services must take precedence over employer paternalism, if union loyalty is to flourish.

Furthering fraternal feelings by expanding union services is limited by available resources. The leader must decide what priority of union services will yield the greatest amount of union identification. Since some membership needs can be met by increased governmental services, many leaders believe that what the union cannot afford the government should provide. This is one reason why unions insist that governmental social security should expand its coverage and provisions.

Business Administrator

The business role of the local union leader is often ignored by students of the labor movement. Plainly, like any other organization the union must keep records, account for funds, prepare contracts, invest money, and staff the office. The larger the local, the greater the preoccupation with business functions. Accountants, auditors, secretaries, treasurers, economists, lawyers, counselors, typists, and others are added to the union pay roll. Placed in business situations union officials are constrained to act like businessmen. They become employers and officials of a supervisory hierarchy; they become imbued with the logic of cost and efficiency; they want a sound financial structure; they worry about the size of the treasury and about useless expenditures. Large locals and international headquarters often have large staffs which are themselves organized. Here unions are placed in the anachronistic situation of having industrial relations problems with their own employees.

[19] Mark Starr, "Role of Union Organization," in William F. Whyte (ed.), *Industry and Society*, McGraw-Hill, 1946; J. B. S. Hardman and Maurice F. Neufeld (eds.), *House of Labor*, Prentice-Hall, 1951.

The primary business function of union officers is to negotiate and administer the contract. This task takes as much skill and knowledge on the part of labor officials as it does for the businessmen. To accomplish it effectively, the labor leader needs to know something about the economics of the industry and the business condition of the company and its competitors. Such knowledge and experience are not quickly acquired upon election, but only with long tenure in office. This fact is not generally appreciated by the rank and file. They believe that the offices should be passed around, and that terms of office should be short. Some older and experienced unions which recognize the need for business experience continually reelect their officials. Other officials manipulate the rank and file to stay in office. In either case, the ability of the official to stay in office depends upon his capacity to play his political role.

Political Chief

An elected official who wants to stay in office must "play politics." Politics is the art of moving others toward particular goals in nonadministrative situations. It normally arises in all institutional sectors where there is competition for leadership. It is inherently neither good nor bad but a normal process of life in nonhereditary social systems. The political process of the union is characterized by the circulation of leaders, which has two phases: getting into office and staying in office. Both depend upon the ability of the office seeker to get support and approval from the membership.

Getting or staying in office is not very difficult in many unions, for the number who aspire for office is often small. In most locals any energetic, ambitious, and moderately intelligent person can, if he wishes, play at least a secondary leadership role. There are three main reasons for the paucity of candidates to office. Most important is the apathy and noninvolvement of the rank and file. Secondly, some employees consider themselves to be temporary union members, for they aspire to become part of management. Third, a large number of members do not feel qualified by knowledge, temperament, or experience to hold office.

In some of the older unions, officers need do little to stay in office. The members are apparently satisfied with their performances, and they perfunctorily reelect them. In newer unions, staying in office may be more difficult. The techniques incumbents use to remain in office depend on the history of the local, current issues, and their past performance. Irrespective of external conditions, however, the candidates must be articulate enough to convince the rank and file that they are doing a good job. Inexperienced and insecure leaders may exhibit a more militant posture toward employers, in the hope of tapping the latent hostility which employees have toward employers. It is therefore sometimes difficult to distinguish when attacks on employers are genuine and when they are motivated by political expediency. Both factors are probably operative.

A mechanic, recently defeated in a local union election, complained, not without some justification:

> It's not what you know or do that counts here. Most of the fellows vote for the guy who makes the most noise. They hear "Joe Smith," "Joe Smith," "Joe Smith." When time comes to vote, they don't know the records of the candidates. They see "Joe Smith" and think, "Oh, yeah, I know him." So they vote for him. The next day, they hear something about Smitty and remember him as the guy that did them dirt. And they say to themselves, "I voted for the wrong guy." See what I mean?

Attention-getting devices have limited utility. If officers don't perform up to expectation they eventually earn the reputation of being "loudmouths." An ex-union official commented on this situation:

> In the long run, the quiet efficient guy makes the best officer. At first the members like the extrovert who wants to be in front. He gets elected to a small committee by making lots of noise. He develops a clique around him which puts him in office. Once there he keeps on making lots of noise to be reelected. Come the negotiations, he doesn't know what to do. So he tells 'em [the bosses] off. After a while the members get sick and tired of these blowhards who go in, and tell 'em off, and come out with nothing. I always say, it's what you come out with that counts. The membership learns the hard way.

The techniques of getting and staying in office are many and varied. A worker must gain popularity to get into office, and he must retain it to stay in office. Getting and retaining popularity take time and effort. In large locals especially, no individual can make himself known to all members. The aspirant to office needs helpers and supporters; he needs a political machine. The machine is so important that the operation of the union cannot be understood without an appreciation of its rise and function.

EMERGENT STRUCTURE: THE POLITICAL MACHINE

In earlier chapters, we demonstrated why informal organization could be thought of as an emergent structure or as a structural response to bureaucracy. It was suggested that from almost any perspective informal organization has both functional and dysfunctional consequences. However it functions, it is an inevitable and necessary ingredient of organizational life. So it is with the political machine of the union. It too is an "informal organization" which emerges as a structural response to the problems confronting a democratic structure in an industrial context.

A political machine is a voluntary organization of people who seek to regulate and control the political process. When formalized it may be a party or a caucus. Whatever its name, the machine is a persistent creature of democratic structures operating in large-scale organizations and comes into being whenever offices and decisions are ultimately dependent upon the consent of large numbers of people. It attempts to organize decisionmaking in the elective, administrative, and legislative processes. There is nothing unusual or insidious about it. A union political machine may be more easly understood if one thinks about its analogous counterpart in the political party of a city, state, or nation. Let us examine how a machine grows in a local union.

Natural History of a Machine

Sam Gibson is a toolmaker in Department 34 of Acme Manufacturing Corporation. Sam is a likable fellow who has the respect and confidence of his fellow workers. He attends union meetings regularly and shows an interest in union affairs. Some of his friends in Department 34 decide that he would make a good steward. He is elected with little opposition. As he makes the rounds as a steward, he sees many people. He discusses union affairs with them and lets them know that he is available for office. An informal group of his co-workers and friends start to talk about running Sam for office. They point to his good record as a steward and get others to "talk up" Sam.

Soon an organized drive is under way. Sam and his associates draw up a program or platform which promises different things to different groups. They gather a list of the unfulfilled promises of incumbents. Armed with handbills, slogans, and informal agreements, Sam's clique goes to work. They buttonhole as many of their friends as possible and ask them to support Sam for office. All the tactics and appeals of local precinct politics are used. If a good job of electioneering is done, Sam is elected to office.

Once in office, Sam naturally appoints his friends and other ardent supporters to important posts and committees. If he likes his job, he may want to stay in office. In the meantime, another group is booming a rival. Sam gets his "heelers" in the plants to campaign for him again. They distribute literature, make new promises, and advance arguments against new candidates. Here is a typical appeal of a heeler:

> You know Sam Gibson has done a fine job in office. He's got a lot of valuable experience. It'd be a shame to change presidents at this critical time. . . . Paul Miller is a good candidate, but he's green. I think he needs more experience. Besides, you know how those guys are in Miller's gang. If they got in power, they'd shove Department 34 around, and you know I'm not kiddin'.

Staying in Power

Obviously, a machine needs fuel and lubrication to keep running. In the union the loyalty of political supporters must be rewarded. Sometimes the machine uses graft, patronage, and threats to stay in power. But in most cases it feeds on the normal motives of its heelers. Some of them are ardent unionists who believe that their candidate and his program will do the most for unionism. They give unstintingly of their time and energy. Others have aspirations for a high appointive job in the union. Lacking the personality qualification for leadership, they work for a machine with the hope that their service and loyalty will be rewarded.

Others are motivated by money to support a machine. They may get a job on the election committee, which pays them a few dollars on election day. The main reward which most machine workers receive is the fun of participating in something exciting and recognition in the form of an office or committee post. A few like to bask in the limelight of their champion, especially if he is rising in the union hierarchy: "Yes, I know Gibson well. He used to work right next to me. About once a month some of the boys who put him where he is get together for a little poker. Sam's a great guy. He's still one of the boys. His job hasn't gone to his head."

Any group in office has some advantages over others aspiring to power. One of the advantages is the quasi-monopoly which officers have over communication channels, the most important of which is the union newspaper. During the membership meetings, the entrenched can emphasize the things that make their administration seem efficient. They may refuse to recognize dissident "agitators" on the floor. They can pack committees with those who are sympathetic to them. They can time the presentation of "bad" reports so that they do little damage. They can use delaying tactics, call meetings at peculiar hours, and take arbitrary actions. In short, they can and do use all the parliamentary tricks known to democratic associations.

As already noted, an important advantage accruing to a machine is the union newspaper. Since many members rarely attend union meetings, the newspaper is their only source of official information. The editor is often hired from the outside. Since he is responsible to the president, he sometimes becomes his personal publicity agent. For example, the president may request "fuller coverage" of his activities in the paper. If he senses a rival for office, he may, by a well-placed editorial, nip a boom in the bud. A typical editorial might read:

> I have been very gratified with the work that brother John Beagle has been doing on the grievance committee. During the year we have settled 138 grievances amicably. The membership may not realize the amount of time and energy we have had to spend on settling grievances. John Beagle has been of invaluable assistance to me in this work. The job of chairman of the grievance committee is going to continue to be critical. We need the skill, energy, and experience of John Beagle on this job.

How elections turn out is the final test of the efficiency of a machine and of an administration. Sayles and Strauss have indicated that there is a complex relationship between events and situations in the plant and final election results.[20] The latter are influenced by intergroup relations, relative wage levels of occupational groups, seniority structure, negotiations, campaign techniques, and so on.

Rarely can a machine retain power for long without responding to the desires of the membership. The workers are prone to feel that success in achieving objectives is more important than conforming to the democratic ideals of a town meeting. Turnover of officials therefore tends to reflect membership dissatisfaction with performance rather than their devotion to democratic principles. Therefore, effective machines often stay in power for long intervals. If they do not result in corrupt administrations, the question may be raised whether they can remain democratic and responsive.

Since the typical situation in American unions is one-party rule, the observer may conclude that democratic government is impossible and that the machine and the hired staff usually have complete charge of union affairs. Indeed, this is sometimes the case.[21] However, several mechanisms may keep the machine responsible. The most common is the existence of factions among actively interested members, and even the existence of factions within the machine. The factions may be based on ideological, economic, and social differences among the membership, or on the personal ambitions of some to secure offices. Whatever their origin, they can threaten the security of a machine and thus make it responsive to membership demands, even though the membership may appear to be apathetic.

In a few instances, American unions have developed formal parties for their internal government with all of the paraphernalia found in the national political scene. Lipset, Trow, and Coleman found that the party system in the Typographical union was based on long-existing cleavages among the members over crucial economic problems and on particular historical factors which stabilized a given structure.[22] The position of the union between

[20] *Ibid.,* pp. 134–149.

[21] As described by Joseph Goldstein, *The Government of a British Trade Union,* Free Press, 1952, pp. 195–228.

[22] Seymour Martin Lipset, Martin A. Trow, and James A. Coleman, *Union Democracy,* Free Press, 1956, pp. 393–412.

the lower and middle classes tended to create permanent radical and moderate parties. The strong occupational cohesion among the printers and the long autonomy of the locals prior to the rise of the international bureaucracy prevented the latter from de-politicizing union affairs. Conflicts, such as the legitimacy of secret societies within the union to control union offices and fore-men's jobs, also promoted permanent political divisions.

Although political factions have less stability than the party system described above, they do serve the same function of imped-ing oligarchic tendencies in the union. Moreover, in such unions as the UAW, officers are committed to democratic principles and at the same time are aware of the tendencies for apathy and oligarchy to develop. They constantly appeal to the members to exert their democratic prerogatives. Moreover, they have estab-lished a mechanism in the Public Review Board by which mem-bers can seek redress against alleged wrongs committed by the union and its officers. Jack Stieber has examined the activities of this board of citizens and found that it has operated as planned. The board has exercised the right to review union actions against members and officers to correct errors which have been made.[23]

In summary, union democracy suffers from many of the same structural problems of all large-scale democracies. Whether unions can realize the ideals of democracy depends in part on the empha-sis placed on those ideals. As long as the ideals remain viable and efforts are continuously made to institute mechanisms (however unsatisfactory) to realize them, the organization need not become oligarchic despite internal strains in that direction.[24]

THE LOCAL AND THE INTERNATIONAL

An important point of segmentation within the union struc-ture develops between the local and the international. Although many unions have locals which are highly autonomous, the gen-eral tendency is for the internationals to centralize functions,

[23] Jack Stieber, "The UAW Public Review Board: An Examination and Evaluation," in *Democracy and Public Review: An Analysis of the UAW Public Review Board,* A Report to the Center for the Study of Democratic Institutions, 1960, pp. 3–28.

[24] William A. Faunce and George Won are studying intensively the func-tion of democratic belief systems among delegates to the UAW convention.

thus weakening local political structures. As in all large-scale bureaucracies, the international may well develop a large corps of experts (a civil service) to perform tasks according to professional standards. Understandably, many union functions are too complex to be performed by untrained amateurs at the local level. Thus, as Wilensky and others have pointed out, the intellectual, the expert, and the bureaucrat in the international obtain greater and greater control over *policy-making*.[25]

Bureaucracies tend to weaken political life by routinizing decision-making in the hands of functionaries. Many local and international officials recognize this tendency and the consequence it has for inducing apathy and alienation in the rank and file. The state and international conventions, with all their color and ritual, serve to reaffirm the belief in the bonds between the state and national officers and membership. If the international can be tied into a political process of the local, the international can become a reality to local members. Efforts are made both by local and by international officials to do this. As indicated earlier, while the ordinary worker has little or no direct contact with the international, officers do, and they can use these contacts to improve their political situation. Although the local is becoming increasingly dependent on the international, local leaders can either facilitate or discourage this trend, depending on their personal motives, aspirations, and ideologies. Career-minded local officers may be classified as those who want to remain in power locally and those who want offices in the international. Those who want to remain in power locally can use the prestige and power of the international to advantage. The mechanism is indirect. Since the reelection of international officers depends in part upon how the officers of the locals evaluate them, and since local officers are involved in selecting delegates to the international conventions, international officers who want to remain in office must lend their prestige to local officers who want to stay in power.

If the job of a local officer is threatened, the international may

[25] Harold L. Wilensky, *Intellectuals in Labor Unions*, Free Press, 1956; Joel Seidman *et al.*, *The Worker Views His Union*, University of Chicago Press, 1958; and Kermit Eby, "The Expert in the Labor Union," *American Journal of Sociology*, July, 1951, pp. 27–32.

give him a "favorable spread" in the newspaper. International officers may visit the local and make speeches on the "good job brother Smith is doing here." They may also furnish the local its best legal talent and negotiators in bargaining sessions, and may appoint local members to jobs in the international. Apart from political expediency, international officers generally encourage long tenure for local officers. They like to deal with experienced men, thus avoiding the task of teaching each new batch of local officers what their duties and responsibilities are toward the international. International officers also find it difficult to keep track of shifting local situations. Like most executives, they prefer stability in their organizations.

Although international officers have longer tenure than local ones, they too are threatened by rivals. Since they soon lose touch with the rank and file, they must depend on their reputations or on a political machine to keep in office. An aggressive head of a large local commands a large number of delegates at the international convention. He can organize a caucus at the convention and threaten the security of international officers or exert pressure on them to change their polices.[26] The local leader can report to the members that there is "dry rot" in the international, that the international is dominated by certain unfriendly locals, that the international is threatening the autonomy of locals, that there is waste, corruption, and plundering of the treasury. These attacks may be used as a cry-wolf technique for officers who wish to remain in power locally, or they may be genuine attacks on the international. Most local officers are sincere and hardworking, and try to cooperate with the international. By considering local and international elections as part of the game, they make possible continuity and order in union government.

UNION LOCALS AND THE COMMUNITY

Strong cleavages may occur not only within the union but also between the internal structure and the community and management. Since conflict with management will be considered in the next chapter, the local's relationships with the community will

[26] See Faunce, *op. cit.*

conclude the internal analysis of the local. Organized labor in the United States is beginning to realize that its general goals cannot be achieved without community support. Labor's reputation in the community is part of a political milieu which has bearing on local, state, and national legislative policies toward labor. In addition to this concern, labor is desirous of securing such local objectives as a fair tax policy, adequate administration of city services to working-class areas, adequate vocational and general educational facilities, adequate financing of social welfare agencies, and other objectives. Just as the Chamber of Commerce is interested in the broad spectrum of city institutional services, so is the AFL–CIO Council.

Serious labor efforts to enter the community arena have been made only during the last twenty years. They may be described as challenges to the virtual monopoly which businessmen and the professionals have had over the community's decision-making apparatus. As might be expected, business has resisted labor's demand for a share of local power and has yielded only when necessary. It is not unrealistic, therefore, to envision the community as a broader sphere of collective bargaining between business, labor, and other interests. The authors have examined this process in detail in their book entitled *Industry, Labor, and Community*.[27] Their purpose here is to refer to this area briefly to complete the analysis of the setting of organized labor on the local level.

Several studies have dealt with the actual activities of organized labor on the local level. James McKee's pioneer study of Steelport (a city of 40,000) showed that the CIO had won formal political control of the community after 1945 but had not altered the basic strength and prestige of business.[28] Moreover, the integration of the Catholic church, ethnic groups, and labor unions into a bloc foreshadowed changes in power alignments. Hart indicated that the UAW in Windsor (population 100,000) was disengaging itself from management-dominated organizations and

[27] Harper, 1960. The following section is taken from pp. 512–573, 584–585, 609–611, 667–677.

[28] "Status and Power in the Industrial Community," *American Journal of Sociology*, January, 1953, pp. 364–370.

was substituting union-sponsored activities to meet the social needs of the workers.[29] In Illini City (population 70,000), Wray found that the unions (despite increased bargaining strength) had not genuinely influenced the programs of city associations. The community representatives of the unions were absorbed into business organizations such as the Chamber of Commerce.[30] In Steeltown (population 40,000), the unions traditionally used their strength to settle economic and grievance problems, but not political, welfare, educational, or other problems. Yet, in a crisis situation, the unions had power resources which had not been manifested earlier.[31] In Jonesville (population 10,000), the unions had not expanded their activities beyond the narrowest limits of collective bargaining and failed to become a significant force in community life.[32] Somewhat the same situation existed in Regional City (population 331,000)[33] and in the satellite city of Cibola (population 20,000).[34]

Union Officials as Community Influentials

Recent findings from a large research project based on studies of community power structures in a group of southwestern (U.S.) and Mexican cities have been reported by Charles P. Loomis and his associates.[35] These findings make a substantial confirmation of the domination of businessmen in community decision-making. The occupations of key influentials were studied for El Paso, Denver, Tucson, Las Cruces, San Diego, McAllen, C. Juarez, and

[29] C. W. M. Hart, "Industrial Relations Research and Social Theory," *Canadian Journal of Economics and Political Science,* February, 1949, pp. 53–73.

[30] Donald E. Wray, "The Community and Labor-Management Relations," *Labor-Management Relations in Illini City,* Institute of Labor and Industrial Relations, University of Illinois, 1953.

[31] Charles R. Walker, *Steeltown,* Harper, 1950, pp. 42–45.

[32] W. L. Warner et al., *Democracy in Jonesville,* Harper, 1949.

[33] Floyd Hunter, *Community Power Structure,* University of North Carolina Press, 1953.

[34] Robert O. Schulze and Leonard Blumberg, "The Determination of Local Power Elites," *American Journal of Sociology,* November, 1957, pp. 291–296.

[35] William V. D'Antonio, William H. Form, Charles P. Loomis, and Eugene C. Erickson, "Institutional and Occupational Representations in Eleven Community Influence Systems," *American Sociological Review,* June, 1961, pp. 440–446.

Tijuana. Comparisons with Pacific City, English City, and Southern City show the following results:

Nine out of the eleven cities reported at least one financier among the key influentials with a total of 39 (almost a quarter) being named in all. Only English City and Las Cruces failed to produce a financier in the top group. Both of the relatively specialized categories of manufacturing and merchandising were represented in nine cities. The merchants (including both wholesale and retail) produced slightly over one-fifth of the key influentials, with English City and El Paso failing to contribute to this category. Among manufacturers, who were almost one-sixth of the total, only Tucson and Las Cruces were not represented, probably because there is a relative absence of manufacturing in the economies of these cities.

The most frequently chosen occupational category outside of business was that of the lawyer, represented eight times in seven cities. It may be that the lawyer is becoming an effective link between business and other sectors of the community. Mayors were chosen as key influentials in five of the eleven cities, whereas other governmental officials and political leaders were chosen nine times in four cities. While it may be argued that the hierarchical structure of local government makes it likely that the mayor will be most often chosen from among governmental officials, the fact that mayors were not chosen in six of the cities suggests the need for further exploration of the place of government in the community power structure.

Labor is notably lacking representation in the influence structure in all communities except English City. In like manner, agriculture is represented only in Las Cruces, by two of the thirteen persons listed; one of the two is at the very top of the list. Religion, education, society and wealth, welfare, and cultural leaders have only scattered representation.

Union Power in the Community: A Case Study

The city of Lansing, Michigan, was selected by the authors for a detailed study of the degree of penetration of organized labor in the main institutional areas of the city.[36] An attempt was made

[36] See William H. Form, "Organized Labor's Place in Community Power Structure," *Industrial and Labor Relations Review*, July, 1959, pp. 526–539.

to assess the relative representation and power of organized labor and management in economic bargaining, local government, political parties, social welfare, education, mass communication, and religion.

Economic bargaining power

Relative economic position of management and labor in Lansing is actually determined in Detroit. The pattern worked out between General Motors and the United Automobile Workers in Detroit is applied almost unilaterally in Lansing. This pattern must then be generally taken over by other locally owned manufacturing plants if they are to retain their labor force. The list of gains which the UAW has wrested from GM since World War II is impressive and suggests a shift in power toward organized labor. While no entirely suitable indices of change in bargaining power are available, obtaining new types of economic gains (fringe benefits), keeping ahead of the rise in cost of living, and raising wages faster than distributed profits probably reflect over-all union bargaining strength.

The UAW has achieved the following gains since World War II: (1) sizable increases in basic wages, (2) share in the growth of productivity, (3) cost-of-living clauses, (4) supplementary unemployment benefits, and (5) other benefits. While GM could probably make these concessions easily from an economic standpoint, they represented a relative loss in bargaining strength. More important, from the point of view of locally owned enterprises, giving workers the "GM package" represented economic concessions relatively greater than those of GM. Within the present framework of ownership, management now has only a slight edge in bargaining power. Interviews with the top thirty business and industry officials in the city revealed that they thought unions had dominant power in economic bargaining, whereas the top forty labor influentials estimated their bargaining power to be almost equal to that of management.

Government

Lansing city government is allegedly nonpartisan, but it is not difficult to identify the party loyalties of those running for office. To determine the influence of organized labor in city government, the occupations and union support of all candidates for mayor, council, and other elective offices were examined for the period of 1948–1957, when labor was most active. Although almost three-tenths of the 185 candidates received moderate support from organized labor, only 4 percent had all-out support. Actually, one-third of all *elected* city officials had moderate backing of labor, although only one union official was actually elected.

Apparently having the backing of labor helped candidates get elected, for almost seven-tenths of those who had such backing were elected, as compared to six-tenths of those who did not have it. These figures must be interpreted within the context of two trends. First, over the decade organized labor tended to back more incumbents who had proved "not unfriendly" to labor, although they were not initially supported when they ran for office. Almost one-quarter of all labor-backed candidates fell into this category. While this technique stimulated incumbents to accept labor backing and decreased the political labeling of candidates, it also reduced the political initiative of organized labor. Although the political strength of labor is increasing, a majority of candidates with explicit union support has not yet been elected.

Municipal boards

There are nineteen boards in the city, members of which are selected by the mayor with the approval of the City Council. The president of the Lansing AFL–CIO Council publicly announced a union policy to have more "working-class people" on municipal boards and commissions. The occupational composition of municipal boards from 1945 to 1957 was examined (about 500 members). If manual, protective, clerical, and service occupations constitute the "working class," only 18 percent of appointed board members were working class.

A closer inspection of the data reveals that no manual workers were appointed to seven boards, less than the average of 9 percent served on eight boards, and more than this average were appointed to four boards. Exactly half of all manual workers on boards were either trustees of the Police and Fire Retirement Board or members of the Traffic Commission. Excluding these, less than 10 percent of city board and commission members were manual workers. Small as this proportion is, it represented a rising trend. Clearly, proprietors primarily and professionals secondarily overwhelmingly dominated municipal boards and commissions. Real estate and insurance agents, typically heavy contributors to political campaigns, were widely represented on the boards.

Political parties

Lansing has been traditionally Republican in state politics. Prior to the New Deal it sent an occasional Democrat to the state legislature. On only three occasions since 1932 has it elected a Democrat to the legislature. Organized labor has virtually no influence on the local Republican party. While the local Democratic party would have no elective potential without the support of organized labor, the latter cannot guarantee the votes of union members. In a poll conducted among workers in the UAW in 1956, the party found that only 40 percent would support Democratic candidates for state and national offices. Only an occasional labor union official was on the county executive, finance, or advisory committee of the party. However, local Democrats help elect a Democratic governor and an occasional congressman. This success gives the unions some political capital which they might otherwise not have.

Education

Unions had little interest in education prior to 1947. With a change in leadership in the local UAW, labor began to show concern for the operation of local educational agencies. There are four areas of interest in local education: school board elections, the joint industry-labor apprentice program, Business-Industry-Education Day, and the adult education program. Analysis of the occupational background of members of the Board of Education reveals that only two union members have been elected to the board since 1935. Only 14 percent of the candidates have been manual or clerical workers. Almost six-tenths of the board members have been proprietors, managers, or officials, and one-third have been professional workers. Two-thirds of the proprietors were in wholesale and retail trade, and the rest were insurance or real estate brokers. Candidates who were managers in the large industries were generally defeated because of insufficient local reputation. A few of the board members who were professionals, government workers, or managers in small home-owned industries were sympathetic to organized labor.[37] On the basis of occupation and residence it appears that less than a fifth of the board members would be sensitive to the educational "needs" of the "working classes."[38]

The joint Apprentice Program Committee in the city school system supervises job training and part-time schooling of those planning to enter the trades. Management and the unions have an equal representation on this committee. Although the participants agree that the program has been administered to their satisfaction, it is clear that industry occupies the dominant position. It can accept or reject any candidates for the program, and the foremen are solely responsible for the reports on the progress of apprentices made to the committee.

The adult education program of the Board of Education has been expanded significantly since World War II. In addition to offering the standard academic and technical courses, the Board has instituted courses "on demand." Almost all of the course requests from labor have been granted by the Board, and in some cases the Board paid instructors to teach courses of interest largely to union members. Each year school administrators have dinner with union officials to discuss problems of mutual concern. This is a far cry from the situation in 1937, when school administrators headed the citizens' committee against the UAW strikes.

Michigan has been in the vanguard of sponsoring Business-Industry-Education Day for over a decade. Since organized labor does not participate in the local program, its officials condemn the annual attempt of businessmen to win the loyalties of the

---

[37] These findings are not untypical. See Roy W. Caughran, "The School Board Member Today," *American School Board Journal,* November and December, 1956.

[38] Of course, some professionals, government workers, and school administrators are often aware of the educational needs of working-class families, and these groups are present in the city. However, when the budget is tight, board members tend to act in terms of the needs of the status groups closest to them. That board composition does not necessarily reflect policy has been indicated by Peter Rossi. See also Alice H. Cook, "Labor's Role in Community Affairs," *Bulletin 32,* New York State School of Industrial and Labor Relations, Cornell University, 1955, pp. 4–15.

teachers. Educational administrators have repeatedly offered to establish a Labor-Education Day, but union officials insist that unions should participate as equal members in the present arrangement.

To summarize, the penetration of labor in various educational agencies has been uneven. Highest influence was found in the adult education program, followed by the apprentice program, membership in the Board of Education, and Business-Industry-Education Day. An arbitrary estimation of penetration of unions into education would be about 35 percent or roughly the extent of labor representation on the Board.

Welfare

Organized labor is attaching increasing importance to the activities of private welfare agencies in the community. Not only do union members normally utilize the services of welfare agencies more heavily than other groups, but these agencies are also called upon to relieve distress of union members during prolonged strikes. Business groups back private welfare efforts to minimize government spending and control in this area. They also use welfare activities as a highly legitimate status platform. Moreover, during prolonged strikes, they want some control over the funds disbursed to striking workers in their industries. Whether other groups would agree that the Community Chest is an important arena of social power is uncertain, but labor is sure that it is.

The history of labor's share in the control of private welfare reflects rather accurately labor's increasing economic power. Thus, in 1927, no union representative sat on the Community Chest Board, and an involuntary pay roll deduction plan was in effect. In 1933, perhaps in an attempt to head off the UAW, representatives of the company unions were placed on the Board. In 1940, two regular union members were hired on the staff of the Community Services Council, and union officers were made co-chairmen of the Industry and Labor Section of the annual Chest drive. At present, six of the thirty-six members of the Board of Directors of the Community Chest are union officials, and one member of the Community Services Council is a union member.

One-third of the Labor Participation Committee members of the Chest are union representatives. In addition, union people are found in twenty-one of the thirty-two agencies participating in the Community Services Council. Through such participation, unions can obtain representation on the huge 152-member budget committee of the Community Chest.

An analysis was made of the occupational composition of all agencies participating in the Community Services Council welfare boards. Labor union officials, manual and clerical workers comprise about one-tenth of all board members. Organized labor is generally dissatisfied with its share of representation on the individual boards, the Community Services Council, and the Community Chest Board of Directors. It has openly announced its intentions to increase its representation in all of these areas.

Four of the twenty-four local welfare agencies do not have a labor representative on their boards. Labor has not succeeded in having one of its members elected to the presidency of the board of directors of the Chest. No union member has ever been the general chairman of the annual campaign committee. Labor has never sponsored "progress" dinners during the annual campaigns. Speakers for these dinners are typically businessmen and professionals. While such positions may represent status rather than power holdings, management is not anxious to relinquish those offices. For example, the president of the Chest board of directors has always been a top influential in the community. The Hospital Expansion Fund Drive and other community projects have usually been organized and led by influentials who have had highest posts in the Council, Chest, and campaign committee.

How can labor's overall position be evaluated in the welfare area? In the Community Chest, labor has one-sixth of the seats on the strategic board of directors, one-third of the members of the Labor Participation Committee, and the co-chairmanship of the important Labor and Industry Section of the annual drive organization. It also has two union members on the staff of the Chest and the support of many professionals in and out of the organization. The strongest card that labor holds is the threat to withhold its contributions. Since it is responsible for collecting about 40 percent of the funds, it can, by withholding support, limit local welfare efforts.[39] Labor is reluctant to take this step because it cannot afford to support welfare activities without outside help. The proportion of union financial support to the Chest (40 percent) maximally represents its power in the welfare sector.

Mass communication

The only daily newspaper and the TV and radio stations in the city are strongly probusiness, if not antilabor. During the past decade the local daily (*State Journal*) has steadily increased the amount of news it reports about local union activities. The acquisition of a "labor reporter" who writes of the doings of local unions indicates some recognition of the power of labor. The *Labor News,* an independent weekly newspaper with a circulation of about 20,000, reaches all members of ex-CIO locals and some members of an ex-AFL local.

The positions taken by the *State Journal* during the decade 1945–1955 on major elections, referenda, and city projects were almost overwhelmingly followed. In two referenda, the *Labor News* successfully opposed the *State Journal*. In the first case, the *News* campaigned vigorously against an increase in bus fares, and in the second it opposed floating a general obligation bond by the city to build parking ramps. On a subsequent referendum taken during the bus strike, the *Journal*'s stand was followed by the voters to double the fares. On the parking ramp bond issue the real estate lobby flooded the *Journal* with paid advertising urging voters to reject the proposal, while the *News* espoused the same position editorially. In the two cases, where the position taken by the *News* was victorious, the voting turnout was comparatively small, less than half of a "good" turnout. While the *News* could not claim even minor responsibility for the "victories," it could be influential in lightly contested campaigns, when it had the support of a major economic interest. In 90 percent of the issues, mass communication agencies would be expected to oppose organized labor.

[39] Labor threatened to boycott the Hospital Expansion Fund Drive for four million dollars in 1954 unless it was assured greater representation and greater participation in overall plans. Key business and civic leaders felt it necessary to visit union halls and sell the program, an unprecedented step. See *Lansing Labor News,* June 3, 1954.

Religion

Religious leaders in the city have generally stayed away from labor-management controversy. Yet representatives of both sides nominated Protestant and Catholic clergy to the top forty influentials of the city. Top businessmen in the city are predominantly Protestants, and so are a majority of the manual workers. Lansing is unlike other cities in that the Catholic clergy cannot be considered strongly prolabor. To be sure, especially in the welfare sector, clergymen have occasionally sided with the unions. In an effort to increase the rapprochement with the clergy, labor has established a permanent liaison organization. Yet in a conflict situation with business groups less than a quarter of the clergy can be counted on to side openly with the unions. This figure is taken as the outside estimate of labor's influence on religious leaders.

Community and key influentials

During the study, a panel of community and labor influentials were interviewed. The community influentials were selected by asking two knowledgeables in seven institutional sectors to provide the names of fifty of the most influential people in the community. Knowledgeables were interviewed from mass communication, business, unions, welfare, education, government, and religion. Forty names on which there was the most consensus were considered community influentials.[40] The people were interviewed and asked, among other things, to select from the list (or add names) the ten most influential people in the community. These were called *key* influentials.

On the list of community influentials appeared two labor officials and three clergymen and one insurance agent who could usually be expected to be neutral and occasionally prolabor. Most of the remainder were businessmen and Republicans. The six "prolabor" influentials comprised about one-seventh of the influentials. They received almost one-fifth of the total votes which they could theoretically receive as key influentials. The two labor officials received 12 percent of the total vote they could receive as key influentials. A generous view of labor's strength

[40] Hunter, *op. cit.*, pp. 8–25.

among community influentials would be about one-seventh of the total.

Conclusions

Prior to 1937, when organized labor had weak bargaining strength, unions had virtually no influence in community-wide agencies. Since that time organized labor has increased its bargaining strength materially. The parallel gains it has made in the community are so dramatic that one may hazard the conclusion that a near equality in bargaining strength was the *sine qua non* of increased community power.

During the decade 1937–1947 labor sought to compete with management in the community in the same style that was effective in bargaining. However, the blunt accusations, the insistent demands, and the disregard of social niceties were not socially acceptable in the community arena. In 1947 a change in union leadership was accompanied by a change in the style of community participation which made it more acceptable to middle- and upper-status groups in the city. The white shirt, the soft-spoken word, and limited community goals became labor's new *modus operandi*. This approach not only enabled labor to penetrate into more community organizations but resulted in two or three "respectable" labor officials' becoming part of the community influence system. Labor developed most strength in areas in which it was guaranteed representation and in areas where it could withhold support, as in the Community Chest. It gained least power in areas where it was denied participation, such as in the mayor's committees and in the area of mass communication. Even within a given institutional area (Community Chest, education, and government), labor's penetration was uneven.

Labor's influence, however, still lags behind its power. Power is least developed in mass communication, city municipal boards, and city government. Without control of the municipal elective offices, labor's penetration into the community power structure will be limited. The question remains: How does labor react to this anomalous position?

In 1957 a slate of the top forty labor influentials in the city was drawn from names provided by a panel of knowledgeables in mass communication, industry, government, and educators interested in organized labor. These influentials were interviewed in order to obtain their assessment of how the local power structure operated and how organized labor fitted into this structure. A summary of the interview results revealed that the labor influentials, while acknowledging management's general dominance of the local community, believed that their own participation was significant. Although they felt excluded from the process of initiating local projects, they insisted they were influential when they entered a contest. The cleavage they saw between themselves and management representatives was not interpreted as an ideological one. Neither was local participation generally viewed as a contest with management and other groups. Moreover, there was little evidence that animosities in collective bargaining were carried over into the community arena.

Labor's primary community objectives are the strengthening and controlling of private health and welfare services and extending its local political influence. While union officials appraise their community participation as effective, they realize that they have not gotten other groups to support labor's other goals. In short, labor has made friends but has not influenced them. This lack of influence has not been fully tested because labor has not pushed for its traditional goals in the community arena; on the contrary, it has generally endorsed the goals set by local business influentials. As suggested, business is not seen in an oppositional context—either in terms of its community goals or in terms of the methods it uses to secure those goals. Many labor influentials suspect that their limited prestige and power result from business's greater interest, activity, and economic concern with community problems.

CONCLUSION

We have completed a structural analysis of American unionism, with primary emphasis on the local. This analysis reveals that the peculiar structure of American unions is due to a simultaneous desire to realize both the principles of democracy and effective bureaucratic organization. The result is a series of internal organizational disjunctures which occur at predictable points. Explication of these points of segmentation may make it appear that

American union structure is weak and inefficient. This, of course, is not the case. Compared to labor movements in other countries the American one is powerful. It is relatively rich, it has a corps of experienced officers, and its members show an unusual degree of solidarity in meeting daily problems at the shop level and collective bargaining problems with management and government. The next chapter focuses on the specific problems.

SELECTED BIBLIOGRAPHY

Barbash, Jack, *The Practice of Unionism,* Harper, 1956.
Form, William H., and Delbert C. Miller, *Industry, Labor, and Community,* Harper, 1960.
Hardman, J. B. S., and Maurice F. Neufeld (eds.), *The House of Labor,* Prentice-Hall, 1951.
Institute of Labor and Industrial Relations, *Labor-Management Relations in Illini City,* University of Illinois, 1953.
Lipset, Seymour Martin, Martin A. Trow, and James A. Coleman, *Union Democracy,* Free Press, 1956.
Ross, Arthur, *Trade Union Wage Policy,* University of California Press, 1948.
Sayles, Leonard R., and George Strauss, *The Local Union: Its Place in the Industrial Plant,* Harper, 1953.
Seidman, Joel, *et al., The Worker Views His Union,* University of Chicago Press, 1958.
Walker, Charles R., *Steeltown,* Harper, 1950.
Wilensky, Harold L., *Intellectuals in Labor Unions,* Free Press, 1956.

CHAPTER 10

Social Conflict
in
the Work Organization

THE CONTEXT OF INDUSTRIAL CONFLICT

The evolution of the labor union has been examined as a power response to managerial authority. It would be naïve to assume that once unions became recognized and evolved adequate internal administrative controls their era of conflict would be terminated. The preceding chapter, which described labor's struggle to share in the control of community institutions, revealed that the contest for power with management and other groups is continuously occurring on several different fronts. This chapter analyzes the union's struggle with management within the work organization.

Unfortunately labor-management conflict is too often seen as formal collective bargaining, which sometimes culminates in the strike. Sociologists, however, are concerned with the broadest dimensions of conflict, of which collective bargaining and the strike represent only two institutionalized forms. For example, Chapter 7 on informal organization revealed that the jockeying between two or more groups for advantages occurs ubiquitously at work. Attempts to control production, setting the pace of work, the recruitment of workers, supervisory behavior, and other activities may take place in the framework of either spontaneously evolved systems or formal organizations. The slowdown, the wildcat strike, the initiation of grievances, the crackdown, and similar devices are as genuine illustrations of collective bargaining (bargaining by collectivities to control the social environment of work) as are negotiations of the wage contract. Moreover, all of these phenomena may be initiated either informally or by officially recognized organizations. For this reason a range of seemingly diverse phenomena are considered together in this chapter.

An uninformed observer scanning the wide range of disruptive or conflict behavior in industry might conclude that only naked force or the necessity for economic survival prevents the collapse of the industrial order. However, a sociological analysis reveals that conflict is usually circumscribed by both custom and law, by necessity and morality.[1] Like other types of collective behavior, social conflict follows discernible patterns which are part of larger social and historical processes. Industrial conflict is often "orderly," in the sense that it arises out of a specific set of conditions; it is set in a particular social and cultural context; it is circumscribed by law; and it is part of a larger process which results in the creation of new social structures. In order to place industrial conflicts within this larger societal framework of emerging power relations, it is well to review briefly the "historical logic" of labor-management relations in the United States. The following section describes the historical development of certain structural features of collective bargaining.

The Rise of Bureaucracy and the Impersonalization of Power

Basic to an understanding of industrial conflict is the realization that it is inevitable in highly industrialized societies which are not centrally and autocratically controlled.[2] In several places we have emphasized that the emergence of large-scale industry destroyed the customary authority relations within smaller enterprises and created new bureaucratic forces which redefined the relationships among interdependent groups. As bureaucracies grew they simultaneously concentrated and delegated authority. They concentrated authority by giving fewer people at the top the right to make policy decisions and they delegated authority by distributing the execution of decisions to numerous function-

---

[1] See Georg Simmel, *Conflict and the Web of Group Affiliation,* trans. by Kurt H. Wolff, Free Press, 1955.

[2] Clark Kerr, "Industrial Conflict and Its Mediation," *American Journal of Sociology,* December, 1954, pp. 244–245.

aries. Thus large enterprises were organized into units which had considerable hierarchical communication but not much communication between different segments on similar levels of authority. This situation resulted in the isolation of large groups at the lower skill levels and fostered in them a sense of self-consciousness. Employees were made aware of their similar working conditions, uniform pay levels, common powerlessness, and common fate. They were easily stimulated to think and act in collective terms and to form such organizations as unions, clubs, or professional societies. In situations involving power and authority these bureaucratically reared people began to turn to their associations for help. The historical shift was from personal influence to group authority, from status relations to contractual ones.

The Emergence of Pressure Organizations

The more groups were formalized within and between enterprises, the more power conscious they became. As pressure groups, they used many of the same rational techniques to reach their goals which their employers had used to organize their work. Pressure groups formed in two areas. First and most obvious, they occurred within the enterprise. The process which segmentalized bureaucracies into subgroups, and the problems which attended the process, has been described above.[3] Secondly, pressure groups arose among similar interest groups in different enterprises. Thus, enterprises with similar problems organized to "promote and protect their mutual interests" against associations of other enterprises. For example, wool manufacturers organized to protect themselves against the inroads of synthetic fibers producers. At the same time, different functional groups in various enterprises banded together "to protect and promote their interests" against other groups in these enterprises. Thus the steelworkers in various enterprises organized unions to protect themselves against employers as a group. Literally thousands of business, professional, and labor lobbies were organized in all large cities. All of them had attributes of collective bargaining associations for they lived in a political atmosphere. Thus labor unions were not the only collective bargaining associations to emerge. Cooperatives, trade associations, professional societies,

[3] See Chapter 5.

and others arose to bargain collectively with various associations.

Formalizing occupational and business associations into power groups was not a new historical development. The guilds and trading leagues of the Middle Ages were the forerunners but not the ancestors of contemporary unions. The distinguishing feature of the contemporary situation is that functionally related groups have relative autonomy. It is not unusual, for example, for a managers' association, an engineering association, a foremen's association, factions of stockholders, labor unions, and perhaps even an organization of customers to coexist *within* a particular enterprise. Each group attempts to manipulate the others to obtain as much advantage as possible.

Group Self-Consciousness and Power Mobilization

The complexity of the current situation is revealed in Fig. 10.1, which shows the large number and variety of formal and informal groups involved in labor-management struggles. In one way or another, owners, managers, the public as consumers, the community, and finally government have become involved.

Since self-conscious groups became keenly aware of power situations, they continually sought new techniques to improve their relative power, or tried more effective methods to mediate their struggles. Since force, violence, and conflict were disesteemed, these associations, especially after World War I, established euphemistic industrial relations programs to bring about "peace and understanding."[4]

Some of the programs which were intended to weaken organized labor were entitled "Multiple Management," "Leadership in Industry," "Profit Sharing," "Community Relations," "Open Door Policy," "The Congressional System of Industrial Government," "Risk Participation," "Safe-Guarding the Right to Work," "Employee Counseling," "The American Plan," and "The Mohawk Valley Plan." Certainly not all plans having these titles were insidious devices to crush organized labor. On the contrary, some were sincere and extremely effective in reducing conflict.

[4] Harold L. Sheppard, "Approaches to Conflict in American Industrial Sociology," *British Journal of Sociology,* December, 1954, pp. 324–341.

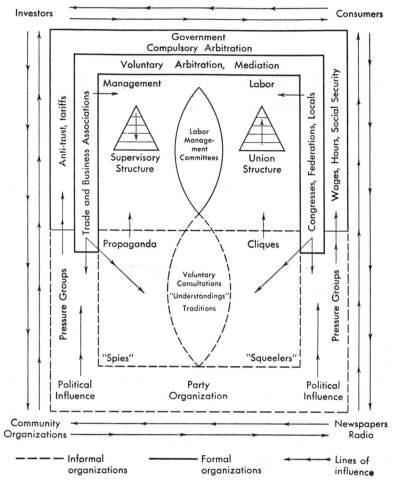

FIG. 10.1. Organizations Within and Without the Work Organization Which Are Drawn into the Struggle for Power.

Organized labor in America was also promulgating plans. It generally sought to reduce the power of management to hire and fire, to have a greater share in the profits of industry, to establish better working conditions, and to weaken the authority of foremen and supervision. The most frequently used title for programs embracing these ideas was "Democracy Within Industry."

Agencies which sought to mediate obdurate types of conflicts were also created. Among these were the American Arbitration Association, the Conciliation Service of the Department of Labor, the National Mediation Board, management-labor committees, and fact-finding committees. In struggles where both parties wanted a fair and impartial settlement of their differences and where neither side wanted a basic change in their power relations, the work of these agencies has been very effective.

Entrance of the State into the Power Struggle

Entrance of a third body into labor relations is inevitable in mature industrial societies where labor and management have nearly equal bargaining strength. Increasingly, the third body is the local, state, or national government. Governmental participation in industrial relations appeared in the United States around the turn of the century and grew rapidly after 1932. In an interdependent society any extended interruption in the operation of the basic industries can bring the entire economy to a standstill. Thus a prolonged interruption in coal mining will, in a relatively short period, reduce the operations of the steel and transportation industries. When these two basic industries are crippled the whole economy suffers. The government, as representative of the entire nation, must step in to reestablish production. The same applies with less force to other "industries," concerned with the "public welfare," broadly interpreted. Thus when the Metropolitan Opera season was canceled in 1961, owing to the inability of management and the musicians' union to arrive at an agreement, President Kennedy expressed his deep concern and sent Labor Secretary Goldberg to help the parties reach an agreement.

The "public interest" theory

Arguments for governmental intervention focus around the so-called "public interest" theory. Its proponents assert that members of the "new middle class" who are not directly identified with management or labor need and desire government intervention to protect the needs of the public. Such an "analysis" is more rhetoric than adequate explanation of governmental intervention. Obviously, the "need" to protect the public in industrial disputes existed before 1932; yet it was generally not forthcoming. The government did not and does not intervene in many cases where the public welfare (however defined) seems to be at stake. Moreover, if the theory is carried to its logical extreme, government intervention would be necessary in many instances because ultimately all industry is interrelated. Last, it appears that the new middle class has not acted in any concerted way to influence governmental behavior in industrial relations.

Obviously, other factors have been operating and continue to operate to induce government to intervene or not intervene in labor-management relations. These factors can best be assessed in a historical context. Traditionally business in the United States had been sovereign over its domain, and the government had no right to interfere except to legitimitize business sovereignty. Repeatedly the courts upheld this position, by ruling that many types of labor organizations and tactics were infringements of property rights.

It was not until labor unionism grew and became politically conscious, not until new laws were passed which sanctioned collective bargaining, not until the judiciary was restrained by new laws redefining the power of property, that government "intervened" in industrial relations. The Great Depression with which business seemed to be unable to cope, occasioned further governmental intervention. Gradually, the legitimacy of governmental intervention became accepted. Government did not necessarily become more antibusiness or more prolabor; it established its right to enter the field of labor-management relations. Once in the field it could be moved in any direction.[5]

Using the power of government

When government intervened the question immediately arose, For whom would it intervene? It is impossible for even the most fair-minded mediating, arbitrating, or regulating agency to operate completely without prejudice. When suspicious and hostile groups were involved, almost no agency decision would be considered fair by both sides. To obtain a "fair" decision the sides attempted to influence legislation and the behavior of govern-

[5] V. O. Key, *Politics, Parties and Pressure Groups*, Crowell, 1953, chap. 9, pp. 268–276.

mental agencies. This direct involvement of labor and business in government is characteristic of contemporary American industrial relations.

To be sure, both business and labor had attempted to influence governmental agencies in the past. Although we cannot review here in detail the political history of business and labor in America, certain trends may be stressed. Certainly the party system was the vehicle through which changes in industrial relations were brought about. It is generally agreed that the parties have not represented radically different programs over the years. The appeals of both the Republicans and the Democrats have been made to the same divergent groups. Inevitably party programs were conservative in reference to property, and no consistent prolabor legislation was enacted.

From the beginning, commercial and propertied interests in America were able to control government to their own advantage. They achieved this position primarily by dominating nongovernmental institutions. By controlling the schools they were able to place men in legislative and judicial offices who were indoctrinated with property and business values. There was not, as some would believe, a calculated conspiracy of the propertied to dominate government. By presiding over the educational system, the press, and other institutions of communication, they indirectly and automatically determined the kind of people that would become legislators, executives, and judges. The latter naturally did "what was right."

With the extension of suffrage, some friends of labor had hoped that labor's numerical dominance might give it control over the legislative bodies. Attempts were made to abandon the two-party system and to form labor parties dedicated to promoting the best interests of the working class. But labor parties, irrespective of their conservative or radical nature, generally failed to attract widespread working-class support.[6] American workers were mobility conscious and they regarded their position in society as temporary. They expected that they, or at least their children,

[6] Henry David, "One Hundred Years of Labor in Politics," in J. B. S. Hardman and Maurice F. Neufeld (eds.)., *The House of Labor,* Prentice-Hall, 1951, pp. 90–113.

would become men of property. While waiting for that day, they were concerned mainly with the size of the pay envelope and what they could buy with it. With few exceptions in city governments, labor never got into power.

Under these conditions, it is understandable why the philosophy of Samuel Gompers held sway for so long a period of time. The essence of this philosophy was that labor should organize politically but not support political parties. Gompers urged that labor first examine the records of legislators in either party, then vote for those who backed labor bills and vote against those who did not. In other words, the usual techniques of a lobby should be used to secure influence in the legislative councils.[7]

The organizing of formal pressure groups

The effect of following this advice was a gradual weakening of the informal monopoly which the commercial and business interests had over government. Business interests which wanted favorable laws or political favors had to organize as *formal pressure groups* to obtain their ends. When labor became politically organized, the era of informal monopoly over government by business was terminated. The struggles of management and organized labor thus became public affairs in which the resources and power of government played crucial roles.

This is the stage in American politics today, with one significant difference. Labor's traditional policy of "Reward your friends and punish your enemies" has been revised because it was basically an after-the-fact strategy. In its stead labor has developed what may be called a "full involvement" program in politics. The present strategy is to become fully involved in politics through the central coordination of the Committee on Political Education (COPE). While not irrevocably tied to the Democratic party COPE has sought to become a strong influence in the party. COPE parallels the party organization from the precinct to the national level and is dedicated to getting union members and sympathizers into active political work. How it relates itself to the Democratic party is a function of the condition of the party locally and labor's relative strength. As Fay Calkins has shown, at times it fights for control of the party at the primaries, at times it seeks to become

[7] *Ibid.*

the balance of power within the party, and, where the party is weak, it may become the party.[8]

As labor's new techniques proved effective, they elicited a strong counteroffensive among business groups. Since World War II the latter have succeeded in restraining the power of the unions by restrictions enacted in the so-called Taft-Hartley laws and their revisions. The laws state that the union cannot use dues to back political candidates for office, it must publish financial statements, it cannot propagandize its members in a political sense, its officers must sign non-Communist affidavits before unions can use the services of the National Labor Relations Board, and so on. Of course, business groups have also used other devices to influence political parties and restrict the power of labor. Labor reacts. And so the struggle goes on.

THE STUDY OF LABOR-MANAGEMENT INTERACTION

From the above it is apparent that broad historical factors which condition industrial relations must be taken into account. Manifestly, the context of industrial relations differs greatly in the United States, western Europe, the Soviet Union, and Latin America. In addition to the historical fabric of industrial relations, one must consider the specific organizations currently involved—that is, the total power structure of management and labor.

Both management and labor are discrete organizations with characteristic structural and cultural attributes. To describe each in isolation would have limited utility because, in reality, they are often interacting. In some areas they stand apart; in other areas each affects the behavior of the other. Thus, it is necessary to study the two houses of labor and management *both in relative isolation and in interaction.*

Several difficulties confront the sociological analysis of industrial relations. First, the action studied may take place on different levels of the interacting organizations. Sometimes labor and management interaction involves only the local structures (as in the wildcat strike and grievance bargaining), sometimes only the

[8] Fay Calkins, *The CIO and the Democratic Party,* University of Chicago Press, 1952, pp. 37–44, *passim.*

larger "external" structures enter into it (e.g., the international union and trade associations in contract negotiations and strikes), and often both local and external organizations are involved. Second, an almost endless diversity of patterns is found among the organizations involved in industrial relations. For example, some large plants must bargain with several different union locals, each of which has worked out a different relationship with management. On the other hand, a particular local may have members in several plants, each of which has different problems. Third, the attitudes which employers and unions have toward each other may vary considerably, ranging from general acceptance to absolute distrust. Fourth, an organizational difference may exist between labor and management. For example, many union locals have almost no autonomy to deal with autonomous employers, while managers of subsidiaries may have no power to bargain with local unions on contract matters.

Obviously, it is neither possible nor desirable to describe all these patterns in detail.

Social scientists are more interested in patterns of relations and emerging processes than they are in specific and unique situations. Obviously, it is neither possible nor desirable to describe all of these patterns in detail. In line with this position, the general model we have in mind in the analysis below is a middle-sized plant with a single union. The latter represents most of the workers, is well entrenched, and maintains an aggressive stance in collective bargaining. Management is also aggressively trying to constrain the area of union power and enlarge its own. Each side has had enough experience with the other to be able to anticipate in some measure the strategy and tactics of the other.

OVERVIEW OF INDUSTRIAL RELATIONS STRUCTURES[9]

The organizations which labor and management build in interaction constitute a complex substructure of both formal and informal systems. Figure 10.2 shows that formal industrial relations are carried on through the collective bargaining committees.

[9] We are indebted to James Rhadigan for his suggestions on an earlier version of this chapter.

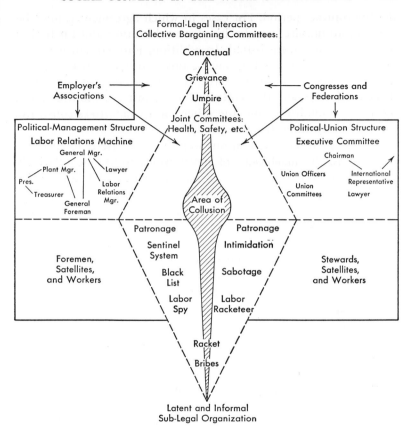

FIG. 10.2. The Power Structures of Management and Labor.

In addition there are parts of the management and union structure which are also concerned primarily with bargaining. Finally, a *latent* structure of sub-legal activities is indicated. This entire organizational complex may be regarded as a cultural pattern of collective bargaining which embraces a wide range of activities. A brief description of each of the component structures follows.

Periodically (every year or two), representatives of the union and management meet as a committee to determine the conditions of their relationship for a period set by the contract. This committee also creates machinery to settle grievances which arise during the contract period. For cases in which agreement cannot be reached, an umpire may be hired, or arbitration and mediation machinery may be instituted. In addition, joint committees may be established—for health, safety, rate setting, recreation, and welfare. These committees have varying degrees of authority. Taken all together, the collective bargaining committees, the grievance committees, and the other joint committees constitute the joint bargaining structure.

If labor-management relations were limited strictly to these organizations, the machinery of negotiations would be relatively simple. However, other parts of management and labor are involved in preparing for the bargaining sessions. For example, in management organization the industrial relations department has grown enormously in size and importance as a response to growth of union power and activities. This department supervises the grievance process and collects materials useful in contract negotiations from several offices including the financial staff, line supervisors, and personnel people. The latter, in turn, must be informed about company industrial relations policies.[10]

Yet the bargaining structures of management and labor should be distinguished from other parts of their organizations. The president and vice-presidents often have nothing to do with industrial relations. Very commonly, there exists a negotiating team composed of the executive vice-president, plant manager, company lawyer, labor relations director, treasurer, and superintendent. Other officials are solicited to supply information and advice as needed. After the contract is signed, the execution of the agreement is carried on by the labor relations director and the supervisors. This execution phase is very important for the general atmosphere of labor relations.

The bargaining corps of labor is a small group of union officials. Unlike their management counterpart, the labor members occupy coordinate positions in reference to each other. Usually bargaining committees are made up of members of the executive committee, the international representative or business agent, and the head of the contract committee. The composition of this

[10] William F. Whyte, "The Impact of the Union on Management Organization," in Conrad M. Arensberg (ed.), *Research in Industrial Human Relations,* Harper, 1957, pp. 171–181.

body is not fixed—and it can be changed as conditions warrant. Once the contract is signed the regular officials and the stewards or committeemen have the responsibility of executing the agreement.

In some cases the decisions of both labor and management are subject to approval by outside agencies. Management may have to conform to the policies of industry-wide associations, and union locals may have to follow the policies of their internationals. Sometimes the central associations enter directly into local bargaining, as in the case of the steel, coal, automobile, and transportation industries. Here the parent bodies are so directly involved that local management and union officials merely execute their directives. As indicated above, the government may enter the bargaining structure under certain conditions, such as national emergencies and in cases involving illegal acts.

In addition to the joint and independent bargaining structures, there exists a latent system which has not received much attention. Figure 10.2 shows how this latent system is intimately bound to larger organizations of both management and labor. Informal agreements are made which may be ultimately formalized in the contract. Illegal methods of persuasion such as bribery, threats, and intimidations may be used by both sides. A patronage system may operate in which each side pays the other for information and unofficial help. In addition, spy or sentinel systems may be instituted by both groups to secure information on the strategy to be used in the power struggles. These sub-legal systems and illegal tactics permeate entire organizations from top to bottom. They even reach into the mediation and arbitration machinery.

In a study of the industrial relations patterns of three factories Dalton documented this latent or unofficial pattern of union-management relations.[11] He found substantial departures from national contracts in the daily industrial relations practices on the local level. First, there were tacit agreements between the union and management to work outside the contract when "necessary." This practice was common where the parties felt that national negotiations did not take into account their local prob-

[11] Melville Dalton, "Unofficial Union-Management Relations," *American Journal of Sociology,* October, 1950, pp. 611–618.

lems. Informal and collusive agreements which sometimes furthered the personal aims of committeemen and supervisors, were also in effect where the workers lacked union consciousness and were willing to abide local practices as long as no problems arose. Further, Dalton found that industrial relations agreements were sometimes sabotaged by foremen who resented management decisions to grant staff experts functions which they had formerly held. The foremen either cooperated with the union informally or failed to cooperate with higher management. Yet at times both management and the union violated economic and production contract provisions. When production pressures were high, the foremen might obtain more than the quota production and later make concessions to the workers and the union through overtime pay or by ignoring minor grievances.

In conclusion, it appears that daily industrial relations in most plants do not strictly adhere to contract rules but represent a shifting mixture of conflict, cooperative, and accommodative behavior on the part of union and management representatives. The next three major sections of this chapter will deal with the power struggles and conflict relations between management, unions, and the workers in three areas: (1) informal collective action, (2) grievance bargaining, and (3) contract bargaining.

INFORMAL COLLECTIVE ACTION

Some Prerequisites of Collective Action

Understandably students of industrial conflict focus most attention on the struggles between the union and management. Yet our earlier examination of informal organization showed that neither management nor the union can attain their goals without the voluntary support of the employees. Under some conditions both the union and management organizations actually subvert the goals of the workers. When this situation persists over a long period of time, a new type of organization may "spontaneously" emerge which exists outside the recognized institutional system. Such emergent organizations are operative during a slowdown, a crackdown, or a wildcat strike. Behavior which occurs outside of formally constituted organizations we shall designate "informal collective action."

It should be readily apparent that many of the early studies of informal organization were inaugurated to understand informal collective action. In general they fell short of their goal because they tended to become ethnographic surveys of the social and cultural life of the factory or office. To be sure, these studies were valuable because they documented a relationship existing between informal organization and such behavior as goldbricking, absenteeism, pace of work, and proclivity toward unionism. Although the studies did not specify the nature of this relationship, they did demonstrate that there was a constant pattern of informal bargaining and that it was a response to continuous pressure of management to control the work environment.[12] The abandonment of the case method of study in favor of testing of hypotheses led to a specification of the conditions which stimulate informal collective action.

Gouldner's studies of bureaucracy and the wildcat strike demonstrate that collective action is likely to emerge when there is an abrupt change in the patterns of formal organization which impinge on worker behavior.[13] Thus, in a gypsum plant and mine, an "indulgency pattern" had evolved over the years in which management permitted workers to take time off for hunting, set their own pace of work, violate some rules (such as the no-smoking rule), and use company equipment for private use. With a change in management, the easygoing social relations ended, as old rules were enforced and new rules were made. Violations of the rules led to changes in personnel and to punishments such as layoffs, demotions, and cuts in pay. In short, a punishment-centered bureaucracy was substituted for the old indulgency patterns. Ultimately this shift elicited collective action in the form of a wildcat strike which lasted for ten days. This case amply demonstrates the importance of taking into account historical factors in the form of *persisting* social systems in the face of instituted change. It also shows the organic relationship between formal organization and informal social systems: changes in one usually elicit changes in another.

More recently, Sayles endeavored to isolate some of the factors

[12] William F. Whyte, *Money and Motivation,* Harper, 1955.
[13] Alvin W. Gouldner, *Patterns of Industrial Bureaucracy,* Free Press, 1954; Alvin W. Gouldner, *Wildcat Strike,* Antioch Press, 1954.

associated with "spontaneous" outbursts of behavior against management and the union. In a survey covering 22 work plants and 300 work groups he found that the incidence and type of disruptive behavior vary according to the type of technology, the type of organizational controls, and the occupational structure of the work group.[14] On the basis of these and other factors, he was able to classify work groups in a convenient typology. The apathetic work group, which was essentially passive, was found in departments with heterogeneous and relatively unskilled job structures and in long assembly lines. Erratic groups, on the other hand, which were highly unstable, demonstrative, and volatile were in departments with homogeneous but relatively unskilled job structures. Strategic groups, which exhibited persistent, calculated self-interest behavior, were found in departments where individuals controlled their work or among homogeneous work crews. Semiskilled workers, for example, whose freedom of action was restricted by technological organization such as the assembly line, were inclined to exhibit more spontaneous outbursts than other types of workers; moreover, they seemed less able to control their behavior and destiny once disruption of work had occurred. Groups made up of skilled workers, however, who controlled their work operations, were not only less susceptible to outbursts but able to maintain their solidarity in order to attain their goals.

There is similar evidence among white-collar workers that the degree of morale, work satisfaction, and collective action is related to such broad structural factors as degree of professionalization and occupational aspiration. Thus, Barnes has shown that engineers with professional training, as opposed to those with technical training, responded less favorably to tight management control and asserted their right to determine the pattern of work.[15]

In an earlier work, Whyte and his associates demonstrated that even individual variations in adhering to group norms in informal bargaining were a function of their social marginality.[16]

[14] Leonard R. Sayles, *Behavior of Industrial Work Groups,* Wiley, 1958, pp. 39–71.

[15] Louis B. Barnes, *Organizational Systems and Engineering Groups,* Harvard University Graduate School of Business Administration, 1960.

[16] Whyte, *Money and Motivation,* especially pp. 39–49.

Workers who refused to work at the informally designated pace, who refused to conspire against the rate setters, who made highest individual earnings, and who cooperated most with management were of upper-lower-class origin, nonethnic, and reared under close parental authority. They were property holders, saved money, and were individualistically oriented. Moreover, they took part in very few social activities in and out of work. The "regulars," who were satisfied with lower wages and who tried to control the pace of work, were of urban lower-class origin, reared in families which practiced loose parental control. They engaged in social activities with their peers at work and outside of work. Understandably, departments which contained both types of workers were incapable of collective action because their mixed social character made arriving at consensus almost impossible.[17]

All of the above studies deal with collective action of workers against management controls. The factors isolated apply equally to the labor union in its attempts to build upon "natural social organization" for purposive collective action.[18] Case studies of propensity of different groups to unionize, to strike, to maintain discipline once a strike is under way, and to respond to union discipline demonstrate the importance of these structural factors.[19] Although more controlled comparative studies are necessary before we can isolate the precise factors associated with variations in union behavior, we can be certain that type of technology, occupational composition, and social background of the worker are among the critical factors.

The Wildcat Strike

One of the most dramatic forms of spontaneous collective action is the wildcat strike. While a completely satisfactory definition of a wildcat strike has not been proposed, the wildcat is a work stoppage which is neither sanctioned nor stimulated by authoritative structures such as management or the union. The stoppage

[17] *Ibid.*

[18] See Joseph H. Downer and Herbert J. Lane, "Shop Society and the Union," *Industrial and Labor Relations Review*, October, 1953, pp. 3–14.

[19] Joel Seidman, Jack London, Bernard Karsh, and Daisy L. Tagliacozzo, *The Worker Views His Union*, University of Chicago Press, 1958; Seymour Martin Lipset, Martin A. Trow, and James A. Coleman, *Union Democracy*, Free Press, 1956.

could be directed against either or both sides or against a generally intolerable situation over which no agency has control: for example, some aspect of informal organization. Some studies of "wildcats" have shown that they were actually directed by the union, in which case they are more accurately termed flash strikes or pseudo wildcats. If an effective union is on the scene, it is almost inconceivable that it would not be aware of "plans" to wildcat, although it might not be able to prevent the strike. The same, of course, applies to management. This is just another way of stating that collective behavior is usually a response to situations involving formal organizations.

To the untrained observer, the wildcat strike has the appearance of a spontaneous, unplanned, capricious act of a leaderless mass. Actually, like all examples of collective behavior, the wildcat represents a response to observable social conditions. From a phenomenological point of view it is not a capricious act; on the contrary, it has elements of planning and leadership. The fact that wildcats recur more frequently at certain times rather than others suggests that broad economic, social, and cultural conditions, as well as the local situation, may be operative.

During World War II, when strikes were prohibited by the no-strike pledge, phenomena similar to the wildcat strike appeared. They took the form of work stoppages several hours long, slowdowns which lasted for days, and heavy absenteeism which resembled group vacations or work boycotts. Such collective behavior, short of a recognizable wildcat, resulted from a number of accumulated grievances which were often unclarified and unresolved. Long work schedules, constant job shifting, no vacations, introduction of new ethnic groups in industry, high turnover, pressure for production, and other situations destroyed the social equilibrium and produced general feelings of tension and dissatisfaction which resulted in quasi wildcats.

After cessation of hostilities, patriotic sentiments no longer constrained individuals and organizations. During the tumultuous and unsettling "reconversion" to peacetime production, a large number of wildcats appeared. The "issues" at that time were more traditional (e.g., work load, job assignments, timing of jobs, and so on). Even though management and the union often worked hard to resolve these issues, wildcat strikes increased. Undoubtedly many of them had a more specific cause than did the walk-outs during the war. In fact, they were often followed by official declarations of strikes and lockouts.

Under more stable economic conditions, and in periods of orderly social change, fewer wildcat strikes appear. Those which do probably result from peculiar situations in the local work organization. The studies of Homans and Scott conclude that wildcats of this type do not occur over issues such as wages, hours, and working conditions which are normally handled by tradi-tional industrial relations machinery.[20] Usually preceding a walk-out there are a number of general grievances which have remained unresolved over a long period of time and have produced general feelings of tension and frustration among the employees. Such issues may be the introduction of new ethnic groups, unexpected promotions or demotions, steady increase in the pace of work, a management reorganization which brings much job changing, re-traction of privileges, inadequate grievance machinery, and so on. All of these situations appeared in the most fully documented case of a wildcat strike available, described by Alvin Gouldner.[21]

The lack of communication over issues and the absence of effective organizational vehicles (union, management, or joint) to handle grievances make employees feel they are "getting the runaround" or that there are no rules or norms. As the number of unresolved incidents accumulate and the tension builds up, group action of unspecified nature is urged. At this point three phe-nomena occur: (1) increased communication within the work group, accompanied by expressions of solidarity and the need for action, (2) the emergence of leaders or spokesmen who help the group arrive at a consensus on grievances and possible courses of action, and (3) the final, often unstated, consensus that nothing short of a walkout can convince authorities to act. An incident often unrelated to past grievances may precipitate the resolution to walk off the job.

Usually the walkout is of brief duration, as union and manage-ment seek to get wildcatters back to work. Before this objective is secured some communication machinery is established to deter-

---

[20] George C. Homans and Jerome F. Scott, "Reflections on the Wildcat Strike," *American Sociological Review,* June, 1947, pp. 278–287.

[21] Gouldner, *op. cit.*

mine the grievances. Often employees return to work with little more than a promise that the causes of the unrest will be found and solutions will be forthcoming. Such a declaration is regarded as a victory by the workers, who feel they have structured a situation to handle their grievances. Unless the basic causes of the grievances are dealt with, a whole series of wildcat strikes may be called within a relatively brief period. A persistence of this type of behavior is evidence of the emergence of a stable organization which takes on formal characteristics. When protracted walkouts occur they are probably flash strikes, provoked by policy conflicts between the union and management.[22] The next section examines the formal institutional means to handle industrial conflicts.

THE STRATEGY AND TACTICS OF GRIEVANCE BARGAINING

There are two major official areas of management and union struggle for power; the first is contractual and the second is grievance bargaining. Bargaining the contract is a more inclusive process because it defines the general relations between the parties for a specific period. Like law, the contract represents a compromise worked out by groups jockeying for power, privilege, and status. Grievance bargaining, on the other hand, is concerned with the daily operation and interpretation of the contract. It may be thought of as an executive and judicial process. It is an important area of labor-management relations because, as many lawyers realize, the execution and interpretation of the law is often as important as the provisions of the law. Moreover, since grievance bargaining is the daily form of union-management relations, it is difficult to overstress its importance. In cases where the contract is made on an industry-wide basis, grievance bargaining is the only area of local bargaining.

Some students of labor argue that the grievance process is not true bargaining.[23] They conceive of the process in the narrow executive and judicial sense of enforcing and testing the law.

[22] See, for example, "Taming a Wildcat," *Business Week*, May, 1944, and "Flash Strikes," *Fortune*, August, 1952.

[23] Neil W. Chamberlain, "Grievance Proceedings and Collective Bargaining," in Richard A. Lester and Joseph Shister (eds.), *Insight into Labor Issues*, Macmillan, 1948.

Sociologically, the grievance process may be thought of as common law and as part of collective bargaining for a number of reasons. First, few laws are so clearly defined that there cannot be room for disagreement on interpretations. Interpretation is a bargaining process sometimes resulting in practices contrary to the original intentions of the lawmakers, in which case it is equivalent to legislation. Second, no matter what the contract specifies, the grievance procedure actually makes the laws of the plant. Industrial jurisprudence, like jurisprudence in general, is built on the principle of precedence and practice. Thus, over a period of time a common practice takes on the aspect of law and may later be included as a contract provision. Third, the arguments used in grievance sessions may forecast a position which will be taken in future bargaining of the general contract. As Kennedy points out, "Grievance negotiation can be the means of creating, aggravating or prolonging conflict. But it contains inherent elements for the reduction of conflict."[24]

The formal process of grievance bargaining is stated in the contract. Although the detailed procedure varies with the contract the general steps are similar. When a worker is aggrieved he is supposed to report his complaint to his foreman or his steward. The other party is summoned and the three make efforts to settle the grievance immediately. If settlement is impossible at this point, the grievance is presented to a committee composed of representatives of management and the union. An unresolved grievance may be referred "upward" three or four times to committees made up of higher echelons of both sides.

These intermediate steps between the foreman-steward level and final arbitration are extremely important. If the first step is usually skipped, the prestige and power of both the foreman and the steward are undermined, and they become merely reporters of incidents. The general result of involving higher echelons is to increase the stability and enforceability of the contract and to increase the size of the staffs needed to process the grievances. Resort to higher levels tends to be disadvantageous to the union because negotiations are likely to take on a more legalistic char-

[24] Van D. Kennedy, "Grievance Negotiation," in Arthur Kornhauser, Robert Dubin, and Arthur M. Ross (eds.), *Industrial Conflict,* McGraw-Hill, 1954, p. 280.

acter and ignore the informal arrangements found among employees. Moreover, higher-level grievances tend to become more like contract bargaining for they increasingly involve principles over which parties are more disposed to fight.[25] Cases which cannot be resolved at the highest level are sent to an arbitrator or umpire for final decision.

Steward-Foreman Bargaining

The formal process

Much of the behavior of foremen and stewards in grievance negotiations follows a pattern. Both are given courses which cover contract provisions and how they should behave on given types of cases. The foremen are trained primarily in the methods of preventing grievances because grievances are costly to process. However, since many foremen are production rather than personnel oriented, they are often in a disadvantageous tactical position. The steward, on the other hand, is taught more aggressive tactics—how to spot grievances and win cases. Since he usually initiates cases, steward-foreman bargaining will be examined primarily from his role perspective.

Duties of the steward

The union recognizes the importance of the steward in the minds both of the employees and of management. He represents the first line of the union just as foremen represent the first line of supervision. The steward manual of the Textile Workers Union of America admonishes its stewards:

> As a shop steward, yours is the job and the opportunity to make this industrial democracy function. You represent your fellow workers in the shop. You are the non-commissioned officer in the union army. As you carry out your duties effectively, you will represent your fellow unionists well, and the union will have value and meaning for them, and will flourish.
>
> You are the representative of the union in the shop. It is within your power to turn a contract from a document of words and clauses into a living protection for the rights of workers. Without you, and others like you, even the best contract is meaningless. You put life in its veins.

[25] See William F. Whyte, *Pattern for Industrial Peace*, Harper, 1951, especially pp. 25–27, 37–45.

You make it work. Because you are in the shop, in immediate contact with both workers and management, you become the basic foundation of the union. The wisest union leader, the most efficient business agent, cannot build the union and make it function effectively without your help. You must deal with management relating to conditions of work, while at the same time you keep the union strong within the shop so that the boss knows that you represent the workers.[26]

The duties of the steward fall into three categories. First, he must see that the general union guarantees provided by law are not violated by the employer. Second, he must insure that specific clauses in the contract with the employer are not violated, including grievance clauses. Third, he carries out general union policies in the plant or office and informs the workers on these policies.

Actually, most of his time is spent in his second duty—seeing that the contract is carried out and that grievance cases are properly handled. The kinds of problems that stewards must deal with are many and varied. Some are plant wide, involving basic policies, and others are imaginary, petty grievances of individuals. Each must be considered, evaluated, and acted upon, for nobody believes that his grievance is unimportant.

The contract, with its legal phrases and clauses, means little to the average employee. He wants the union to do things for him irrespective of the contract. The kinds of problems he brings to his steward represent his aspirations and his fears concerning his position. For example, he wants good working conditions in terms of light, ventilation, and safety. The union's ability to do something about these is vital, as the following illustration proves. A young worker reported, "When I was working at the factory, the foreman put a bunch of us to work, piling up boxes containing the finished product. Above our heads was a conveyor belt carrying steel from one department to another. Because of the danger of this steel slipping off the conveyor belt and falling on us, we refused to work. We reported this to the steward who reported it to the foreman. Action was swift. A group of maintenance men arrived and soon a steel screen was built to catch any steel which might fall from the conveyor belt. We resumed our job of piling boxes."

[26] "So You're a Steward," Textile Workers of America, C.I.O., New York, undated.

Probably the most frequent complaints the steward must handle concern income, job rates, and promotions. Although there may be nothing in the contract stipulating an advance in pay after a specific length of service, workers may ask the steward to do something about the situation. Employees get to know the informal pattern of advancement in pay and position. They are constantly comparing their pay with that of other workers. If they are not advanced as rapidly as they believe proper, they feel discriminated against. Thus, the steward is asked to do something for which he has no legal power. A steward summarized his peculiar position in such a case: "Pete Fisher asked the supervisor for a raise twice but got nowhere. He asked me to file a grievance because his brother-in-law in Department 14 has been with the company less time and he's making more money. Pete's got a right to gripe because they're both doing the same kind of work. But there's nothing I can do. The foreman hasn't violated the agreement. Pete's just unlucky. Yesterday I told him the situation, and now he's sore at me. You just can't win with these guys."

More common grievances concern a change of rate which affects the entire department. Here, too, the steward is placed in a difficult position because he is pitted against managers and engineers who bombard him with a mass of technical evidence that the new rates will actually be better than the old ones. At the same time employees have a deep-seated suspicion of any changes in wage rates. To be reasonable with management and to protect the men at the same time is a difficult task.

Employees develop a sense of proprietorship around their jobs. They resist being moved from one job to another because they then feel that they don't belong to a job. They want to feel that they are indispensable to a particular job or machine. In short, they want security, and they press this fact on the steward. In some work organizations transferability is necessary because of rapid changes in operations. In this case the steward's job is a trying one. The following complaint illustrates how the position of the steward may be undermined when he cannot deal with the problems of job security:

> Our union was very weak in taking care of grievances on the job. It seemed as if our grievance committee was afraid of the company officials. I'll take my case as an example. I was an automatic screw machine

operator. I was not supposed to whell chips as a regular job; however, this was the kind of work that I did for two months. I took my complaint to the steward, and after fumbling for words, he said that there was nothing that could be done about the situation. This was the first and last time I ever took up a grievance through the union. Other complaints which I placed directly before the company officials got much more satisfactory results.

In such cases, where employees get action from management rather than the union, the security of the union is threatened. Even when management offers something deeply desired, the union is suspicious. It may interpret employer welfare efforts as a wedge to separate the member from his union. It wants the worker to think of the union as the only source of his welfare.

Another goal of the union steward is securing uniformity of working conditions. The union is thoroughly suspicious of differential treatment because this, too, can become a weapon to separate the union from its members. Securing uniformity in treatment is based on the notion that employers should be related to employees as a group and not as individuals. It is the steward's job to see that even minute violations in this code do not occur, for employees are not immune to accepting favored treatment.

Uniformity in practice covers such areas as wages, methods of upgrading and transferring, rest pauses, starting and quitting time. Insistence on uniform treatment of workers means that companies are reluctant to introduce new changes, even on an experimental basis. If they want to adopt a new practice, it must be adopted in all departments simultaneously with union consent.

Orientations of the Steward

How the steward performs his duties depends upon his orientation, how he interprets his role, and the social situation in his department.

The job- or management-oriented steward

Some workers are not stewards by choice. The men in a department may regard the steward's job as a thankless one and force it upon an individual. Occasionally this person is not an ardent unionist. He may even hope to get a foreman's job. But in the meantime he must be "one of the boys" and must demonstrate to management his ability to get along with people.

The job-oriented steward may play his role in one of two ways. First, he may do as little as he can for the union, yielding only to strong pressure from employees. When conferring with the supervisor or management, he may display his "reasonableness, fairness, and intelligence." Stewardship for him is an avenue for meeting and conferring with management. If astute enough, he can impress both management and the workers with his ability. However, he may arouse the suspicion of both.

Second, the job- or management-oriented steward may play a very vociferous role. So concerned is he with convincing management of his ability that he presents workers' grievances with special zeal. He hopes to impress management with the idea that he could do an equally good job if he were a foreman and had to fight grievances. This type may regard the steward's job as a game, a battle of wits with management. He does not get angry, or even believe in his own tactics. His purpose is to do such an effective job that management feels it cannot do without his services.

A sales manager reminisced on his days as a union man:

I had a lot of fun in the union. I wanted to be a mechanic but I really wasn't any good. As a joke the fellows elected me their steward. But I surprised them by being one of the best stewards they ever had. I guess I have the gift of gab, and that's what a steward needs. Anyway, I remember one time on an almost hopeless grievance case, I bet the superintendent ten dollars I'd win. And I even told him the way I'd do it.

Of course, he wouldn't believe me. When we met I gave it to the board just as I said, and the superintendent wasn't prepared for a defense. Of course, I was ready for an entirely different attack if he did believe me. But there was no bad blood. Not long after that he recommended me for a job in personnel.

The union-oriented steward

Other stewards are certain that their future rests not with the company but with the union. By being effective stewards they hope to build a machine that will boost them into an office of the local. They also may hope for a full-time paid job in the international organization. This type of steward is immersed in union ideology. He takes up many doubtful cases and does his best to

win them. The image he wants employees to have is that of someone who will do everything in his power to help anyone. Frequently he is a vocal and colorful person. He gets steward training, reads union literature, attends union meetings, and practices
the philosophy that the union is always right.

Sometimes this philosophy yields unforeseen problems. Gardner
describes the case of an overly zealous steward who not only increased tension in the union but got into a difficult personal
position.

> . . . In a department working on shifts, the morning shift started at
> 6:00 A.M. and the second shift ended at midnight. Some of the people
> on the first shift complained that they had to get up too early in the
> morning and wanted to change their starting hour to 7 o'clock. This
> seemed reasonable until the steward discussed it with workers on the
> second shift. They were strongly opposed to the change because they
> would not get through work until 1 o'clock instead of midnight. If the
> steward then officially requested the change, the second shift would be
> down on him; but if he did not, the first shift would feel that he was
> not representing them properly.[27]

Ambitious stewards as they climb the union ladder are inclined
to regard each job as a stepping stone to another. Consequently,
they tend to lose touch with the problems and sentiments of
workers at the lower levels. They also tend to fray the fabric of
social relations by emphasizing existing antagonism between officers and the rank and file. Career-bent unionists become known
as "porkchoppers," i.e., men who are more concerned with their
jobs than with the welfare of the workers.

The employee-oriented steward

Most commonly the steward is an ordinary employee who has
the confidence of the men in his department. He is secure in his
job and has no burning ambition to advance in either the management or the union hierarchy. The job of steward usually does
not consume much of his time because he has organized it effectively.

Employee-oriented stewards interpret their role as one of "helping out the boys." They know how to handle the chronic com-
plainers, how to push a case which has merit, and how to deal with

[27] Burleigh B. Gardner and David G. Moore, *Human Relations in Industry*,
Irwin, 1955, p. 161.

the supervisor. This kind of steward is frequently reelected because the men have confidence in him. Also, management would rather work with him than with a new steward every year. The experienced steward comes to see that some of management's problems are real and not susceptible of easy solution.

The men, on the other hand, also prefer the worker-oriented steward who is reasonable and who at times even resists mandates from union officials. Therefore, a steward who works for them against management and sometimes against the union is trusted, for he represents both the beliefs and the fears of his men.

The employee-oriented steward is not necessarily the most effective steward. But he is more acceptable because he does not threaten anyone's status. Since he tends to be the kind of stable "workhorse" who is reelected year after year, the problem of adjusting to a continuous change of stewards is avoided by the workers in his department. The men are unsure of a new steward until they test him out. Being on trial tends to make the steward overplay his role, to the irritation of the supervisor. Since all work relations have a strain toward stabilization, foremen and workers prefer to deal with the same steward, who, whatever his other shortcoming, is sincere and reliable.

Roles of the steward

To win cases stewards must know the art of politics. Some are very good politicians; others are very mediocre. In small plants where relations are amicable, the union is accepted, and the power situation is stable, grievance bargaining tends to correspond closely to the formal code. Whenever labor relations get tense, a more dynamic pattern of bargaining evolves. The company tries to enforce a literal or "tight" interpretation of the contract, while the union wants a liberal or "loose" interpretation. A conflict situation results, the contour of which depends upon how the steward and the foreman play their respective roles. The emphasis in the section below is on the steward because his position makes him take a more aggressive posture.

THE DETECTIVE

A steward plays a number of roles, sometimes emphasizing one and sometimes another. His main role is that of detective. He should try to get around to see whether the contract is being violated, and whether employees have grievances. He needs to get acquainted with all new men in his department and find out if they carry union cards. Through observation, personal contact, and use of the "grapevine" he must secure information on all significant occurrences in his district. If he has a stationary job, and if the aggrieved parties must report to the foreman first, he will find it difficult in a large department to spot incipient grievances and to get his defense set. The ambitious steward tries to get a job which gives him mobility. Failing this, he seeks permission to roam the plant one or two hours a day to inform himself on local grievances. Ordinarily, the contract states that the steward should not leave his job unless he is called. He is usually allotted (in the contract) an hour or two off the job to take care of union affairs.

An ambitious, inquiring steward is considered dangerous by a foreman. The struggle of power may begin at this level. The foreman may impose too high standards of work performance on the steward and restrict the latter's mobility to those cases in which he is officially summoned. The tactics of a foreman and a steward in such a situation were reported by a steward in an automobile plant in Detroit. The following is a wire recording of the interview:

There's a place where I'd say your average steward is—I'll say stupid. They don't use two hours [daily allotted to them in the contract]. When I don't use up my two hours one night, the next night I use up four hours. . . . Because I know throughout the GM family if most of us don't use those two hours, with the next contract we get—which they tried last time—they'll try to cut the time down to one hour.

As soon as management found out I was aggressive they put the heat on me. O.K., they tell that foreman, "That guy doesn't leave the department until he's called." I had a hell of a time getting my system set up. I finally every time I got called out I used my two hours and I go throughout the whole district. So I made a few contacts—I tell the guys, "If you work with me I'll work with you, see." Well they kept putting the thumb down on me. I couldn't get out of that department. Foreman was watching me all the time. So I got my contract out—so I said, "John, tonight you call me at eight o'clock; Pete, tomorrow night you call me at 7:30." I not only used my two hours, I used two and a half to three hours. Then they said "Jesus—you're using 2½ to 3 hours a night." I said, "Yep, I can't figure that out. Boy there's a lot of grievances!"

Instead of fixing things up on the floor like, "You can't do this. Let's do it this way," I wouldn't do that. I'd say, "Nothing I can do about it" and fill out a lot of grievances. Then labor relations noticed all the grievances from me. Two big guys came down to see me. They says, "What's the matter?" I says, "Not a damned thing." They says, "Well, gees, you got more grievances than any other guy in the plant." I says, "I can't figure it out. Lots of this stuff could be settled on the floor if we'd cut out this baloney." I says, "Look right here, we got a little grievance down here right now. I don't want to use your valuable time. But, by God, you guys don't want to cooperate." They couldn't understand that and I told them. "My job is just like yours, as a matter of fact if it wasn't for us god-damn committee men, you guys would have a hell of a job. As long as you guys keep me away from my duty, you're going to get grievance after grievance after grievance."

That night, the foreman came up to me and said, "Well—look, if you want to leave your department for 2 hours, it's all right as long as you turn in your time." I said, "That's good."

You see, it had to be that way. They were setting up a new department, new men being hired. I had to find out who the guys are, and introduce myself, and get them into the union.

This case illustrates the importance of the detective role to the steward. Unless he has mobility to ferret out the grievances, to get to know the men in his district, his effectiveness will be diminished. There is a jockeying for power on this basic level—to keep the steward from doing his best job and to exert pressure on the company to allow union activities free reign. Even more fundamental is the relationship of contract to custom. Every right and privilege in the contract is in danger of being abolished if the union doesn't show cause for its continuance. The reverse also holds. If either side can prove that a contract clause does not correspond to custom, there is danger that the clause may be removed. If, as in this case, the time allowed stewards for union activity were reduced, the detective role might be seriously impaired. Obviously the foreman also has a parallel detective role, but his mobility is not as constrained as the steward's.

THE LAWYER

Not only must the steward know the contract in detail, but he should know how to interpret it. A good steward carries a contract with him all the time. He constantly consults it and, when necessary, shows it to the foreman or aggrieved workers. The foreman, of course, also shares the legal role with the steward.

Aside from finding the legal basis for action, the steward has to present the case to the foreman or higher officials. Many of the legal techniques of testimony, presenting evidence, examination, and cross-examination may be used. The following account by a steward illustrates the legal complexities involved in some grievances.

This fella I'm telling you about got a really rotten deal with the company once. Well, he had an opportunity to do some carpentry work one summer and he took a week off. He contacted the supervisor, now that's something he shouldn't a done, and asked for a 90-day leave. The supervisor said, "I don't think you can get it but you come and work Monday and I'll see what I can do." Monday he told him, "I can't give you the time off because I can't find a replacement for you." This fellow makes a statement, "I'll find a replacement for you," and he walks off. Now we're not puttin' that in the minutes naturally. Management's contention was that he didn't notify them that he was going to leave.

So he takes off. Management was a little lenient, waiting eight days before they notified him that he's considered a voluntary quit. This fellow, instead of making a move right then, waits several more days before he notified the union that the company notified him that he's out of work. So we filed a grievance.

We take our grievance down to the foreman, but he couldn't make a decision on a case like this. So we went to the general foreman. We pounded home the fact that this fellow is a good employee, was with the company for 15 years. We wanted to know why he'd fired a guy like this. He says, "It's not a fire, it's a quit!" We says, "Yeah, but the fellow wants his job back. You're the guy who can give it to him or not." "Well," he says, "I can't do it." That meant that he got labor relations standing on the case.

Well, we pound labor relations. We use all our resources going on past practice. We brought up a case like this where a guy was fired even when he told management that he'd be back by a certain day. If this fellow here would have told the boss he wouldn't be in by a certain date, we'd had a good case. Now we had to lie like hell to get him back in. But after a lot of finagling we got him back all right. We really got management's crow on that one.

THE POLITICIAN

Playing a political role is almost inescapable for steward and foreman. Each is on the lowest rung of his organizational ladder. In a sense, they may be thought of as ward or precinct captains. Their main duties are to act as listening posts, organize favorable opinion, root out sources of discontent, help build a following for themselves or for some other person, propagandize a particular policy, exert pressure on their own members, threaten the opposition, and distribute favors or patronage.

Some of the techniques used in the political role are legal, some are sub-legal, and others are criminal or illegal. Any or all of these techniques will be used in different situations. Occasionally, foremen and stewards use their position to extort money for personal ends. They are rugged individualists who espouse any cause for personal gain. Not infrequently they jump from one side to another seeking the best opportunity to ply their trade.

Tactics and Weapons

The tactics and weapons used by stewards and foremen in grievance bargaining depend upon their roles and orientations, the history of local labor-management relations, and the wider strategy of the two groups.

Gaining acceptance

Both foremen and stewards are taught that they are most effective if they get accepted as likable people, who are reasonable to deal with. They are told to win each other's confidence, to act sincerely, and to be friendly. A steward relates how he gets acceptance by foremen.

> Well, I go to the employee and get all the information from him. Then I'll say, "Now look, don't lie to me. If there's any lying let me do it. Now go ahead and repeat what you just told me." By the time he repeats it it's all a little bit different. So then I take notes and go in to the foreman and start talking to him. Naturally, each foreman I use a little bit different approach. Now there's one foreman who's very much of a fisherman. Well I go fishing with him for maybe twenty minutes before I go to work on a case. Now there's another who's a gentleman farmer. I garden with him a little bit, and so on down the line. I use each one different. I have one I can go in and hit the desk with my fist a couple of times and he'll sit and shake. Another you couldn't scare—they're union haters. There's where lots of stewards are weak. They don't know how to handle different foremen. They go in and say, "According to the contract you gotta do this or you can't do this." The contract gives you very little ammunition or support. If you had to use your contract, you might as well leave the committeemen out and just forget about the union, because you have nothing there.

Establishing dominance

A tactic frequently used by both sides is establishing and maintaining the initiative. The foreman is urged to anticipate grievances at their source. Many grievances, for example, may arise over accidents. Safety is usually the foreman's responsibility. By repeatedly insisting on the use of safety devices (safety glasses, for instance), he may establish dominance. The more the foreman anticipates grievances, the greater the likelihood that the steward will lose interest in his responsibilities and let the foreman have a free hand. The same tactic may be used by the steward. He may be alert for every picayune violation of the contract. At every opportunity he may jump the foreman until the latter gets into the pattern of consulting the steward before he makes any important decision.

Intimidation

Intimidation is usually a more useful weapon to the steward than to the foreman. Since the steward's job is usually protected by the contract, there is little that the foreman can do as long as a union exists. However, the security of the foreman is dependent on the cooperation he secures from those in his department. Foremen are rated by higher managers on their ability to settle grievances on the floor and on their ability to get out production. If the steward decides to push grievances up the channel for settlement, and if he can organize the department to sabotage the foreman's effort for high productivity, the latter's tenure is at stake. The "squeeze play" on the foreman usually "brings him around." This is a form of intimidation which works as long as management does not actively enter the struggle at the first-line level. If it does, a "squeeze" may be applied to the steward as a way to discredit his efforts. A steward relates how a foreman is dependent on the workers and the process they use to intimidate him:

A short time ago we had a lot of trouble with a certain foreman. He was an ex-committeeman by the way. He started out all right, was a good boy, but the guys took advantage of him. So he had to get back at them. He was making them toe the line . . . no quitting early, work from whistle to whistle, no sitting down, no horseplay, this and that. I told the committeeman there, "You do the same thing. Every time he does any work, even if he picks up a box, write a grievance, violation of paragraph 66, violation of paragraph 32, violation of paragraph so and so." The first thing you know grievances started mounting—finally had a pile like that.

Things got so bad that they called a meeting of the top committee. I told them that the guys naturally jump at a foreman when he gets that way. This foreman was removed from that department. He was moved to our department and it's his last chance. If he doesn't do good in this department out he goes. So I went to the guy and told him. "It's your last chance here and you know it. You cooperate with us and we'll co-operate with you. If you don't, we'll put the screws on you and out you go." Things are working out pretty good so far.

Sometimes union intimidation does not work, as the following quotation from a labor relations official reveals.

The committeemen are the filthiest talking, most intolerant, and hardest men to get along with in the plant. They were picked for this reason. Their job is to continuously goad supervision into grievances. They abuse, insult, and all but commit libel against the foreman trying to browbeat him into a grievance settlement. They try to find a man's weakness and his area of sensitivity—like his religion, education, nationality, eyeglasses, wife or family—and throw it into a case just to goad the foreman into an unfair practice or to give in on a grievance. If the foreman raises his voice, swears at, or even threatens to strike a union member, the union screams management abuse. I tell the foremen to always keep their temper and act like gentlemen. In the long run, the men in the shop find out what's going on and they lose faith in the union. This is already happening.

Indebtedness

A common technique of influencing an agent or officer is to get him in a state of indebtedness. Foremen and stewards may do each other favors which eventually lead to intimate and dependent relationships. Instead of regarding each other as representatives of organizations, they come to think of each other as people who have common problems. If the relations of company and union are cordial, friendliness is no deterrent to effective cooperation. If relations are tense or in a state of transition, friendliness and indebtedness may lead to greater eventual difficulties in grievance bargaining. For this reason militant unions discourage friendliness with management. They feel that the higher prestige of management may lead to fawning on the part of union members. A steward's report illustrates a tactic of indebtedness used by a foreman:

> Two or three times the foreman came up to me and I noticed he had a funny look on his face. Finally at five o'clock I says, "Hans, I'd like to get a pass to go to the union meeting. I'll be back around 7:30 to pick it up. I'll be back at work about ten o'clock." "Okay," he says. He didn't have to do it, mind you. I was going on his better graces. So at 7:30 I asked,
>
> "You got my pass ready, Hans?"
>
> "Yeah," he says. "Come on in the office. Look!" he says. "You don't have to punch out."
>
> Naturally I acted dumb and said, "Whad'ya mean? I gotta punch out."
>
> "No, that's all right, just go on and I'll take care of it."
>
> "Whad'ya mean take care of it?"
>
> "Why," he says, "you lose two or three hours every time you go out of here."
>
> "Yeah, I know that."
>
> "Well, that's three or four dollars every time you go."
>
> "Yeah, I know that." I played dumb as hell.
>
> "Look, you just go ahead. Just leave the card in the rack, don't punch it."
>
> I said, "No," and he got mad.
>
> I got back about 9:30. To get back you gotta take the card to the foreman and he writes the time you get in on the back.
>
> He says, "Go ahead, I can okay this here."
>
> I said, "No, you better not."
>
> "Look," he said, "why don't you want me to do that?"
>
> "Do you really want to know? Maybe some of these days one of these guys will be on the carpet. He'll call his committeeman and I'll come in here, and I'll get the case, and maybe say to you,
>
> "'Hans, what in the hell are you doing this for?' And you'll give me a song and dance about how rotten the employee is. Finally, if I keep on bargaining you'll say,
>
> "'Look, for Christ sake, don't you remember the time when I okayed your card?'"
>
> I say, "For a lousy three or four dollars I leave some poor bastard idle." That foreman got redder than a goddam beet.

The steward may do a foreman a good turn by urging high productivity when the foreman is under pressure from the plant manager. He may give him a ride home, mow or water his grass. All this may be done in friendliness, but it also affects grievance bargaining.

One of the weapons that a foreman can use effectively to win support among his workers is distribution of overtime work. Most contracts state that management shall "equalize hours as far as practicable." What is practicable is determined by the foreman. Therefore, grievance cases on equalization are hard to win. The only way a steward can overcome this advantage of the foreman is to make the workers very conscious of the number of hours each of them works. Then they will insist that the foreman be just in distribution of overtime. Many so-called wildcat strikes are engineered by stewards as a protest to such unenforceable violations on the part of the foreman and company.

When overtime is distributed with an eye to getting loyalty, it is, of course, a form of patronage. Patronage is an accepted technique of gaining support in American culture. It is used both by the union and by management. Bribery is occasionally practiced, especially in racket-ridden unions and businesses.

CONTRACT BARGAINING

A Process in Power Definition

Contract bargaining is, by its nature, an intermittent process. Every year or two the executives of management and the union meet to determine their relations for the next fixed period. The agreements they legislate at the bargaining table can alter previous relations and establish new ones. The stakes are high: the economic well-being of the company, job security, the size of the pay envelope. the social climate of the office or factory, and the relative power and prestige of the parties. The agreements reached represent the final stages of a long and involved process. Thus, although the period in between negotiations is one of relative accommodation, it is also a period of preparation for the oncoming contest. The analysis of the grievance process revealed that it was also concerned with definitions of relative union and management strength. The accumulated experience with grievances, the collection of data by both sides, and evaluation of the previous contract are all part of the process of preparing for negotiations.

Unlike grievance bargaining, contract bargaining involves the total organizations of labor and management. Increasingly, more outside agencies are concerned with contract negotiations. Among the most important of these are the employees' associations, the international unions, and governmental agencies on the state and national levels.

Stages in Contract Bargaining

Agreement on the final contract is the last in a series of steps. Some authors indicate that there are as many as ten steps in contract bargaining while others stress as few as four. The number of stages is less important than understanding the process through which negotiations move and the factors affecting it. Moreover, the process may be analyzed along several dimensions: in terms of temporal stages, in terms of human relations problems, or in terms of a power process.

In a series of excellent articles Garfield and Whyte have shown that collective bargaining is a human relations process.[28] The ceremonies associated with contract negotiations have the important function of mobilizing emotions and forming attitudes which are necessary to support appropriate social behavior of the negotiators and their respective audiences. Thus the ceremonial blue-sky proposals which unions submit at the first meeting inform the rank and file of the intent of their negotiators to do their best for them. Management's rock-bottom proposals serve the same function for the stockholders. The ceremony surrounding the signing of the final contract gives the union a needed status platform and commits it before the public and before management to live by a document which they agree is a good bargain. The friendly teasing and expressions of good faith serve to reduce the acrimony of earlier negotiations.

The following analysis endeavors to follow the temporal stages usually associated with contract negotiations.[29] An attempt is also made to interpret the human relations problems which occur at different stages. In some situations a different sequence undoubtedly occurs or certain stages may be omitted. A deeper under-

[28] See Sidney Garfield and William F. Whyte, "The Collective Bargaining Process: A Human Relations Analysis," *Human Organization,* Summer, Fall, Winter, Spring, 1950–1951.

[29] Many of the ideas in this section were inspired by Neil W. Chamberlain's *Collective Bargaining Procedures,* American Council on Public Affairs, 1944.

standing of bargaining is obtained if we have as a model a situation marked by general aggressiveness by both parties.

1. *Gathering of ideas for the new contract*

Almost as soon as the contract is signed the union starts to gather from the members ideas on what is "wrong" with it. For example, grievance cases come up which are lost. Plans are therefore made to change the contract in the future so that such cases may be won. Changes in wage rates which at first appeared reasonable turn out to be harmful. An effort must be made to change the rates in the new contract. On the other hand, certain clauses in the old contract may have proved to bring unexpected windfalls. Sentiment for their retention is indicated.

Thus, the proposals for the new contract usually reflect the frustrations of the old contract, the long-term desires of the membership, and certain other objectives which the union believes it can secure. The new contract is often privately drawn up by the union officers. However, proposals must be discussed in the international convention, in the executive committee, or in open meetings of the membership. It is a vital sociological document which embodies the opinion of the workers. It also reflects the compromises of factions within the union.

Larger unions make provision for regional or national meetings to gather the proposals of their locals. But the more highly centralized the unions, the smaller is the probability that ideas of local groups will be represented. Where bargaining occurs on an industry-wide basis, sentiments of particular locals must be either compromised or ignored. This is one reason for strong home-rule sentiment in the larger democratic unions.

Contract changes are considered by management a couple of months before negotiations begin. The experience of living with a particular agreement gives executives ideas about what they like and don't like in the contract. Efforts are made by intelligent managers to get the feelings of the supervisors on the shortcomings of the present contract and their suggestions for the new one. However, there is no compulsion in this matter, and more frequently the board of directors or top line officials determine what kind of contract is needed.

2. Drafting the proposal and counterproposal

A formal contract proposal or counterproposal, whether it is to be given orally or in written terms, is drafted by both sides before negotiations begin. In the local union the executive or contract committee usually drafts its first proposal, which is then submitted to the membership for ratification or amendment. Strong factions may attack the proposal as weak, in which case demands are raised. Leaders must take these demands to the bargaining table whether they believe them capable of realization or not. Where bargaining is on an industry-wide basis, drafting is done by regional or national panels and leaders responsible to the international union.

By custom, at the first bargaining session the union states its proposals first. In the meantime, company officials seek to anticipate what the union will demand. On the surface this does not appear to be difficult because once the union submits its proposals to the membership there is little possibility of keeping them secret. However, executives are aware that these public proposals are expressions of what the membership ideally wants; they are not certain of the terms which the union will finally accept. Of course, union officers have private notions of what their final offer will be, but since they are not sure what they can finally secure, they keep their minimum demands secret. Company negotiators, having arrived at an opinion of what the union will accept and what the company will offer, draft a counterproposal. Not infrequently they consult trade associations to be assured that their counterproposal will not deviate from the pattern desired by the industry. Indeed, as in the steel industry, the associations often determine the exact content of the individual proposals.

3. The first meeting

The first meeting of the joint negotiating committees is usually regarded as important, for it may set the tone of following negotiations. Although the union proposal is regarded as an offensive instrument, the manner of its delivery is often set by tradition. Many unions, for example, make eloquent, blue-sky proposals at the first session. They demand fantastic wages, hours, and other concessions and attempt to justify their position. Both union and management realize that the final contract will be much closer to the present one than to the proposals. Unrealistic union demands flow from the political nature of the union. They are presented to convince factions in the membership that the officers are out to get everything possible. Blue-sky proposals may indicate that the union will not be satisfied with ordinary concessions. From the presentation at the meeting and from the "grapevine," management must guess whether the "union boys are putting on an act" or really mean business.

At either the same or the following meeting, management submits counterproposals. They are often exaggerated in character, but they may reveal the pattern of the attack to be used in future meetings.[30] An elaborate justification for the position is presented in the hope of putting the union on the defensive. The company proposals are often as unrealistic and ritualistic as the blue-sky demands. They are made to secure a tactical advantage and to suggest to the union some of the concessions it must make.

4. *The bargaining sessions*

The day-to-day atmosphere of negotiations may vary considerably. Barbash comments on this point: "One kind of union negotiator comes to the collective bargaining conference all set to thump the table, another makes his point serenely; still others alternate between serenity and toughness, as the occasion demands. Sometimes the union bargaining committee is chosen to represent the diverse temperaments that have their special purpose at a negotiations conference. When the table thumper has issued his ultimatum, the situation is 'rescued' from a state of impasse by the committee member who specializes in 'pouring oil on troubled waters.' "[31]

Although union negotiators are chosen more for their bargaining ability than are management negotiators, the latter also vary in their approach to bargaining. Some are quiet and dignified; others are aggressive and dynamic.

Obviously one purpose of the meetings subsequent to the first is for each side to ascertain what are the real as opposed to the

---

[30] *How to Handle Collective Bargaining,* National Foreman's Institute, 1944, p. 8.

[31] Jack Barbash, *Labor in Action,* Harper, 1948, p. 102.

expressed demands of the other party. In the most extended and insightful description of this process Dubin stresses that the task of the negotiators is to arrive at "equivalent concessions" between nonsimilar demands.[32]

5. Bargaining tactics

To have true collective bargaining there must be a rough equality of power. When one party can dictate terms of an agreement, there is no chance for a bargain. Implicit in bargaining is the threat of the ultimate use of force. Where force is absent, concessions rest on the mercy of the opponent, of which there is precious little. Tactics are useless when both parties are aware that a significant difference in power exists between them. Tactics are useful when power relations are unclear and when there is an approximate equality of power.

Successful bargaining has been called an art because the ingredients of influence have not been scientifically analyzed. Bluffing, the using of facts, leaving the door open, retiring gracefully, pursuing an advantage, threatening to use force, laying a trap, and confusing the opponent are common tactics in bargaining. Some negotiators are more successful with some techniques than with others. Whatever methods are employed, effective bargaining certainly rests on the use of the right techniques at the right time. Knowledge of personalities, social situation, and market conditions is also necessary for success in this area.

REDUCING DISAGREEMENT

The process of collective bargaining is one of reducing the issues of disagreement. This is done by both parties as they come to concern themselves with specific issues rather than with the general contract. The conference chairman may propose that each point be taken up individually, or in a particular order. If this is the procedure, a number of items may be taken care of quickly. There tends to be a ready agreement on the traditional prerogatives of both groups which were embodied in the previous contract. Other items, on which the parties are not far apart, are con-

[32] Robert Dubin, *Working Union-Management Relations—The Sociology of Industrial Relations,* Prentice-Hall, 1958.

sidered next and settled. When long and heated arguments focus on an issue, progress may be made by postponing a decision on it and moving to another item on the agenda. In the meantime, each party may conduct a caucus and decide upon future concessions and tactics. Sometimes this order is reversed, and the tough issues are taken up first.

FROM PRINCIPLES TO PRACTICES

Each party usually feels that it has some rights and principles which it must protect at all costs. For management these are its "prerogatives"; for the union, its "rights." Obstacles to agreement usually arise when prerogatives or rights are challenged as such. It is virtually impossible to settle controversy on principles. For example, union negotiators may argue that profits are too high. This is an area of decision in which management feels it should have complete control. A compromise on how profits should be distributed is impossible. The tactic used to resolve the deadlock is to pass from principle to practice. In this case it would be to negotiate specific wages for specific jobs in the light of the company's ability to pay. Obviously, this is just another way of deciding how to distribute profits. However, men fight to protect semantic idols. In practice, the idol may be chipped away without anyone's decrying it.

APPEAL TO FACTS

Almost all negotiators use economic data in the presentation or refutation of an argument. Charts may be made depicting trends in average wages in the industry, profit position, cost of living, prices, costs, and so on. How effective this practice is in influencing the opposing party is open to question. Arguments invariably develop as to the "validity" of the statistics, and charges are made that they are "loaded" to prove a point.

Facts influence men if they are rational and if they share common ends. When this is not the case, an appeal to statistics assumes the form of a ritual. This does not mean that the ritual has no function. The presentation of data may serve to reduce the blue-sky demands. It may indicate that the group was concerned enough about the issue to spend much time and money gathering facts, and that it will not yield easily. Moreover, the newspaper may print the data and swing public opinion to one side or the other. In general, while tactics can be influenced by statistics, the battles are won with other devices.

IMPASSES

In some cases negotiations do not move according to the principles described above. After the agendum of demands and counterproposals has been hammered out, a period of relative inflexibility may occur as each side seeks to discover what the other side will actually yield without revealing its own position. The elliptical talk, the vague threats, and the pointless discussions, as they continue without decision, serve to heighten the atmosphere of frustration and hostility. Periodically the sessions are broken off, as each side consults privately on what it seems to see as a concession or an offer. If discussions remain on a dead level too long, disagreement spills onto the public stage. Each side publicly castigates the other for refusal to bargain or for making unreasonable demands, while it presents its own position as one of sweet reasonableness. Such behavior serves not only to release tension but also to stimulate both sides to conclude the negotiations.

Public discussion is fraught with the danger of governmental intervention. Usually this is avoided in the United States and used only as a last resort. Management sees governmental intervention as an improper assertion of authority, and the unions feel that some governmental agencies are antilabor. Both consider it better to resolve their differences privately than to have an unfair decision forced on them.

Eventually the negotiators must return to the task of "driving the bargain." Dubin indicates that they settle down to this with notable rationality and calm. Both sides tacitly agree they need to end the discussions as they both know the true intentions of the other side. It is rare that new issues arise at this point. The remaining differences may be compromised either by splitting the difference or by a more complex pattern of give-and-take. Trading off different concessions seems to be practiced more frequently in the United States. Slowly the contract is written and prepared for signing. Union members are usually expected to go along with the instrument their negotiators have prepared. If they do not, a crisis is provoked which may end in a strike.

6. Signing the contract

The final contract is signed in a joyous atmosphere of hand-shaking, congratulations over the success of the negotiations, and even horseplay and teasing. Often newspaper reporters and photographers are on the scene to witness the signing of the agreement and to record utterances on the great statesmanship exhibited by both sides. Such expressions of cordiality and good will may appear anomalous so soon after the often bitter and acrimonious sessions. As Garfield and Whyte explain, this is essentially a ceremony of reconciliation which is a necesssary transition from a climate of conflict to a climate of peaceful coexistence.[33] It announces to both the parties and to the general public the intentions of both sides to get along for the duration of the contract.

Factors Influencing the Contract

The human drama of the collective bargaining process may obscure an understanding of the elements which ultimately affect the resolution of the power struggle. Important elements are found on both the social psychological and broader institutional levels. Chamberlain suggests that among the former are the character and talents of the bargainers and the nature of their authority, and among the latter are the types of organizations involved.[34] Obviously, a committee of like-minded professional union bargainers who have the authority to make a settlement and representatives of a local bargaining committee made up of different factions which have no authority to make a final agreement will bargain differently. Similarly, the behavior of the management negotiators will vary in reference to these factors.

In addition, bargaining will be greatly affected by the historical framework of union-management relations. For example, negotiations in the automobile industry tend to be rather acrimonious while those in the building industry are usually more tempered.

---

[33] Garfield and Whyte, op. cit., Spring 1951 issue.
[34] Chamberlain, Collective Bargaining Procedures, p. 26.

The negotiator's tactics will vary with the traditional goals of his side and the goals he imputes to the other side. Harbison and Dubin illustrate this point by contrasting the negotiations patterns which used to exist between the United Automobile Workers union and General Motors and Studebaker.[35] General Motors took the position that managerial prerogatives had to be protected at all costs. This was based on the corporation's conviction that the realization of the union's economic objectives would eventually destroy private enterprise and undermine the authority and status of management.[36] Union officials, on the other hand, believed that full production and full employment could not be achieved in the industry unless government and the union restrained the avarice of the corporation.

The patterns exhibited by the union and Studebaker were cooperative rather than antagonistic because bargaining centered around problems rather than principles.[37] The union operated within an atmosphere of security fostered by company policies. Management had its own prerogatives, which were not challenged by the union. Both groups shared in making and administering work rules. As a result, the balance of power between management and the union was rather stable.

Another important factor conditioning bargaining is the type of labor-management pattern that exists in the industry in question. Three general patterns have been suggested.[38] The first is the *generating type,* represented by General Motors and the UAW and United States Steel and the United Steel Workers among others. These powerful management and union complexes set the pattern of wages and conditions of employment in the entire industry. The decisions of thousands of smaller employers are influenced by the pattern set by the leaders. These smaller employers constitute the *satellite type.* The third type, the *semi-isolated,* are not large enough or powerful enough to influence other groups. At the same time, they are not directly influenced by patterns set

[35] Frederick H. Harbison and Robert Dubin, *Union-Management Relations,* Science Research, 1937, p. 65.

[36] *Ibid.,* p. 67.

[37] *Ibid.,* p. 133.

[38] See Frederick H. Harbison, Robert R. Burns, and Robert Dubin, "Toward a Theory of Labor Management Relations," in Lester and Shister, *op. cit.,* pp. 21–23.

by the generating type. Relations between union and management are more or less self-contained in this type.

In bargaining sessions the negotiators in the generating and semi-isolated patterns have greater independence. Their sessions are likely to be strategic in nature. Sessions in the satellite pattern will be tactical because the participants realize that the general pattern has been set, and they can only gain an advantage on a local or fringe issue.

Other factors of a structural character influence the relative power of labor and management in the bargaining situation. Schneider lists four of basic importance.[39] The first is the degree of skilled labor in the union. In case of an impasse, since skilled workers would be harder to replace than semiskilled or unskilled workers, the union with more skilled workers has greater bargaining power. Second, no matter how powerful a union is, its gains are limited by the capital and competitive situation of the industry. A monopoly generally can hold off union demands longer than a company in a highly competitve industry. The relative weakness of the latter drives it to seek industry-wide agreements to stave off having the union play one off against the other. The stage in the business cycle is the third factor affecting the outcome of negotiations. In prosperous times, when labor supply is short, the union has a relative advantage; during depressed periods the employer has an advantage. Other important factors include the political situation of the nation and the history of the bargaining relationship.

Almost all of the factors cited by Schneider are structural in character and cannot be influenced by the negotiators. One might be tempted to conclude that the whole bargaining pattern is a gigantic ritual over which the negotiators have no control. Such a conclusion would be overdrawn because each of the structural factors actually represents a range and not a fixed boundary. Negotiations determine just what the point of settlement will be within a given range. When negotiators cannot determine this and do not want an ultimate test of strength, they resort to media-

[39] Eugene V. Schneider, *Industrial Sociology, The Social Relations of Industry and Community,* McGraw-Hill, 1957. See also Wilbert E. Moore, "Occupational Structure and Industrial Conflict," in Kornhauser, Dubin, and Ross, *op. cit.,* pp. 221–231.

tion or arbitration. The ultimate test of power is the srike situation.

THE STRIKE

Varieties of Strikes

The strike may be defined as a more or less temporary abandonment of jobs by the work force of an organization with the intention of forcing management to accept a particular goal. Since workers do not want others to replace them, a strike implies action against the employer or any other group which threatens job ownership. Under this loose rubric, a great variety of phenomena are included: the wildcat strike, the flash strike, the sit-down, the bargaining strike, and related actions.

Ross emphasizes that the nature of the "strike as a weapon of labor is largely dependent on the nature of the organization sponsoring it."[40] From his brief historical analysis he concludes that the strike was not always—and is not always today—associated with a formal labor union. The earliest strikes in the United States were called and directed by *ad hoc* organizations which died with the termination of the strike. Ross estimates that up to 1900 about one-third of the strikes in the United States were not sponsored by labor unions but were spontaneous acts of *ad hoc* organizations. He suggests that the degree of violence associated with the strike is in inverse proportion to the degree of its association with a permanent organization. The more institutionalized the sponsoring organization, the less it resorts to violence as a tactic for achieving its goals.

Several factors obviously influence the incidence and character of the strike as a union weapon. Certainly, broad social and economic conditions are always operating. When a country is in the early stages of industrialization and the work force is experiencing problems of social adjustment and economic insecurity, "spontaneous strikes," often of a violent character, seem to be the rule, whereas fewer and less violent strikes seem to be associated with a mature industrial society whose workers are experiencing

[40] Arthur M. Ross, "The Natural History of the Strike," in Kornhauser, Dubin, and Ross, *op. cit.*, p. 23.

a rising level of living. The diverse aims of strikes obviously affect the tactics which are selected. Thus a political strike takes on a different pattern from that of an economic bargaining strike. Last, the type of organization sponsoring the strike affects the pattern of behavior. The craft union, for example, which often monopolizes the skill of an industry, does not behave the same way during a strike as the industrial union.

Obviously a good typology of strikes should be created which takes into account the variables cited above, such as organizational sponsorship and degree of industrial maturity. Since sufficient comparative studies of strikes are lacking, only a suggestive typology may be offered. The first type of strike, the *wildcat,* occurs under widely varying conditions. As indicated above, it is associated with unique problems in a work organization which are not resolved by available institutional resources. Wildcats take the form of collective protests to force authoritative structures to concern themselves with the neglected problems of the employees. A second type of strike, often associated with ideological and political unions, is the *agitational* strike. It is concerned not with specific employee grievances but with causing widespread social disorder for the purpose of bringing about a societal or governmental change which harmonizes with the ideology of the workers or their officers. The strike is thus directed against the employer only incidentally, to the extent that he is part of a larger social and economic system which is considered odious. In its extreme form, the agitational strike takes on the character of a general strike.

The third type of strike may be called, for lack of a better name, the *economic* strike. It is usually associated with business unions which want mainly to improve the general position of workers by gaining specific concessions from a specific employer. Such a strike is, therefore, a weapon of bargaining and a test of the relative power of the union and the employer. It is most frequently found in the United States.[41] A fourth type of strike may be called, simply, the *sympathetic* strike. It may be associated with any of the above types, for its sole characteristic is a display of solidarity on the part of workers in one organization with the employees of another organization who are engaged in a strike.

[41] *Ibid.,* pp. 35–36.

The Economic Strike

The typical strike in the United States today is called by a labor union against a specific employer to achieve concrete concessions. As part and parcel of the larger collective bargaining process, it may be considered an ultimate test of strength on both sides. The aim of the union is to so deprive the employer of the profits of production that he will accept the union's terms. On the other hand, the employer uses the strike to so deprive employees of income that they will accept terms suitable to him. Thus, if the strike is an available institutional weapon, it may be called or provoked by either side when the other side makes unacceptable demands.

Dubin cogently explains that the emphasis placed on the disruptive aspects of the strike has led many observers to overlook the common goals which both union and management have even during the strike.[42] Both want the same workers to return to the same jobs they have left, both expect the strike to be short, and both expect the strike to be settled. In short, neither wants to destroy the other and each expects to get along with the other after the strike.

Natural History of the Strike

Unfortunately, since there are so few well-documented histories of strikes, it is difficult to ascertain their common social processes. However, Karsh, Warner and Low, Chamberlain, and Hiller, among others, have provided good descriptions of actual strikes in the United States from different perspectives.[43] Karsh's study is particularly noteworthy because it is based on actual interviews with union officials, strikers, and nonstrikers both during and after the strike. The description of the natural history of the strike below is partial and only suggestive.

At some point in the negotiations the union feels or is driven to feel that it cannot gain in bargaining objectives without resort to a strike. Usually the employees have been made aware of this

---

[42] Dubin, *op. cit.*, pp. 209–210.

[43] Bernard Karsh, *Diary of a Strike,* University of Illinois Press, 1958; W. Lloyd Warner and J. O. Low, *The Social System of the Modern Factory,* Yale, 1947; Neil W. Chamberlain, *Social Responsibility and Strikes,* Harper, 1953; E. T. Hiller, *The Strike,* University of Chicago Press, 1928.

possibility by the union officials, who stress the obdurate, unreasonable, inflexible, and selfish stand of the employers. Often the strike vote has been taken before the negotiations, so officials need only determine the most opportune time to strike. At the appointed time, the rank and file walk out of the plant, usually with a sense of determination, enthusiasm, and euphoria. Morale is high as all workers are given a function such as picketing, serving in the soup kitchen, working in the makeshift office, passing out handbills, and so on. During the first days of a strike a holiday atmosphere prevails as old routines are broken and new experiences are welcomed.

The sense of optimism diminishes as the strike drags on, as economic resources are strained, and as strike assignments take on a monotonous and routine character. At this point the employer attempts to instigate a back-to-work movement and the union seeks displays of commitment on the part of the workers. The longer the strike, the greater its economic and social impact on the community, the greater is the tendency for both the union and management to bring their cases before the public. The involvement of outside publics increases as the strike persists. At first official governmental agencies become involved and later citizen committees of all types.[44] It is during this tense stage that the threat of violence is highest.

When the community is brought in, both sides are usually willing to concede something. Often only a legitimate and neutral sponsor is needed to get the two sides together. He must not violate their sense of dignity and their need not to admit defeat. Once negotiations are resumed, differences are usually settled quickly. After the contract is signed both parties claim a victory. However, the ceremonies signaling the end of the struggle are not as warm as those associated with the cessation of nonstrike bargaining sessions. When strikes are protracted, especially when part of the work force either did not strike or when part of it returned to work before the end of the strike, feelings of hostility persist for a long time and disrupt the orderly resumption of work.[45] However, as Karsh's interviews with workers four years

[44] See the sequence pattern elaborated in William H. Form and Delbert C. Miller, *Industry, Labor, and Community,* Harper, 1960, pp. 109–110.
[45] Saul Pett, "Kohler and the UAW: All That Remains Is Hate," in Jack Barbash (ed.), *Unions and Union Leadership,* Harper, 1959, pp. 270–276.

after the strike reveal, hostilities cannot be kept at a high pitch forever, and workers and managers gradually reestablish orderly if not friendly relations.

Institutionalization and Strikes

The dramatic character of strikes is perhaps responsible for the widespread belief that strikes are frequent and violent. Even during the most turbulent periods the proportion of total work time lost by strikes is negligible—probably under 2 percent of the time worked. Moreover, resort to violence and force is exceedingly rare. As a technique of collective bargaining, the strike is susceptible to the institutionalization tendency of other phenomena. Ross and Irwin, in a study of the strike in five countries, showed that, except possibly in the United States, the frequency and duration of strikes are declining.[46] This trend has been occurring despite the fact that labor unions have grown in size and strength. A similar conclusion is indicated by the studies of Kerr and Siegel in several countries.[47] Kerr proposes a generalization which fits admirably into general sociological theory: "The most general explanation of the interindustry propensity to strike is the nature of the industrial environment and in particular, its tendency to direct workers into isolated masses or to integrate them into the general community."[48] Whether this integration is forced or voluntary, its consequences seem to be the same. With industrial maturity, with the appearance of large markets, with the acceptance of unionism as a permanent part of industrial relations, strikes seem to decline.

UNION–MANAGEMENT COOPERATION

Voluntary Cooperation

Many people who regard interruption in production as "the labor problem" dream of the day when cooperation will characterize all labor-management relations. They seem unaware that

[46] Arthur M. Ross and Donald Irwin, "Strike Experiences in Five Countries, 1927–1947: An Interpretation," *Industrial and Labor Relations Review*, April, 1951, pp. 323–342.
[47] Clark Kerr and Abraham Siegel, "The Interindustry Propensity to Strike —An International Comparison," in Kornhauser, Dubin, and Ross, *op. cit.*
[48] Kerr, *op. cit.*

large areas of cooperation already exist, among them the grievance and collective bargaining procedures. They cannot see that antagonism and cooperation may coexist as institutionalized procedures. They want to eliminate strikes, the waste of restrictive practices, and the antagonisms which exist among industrial groups. Such complete "cooperation" is probably neither possible nor desirable in a free society.

The economic setting

Shister found, in surveying cases in which union-management cooperation had been successful in reducing unit costs, that it rarely occurred in prosperous times or in prosperous industries.[49] General economic depression has been partly responsible for cooperation in reducing cost, lowering wages, or rationalizing production and not the *intellectual acceptance of the principles of union-labor cooperation.* The men's clothing industry is the classic case in point. In the 1920s, costs in the industry were reduced by wage cuts, introduction of the piece-rate system, and elimination of restrictive rules. These concessions were made with the understanding that management would also cut costs by modernizing equipment, seeking new markets, and raising wages as efficiency increased.

Instances of cooperation are found when a unionized company is competing disadvantageously with nonunionized plants. They are also evident when an industry is adversely affected by competition from a substitute product. For a time, the railroad industry was stimulated to cooperative practices by the threats of new transportation media such as planes, buses, and automobiles. A similar situation was found as demand shifted from cotton to silk and rayon.[50] The UAW did not make as high demands on the small auto supply firms during the recession of 1958 as it made on the Big Three.

Depressed economic conditions either of a general character or confined to a specific industry do not automatically lead to co-

[49] Joseph Shister, "Union-Management Cooperation: An Analysis," in Lester and Shister, *op. cit.,* pp. 87–115.

[50] S. H. Slichter, *Union Policies and Industrial Management,* Brookings, 1941, chaps. 17 and 18.

operation. The types of industrial relations which will emerge in depressed industries depend upon the union objectives, the sentiments of the workers, the type of union leadership, and management's attitudes.[51] Union objectives may be to maintain wage rates as high as possible even though they result in greater unemployment. This has been the policy selected by the United Mine Workers, who have accepted technological changes and decreased employment with greater welfare contributions from the employers.

Opposition to cooperation

The union or management may be opposed in principle to collaboration. Employees may resist incentive systems or cooperative schemes on the basis of sentiment alone, irrespective of the effects which such schemes might have on the size of the pay envelope. Union leaders may not be able to educate the rank and file on the reality of nonunion competition and the inevitability of industrial rationalization. To the worker, unemployment is unemployment irrespective of cause.

Stimulated Cooperation

In general, American unions and businesses prefer collective bargaining to forced cooperation. Management considers losses incurred by restrictive practices a constant cost of production, and unions feel that possible wage losses resulting from noncooperation are worth the price of independence. Foreign experiences, such as codetermination in Germany and compulsory arbitration, have not won widespread support in the United States. It is only during wars and national emergencies that extensive cooperation has been sustained.

Labor-management committees

During both world wars the government encouraged the formation of joint labor-management committees to assure sustained production. Early in 1942 the War Production Board urged representatives of the union, management, and the government to form shop committees which would stimulate the highest produc-

[51] Shister, op. cit., pp. 91–105.

tion possible.[52] These committees were not substitutes for the bargaining committees already in existence; they employed suggestion systems to find ways to improve production. Salvage and conservation programs were inaugurated, and improved systems of caring for tools and equipment were organized. The committees also encouraged improvement of the quality of work. Health, safety, and transportation facilities were improved to decrease absenteeism and tardiness. Housing bureaus, job training, and other programs were also jointly sponsored to raise morale and productivity.

During the war management and union leaders successfully cooperated, and very few strikes were called. Although in some cases cooperation was little more than window dressing, the committees did achieve their general objectives. However, with the cessation of hostilities, most of these committees collapsed. The relations between union and management which existed prior to the war were soon resumed. It is unlikely that such widespread cooperation will return during peacetime. A powerful government may encourage it, a totalitarian government may insist on it, but free unions and businesses will comply only when they have no other alternative.

After the war many felt that compulsory arbitration should be extended to certain industries such as public utilities and "necessary" services such as supplying milk and food. The evidence suggests that legislation in this area does not achieve its purpose and that, in general, disputes in such industries are best handled either through mediation machinery or through routine collective bargaining. If order as well as free collective bargaining are desired goals in industrial relations, responsible institutional mechanisms may be stimulated, as Kerr suggests, by integrating workers and employers into the wider society, by general societal stability, by ideological compatibility, by responsible leadership, and by the orderly dispersion of grievances.[53] These conditions are not easily achieved by conscious planning. They grow out of interaction and common sentiments which arise in the process.

[52] Clyde E. Dankert, *Contemporary Unionism in the United States,* Prentice-Hall, 1948, pp. 473–475.
[53] Kerr, *op. cit.*

The Scanlon Plan

An interesting experiment to build a responsible mechanism of industrial cooperation was initiated after the war by the late Joseph Scanlon. The plan has two simple but interrelated features. They may be summarized in a slogan: "Cost reduction sharing through effective participation." As McGregor points out, cost reduction sharing is not simply profit sharing but a method of savings which "utilizes a ratio between total manpower costs of the organization and a measure of output such as total sales or value added by manufacture."[54] Improvement of the ratio is considered a profit gain for the organization. Some proportion of the savings, usually 50 percent, is returned to participants on a monthly basis as a percentage of their basic earnings. Top management does not ordinarily participate in the savings. Thus the plan seeks to improve the *overall* economic success of the organization and make the impact of successful change immediately apparent to the members.

McGregor feels that the distinguishing feature of the plan is that it couples incentives to a formal group method of assuring every employee an opportunity to contribute directly to organizational effectiveness. A series of committees which represent every group and function are constituted at all levels of the organization to receive, discuss, and evaluate anybody's ideas to improve the ratio. "Departmental committees of workers and lower-level supervision are empowered to put into effect ideas appropriate to their level. . . ."[55] Suggestions having organization-wide implications are evaluated and implemented by a higher-level screening committee made up of representatives of the work force and top management.

The manner in which the committees function is important. Committee meetings of any size may be held almost spontaneously to discuss any idea. However, formal minutes of these meetings are always kept so that ideas are not lost either locally or on the screening committee. People are encouraged to share ideas and seek the help of others in different parts of the organization.

[54] Douglas McGregor, *The Human Side of Enterprise*, McGraw-Hill, 1960, p. 111.
[55] *Ibid.*, p. 114.

Thus the system is designed to increase economic gains and give social and ego satisfactions at the same time.

As might be anticipated, the plan may be most easily established in small-scale organizations which can respond quickly and directly to the ideas submitted. Although the plan has not been widely accepted it does offer suggestive directions for formal cooperation among otherwise isolated groups.

Informal Cooperation

Dual loyalty

Despite the general rejection of enforced cooperation by management and the unions, a certain amount of spontaneous cooperation is necessary if an enterprise is going to survive. Even where antagonism appears to be rampant, certain common sentiments bind the two sides together. The most important of these is identification with the plant, its products, and its prestige in the community. It is difficult to spend half one's waking hours in an organization and have no emotional attachment to it. Even antimanagement employees usually derive pleasure from showing their families where they work and what they do. To stimulate this sense of identification several companies have inaugurated "family days." The employees' families are taken on a tour of the plant, shown where the family member works, and then entertained and fed. All animosities are temporarily forgotten.

Function of the holiday

Where antagonisms do not exist employees display loyalty both to the employer and to the union. Research evidence supports the generalization that dual loyalty is the rule rather than the exception.[56] Joint celebration of holidays tends to promote sentiments of solidarity, common ideals, and values. This is especially the case when holidays are observed in the plant. Since holidays in America are becoming less and less holy days and increasingly days "to have fun," an approaching holiday signifies a cessation of both work routines and routine animosities.

[56] See "Dual Allegiance to Union and Management, A Symposium," Institute of Labor and Industrial Relations, Reprint Series No. 25, University of Illinois, 1954.

The holidays most commonly observed in work plants are Christmas and New Year's. Celebrations vary in their elaborateness from playing appropriate music during lunch hour to staging special programs. Not infrequently the annual bonus is given during these celebrations. Significantly, the bonus is given when it is most needed and when good will is most likely to abound. Newspapers emphasize the joy and good cheer of the season. A typical report reads:

2,500 CHILDREN SEE SANTA CLAUS AT PRE-CHRISTMAS PARTIES
AND ADULTS ARE FETED, TOO, AT AFFAIRS IN ROCHESTER

Christmas may be officially celebrated Dec. 25, but some 2,500 screaming, happy kids had a different answer yesterday as a flurry of pre-Christmas parties blanketed the Rochester area. And to prove that the festive holiday isn't solely for children, countless other parties, for adults only, were held in local hotels, hospitals and private homes.

Top afternoon crowd was counted at the Bausch and Lomb Co. children's party where nearly 1,800 youngsters and sons and daughters of plant employees, jammed their way into the auditorium to join in the merriment. Other local industries and veteran and fraternal organizations collaborated to make Saturday, Dec. 18 glow in every tot's memory.

A premature Christmas celebration was also observed at Whiting-Buick where 78 children of the firm's employees gathered to talk to Santa and to receive gifts. A dinner was followed by entertainment and dancing. One highlight was the presentation of the more than 100 bonus checks to the kiddies' fathers.[57]

Occasionally, other opportunities for joint celebrations occur. A factory may want to celebrate an anniversary of twenty-five, fifty, or a hundred years in a community. Managers try to make the celebration take on the characteristics of a general holiday. Leaders from labor, business, government, and religion are asked to play a role. A presser in a clothing factory tells of a centennial anniversary dinner given by the company.

What a party we had yesterday at the Iroquois Hotel! Jesus, there must a been about 2,000 people in the ballroom. What a feed we had—turkey, chicken, salad, steak, pie—everything you could eat, and boy, there was everything to drink—wine, beer, whiskey, everything!

Everybody had a wonderful time.

All the big shots in the city were there. There was the mayor, the Bishop, the president of the company, the president of the Interna-

[57] *Rochester Democrat and Chronicle,* December 19, 1948.

tional, newspaper photographers, and lots of other people. After the dinner, the mayor, Mr. ——— [president of the company] and Mr. ——— [president of the union] made speeches. . . . What did they say? Oh, I don't know, they talked about the company being in business for a hundred years . . . what a good name the company has . . . there's going to be lots of work ahead . . . we gotta keep up quality work . . . what a good union we got . . . season's greetings . . . and things like that.

After the speeches there were drinks. Everybody was walking around drinking, visiting, and having a good time. The mayor, the Bishop, and the union big shots were drinking in a little room on the side. I went in there 'cause I was feeling a little rocky I guess. But they were very nice. They offered me a drink and I talked a while, and then joined the boys. . . . I'll bet that party cost the company more than ten thousand bucks.

THE FUTURE OF INDUSTRIAL RELATIONS

We have analyzed both the conflict and the cooperative dimensions of industrial relations. On balance, it appears that the industrial structure is becoming institutionalized and that less open conflict is the result. Yet it would be erroneous to conclude that only minor changes are in store for the future. As in the past, changes in the technology of industry will alter the social organization of management, unions, and their relations. Among the most dramatic changes resulting from increasing mechanization and automation will be those in the occupational composition of the labor force. In the future a larger proportion of workers will be white collar, technical, and professional workers. As the proportion of manual workers is reduced, the educational level of employees will rise. As rational techniques are applied to decision-making, the managerial styles of company and union officers will also change. Already, planning and programming in industry are not left to individual caprice but to the mathematical scrutiny of computers.

Karsh and Levine have made a penetrating analysis of how changes in technology, occupational composition, and decision-making will affect industrial relations.[58] They believe that unions will meet the challenge of the changing composition of the labor force by organizing more clerical, technical, and professional

[58] Bernard Karsh and Solomon B. Levine, "The Coming Revolution in Labor Relations," *Mill and Factory*, December, 1960, pp. 1–6.

workers. This, they feel, will not be as difficult as some believe because large-scale industry is already subjecting these workers to the same alienating tendencies previously inflicted on the manual workers. For example, hundreds of engineers working for the same company and exposed to similar technology and similar working conditions should respond as a collectivity to improve their situation. Whether these white-collar workers will join present unions or form independent associations is not clear. The important thing is that they will organize on a colleague basis and bargain collectively.

Karsh and Levine believe these new and expanded unions will be organized less around specific products as at present and more around process technologies.[59] Just as companies are currently diversifying their products around certain processes in chemicals and electronics, so will unions respond in the future to these trends by organizing all types of workers in industries involved in these processes. Industrial relations structures will be modified in this new environment. For example, industrial relations staffs will be composed increasingly of experts cognizant of the new technologies of product processing and the new technologies of the social sciences. Both unions and management will have to hire professional engineers and social scientists to help them make complex industrial relations decisions.

In this new industrial climate, the union local and the management of small plants will be able to make fewer independent decisions because bargaining teams from related unions and related companies will be making the significant decisions. The function of the union local and local management will be to provide local information to national bargaining teams and interpret national decisions to the local units.

What kind of contracts will these teams devise? Certainly they will be more complex, longer, and wider in range of problems covered than current contracts. Consequently they will be in effect for longer periods. Moreover, their complexity will necessitate a longer period of preparation, so that bargaining will be a more continuous process. In short, the decisions on contracts will be subject to constant study and will stimulate other types of decision-making in the industry.

[59] *Ibid.*

The actual content of bargaining will probably include areas now considered to be management prerogatives or areas over which there is no sovereignty.[60] There will be more bargaining on job evaluation, job displacement, job retraining, and other matters directly affected by technology. Very probably bargaining will cover new areas such as industrial policies, pricing policies, plant construction, and even community philanthropy.[61]

With more complex and wider areas of bargaining, differences of opinion between management and labor will not disappear. While the strike may be resorted to less frequently, it will not disappear either, for it is a weapon which labor must have in a free society.[62] However, since the impact of the strikes may be even greater than at present, governmental concern with industrial relations will increase rather than decrease. Therefore, we can expect governmental agencies to keep closer and more continuous contact with collective bargaining at all of its stages and not only at the crisis stage.

The above forecasts hold mostly for societies not having unions which intend changing the entire social order. Certainly, as is the case of certain ideological unions in Europe and Asia, institutionalization of collective bargaining will not flow automatically from changes in the technological system, the occupational structure, and managerial styles. Neither will these changes occur if the threat of war restricts free collective bargaining.

SELECTED BIBLIOGRAPHY

Dubin, Robert, *Working Union-Management Relations—The Sociology of Industrial Relations,* Prentice-Hall, 1958.

Garfield, Sidney, and William F. Whyte, "The Collective Bargaining Process: A Human Relations Analysis," *Human Organization,* Summer, Fall, Winter, Spring, 1950–1951.

Gouldner, Alvin W., *Wildcat Strike.* Antioch Press, 1954.

Karsh, Bernard, *Diary of a Strike,* University of Illinois Press, 1958.

[60] Contrasting views on this problem are found in Jack Stieber (ed.), *U.S. Industrial Relations: The Next Twenty Years,* Michigan State University Press, 1958.

[61] Karsh and Levine, *op. cit.*

[62] A. Kornhauser, "The Undetermined Future of Industrial Conflict," in Kornhauser, Dubin, and Ross, *op. cit.,* pp. 519–526.

Kerr, Clark, "Industrial Conflict and Its Mediation," *American Journal of Sociology,* November, 1954, pp. 230–245.

Kornhauser, Arthur, *et al.* (eds.), *Industrial Conflict,* McGraw-Hill, 1954.

Sayles, Leonard R., *Behavior of Industrial Work Groups,* Wiley, 1958.

Seidman, Joel, *et al., The Worker Views His Union,* University of Chicago Press, 1958.

Simmel, Georg, *Conflict and the Web of Group Affiliation,* trans. by Kurt H. Wolff, Free Press, 1955.

Warner, W. Lloyd, and J. O. Low, *The Social System of the Modern Factory,* Yale, 1947.

Whyte, William F., *Pattern for Industrial Peace,* Harper, 1951.

CHAPTER 11

Income, Class, and Social Structure

THE NATURE OF CLASS

In the long run, groups which accumulate the greatest amount of power also receive the greatest amount of income and property and are also accorded the greatest degree of social honor or prestige. In sociological terms, and using Max Weber's concepts, we may say that power, class, and status orders have a tendency to converge.[1] This is to be expected because groups or parties pursue power in order to realize certain material and nonmaterial goals. The preceding chapter was devoted to the power or political order and the struggle of labor and management as parties to secure specific ends. This chapter examines the economic results of this struggle in American society.

Union-management bargaining represents only one level of the economic struggle. Individuals also bargain to improve their economic situations. Moreover, groups which have successfully acquired power in the past erect mechanisms that become institutionalized to maintain their position of economic dominance. That is to say, certain groups succeed in legitimizing their power as part of the "natural order of things." Their security is not bargainable because it has become a part of the generally accepted social order. The purpose of this chapter is to illuminate the operations of the formal and informal controls in the economic order.

[1] *From Max Weber: Essays in Sociology,* trans. by H. H. Gerth and C. W. Mills, Oxford University Press, 1946, pp. 180–195.

Economic inequality has many important consequences especially in industrial societies. For purposes of terminological clarity, people who are in the same economic situation shall be designated as a "class." As Weber indicates, a class is a category of persons who have similar chances of receiving those things which are valued in a society and which are obtainable only by income or property. These "life chances" obviously vary in content from one society to another.

Since we are concerned with industrial societies in which markets are the main distributional mechanisms, most of the things which are socially and culturally valued are obtainable with money. Highly developed market societies, by their very nature, are "materialistic" societies in the sense that the acquisition of almost any end (even nonmaterial) becomes cost and price conditioned. Unless the accumulation of money and property is limited by strong social and/or governmental sanctions, industrial societies also tend to develop gross economic inequalities. Such inequalities, by definition, constitute the basis for developing an economic class system.

Relevance of Class for Social Action

The followers of Marx and others believe that inequalities in property and income inevitably result in the formation of classes *as parties* which ultimately fight to control the economic and political orders. This may happen and indeed has sometimes happened. However, Weber and others take the position that economic classes do not necessarily become politically organized to seize power. The task of the sociologist is to ascertain under what types of historical, social, and cultural conditions economic classes do become politically organized, and what types of behavior follow under various conditions.

Although types of economic relations which condition the socialization and politicization of economic classes depend on local historical and social conditions, some types of economic relations exert influence in all industrial societies. For example, Marx's contention that ownership of productive facilities is an important dividing line for the formation of political as well as economic classes probably has universal validity, although his specific prognosis on the form of subsequent behavior has not been universally validated. Thus the emerging industrial societies in Asia and Africa today have mixed property forms—e.g., individual, governmental, and cooperative. The formation and behavior of economic classes in these societies seem to be taking different paths. Other important economic factors affecting class formation and behavior are: types of creditor-debtor relationships, types of income received, laws regarding property rights, size and organization of markets, amount of occupational specialization, and so on. These factors affect income accumulation, economic security, social rights, privileges, and honor.

Three Problems of Class for Industrial Societies

The sociological study of economic distinctions leads to the general study of social stratification. In this area the sociologist is equally interested in the impact which the general society, its institutions, and its norms have on the operation of the economic system and the formation of classes. This orientation distinguishes the sociological from the purely economic interest in income and property distribution.

Sociologists are interested in three areas relating to economic class. The first deals with the effect of industrialization on the distribution of income and property. How does industrialization affect the life chances of people in different economic classes? What kinds of behavior may be expected of the different classes? Chapter 1, 2, and 3 partially answered these questions. There we reviewed how industrialization in the West changed the economic and social order of an earlier society, how it affected the life chances of workers in the new cities and factories, how it forged new occupational groups, and how these groups sought to alter their conditions. We also reviewed occupational trends at different phases of the industrialization process and the relevance of these trends for economic well-being.

The second area is the general problem of whether industrialization fashions a uniform value system in which life chances and life goals become universally defined as similar. This is a question which is yet unanswered and needs to be attacked by both cultural anthropologists and sociologists. As we shall illustrate later, certainly in the American situation industrialization has been paralleled by monetary and material definitions of life goals. The scanty evidence now available tends to support the generalization that industrialization all over the world leads to a rejection of traditional particularistic values and the substitution of materialistic values. Moreover, as Engels, Polanyi, Zimmerman, and others have pointed out, priorities in areas of consumption (food, clothing, amusements, savings, etc.) tend to be satisfied in similar ways the world over.[2] It appears that changes in consumption patterns occur in an orderly way, first in some areas and then in others. The consumption patterns of a society may well reflect its level of industrialization.

The third general area of sociological interest is how the organization and values of a society affect and control the distributive order. The questions which arise here are: How much economic inequality exists in American society? How are certain categories of persons and groups favored or disfavored by the distribution system? How are economic rewards and deprivations socially distributed? How does a society reconcile conflicting economic and noneconomic values which affect life chances of classes? How are occupational and community markets organized to perpetuate a given class arrangement?

THE AMERICAN INCOME VALUE SCHEME

Foreigners have always been impressed by the American passion to accumulate money and property. Unlike European societies, which have continuities with historical eras when religion, government, and the arts were important, Americans see their past as a continuous struggle for economic improvement. The break with tradition which attended migration to the United States, the two-century collective problem of subduing a rich but wild continent, and the fact that the major part of the settlers had an individualistic Protestant faith help account for the emphasis on material values.

Material values in the United States are the basis of self-evaluation, the evaluation of others, and the evaluation of organizations and societies. Men are evaluated on how "successful" they

[2] F. Engels, *The Conditions of the Working Class in England in 1844*, trans. by F. L. Wischenwetsky, G. Allen, 1922; K. Polanyi, *The Great Transformation*, Holt, 1944; C. C. Zimmerman, *Family and Civilization*, Harper, 1947.

are and institutions and nations on how much "progress" they have made. Both success and progress are measured in terms of accumulated economic wealth. Individual "success" is measured by level of income, amount of savings, and property accumulated. At all organizational levels, from worker to top manager, ubiquitous comparisons of income and property are made. Such insistent questions cannot be avoided: Am I more or less successful than others? What are my chances to increase my wealth and security? How can I best communicate to others an advantageous economic position?

The answers to these questions have relevance for noneconomic behavior. Monetary success is so important that it is almost equated to moral stature.[3] The "worth" of men and institutions is measured by their financial strength, their financial stability, their economic prospects, and the size of their debts. Organizations are established to determine the "credit ratings" of men and private and public corporations. A man's (or a company's) "integrity" is determined by his credit rating.

Money is an important personal value in American society. Since it is easy to apply a monetary yardstick to compare people and institutions, a great deal of secrecy or publicity develops around money, depending on the circumstances. If an institution feels economically successful, it publicizes its earnings, savings, and property. If its economic position is insecure, complex mechanisms are erected to hide this knowledge. Some degree of financial dissatisfaction is usually present at all income levels. At the lower end of the class scale, increased income is desired primarily to increase consumption of the basic necessities of life; at the middle income levels, increases are desired to improve the style of consumption; and at the highest levels, increases are motivated to display the breadth of influence and control over men and associations. Only the operation of strong status and power incentives can account for the desire to accumulate more money than can possibly be consumed by future generations.

Prior to World War II, middle- and lower-class Americans

---

[3] In fact, in the Calvinistic code, economic success was interpreted as evidence of God's grace. The code still survives in American culture. See Max Weber, *The Protestant Ethic and the Spirit of Capitalism*, trans. by Talcott Parsons, G. Allen, 1930.

tended to limit conspicuous consumption in favor of savings. Under the influence of aggressive marketing, changed patterns of social mobility, and easing credit, saving has become less of a virtue. It has become fashionable to go into debt to purchase articles for visible consumption. Even companies have become "other directed" and have increased their "display expenditures" in the form of exotic advertising, sumptuous buildings, and "client development."

LIFE CHANCES OF LOWER CLASSES

The shift from the Protestant to the social ethic has been sometimes interpreted as a phenomenon of general high prosperity. However, American society is far from affluent, and the expenditures of the common man have not yet reached the "wasteful levels" publicized by some. For example, almost three-tenths of the American consuming units in 1950 received incomes below the emergency standard established by the Bureau of Labor Statistics.[4] Studies of health reveal that at least one-fifth of the population needs immediate medical care and that the level of health and life expectancy is directly related to income.[5] One-quarter of the city dwellings have been found to be substandard, and these, of course, are occupied by low-income groups.[6] An increasing proportion of the population is experiencing mental ill health. Clark has documented that psychosis rates, for example, are highly and inversely correlated ($-.85$) to occupational and income levels.[7] Hollingshead and Redlich have observed the same phenomenon and have shown that lower-income people receive tardy and less adequate psychiatric treatment than higher-income people.[8] And Streib has shown in a nation-wide study of

[4] *Statistical Abstract, 1952*, Chart 320, GPO, 1953.

[5] "Illness and Medical Care in Relation to Economic Status," *The National Health Survey, 1935–36*, Bulletin No. 2, GPO, 1938; J. Frederic Dewhurst and associates, *America's Needs and Resources*, Twentieth Century Fund, 1947, chap. 11, "Medical Care."

[6] A. Handler, L. N. Bloomberg, and H. G. Brunsman, "Housing," in Dewhurst, *op. cit.*, p. 224.

[7] Robert E. Clark, "Psychosis, Income, and Occupational Prestige," *American Journal of Sociology*, March, 1949, pp. 438.

[8] A. B. Hollingshead and F. C. Redlich, *Social Class and Mental Illness*, Wiley, 1958.

morale among the aged that a greater proportion of people in impoverished circumstances have lower morale than the more well-to-do.[9] It can be easily demonstrated with other items that "the good life" is unequally distributed in the population and that the "alleged compensations" for being poor are nonexistent.

SOCIAL AND FUNCTIONAL THEORIES OF PAYMENT

Each society has its set of rationalizations for its distributional system. In the United States, a person's income and economic level are supposed to represent his achievement in the economic arena. Income represents payment for the exercise of a man's economic function, his efforts, skills, and economic risks. Greatest returns are awarded to people who own property, who direct the work of others, who exercise a hard-to-learn skill, who are willing to risk property, and so on. In short, income and payment are supposed to be determined by the application of a set of impersonal norms universalistically applied.[10] This "functional theory of payment" is in sharp contrast with a "status theory of payment," which rewards a man according to his social status, the status of his family, and his social obligation to kin, employees, and others.

Industrial societies evolving out of traditional patterns tend to recognize explicitly the social status of the worker in determining his wages and employment. Iwao Ishino points out that in industrial Japan the Oyabun-Kobun system of mutual dependency relations retains its feudal patterns.[11] Thus the system of reciprocal relations influences one's ability to get a permanent job, one's salary, and other economic matters. Abegglen also documented the persistence of a feudal system of rights and obligations in the Japanese factory.[12] Once an employee is accepted as a regular worker both he and the employer expect the relationship to be a lifetime one. Moreover, the worker is retained even if he

[9] Gordon F. Streib, "Morale of the Retired," *Social Problems,* April, 1956, pp. 270–275.

[10] Kingsley Davis and Wilbert E. Moore, "Some Principles of Stratification," *American Sociological Review,* April, 1945, pp. 242–248.

[11] Iwao Ishino, "The 'Oyabun-Kobun': A Japanese Ritual Kinship Institution," *American Anthropologist,* December, 1953, pp. 695–707.

[12] James C. Abegglen, *The Japanese Factory,* Free Press, 1958.

is nonproductive. In general the employer's kin are assigned positions which befit their social status and technical qualifications. In turn, employees are expected to be loyal to the employer in face of adversity. Recognition of the social status of the worker is reflected in the categories used to determine his monthly income. Table 11.1 reveals several nonperformance categories in

TABLE 11.1 Monthly Wages and Type of Payment

Type of Payment	Shokuin Percent	Kain Percent
Base pay	27.5	26.7
Work allowance	33.1	25.8
Temporary allowance	24.8	
Productivity allowance		28.2
Age allowance	7.9	11.1
Family allowance	4.1	7.7
Attendance allowance	2.9	3.9
Deductions	−0.3	−5.5
Miscellaneous		2.1
Subtotal	100.0	100.0
Yen	23,204	17,812
Overtime	15.1	27.2
Total	26,702	22,659

SOURCE: James C. Abegglen, *The Japanese Factory*, Free Press, 1958, p. 52.

the pay check, such as age, size of family, and work status. Other factors such as food, housing, clothing, and services which the employer may furnish are not revealed but are considered part of the payment system.

American Compensation Values

Probably a "status" pay check is easier to justify than a "productivity" pay check. It is extremely difficult to apply the functional theory of rewards in a society or in a work organization because disagreements usually arise concerning the importance of particular types of work, especially at the managerial level.[13] It is precisely such disagreements, such deviations from the func-

[13] Melvin Tumin, "Some Principles of Stratification, a Critical Analysis," *American Sociological Review*, August, 1953, pp. 387–394.

tional-universalistic theory, that constitute the basis of a socio-logical theory of rewards. While preliterate and most industrial societies explicitly recognize some social criteria for income payments, American society makes few concessions to the economic and social status of the employee.

For example, an income ceiling has never been applied. Only higher tax rates at high income levels blunt the ideal of unlimited earnings. At the other end of the scale, income tax exemptions for dependents permit a man to pay lower taxes than he might otherwise pay. The function of the tax is to obtain funds from those most able to pay and not to redistribute income according to a set of preconceived norms.

However, a few concessions to the functional income theory have survived in American society. Normally a more seasoned employee is paid a higher wage rate than a less seasoned worker even if both do the same job at the same performance level. Women and children have been traditionally paid lower salaries than men. Seniority has been recognized by giving long-tenure workers priority in promotions. Men, older workers, and the most experienced are usually last to be released during production cutbacks even though they may not be the most productive employees. The norms underlying these exceptions are that the employer should recognize the greater responsibilities which older and married men usually have. In addition, older employees are thought to be more loyal to the company and, in the long run, more productive.

SOCIAL STATUS AND THE LABOR MARKET

While these exceptions are sometimes explicitly recognized, others are not, even though they may be more systematically applied. "Pull" and "prejudice" are explicit violations of universalistic earning norms. Pull refers to the use of personal ties (family, friendship, etc.) as the basis for a wage increase or a promotion. Prejudice refers to the differential distribution of advantages or disadvantages to a particular category of persons. That is, a stratification principle is applied by the employer or supervisor to distribute rewards according to the "social nearness or distance" of the employees. In other words, employees who have the values, style of life, social attitudes, and beliefs similar to those of the group in power are given economic advantages (raises, promotions) irrespective of their economic contribution to the enterprise. Although culturally similar groups, e.g., people of similar *social* class orientations, may be able to work together better than people with diverse backgrounds, it does not follow that the latter will contribute less to the enterprise. For example, rural migrants who work in factories are often more productive than urban workers who are culturally closer to the employer.

The types of "social tests" which employers may apply to distribute rewards differentially vary according to such factors as the economic condition of the enterprise, the stratification composition of the labor force, traditional employment patterns, the power situation relative to the unions, and the political situation. In one country the main test may be political loyalty; in another, kinship ties; in others, race, nationality, or religious background; and in still others, social class background. In all cases a vicious circle of self-fulfilling prophecy operates. Workers of a given background are denied access to higher incomes and occupations, the denial makes them unfit for upward mobility, and they then fail functional tests for mobility. Let us examine how the normative system functions in the American labor market.

Relevance of Status to Industrial Distribution

In the study of local labor markets the researcher is able to see most clearly how social norms are applied in industry. Some labor economists ignore these norms or regard them as "imperfections," "contradictions," or inexplicable findings. For the sociologist these "imperfections" constitute important data for the study of market behavior. The research of Nosow demonstrates the point.[14] He studied the industrial distribution of various "origin groups" in a Michigan city. The industries were classified by type, size, and pattern of ownership (local or absentee). He hypothesized that the various origin groups (Negroes, foreign born, southern born, and locally born) would be differentially distributed in various types of industries.

Table 11.2 demonstrates that the operation of normative patterns is more forcibly seen in the case of Negroes, foreigners, and the southern born. Negroes were disproportionately concentrated

[14] Sigmund Nosow, "Labor Distribution and the Normative Order," *Social Forces*, October, 1956, pp. 25–33.

TABLE 11.2. Industrial Distribution of Workers in Lansing, Michigan,
According to Origin, in Percentages

Industry	Michigan	Nearby State	Lansing	Other State	Foreign	South	Negro	Mean
Forge and foundry	7.8	5.6	2.8	8.8	16.0	14.3	26.8	9.2
Automotive	50.2	60.6	57.9	44.1	60.0	42.0	58.5	53.4
Other manufacturing	8.2	14.1	15.0	17.6	12.0	14.2	4.9	11.2
Transportation, etc.	10.7	2.8	6.5	5.9	2.0	2.4	—	6.6
Business and repair service	7.4	5.6	8.4	11.8	2.0	16.7	2.4	7.5
Wholesale and retail trade	5.3	2.8	2.8	—	2.0	2.4	—	3.4
Other service	2.5	1.4	2.8	2.9	2.0	—	4.9	2.4
Construction	7.8	7.0	3.7	8.8	4.0	7.1	2.4	6.3

Chi—square = 61.97; d.f. = 30; p = less than .001. (Some of the small cells were combined.)

SOURCE: Sigmund Nosow, "Labor Distribution and the Normative Order," *Social Forces,* October, 1956, p. 29.

in the large absentee-owned plants, in the forges, foundries, automotive industries, and "other service" industries. A somewhat similar pattern characterized the foreign born. Negroes and foreigners tended to be underrepresented in transportation, wholesale and retail trade, and "other manufacturing." These plants were usually small and locally owned. Since variations in skill level and education among the origin groups were not related to their industrial distribution, obviously selective hiring policies were operative. Moreover, since different industries have different skill requirements, wage levels, and opportunity structures, it follows that the life chances of workers were affected by the operation of the local community hiring norms.

Occupational Distribution and Status

In a pioneer study Warner and Low examined the wage structure of the shoe industry of a small New England city and found that previous to unionization the degree of a job skill bore no predictable relation to rate of pay or to the evaluation of the job by workers or the community.[15] There were large differences in

[15] W. Lloyd Warner and J. O. Low, *The Social System of the Modern Factory,* Yale, 1947, chap. VI.

the wages paid to men and women, which, even if they did not reflect skill level, were accepted by all workers when they agreed that the jobs were in fact "men's jobs" or "women's jobs." Moreover, the ethnic work groups which had greatest internal solidarity (the Riverbrookers and other native Yankee departments) also had higher hourly wages, irrespective of their functions. Mixed ethnic groups and those of lower ethnic status had significantly lower wages.

Several other studies reveal the operation of particularistic norms in the labor market. Orvis Collins demonstrated that an informal ethnic system of job occupancy and promotion existed in a New England plant, and that the violations of this system induced an industrial relations dispute.[16] Charles S. Johnson has documented how the changing patterns of job segregation among Negroes and whites in the southern tobacco industry represent a delicate balance between the factors of traditional job assignments, unemployment conditions, and cost concerns of employers.[17] Cayton and Drake have made a detailed analysis of the racial composition of the occupational structure of Chicago and established a method to measure the *extent* to which "job ceilings" are imposed for Negroes.[18] Richard R. Myers studied the building industry, where labor turnover is very high, and demonstrated the importance of personal choice in employment on the part of the foreman and journeymen.[19] These choices are made in terms of the religion, race, and ethnic identification of the worker, as well as by more subtle criteria such as "sociability," "good judgment," and "initiative." The operation of these criteria resulted in primary work groups which had considerable internal stability.

In general, social norms are more easily applied in smaller isolated towns which have one or few industries. Where no labor unions exist, where ethnic groups are strong and segregated, and

[16] Orvis Collins, "Ethnic Behavior in Industry: Sponsorship and Rejection in a New England Factory," *American Journal of Sociology,* January, 1946, pp. 293–298.

[17] Charles S. Johnson, "The Conflict of Caste and Class in American Industry," *American Journal of Sociology,* July, 1936, pp. 55–56.

[18] H. R. Cayton and St. C. Drake, *Black Metropolis,* Harcourt, Brace, 1945, chap. 9.

[19] Richard R. Myers, "Interpersonal Relations in the Building Industry," *Human Organization,* Spring, 1946, pp. 1–7.

where industrialism is just beginning, the social characteristics of employees count most heavily in shaping their economic destinies. The research of Noland and Bakke presents supporting evidence.[20] They systematically studied the qualifications which employers thought were important in hiring new workers and the criteria they applied in actual hiring. The research was done in two communities: New Haven, Connecticut, which is in a mature industrial region, and Charlotte, North Carolina, which is in an emerging industrial area. All employers in both communities indicated that, in addition to technical qualifications, they preferred workers of a particular character, personality, physique, and nationality. More than half also expressed preference in terms of sex, color, age, church attendance, citizenship, residence, and political leanings. Family status and religious affiliation were qualifications for employment mentioned by less than half of the employers.

In accord with our earlier observation, a larger percentage of Charlotte employers than New Haven employers expressed preference for workers with particular social characteristics. Noland and Bakke also showed that under some conditions employers were able to apply both social *and* technical qualifications of employment, and under other conditions they had to yield on *both* scores. It appears that the insistence on *both* social and technical qualifications of work is greater for white-collar than for manual workers.[21] However, the conclusion is clear that technical and social norms are both important. They form part of a single system which affects the economic fate of all workers.

SOCIAL ALLOCATIONS IN THE MARKET AND LIFE CHANCES

Occupation and Income

Income, security, and economic opportunity are affected by the same kind of particularistic norms as affect job distribution, for the level of income and life chances are highly dependent on the occupational level. Table 11.3 presents data on annual income for

[20] E. William Noland and E. Wight Bakke, *Workers Wanted,* Harper, 1949.
[21] *Ibid.,* p. 128.

TABLE 11.3. Percent of Employed Persons in Each Occupation Group, and Percent of Aggregate Income in 1951 and 1958 Received by Each Occupation Group, By Sex

Major Occupation Group in April, 1952	Male Income, 1951					Female Income, 1951				
	Recipients, Percent	Percent of Total	Median	Arithmetic Mean	1958 Median	Recipients, Percent	Percent of Total	Median	Arithmetic Mean	1958 Median
Total employed	100.1	100.1	$3,193	$3,640	—	99.9	100.0	$1,718	$1,802	—
Professional, technical, and kindred workers	7.7	11.1	4,250	5,271	$5,956	11.6	16.6	2,517	2,579	3,501
Self-employed	1.3	2.9	6,167	8,390		0.5	0.6			
Salaried	6.4	8.2	4.176	4,689		11.1	16.0	2,556	2,601	
Managers, officials, and proprietors, exc. farm	12.2	19.8	4,100	5,915	6,034	5.4	6.9	2,070	2,309	3,313
Self-employed	6.7	10.5	3,529	5,706		3.1	3.2	1,313	1,843	
Salaried	5.5	9.3	4,547	6,148		2.3	3.7			
Clerical and kindred workers	6.8	6.4	3,424	3,424	4,398	30.5	36.5	2,165	2,152	2,943
Sales workers	5.3	6.1	3,628	4,132	4,291	7.2	5.8	1,281	1,463	1,604
Craftsmen, foremen, and kindred workers	20.7	21.5	3,656	3,783	4,970	1.5	1.6			
Operatives and kindred workers	21.0	17.9	3,108	3,101	3,909	20.4	19.6	1,758	1,739	2,075
Private household workers	0.1	0.1				9.5	3.3	492	622	467
Service workers, exc. private household	6.0	4.2	2,474	2,562	3,090	11.7	8.5	1,106	1,311	1,255
Laborers, exc. farm and mine	8.3	5.2	2,281	2,272	2,486	0.7	0.5			
Farmers and farm managers	9.3	6.7	1,518	2,626		1.0	0.4			
Farm laborers and foremen	2.7	1.1	1,057	1,505		0.5	0.2			

SOURCE: U.S. Bureau of the Census, Current Population Reports—Consumer Income, Series P-60, No 11, Table 1.1. The arithmetic means and the distribution of the aggregates between self-employed and salaried workers within the professional and managerial groups were derived from Table 5 of the same report. Data for 1958 are also from Bureau of the Census.

occupational groups in the United States by sex for 1951 and 1958. Several important conclusions may be drawn. First, the occupational compensations for women are significantly lower than for men on the same occupational level. Second, wide differences in income are found between occupational groups, especially when the mean rather than the median incomes are considered. Professional and managerial incomes are substantially higher than the others. Thus, although the two categories comprise 20 percent of the employed men, they received nearly one-third of the total income. Clerical, sales, and skilled workers received a share of income proportionate to their number, while operatives, service workers, and laborers received less than a proportionate share. Although some income differences are no doubt due to educational age (experience) differences among the occupational groups, Miller found that income differences remained "after both of these factors have been eliminated. The clerical and sales groups and the craftsmen have considerably higher incomes than operatives who in turn have higher incomes than service workers and laborers of the same age and educational attainment."[22]

Differential Economic Risks

Economic risks also fall differentially on occupational groups particularly in the form of unemployment or underemployment. Data in Table 11.4 demonstrate that there is almost a unilateral correlation between socioeconomic level of the occupation and the percentage of unemployment. Thus in 1961, while only about 2 percent of the professional and managerial workers were unemployed, about 5 percent of the clerical workers, 10 percent of the skilled and semiskilled workers, and 20 percent of the laborers were unemployed. Expressed differently, whereas manual workers comprise almost six-tenths of the labor force they made up eight-tenths of the unemployed.

This same Labor Department report presented data on duration of unemployment during "the recession." About one-half of all jobless blue-collar workers, as compared with one-third or less of jobless white-collar and service workers, had been out of work fifteen weeks or longer. "Extended periods of joblessness are more common among blue-collar groups under all economic conditions.

[22] Herman P. Miller, *Income of the American People*, Wiley, 1955, p. 253.

In addition, over the past year their long-term unemployment rates have risen sharply, while rates for white-collar and service workers have increased only slightly."[23]

TABLE 11.4. Unemployment Percentages in Civilian Labor Force, By Occupation

Occupation	Percent in Each Category Unemployed, February, 1961	Percent Distribution of Total Unemployment by Occupation
Total unemployed	8.1	99.9
Professional, technical, and kindred workers	2.0	2.8
Farmers and farm managers	.5	.2
Managers, officials, and proprietors, except farm	2.4	3.1
Clerical and kindred workers	4.9	8.8
Sales workers	5.3	4.2
Craftsmen, foremen, and kindred workers	10.1	15.9
Operatives and kindred workers	12.9	29.3
Private household workers	6.8	3.0
Service workers, except private household	7.9	9.2
Farm laborers and foremen	10.1	3.5
Laborers, except farm and mine	19.3	12.4
No previous work experience	—	7.5

NOTE: No seasonal adjustment of these figures is available. The category of craftsmen, foremen, and kindred workers is probably more affected by seasonal unemployment during February than other groups except farm labor.

SOURCE: *Monthly Report on the Labor Force,* U.S. Department of Labor, April, 1961.

Even when workers are injured on the job, the compensation system of some states takes into account their past occupational level. For example, in Michigan an injured unskilled worker is entitled to two-thirds of the difference between the weekly salary he earned at the time of injury and the weekly wage earned thereafter, while skilled workers are entitled the full difference in pay.[24]

[23] *Monthly Report on the Labor Force,* U.S. Department of Labor, Bureau of Labor Statistics, April, 1961, p. 7.
[24] *Workmen's Compensation Rights, 1960,* Michigan AFL–CIO, p. 8.

Indirect Payments

The distribution of economic privileges and rewards is manifested in less direct ways. For example, almost all medium- and large-scale enterprises have rules and privileges which are applied differentially to various occupational categories. These rules deal, for example, with length of time required for dismissal notice, granting of severance pay, amount of discount given for the purchase of company-made articles, unemployment protection, seniority rights, amount of vacation, use of company facilities or services (e.g., medical, recreational, transportation), gifts and grants (educational allowances, scholarships for children, Christmas gifts), health, welfare, and retirement schemes, credit facilities, discounts on purchase of company stocks and bonds, and so on. It is difficult to measure the precise value of such indirect payments, but they may constitute as much as one-half of the actual monetary income received. As Fig. 11.1 reveals, these non-monetary payments are typically as unequally distributed as are the monetary ones. Workers who receive salaries also receive more indirect payments. Organized labor, of course, is cognizant of these inequities in risks and nonmonetary payments and has increasingly bargained for "fringe" payments.

The Place of Negroes in the Job Market

Selective discrimination in the job market is most clearly seen in the case of Negroes. In September, 1956, *Fortune* reported that "not since Emancipation has the Negro known a moment more hopeful—and crucial—than today."[25] The article proceded to document that Negro gains were made on all fronts: in occupational mobility, in real income, in savings, home ownership, and education. Optimistic Negro business leaders, who were stimulating the growth of a mass Negro market, felt that they were "developing a true American middle class." Unquestionably, Negroes did participate in the general upsurge of prosperity. The crucial question, of course, is whether Negroes were beginning to close the gap which long existed between them and the white population. The most important favorable evidence was the rising per

[25] Emmet John Hughes, "The Negro's New Economic Life," *Fortune*, July, 1958, pp. 127 ff.

capita Negro income as a percentage of the white per capita income. In the pre-World War II period, it was 30 percent compared to the 1956 figure of 53 percent.

Fortune warned that these gains might be temporary and even reversible. Indeed, two years later Daniel Bell documented in *Fortune* the selective effects of the 1958 recession.[26] He stressed the fact that the recession was peculiarly stratified, hitting the industrial blue-collar workers rather than the working force as a whole. He further revealed that the 1958 recession impressed on younger employees the fact that they do not have middle-class security. Moreover, the heaviest burden of the recession fell upon Negroes, for one of every seven were jobless compared to one in fifteen of the whites. With low skills and low seniority, they were unemployed first and longest.

Nissen made a detailed study of Negro-white income and wage differentials for the period 1949–1958.[27] He focused primarily on industrial wage earners because the vast majority of the Negroes are employed in industry. In a year-by-year analysis he found no change in the relative proportion of Negroes employed as operatives and kindred workers. More important, he discovered that the unemployment rate for Negroes was always higher than for whites, and it fluctuated more widely. Fluctuations in Negro incomes were also greater than in white incomes. Income differences between the two groups, expressed in terms of Negro percentage of income for whites showed a slight tendency to *widen*. These findings support those of Scott Greer, who demonstrated that Negroes are the last to be assured of economic benefits and the protection of the unions.[28]

John H. Douglass completed the most detailed comparison of the relative economic position of Negroes and whites in the United States.[29] He showed that in 1955 only two-tenths of the Negroes, compared to six-tenths of the whites, had occupations at

[26] "The Invisible Unemployed," *Fortune*, July, 1958, pp. 105 ff.
[27] Tony Nissen, "A Study of White-Non-white Wage and Employment Differentials, 1949–58," unpublished manuscript, 1960.
[28] Scott Greer, *Last Man In*, Free Press, 1959.
[29] Addendum, *Tables and Some Explanations Relating to the Negro Family's Search for Economic Security*, U.S. Department of Health, Education and Welfare, August 27, 1956.

Areas of Economic and Social Security	Managers
Hiring and Firing	3 months dismissal notice Preference for white married man or single career woman No severance pay
Economic Payment	Monthly salary and executive bonus Stock participation
Work Scheduling	Permissive and flexible Day shift only Leaves of absence granted
Seniority Rights	None specified
Leisure	1 month vacation with pay Special travel service provided Social, professional managerial memberships paid Summer picnic, Thanksgiving, and Christmas gifts
Health and Welfare	Executive retirement plan Group life insurance program
Education	Supervisor and management training at plant and college Conference expenses, paid scholarship program

FIG. 11.1. Provisions for Managers, White-Collar Clerical Workers and Delbert C. Miller, *Industry, Labor, and Community*, Harper,

or above the manual skill level. Negroes were concentrated in larger proportions in farming and in personal and domestic services. While the Negro median annual income in this period was $2410, the figure for whites was almost double that. This difference reflected not only the fewer hours Negroes worked but also a greater amount of unemployment. In fact, whites worked on the

White-Collar Clerical Workers	Manual Workers
2 weeks dismissal notice Preference for white woman worker 1 week severance pay	1 day dismissal notice Preference for white married man or woman No severance pay Open shop
Salary paid every 2 weeks 30 percent discount on purchases	Hourly wage set by personnel department 20 percent discount on purchases
Strict daily schedule Scheduled day shift only Lay-offs under manager's discretion	Dictated pace of work with rigorous time schedule 3 shifts Lay-offs under manager's discretion
None specified but informal system operates	Seniority rights function according to custom and economic circumstances; foreman has broad discretionary authority
Union-matched vacation plan of 1–2 weeks with pay based on length of service Ball teams and bowling leagues Summer picnic, Thanksgiving and Christmas gifts	1–2 weeks vacation based on length of service Bowling and baseball leagues Summer picnic, Thanksgiving and Christmas gifts
Group health and life insurance available for purchase Company credit union	Group health and life insurance available for purchase Company credit union
Job up-grading Induction and economic education Some scholarships for children of employees based on examination	Job training Induction and economic education Some scholarships for children of employees based on examination

and Manual Workers in a Small Manufacturing Plant. (From William H. Form 1960, pp. 402–404.)

average almost five hours more a week and were unemployed about half the rate of the Negroes.

These variations are directly reflected in life chances. Thus even in 1954 the infant mortality rate of nonwhites was 1.8 times that of the whites, and the maternal mortality rate (resulting from deliveries, complications of pregnancy, childbirth, and the puerperium) was almost four times that of white mothers. Moreover, Negro infants had an estimated average length of life of 63.1 years compared to 70.3 years for whites. The age-adjusted death rate for all causes for nonwhites was 148 percent of the rate for whites.[30]

INDUSTRIAL CHANGES AND ECONOMIC SECURITY

Modern industry is characterized by change. Collapse of industries, plant relocations, and modernization are common phenomena. Some changes result from internal technological or organizational innovations, others from shifting market conditions. The consequences of changes for the workers can be either positive or negative. They take the form of promotions, demotions, unemployment, migration, or retirement. While it is difficult to be certain, the evidence suggests that the deleterious effects of industrial changes have greatest impact on lower occupational levels and on marginal social groups in those levels.

There is general consensus that the long-run effects of technological change in a mature industrial society offer increasing job opportunities for highly trained white-collar, skilled, professional, and managerial workers. Interpreted from another point of view, technological change in a manufacturing industry decreases the employment and economic opportunities of relatively unskilled manual workers. Over the short run at least, automation has greater negative consequences on the lower half of the occupational structure. As Wilcox points out, unemployment in 1959 was concentrated in manufacturing with the result that two out of five of the unemployed were laborers and semiskilled operatives. Moreover, these occupational levels experienced a decrease in income prior to unemployment in the form of fewer hours worked in the work week.[31]

The ability to migrate may be crucial in situations where economic opportunity is limited. Here again, those with greatest skill and education, i.e., those who generally make higher incomes, are

---

[30] Ibid.

[31] Richard C. Wilcox, "Fast Changing Technology—Its Impact on Labor Problems," *Pennsylvania Business Survey*, Pennsylvania State University, December, 1959, pp. 4–5.

forced to move the least and, when they do move, tend to experience relatively few economic losses.[32] The reverse seems to operate for those on the bottom half of the economic ladder. In a study of the relocation of an automobile factory on the west coast, Gordon and McCrorry found that workers who had reason to feel apprehensive about their chances of finding another job in the Bay area elected to transfer.[33] In general, the transfer rate was inversely related to skill, status, and pay level. Thus a relatively large proportion of Negroes elected to transfer, despite their low seniority. Older men, who considered their age a barrier to re-employment, elected to transfer, as did men with large families. Form and Bloch discovered, in similar research dealing with the transfer of a department of an automobile industry to another city, that greatest economic losses were experienced by low-seniority workers who remained in the community and gambled on being reemployed by the industry.[34] Most frequently they were working wives whose income was sorely needed to maintain a given level of consumption. In an investigation of a plant shutdown in a depressed area Wilcox found that the earnings of workers who sought only local job opportunities were inferior to those who moved out of town or who commuted to other towns to work.[35] In an important study of the relation of occupational mobility to income in Detroit, Curtis found that occupationally stable men earned consistently higher incomes than either upwardly or downwardly mobile men on the same level.[36]

SOCIAL-ECONOMIC TYPES OF MARKETS

The above discussion on the relation of income, economic privilege, and risk suggests that different types of markets are

[32] Harold L. Sheppard, Louis A. Ferman, and Seymour Forber, *Too Old to Work—Too Young to Retire: A Case Study of a Permanent Plant Shutdown,* Special Committee on Unemployment Problems, U.S. Senate, GPO, 1960.

[33] Margaret S. Gordon and Ann H. McCrorry, "Plant Relocation and Job Security: A Case Study," *Industrial and Labor Relations Review,* October, 1957, p. 34.

[34] William H. Form and Heinz Bloch, "The Economic and Social Effects of a Departmental Transfer," unpublished manuscript, 1961.

[35] Richard C. Wilcox, "Employment Effects of a Plant Shutdown in a Depressed Area," *Monthly Labor Review,* September, 1957, p. 1051.

[36] See Richard F. Curtis, "Income and Occupational Mobility," *American Sociological Review,* October, 1960, pp. 727–730.

operating in the economies similar to those in the United States. These markets are social as well as economic phenomena and tend to parallel economic classes. For purposes of simplification we have classified markets into five types: (1) self-controlled, (2) traditional, (3) administered, (4) contested, and (5) free or marginal. Although these are not mutually exclusive, they can be distinguished on the basis of the following characteristics: occupational composition, power to fix income rates, level of income, degree of particularism in setting incomes, amount of nonmonetary income, and types of mechanisms used to change income levels.

1. The *self-controlled market* is ideally comprised of owners and managers of large enterprises who make income decisions not only for others but also for themselves. If the enterprise is moderately prosperous their salaries are determined only by self-restraint, vague guidelines from the past, and impressions of their own worth and what others might pay them. Thus they assign themselves the highest incomes possible commensurate with fiscal policies which they themselves set for the company. They also assign themselves the highest types of noncash payments available. Since they experience no unemployment, their incomes change according to their general evaluation of the economic and social conditions of the enterprise. In short, their market is the result of decisions they make concerning themselves and a few intimate peers. The decisions therefore tend to be highly particularistic and nonrational.

2. *Traditional markets* are found among the old-line independent professionals, independent artisans, and service workers —i.e., in occupations which have traditions and institutions to maintain them. Doctors, lawyers, prostitutes, watchsmiths, and similar persons have skill monopolies and an ethic dealing with their market relations. Their income is determined by self-imposed collective agreements, often of an informal character, which take into account the status level of the occupation, the status level of individual clients, customs of the occupations, and economic conditions. Although incomes in these markets vary considerably, they tend to be moderate to high. Noneconomic privileges have a persistent quality, and "bargaining" is affected by particular relationships with clients. Since drastic changes in

income are unusual, job tenure tends to be high. As some of these occupations become absorbed into large bureaucracies (such as hospitals and law offices), incomes become administered as salaries, and privileges become almost a part of the common law.[37]

3. The *administered market* is a phenomenon of large-scale governmental and business bureaucracies. Although they contain the full range of occupational workers from professionals to unskilled laborers, they are primarily comprised of white-collar office workers. Large-scale organizations try to rationalize salary scales according to a "scientific" theory of job classification based on the complexity of job functions. Thus personal contact and traditional factors in the determination of salaries are likely to be minimized in the face of civil service rules and salary schedules.

Typically, incomes in the administered market tend toward an average which avoids the high and low points of incomes in the "free market." In exchange for sometimes lower salaries, workers are assured greater security in the form of more stabilized employment and nonsalary benefits (sick leaves, longer vacations, insurance, credit unions, and pensions). Legal or quasi-legal clauses restrict bargaining behavior in the form of no-strike pledges, limit bargaining spheres, limit political participation, require longer notifications for quitting, force contributions to enterprise activities, and so on. In short, the sociological factors which restrict the free play of economic forces are formally recognized in this type of market whereas in the two previous types of markets they are informally recognized.

4. *Contested markets* are characterized by the presence of labor unions which bargain with management to fix wage rates for classes of employees. The power to set wages is circumscribed by the strength of the parties, the general economic situation, and some traditional forces. Custom and tradition in wage determination tend to be limited as both parties seek to arrive at rational income schedules.[38] Thus unions want equal pay for equal work, irrespective of the race, sex, or background of the employee. How-

[37] See C. Wright Mills, *White Collar*, Oxford University Press, 1956.

[38] On this basis Orme W. Phelps classified the administered and the contested markets as "structured" and other markets as "unstructured." In the sociological sense all types of markets have "structure." See O. W. Phelps, "A Structural Model of the U.S. Labor Market," *Industrial and Labor Relations Review*, April, 1957, pp. 402–423.

ever, unions sometimes face dilemmas when they insist that wages should take into account such noneconomic factors as length of employment. Unions sometimes have contradictory positions toward technological change; they may resist technological change and at the same time demand higher wages which result from the increased productivity of new machines. "Fringe" benefit demands and plans to increase the security of the workers also mitigate the free play of economic forces.

In general, incomes in the contested markets usually run from moderate to low. Since the economic situation of workers tends to be insecure, the aim of unions is to limit the deleterious effects of free market forces on wages. In the authors' opinion there is little doubt that unions have had a positive effect on wage levels. Robert Ozanne's study has shown that unions maintained the relative income position of workers in the face of simultaneous unemployment and inflation during the 1958 recession. His examination of the nonunion period of 1923–1929 and the unionized period of 1947–1956 reveals a considerable increase in earnings (holding prices constant) during the union period.[39]

5. The *free or marginal market* may be thought of as existing where sociological forces (custom, tradition, and union organization) are virtually nonexistent. The free market flourishes where individuals and economic units are not organized, so that the free play of economic forces is permitted. Typically, the economic units are small and the employees tend to be marginal. The ideal type here might be the small retailer or manufacturer who is on the edge of economic survival, hiring workers who do not find a place in other, more secure markets.

This is the market of the classical economists, where income levels are determined by the individual's ability to anticipate and adjust to the operation of the forces of supply and demand. He may become rich or he may remain destitute; he may exploit or be exploited; he may be rich today and poor tomorrow. His life chances and security are set by his ability, luck, and forces which he cannot control. Obviously this type of market, which operates in an economic but not in a social system, does not accurately portray the general situation. It is the rule rather than the excep-

---

[39] Robert Ozanne, "Impact of Unions on Wage Levels and Income Distribution," *Quarterly Journal of Economics,* May, 1959, pp. 177–196.

tion for markets to be socially and culturally as well as economically organized. Although we have described some of the social variables which affect labor market behavior, we do not yet have an adequate sociological labor market theory.

THE AMERICAN INCOME STRUCTURE

An important question is whether the increasing self-conscious application of controls in the market has consequences for the distribution of economic classes in the United States. Put differently, Are changes occurring in the relative position of income groups? Are incomes verging toward a mean or are the differences as great as or greater than in the past?

There can be little doubt that real incomes in the United States have generally risen for all economic classes over the past twenty-five years. The evidence also suggests that income differences among the manual workers have been diminished somewhat. The spread of national markets has reduced some of the price differences among the regions, and the growth of unionism has decreased some of the wage differences between the unskilled, semiskilled, and skilled workers.

A number of observers feel that such trends are part of a general flattening of the income structure. They believe that the American economy is forging a vast middle class by reducing high incomes and raising low incomes. They claim that high taxes on high incomes, minimum wage legislation, social security for the aged, widespread union agreements, and the explosion of the white-collar sector are creating a middle-income society. Other theories dealing with the mass man, the organization man, mass consumption, and "other-directed" character structures are postulated on decreasing income disparities.[40]

Documentation for these trends is not conclusive. In an extensive historical study of American income distribution over the last half-century, Kolko concluded that no drastic shift has occurred.[41] Ranking earning groups into tenths from highest to

[40] Ortega y Gasset, *The Revolt of the Masses*, Norton, 1932; William H. Whyte, Jr., *The Organization Man*, Simon and Schuster, 1956; David Riesman, *The Lonely Crowd*, Yale, 1950.

[41] Gabriel Kolko, "The American Income Revolution," *Dissent*, Winter, 1957, pp. 35–55.

lowest, as in Table 11.5, he concluded that one cannot find even a remote approximation of a radical shift in any category. The two highest tenths have consistently received since 1910 over 45 percent of the national money income, and the lower five tenths have continually received around one-quarter or less of the total

TABLE 11.5 Percentage of National (Money) Income Received by Each Tenth of Recipients, Before Taxes

	Highest Tenth	2nd	3rd	4th	5th	6th	7th	8th	9th	Lowest Tenth
1910	34	12	10	9	8	7	6	6	5	3
1918	34	13	10	9	8	7	7	6	4	2
1929	39	12	10	9	8	6	5	5	4	2
1937	34	14	12	10	9	7	6	4	3	1
1941	34	16	12	10	9	7	5	4	2	1
1945	29	16	13	11	9	7	6	5	3	1
1947	33	15	12	10	9	7	6	4	3	1
1950	29	15	13	11	9	8	6	5	3	1
1953	31	15	12	10	9	8	6	5	3	1
1955	29	16	13	11	9	8	6	4	3	1

SOURCE: Gabriel Kolko, "The American Revolution," *Dissent*, Winter, 1957, p. 38. The figures for 1910 through 1937 are taken from U.S. Bureau of the Census, *Historical Statistics of the United States, 1789–1945*, 1949, Series A 185-194. They are the only reliable figures for this period available. Figures for 1941 through 1951 are taken from the *Federal Reserve Bulletin*, August, 1948, p. 923, and September, 1951, p. 1067. Subsequent figures are from the *Federal Reserve Bulletin*, June, 1956, p. 569.

national income. This uneven distribution remains even after one takes into account the after-tax distribution of income, income-in-kind, savings, and tangible holdings of economic wealth. The economic elite has maintained its income and standards of living by avoiding the highest tax rates, resorting to "deferred tax plans," dispersal of ownership among family members, receiving payments in kind, receiving unpaid services, purchasing stock below market value, and so on.

Kolko also raises the question of whether spectacular rises in standards of living have occurred for the population as a whole. In 1951, the Bureau of Labor Statistics found that an average urban family needed $4166 per year to maintain an adequate standard of living. Defining 70 percent of this figure or below as an emergency or poverty level, Kolko concluded that the proportion of large families living at emergency levels has remained unchanged since 1935. During this period about three-tenths of the "national consumer units" have been below the emergency level.

These findings, of course, do not mean that no changes are occurring within the American class structure. While the total profile of income may not have been altered, internal changes are taking place. We have already noted that the range in the wage levels of manual workers has been reduced with the growth of national union contracts and with labor's insistence that the wages of unskilled and semiskilled workers be raised. At the same time, income differences between organized and unorganized workers may have increased.

Historical analysis of income changes also reveals increasing discrepancies between the social and economic statuses of some occupations. Thus although the proportion of white-collar workers in large organizations has grown, their income superiority over manual workers has decreased. Relative income declines have also been experienced by some dependent professionals such as nurses, teachers, accountants, and others. Such status inconsistencies may well increase in the future as workers press for secure (but often lower) incomes to replace higher and fluctuating incomes.

Clearly, the universalism–particularism dilemma in income determination is not being quietly resolved. Labor unions, governmental legislation, and personal dedication to the values of equality have decreased income differences between age, sex, and racial groups in the same occupations, but the demand for income inequalities along status lines persists. In the following section we shall continue the income-class analysis on the work plant level.

CLASS STRUCTURE IN THE WORK PLANT

The focus of the economic struggle lies in the social structure of the work plant. Its results are reflected in the class systems of the work plant, and in its salary and wage schedule. In large industries where ownership is absentee, the managers constitute the highest class. Since they have so much autonomous control, they participate directly in the profits as well as drawing salaries. Below the managers and owners are the minor executives, supervisory personnel, and clerical workers. Their incomes usually are in the form of salaries and bonuses. Below them are the wage workers, whose incomes reputedly vary with their skills and the demand for their skills in the labor market.

It is evident that several income strata exist in most plants. Where one stratum begins and another ends is in part a matter of the researcher's decision. If there are convenient breaks in the amount of income received or if different kinds of income are given at particular pay levels, the classes may be divided at these points. In Fig. 11.2 which presents the income structure of the Midwestern Compressor Company, the classes were drawn where the largest breaks in income occurred and where the type of payment changed.

Classes I, II, and III are comprised mainly of managerial groups who receive salaries, bonuses, and dividends. Class IV is made up mostly of salary and wage workers, as is the lowest class, VI. Class V is made up of salaried and wage workers who also receive bonuses. The most important break in the class system is between Classes III and IV. Those in the first three classes are the managers, who received highest incomes and different kinds of payment. Classes IV, V, and VI are made up of dependent salaried and wage workers. Vertical mobility between the top and bottom three classes was very rare, as was mobility between adjacent classes. The greatest amount of movement occurred between Classes IV and V, and the lowest-tenure rates were found in Classes V and VI, which were mostly semiskilled workers and women clerks.

Fluidities and Rigidities

There is always some movement up and down the economic ladder, but it is generally restricted in volume and range. Studies of vertical occupational mobility point to the existence of two separate substructures—the white-collar and the blue-shirt. Mobility within the structures is possible and recurrent, but mobility between them is rare.[42] Thus, the chance that a low-paid office

[42] See the studies presented in Sigmund Nosow and William H. Form, *Man, Work and Society*, Basic books, 1961, chap. X, "Occupational Mobility."

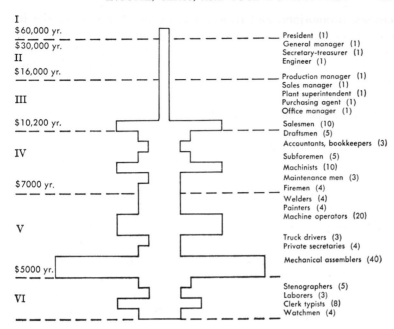

FIG. 11.2. A Profile of the Class Structure in the Midwestern Compressor Company. All incomes are on a yearly basis; bonus is not added to income; Classes I, II, III also are stockholders, but income from stock is not included. The lengths of the bars indicate the relative number of people in the occupation.

worker will become a manager and earn a large salary is higher than that for a skilled manual worker.

Several norms tend to block occupational and class mobility in work organizations. For example, in the Midwestern Compressor Company, Negroes could never aspire to a job higher than that of maintenance man or semiskilled worker. Assemblers might become skilled workers after a long waiting period. Draftsmen were in dead-end jobs. Managers were typically brought in from other plants. Being a shop steward automatically blocked upward economic mobility. Union contracts, salary schedules, informal agreements, "traditional" wages or salaries tended to rigidify the class structure.

On the other hand, the possibilities for a worker to increase his income within his class range were relatively numerous. Rate increases, promotions, and transfers accounted for most of the increases. Long-tenure workers constantly surveyed the wage structure and sought the best jobs. They got to know which jobs paid the most, had most stable employment, received most overtime, and so on.

Although the difference between highest and lowest wages for manual workers may be small, a highly graded wage structure exists in most plants, and workers try to move up this structure. Thus, the steel industry in 1947 had thirty job classes.[43] Climbing the wage ladder gives many workers a feeling of economic improvement. Other economic incentives offered by management include the piece-price system, group incentive plans, profit sharing, bonuses, and prizes. However, such devices have limited applicability because management must maintain a "proper balance" of incomes among different classes of workers.

Management is sometimes caught on the horns of a dilemma. It realizes that, although some workers will respond to wage incentives, the incentive system itself may upset the social equilibrium necessary for smooth production. William F. Whyte and his associates found that incentive systems which are applied in departments with socially heterogeneous workers stimulate social cleavages.[44] Thus workers who were reared on farms or in urban lower-middle-class families believed more strongly in economic individualism. They were not socially active in or outside of the department, largely because they avoided money-spending activities and hobbies. They tended to be Protestants, Republicans, homeowners, and savers. In conformity with their economic and social orientations, they were the *rate busters* in the department and earned the highest incomes. The *restricters,* on the other hand, were sons of urban workers. They led active social lives in and out of the department, rented their homes, pursued money-spending hobbies, and voted Democratic. Obviously, the rate busters were closer to the norms of management than the restricters and believed more in individual bargaining.

As long as individual bargaining is rewarded according to the production, skill, and age of the worker, it is tolerated. However,

---

[43] See Jack Stieber, *Steel Industry Wage Structure,* Harvard, 1959, especially pp. 253–272.

[44] William F. Whyte, *Money and Motivation,* Harper, 1955, pp. 39–49.

whereas it is considered proper and even advisable for white-collar or professional workers to seek "social" contacts with their supervisors, manual workers regard such action with scorn. The worker who is known as the foreman's "pet" spends an unpleasant life on the plant floor. He is the object of all types of sanctions, from silent censure and razzing even to physical violence. Norms regarding behavior toward supervision are usually rather clearly specified; a worker may send his foreman a Christmas card, contribute toward a birthday present, and ask about the health of his family, period.

Not all the pressure to avoid particularism comes from the workers. Managers recognize that worker morale cannot be maintained if management violates its own universalistic norms. Moreover, they realize that equal status and equal power jobs must have approximately equal incomes. When semiskilled workers earn more than foremen, when accountants make more than superintendents, the anomalies in the reward system may result in lowered morale, high employee turnover, and other undesirable actions.

Problems Raised by Income Inequities

Employees are usually aware of how their incomes compare with those of their fellow workers. Often small differences in pay are magnified to an inordinate degree. They will spend many anxious hours trying to account for their inferior pay. They will worry about whether they should approach the boss for a raise, whether they should "tell the supervisor off," and whether their chances of "improving themselves" are good or bad.

Administrators also worry about gross inequalities in incomes. In a study of personnel problems in a library, all staff members were asked to "guess" the salaries of their fellow employees. It was discovered that they had accurate knowledge of everyone's salary despite the fact that salaries were allegedly confidential. Many of the staff tensions resulted from the generally known fact that the actual salaries did not conform to what the librarians and the administration thought they should be. In fact, the published salary schedule followed a designated and existing hierarchy of authority and responsibilities, whereas the actual one reflected a previously existing hierarchy.

Position	Theoretical Salaries	Actual Salaries
Librarian	$13,500	$13,500
Chief of processing	12,000	7,500
Chief of service	12,000	8,000
Order librarian	7,500	6,325
Cataloguer	7,500	8,250
Circulation librarian	7,000	6,000
Readers' adviser	7,000	6,000
Junior cataloguer	6,250	vacant
Accessions librarian	6,250	8,325
Circulation assistant	5,400	5,350
Circulation assistant	5,400	4,200
Periodicals librarian	5,400	4,000
Juvenile librarian	5,400	4,050
Janitors	—	4,050
Student assistant	1.25 per hour	1.65 per hour
Student assistant	1.00–1.25 per hour	1.00–1.65 per hour

General tensions arose from the feeling that salaries should be raised to conform with the theoretical schedule. Deep antagonisms developed among those who thought their salaries were "out of line." For example, the chief of processing and the chief of service had lower salaries than their subordinates, the cataloguer and the accessions librarian. Newer workers who felt that they had more training than older workers, and did more important jobs, received lower salaries. Circulation assistants did the same jobs, yet their salaries differed markedly. Student assistants got higher wages than was theoretically possible. Such situations are not uncommon in other types of work organizations and they create problems among employers and for supervision.

Class Position and In-Plant Mobility

One of the prevailing beliefs of American society is that the individual is responsible for his economic position. It is held that unemployment, income level, independence, and job mobility are conditions for which the individual is largely accountable.[45] This doctrine of personal responsibility in an impersonally directed world survives despite the fact that a continually smaller proportion of employees are able to achieve independent occupational

[45] Robin Williams, *American Society,* Knopf, 1956, pp. 136–149.

status. Yet workers at all levels want to become independent busi-nessmen.[46] Failing this they want jobs with a large amount of authority and independence. In short, they want an opportunity to control the conditions which affect their economic well-being and that of their families. Inability to achieve economic inde-pendence and mobility leads to mass frustration.

Obstacles to mobility are epitomized in two current aphorisms: "You've got to have money to make money," and "To get to the top you've got to act like the top." Two cases illustrate the prob-lem. Joe Doakes carries a sack lunch to work. No matter how good a lunch it is, he thinks he would "get farther" if he could afford to eat in the cafeteria, or perhaps in the "exclusive" restau-rant a few blocks away. He feels that he cannot associate with people of greater influence if he eats his lunch in the department. He would gain prestige and a greater chance for advancement if he could eat with "higher-ups" in the cafeteria or restaurant. But his income is not high enough to allow him to do this.

Managers and staff personnel often stop for a cocktail on the way home. Participating in this ritual calls for economic power. To belong to the same social organization as the "men of influ-ence" in the plant likewise demands economic power. The com-ments of a clerical worker in an optical company demonstrate this point.

I began to wonder how it was that some people became supervisors. I worked as hard as anybody else, yet I never got any place, I asked Joe, and he says, "It's all a racket; you've got to be a Mason. All of the Masons help each other out. Look at Bob, at Jim, and Bill. They're all Masons, and they haven't been here more than two years, yet they're supervisors." I tried to join the Masons when I found this out, but you can't join—you've got to be invited. So I asked my uncle to invite me. But things are not so simple. I started to hang around a bunch of Masons. I found out it costs seventy-five dollars to join. Then, there are dues. But that's just the beginning. You must do the things every-body else does. Thirty cents for every game of bowling, seventy-five

[46] In the white-collar suburb of Greenbelt, Md., 40 percent of the heads of families expressed a desire to become independent businessmen or inde-pendent professionals. See William H. Form, "Status Stratification in a Planned Community," *American Sociological Review*, October, 1945, pp. 605–613. Ely Chinoy found the persistent belief among automobile workers in the possibility of achieving independent business status. See *Automobile Workers and the American Dream*, Doubleday, 1955.

cents for every glass of whiskey. And you've got to treat like everybody else. Of course, if you are a supervisor you can do these things—which I admit I enjoy. But how long can you stand it on a clerk's pay? I gave up the idea.

The frustration that many employees feel arises from their lower economic position and their inability to match the style of living of higher classes. A vicious circle is set up—social contacts are needed to raise one's economic class level, yet one's class position prevents him from pursuing social contacts. This restriction increases feelings of deprivation in the lower classes, which serve, in turn, to augment feelings of insecurity and inferiority. It is probably this syndrome that forces many families into debt for articles of conspicuous display. The isolation from higher groups forces them to make "errors in taste," which are quickly noted by others.[47]

Social-Psychological Correlates of Class Mobility

Class position is a dynamic and changing thing, for salaries and wages constantly rise and fall. It is important, therefore, to appraise the economic or class position of workers over a period of time. If increases in income were the only factors which motivated workers to work, many would not work so hard, because changes in income are not necessarily transformed directly and proportionately into changes in life chances. A difference in income of a few hundred dollars a year is of immense significance at the lower end of the economic scale. Small increases in income yield greater personal comfort, appreciably better food, housing, clothing, personal grooming, and so on. At the lower end of the economic scale, life chances probably rise faster than increases in income. Then, as income continues to rise, there is a period of proportionate rise in life chances. Obviously the rate of consumption must decline with very high incomes, with the consequence that the style of living of the moderately wealthy and the extremely wealthy may not differ appreciably.

As industrial society grows in size and complexity, as it becomes

---

[47] William H. Form and Gregory P. Stone found that different economic levels in the city used different criteria to identify the status level of different classes, so that the possibility of "taste errors" emerged. See "Urbanism, Anonymity, and Status Symbolism," *American Journal of Sociology,* March, 1957, pp. 504–514.

more bureaucratic, as businesses grow, money is more frequently used to measure the general worth of individuals and institutions. The need for impersonal criteria to gauge social status in an impersonal world increases rather than decreases, and new symbols of status must be created. Thorstein Veblen dramatically demonstrated the dependence of these symbols of invidious and conspicuous display upon economic power.[48] Frequently, then, personal economic security is less important than the ability to display a superior economic position. Psychologically, the important question becomes: Is my income increasing or decreasing faster than that of those whose approval I expect and desire?

Dreyfuss contended that the aim of men in power is to accentuate rather than to gloss over income differences among workers in similar occupations.[49] They create envy by instituting highly stratified income schedules and by giving similar jobs different names. Thus an assistant and an associate chief clerk may have very similar duties but receive an income difference of $100 a year. This situation makes them more conscious of their income and status differences and decreases their collaboration in the struggle against management. As they climb the small steps of the economic and status ladders, they feel optimistic of the future and become inclined to support the prevailing economic system. Unfortunately most of the literature on wage and incentive systems almost completely ignores the social and political meaning of income differences.

TYPES OF CLASS WORK HISTORIES

It has been observed that Americans are reared in a culture that stresses individual economic mobility. Since both occupational and income upward mobility is the expected pattern, and since all workers cannot realize it, variations in self-estimation, the appraisal of others, and political ideology attend different mobility experiences. This section examines several types of work histories which involve changes in income, and the social-psycho-

[48] Thorstein Veblen, *The Theory of the Leisure Class,* Viking, 1931. For a popularized version of similar themes, see Vance Oakley Packard, *The Status Seekers,* McKay, 1959, and *The Wastemakers,* McKay, 1960.

[49] Carl Dreyfuss, *Ideology and Occupation of the Salaried Employee,* trans. by Ernst E. Warburg, Columbia, 1938.

logical consequences of such changes. Of the many possible varieties of careers six types have been selected:

1. The climbers: slow, steady progress from lower to higher levels.
2. The Brahmin: total work career is at upper income level.
3. The proletariat: total work career is at the lowest income level.
4. The skidders: steady deterioration of class position.
5. Wanderers: regular fluctuation in class position between any levels.
6. Irregulars: shifts from any level to any other.

These types of class experiences or economic biographies are illustrated in Fig. 11.3. The observations on the relations between

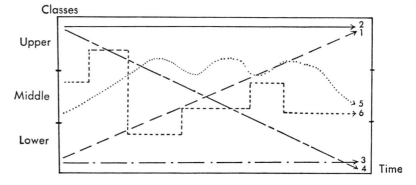

FIG. 11.3. Types of Class Work Histories.

mobility experience and the workers' attitudes toward themselves, their work, their fellow employees, and their politics should be regarded as hypotheses and not conclusions. Each class experience is not necessarily accompanied by a distinctive social-psychological syndrome. For example, a worker may fall from high to middle income level, and another may fall from middle to lower class. Both may react in essentially the same way. Also it is possible for all workers who experience similar mobility not to exhibit the same behavior. However, we shall describe the most frequently recurring responses in each type of class career. Many of our ob-servations are really imputations from social stratification theory[50] because very few studies exist which measure the social-psychological correlates of class mobility.

The Climbers

Those who begin at low income levels and move continually to higher levels, that is, the "climbers," have a middle social class ideology. They are proud of their mobility and they want to advertise their status by consuming according to the style of the times. They can see no advantage to group organization or unionism for they attribute their "success" to hard work, ability, and initiative. Although they prefer to associate with those in higher income classes they are attracted to able, aggressive, and efficient individuals who are rising occupationally. Their overt feelings of security tend to be rather strong, their economic convictions conservative. They are inclined to retain a highly developed work drive, even after the need for it is no longer evident. This may be in part due to the retention of earlier work habits, but it may also reflect some anxieties about falling. The following quotation of a steel mill superintendent illustrates the type:

> I attribute my success to hard work, nothing more, nothing less. I don't believe I'm more capable than the ordinary man, but I've gone farther. I always tell my workers that any man who works by the clock will never get any place. I've never looked at the clock, as long as I've worked. I've put in extra time and I've done more than was expected. And I've been amply rewarded. I've always been able to hold my head high and look any man straight in the eye. My family has never lacked anything. It was difficult the first few years—skimping and all; but we've always had enough to appear decent. And now we can afford some luxuries. I own a big home in a good section of town, my children are going to college, I have a responsible job, and I don't have to worry about another depression. In a few years, I'll be able to retire and do things that I've always wanted to do.

The Brahmin

The second type are individuals who begin at a high class level and remain there. These people often have inherited a business which is stable and rather profitable. They may also be well-trained managers, most of whose work experience has been on top echelons. In either case, they are the best-paid workers in the

---

[50] See Reinhard Bendix and Seymour Martin Lipset, *Class, Status and Power, A Reader in Social Stratification,* Free Press, 1954.

plant. Their material consumption is also high but less "fashionable" than that of the climbers. Like the latter, they believe in their inherent individual worth and ability. They are also conservative politically.

They differ from the climbers in one important aspect: they have greater feelings of security, both economically and socially, which affect their relations with other employees. For example, their contacts with subordinates tend to be fewer, less personal, and accomplished through intermediaries. Although they have less hostility toward lower-class employees than the climbers do, they also feel that working-class people are likely to be incapable, unambitious, and irresponsible. The Brahmin readily admit they are not democratic in their associations, and they assume a bearing of impersonal superiority and self-confidence.

Although the Brahmin are sometimes indistinguishable from the climbers economically, they usually have a broader education and cultural background. The climbers resent the self-assurance and the condescending air of the Brahmin, who have not had to buck obstacles to achieve their status. Below is part of an interview held with an executive of a large shoe manufacturing company.

Some of the young engineers and even some of the old-timers irritate me occasionally. My grandfather started this company, and my father is running it now. I imagine I'll have to carry on in a few more years myself. One of the first things I'll do is get rid of some of these eager-beavers. Half of my father's time is consumed turning down some of the "bright ideas" of the young squirt engineers and the suggestions of the old-timers who think they own the place. The old-timers are the superintendents, and they aren't so bad; but they annoy me with their eternal politeness. We couldn't really run the place without them, for they know how to handle the men in the shop.

It's a funny situation; the engineers are trained, but they have little experience; the old-timers have the experience but they don't have much native capacity. I've been raised in the shoe business, and I've had good training besides. I don't have to think of new ideas just to insure my security. A family enterprise such as this is good, because it is guided with balance and reason.

The Proletariat

The case of the lower-class worker who begins and remains on that level is perhaps the most common and the least known (see

Fig. 11.3). Americans have been so preoccupied with upward economic mobility that they have failed to study systematically their own proletariat. Yet it is known that occupational inheritance at the bottom is the rule rather than the exception.[51] Also, Clark has shown that relative life earnings of various occupations tend to remain constant despite price changes.[52] Thus, unskilled workers and farm laborers have remained at the bottom of the income heap over the years. Often they live below the minimum standards of health, even though most of their income is used to buy the basic essentials of food and housing.

The reactions of lower-class workers to nonmobility is of interest because they also have been socialized to expect economic improvement. The scanty evidence suggests that after a few years they abandon aspirations and hope to make enough money to satisfy their immediate physical needs. Unconcerned about becoming wealthy and secure, they expect to do the same kind of work until their physical strength ebbs. Although work is not considered socially rewarding, they feel they *really* labor, and that they really earn their money. They would like to "do something" to improve their economic position, but their fatalism makes any such attempt difficult. In fact, they withdraw from all organizational activity before the age of forty.[53]

Part of a conversation with a worker of foreign original reveals some of the typical attitudes:

You ask me what I want most out of life. Not much. Most of all I want to have my health and my strength, for without these a man cannot work. All my life I've worked hard, and if God gives me the strength, I must continue. You see, I did not get much education, for my father was not one to do much for his children. I began working at the age of seven, and I know nothing but work. I only hope that I won't have to depend on my children for anything in my old age. Maybe I can even leave them something, who knows? When I first came to America, I made only a dollar a day working, now I make almost nine dollars a

[51] Nosow and Form, *op. cit.* chap. 10.

[52] H. F. Clark, *Life Earnings of Selected Occupations,* Harper, 1937, Table 3, p. 7.

[53] Harold L. Wilensky, "Life Cycle, Work Situation, and Participation in Formal Associations," in Robert W. Kleemeier (ed.), *Aging and Leisure,* Oxford University Press, 1961, pp. 234–235; Genevieve Knupfer, "Portrait of the Underdog," *Public Opinion Quarterly,* Spring, 1947, pp. 103–114; Simone Weil, "Factory Work," trans. by F. Giovanelli, *Politics,* December, 1946, pp. 369–373.

day. But it's always the same for the workingman. Yes, the union helped a little, but the worker is always the same. What do I do with my free time? I rest, for I tire easier now than I used to.

In the work plant the proletariat are inclined to be resentful against those who have "easier" jobs with more pay. They define the job as easy if physical exertion is minimal. For them, foremen or clerical employees do "nothing," and yet they earn more money.

The lower-class worker is released with the first sign of declining production. He therefore does not develop, as do others, a sense of loyalty to the job, the firm, the boss, or even his work associates. He realizes that "his labor is worth just so much an hour." Raises are few and far between and seniority has a limited meaning. If, therefore, he learns of another job which pays slightly more, he does not hesitate to accept it. Also, since he has little to lose, he quits a job for what others may regard as petty reasons.

The nonmobile worker "puts in his time." He does not do anything "extra," for extras are not rewarded. He is inclined to resist innovations on the job, which he interprets as "exploitative." He has, in short, adjusted to the notion of nonmobility. Such a pattern reinforces the belief among managers that laborers are untractable, unreliable, and unpredictable.

The Skidders

The career of class-falling is perhaps the most interesting and the most difficult to understand. A "has-been" is in a particularly difficult position, for he has to explain to himself and to others the reasons for his fall. If a long history of decline is noted, an elaborate defense must be erected. In fact, Wilensky and Edwards found in a study of the downwardly mobile in a sample of 500 workers that they denied failure and continued to retain their middle-class perspectives.[54]

An individual will rarely totally accept the doctrine of individual responsibility as applying to himself, especially when he has fallen in class position. He prefers an impersonal explanation such as the depression, chance, or fate. A common expression is

[54] Harold L. Wilensky and Hugh Edwards, "The Skidder: Ideological Adjustment of Downwardly Mobile Workers," *American Sociological Review,* April, 1959, pp. 215–231.

"I had just one bad break after another." Often, unscrupulous persons are blamed for the fall: "My boss had it in for me," or "They are prejudiced against people of my religion or my nationality." Such explanations personalize the situation and make it more acceptable.

The skidder is rarely one who takes his fall nonchalantly or with a high degree of fatalism. He may borrow prestige from the past, alluding to his former association with the "big shots." He has the "inside" story of how decisions are made, and feels superior because of it. Some skidders may refuse to talk about their past and continually attempt to regain favor in order to climb. The skidder often disdains ordinary workers and may never identify himself with them. Wilensky and Edwards found that skidders tend to be more conservative politically than their peers, which attitude is a form of rejection.[55] However, a few do become completely alienated from higher classes and develop a strong sense of identification with the lower classes. Since they do not share the typical fatalistic reactions of their peers, they sometimes become leaders in the unions and other worker organizations. The following case demonstrates this type of reaction:

> My father was an engineer who made pretty good money. He wanted me to become an engineer too. I suppose I would have become one if it weren't for the war—World War I, I mean. I left high school in my senior year to "join up." I had all the action I wanted. When I got back I went to work in my father's firm. But that's a long story. The firm got in a financial mess, my father died, and I looked for another job. With my inheritance I started an electrical appliance business. I lost my shirt in it. Then I did some selling, and did pretty well for a while. I invested all of my savings in the company I was working for. The depression soon liquidated that, and my job. I took all kinds of jobs, and now I'm an inspector of electric motors. That's a fancy title, but actually the job is easy and it doesn't pay much. I've been trying to stir the boys up to join the union. The fools don't know that you can't win unless you get organized like the bosses.

The Wanderers

A fluctuating class experience may occur on any level or between levels (see class work history 5, Fig. 11.3). This phenomenon is rarer than most people suspect because the great majority of

[55] *Ibid.*

workers do not experience class mobility. Since most mobility occurs within the first ten or fifteen years of work life, those who exhibit the cyclical mobility pattern tend to be older workers. Their attitudes and behavior depend upon whether they are at a high or a low phase in the cycle, and their past experiences. The one thing they have in common is experience in at least two periods of relative prosperity and one period of depression, or the reverse: two periods of depression and one of prosperity. We can anticipate three types of response: the hopeful, the fatalistic, and the confused. Research is needed to discover which of these is most recurrent on different class levels and the conditions that give rise to them.

The *hopeful reaction* obviously is found among those who are currently at the low phase of an economic cycle. The subject feels that uncontrollable circumstances are the cause for his present plight, but with tenacity, optimism, and faith in the system, and in himself, he will see better times. Probably hopeful responses occur more frequently among workers who fluctuate between the middle and upper levels and among those who have accumulated substantial economic reserves. Past experiences of "success" buttress their hopes for the future. Said a rather prosperous life insurance salesman in a heated political argument:

> The trouble with you liberals is that you don't have faith in yourselves and in the economic system. Sure, life is tough, but those who are persistent will get there. Take Mr. Taylor, for instance. He's got a good business in that garage. He's got twenty men working for him. He's set now, but how do you suppose he got there? The other day when I sold him some insurance, he told me that he started in business fourteen times. He's been through bankruptcy five times. But did he quit or lose faith? No, he was building up experience. He doesn't have to work any more, but he does. He's naturally an energetic and nervous man. He'll retire in a few years and he won't have to worry about the future. Sure he's an independent cuss, but who wouldn't be after what he's gone through? You've got to give him credit, boy. He's not waiting for handouts.

The *fatalistic pattern* is more typical of those whose class position fluctuates at the lower range. It is essentially a passive response to continuous economic setbacks. The individual acknowledges that his fate is beyond his control. He refuses to fight or to falter. His emotional involvement with his work is reduced by repeated and unsuccessful attempts to maintain a higher class position. Yet he tends to be somewhat opportunistic and takes advantage of a good situation if it arises. Since success is explained in terms of luck or "breaks" and not individual effort, he tends to be apathetic toward group efforts to improve his economic situation. A garrulous barber explained:

> Oh, we barbers are used to this kind of thing. You know, barbers never make much money. At the union meeting, we decided to raise our price for haircuts to two dollars. There wasn't much fuss about it. We know that in a little while we'll have to lower our prices again, and it's better to lower them from higher prices than from lower prices. So we take things as they come, the good with the bad. . . . Yep, I've been barbering now for fifteen years. Just when I get enough saved to buy a good shop at a good location, a depression hits us. I suppose me and Jack will stay here the rest of our lives. I just hope my legs and hand hold out a few more years. You know your hands and legs are the first things that go on a barber—arthritis.

The third pattern, the *confused or mixed reaction,* is really a combination of the hopeful and fatalistic responses. Here the individual worker either has ambivalent attitudes toward himself and the situation in which he is working or swings toward one pole or another, depending on external circumstances. The cultural impetus in our society is toward optimism, so we may presume that this is the more recurrent pattern.

The mixed reaction is perhaps the least adjustive psychologically. When his class position is "satisfactory," the worker feels successful and optimistic. At another time, he may feel pessimistic and unsuccessful. At one moment he identifies with higher classes; at another he may feel intense hatred. Ambivalent reactions also manifest themselves toward fellow workers. With a murky self-conception he is not sure whether he is a success or a failure in his eyes or in the eyes of others. Neither can he decide whether he is responsible for his present position or whether circumstances are. This uncertainty affects his social relations with his fellow workers. Thus, many regard him as unpredictable, irresponsible, "queer," "nervous," "untrustworthy," or "nutty." A student reports a conversation with a workmate of his brother:

> You know, your brother Jerry is a peculiar guy. He's been workin' at the [radio] plant with us now for four years. I know he's a pretty bright

guy—he knows a lot about radio. But he can't forget that he once used to use that stuff he knows. After all, he does the same things like us—you know—assemble parts. He tried to start a union when he worked for Warner's, didn't he? Now, he's changed and he won't even join the union. What's he trying to do, become a foreman again? I tell you he's kind of peculiar. . . . You know, he talks down the union and then tells us that we're saps because we ain't radical enough. We know he ain't a stoolpigeon, but he's always stirring up some argument and he's talking all the time. He don't belong in a factory. He shoulda been a lawyer.

CONCLUSION

This chapter has attempted to demonstrate how the economic status and the destinies of employees are affected by the operation of noneconomic forces in the society. The basic objective has been to show that the labor market is everywhere both an economic and a social phenomenon and must be analyzed from both perspectives. The chapter has shown that the economic position of employees is the result not only of formal bargaining but also of social organizations functioning in accordance with traditional norms.

In technologically advanced societies, the economic fate of workers is typically stratified. The life chances of men are typically unequal because men have unequal facilities to control others. While Chapter 10 analyzed the relevance of power relations and bargaining in the distribution of economic and noneconomic values, the following chapter will analyze the function of social honor in fashioning the fate of men at work.

SELECTED BIBLIOGRAPHY

Clark, H. F., *Life Earnings of Selected Occupations,* Harper, 1937.

Curtis, Richard F., "Income and Occupational Mobility," *American Sociological Review,* October, 1960, pp. 727–730.

Dewhurst, J. Frederic, and associates, *America's Needs and Resources: A New Survey,* Twentieth Century Fund, 1955.

Greer, Scott, *Last Man In,* Free Press, 1959.

Hollingshead, A. B., and F. C. Redlich, *Social Class and Mental Illness,* Wiley, 1958.

Kolko, Gabriel, "The American Income Revolution," *Dissent,* Winter, 1957, pp. 35–55.

Miller, Herman P., *Income of the American People,* Wiley, 1955.

Sheppard, Harold L., Louis A. Ferman, and Seymour Forber, *Too Old to Work—Too Young to Retire: A Case Study of a Permanent Plant Shutdown,* Special Committee on Unemployment Problems, U.S. Senate, GPO, 1960.

Whyte, William F., *Money and Motivation,* Harper, 1955.

CHAPTER 12

Status and Prestige in the Work Organization

THEORETICAL CONSIDERATIONS

Concept of Status Organization

Every position in a social organization is evaluated by people in it, by those interacting with it, and by many who merely know of its existence. This evaluative component of social relations applies to entire groups, to their positions, and to the people who occupy the positions. Moreover, there is a universal tendency to rank evaluations, with the result that an evaluation structure emerges. In the previous chapters we analyzed two different ranking structures, one dealing with power and the other with economic reward. Ranking within these structures can be independently determined by outside observers. That is, there are clear tests whether a person, position, or group has greater or less power and income than another person, position, or group. The distinguishing feature of a status structure is that rank assignment is dependent on personal evaluation of the prestige or social honor of others. As Robert Dubin has indicated, status structures are rewarding, not operating, features of organization.[1] Whereas class organization reflects material distribution of economic reward, status organization deals with the allocation of esteem, prestige, and social honor.[2] All people and groups may be thought of as living in status situations which continually test,

---

[1] Robert Dubin, *The World of Work*, Prentice-Hall, 1958, pp. 55.

[2] Esteem, prestige, and social honor are used in different senses. See, for example, Kingsley Davis, *Human Society*, Macmillan, 1949, chap. IV.

validate, and legitimize a given level of social prestige or honor. It is important that status organization be studied separately from other aspects of social organization in industry because, as C. I. Barnard early indicated, status organizations have a considerable degree of independence from other structural aspects of organization.[3] Although status may be closely associated with functions of a position, its power, and economic reward, it is wise to analyze the status system independently. For as Weber has clearly shown, these three stratification orders need not and do not necessarily converge either in society as a whole or within industry.[4] It is the very nonconvergence of power, class, and status that gives modern society and modern industry its dynamic quality, as we shall see. In this chapter we shall examine the status organization of industry in detail, referring, in the process, to its changing relations to the other orders of stratification.

Components of Status Organization

The social organization which revolves around status is usually extensive. Some aspects of it are formally recognized; others remain latent. Traditionally, Americans, in contrast to other, historically oriented societies, have paid comparatively little attention to status. It might be more accurate to say that Americans have been less aware of the status dimension of their society. Their lack of awareness is part of a general tendency to underplay the existence and importance of social class. However, sociological analysis in the last two decades has exposed to Americans the elaborate status structures they have built up in industry and society.[5] Many management and union leaders today are willing to face up to the existence and importance of social honor in the work situation.

Some of the components of status organization suggested by Barnard are as follows:

[3] C. I. Barnard, "Functions and Pathology of Status Systems in Formal Organizations," in William Foote Whyte, *Industry and Society*, McGraw-Hill, 1946, p. 46.

[4] *From Max Weber: Essays in Sociology*, trans. H. H. Gerth and C. W. Mills, Oxford University Press, 1946, pp. 180–195.

[5] See the many studies reported in Reinhard Bendix and Seymour Martin Lipset (eds.), *Class, Status, and Power, a Reader in Social Stratification*, Free Press, 1953.

1. Ceremonies of induction, transfer, retirement, and others. These take the form of formal dinners, parties, admonitions, giving of gifts, and taking oaths. In the informal relations in the work situation, ceremonies are less reserved and are expressed in joking, "razzing," horseplay, and "speechifying."

2. Symbols of status such as titles, name plates, emblems, stationery, and equipment.

3. Differential distribution of emoluments, perquisites, and privileges. Included here are bonuses, larger offices, more helpers, travel expenses, and special equipment and services. If visible, these privileges also serve as status symbols.

4. Restrictions and limitations of behavior. Along with prerogatives granted to certain positions, a number of proscriptions are also associated with status positions. Just as the adult cannot retain some of the privileges of the child, so people in higher status positions cannot enjoy the privileges of lower positions, and vice versa. The manager, for example, may never abandon his white shirt and tie in formal meetings. These prohibitions are as much a part of the status system as his prerogatives.

Functions of the Status Structure

The universality of status distinctions in all societies attests to their functional importance. Status structures arise in industry for the same reasons that they arise in society in general. While this statement is undoubtedly true, the problems it poses are complex, and precise knowledge of the causes of status structures is limited. However, three or four main factors may be singled out.

1. The very nature of the human animal and human society makes an evaluation structure almost inevitable in all activities. The mere fact that man is a social animal reared in a society with ideals, norms, and values means that he will try to realize the norms in his behavior as a basis of social approval and recognition. Differential approximations of the social ideals and norms result in a status rank-structure. Industry, as well as society, has a normative structure which constitutes the mudsill of a status structure.

2. Social differentiation fosters social stratification. Thus the larger the number of positions, the greater the probability that the positions will be status-ranked. Contemporary industry is *par*

excellence a highly functionally differentiated structure which fosters status distinctions.

3. Positions which have complex functions, which call for extensive training, and which have greater authority usually are accorded greater prestige or status. Such rewards constitute motivations to seek training and make the necessary sacrifices to perform difficult tasks effectively.[6]

4. Status distinctions tend to legitimize and validate a given social order, giving it a traditional justification, primarily with the use of status symbols. Thus in anonymous situations an employee need not question the right of a person unknown to him to issue orders if he possesses a symbol of authority, for example, a badge, a particular type of dress, or special equipment. Soon after the Revolution, the Soviets, in an attempt to "democratize" the Army, abolished symbols and prerogatives of rank. After a short interval titles, the salute, the distinctive uniforms, and other status symbols were reinstituted as necessary to legitimize the authority structure so fundamental to military discipline.

5. The legitimizing function of status distinctions is closely linked to their function of facilitating organizational effectiveness and communcation. In complex organizations, which are commonplace in industry, status distinctions facilitate the articulation of various positions. Inevitably, prestige distinctions based on function become generalized to include other types of behavior.

6. Status structures also serve to integrate organizations into the broader society. Since industry is linked functionally to other community institutions, it must share in their norms, values, and status distinctions. In this manner, for example, the social class system of the community is extended into industry, providing a continuity of experience and expectations for all concerned.

It would be erroneous to conclude that the functions of the status structure *insure* an effective and efficient organization. As Barnard has suggested, the functions may also become the basis for pathological developments. Thus, it is easy for a status system to become so rigid, so stable, and so important as to block organizational changes. Where status becomes an end rather than a

[6] Kingsley Davis and Wilbert E. Moore, "Some Principles of Stratification," *American Sociological Review,* April, 1945, pp. 242–249.

means, social mobility is halted, so that a given order assumes a sacred character, as in the caste system.

Requisites of Status Situations

Two case histories are presented below to document the reality and the complexity of status situations in industry. The first is that of a girl who had just entered college after her first job experience.

Last summer was the first time in my life that I had ever worked for pay. The place was a large department store. I was put in hosiery. My first day was a hectic one. I tried to learn the job, become acquainted with the other clerks, find time for lunch, and become an expert on salesmanship the first day.

As time went on, I became more settled in the routine duties of a salesgirl and began to notice what went on among the personnel.

A large department store hires many different types of people. The main floor consists mostly of high school girls. In the gown department and fur department are the older, more experienced women. Then, of course, there are the supervisors, floor walkers, stock people, and many others that make up the store. All these people belong to different cliques. The members are interested in their own welfare and not in the clerks as a whole.

The whole matter depends on the supervisor. For instance, in our store the supervisor was a very attractive woman of about forty years of age. She dressed perfectly and had a charming personality. Her one fault was intolerable. It was nationality prejudice. It seems that her ancestors came over on the *Mayflower*. She had a great dislike for Italians and Jews. Anything that went wrong was blamed on them. When one of the Italian or Jewish girls wanted a day off, they were refused, though the other clerks were granted days off for less serious purposes than theirs. And so it went, those who had social prestige and those who had none, the haves against the have-nots!

Social snobbery on the job is one of the many faults we have in America. We may read and hear about American Democracy, but when we come right down to the facts, we haven't much.

A male college freshman discusses his irritations over a particular status situation:

It is very easy to say that there can't be such a thing as social snobbery. A job is a job and every person who has anything to do with that job should do it at his very best. This statement, however true it may be, is not always just so. I have had the experience where it has been entirely different.

A few years ago, I worked on a job that paid quite a bit per hour, but it was at the same time a dirty job. I worked with two other boys as a cleanup crew. One of the boys was from a family of about the same caliber in social standing as my family. The other boy was older than we were and he was from a better family. I didn't mean better in a sense of perfectness but his father was well-to-do for he had a good job as the president of a small factory. The three of us working together could have been almost excellent on the job. As it was, we were not working together, for the boy whose dad was rich had an exalted opinion of himself.

Our job as a cleanup crew was to keep the floors clean, bale scrap paper, and to keep the machines clean. We had decided to divide the work among ourselves and make it easier for us. The rich boy was very much turned against this idea for he didn't want to clean any of the machines when it was his turn. He shirked all his duties with a fear of getting a little dirt on his hands. He came to work in his suit of good clothes when we came in our overalls. I slowly took an attitude toward him which wasn't very nice but which I knew the other boys also took. When we were asked to do things out of our line of work, our friend, the rich boy, did not take his share, but we dropped our other jobs, finished what we were asked to do and went back and picked up where we had stopped.

The man who had charge of keeping us busy began to notice what was going on so he went to the boss about it. We found out that he had gone in and as we waited for his return we hoped that this wouldn't cost us a job. When he came out, he took us into a corner and explained the situation. The rich boy's father had done a lot of business for this particular company and had gotten his son the job there. Our boss was obligated to the boy's father for many things, and therefore, he was in no place or position to fire him. He could not and did not. We had to learn to get along ourselves and let our rich friend keep on at his usual rate of loafing. We were never friends, and I doubt if we ever will be. I only hope that someday for his sake somebody will be in a position to make him see the light.

There is snobbery over a job as long as one person, it only takes one, among the whole group of people has an exalted opinion of himself. People who are doing a job should do it with a feeling of helping somebody else and not just themselves.

These two histories illustrate some pathological aspects of status situations. However, they point up the four requisites of a status situation: the bearer of status or the claimant, the symbol, the audience, and the deference pattern.[7] The claim is simply an expectation which an individual or a collectivity has for deferential behavior on the part of others. A claim may take the form of an

[7] See Hans Speier, "Honor and the Social Structure," *Social Research,* February, 1933, pp. 74–97.

assertion of a special privilege, such as refusing to do dirty work, occupying a favored location, being consulted first, receiving higher pay, or being addressed by a particular title. A claim which is not honored or validated by an audience is empty and leads to status frustration. The audience is therefore part and parcel of the status situation, although its presence may not be readily apparent. If the person or audience is forced to defer, it is an empty ritual devoid of satisfaction to the claimant. Therefore, in genuine status situations the deference must be voluntary, because the bestower of status shares the ends, norms, and values of the claimant. Deference behavior may vary from a simple assent to the claim to complex rituals. In rare situations deference is given even though no claim has been made. This may result in embarrassment, but more often it brings a change in the status structure because deference is rarely refused.

To facilitate social interaction in status situations, symbols are devised and agreed upon by the claimant and the audience. Americans are verbal equalitarians who dismiss status claims and elaborate status symbols as undemocratic on the organizational level and as social snobbery on the individual level. Yet, as Fig. 12.1 shows, modern industry has elaborated a vast and complex system of status symbols to parallel bureaucratic levels of authority. This is most readily apparent in the white-collar and managerial sectors of bureaucracies because status symbols there are consciously and rationally developed as part of the reward system. However, the pursuit of status symbols is also highly developed on the plant floor, although its manifestations are different, as we shall see.

Symbols are a form of advertising and a request for deference. Workers strive as much for the symbols of status as they do for the factors that underlie status. Not infrequently, managers underestimate the importance of status to others. Their preoccupation with salaries, wages, and other such items makes them unaware that many dissatisfactions can be traced to their unwillingness or failure to grant status to lower-income groups. The Negro laborer, for example, would rather be called "mister" than receive a raise of five cents an hour. Sometimes a status symbol brings its bearer considerable inconvenience, such as having to travel to the top-floor office and being unable to shed one's coat.

Yet workers would rather be inconvenienced than abandon their symbols of status.

Different occupations and work plants evolve unique symbols of status. One of the most common is clothing. It is well known that people who work in their "going-out" clothes generally have higher status than those who wear occupational garbs. Thus the white-collar worker has greater prestige than the worker in overalls. Clothing distinctions may be carred to a ludicrous point. In a small garage that the authors studied a wide variation in clothing symbolized gradations of status. The owner worked in his "business" suit. The stock and order clerks wore no special uniform but had to remove their coats and worked in their shirt sleeves. The supervisor of the mechanics also removed his coat, but he wore a nonfunctional white smock. The mechanics wore full-length blue jumpers, and the apprentices and cleanup men wore overalls or discarded clothing. Although this hierarchy of garb was not formally instituted, it was nonetheless scrupulously observed.

Uniforms, with some notable exceptions, indicate lower-status jobs. They are common among personal and domestic service workers, truck drivers, and public service workers. Some corporations have found the status struggle via clothing so intense that they have instituted uniforms. But the uniform may also be used to signify status distinctions. The military forces have, with the use of gold braid, developed symbols to indicate both status and power. The uniforms of policemen, firemen, movie ushers, nurses, and waitresses and the academic robes of college professors follow a similar pattern.

The hours of work symbolize prestige position. Usually the later the worker arrives and the earlier he leaves his job, the higher his status. Whether he punches a time clock or not is also a matter of prestige. (It is interesting to note the rationalizations of office workers against installing time clocks.) Usually, the longer and later the lunch hour, the higher the status; the night shift is less prestigious than the day shift; and so on.

The place one dines or lunches also reflects status—whether on the plant floor, in the cafeteria, in nearby restaurants, or downtown. The length of the vacation, the opportunity to choose the time of year off, and the number of vacations and holidays off all

Visible Appurtenances	Top Dogs	V. I. P.s	Brass	No. 2s	Eager Beavers	Hoi Polloi
Brief cases	None—they ask the questions	Use backs of envelopes	Someone goes along to carry theirs	Carry their own—empty	Daily—carry their own—filled with work	Too poor to own one
Desks, office	Custom made (to order)	Executive style (to order)	Type A "Director"	Type B "Manager"	Cast-offs from No. 2s	Yellow oak—or cast-offs from Eager Beavers
Tables, office	Coffee tables	End tables or decorative wall tables	Matching tables Type A	Matching tables Type B	Plain work table	None—lucky to have own desk
Carpeting	Nylon—1 inch pile	Nylon—1 inch pile	Wool-Twist (with pad)	Wool-Twist (without pad)	Used wool pieces —sewed	Asphalt tile
Plant stands	Several—kept filled with strange exotic plants		Two—repotted whenever they take a trip	One medium-sized Repotted annually during vacation	Small Repotted when plant dies	May have one in the department or bring their own from home

	Silver	Silver	Chromium	Plain painted	Coke machine	Water fountains
Vacuum water bottles						
Library	Private collection	Autographed or complimentary books and reports	Selected references	Impressive titles on covers	Books everywhere	Dictionary
Shoe shine service	Every morning at 10:00	Every morning at 10:15	Every day at 9:00 or 11:00	Every other day	Once a week	Shine their own
Parking space	Private in front of office	In plant garage	In company garage —if enough seniority	In company properties— somewhere	On the parking lot	Anywhere they can find a space— if they can afford a car
Luncheon menu	Cream Cheese on Whole Wheat Buttermilk and Indigestion Tablets	Cream of Celery Soup Chicken Sandwich (White Meat) Milk	Fruit Cup— Spinach Lamb Chop—Peas Ice Cream—Tea	Orange Juice Minute Steak French Fries— salad Fruit Cup— Coffee	Tomato Juice Chicken Croquettes Mashed Potatoes Peas—Bread Chocolate Cream Pie Coffee	Clam Chowder Frankfurter and Beans Rolls and butter Raisin Pie à la Mode Two Cups of Coffee

FIG. 12.1. Exec-Chart: A Ready Guide for Evaluating Executives. (From Meyer Weinberg and Oscar E. Shabat, Society and Man, Prentice-Hall, 1956, p. 150.)

are indicative of prestige rank. A winter vacation in Florida or abroad reflects the acme of status.

Other things around the office show status, as Fig. 12.1 reveals. The size of the desk, the location of the desk, the display of a name plate, the private office, the size of the office, the number of secretaries, the proximity to the chief executive, the rug on the floor, paintings on the wall, private entrances, private telephone, reception room, private washroom, display of magazines—all are symbolic of relative prestige. White-collar workers develop many status symbols. One hypothesis which may account for this is that their work is not easily distinguishable. They all work with paper, and all papers look alike to the outsider. Therefore, symbols must be used to inform observers of the exact status of individual workers.

Some corporations have evolved elaborate systems of status symbols. With each job promotion the company may specify the use of an additional symbol, such as a secretary, a larger office, a larger desk, the use of a name plate, being listed in the company directory, a change in the title, and so on. In the absence of such consciously erected systems, workers informally create their own and observe them as scrupulously as the formal ones.

Of course, manual workers also develop status symbols, many of which are similar to those associated with white-collar occupations. Some of these are the use of job titles, the location of the bench, and type of clothing worn on the job. Perhaps the most important sign of status is to be consulted by supervisors. No matter how well management has coordinated production, bottlenecks arise which can be eliminated only by utilizing the experiences of the workers. The frequency of the consultation, therefore, is symbolic of status.

THE ORGANIZATION OF STATUS

The Traditional Model

Traditional societies, made up of artisans and craftsmen, develop characteristic status structures quite different from those found in contemporary industrial societies. It would be erroneous to conclude that a highly developed status system is absent in artisan enterprises. The status distinctions between master, journeyman, apprentice, merchant, and others during the Middle Ages were clear and distinct. Elaborate status marks or symbols, primarily in the area of clothing, were devised to parallel status distinctions. Moreover, these distinctions were accompanied by a complex and differentiating system of privileges, obligations, and rewards.[8]

The main feature of this system was its clarity. There was little disagreement on the ranking of the bearers of status, the bestowers of status, the symbols of status, and the appropriate deferential behavior. Moreover, since the entire economic system was stable, its status segment also had an enduring quality. This stability was easily maintained because the market was primarily local and because the wider community was organically linked to it. Since the status structure of industry was part of the wider community status structure, the two reinforced each other.

The Contemporary Model

Each of the factors used to characterize the traditional status model may be used to describe the contemporary situation. These factors deal with the

1. Requisites of the status situation.
2. Stability of the status structure.
3. Internal mobility in the structure.
4. Multiplicity and overlapping of structures.
5. Convergence or dissonance of structures.

The contemporary scene provides a wide range in each of these factors, which are discussed below.

Change in status

The two chief external characteristics of modern industry which differentiate it from its predecessors are its larger size and its greater internal complexity. Although the principles of large-scale organization and minute division of labor were originally found in government, the military, and religion, manufacturing extended them to an inordinately high degree. The main reason for these developments, as we have seen in Chapter 2, was the

[8] See Chapter 2.

systematic application of rationality and science to production. Since the status system of modern industry is based primarily on technical specialization, constant changes in specialization force constant readjustments in the status system.

Specifically this means that the status position of many people is not stationary, that various audiences are constantly reevaluating status situations, that the symbols of status are changing with technological and organizational changes, and that the patterns of social deference are also changing.

The impact of technological and organizational change on the status structure has been variously reported. Smith and Nyman note that changes in the technology of cloth making altered the entire status structure of the factory.[9] Engineering specialists were placed in positions of authority over old skilled spinners, whose skills were gradually taken over by new machines. In the meantime, young untrained workers were hired at the same wage levels as the oldsters. These changes not only created a new status elite but lowered an old one and deprived it of a traditional audience, the younger workers. Warner and Low reported a similar process in the shoe industry of a small Massachusetts town. In this case not only did the deletion of skills destroy the traditional status hierarchy in the plant, but the change from local to absentee ownership literally deprived the new owners and managers of a status audience. Workers abandoned their traditional loyalties to the owners or their surrogates and transferred their loyalties to union leaders.[10]

Faunce reports similar evidence in the area of automation. Skilled workers were transferred from old plants to newly automated plants.[11] Although transfer to the new jobs was considered upgrading, many workers reported dissatisfactions. The isolation foisted on them by the greater space the machines occupied reduced their social interaction with others and deprived them of their customary recognition. The new technology also reduced the function of the foremen because they could neither teach the

[9] Elliott Dunlap Smith and Richmond Carter Nyman, *Technology and Labor*, Yale, 1939.

[10] W. Lloyd Warner and J. O. Low, *The Social System of the Modern Factory*, Yale, 1947, pp. 66–89.

[11] William A. Faunce, "Automation and the Automobile Worker," *Social Problems*, Summer, 1958, pp. 68–77.

specialty once it was learned nor supervise its execution. They tended to become watchers of watchers.

Of course, organizational and technological changes also create new status structures with new symbols and new audiences. For a time at least, the computer installer, the designer of new operations, and the systems analyst may occupy exalted positions in a changing enterprise. The space or atomic physicist or the electronics expert is fashioning not only a new technology but a new status system. Such changes were rare in the pre-industrial enterprise.

Mobility in status structures

Whenever fluidity is the constant condition of an organization, the chance of social mobility on the part of its incumbents is increased. In modern industry this means that increased technological and organizational changes foster increased vertical occupational mobility, and with this condition increased status mobility. While the relation between occupational and status mobility is not direct, it is nonetheless high because occupational changes tend to shatter the traditional segments of status structures. That is, the nontask and nonauthoritative aspects of status (e.g., ritual) tend to wither fastest under the impact of technological and occupational changes.

Obviously all such changes do not have a uniform impact on status. We do know that the changes in occupational and status mobility are more dependent on the stage of technological development than on the social class structure. Lipset and Bendix have shown that, despite the alleged difference between the open and closed social class structure in the United States and Europe, the amount of occupational mobility in both areas is related directly to the stage of industrial development.[12] That is, the same amount of vertical occupational mobility tends to be found in all economies at the same level of industrialization. The precise points where greatest mobility occurs are not certain, but scanty evidence suggests that it occurs where there is a basic change in type of economy.

Pirenne has shown that in the various stages in the evolution of

[12] Seymour Martin Lipset and Reinhard Bendix, *Social Mobility in Industrial Society,* University of California Press, 1959.

capitalism new types of capitalists emerged, and that there was not a simple hereditary transfer of capitalistic generations.[13] To be sure, while earlier generations erected complex trappings to glorify their honor, they were unable to utilize status mechanisms to maintain and extend their honor in competition with rising new types of capitalists. The latter either challenged the legitimacy of the older generation or proceeded to erect independent systems with new claims, new symbols, new audiences, and new deference rituals. A similar process may be expected to occur in the emerging economies of Africa, Asia, and Latin America. Hereditary tribal chiefs, for example, will probably not become the managers of the new society. Despite the legitimacy of their ancient honor, they will not be able to command the respect of the new urban masses, who will respond to other symbols in the new economy.

Illustrations of the change of entire structures in the face of industrialism may be found even in mature industrial societies. Stone and Form studied the status structure of a midwestern town of 10,000 people in the corn belt.[14] They found the coexistence of two status structures, one built upon the traditional agricultural and trade economy and another on the new invading industrial economy. The managers of the new industries, who were reared in large cities, and their satellites did not attempt to find a place in the traditional structure dominated by the "old families," who had built their position on land ownership and trade. Neither did the old families accept the newcomers, who insisted on drinking "standing up" and who modeled their style of living after the cosmopolitan pattern in nearby cities. As a result, parallel status structures emerged, highly differentiated at the top. Undoubtedly the situation was transitional, with the probable outcome that the invading status system would eventually triumph. As a matter of fact, young people began to abandon the oldsters and sought entry into the new factories.

Confirming evidence of status mobility in contemporary industry is provided in the recent reanalysis of the North-Hatt occu-

[13] Henri Pirenne, "The Stages in the Social History of Capitalism," *American Historical Review,* April, 1914, pp. 494–515.

[14] Gregory F. Stone and William H. Form, "Instabilities in Status: The Problem of Hierarchy in the Community Study of Status Arrangements," *American Sociological Review,* April, 1953, pp. 149–162.

pational prestige scale. Whereas the owners of large industry occupied a position superior to the managers of large industry in the first administration, the positions were reversed in the recent reanalysis.[15]

OPEN AND CLOSED STATUS STRUCTURES

While contemporary industry evidences more mobility than its forebears, equal mobility opportunities are not available to all. Not only do some industries have more fluid status structures than others, but all industries have greater or lesser opportunities in various parts of the organization. The accumulated research suggests that there is less opportunity for mobility for manual workers than for white-collar workers. Several forces serve to solidify or shatter status structures of work plants.

Perhaps the strongest force keeping status structures open is the ideology of free mobility. Since workers believe in free mobility, managers are constrained to put it in practice. This pressure cannot be resisted too long without impairment of morale. It is also reasonable to assume that if status circulation is unduly restricted, plant efficiency is lowered. An organization can absorb only so much "dead wood" and still function adequately. Only a limited number can be "kicked upstairs." "Shakedowns" are inevitable and "new blood" must be transfused into the system. The introduction of new machines demands changes in the technical organization and therefore in the status organization of the work plant. Cost accounting methods reveal inefficiencies that can be removed only by changing personnel.

The forces solidifying the status structures are many. The mere inertia of an organization makes changes difficult. Barnard agrees that "the resistance to loss of status is in general stronger than the desire to achieve higher status."[16] Thus the organization must be protected against inherent disruptive tendencies. The problem that the administrator faces is whether or not to replace inferior men who have knowledge of the local work situation with superior men who do not have the support of the workers.[17] Gardner

---

[15] Albert J. Reiss, Jr., *Occupations and Social Status,* Free Press, 1961, pp. 202–203.

[16] Barnard, *op. cit.,* p. 78.

[17] *Ibid.,* p. 76.

suggests another obstacle to mobility: "In many cases the one who works hardest or is best at the lower level is not the one who can do the best at the next level. . . . The best mechanic or the most efficient operator does not always make the best foreman, the ability to handle a group does not develop naturally out of the ability to handle machines."[18]

The very hierarchical nature of enterprises means that there are relatively few jobs available to aspirants at the highest levels. However, the growing proportion of middle-management jobs and the elongation of hourly wage schedules provide mobility hopes for many. Yet, many jobs lead to blind alleys, and increased educational qualifications for jobs will allow highly trained younger workers to take positions previously available to employees who climbed the local job ladder. Fortunately other channels of status mobility are available than through the job route.

Multiplicity of status structures

In traditional work plants the interpersonal relations were so intimately interlocked with tasks that a single social and status system could be said to exist. An important feature of modern industrialism is the proliferation of systems in which the worker may and often must participate. There are as many status systems as there are areas for participation. The typical employee must participate in the formal job structure of the enterprise, but he may also participate in the systems of human relations which emerge in his department, in the wider plant, in the labor union, and in the organizations sponsored by labor, management, and the community. Obviously, these areas of participation may be more or less integrated or disparate, depending on various conditions.

FORMAL STATUS STRUCTURES

In general, the formal status structure of a work plant corresponds to the lines of authority in the organization chart. The president is accorded the highest prestige, then the general manager, and so on down the line. The compensation associated with

[18] Burleigh B. Gardner and David G. Moore, *Human Relations in Industry,* Irwin, 1955, pp. 265–266.

the position and its authority tends to correspond with the levels of the supervisory structure. This correlation is most apparent in military organizations, where extreme care is taken to assure a conversion of power, income, and prestige. The symbolic manifestation of the entire stratification system is reflected in the uniforms assigned to various levels as well as the privileges, e.g., the salute, the separate facilities, the titles, and so on.

Although status symbols may be less clear in industry, they are nonetheless present. Long tenure is typically and formally recognized by gifts, medals of service, dinners, and special privileges. Promotions, transfers, and resignations are typically accompanied by rites which recognize the honor of the person. Two other important aspects of the status structure are often overlooked. The first deals with the use of publicity in the company or local newspaper. Whenever it is deemed desirable, management may boost the prestige of a person or office by giving favorable and extensive publicity. This often appears prior to a promotion or a reorganization which will raise the importance of an office. The second mechanism is appointment to boards of prestigious community associations. Ross and others have shown that community participation is not only under the control of business but considered part of normal business life. Since board memberships are as status-ranked as jobs, an employee's status usually includes his community activities.[19]

Not much is known about the mechanisms to deprive people of their status. In the military they are clear: demotion, tearing off of insignia, dishonorable discharge, confinement, and reduction of privileges. Parallel mechanisms are undoubtedly found in industry.

In large and complex enterprises it is difficult to design rationally a status system that arranges all positions in a hierarchical order. Research specialists, "permanent" consultants, and administrative assistants do not easily fit into a hierarchical scheme, and they are given material and status awards which many consider "out of line." In addition, job assignments are gradually altered to meet specific exigencies, with the result that unintended status differences emerge.

[19] Aileen D. Ross, "Philanthropic Activity and the Business Career," *Social Forces*, March, 1954, pp. 274–280.

Such was the case in a telephone accounting office studied by the authors. A middle-aged woman (Bertha) had been district clerk for a number of years. She was an efficient worker highly respected by management and co-workers alike. During a revisit to the plant, we discovered that Bertha had quit her job in a salary row. An investigation revealed that Bertha's salary was exactly that of the bookkeeper and that both were at the top level of their salary scales. However, owing to Bertha's efficiency and the supervisor's confidence in her, Bertha's job had become a "catchall" which included some supervisory responsibilities. When Bertha found she made the same salary as the bookkeeper she demanded a raise above the official ceiling, which was denied. After she left, management redistributed job assignments in the department. Nevertheless, the job of district clerk continued to have high prestige, and many girls competed for it.

Labor unions also have formal status structures, which bear some resemblance to those of management. As with the latter, union offices are granted respect according to their power and income. Although it is not as elaborately developed as in management, unions also grant formal recognition to their officers in the form of awards, banquets, plaques, and special privileges. Unions have newspapers, too, which are used to accord honors to officers and members. And, like management, union officials are assigned memberships on community boards as recognition of their status.

However, there is one important feature that distinguishes the union status situation from the management one: the popular election of officers. At the risk of oversimplification, the generalization may be made that the management status structure is more consciously engineered and supported by accumulated power, while the union structure is a genuine reflection of member evaluations. That is, the union has greater assurance that the status audience (the members) grants deference voluntarily, through the election process. The same generalization applies to the mechanism of status disqualification—the defeat of nonrespected candidates for office.

PARTICULARISTIC STATUS STRUCTURES

Prestige is also accorded individuals, positions, and groups on bases not recognized by the formal union and management organizations. However, even in such nonformal situations the dynamics of status have bearing on the functions of formal organizations. If they did not, they would be of no concern to industrial sociology. Our concern is with status phenomena referring to particular workers, to particular departments, and to particular situations not covered by the rules. The very specificity of these phenomena make generalizations difficult. However, a few generalizations may be hazarded.

First of all, there may be disagreements on the prestige, salary, and authority levels assigned to particular jobs and their incumbents. Occupational sociology is replete with illustrations of jobs which are classified by workers as "morally dirty" or desirable in opposition to management definition.[20] Rate setters are a case in point. They represent a threat to the workers' informal control system and are, therefore, despised despite management's high evaluation of them. In contrast, a job which gives the worker independence frees him from authority and is highly valued, whatever management's evaluation. All jobs are ranked in terms of the degree to which they approximate the norms of the informal system.

Job incumbents also may be ranked on performance standards not set by management. An engineer who makes a quick concise report to meet a deadline may be disesteemed for not following the traditional niceties and rituals of the occupation. The high producer who cuts corners is not honored despite his larger pay check. Similar illustrations may be found in union organization. The "porkchopper" is disesteemed in spite of his high office because he uses the union as a vehicle for escaping the factory and neglects the "union guy," while the conscientious steward may be highly respected. If such evaluations endure they become part of particularistic status structures. If they are contingent on personalities they represent simply informal leadership.

A second basis of nonformalized status is the extension of community status in the plant. If this has no bearing on union or management functions or relations it is not part of the plant structure. For example, if different ethnic groups are found in an office, but ethnicity has no bearing on job assignment, union politics, attitudes toward management, morale, work cliques, and related

[20] See Everett C. Hughes, "Work and the Self," in J. H. Rohrer and M. Sherif (eds.), *Social Psychology at the Crossroads*, Harper, 1951, pp. 313–323.

phenomena, we are not interested in it. However, this is rarely the case. Typically the factors which underlie status in the community are expressed in both the informal and the formal structures in the plant. The most important of these are social class, ethnicity, age, and sex. Figure 7.3 in the chapter on informal organization illustrates the overlapping of these factors on job ecology. Other research shows that ethnic status, for example, affects group membership, productivity, morale, and job satisfaction.[21]

Hughes reports that the status distribution of a particular plant was reflected in the informal seating arrangement in the company cafeteria.[22] Figure 12.2 reveals a segregated seating arrangement by occupation, race, and sex. The office personnel customarily sat in the northern half of the room and the male supervisors in one corner. Next to them were the white female office workers. The plant workers sat at the tables in the southern half of the cafeteria. The status order is clearly reflected in space: the white males coming first, then the white females, followed by Negro males and females. Although such clear patterns are not typical in work organizations, some manifestations are usually present. Shifting workers around affects not only production but also status arrangements and related phenomena.

Many work-related activities both inside and outside the plant have been found to be extensions of the particularistic status system. The car pool, card playing during lunch, betting, visiting, recreational doings (bowling, fishing, hobbies) are often status stratified.[23] These work-linked activities have a bearing on union and management activities alike.

Union politics is similarly affected by the extension of community status relations. The rise of union factions, the heated contests for office, the turnover of officials and related events are often little more than struggles of different status groups (occupational, ethnic, or religious) to maintain or change a given

---

[21] A. Zaleznik, C. R. Christensen, and F. J. Roethlisberger, with the collaboration of George C. Homans, *The Motivation, Productivity, and Satisfaction of Workers: A Prediction Study*, Harvard University Graduate School of Business, 1958.

[22] Everett C. Hughes, "The Knitting of Racial Groups in Industry," *American Sociological Review*, October, 1946, p. 514.

[23] Zaleznik *et al., op. cit.*

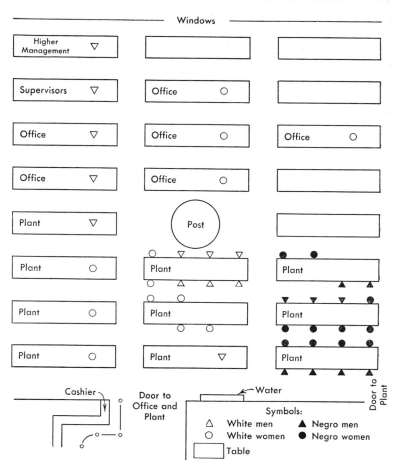

FIG. 12.2. Seating by Age, Sex, and Race in a Factory Cafeteria. (From E. C. Hughes, "The Knitting of Racial Groups in Industry," *American Sociological Review*, October, 1946, p. 514.)

status arrangement. Such phenomena are exactly parallel to those found in the internal politics of metropolitan political party machines. Indeed, labor union and party struggles are often parallel if not identical phenomena. The United States has witnessed in some areas a shift in union and party leadership away from Protestant, Anglo-Saxon control to a multi-religious, multi-ethnic pattern of control. The dynamics of the status revolution know no boundaries.

Mechanisms used to maintain particularistic status systems are the same as those used to maintain informal organizations generally: initiation, rituals, rewards, sanctions, and so on. The objective is in all cases to so integrate the person in a network of personal obligations that he cannot violate local norms without dishonor. Later in this chapter the factors underlying the status system will be more systematically explored.

LOCAL AND WIDER STRUCTURES

As we have seen, the status of a person is highly dependent on his interaction with others and their evaluations of him. Therefore, social participation is required first for acceptance and then for prestige. Four types of participation may be found in the work plant: (1) the isolation pattern, (2) the local pattern, (3) cosmopolitan, and (4) marginal.

1. *The isolates.* Incredible as it may appear, for a significant proportion of the workers (probably a tenth) the work plant is not a source of self-identification or recognition. Some workers literally cut themselves off from every type of contact which is not necessary for job performance. They travel to work alone, eat alone, participate in none of the local social life, do not attend union meetings, and so on. The isolates typically do not take part in social activities in their neighborhoods or in community organizations. Their source of social approval appears to be limited to the family. Since they are literally outside the status system of the department, they do not share the norms of their co-workers, who generally regard them as "queer birds interested only in the buck." They have negative prestige at worst and are tolerated at best.

Little is known about isolates. There are probably two types: the unintegrated and the alienated. The former tend to be migrants who have not become assimilated to industrial life or who insist on maintaining their earlier traditions. Some are foreign born who have not learned the language, and others are rural migrants or members of religious sects who want to maintain their isolation and way of life. They are serious hard workers and sometimes rate busters.[24] Their low esteem does not bother them. The other type are alienated workers who have consciously rejected the values of local society. Often they are downwardly mobile workers who share the norms of the managers, or occasionally technicians or professionals who ideologically reject the society.

2. *The localites.* The vast majority of workers seek recognition mainly from the immediate work group or from co-workers in the department. They try to meet all the norms of the group—in production, union participation, and social activities in and out of the plant. Localites are more commonly found among manual workers who have few organizational contacts. They find more satisfaction in bowling with the boys, visiting a sick friend, or contributing to a gift than attending a shop or union committee meeting.[25] Leaders among the localites may become union stewards and occasionally foremen. In both cases, they are oriented toward the particularistic status systems and not the formal organizations.

3. *The cosmopolites.* A few workers seek recognition on a larger stage, in the *work plant society,* in the union, or in the broader community. They try to become leaders in the occupational, professional, managerial, or union organizations. Newspaper publicity is more satisfying to them than recognition from their colleagues. They are more commonly found among skilled, white-collar, managerial, and professional workers. Although they have personal contacts among co-workers they are interested in larger organizations or in positions which give them many contacts.

4. *Bridgemen or system-linkers.*[26] A few workers seek and find recognition both from their immediate work associates and from the wider society. When unsuccessful they may remain socially marginal persons; when successful they become true leaders or officers who link local structures to hierarchical ones. For exam-

[24] Suggested by William F. Whyte, *Money and Motivation,* Harper, 1955.
[25] Pattern suggested by Robert K. Merton, "Social Psychology of Housing," in Wayne Dennis (ed.), *Current Trends in Psychology,* University of Pittsburgh Press, 1948.
[26] The concept system-linkage is developed and elaborated by Charles P. Loomis in *Social Systems, Essays on Their Persistence and Change,* Van Nostrand, 1960, especially pp. 32–35.

ple, in university life the bridgeman is a professor who is a respected scholar in his department and a good administrator. In the factory, he is a grass-roots union leader or a "good foreman all the way around." These people receive recognition from several sources as they link systems.

A different social orientation characterizes each of the above types. The isolates dismiss the entire status situation as unimportant and sometimes even immoral. The localites want to preserve the particularistic status system. Being nonmobile, they regard the restless pursuit of status on the part of cosmopolites as almost pathological if not unethical. Since the localites do not see the cosmopolites spend the time of day, have a glass of beer, and enjoy good fellowship, they consider them diffident, humorless, and unbending. They are surprised when they see "the human side" of the cosmopolites. Grief occasioned by their children's misfortune, laughter unexpectedly aroused, or the rare sharing of gossip elicits the comment, "Maybe he's a regular fellow after all."

The cosmopolites are inclined to consider the localites gossipy old women and are irritated by their petty status problems. Such was the case of a manager who asked a new man in his department to organize the collection of Community Chest pledges. Since the oldest worker was traditionally given this job, resistance to collections was encountered. Although the manager later promised to observe the tradition, he regarded the entire affair as "stuff and nonsense." Cosmopolites are often upwardly mobile or upwardly oriented persons who are able to see the status situation of superior reference groups but not of inferior ones. Perhaps a reason for this blindness is that the particularistic and formal status structures in the highest echelons tend to merge, while in lower echelons of organization they tend to separate.

Unsuccessful bridgemen become marginal people and exhibit the social psychology of marginal people generally. Unable to reconcile conflicting status demands of different groups, they become suspected and disesteemed on all sides. The "climber" is sometimes put in the position of violating local norms and assuming "airs" and adopting illegitimately and prematurely the status symbols of higher status groups. Successful bridgemen, as indicated above, have unusual social insights and skills. They are able to see the status problems of different groups, appreciate them for what they are, and find common linkages where they exist.

Congruence and dissonance of status structures

The analysis of types of status structures is now complete. It has been demonstrated that the primary difference between the traditional and contemporary work plant status structures is that the latter is composed of several substructures which do not necessarily converge. Union and management, formal and personalistic, local and cosmopolitan structures which may be more or less fluid or rigid function simultaneously. Two main problems of the social analyst are (1) to determine how these structures are articulated and (2) to determine how the workers behave in the situations they confront. Obviously in plants marked by intense labor-management conflict, traditional hostility, and strong departmental rivalries there will be a lack of convergence in the status structures. A situation of status dissonance presents the employee with definite alternatives from which he must choose.[27] He cannot, for example, seek recognition from both management and the union, from all ethnic groups, from all departments. A selection of one route automatically qualifies him for status in one area and disqualifies him for status in another.

Such extreme situations endure for long periods in situations marked by ideological cleavage. Status cleavage persists where labor and management represent different ethnic groups and where labor unions are ideologically oriented. Such is the situation in the mines and refineries of the American Southwest, where the labor force is Spanish speaking and committed to the United Mine and Mill Workers of America.[28] It is the same among the longshoremen in the United States, where unions are ideologically hardened, and in colonial situations where management and labor represent different cultural groups. Even here, however, workers may have problems of selecting status audiences with possibly conflicting norms, as between local and larger

[27] Closely related to the concept developed by Gerhard E. Lenski, "Status Crystallization: A Non-Vertical Dimension of Social Status," *American Sociological Review*, August, 1954, pp. 405–413.

[28] See William H. Form and Delbert C. Miller, *Industry, Labor, and Community*, Harper, 1960, pp. 376–379.

structures in management and labor. In general, however, status anxiety emanating from choice problems in dissonant situations is nominal, for choice itself is limited. Once the choice is made, social acceptance usually follows and the special prestige roads are clearly marked.

It is in the less well-defined situations that problems of status dissonance and status anxiety arise. For example, research evidence suggests that in the United States workers may be loyal to both management and the union without experiencing conflict[29] Employees may commit their identities or seek recognition from one side or the other without traumatic results. Yet industrial relations are sometimes volatile, for sudden conflict may appear after long periods of industrial peace. During conflict periods, loyalties become hardened, past behavior is reviewed, and commitments are demanded. Some may find that they can no longer be respected by both sides, or by people in various departments. During an organizing campaign, during a protracted strike, in a thorough reorganization, status careers are put on the block, and many experience status anxiety because they cannot reconcile demands emanating from conflicting status groups in the plant and community.[30] Even the isolate may be forced to make a choice during crisis periods; indeed, this is one way of forcing him to become a status-relevant person.

Status anxiety is a pattern of consistent concern which a person has about his status definition. While dissatisfaction inevitably accompanies anxiety, dissatisfaction is not equivalent to anxiety. Many workers are dissatisfied but not anxious about their status. Anxiety generally results from either a structural situation or an autobiographical one. In the former, the person or group is confronted with a dilemma which is an unresolvable feature of a dissonant situation. The downward mobility of an entire occupational group constitutes a case in point. Mills aptly described the "status panic" exhibited by the old middle class as its traditional status became undermined by corporate capitalism.[31] Similar experiences may be confronting occupations threatened by automation.

[29] See, for example, "Dual Allegiance to Union and Management, A Symposium," *Personnel Psychology,* March, 1954, pp. 41–80.

[30] Bernard Karsh, *Diary of a Strike,* University of Illinois Press, 1958.

[31] C. Wright Mills, *White Collar,* Oxford University Press, 1956, pp. 239–258.

Autobiographical anxiety typically results from dissatisfaction with mobility experiences. There are many poignant examples of suffering over a threatened or actual loss of status, over status upgrading, and over status immobility. Gardner and Moore cite a case of a capable engineer who developed a severe neurosis because he was not promoted as rapidly as he thought he should be. Although the situation was due to adverse economic conditions, he felt his work was inadequate and experienced breakdown.[32]

Although occupational downgrading induces personal trauma, it is not very frequent because, as Barnard indicates, "Some degree of recognition of a right to retain status . . . is felt to be generally just, even though in particular cases the effect may not be thought so. The sentiments supporting conservation with respect to status are developed and maintained by rationalizations, ceremonies, and symbolism."[33] Devices are therefore created to ease downward mobility. These include "kicking a person upstairs," speeded retirement, transfer to a less important post but with the same title, changing the title, making "temporary" arrangements, and so on.

Promotions may also precipitate anxiety on two levels: worry about finding a place in the "new" status system and desire to maintain the respect of former co-workers. Obviously the whole status pattern changes with promotion to a new level or to supervision. The retention of old friendships and the necessary acquisition of a new set makes the "economy of friendships" too large, with the usual result that old friends are dropped. Guilt feelings and accusations of "going high-hat" compound the suffering. Under these circumstances it is understandable why some workers refuse promotions, especially if offered late in their careers.

In conclusion, status anxiety arises from structural incompatibilities among the various systems in which the worker participates, his expectations, and his mobility experiences.

FACTORS UNDERLYING STATUS ORGANIZATION

The allocation of status either to individuals or to categories in union or management follows predictable patterns based on the normative patterns of a society. The most important factor

[32] *Op. cit.*, p. 260.
[33] *Op. cit.*, p. 79.

underlying status is the evaluation of functions performed. In addition, as we have shown, factors which underlie status in the community or wider society also operate in the work plant. Among the most important of these in American society are age, sex, and national or racial origin. Last, individuals and groups are assigned prestige according to their style of performance; that is, those who most nearly approximate ideal role performance are granted highest status. The roles include, of course, those in the system of interpersonal relations as well as occupational roles.

Occupation and Status

The most general index of social status in Western societies is probably social class. Although the meaningfulness of this concept is limited in urban society, it does reveal in a crude way the general rank of a person in different contexts. W. Lloyd Warner and associates, who have made the most exhaustive studies of social class in various communities, have found a high correlation between social class level and occupation. In fact, they have created an occupational scale which may be used to reveal a person's general social class level.[34] The high correlation undoubtedly points to the fundamental importance of occupation for general ranking in industrial society. Although other factors are also important in fixing status, they too tend to be circumscribed by occupation. Thus, family background, breeding, and social participation are highly related to occupation. As discussed elsewhere, the income, power, and style of life of the occupation have consequences for general social status in the broader community.

Occupations themselves conform to a prestige hierarchy of their own in a society. The hierarchy of a particular factory or bureau cannot deviate significantly from the general societal occupational hierarchy without negative consequences. Social scientists have created scales of occupational prestige designed for various purposes. In general, the findings of these scales confirm each other to such a high degree that we may be certain they reflect a societal value system. Perhaps the most widely accepted occupational prestige scale is that devised by North and Hatt. In 1947 a

[34] W. Lloyd Warner, Marcia Meeker, and Kenneth Eells, *Social Class in America,* Science Research, 1949, pp. 140–141.

nation-wide sample of persons were asked to rank ninety representative occupations for their prestige. Respondents were asked to judge whether the jobs had a standing that was excellent, good, average, below average, or poor. The rating of "excellent" was given 100 points; "good," 80 points; "average," 60 points; and so on. The results were then averaged to produce the ranking found in Table 12.1.

Broad occupational classes used by the United States Census Bureau were ranked from high to low in the following order: Governmental officials; professionals; proprietors, managers, and officials; clerical workers in offices and stores; craftsmen; farmers and farm managers; protective service workers; operatives; farm laborers; service workers; laborers. Although the scores of the last four categories were very close, the census occupational scale was confirmed.

From a sociological point of view, it is important to ask what priority of values is reflected in job scales. Since high governmental offices are granted the highest prestige, it would seem that the most important value attached to occupations is the amount of their legitimate power. Professional workers are next highest in prestige, and are concentrated in the upper quarter of the North-Hatt and Smith scales.[35] This position reflects the general importance of knowledge and highly developed mental skills in industrial society. The prestige of property apparently depends upon the amount held, because proprietors are scattered in the top half of both scales. Since only two proprietary occupations are found in the upper quarter of the North-Hatt scale, the prestige of income and property seems to be of tertiary importance.

The hierarchical character of values seems to break down in the middle part of the scale, for here are found some professionals, small businessmen, and white-collar workers. If any value is operative it appears to be nonmanual or nonmenial services to people, often involving paper work. Generally speaking, occupations below the middle are manual in nature, i.e., they represent a skill hierarchy in the handling of material things. At the top of this broad class are the skilled craftsmen, followed by semi-

[35] Mapheus Smith, "An Empirical Scale of Prestige Status of Occupations," *American Sociological Review*, April, 1943, pp. 185–192.

TABLE 12.1 Prestige Ratings

1. U. S. Supreme Court justice	96
2. Physician	93
3. State governor	93
4. Cabinet member in federal government	92
5. Diplomat in the U. S. foreign service	92
6. Mayor of a large city	90
7. College professor	89
8. Scientist	89
9. U. S. representative in Congress	89
10. Banker	88
11. Government scientist	88
12. County judge	87
13. Head of department in state government	87
14. Minister	87
15. Architect	86
16. Chemist	86
17. Dentist	86
18. Lawyer	86
19. Member of board of large corporation	86
20. Nuclear physicist	86
21. Priest	86
22. Psychologist	85
23. Civil engineer	84
24. Airline pilot	83
25. Artist who paints pictures that are exhibited in galleries	83
26. Owner of factory that employs about 100 people	82
27. Sociologist	82
28. Accountant for a large business	81
29. Biologist	81
30. Musician in symphony orchestra	81
31. Author of novels	80
32. Captain in the regular army	80
33. Building contractor	79
34. Economist	79
35. Instructor in public schools	79
36. Public-school teacher	78
37. County agricultural agent	77
38. Railroad engineer	77
39. Farm owner and operator	76
40. Official of an international labor union	75
41. Radio announcer	75
42. Newspaper columnist	74
43. Owner-operator of printing shop	74
44. Electrician	73
45. Trainer machinist	73
46. Welfare worker for city government	73
47. Undertaker	72
48. Reporter on daily newspaper	71

skilled workers and those who operate simple machines (automobiles and automatic machines). Unskilled laborers in factory and farm fall at the bottom of the manual hierarchy. Apparently domestic and personal services for people are valued even less than handling material goods. Persons in these occupations are subject not to the rational authority of supervisors as are factory workers, for example, but to the personal whims of employers. However, in the lowest occupations are those who work against people or express opposition to societal values: the criminal, the prostitute, and the bum.

Of special interest is the prestige rank of the union official. In the North-Hatt scale officials of international unions ranked some-of Selected Occupations: 1947

49. Manager of a small store in a city	69	70. Milk-route man	54
		71. Restaurant cook	54
50. Bookkeeper	68	72. Truck driver	54
51. Insurance agent	68	73. Lumberjack	53
52. Tenant farmer—one who owns livestock and machinery and manages the farm	68	74. Filling-station attendant	52
		75. Singer in a night club	52
		76. Farm hand	50
		77. Coal miner	49
53. Traveling salesman for a wholesale concern	68	78. Taxi driver	49
54. Playground director	67	79. Railroad section hand	48
55. Policeman	67	80. Restaurant waiter	48
56. Railroad conductor	67	81. Dock worker	47
57. Mail carrier	66	82. Night watchman	47
58. Carpenter	65	83. Clothes presser in a laundry	46
59. Automobile repairman	63	84. Soda-fountain clerk	45
60. Plumber	63	85. Bartender	44
61. Garage mechanic	62	86. Janitor	44
62. Local official of a labor union	62	87. Share cropper—one who owns no livestock and equipment and does not manage farm	40
63. Owner-operator of a lunch stand	62		
64. Corporal in the regular army	60		
65. Machine operator in a factory	60	88. Garbage collector	35
66. Barber	59	89. Street sweeper	34
67. Clerk in a store	58	90. Shoe shiner	33
68. Fisherman who owns his own boat	58		
69. Streetcar motorman	58	AVERAGE	69.8

SOURCE: Cecil C. North and Paul K. Hatt, "Jobs and Occupations: A Popular Evaluation," Opinion News, September 1, 1947, pp. 4 and 5.

what above the middle, position 40 out of ninety occupations. While international officers ranked slightly higher than skilled craftsmen, local union officials ranked in position 62, roughly the lower boundary of skilled jobs and two-thirds from the top.

Probably various groups rank various jobs differently. Probably ardent union members would place an international union official at the same level as the manager of a large business. Undoubtedly some degree of job involvement and job ethnocentrism is operative. In a study of prestige rank of thirteen common jobs Form found that manual workers tended to rank their own jobs higher than clerical jobs. Clerical workers, on the other hand, ranked their jobs higher than manual jobs.[36] There is also some evidence that the managers of large absentee-owned enterprises now have higher status than proprietors and owners of business. Various groups, under the banner of "professionalization," have engineered increases in the status of their occupations: e.g., realtors, morticians, and accountants. The inflated prestige of the airline hostess illustrates the same phenomenon at another level. Historically, occupational heroes have changed. As Mills has pointed out, the business hero of Horatio Alger has been replaced by heroes of sports and screen.[37] The status of the moneylender, the foreman, and the physician has also changed over time.

However, these changes and disagreements seem to be minor when compared with the stabilities in occupational rank. According to Davies, in a review of the literature on occupational prestige, studies show that relatively little occupational ethnocentrism exists—people know where they stand and how others rank them.[38] Also the few systematic studies of changes in occupational rank over time, such as that of Deeg and Patterson, show only minor changes.[39] Persistence of prestige stabilities suggests that there are functional reasons for the prestige structure. If this is the case, we should find similar occupations similarly ranked in different societies which have similar occupational structures. Indeed, there may even be some parallelisms in occupational ranking in societies with different economic systems.

Inkeles and Rossi attempted to weigh the structural as opposed to the cultural factors underlying occupational prestige in six industrially advanced nations. Although the studies were done with different techniques and at different periods in the various countries, the intercorrelations of occupational ranks were surprisingly high: $+.84$ and above. While the data in Table 12.2 reveal that the highest intercorrelations were among countries with the greatest cultural similarities—Great Britain, the United

---

[36] William H. Form, "Toward an Occupational Social Psychology," *Journal of Social Psychology,* August, 1946, pp. 85–99.

[37] *Op. cit.,* pp. 336 ff.

[38] A. F. Davies, "The Prestige of Occupations," *British Journal of Sociology,* June, 1957, pp. 134–147.

[39] M. E. Deeg and D. G. Patterson, "Changes in the Social Status of Occupations," *Occupations,* January, 1947, pp. 265–268.

States, New Zealand, and Germany—all correlations were high.[40]

Comparing occupational prestige in countries at different levels of industrialization is fraught with dangers, the most important of which is that the same occupations are not present or that the proportions in similar occupations vary. Thus, Tiryakian found in the Philippines occupations not found in the United States.

TABLE 12.2 Correlations Between Prestige Scores (or Ranks) Given to Comparable Occupations in Six National Studies

	U.S.S.R.	Japan	Great Britain	New Zealand	U.S.	Germany
U.S.S.R.		.74	.83	.83	.90	.90
Japan			.92	.91	.93	.93
Great Britain				.97	.94	.97
New Zealand					.97	.96
United States						.96
Average correlation	.84	.89	.93	.93	.94	.94

SOURCE: Alex Inkeles, and Peter H. Rossi, "National Comparisons of Occupational Prestige," *American Journal of Sociology,* January, 1956, p. 332.

He also noted that while farmers are 80 percent of the labor force in the Philippines, they constitute a small minority in the United States and other technologically advanced countries. Obviously nonagricultural occupations have a scarcity value in the Philippines. Yet comparable occupations found in the Philippines, Great Britain, New Zealand, Japan, and Germany showed rank correlation coefficients above +.90.[41]

Obviously similarities in occupational prestige rank in culturally diverse societies suggest that similar underlying forces are operating in all of them. Unfortunately, an adequate theory to explain this phenomenon is lacking. However, as suggested above,

[40] Alex Inkeles and Peter H. Rossi, "National Comparisons of Occupational Prestige," *American Journal of Sociology,* January, 1956, pp. 329–339. See also Charles E. Ramsey and Robert J. Smith, "Japanese and American Perceptions of Occupations," *American Journal of Sociology,* March, 1960, pp. 475–482.

[41] Edward A. Tiryakian, "The Prestige Evaluation of Occupations in an Underdeveloped Country: The Philippines," *American Journal of Sociology,* January, 1958, pp. 390–399.

two or three factors may be clearly seen. Probably, as Davis and Moore observe, the occupations which have greatest "functional importance" and require greatest training or skill universally rank high.[42] The problem is to explain the meaning of functional importance in various contexts. Certainly in societies with a highly articulated division of labor the positions and occupations which coordinate the structure, which are necessary to keep the technology functioning, which can be withheld only with severe damage to the entire population, tend to be those having the most amount of power, income, and social status. Thus, highest governmental officials, the professions, high administrators, and skilled craftsmen generally rank high in occupational prestige no matter what the local cultural variations. What holds true for entire societies also holds true in specific work plants—in factories, hospitals, government offices, armies, restaurants, and universities. Considerably more work needs to be done, however, before the above observations are refined and verified.

Sex Typing and Job Prestige

Every society exhibits a sexual division of labor with status distinctions. Traditional societies the world over tend, with few exceptions, to grant higher status to occupations assigned to men. With industrialization and rationalization of production there is a universal inclination to absorb women into the labor force in jobs closely related to their traditional roles. At first these tend to be at lower income, status, and authority levels. Thus in 1860, one-half of the women in Turin, Italy, were employed primarily in the textile industry and in domestic service while the men dominated in manufacturing. One century later only a third of the women were employed because the textile industry had declined, and men continued to dominate in manufacturing.

However, with time, women penetrate the occupational structure at various prestige levels in special occupations, which at first are extensions of their normal roles of family service. Teaching, nursing, social work, and domestic service illustrate this trend. In this case the status and income levels of the occupations tend to decline, especially if the women replace men, as has happened, for example, in teaching and office work. The rationaliza-

[42] *Op. cit.*

tion given for the decline has been that women are not chief wage earners and have fewer economic obligations. This is nonsense. Women have also been excluded from jobs demanding heavy physical exertion such as mining and steel manufacturing.

Table 12.3 reveals the sex breakdown for main occupational groups in the United States in 1960. Numerically the women out-

TABLE 12.3 Occupational Composition of the Employed U.S. Labor Force, by Sex: 1960

Occupations	Male	Female
Professional, technical, and kindred workers	11.0	13.8
Farmers and farm managers	5.6	.5
Managers, officials, and proprietors except farm	11.5	4.0
Clerical and kindred workers	7.1	32.7
Sales workers	7.4	8.7
Craftsmen, foremen, and kindred workers	20.5	1.3
Operatives and kindred workers	19.5	15.7
Private household workers	0.1	4.1
Service workers, except private household	5.2	12.4
Farm laborers and foremen	2.3	.9
Laborers, except farm and mine	5.6	.5
Occupation not reported	4.2	5.4
Total	100.0	100.0
Numbers	43,466,946	21,172,301

SOURCE: Bureau of the Census, *U.S. Census of Population*, U.S. Summary, 1960, General Social and Economic Characteristics, Tables 88 and 89.

number the men only in clerical office work and in domestic and service work. These occupations usually have lowest status in the white-collar and manual hierarchies. Comparing the occupational distributions of men and women, we find a larger proportion of white-collar women in the professions and clerical (office and sales) jobs, while more men are proprietors, managers, and officials. In the manual area a greater percentage of the men are found among craftsmen, operatives, and laborers.

Within these broad categories certain specific occupations tend to be assigned to one sex or another, as is seen in Table 12.4. Thus women are dominant as welfare workers, teachers, librarians, office machine operators, milliners, and operatives in tobacco manufacturing and apparel industries. Men and women are found about equally as actors, bookkeepers, accountants, ticket agents, and operatives in textile mills. Women are greatly under-represented among dentists, accountants, purchasing agents, and in many other occupations.

TABLE 12.4 Percentage of Employed Males in Selected Occupations: 1950

Occupation	Percent
Mine operatives and laborers	99.2
Engineers	98.8
Physicians and surgeons	93.6
Accountants and auditors	85.1
Proprietors (retail trade)	84.0
Actors	62.3
Salesmen and sales clerks	61.7
Postmasters	55.2
Textile mill products all workers	46.7
Hospital and institution attendants	40.5
Social and welfare workers	30.8
Teachers	25.5
Bookkeepers	22.4
Office machine operators	18.4
Waiters	18.1
Milliners	10.3
Stenographers, typists, secretaries	5.4
Nurses	2.3

SOURCE: Bureau of the Census, *U.S. Census of the Population*, Advanced Reports, General Social and Economic Characteristics, PC (A3-1) 1960.

Women invade the jobs traditionally held by men during periods of labor shortage and in situations where cheap labor is desired. During World War II not only did they replace men as semiskilled operatives in manufacturing, but many became skilled craftsmen such as machinists and welders, inspectors, and foremen. To be sure, some of these jobs were "broken down" into simpler operations. Although stimulated by war, the invasion of women into manufacturing was part of a long-term trend showing that more women remain in the labor force for longer periods of time. This has the effect of further shattering the status system of industry and breaking down the sex typing of jobs. The recognition that women are a permanent part of the labor force and will continue to compete with men for jobs is largely responsible for the insistence of labor unions and governments on equal pay for equal work, antidiscrimination clauses in labor contracts, and observance of seniority rules covering both men and women.

Certainly every type of device is still being used to stop women from taking over men's jobs and to prevent jobs from becoming defined as women's jobs. However, the alleged threat to male job status by the ingress of women in industry is probably exaggerated. Since women tend to enter industry at the lowest levels and accept menial and routine jobs, they may have the indirect effect of upgrading men. In an expanding labor force, men are upgraded as women take the least desirable jobs. In a sense, women are replacing immigrants and rural migrants by taking the worst jobs and upgrading the stable male workers.

The barrier to upward occupational mobility of women is reflected in the very small proportion who become supervisors. While both sexes spurn women as supervisors, men especially feel that women supervisors lower their job status. Even where men adjust to the situation, other men gibe them about being bossed by women both at home and on the job. Women supervisors are accused of being too emotional, autocratic, partial, sensitive, and overdemanding. Although some women supervisors undoubtedly exhibit such behavior, Gardner and Moore believe that it is due to the new social role they are playing. Their alleged limitations are for the most part mythical, and, where not mythical, the result of a difficult social situation and not of their inherent nature.[43]

Age and Work Status

Traditionally, age and its twin seniority have been fundamental factors underlying status orders. Prestige has been associated with the older worker because he has had time to acquire skills. In an economy dominated by manual skills, the old hand was the most efficient and stable worker. Helpers and apprentices had to wait patiently for him to teach them new skills and allow them to do new operations. Apprentices had to defer to the masters, on whom they depended for acceptance and mobility. The

[43] Gardner and Moore, *op. cit.*, p. 286.

literature on the guilds and early craft unions stresses the importance of age in the acquisition of skill and status.[44]

Within broad occupational categories, specific jobs are dominated by younger and older workers for each sex, as Tables 12.5

TABLE 12.5   Median Ages for Males in Selected Occupations: 1950

Older Workers	Age	Younger Workers	Age
Local public administration	52.5	Chemists	35.0
Clergymen	43.8	Athletes	24.2
Postmasters	52.1	Draftsmen	31.4
Proprietors, managers, officials		Surveyors	32.1
Salaried	42.8	Telegraph messengers	18.4
Self-employed	45.7	Office machine operators	28.3
Real estate agents and brokers	50.8	Shipping, receiving clerks	34.4
Locomotive engineers	55.0	Truck and tractor drivers	34.1
Tailors	55.4	Members of armed forces	23.7
Paperhangers	50.4	Farm laborers (wage workers)	32.0
Guards, watchmen, and door-		Sailors and deckhands	34.3
keepers	55.1	Laborers (manufacturing)	35.5
Boarding and lodging-house		Attendants, recreation and amuse-	
keepers	56.2	ment	19.8
Marshals and constables	52.6	Bootblacks	24.7
Railroaders and railway express		Messengers and office boys	22.3
service	44.8		
Watchmen, crossing and bridge			
tenders	52.7		
Barbers, beauticians, and mani-			
curists	48.0		
Janitors and sextons	52.9		

SOURCE: U.S. Bureau of the Census, *U.S. Census of Population: 1950*, Vol. IV, *Special Reports*, Part 1, Chapter B, Occupational Characteristics, GPO, 1956, Table IV, pp. 37–44.

and 12.6 show. Young men predominate as soldiers, sailors, truck drivers, laborers in manufacturing and agriculture, office machine operators, dancers, athletes, and teachers. With the exception of a few professions these tend to be low-status and temporary jobs and jobs which require strength and dexterity. Older men predominate among clergymen, veterinarians, conductors, postmas-

[44] See, for example, Henri Pirenne, "Guilds, European," *Encyclopedia of the Social Sciences,* Macmillan, 1930.

ters, baggagemen, real estate agents and brokers, railroaders, tailors, guards, watchmen, janitors, and boarding-house keepers. With some exceptions these tend to be high-tenure, medium-skill or low-skill dead-end jobs. Younger women take jobs as nurses,

TABLE 12.6 Median Ages for Women in Selected Occupations: 1950

Older Workers	Age	Younger Workers	Age
Authors	44.1	Chemists	28.0
Librarians	42.4	Dancers and dancing teachers	27.4
Religious workers	46.2	Draftsmen	28.8
Teachers	41.4	Nurses, student professional	20.3
Farmers, owners and tenants	50.5	Technicians, medical and dental	28.1
Managers and superintendents of		Bank tellers	29.2
buildings	54.6	Messengers	22.3
Local public administration	47.3	Office machine operators	27.7
Real estate agents and brokers	48.8	Stenographers, typists and secre-	
Dressmakers and seamstresses except		taries	28.0
factory	52.4	Counter and fountain workers	26.8
Boarding- and lodging-house		Elevator operators	30.8
keepers	58.9	Ushers, recreation and amusement	18.1
Charwomen and cleaners	48.1		
Guards, watchmen, and door-			
keepers	58.9		

SOURCE: U.S. Bureau of the Census, *U.S. Census of Population: 1950*, Vol. IV, *Special Reports*, Part 1, Chapter B, Occupational Characteristics, GPO, 1956, Table IV, pp. 45–63.

typists, office machine operators, ushers, elevator operators, and waitresses. Older women are religious workers, teachers, librarians, real estate agents, dressmakers, housekeepers, and charwomen. Thus the younger women tend to dominate in lower-status white-collar and service occupations, while older women are concentrated in professional work and stable service occupations, with some important exceptions.

In general, the younger the age level of those in an occupation, the lower its prestige. Low status is tolerable for the young worker because the job is often considered temporary. Difficulties in adjustment are evident when the age of a worker does not correspond to the age expectation of his job. If he is too young for the job, he must struggle to attain status and to carry out the associated responsibilities. This is not infrequently the situation in business where young, well-trained men are called to assume supervisory positions.

Age prestige still survives in American industry. The average age of the craftsman is five years higher than that of the operative. The old-timer still looks down on the neophyte as a "young punk who doesn't know what the score is." The former feels more secure because he knows the "bugs" in learning a new job, how to save his energy, how to cut corners, how to loaf without being caught, how to shift blame, what the pace of the work should be, and how to get along with the idiosyncracies of his fellow workers and the foreman. Yet he regards the newcomer with a mixture of anxiety and self-assurance.

The younger worker hopes to compensate for his lack of skill and experience by using his abundant energy. The "cagey old-timers" who have control of the informal social organization admonish younger workers to "take it easy" or "do it this way." The oldsters tend to receive the support of the supervisors because the latter usually do not want to disturb the prevailing work patterns or alienate the dependable and stable workers.

Recognition is formally given to age and length of service. Thus old hands are frequently kept on the job because of their past loyalty to the company. They are given watches, awards, and testimonials as tokens of appreciation. Employers sometimes prefer older workers because (1) they already know the job, (2) they are more dependable and accept responsibility better than younger workers, (3) they have greater family responsibilities which make them cautious about losing time, moving to another job, or "falling" for agitators.[45] Promotion also is offered to the older workers and to those who have longer service. Seniority rules in union contracts formally recognize the status and prerogatives of age.

However, the prestige of age is being undermined by the "accent on youth" and the "leveling forces" in industry. As skills become diluted by automatic and semiautomatic machinery, reliance on skilled labor is decreased. It becomes easier to transfer from one job to another, from one plant to another, and from one department to another. "Playing the job market" reduces senior-

[45] E. W. Bakke, *The Unemployed Worker,* Yale, 1940, p. 244.

ity and age grading. As the "speedup" system spreads and jobs are broken down, young men who can stand the pace are sought increasingly. They are in demand particularly during depressed economic periods when a man of forty-five is "too old to work and too young to retire or die."

Yet despite these forces certain jobs still tend to be age-graded. Table 12.7, which gives the median ages of various occupational

TABLE 12.7 Median Age of Men and Women by Occupational Level: 1950

Occupation	Males	Females
Professional, technical, and kindred workers	38.7	38.3
Farmers and farm managers	45.8	50.6
Managers, officials, and proprietors, except farm	44.6	44.8
Clerical and kindred workers	36.0	29.6
Sales workers	36.6	36.9
Craftsmen, foremen, and kindred workers	40.6	38.9
Operatives and kindred workers	35.8	36.5
Private household workers	46.1	40.8
Service workers, except private household	43.9	38.4
Farm laborers and foremen	26.6	36.0
Laborers, except farm and mine	36.9	36.1
Total	39.2	36.2

Source: U.S. Bureau of the Census, *U.S. Census of Population: 1950,* Vol. IV, *Special Reports,* Part 1, Chapter B, Occupational Characteristics, GPO, 1956, Table IV, pp. 37–53.

levels by sex, reveals that the youngest workers are found among the unskilled, laborers, operatives, and clerical workers. The middle-aged predominate among the professionals, craftsmen, and service workers. Older workers are found among farmers, proprietors, managers, and officials. The general age distribution by occupational levels is strikingly similar for both men and women. Also the difference between the median ages of working men and women is not as great as is commonly supposed: 39.2 years for the men, 36.2 for the women—a difference of three years. This difference has decreased by three years during the past decade.

Several factors may account for the age stratification in Table 12.7:

1. The unskilled jobs are usually the heaviest and are most efficiently done by young people.
2. Young manual workers usually enter the bottom of the occupational ladder. After a period of testing and apprenticeship some may move into semiskilled and skilled labor. Hence the low median age for laborers.
3. Clerical work, both sales and office, is often temporary for young workers, especially for women. Since clerical jobs are the lowest-status white-collar jobs, they are often assigned to the youngest workers.
4. Domestic and service jobs provide no mobility opportunity. A great proportion of their incumbents are Negroes and foreign born who cannot find other jobs. Thus they are likely to be older than the manual laborers.
5. Since professional work requires longer formal education, and since skilled labor requires experience, these occupational levels tend toward greater stability, and their members are usually middle aged.
6. Farmers, proprietors, managers, and officials are at the top of the white-collar and property ladders. The fact that time is required to acquire property and to move to supervisory positions helps account for the older age of these categories.

Older members are reluctant to defer to their "inexperienced" colleagues. The latter resort to bureaucratic devices to insulate themselves against the attempts of older members to demonstrate their status equality or superioriy. Since this conflict disturbs the organization, administrators sometime feel justified in keeping older people in high-ranking jobs. A new problem is then created because younger men feel impatient about blocks to upward mobility.

When workers do not advance rapidly enough, they may feel they are too old for the job. A supervisor of a newspaper office told the authors,

> Benny has been with the *Journal* for fourteen years now. He came to us as a messenger boy when he was almost twenty. He's still a messenger boy. He told us when he came that he wanted to become a reporter. Every now and then he does give us some news, but he'll never make the grade. Most of the boys feel sorry for Benny, even though he is hard to get along with. I told him to look for another job because he has no

future here, but he claims that he can't find work and that the *Journal* needs him.

Someimes old people are kept on the job "just to give them something to do." Being called "boy" and asked to do dirty jobs, dreaming of their past importance, having "to take stuff from the young punks"—all this produces an embittered and estranged worker.

Ethnicity and Status

In no major industrial region of the world, Hughes indicates, has one ethnic group furnished the whole labor force, from managers down to unskilled workers.[46] The ethnic mixing may be small, as in the case of the Irish, Welsh, and Scotch in England, or it may be extreme, as with the East Indians, Negroes, and British in Africa. In any case, industry is almost universally a prime agent of racial, ethnic, and religious segregation. Although it brings people together, it also segregates them in different types of work. Almost invariably the segregation is a form of discrimination, for ethnic groups are not allowed equal chances to obtain highest industrial positions. To be sure, ethnic groups introduced at the lower levels of industry are not qualified technically and culturally to assume high positions. Similarly, ethnic groups introduced at the top, e.g., managers and professionals in underdeveloped areas, are not permitted to fall in the industrial hierarchy even after many generations. In either case, the operation of status factors, which are at the heart of ethnic relations, prevents equality of access to jobs.

Once an ethnic job structure has been established it is almost impossible to eradicate. The subordinate position of the French in Canada, the Negroes in the United States, the Polish in Germany, and the Indians in Latin America has endured for centuries. Johnson has documented the complex process of racial segregation and discrimination in the tobacco industry.[47] Prior to the Civil War and for a period thereafter, the Negro had come

[46] Everett C. Hughes, "Queries Concerning Industry and Society Growing Out of Ethnic Relations in Industry," *American Sociological Review*, April, 1949, pp. 211–220.

[47] Charles S. Johnson, "The Conflict of Caste and Class in an American Industry," *American Journal of Sociology*, July, 1936, pp. 55–65.

to hold a job monopoly in the manufacture of tobacco. Many Negroes were highly skilled and earned high wages. However, as each piece of industrial machinery was introduced, white workers became operators and Negroes were assigned the lower-skilled, dirtier, and heavier type of work. With advanced technology and work organization, it has been more difficult to maintain a racial division of function. Yet race tradition with its insistence on segregation has kept the races in perpetual and unresolved conflict.

Multi-ethnic systems are perpetuated not only by the dominant group but also by the subordinate groups. Status distinctions are used to perpetuate any economic or political advantages secured. In a study of Spanish-speaking minorities in a Utah mining town, Blair found that all Mexican and Puerto Rican men worked on the track or powder gang.[48] The track gang members received the lowest pay, and the normal promotion route was to the powder gang. Although promotion was allegedly based on seniority, job performance, and English proficiency, no Puerto Rican had been promoted to the powder gang in five years. The Mexicans who dominated the powder gang regarded themselves as definitely superior to the Puerto Ricans and rejected them as "foreigners" and "partly Negro."

Many employers recognize the existence of ethnic antagonisms and attempt to promote or diminish them according to their ends. If the economic position of the industry is secure, they usually observe community and work group norms by segregating antagonistic groups and maintaining their "traditional" relationships. Under some conditions ethnic groups may bury their traditional rivalries and present a united front to the employers by joining a union and presenting demands. This process of solidarity occurred in the United States during the organizing campaign prior to and following World War II. Warner and Low have demonstrated that under common adverse economic pressure, ethnic groups combined to strike against their employers.[49] However, collective action follows economic deprivation only

[48] William C. Blair, "Spanish-Speaking Minorities in a Utah Mining Town," *Journal of Social Issues*, 1952, vol. 8, pp. 4–9.
[49] Warner and Low, *op. cit.*

when other conditions facilitate it. In Yankee City these conditions were: a generation of industrial experience on the part of the workers, a parallel dilution of their skills, a shift from local to absentee ownership, and a change in community sentiments favoring the workers. In similar situations employers may stimulate ethnic conflict to prevent the solidarity required for union organization. In the United States this device was employed in the twenties when employers defined unionization as an un-American activity sponsored by foreign radical groups.

Two additional observations need to be mentioned. First, under some conditions managers want to abolish ethnic job structures with their often troublesome status problems. This situation arises when management cannot observe traditional job monopolies and at the same time introduce needed technological and organizational changes in line with economic necessity. It also occurs in an expanding economy when the usual sources of labor are not available and the only alternative is to introduce a new ethnic group. Second, even when competing ethnic groups exhibit solidarity against the employer on an issue such as union recognition or wage demands, this solidarity does not signify the destruction of an ethnic job structure. Unions, as well as management, may be confronted with ethnic job claims which are resistant to change.

"This is a white man's job, this a Negro's job, this a woman's job, this a new man's job" may often be heard in the work plant. These words reveal sentiments that some jobs are the monopoly of specific groups, that the status of the job and the worker should be fixed, that normally each race should not compete for the same jobs, and that the job identifies the status of the worker. Thus, in some plants certain jobs are assigned to Negroes, others to native born, foreign born, old immigrants, or new immigrants, as the case may be. When these ethnic job expectations are threatened, conflict may ensue. Collins describes a strong ethnic status structure in a New England factory. The management and personnel officials were Yankees, the foreman Irish, the workers of other ethnic backgrounds. When a Yankee was appointed foreman, a wildcat strike was called because management had violated the ethnic pattern of promotion. Only when management changed the job title did it succeed in giving the Yankee a job commensurate with the foreman's job.[50]

The breakdown of ethnic and racial job statuses

A two-way process occurs in a breakdown of the ethnic job status structure. One phase is that of invasion. Jobs that traditionally "belong" to one group are invaded by foreign born and Negroes. Although the process is gradual, its accumulated results are spectacular. For example, Negroes have been invading industrial occupations for decades. Of course, they started at the bottom of the ladder, but during war and prosperous periods they climbed to jobs which required greater skills. As industry needed fewer unskilled and more semiskilled workers, there was no other place for the unskilled Negroes and others to go but upward. Thus, technological forces are throwing people of different ethnic and racial backgrounds together.

The second phase in the breakdown of an ethnic job structure occurs during periods of economic depression and retrenchment. Pressure is then exerted on invaders to go back to their previous lower-status jobs. This they resist violently, as do those who are threatened by a backwash of competitors. Management has recognized but often underestimated the power of informal work groups to control their membership. Hughes has studied this process. He relates,

In a certain plant, Negroes were first hired in a department that, though dirty and smelly, and without prestige, has a very stable working force. The men in it, mostly elderly Poles, work in groups of three that produce as units and are paid so as to make teamwork the key to a good income. It was thought that these men would not have much prejudice and that isolation of the department would allow the hiring of Negroes without much comment. Of several Negroes hired, none stayed more than a few days. The management was disturbed, for it thought the Negroes were confirming the common opinion that they are unreliable. Interviews with these Negro men brought out a consistent and simple story. The workers in the department had practiced every obvious and subtle art to let the newcomers know that they would never learn (i.e., be taught) the work. Upon hearing all this an aged member of the management, now retired, snorted that no one had ever

[50] Orvis Collins, "Ethnic Behavior in Industry: Sponsorship and Rejection in a New England Factory," *American Journal of Sociology,* January, 1946, pp. 293–298.

succeeded in 40 years in putting in that department any new man not chosen by the men already there.[51]

In this case, management apparently considered the status of the Polish and Negro workers roughly equal. Possibly the Polish workers did not have feelings of racial animosity. Yet they realized that management had assigned them the lowest status possible and they were unwilling to accept this definition.

The pattern of resistance to the Negro is similar to the pattern of resistance to women as status equals. Personnel officers rarely admit that prejudice prevents them from employing Negroes in higher jobs. They insist that Negroes do not have the required skills, that they are not motivated to perform, and that they are unreliable workers. Like the foreign born, poor whites, and other groups they have high rates of absenteeism, do not respond to financial incentives, refuse to be educated, are irresponsible, and lack ambition. A superficial analysis supports this position. Negroes and foreign born often represent a new and inexperienced labor force not yet acclimated to modern industry. It is surprising that they do as well as they do, and not that they do badly. Wilson and Gilmore have shown that industries that appreciate this point of view have been able to integrate Negroes into their labor forces.[52]

Allison Davis has also investigated this problem.[53] He concludes that management has the attitude, habits, and values of America's middle class, which emphasizes punctuality and responsibility. However, ethnic groups in lower social and economic levels do not respond to the same norms. The low income, the terrible pressure for physical survival, the responsibility of the family-clan for the individual, the practice of communal rather than individual living, the low level of health which results from inadequate housing, the lack of motivating rewards in the educational system, biological enjoyment compensating for the absence of pleasure in the work and participation in the larger society, and the lack of economic security all serve to create a culture

[51] Everett C. Hughes, "Race Relations in Industry," in Whyte, *Industry and Society, op. cit.,* pp. 113–114.

[52] L. Wilson and H. Gilmore, "White Employers and Negro Workers," *American Sociological Review,* December, 1943, pp. 698–705.

[53] "The Motivation of Underprivileged Workers in Industry," in Whyte, *Industry and Society, op. cit.,* pp. 84–103.

which is antithetical to middle-class rewards. The real "problem," some believe, is to change the social structure, to make the attainment of middle-class values open to all. Whether changes in our socioeconomic system will make this possible is finally a question which lies in the realm of national social policies.

Introduction of Negro workers in industry

Gardner and Moore describe the introduction of Negroes into a particular department of a factory during the war.[54] When they were hired as underlings, sweepers, and janitors, no "social" preparations were considered necessary. When the decision was made to move them in as operatives, preliminary discussions were held with union leaders, supervisors, and some workers. At first Negroes were carefully selected according to looks, cleanliness, and other desirable attributes. They were introduced gradually and individually, so as not to produce much antagonism. As the war progressed, the "best type" was soon exhausted, and it was necessary to be less "discriminating" about the new recruits. They were introduced more rapidly and in larger numbers. The problems of assimilating them under the unusual pressures of war living were fraught with danger. The tensions wrought from long working hours, crowded washrooms, high production demands, and no vacations spilled over into race conflict. The frustrations produced by these abnormal conditions were directed toward the Negro. He was accused of avoiding the draft, holding down departmental quotas, stealing a white man's job, high absenteeism, and disloyalty. On occasion the tensions resulted in fights and riots. It took great social skill on the part of personnel administrators and supervisors to control these conflicts.

Since the war it appears that the resistance of white employees to the induction of Negro workers has been broken under given conditions. Killian studied an extreme situation, the effect of southern white workers on race relations in a northern plant.[55] He found that despite predictions to the contrary, Negro coworkers were tolerated by southern whites if management took a determined stand. Reed found substantiating evidence in the

---

[54] Gardner and Moore, op. cit., pp. 279 ff.

[55] Lewis M. Killian, "Effect of Southern White Workers on Race Relations in a Northern Plant," American Sociological Review, June, 1952, pp. 327–331.

west coast aircraft industry.[56] A survey of employee attitudes revealed that 40 percent were opposed to the entry of Negroes. Yet after Negroes were employed no opposition developed. In fact, many interracial friendships were formed within the plant, but these did not generally carry over into the community.

Scott studied the conditions of ethnic cooperation among work groups and found that a balanced work group made up of about equal numbers of persons from different ethnic backgrounds tended to develop more friendships, more cooperative attitudes, and less conflicts than ethnically unbalanced groups.[57] Probably more important than ethnic balance is the factor of equal-status work contracts. Hardin, and Hogrefe found almost no instance in which white-collar employees protested or quit their jobs when Negro co-workers were introduced. Further, white employees showed little or no differences in their behavior toward Negro and white fellow workers when management set clear standards of behavior. However, as in other studies, work relations did not carry over into the community.[58]

Glaser suggests that there is a continuum in identification patterns in ethnic relations. He says that "the initially prejudiced white may first admit that Joe, his co-worker, is an exception to the Negro stereotype, then that Negroes are all right in the plant but he wouldn't want them as neighbors, and finally that they are good neighbors but he wouldn't want one for a son-in-law."[59] Many workers are passing through this continuum, as has been demonstrated in part by a study of attitudes of southern-born workers in Detroit. Kornhauser found that southern workers who had resided in the city for fifteen years had attitudes not distinguishable from those held by native-born Detroiters.[60]

[56] Bernice Anita Reed, "Accommodation Between Negro and White Employees in a West Coast Aircraft Industry," *Social Forces,* October, 1947, pp. 76–84.

[57] Woodrow W. Scott, "The Balanced Ethnic Work Group," *Sociology and Social Research,* January, 1961, pp. 196–201.

[58] John Hardin and Russell Hogrefe, "Attitudes of White Department Store Employees Toward Negro Co-Workers," *Journal of Social Issues,* 1952, vol. 8, pp. 18–26.

[59] Daniel Glaser, "Dynamics of Ethnic Identification," *American Sociological Review,* February, 1958, pp. 31–40.

[60] Arthur Kornhauser, *Detroit as the People See It,* Wayne University Press, 1952, p. 89.

There is little doubt that the long-term effect of successfully mixing ethnic groups in industry leads to expanding cooperative relations in the broader community. This will be the result whether or not it is the policy of labor, management, or governmental groups. There is generally little pressure by management to encourage workers to expand interethnic contacts. It is being exerted primarily by labor unions and some governmental agencies.

The union and ethnic status

The history of ethnic relations within organized labor is voluminous and can only be briefly alluded to here. As in the case of management, the circumstances involving the breakdown of ethnic status barriers in unions have been more a response to external forces than to humanitarian motives. Clearly the early craft unions in the United States found it easy to accommodate to the ethnic structure of the community. They were not only occupationally homogeneous but also socially and culturally closed organizations. Indeed, unions in many instances became instruments to protect the secure status of their members.

With increasing industrialization, the union as well as management had to respond to the changing market demands. Management needed large numbers of semiskilled and unskilled workers and was willing to hire any type—women, children, immigrants, racial groups—whatever. Most craft unions were unwilling to organize the relatively unskilled workers, who were often ethnically different. However, the union became a model of action for the unorganized workers who were being transformed into self-conscious entities by the factory system. Also, blurring craft jurisdictions, the disappearance of some occupations, and the threat of job displacement convinced many that all workers, irrespective of occupation and ethnicity, had to be organized. In fact, this became the recognized policy of most industrial-type American unions and was adopted by many craft unions too.[61]

Scott Greer's study of labor unions in Los Angeles revealed that different types of unions contained varying proportions of

[61] H. R. Northrup, *Organized Labor and the Negro,* Harper, 1944.

Mexicans and Negroes. Unions having the largest proportions of these groups were of the "industrial-operative" and the "one-job laborer" type, while craft unions, customer service, and clerical unions had smaller proportions.[62] Greer also found that "the chief agency of change in ethnic composition of the unions is the supply and character of labor in relation to effective demand. Once men are working the union must organize them, no matter what their ethnic identification."[63] Moreover, the dispersion of ethnic groups in the entire occupational structure was achieved easiest in the industrial-type locals.

Unionization almost inevitably changes the status of ethnic groups, even under the most adverse conditions. Broom and Shevsky point out that the Mexican workers in the United States have typically been migratory common laborers, in mass employment situations. No other group has experienced such large-scale gang employment and isolation from other native and ethnic workers. And no other secular organization appears more capable of affecting the Mexicans' isolation pattern and their rate of acculturation than the labor union.[64]

Part of this acculturation process is a result of union policy and part of it derives from the dynamics of union organization itself. Since World War II many unions have lobbied to get the federal and state governments to continue the Fair Employment Practices provisions which were included in the defense contracts. In addition, they have inserted analogous provisions in specific labor contracts. Obviously, when such a provision is followed, ethnic group members receive the benefits of seniority provision and are promoted to better jobs. The resultant mobility increases status-equal contacts with other ethnic and nonethnic groups and reduces ethnic conflict, cultural isolation, and status distinctions.[65]

Moreover, labor unions have embarked since the war on a conscious policy of participating in all community-wide associations

[62] Scott Greer, *Last Man In*, Free Press, 1959, p. 26
[63] *Ibid.*, p. 29.
[64] Leonard Broom and Eshref Shevsky, "Mexicans in the United States," *Sociology and Social Research,* January, 1952, pp. 150–158.
[65] Jack London and Richard Hammett, "Impact of Company Policy on Discrimination," *Sociology and Social Research,* 1954, pp. 88–91.

and activities. Perhaps the most important aspect of this involvement is political participation. If these activities have not actually thrust ethnic group members into the community arena, reducing their isolation, labor has "spoken for" minority groups and insisted that they are part of the body politic. To be sure, such programs are not found in all communities and regions of the nation. Yet the avowed union objective of integrating ethnic groups in national political life reduces their sense of isolation and status deprivation.

The union itself is a political body, participation in which has status consequences. In industrial locals which span the job hierarchy, participation and office holding are highest among the skilled workers, who are primarily nonethnics. In one-job locals, ethnic groups often make up the dominant bloc of voters, and they often control the offices.[66] Mobility within these unions increases not only the power and status of ethnics but their contacts with the broader labor movement and its ancillary activities.

STATUS MOBILITY RESPONSES

It is not altogether clear whether upward status mobility is increasing or decreasing in contemporary industrial society. If the rate of upward occupational mobility is taken as the basic measure of status mobility, it may well be that there is relatively more status mobility today.[67] Yet it appears that there is greater status anxiety now than formerly. This condition is probably due to the greater importance attached to upward mobility today and not to blocked mobility itself. Obviously everybody cannot climb regardless of the objective opportunities. But many may have the desire to climb and, not doing so, experience a sense of futility. While the great majority of workers at all levels eventually adjust to the idea of status immobility, they adjust differently. Both individualistic and group patterns may be singled out. The former are more commonly found among white-collar workers and the latter among manual workers, with some outstanding exceptions.

[66] Greer. op. cit., p. 63.
[67] W. Lloyd Warner and James C. Abegglen, Occupational Mobility in American Business and Industry, University of Minnesota Press, 1955.

Individualistic Patterns

Self-improvement

Traditionally self-improvement in the United States has meant becoming an independent businessman or perhaps an independent professional worker. "To be one's own boss" still exerts a powerful pull, and it is still the ambition among American manual and white-collar workers. Chinoy found that automobile workers still dream of the possibility of leaving the factory to set up their own businesses.[68] However, white-collar workers and college students are aware that it is increasingly difficult to become an independent proprietor. They now aim at becoming a manager of a large enterprise.

There is evidence that the prestige of independent business and high authority is weakening. Rosenberg found in his study of Cornell University students that many sons of businessmen did not want to follow in their fathers' footsteps but preferred to become professionals.[69] Another group selected business administration courses with reluctance and without enthusiasm. Many workers now seek jobs which remove them from direct supervision; they prefer independent jobs. It is fashionable in some large business and government bureaucracies to turn down the big jobs so that one can live with a minimum of anxiety and be able to realize other values. Many university administrators are giving up their positions to pursue academic work. These signs point to a change in the sources of status achievement away from ownership, high authority, and high income.

At the middle levels of business mobility aspirations are strong. With the growing realization that many jobs are "dead ends," self-improvement is interpreted to mean training oneself in another job which offers a better road to mobility. Going to night school has been a favorite path of the ambitious status seeker. The purpose of getting additional training is not only to learn but to gain favorable attention from supervisors. It is a way of informing authority of the strong desire to climb. Businessmen often encourage their employees to obtain additional education

[68] Eli Chinoy, *Automobile Workers and the American Dream,* Doubleday, 1955, chap. VII.

[69] Morris Rosenberg, *Occupations and Values,* Free Press, 1957, chap. IX.

by paying all or part of the expenses. The worker may think, "The company is interested in me, and when my chance comes I'll be prepared."

Many businesses have inaugurated internal training programs. Usually employees are given time off during working hours to attend classes. Thousands of workers are annually given rudimentary training of one type or another. They jump at the chance to secure recognition as good students. Obviously, no more than a small proportion of trainees will secure job advancement and the recognition that goes with it. The higher the goals, the fewer the jobs and the more numerous the candidates. Fortunately, many continue to feel that "Education is never wasted." The fact that a small proportion are upgraded and receive formal recognition keeps hope alive in many workers. Such training programs sometimes serve a double purpose; they drain off frustrations of status seekers and increase their transferability potential.

Status emulation

Another individualistic response to mobility blockage is to try to improve "social" contacts on the job. The worker tries to ingratiate himself with the foreman and avoids association with his fellow workers. If he is "snooty," an "eager beaver," or the "foreman's pet," he must be able to endure the barbs of his fellow workers.

Status emulation is more prevalent among white-collar workers, petty managers, and officials than among manual workers. The former seek status by demonstrating that they already belong to a higher-status level. The family budget is strained to permit the display of a style of life similar to that of status superiors. The worker feels that he must buy a tailor-made, double-breasted suit, join certain clubs, serve Scotch rather than beer, move to another section of town, shift church membership, acquire impressive sterling tableware, or buy the Mrs. an expensive evening gown for the next dance.[70]

Supervisors and minor executives are especially concerned

[70] See the classic Thorstein Veblen, *Theory of the Leisure Class,* Modern Library, 1931, chap. 4, "Conspicuous Consumption."

about appropriate behavior. The training they seek is often "personality development." "How to win friends and influence people" has much more appeal to the white-collar male workers than courses in bookkeeping and accounting. Learning how to get along in the personality market,[71] making yourself well liked, developing a dynamic, expansive personality, making people feel comfortable, and having savoir-faire are necessary (so the belief goes) to status acceptance and climbing.

Displacement of the status struggle

The third type of reaction to status blocking is to abandon hope of gaining prestige from the job. The individual seeks to gain esteem in his off-job relationships in the plant. The sources of status gratification arise both from informal interaction among the workers and from organizations sponsored by management and the union. Many informal activities provide opportunities for recognition. Someone acquires the reputation of a cardsharp, another is lauded because he can defy authority, still another has a knack of pacifying antagonists, another is a good story-teller or jokester, another is a good labor man, another is a group spokesman. They do their work adequately, but their chief satis-factions derive from their nonwork activities.

Status may also be attained from company-sponsored after-work programs. Many businesses, offices, hospitals, and schools sponsor athletic teams for their employees. All kinds of clubs are formed—camera, hiking, band, orchestra, choir, and others. Dances, banquets, and dinners are given. All these activities multiply contacts and create new social organizations. The greater the amount and complexity of social organization, the greater are the chances for active social participation and for personal recognition. Since such organizations increase the area of acquaintance of the individual, they are an additional source of prestige. They make possible the anachronism of low income, low formal recognition, but plant-wide informal status. "You pitched a fine game last night, Walt"; "Congratulations for being elected chairman of the local, Bob!" "How much did we make from the

[71] C. Wright Mills, "The Competitive Personality," *Partisan Review*, September–October, 1946, pp. 433–441.

dance, Betty?" "That's a beautiful watch the company gave you last night, Pop"; "That's a beautiful snapshot, Dick"; "You've been chosen chairman of the flower committee, Mona."

It has been suggested that these plant-sponsored activities are designed to drain off frustrations arising from the blocks to status advancement. Management may or may not consciously realize that its programs have this effect. Gardner and Moore report an excellent illustration of this mechanism at work:

> In another concern there was a large engineering staff with many young graduate engineers in the lowest-status engineering jobs. While these were good jobs and fairly well paid as compared to shop jobs, they were, nevertheless, at the bottom of the engineering hierarchy and advancement was often slow. Among the employees of the company a very active camera club was developed in which many of these young engineers participated and there was a great deal of competition for recognition in the photographic exhibits and for positions as officers of the club. Through this club they apparently received the recognition which they felt was lacking in their jobs. As soon as they began to advance in the supervisory hierarchy or otherwise gain status on the job, they began to lose interest in the club; they found they did not have time to compete in exhibits, and often would practically give up the hobby.[72]

Achieving status in the community is a less direct method of securing status at work. Recognition in the community usually derives from participation in its social organizations. To be grand master of the lodge, head of the World-Wide Service League, organizer of the Jay-Teen Club, deacon of the church, or head of the Parent-Teacher Association usually brings recognition from one's fellow workers. However, this channel is not always open to workers when management wants to use the community either as a testing ground for administrative ability or as a reward for status achieved at work.[73]

Group Responses

Many observers have felt that modern industrialism has removed "dignity" from the worker. The dissipation of skills and the rationalization of production have removed much of the "individuality" from the job. These processes reduce the differen-

[72] Gardner and Moore, *op. cit.*, pp. 258–259.
[73] Ross, *op. cit.*

tiation which is basic to stratification in general and status stratification in particular. Many workers find themselves one of a mass—performing the same routines, taking the same orders from the same supervisors, and receiving the same rate of pay. The tendency, therefore, is to reward not skill or production (which is geared to the average worker) but length of service, regularity of work habits, good attendance, cooperation with management, making "contacts" on and off the job, and "good personality." Since large numbers of people satisfy these requisites, gradations of income and status become based more and more on group affiliation and group membership. The status of the individual becomes increasingly determined by the relative status of the group of which he is a member, rather than by the technical skill displayed in his job.

Plainly, the organization which is most concerned about the economic and social status of the worker is the labor union. The history of trade unionism reveals a gradual growth in the interests and areas of bargaining. Increasingly, unions are providing their members recreational, cultural, and, more recently, political training. Although many of these activities (camps, picnics, recreation, counseling programs) are motivated by the desire to secure greater solidarity for economic struggles, they provide at the same time another area for social participation, another avenue for status mobility. Life is given new meaning because a career, a faith, an ideology, an opportunity for recognition are now available. C. W. M. Hart expressed the thought that the labor union is replacing business as the primary source of social status for the worker in the community.[74]

The replacement of individual status striving by group status striving is not new in industrial organization. What is new is the greater emphasis on group status, and the efforts of management and labor to promote it. This is a difficult task because some group identifications have been lost in the urbanization process. Hence, conscious effort must be exerted to make groups aware of themselves and to make them compete for status. Many of the battles between organized employers and employees can only be understood as battles for income and status.

[74] C. W. M. Hart, "Industrial Relations Research and Social Theory," *Canadian Journal of Economics and Political Science,* February, 1949, p. 73.

The public often does not understand why labor and management will not come to agreement on a wage scale, especially when they are close to a settlement—often a matter of two or three cents an hour. This is especially the case during a strike, when both sides are losing and stand to lose more than they can possibly gain. Each side calls the other side "pigheaded," "unreasonable," and the "public" invokes "a plague on both your houses." Although such impasses are tests of power and endurance, the antagonists would be better off to nurse their strength for a showdown on more important issues. Since they do not do this, it is reasonable to conclude that such battles are not motivated by economic reasons alone but by the demand for recognition and status.

The continuous demands of organized labor also are motivated by the desire for greater recognition. The ceaseless push for better working conditions, cleaner washrooms, higher pay, more effective grievance machinery, better promotion and security plans, protective devices, and special clothing is undoubtedly sincere, but it is also an attention-getting device. Labor is strongly motivated to be accepted as having a status equal to management's. The new "dignity" of labor is a concept which envisions labor as a copartner, equal in every way with management.

Labor is making a final assault on the last barrier to status equality, an assault on management prerogatives. Management has received perennial recognition because it has made the important decisions in industry. Labor leaders are pointing out that all men should participate in making decisions that affect their welfare. Management, on the other hand, says that decision-making goes with ownership. It claims that labor is unfit technically to play the role of management and that such a role is unjustified ethically.

However, to be master of one's destiny is a strong motivating force in America. Labor's demands may be interpreted as attempts to gain this kind of self-respect. Workers may be easily replaceable, workers may be part of a productive machine, but workers want to feel and want others to know that they are an important part of industry. They are girding their power and organization to prove it.

CONCLUSION

Status has been traditionally conceived as an individual attribute. We have demonstrated that it must be considered a social group phenomenon. In fact, every work plant has a status organization somewhat independent from the supervisory and other organizations. Like other structures, status may be formally and informally organized; its structure may be rigid or fluid. In any case, workers are much concerned about their status positions in their work groups. They are constantly trying to obtain those symbols which lead others to accord them recognition.

One of the main attributes of the modern industrial system is its tendency to reduce the social differences among workers. Workers evolve many adjustments to this leveling process, the most important of which is the creation of pressure groups. Workers and unions feel that when they get power equal to management's, status equality will automatically follow.

SELECTED BIBLIOGRAPHY

Barnard, Chester I., "Functions and Pathology of Status Systems in Formal Organizations," in William F. Whyte (ed.), *Industry and Society*, McGraw-Hill, 1946.

Greer, Scott, *Last Man In*, Free Press, 1959.

Hughes, Everett C., *Men and Their Work*, Free Press, 1958.

Lenski, Gerhard E., "Status Crystallization: A Non-Vertical Dimension of Social Status," *American Sociological Review*, August, 1954.

Lipset, Seymour Martin, and Reinhard Bendix, *Social Mobility in Industrial Society*, University of California Press, 1959.

Mills, C. Wright, *White Collar*, Oxford University Press, 1956.

Northrup, H. R., *Organized Labor and the Negro*, Harper, 1944.

Nosow, Sigmund, and William H. Form, *Man, Work, and Society*, Basic Books, 1962.

Reiss, Albert J. Jr., *et al.*, *Occupations and Social Structure*, Free Press, 1961.

Veblen, Thorstein, *Theory of the Leisure Class*, Modern Library, 1931.

Weber, Max, "Class, Status and Power," in H. H. Gerth and C. W. Mills (trans.), *From Max Weber: Essays in Sociology*, Oxford University Press, 1946.

PART III · The Individual in the World of Work

This has been called the employee society. Work remains as a central interest in life and each new person is expected to get ready for a work life. Moreover, since large-scale organizations are the largest employers each person tends to become dependent on property owned by others for his means of livelihood. Part III begins with the career and occupational mobility patterns that distinguish persons who are moving through the labor force. The socialization of the child to the work patterns of American society is described. Then the initial, trial, and stable periods of active work life are traced, with their cultural and social attributes and the social adjustments required in each period.

In Chapter 14, "Personality and Organization," the conflict between individual aspirations and organizational constraints is set forth as one of the enduring themes of social adjustment. Modern education and mass communication combine to create high aspirations in parents, which are transmitted to their children. Our dynamic society produces millions of persons who seek much more than they attain within the organizational structure of their lives. Achievement and frustration are common companions in such a society, and no one escapes the wounds of ego.

CHAPTER 13

Career
and
Occupational Mobility

"HOLDING A JOB"—ITS SOCIAL
AND ECONOMIC DEFINITIONS

In the adult world any effort which does not receive a direct payment in money, goods, or services is not regarded in the same way as work which is so rewarded. Thus, the student or housewife is considered outside the market—indeed, more a part of the leisure class than of the population making up the labor force. However, any part-time or full-time worker in a factory, store, or office is said to be "holding a job," i.e., shouldering a part of the world's productive work.

This distinction was nurtured for many years by the traditional economists, who refused to consider students and housewives as producers of wealth. The economist likewise excluded merchants, sailors, carpenters, actors, and domestic workers as productive workers—in fact, any who failed to produce material wealth. Alfred Marshall was considered revolutionary when he first defined "labour as any exertion of mind or body undergone partly or wholly with a view to some good other than the pleasure derived directly from the work." He proposed that all labor be regarded "as productive except that which failed to promote the aim towards which it was directed."[1] Service employment has since been accepted by economists and constitutes a base upon which to examine the economic operation of home, school, hospital, church, and service fields with the same standards as might be

[1] Alfred Marshall, *Principles of Economics,* Macmillan, 8th ed., 1930.

applied to factory, office, store, and insurance route. It is this perspective that the writers are trying to interpret in the social analysis of various work plants and in the adjustment of the worker to them.

Yet there remains in popular thinking economic and social differences between nonmonetary work positions in the home and school and monetary work positions in the factory or store. As we have pointed out in an earlier chapter, these differences are largely explained by the identification of the *market*. The *market* is defined as a physical location characterized by buying and selling of goods and services, with prices determined according to the supply and demand for such goods and services. Unless the worker is hired in a labor market—which is to say, employed by an employer who can choose his workers from an available supply and pay them according to a competitively determined rate—his work assignment is not a "job." Ordinarily a boy or girl gets his first "job" only when a work assignment is secured outside the home or school. Getting a job is regarded as taking a step out into the adult world. Sometimes the skills required in these first jobs are very simple, yet the collective responsibility is often great. A large city newspaper would find itself much embarrassed if its newsboys failed to appear at their appointed time. It is not entirely "palaver" when the newspaper publisher tells his newsboys, "We are in business together."

Entrance into this job world provides status not alone because of the responsibility and monetary return but also because the great American legend regards every worker as launching on an upward course toward success. The very young worker is never regarded as "stuck" in a job; he is merely proving himself for the day when he may climb from the bottom to the top ranks of fame and fortune. Indeed, the worker can perform most distasteful work with adequate spirit if he knows that he is merely doing temporary work which will eventually lead to better things— and especially if he knows that his family and friends regard his present job as only a temporary step to a more responsible one.

The adjustment phase we are about to examine begins when the boy or girl finds his first part-time job while enrolled in school. This takes the young person into the initial period of work adjustment. It is called the initial period, since it marks the beginning of work behavior in the work market. Entrance into the work market is actually the second of a fivefold work pattern which the individual may live to experience. Since the five periods of work adjustment are knit together in most occupational histories, our first task will be to define and illustrate each period.

FIVE PERIODS OF THE LIFEWORK PATTERN

Preparatory, Initial, Trial, Stable, and Retirement Periods of Work Adjustment

In a full life, five spans of work adjustment bridge the beginning and end of working. These may be called (1) preparatory, (2) initial, (3) trial, (4) stable, and (5) retirement. Figure 13.1

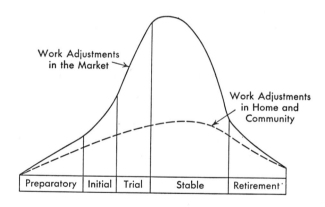

FIG. 13.1. Five Periods of the Lifework Pattern.

illustrates the lifework pattern of the typical worker. It can be seen that the initial, trial, and stable periods encompass most of the work adjustments made in the work market. These three periods represent what is often referred to as the "active work life." It should be noted that many work adjustments in the home and the community are part of the active work life. There are the manifold tasks of household maintenance, child rearing, and the "organization work" which the alert citizen and businessman find themselves obliged to undertake. The work adjustments of home and community are present in every one of the work periods. The preparatory period represents early experiences and adjustments in the home, school, and community as the young person develops physical and mental maturity. The end of life is marked by a retirement period which demands new adjustments in the home and community as the work position in the market place is relinquished. Our attention will be focused especially on the three periods which make up the "active work life."

The worker begins his active work life when he accepts his first job in the work market. With this step, he enters the initial period—*a period of job impermanence beginning when the worker seeks his first jobs during his span of school enrollment and continuing until he has terminated his education.* The worker accepts jobs knowing full well that he intends to fill them only temporarily. His main job is the completion of his education, and his life is oriented largely to the school. The part-time or full-time jobs which he takes are stopgaps for him. It is true that the young worker may perform them with conscientious and serious zeal, but such earnestness is almost always accompanied by the belief that the present job is only a stepping stone to a better one. He takes for granted that he is on a temporary job, although he may look forward to a permanent job with his employer at a later time.

Compulsory education laws place the accent upon the school as the main preoccupation of childhood and much of youth. Only when formal education is terminated does the young worker feel the demand for a permanent job. If he is to find a new orientation, he must discover a satisfying substitute for the status he had while permanently occupied in the school. His culture requires that he "make good." For both the young man and the young woman, this means that a full-time permanent job must be secured in some work plant. The trial period begins when school days are over and youth "goes to work." It may be defined as *a period of job transition beginning when the worker seeks his first full-time work position and continuing until he has secured a work position in which he remains more or less permanently (three years or more).*

The trial period is usually marked by considerable changing of jobs. The worker tries out numerous jobs by moving within work plants via transfer and promotion, and by leaving one work plant for another, seeking a work position with which he intends to remain. Finally he "finds himself," "steadies himself," or perhaps just "resigns himself" and thus enters into a period of stable work adjustment. The stable period may be defined as *a period of job persistence beginning when the worker finds a work position in which he remains more or less permanently (three years or more) and continuing until retirement, death, or until he enters another trial period.* Stability is most secure when the worker is satisfied that he is performing in his "chosen" occupation and within a given work plant in which he intends to remain during the rest of his work life.

Figure 13.2 summarizes some of the characteristics of the three periods of "active work life." The worker is shown progressing from the intial period, when he works only temporarily at the jobs he secures, to the trial period, when he "gets started" in earnest on a full-time job which he "tries out." The stable period is shown as a stage of job persistence when the worker has become relatively fixed in a given occupation and in a given work plant. The feelings and attitudes of the worker during these periods reflect the kind of adjustments which characterize each period.

A consideration of these three periods of active work life raises many questions. What are the first jobs which the worker finds? How do they affect his later work life? How does the school prepare for monetary work positions? How does the worker get his first permanent job? Is there any order or plan by which workers get jobs and then progress? Can workers still climb from the bottom to the top? When does a worker become stable? What happens to the worker's outlook on life when he reaches the stable period? These and many other questions must be answered before we have completed an analysis of the lifework pattern. We shall not find that all workers are destined to gain stable work lives. All that can be said is that the normal thrust for a stable work life is a strain for that job (or occupation) which the worker conceives as "the job, or kind of job, I've always wanted." The worker may fail of his mark and accept a compromise for less than he aspired. He may stay on a job because of the necessity of making a living although his work brings no satisfying reward except the means of livelihood. Yet the struggle for vocational satisfaction sets up tensions that are dynamic. When the "right" job cannot be secured, changes in jobs or changes in work organization dot the occupational history. Life histories are affected by larger social and economic changes as well as by the indeterminate forces of personal health and fortune. It should be understood, therefore,

Periods of Work Adjustment	Initial Period	Trial Period	Stable Period
Nature of job	Part-time and summer employment	Full-time employment	Full-time employment
Mobility	High occupational and work plant mobility	High occupational and work plant mobility	Low occupational and work plant mobility
Worker's occupational history is characterized by:	Job impermanence	Job transition	Job persistence
Psychological components: I. Feelings of the worker	Worker feels that he is only working temporarily and that his performance on the job is secondary to his school life.	Worker feels that he is working at a job (1) in preparation for a more responsible job or (2) to find out if he wants to remain at his present job or work plant, or is merely (3) holding on until he can make a change.	Worker feels that he has found the job and the work plant in which he intends to remain, or finds himself unable to move from the job or the work plant.
II. Attitudes of worker and observers as described by common folk expressions	"Making some spending money" "Preparing himself" "Helping out" "Working temporarily"	"Getting started" "Moving around" "Trying to find out what he likes" "Staying until the first of the year" "It's a living for a while"	"A fixture" "Old-timer" "Intends to stick here" "He likes his job" "He's stuck in that rut"

FIG. 13.2. Periods of Active Work Life.

that the periods of the lifework pattern reflect the anticipated road of work socialization as the hopes and ambitions of young workers point toward the future. It must be recognized, too, that these constructed types are modal and that considerable variation occurs, especially among manual workers who lack job security.[2]

Lifework Pattern for Women

For women workers there is a more intermittent character to their work in the labor market. Carr has projected the lifework pattern of the housewife and suggests eight different periods: (1) the preparatory period; (2) the transitional and mixed period, when she is dating and working; (3) the period of marriage, withdrawal from the labor market, and establishment of a home; (4) the period of marriage adjustment; (5) the period of settled domesticity; (6) the period of divided interests, when the woman re-enters the labor market; (7) the period of increasing biological risk, when the husband may die and when she is getting ready to leave the labor market; (8) the period of retirement and widowhood.[3] In this chapter the three work periods selected for description are those common to the male worker and to the career woman. In marriage both partners must learn to make adjustments to these work periods whether the woman is directly involved or not. Increasingly, as more married women enter the labor market and as they come in sooner after their children are born, the three periods of active work life will become common to both.

THE CULTURAL EXPECTATIONS OF THE INITIAL WORK PERIOD

Social Weaning

The initial work period might be considered part of the *social weaning* process. The child's dependence upon the home must be broken. However, the habits and emotional ties which have so long provided a shelter for him are not easily unhinged. The

---

[2] Howard Becker, "Constructive Typology in the Social Sciences," in Harry E. Barnes, Howard Becker, and Frances Bennett Becker (eds.), *Contemporary Social Theory*, Appleton-Century-Crofts, 1940, pp. 17–46.

[3] Lowell J. Carr, *Analytical Sociology*, Harper, 1948, pp. 505–517.

child must be slowly prepared for the independence he must learn to assert, for there is no innate drive which will automatically direct him to such maturity. This is demonstrated by the following description given by a college man in his freshman year: "During the last two years in high school, I found that I would have to go to work in order to keep myself in spending money. How I hated the thought of going to work! The mere thought of going to work would send chills running up and down my spine. I had always helped in the garden at home and I always helped my mother clean house, but the thought of going some place else to work seemed different to me. I finally summoned up enough courage to start looking for a job."

Indoctrination of Work Values

Maturity is acquired; its achievement is recognized when the social norms which define it are satisfactorily approximated. The index of achievement is made up of the opinions of interested adults who watch the progress of the young person. Their judgments will be expressed invariably in terms of cultural expectations. Some of the most compelling imperatives are as follows:

1. You have to learn to accept responsibility.
2. You have to learn to work hard.
3. You have to learn to get along with people.
4. You have to learn the value of money.
5. You have to learn to hold a job and build a reputation for being a good worker.

These cultural expectations are indoctrinated into the child by the family and other institutions. The child hears his father and mother and his older brothers and sisters appraise the conduct of friends and outsiders in terms of these standards; the school reiterates and emphasizes them; the church gives its moral sanction to them.

THE CULTURAL BACKGROUND OF TRADITIONAL WORK VALUES

Our traditional work values spring from a historic background which includes the experiences of survival on the frontier as well as a compelling interpretation of life called Puritanism. If we are to understand the patterns of work behavior expected of young people in our culture, we must examine the traditional work values. An understanding of the origins of these values will provide an opportunity to appraise their present usefulness. It will also help us to evaluate some of the conflicts and failures of the traditional values in modern life. The experiences of frontier life constitute the first source for explaining the cultural background of these work values.

Frontier Life

The frontier required hard work by everybody. Wright and Corbett put it: 'Childhood was not long on the frontier, and youth was little different from manhood and womanhood."[4]

Children were important citizens. They lightened the labors of both men and women. And at fourteen a boy was given a rifle and assigned his loophole in the fort, where he stood shoulder to shoulder with the men. A boy's life or a girl's was filled with chores that were half work, half play. Getting in wood, making fires, feeding stock, and going to the mill were parts of the daily round and could themselves have filled any average day. But these were not all. Other tasks were the grating and pounding of corn, bringing water from the spring, and carrying clothes to and from the pond on wash days. There was the churning, the Saturday scrubbing and scouring with split brooms. . . . Children helped at all stages of woolen clothmaking from the shearing of sheep to the sewing of garments. . . . Girls were kept busy with skillet and spoon stirring and turning and mixing. They helped bake the johnny cake. They peeled turnips and potatoes. They helped with the washing at the pond or at the hollowed log trough and with the milking and churning. . . . At spinning, weaving, and knitting their fingers were as skilled and delicate as their brother's with his barlow knife.[5]

Puritan Values

Life on the frontier made hard work a *necessity;* the influence of Puritanism made hard work a *virtue.* Puritanism may be described as a philosophy of life or that code of values which was carried to New England by the first settlers in the early seventeenth century. Any inventory of American traditions would have

---

[4] J. E. Wright and Doris S. Corbett, *Pioneer Life,* University of Pittsburgh Press, 1940, p. 98.

[5] *Ibid.,* pp. 86–88.

to commence with Puritanism. Miller and Johnson, in their comprehensive study of Puritanism, state,

> Its role in American thought has been almost the dominant one, for the descendants of Puritans have carried at least some habits of the Puritan mind into a variety of pursuits, have spread across the country, and in many fields of activity have played a leading part. The force of Puritanism, furthermore, has been accentuated because it was the first of these traditions to be fully articulated, and because it has inspired certain traits which have persisted long after the vanishing of the original creed. Without some understanding of Puritanism, it may safely be said, there is no understanding of America.[6]

There are four values of Puritanism which have special reference to work. These might be described thus:

1. It is man's duty to know *how* to work and how to work *hard*.
2. Success in work is evidence of God's favor.
3. The measure of success is money and property.
4. The way to success is through industry and thrift.

Each of these values has left its mark on the passing generations of Americans. They live on in the tradition of America today.

THE SOCIAL PSYCHOLOGY OF THE INITIAL WORK PERIOD

The success of socialization is complete when the values of the group become attitudes in the personality. To be a nonconformist is to be self-reliant, says Emerson, but few individuals escape the force which our social groups exercise to compel conformity. In a contest between individuality and conformity, the strongest forces lie with conformity; for the group will provide its approval and praise for conformity and offer scorn and censure for nonconformity. *Thus the normal processes of socialization convert the cultural expectations of the initial work period into active wishes within the individual.* Five wishes normally arise as end products of the cultural expectations: (1) the wish for independence, (2) the wish to demonstrate ability to work hard, (3) the wish to determine ability to get along with people, (4) the wish to have and manage money, and (5) the wish to make a good job record.

[6] Perry Miller and Thomas H. Johnson, *The Puritans,* American Book, 1938, p. 1.

THE FAILURE OF SOCIALIZATION TO INCULCATE TRADITIONAL WORK VALUES

Changing Work Attitudes of Youth

Socialization does not always succeed in transforming the cultural expectations into personal attitudes. Older adults often say, "I don't know what's got into young people today. They don't want to do anything that requires hard physical labor. You can't get them to accept responsibility, and they think it will kill them if you ask them to work more than eight hours a day. They spend their money like water and some of them are so discourteous you feel like taking a paddle to them. They all think that someone will take care of them."

Contradictions in Work Values

These anguished complaints reflect a culture containing new values which have arisen in contradiction to the old. The cultural contradictions exist side by side in the same society. As persons strive to "belong" to the social groups in which they participate and to seek out recognition and prestige, they find ambiguous guides. They learn that

1. You have to learn to accept responsibility. *But:* It takes a long time before you can get a job that calls for much responsibility.

2. You have to learn to work hard. *But:* A man doesn't have to risk his money and worry over a business, do hard physical labor, or work long hours in order to make a good living any more. There are lots of softer jobs which pay good money and you don't have to kill yourself. It is more important to get located right and make good contacts.

3. You have to learn to get along with people. *But:* You have to learn to be aggressive and push yourself or you won't ever get ahead. You have to step on some people's toes or you will never get things done.

4. You have to learn the value of money. *But:* Nobody gets rich these days by pinching pennies. If you want to make money, you must look and act as if you have money. The most important thing is to know the right people, belong to the right clubs, and get invited to the right social functions.

5. You have to learn to hold a job and build a reputation for being a good worker. *But:* You are not going to live your life in one company or one town. The way to get ahead is to keep moving around. You should be able to get a better job and more money on every move.

The existence of such contradictions results in a socialization of many differing work attitudes. Traditional work values have a strong hold over rural and small-town life. It is in urban life that the conflict between traditional values and the new values is greatest. Young people are caught in this conflict, and many become confused as to what work role they should play. Some march on in conformance with the traditional values. Others turn to the new values and, with a feeling that they are wise in the ways of the world, assume work roles which aim for the big money.

A number of social forces have combined to frustrate the indoctrination of traditional values. The major forces operating to disorganize traditional expectations and to create new work values are (1) manifold aspects of the industrial revolution, (2) the decay of the religious view of work, (3) the definition of formal education as vocational and professional training, (4) the growth of get-rich-quick opportunities and white-collar criminality, (5) the disappearance of social stability and confidence in long-run goals, (6) the disappearance of apprenticeship work experiences.

Major forces operating to disorganize traditional work values

1. MANIFOLD ASPECTS OF THE INDUSTRIAL REVOLUTION

The effects of the industrial revolution upon work motives and habits are far-reaching. Prominent cause-and-effect relationships may be identified.

	Cause	*Effect*
The industrial revolution:	1. Transferred an increasingly large number of persons from rural to urban life. Secondary group participation increasingly comes to predominate within the growing corporate structures.	Introduced impersonality and weakened the social controls supporting traditional work values.

Cause	*Effect*
2. Replaced independent proprietorship with dependence upon an employer.	Brought about decline in motivation and sense of personal responsibility.
3. Set work performance within highly specialized or highly routinized limits.	Weakened purposive effort as end product was obscured and the individual's part became unidentifiable.
4. Created an impersonal market in which demands for labor were subjected to extreme cyclical variations during which large groups of workers were exposed to economic insecurity and suffering.	Aroused feelings of insecurity and insignificance. "Nobody is indispensable."
5. Stimulated an increasingly restricted market as monopolistic practices of management and unions multiplied.	Formed motives and habits in which attempts to gain by producing less were seen to be rewarded.
6. Raised the standard of living by increased mechanization of work tasks.	Stimulated motive to reduce efforts of manual labor by "letting a machine do it."

2. THE DECAY OF THE RELIGIOUS VIEW OF WORK

The Christian view of work holds that all work and property belong to God. Man is the steward who is called to serve God through work. All work is of equal moral worth in His eyes.

This view placed each man in a position of duty to his fellow men as well as to his God. Where it prevailed, a sense of moral worth and economic justice accompanied the distribution of work tasks.

Secular thinking has largely supplanted this concept. Distinct status rankings are now assigned to the occupational classifications which define "superior" and "inferior" work. The industrial revolution accentuated these status differentials as manual workers, particularly, were exposed to the insecurity and deprivation of economic depressions. A weakening of the moral view of work destroyed a sense of economic justice. Workers came to believe that they did not have a moral obligation to their employer.

3. THE DEFINITION OF FORMAL EDUCATION AS VOCATIONAL AND PROFESSIONAL TRAINING

The belief that each step reached on the educational ladder is at the same time a step taken toward a higher-status, better-paying job has stimulated greatly the aspiration for white-collar jobs. It explains why so many young people expect to avoid manual labor and why they often look with disdain upon workers engaged in manual labor.

4. THE GROWTH OF GET-RICH-QUICK OPPORTUNITIES AND WHITE-COLLAR CRIMINALITY

This is the country of bonanzas, rackets, and stock market fortunes. As one young man put it, "The guy that gets money is the one that figures the angles." The widespread pattern of adult participation in get-rich-quick schemes ranging from chain-letter crazes to stock and land speculation has stimulated young workers to look for short cuts to "success."

5. THE DISAPPEARANCE OF SOCIAL STABILITY AND CONFIDENCE IN LONG-RUN GOALS

War, depression, and inflation shake the fabric of life plans and weaken confidence in long-run goals. This atmosphere places more value on what the worker can get now than on what he may attain later.

6. THE DISAPPEARANCE OF APPRENTICESHIP WORK EXPERIENCES

The urban child has become an economic liability. He is not wanted permanently in the work market until he has, at least, a high school education. There is but a limited range of work experiences open to him before that time. He is uncertain as to what occupation he shall follow for he understands what few of them entail. Within the rural environment his life as farmer would have been prepared for him by a long apprenticeship in which his work would be wanted and needed.

These and other forces have brought disorganization to traditional work values. Society shares a responsibility for the work habits and attitudes that it sees laid down in the young people. It is perhaps not so amazing that traditional values have become as disorganized as that, in the midst of the forces recounted, they have held such continued vitality.

Three competing work ethics in modern society

Max Weber gave the name "Protestant Ethic" to the traditional set of Puritan work values. Transition to an industrial civilization has brought two other major sets of competing work values. A "labor ethic" has accompanied the rise of unionization. It stresses that enduring individual gains are best achieved through collective bargaining achievements shared by the group; that group loyalty, in turn, is more important than individual career or wage advances; and that group security has the highest value and that it may be necessary to impose strict discipline upon the group, including restriction of output, denial of piece rates, and strike action when necessary to protect jobs. William H. Whyte, Jr., claims that the influence of the corporation and modern life is giving rise to a bureaucratic or managerial set of values which he calls the "Social Ethic." Its major propositions are three: a belief in the group as a source of creativity, a belief in "belongingness" as the ultimate need of the individual, and a belief in the application of science to achieve "belongingness." Child sociology in the home and progressive education in the school may be regarded as complements of the Social Ethic.

These three work ethics thread their way through work habits and attitudes. Individual attachments can be explained by the social background of the individual and the reference group identity which he has with a work group. If there is confusion, social heterogeneity has created it.

THE TRIAL WORK PERIOD
AS A SOCIAL EXPERIENCE

The trial work period can be defined arbitrarily as the first ten or fifteen years of the individual's full-time work experience. We might agree upon the age span of 18 years to 34 years inclusive as that of the trial period. A precise section of work history would then be available for study.

However, it should be understood that the trial work period represents a type of social experience. It is during the trial period that the individual tries out jobs, tests his ability and interest, and sizes up his chances of advancement. The trial period becomes a struggle to find oneself and to place oneself in a relatively secure work position. For some, it is the climb to the desired vocational goal, to the career that has long been cherished in imagination and expectation. For others, it is a day-by-day struggle against insecurity and boredom. Yet all who participate in work must in varying degree live through a trial period. It will be but a very short period for some workers until a stable work life is achieved. For others, the trial period as a social experience will continue throughout the entire work life. Still others will find that their work life is but an alternation of trial and stable work periods.

DEFINITION AND CHARACTERISTICS
OF THE TRIAL WORK PERIOD

The trial work period has been defined as the period of job transition beginning when the worker seeks his first full-time job and continuing until he has secured a work position in which he remains more or less permanently (three years or more). It is a period of high occupational and work plant mobility. The worker is trying to find and secure that "job" which satisfies his needs for expression, for security, and for recognition. Elmo Roper reported to the American Management Association that his experience in public opinion polling had shown that the average worker has four major wants, in this order: (1) security, (2) a chance to advance, (3) to be treated like a human being, (4) to feel important.[7] The trial work period commonly represents the personal struggles to find an occupation and a work plant where the worker feels these wants may be gratified.

Workers seldom look upon their first full-time jobs as those in which they will remain. More often the worker feels that he is working at a job in preparation for a more responsible one or to

[7] Address before the American Management Association, Conference on Manpower Stabilization, New York, September 28, 1943. See also Elmo Roper, in American Mercury, February, 1944.

find out whether he wants to remain at his present job or work plant; or he may be merely holding on until he can make a change. To secure information about the trial period the writers have examined the work histories of Ohio workers who make up a sample which matches the Ohio labor force in such characteristics as occupational distribution, age, and sex.[8] Interviews with workers in the states of Washington and Michigan have been conducted. All of these efforts have been centered upon the discovery of the nature of the occupational progression, and the accompanying attitudes and roles which the worker exhibits.

SIX DISTINCT TYPES OF CAREER ORIENTATION

The types of career orientation which have been discovered among the workers in the 18-year to 34-year span are attitudinal sets which may be distinguished as (1) ambitious, (2) responsive, (3) fulfilled, (4) confused, (5) frustrated, (6) defeated. Figure 13.3 illustrates these types. The figure also indicates the kind of work progression patterns which are commonly associated with the six orientations. These orientations and work progression patterns will be described.

1. Ambitious

The ambitious worker is one who has a feeling of hope and confidence that he can reach higher occupational goals. He usually seeks higher occupational goals in order to attain greater authority, status, or income.

The ambitious worker possesses a strong motivating drive that engages him in the competitive struggle to get ahead. Our culture smiles upon such behavior, stressing initiative and defining success as a job movement that progressively lifts the individual into positions of greater responsibility. Parents, relatives, friends, and teachers of middle-class society encourage the young worker to fulfill the American career stereotype. One man told us:

---

[8] Delbert C. Miller and William H. Form, "Occupational Mobility and the Measurement of Occupational Adjustment," in Robert O'Brien (ed), *Readings in General Sociology,* Pacific Books, 1947, pp. 221–228; "Measuring Patterns of Occupational Security," *Sociometry,* November, 1947, pp. 362–375; "The Career Pattern as a Sociological Instrument," *American Journal of Sociology,* January, 1949, pp. 317–329.

Career Orientation	1. Ambitious	2. Responsive	3. Fulfilled
Character of Aspiration	Feeling of hope and confidence that higher occupational goals can be attained	Feeling of acceptance with job progression which parents or relatives expect worker to follow	Feeling of satisfaction upon attainment of desired occupational goal
	4. Confused	5. Frustrated	6. Defeated
	Feeling of uncertainty regarding past and present work progress and indecision regarding further moves	Feeling of being thwarted in occupational aspiration but desirous of moving toward another goal	Feeling of resignation and hopelessness with work progress
Progression Associated Kind of Work	1. Rising	2. Repeating and Paralleling	3. Completed
Identified by:	Evidence of movement involving successive increase of income or status or both	Evidence of acceptance of a job previously followed by a parent or relative; evidence that steps are planned more or less in advance by others, usually parents or relatives	Evidence that desired occupational goal was attained and the holder is now satisfied to remain in the occupation and at the level he has attained
	4. Erratic	5. Blocked	6. Regressive
	Evidence of erratic horizontal and vertical occupational mobility	Evidence that desired occupational goal was not attained and that holder is now unable, temporarily at least, to move to another goal	Evidence of movement involving successive loss of income or status or both

FIG. 13.3. Six Types of Career Orientation Found in the Trial Work Period.

It seems to me that I have always felt I had to make good. My father used to tell us that the people who live in the hilly north section of the country were poor because they were lazy and lacked ambition to get ahead. He said they could have good farms and a house as good as ours if they would save and work. He called the hill section people, "white trash." The thought of becoming "white trash" came to be more odious than the thought of being cast into Hell itself. It was unthinkable that anyone in our family should ever slip to the place where he would have to live in the hill section among such people.

I learned that I had to work hard. Every time that my father felt I was not working hard enough he would say, "You are getting more like that white trash every day you live." This would make me so mad that I did not dare to speak back. I resolved that I would show my father something about my ability to get ahead that would make him take back those words. I think that is partly the source of my ambition to make big money.

Work histories of those with ambitious career orientations are records of job movement that lift the worker from one income or status position to another. These work progressions are characterized by rising. The ambitious workers often have the attributes which are described for the "climbers" in Chapter 11.

2. Responsive

The responsive worker is identified as one who is fulfilling the career which others expect him to assume. The most common of all occupational patterns is that of the son following an occupation on the same or an adjacent socioeconomic level as that of the father. All research studies show that a majority of the recorded regular occupations of the sons fall upon or are adjacent to the level of their fathers' regular occupations on *all occupational levels*. The workers who "inherit" occupations in the same socioeconomic level are called responsive. Some may be characterized by strong motivating drives as they feel compelled to match the father's achievement. Others find that the circumstances of life lead them with less effort in almost automatic progression to their lifework. The latter cases are commonly observed among owners who plan that their sons will eventually assume the responsibilities of their business or professional practice. Both the final job and the intervening steps of education and apprenticeship may be planned, and the worker is simply expected to fulfill his destiny by following the plan.[9]

[9] The reader will recall the attitudes of the Brahmin in Chapter 11.

Interesting cases for study are those of sons who are catapulted into positions of major responsibility at a relatively early age. Henry Ford II inherited the presidency of the giant Ford Motor Company in 1945 at twenty-nine years of age. Robert M. Hutchins attained the presidency of the University of Chicago at thirty-one years of age. The first repeated his father's career by assuming the identical position in the work plant; the second paralleled the career of his father, William J. Hutchins of Berea College.

Although these cases have involved sons of an owner and a professional, responsive workers may be found also among clerical, skilled, and unskilled workers. Here the observable pattern is one of attitudes oriented in such a way that the son expects to continue in the occupation of the father. Bakke has pointed out that among working-class individuals one is regarded as successful when he has attained the sort of job and standard of living customary among his associates.[10] Therefore, the occupational expectation of sons and daughters seldom soars ahead of the standards attained by the father and other members in their social class. Where families have striven to provide children with the education and training that might equip them to climb from the working class, the desire has been commonly shared by the children *until they took their first job.* Once they have made a start as manual workers, ambition has become stifled and with each passing year the likelihood of advancement beyond working-class status becomes less probable. Bakke puts the orientation this way: "The best summary which characterizes the standards of many of those with whom we had contact was this, 'All that I ask now is a chance to pay my bills and be able not to worry.' "[11]

3. Fulfilled

The fulfilled worker is characterized by a feeling of satisfaction upon attainment of a desired occupational goal. He may have been extremely ambitious in earlier stages of his work life when he was struggling to achieve his present work position. Now that he occupies that position, he wants nothing more than a successful tenure within it. The work history commonly associated is one that might be called *completed.* There is evidence of a work

[10] E. Wight Bakke, *The Unemployed Worker,* Yale, p. 20.
[11] *Ibid.,* p. 26.

progression from less responsible to more responsible jobs. The fulfilled worker may seek more money and more prestige, but he is satisfied with his choice of occupation and has no ambition to move in any different direction.

4. Confused

The confused worker has a feeling of uncertainty regarding past and present work progress and indecision regarding future moves. The work history is commonly marked by evidence of *erratic* horizontal and vertical occupational mobility; it is a chronicle of floundering or of adventuresome floating. Two components seem to explain the apparent aimlessness of the pattern: personality characteristics of the worker and the unstable nature of the jobs occupied. Such personal characteristics as desire for adventure or difficulty in getting along with people show up in high, erratic occupational mobility. The instability of jobs themselves within semiskilled and unskilled classifications reveals still another frequent cause of high occupational mobility.

The struggle to find an emotionally secure and satisfying place within work groups is universal. Most job histories reveal evidence of this struggle in the patterns of vertical and horizontal mobility or in the earlier shifts of educational training. It has been pointed out that the intense specialization of our contemporary world has heightened the difficulty of finding one's "place." Moreover, secondary group life in large work groups may stifle emotional satisfactions even when the individual is thoroughly competent in the work position. Thus, the search for a work position in which the individual feels competent technically and secure emotionally is not an easy one.[12]

5. Frustrated

The frustrated worker feels that he has been thwarted in his occupational aspirations. He desires to move to another occupational goal but finds himself blocked. He is in an occupational

---

[12] The reader will recall that other main types of reactions to fluctuating class histories were identified in Chapter 11. These were (1) hope-springs-eternal reaction, (2) ride-with-the-tide fatalism, and (3) confused, mixed, and alternating responses. Insofar as the work history involves fluctuating movements between classes it will be useful to refer to Chapter 11 for further insights regarding floundering work histories.

rut. He knows he is blocked and is anxious to get out of his present job. The work history of the frustrated worker is identified by evidence that the desired occupational goal was not attained and that the worker is now unable to move to another goal.

6. Defeated

The defeated worker possesses a feeling of resignation and hopelessness as regards work progress. His most common reaction is to see himself as a failure.[13] His work history is commonly identified by a *regressive* work record involving successive loss of income or status or both. It may be that during the early part of the career there is upward movement, which becomes halted, and then the downward movement sets in. The "fall" may be small or great. The variations are not of significance to us except as they contribute to better understanding of the social adjustments of the defeated worker. What is of major interest is the emotional impact of the occupational descent and its ramifications in the social life of the worker and his family.

Six types of career orientation have been presented as significant attitude sets of the worker in the trial work period. Only limited research has been done to trace out the full social ramifications of career histories. However, it is well known that important social effects are associated with each type of career orientation. Career patterns are profoundly influenced by career orientations. Robert Merton has emphasized that there is a "self-fulfilling prophecy" which often brings into being those future events in which the believer has devout faith. Many careers are but the objective products of subjective perceptions.

CAREER PATTERNS DURING THE TRIAL WORK PERIOD

The trial period has been defined as the period of job transition beginning when the worker seeks his first full-time job and continuing until he has secured an occupation in which he intends

---

[13] Bakke, *op. cit.*, pp. 363–365; cf. Harold L. Wilensky and Hugh Edwards, "The Skidder: Ideological Adjustments of Downward Mobile Workers," *American Sociological Review*, April, 1959, pp. 215–231.

to remain for the rest of his work life. In research practice it has been our habit to regard any worker who has not remained for at least three years on a job as holding a trial job. A worker who has remained more than three years in a given work position has been regarded as on a stable job.

The assumption has been made that every worker enters the trial work period when he begins to search for his first full-time job. The early years of work life are observed to be years of testing when the individual may be called upon to make new adjustments as worker, marital partner, home builder, and parent. The brunt of these adjustments may be best seen in the age span beginning around 16 to 20 and continuing to about 30 to 34 years. The span 18 years to 34 years has been arbitrarily selected in order to focus attention upon the age period when most workers will be struggling with common problems of adjustment.

It is always understood that the trial work period is meaningful only as it corresponds to a social experience. Therefore, some workers may be expected to achieve stability early in their work life and others late or not at all. What, then, is the history of workers when they embark on full-time work life? To gain insight into the meaning of such history it is necessary to clarify the kind of mobility that can be observed.

The Occupational Mobility of Workers

The occupational histories of workers show two major types of mobility: horizontal occupational movement and vertical occupational mobility. *Horizontal occupational movement* refers here to any job movement which involves a transition from one work position to another work position. When we are interested in horizontal movement we examine career patterns for the number of jobs held and the duration of each job. Such movement may be observed when a worker moves from (1) one job to another job within the same company (transfer or promotion), (2) one company to another company within the same local community, (3) one company to another company in another community. Therefore, horizontal occupational movement describes all job moves *without regard for their socioeconomic classification*.

Vertical occupational mobility refers to job movement between socioeconomic levels. A semiskilled drill press operator who assumes the work of a skilled turret lathe mechanic is considered as moving from a semiskilled to a skilled work classification, thus raising his socioeconomic classification. Obviously, vertical movement can be downward as well as upward on the socioeconomic ladder.

The recording of vertical mobility is hampered by the fact that it is difficult to establish the relative socioeconomic level of each job classification. Before any scale could have validity each occupation would need to be examined against such criteria as scale of living, occupation, income, wealth and savings, marital and family circumstances, social repute, schooling of parents and children, political character and influence, and, perhaps, recreational conditions. Since the degree of correlation between these conditions and given job classifications has never been determined with precision, no present scale of socioeconomic levels is entirely satisfactory. Research workers have made serious attempts to secure a good scale.[14]

The most widely known scale is that of Dr. Alba Edwards of the United States Census Bureau.[15] His scale lists the following "socioeconomic" groupings:

[14] W. L. Warner, M. Meeker, and K. Eels, *Social Class in America*, Science Research, 1949; Paul Hatt and C. C. North, "Jobs and Occupations," *Opinion News*, 1947, vol. 9, p. 13; C. Burt, *A Study in Vocational Guidance*, Industrial Research Board Report No. 33, London, 1926; F. E. Barr, "A Scale for Measuring Mental Ability in Vocations and Some of Its Implications," M. A. thesis, Stanford University, 1918, reprinted by L. M. Terman in *Genetic Studies of Genius*, Vol. 1, Stanford, 1925, p. 66; E. S. Brussell, "A Revision of the Barr-Taussig Scale," University of Minnesota (unpublished); G. S. Counts, *The Selective Character of American Secondary Education*, University of Chicago Supplementary Education Monographs, No. 19, May, 1922; G. N. Kefauver, V. H. Noll, and E. E. Drake, *The Secondary School Population*, National Survey of Secondary Education, Bulletin No. 17, 1932, Monograph No. 4, GPO, 1933; R. O. Beckman, "A New Scale for Gauging Occupational Rank," *Personnel Journal*, December, 1934, pp. 225–233; F. Goodenough and E. J. Anderson, *Experimental Child Study*, University of Minnesota Press, 1931, pp. 243–244; Ethel Kawin, *Children of Pre-School Age*, University of Chicago Press, 1934, pp. 164–69; Theodore Caplow, *The Sociology of Work*, University of Minnesota Press, 1954.

[15] Alba M. Edwards, "A Social-Economic Grouping of the Gainful Workers in the United States," *Journal of the American Statistical Association*, December, 1933, pp. 377–387; Alba M. Edwards, *Sixteenth Census of the United States, Comparative Occupation Statistics for the United States*, GPO, 1940, p. 176; cf. Edward Gross, "The Occupational Variable as a Research Category," *American Sociological Review*, October, 1959, pp. 640–649.

1. Professional persons.
2. Proprietors, managers, and officials.
   a. Farmers (owners and tenants).
   b. Wholesale and retail dealers.
   c. Other proprietors, managers, and officials.
3. Clerks and kindred workers.
4. Skilled workers and foremen.
5. Semiskilled workers.
6. Unskilled workers.
   a. Farm laborers.
   b. Laborers, except farm.
   c. Servant classes.

Dr. Edwards defends his classifications by pointing out that each of the six groups has a somewhat distinct standard of life economically, and to a considerable extent intellectually and socially. Table 3.5 in Chapter 3 depicts salary income and years of school completed. When considered together, these two measures indicate that the socioeconomic groups so classified are arranged in a descending order of social-economic status and that they do constitute a ranking scale.

These groupings, with some refinements, have been employed in classifying the gainfully employed workers in the United States Census since 1930. Most occupational research has followed either these classifications or a set very similar to them. Vertical mobility of workers will be recorded in terms of the Edwards scale in this chapter.

Horizontal Occupational Movement of Workers During the Trial Work Period

There is no complete record of the occupational histories of the gainfully employed workers in the United States. The Census Bureau makes a survey once each decade to assess changes that have taken place within *occupational classifications,* but this record tells nothing about individual work histories. Few work institutions or associations have kept records of *individual work histories* after the workers have severed their relationship with the institution. Most schools know very little about their graduates five or ten years after graduation. Business firms either destroy their terminated employee records or place them in their "dead" file and usually make no further follow-up. Social workers keep

elaborate records on their active "cases" but seldom maintain
follow-up records after a client has become rehabilitated. The
result is an abundance of *cross-sectional* work records but a limited number of *longitudinal* histories. The study of work adjustment requires an ample body of continuous records following
work histories from birth until death. Such histories are not now
available. However, sample studies enable us to begin the analysis of work life and the adjustment problems related to it. Most
of the studies have been made by researchers who were interested
in following up the careers of students who had graduated from
high school[16] or from college.[17]

The research studies vary greatly in the number of years of
follow-up and the care which was given in ascertaining experiences between the time of graduation and the terminal time used
in the study. Despite the lack of continuous study of a given population there is a growing body of fact upon which to draw conclusions. Especially useful are the few studies which describe a
sample of workers representative of the total labor force.[18] Lip-

[16] Howard M. Bell, *Youth Tell Their Story*, American Council on Educa-
tion, 1938; Herbert W. Benedict, *Canton Vocational Survey*, Canton Board of
Education, Canton, Ohio, 1938; W. L. Richey, *Youngstown Occupational
Survey*, Youngstown, Ohio, 1938; Don J. Bogue and H. Ashley Weeks, "Factors in the Occupational Adjustment of Male Youth in Whitman County,
Washington," *Research Studies of the State College of Washington*, 1941,
vol. IX, pp. 119–133; Paul H. Landis, *Six Months After Commencement*,
Bulletin No. 420, Agricultural Experiment Station, State College of Wash-
ington, 1942; Paul H. Landis, *Washington High School Graduates in Depres-
sion and in War Years*, Bulletin No. 463, Agricultural Experiment Station,
State College of Washington, 1945; Howard C. Seymour and Carl E. Tremer,
We Left School a Year Ago, Rochester Public Schools, Rochester, N.Y., 1941;
R. F. Berdie, *After High School, What?* Univ. of Minnesota Press, 1954.

[17] John R. Tunis, *Was College Worth While?* Harcourt, Brace, 1936; Alvin
C. Eurich and C. Robert Pace, *A Follow-Up Study of Minnesota Graduates
from 1928 to 1936*, University of Minnesota, Committee on Educational Research, 1938; Walter J. Greenleaf, *Economic Status of College Alumni*, GPO,
1939; F. Lawrence Babcock, *The United States College Graduate*, Macmillan,
1941; C. Robert Pace, *They Went to College*, University of Minnesota Press,
1941; Maitland Edey, "The Class of '32," *Life*, June 16, 1947, pp. 51–60; Ernest
Havemann and Patricia Salter West, *They Went to College*, Harcourt, Brace,
1952.

[18] Percy E. Davidson and H. Dewey Anderson, *Occupational Mobility in an
American Community*, Stanford, 1937; William H. Form, "The Sociology of a
White Collar Suburb: Greenbelt, Maryland," unpublished doctoral thesis,
University of Maryland, 1944; Delbert C. Miller and William H. Form,
"Measuring Patterns of Occupational Security," *Sociometry*, November, 1947,

set and Bendix studied a representative sample of 935 working heads of families in Oakland, California, in 1949–1950, gathering job histories from their first job to the present one. They found that the workers change jobs most frequently during their early years in the labor force while the older workers settle down. Job mobility clearly decreases as age increases. Table 13.1 demonstrates the job mobility by age groups. "Low mobility" has been designated as 0–1.9 job changes on the average during every decade in the labor force. "Medium mobility" has been designated as 2–4.9 job changes, and "high mobility" means five or more job changes. Shifts in occupations or communities were also taken into account. It can be clearly seen that the age group 21–30 is characterized by a markedly high job mobility with 66.3 percent of the group falling in that category. By age 31–40 the percentage in the high-mobility category has dropped to 30.7 percent.

TABLE 13.1   Job Mobility by Age Groups

Age Groups	Low		Medium		High		Total	
	Number	Percent	Number	Percent	Number	Percent	Number	Percent
21–30	10	5.7	49	28.0	116	66.3	175	100.0
31–40	57	23.9	108	45.4	73	30.7	238	100.0
41–50	89	39.7	109	48.7	26	11.6	224	100.0
51–60	88	56.4	62	39.8	6	3.8	156	100.0
61–70	59	62.1	31	32.7	5	5.2	95	100.0
70 and over	36	76.6	11	23.4	0	0.0	47	100.0

SOURCE: Seymour M. Lipset and Reinhard Bendix, "Social Mobility and Occupational Career Patterns," *American Journal of Sociology*, January, 1952, p. 367.

These findings confirm an earlier study by Davidson and Anderson, who have shown that young adults have relatively high horizontal occupational movement. When 466 San Jose respondents in the age group *20 to 34 years* inclusive were asked how

pp. 362–375; W. H. Form and D. C. Miller, "The Career Pattern as a Sociological Instrument," *American Journal of Sociology*, January, 1949, pp. 317–329; Richard Centers, "Occupational Mobility of Urban Occupational Strata," *American Sociological Review*, April, 1948, pp. 197–206; Seymour Martin Lipset and Reinhard Bendix, *Social Mobility in Industrial Society*, University of California Press, 1959, pp. 147–199.

many different occupations they had followed for eight months or more, the results showed an average of three different occupations.[19] Figure 13.4 shows the percentage of different occupations specified for ages 20 to 34 years.

The study of Princeton graduates in the class of 1932 shows that *after fifteen years out of college* the average number of different jobs is 3.3 per graduate.[20]

The relatively high job movement of the trial work period con-

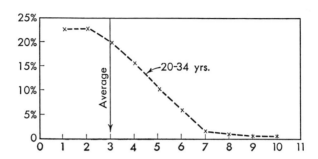

FIG. 13.4. The Percentage of Different Occupations Followed for Eight Months or More for 466 Workers Between 20 and 34 Years. (Reprinted from *Occupational Mobility in an American Community,* by Percy E. Davidson and Dewey Anderson with the permission of the authors and of the publishers, Stanford University Press, 1937, p. 73.)

trasts with the more stable years of later work life. Davidson and Anderson report that workers in the age spans 35 to 54 years, and 55 years and over have held an average of 4.1 different jobs in their lifetime;[21] that is, on the average only one more job move is made after 35 years of age. It can be said that there is *three times as much horizontal occupational movement before 35 years of age as after that age.* This finding must be considered as pertinent only to the San Jose population of this study. The figures cited apply to the 1165 respondents 20 years of age and over. It is to be remembered, too, that the occupational mobility has been

[19] Davidson and Anderson, *op. cit.,* p. 73.

[20] Edey, *op. cit.,* p. 52.

[21] Davidson and Anderson, *op. cit.,* p. 73. Robert Dubin, using data gathered in the 1950s, estimates that the average worker will hold nine jobs in forty-six years of working. See *The World of Work,* Prentice-Hall, 1958, p. 266.

expressed in *average* terms. Actually there is a wide variation in the jobs held if individual careers are examined. In the trial period workers of San Jose have held from *one to ten* different jobs for eight months or more. One out of five says that he has never had more than one job. At the same time, one out of five says he has had five or more different occupations.

In the Princeton study all respondents have completed fifteen years of work life. One graduate reports fourteen different jobs during his trial work period. At the stable end of the range more than one out of four says he has been on one job only during his fifteen years.

These studies are among the very few to reveal the horizontal occupational movement of workers by age. They leave much to be desired. The San Jose study does not tell us about the job moves where the respondent had spent *less than eight months on* the job. It fails to give us a picture of work histories at the *end* of a given number of years but tells only about workers within an age span. The weakness of the Princeton study appears in the unrepresentativeness of the sample. This is no fault of the researcher but grows out of the fact that Princeton graduates have family backgrounds which reflect higher income and educational level than is true of either the average young male worker of the United States or the average college graduate.

The picture of the trial work period does begin to emerge in spite of the lack of complete detail. It is a period of relatively high occupational movement and of high residential mobility. In an ingenious study of the mobility of insurance policy holders Moore demonstrated the current movement of people.[22] Using the 4103 active policies of an insurance company written by the company during the years 1922, 1923, 1924, and 1934, Moore checked the changes in the addresses of these insurance holders to discover their residential mobility. Figure 13.5 is a graph of the moves for each age group.

Moore states that "The highest adult mobility incidence is found for ages 24–27, when nearly one in three annually change their residence. The later thirties reduce the mobility to one in six. In the forties, the average is nearer to one in nine. Through-

[22] Elon H. Moore, "Mobility of Insurance Policy Holders," *American Sociological Review,* February, 1938, pp. 63–77.

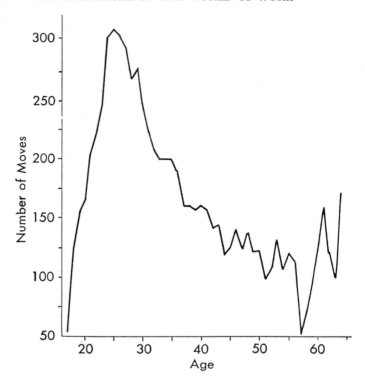

FIG. 13.5. The Residential Mobility of 4103 Insurance Policy Holders by Age. (Adapted from Elon H. Moore, "Mobility of Insurance Holders," *American Sociological Review,* February, 1938, p. 68.)

out the years the heaviest mobility rates appear to be associated with social and job adjustment. If one accepts this hypothesis, then the process of adjusting appears greatest at about the age of 25—and most stable . . . adjustment occurs in their fifties."[23]

The overall pattern of the trial period can now be described. Relatively high occupational and residential mobility is characteristic. Manifold social adjustments are enforced as the demands of marriage and parenthood are encountered and new requirements of housing, transportation, and community life are met. The important facts of vertical mobility have not yet been explored. It has been assumed that the trial work period is a time

[23] *Ibid.,* p. 68.

of testing and of struggle to establish oneself. In America, workers have free choice of vocation and a large measure of educational opportunity. It is to be expected that there will be considerable movement up and down the socioeconomic ladder. What do the work histories of young workers reveal?

Vertical Occupational Mobility of Workers During the Trial Work Period

The 466 San Jose workers in the *20–34-year age group* investigated by Davidson and Anderson showed 974 job moves in occupations they had held eight months or more. Figure 13.6 shows the steps moved *upward* and *downward* on the occupational ladder. A step is a movement upward or downward from the present regular occupation of the respondent. Job moves that were upward on the socioeconomic scale were reported by 36.1 percent of the respondents; 24.7 percent of the job moves were reported as downward. The largest percentage of moves, 43.0 percent, are on the same level. What, then, can be said about the upward movement of workers as they struggle for higher socioeco-

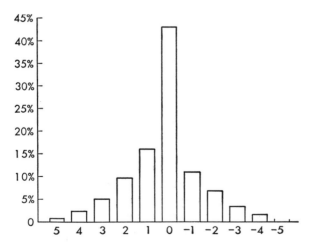

FIG. 13.6. Vertical Occupational Mobility of Workers 20 to 34 Years of Age, for All Their Occupations Held for Eight Months or More. (Reprinted from *Occupational Mobility in an American Community*, by Percy E. Davidson and Dewey Anderson with the permission of the authors and of the publishers, Stanford University Press, 1937, p. 91.)

nomic levels? The figures show that the mean number of steps moved is just one. The overall direction for the total group is very slightly upward (+.20).

Three national surveys which have been made of occupational mobility in the urban labor force of the United States show that most sons stay in the same manual or white-collar status as their fathers' occupation before them. Table 13.2 shows the results of the three surveys. "Upward mobile" includes men in nonmanual occupations whose fathers were in manual occupations; "downward mobile" includes men in manual occupations whose fathers were in nonmanual occupations. Note that there is more upward mobility than downward mobility which is accounted for, in part, by the expansion of the nonmanual sector of the labor force.

TABLE 13.2 Percentage of Men in Urban Occupations with Fathers in Urban Occupations Who Have Been Mobile Upward or Downward

Category	Centers 1945	NORC 1947	Survey Research Center 1952
Upward mobile	17	21	19
Downward mobile	8	11	13
Stationary	75	68	67
Number in sample	598	719	463

SOURCE: Seymour Martin Lipset and Reinhard Bendix, *Social Mobility in Industrial Society,* University of Caifornia Press, 1959, p. 88.

However, most sons of urban dwellers have not changed their class position, as defined by a shift across the manual-nonmanual line, and approximately 10 percent have fallen in status.

The detailed picture of the mobility of American males presented in Fig. 13.7 shows that the majority of the sons of professionals, semiprofessionals, proprietors, managers, and officials —the most privileged occupations—are not able to maintain the rank of their fathers, and that about one-third of them are actually in manual employment. Taking all occupations into account, the picture that emerges is one of limited upward occupational mobility. This does not mean that the individual position in the

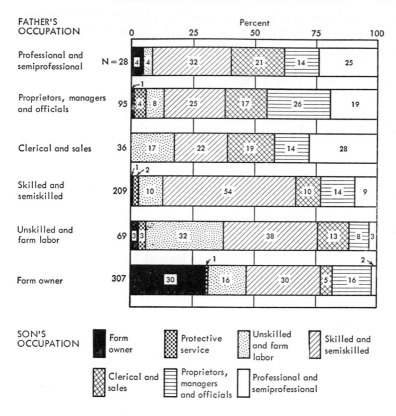

FIG. 13.7. Occupational Distribution of a Sample of American Males, by Their Fathers' Occupation. (From data of the Michigan Survey Research Center study of the 1952 presidential election. Protective Service omitted from "father's occupation" because of too few cases.)

labor force is destined to be without occupational variety or vertical movement. Movement into a higher social class or from the slums to the suburbs in one generation is attainable for millions. A still larger proportion of all workers will have worked in different jobs and in different communities. But vertical mobility is largely confined to mobility on either side of the dividing line between manual work and the nonmanual occupations. There is little permanent occupational movement across this basic line. Although persons may have experience in a wide variety of occupations, most of it will be either manual or nonmanual. Two major types of departures may be observed: (1) Individuals whose occupational career is predominantly manual may have brief experience in nonmanual occupations, especially in small business, sales, and lower white-collar positions. (2) Individuals whose career is predominantly nonmanual quite often have spent some time in manual positions, generally briefly and early in their career.[24]

Five to twenty-five more years of additional work experience does not alter these facts. A comparison among age groups 20 to 34, 35 to 54, and 55 years and over shows that they are much alike in the type of vertical movement their members have experienced. The mean number of steps per change of occupation for all 1165 respondents in all age groups is +.19.[25] It appears that stablizing forces have already formed by the time the individual is ready to embark on his first job. The writers sought to verify this finding in their study of a representative sample (276 cases) of the Ohio labor force. We set up the hypothesis that occupational careers of all workers tend to remain on the same occupational level from the first part-time job to the last job held. The problem was to determine whether the last job in the occupational career was related to the jobs held in the initial, trial, and stable work periods. Our desire was to attempt to measure the relationship along the historic route of job changes so that all jobs held by the worker were included.

To accomplish our aim we found the occupational distribution for the last job held. Then, taking each occupational level individually, we reconstructed the occupational distribution for all first jobs in the initial, trial, and stable work periods. Coefficients of contingency were computed showing .54 for the initial period, .71 for the trial period, and .87 for the stable period.[26] When we recall that the highest possible contingency coefficient for a 7×7 table is .926, it is evident that strong and significant relationships exist. These statistics support the hypothesis that

[24] Lipset and Bendix, *op. cit.*, p. 180 (based on their Oakland, California, Labor Study).

[25] Davidson and Anderson, *op. cit.*, p. 91.

[26] Delbert C. Miller and William H. Form, "Measuring Patterns of Occupational Security," *Sociometry*, November, 1947, pp. 362–375.

job histories have a *strong internal strain toward consistency.*[27] This finding has been confirmed since by Lipset and Malm, who have shown that the first job is clearly the most important single predictor—more important than education and father's occupation—of present occupational status.[28] Apparently, from the very beginning of the work career of the job, orientation paths are partially predetermined. At no stage of their careers do people wander aimlessly and accidentally from one occupational level to another. Once started on an occupational level, a worker tends to remain on that level or an adjacent one. There seem to be social factors of education, occupation of father, "connections," and pressures that direct occupational choices along fairly predictable lines.[29]

The trial work period can now be described as *a period of proportionately high occupational movement and residential mobility but with limited vertical mobility.* Vertical mobility in the San Jose age group 20 to 34 years was shown to be characterized by a very slight upward movement (less than one step) when the present regular occupation of each respondent was compared with all other jobs held for eight months or more. The direction and distance of the job moves appear to be less the result of a preconceived plan than the product of impersonal social forces. Definite factors outside the range of individual option are seen to be directing the flow of workers from one occupation to another.

THE CHARACTER OF THE STABLE WORK PERIOD

It can be noted as one examines the career patterns of both young and older workers that there is a wide range of possible job histories. However, equally demonstrable is the fact that for many workers the age span 35 years to 60 years covers a stable work period. The worker finds a relatively permanent job and "settles down." He develops social roots in the work plant and in the local community. This period may be characterized by a

---

[27] For a discussion of the contingency coefficient see G. U. Yule and N. G. Kendall, *An Introduction to the Theory of Statistics,* Griffin, 1937, p. 69.

[28] S. M. Lipset and F. Theodore Malm, "First Jobs and Career Patterns," *American Journal of Sociology and Economics,* 1955, vol. 14, pp. 247–261.

[29] Davidson and Anderson, *op. cit.,* pp. 84–102.

relative absence of work tension and the development of a feeling of belonging to the groups in which the worker participates. *The stable period may be defined as a period of job persistence beginning when the worker finds a work position in which he remains more or less permanently (three years or more) and continuing until retirement, death, or until he enters another trial period.* Stability is most secure when the worker is satisfied that he is performing in his "chosen" occupation and within a given work plant in which he intends to remain during the rest of his working life.

The stable period may be the result of freely chosen or constrained action. The worker may remain on a job because he is satisfied to make it a permanent one. On the other hand, he may remain on a job, hoping to move, only because he cannot find an acceptable alternative. In either case, he probably becomes knit to the social life of the work plant and the community. Seniority or tenure gives him an increased measure of security. The family and the community exert pressures which dampen residential and occupational mobility.

Even if occupational stability is not achieved, the expectations of associates and of the community surround the mature worker and exert subtle but real pressures upon him. He is expected to marry and establish a home. He is expected to send his children to school, to vote, pay his taxes, and participate in community life. He is expected, in short, to become a stable worker. The social forces which grip him tend to move him toward such a status. One bit of evidence is the decline in occupational and residential movement which the average worker experiences between 35 and 60 years of age.

Davidson and Anderson's study of occupational movement shows this tendency toward occupational stability in later work life. Figure 13.8 is a graphic representation of the time spent in the present occupation by 749 representative San Jose respondents. The first curve represents the respondents in the 20–34-year span; the second curve illustrates the group 35 years and over. The median years spent on the present job for the 20–34-year group is 5.1; the 35-year-and-over group have had 13.1 median years on their present job. Obviously there is more chance for the older workers to have a greater number of years on their present

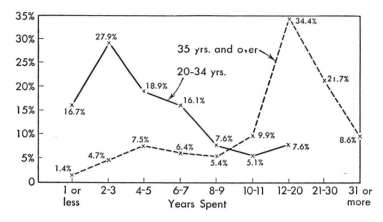

FIG. 13.8. Years Spent in Present Occupation by 749 Respondents Classified by Two Age Groups, 20 to 34 Years of Age and 35 Years of Age and Over. (Reprinted from *Occupational Mobility in an American Community*, by Percy E. Davidson and Dewey Anderson with the permission of the authors and of the publishers, Stanford University Press, 1937, p. 81.)

job. However, the fact that the 35-year-and-over group have a much greater span of time on the present job strengthens the concept of stability. It demonstrates that the stable work period is characterized by the slowing down of horizontal occupational movement.

It can be shown that residential movement also slows down. If the reader will refer to Fig. 13.5 he can again compare residential mobility with age. Moore's study showed that

the highest adult mobility incidence is for ages 24–27, when nearly one in three annually change their residence. The latter thirties reduce the mobility to one in six. In the forties the ratio of moving falls to one in eight while in the fifties the average is nearer to one in nine. One may assume that the upward change found in the sixties is doubtless mobility occasioned by ill-health or made possible by retirement.[30]

These two studies indicate that a stable work period is probably experienced by large groups of workers. Many other indices, such as income, home ownership, marital status, and parenthood could be explored to find additional evidence for increased stability in the age group 35 years and over.

[30] Moore, *op. cit.*, p. 67.

OCCUPATIONAL MOBILITY AND SECURITY

A work history, as we have conceptualized it, contains two interrelated factors; one is the amount of vertical mobility and the other is the amount of occupational stability and security as determined by a special analysis of the horizontal movements. In order to examine the relationship between these two factors we charted the changes in the initial, trial, and stable work periods against the occupational levels in which these changes occurred. The result is a gridlike pattern revealing the vertical mobility of a worker in a given occupational grouping. An example of the charting for a single professional worker is shown in Fig. 13.9.

R-19 began his work life with a part-time job as a soda jerk in a drugstore. After finishing college his first job was teaching. Following a brief trial on this job he entered into a partnership with his uncle as an auto dealer (proprietor). Within two years he was back in teaching, holding the first such job five years, and the second eight years—both stable jobs.

This chart portrays two kinds of changes: (1) changes in the tenure and nature of work positions as described by the initial, trial, and stable jobs within a work history; (2) changes in the occupational classification of the worker as he moves vertically on the grid. This graphic device can be employed to exhibit the work life of groups of workers in each occupational classification. The last job on which the worker is employed is always used as the criterion to place him in an occupational grouping. The charts selected for the occupational groupings reveal modal patterns that distinguish the work histories of persons associated with different occupational levels. The career patterns for the majority of workers in each occupational level are reproduced in Figs. 13.10 through 13.16, inclusive.

CAREER PATTERNS

Certain conclusions may be drawn from inspecting the varied career patterns in each level. We shall comment only on the central tendencies.

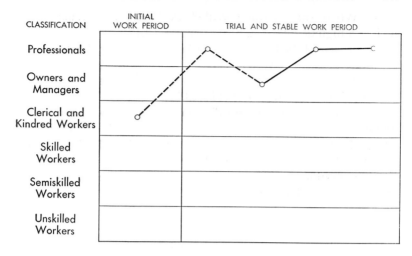

FIG. 13.9. Work History of a Single Professional Worker.

1. Figure 13.10 shows that professional workers start their initial work on many different levels but soon move to the professional level without much intervening experience in other occupations. Once they become professionals, only a few risk trying other jobs. Those who do usually have trial jobs in the proprietary or managerial occupations, or both.

2. The proprietors, managers, and officials show histories of much vertical mobility in the initial and trial periods but also show surprising stability in the stable period of their work lives (see Fig. 13.11).

3. Clerical workers (Fig. 13.12) exhibit some vertical movement before reaching the clerical level but little movement thereafter. An examination of the work histories of business owners and managers shows that in some cases clerical work was a stepping stone. As far as we can determine here and on the basis of other research these cases of climbing are exemplary of a small minority, not a majority of clerical workers.[31]

4. The patterns for the skilled workers and foremen indicate that their work origins are largely in unskilled and semiskilled

[31] See Davidson and Anderson, *op. cit.,* pp. 105–113.

labor. When they become skilled workers and foremen they achieve a high degree of stability (see Fig. 13.13).

5. The semiskilled workers display some vertical movement, for many of them have had early jobs as personal and domestic service workers. Mobility above the semiskilled level, once it is attained, is rather infrequent (Fig. 13.14).

6. The immobility of unskilled and domestic workers is pronounced. Many of them begin their work lives in domestic and personal service jobs. Some move to the unskilled labor classification and there remain; the others never budge from their beginning classification. Both groups experience many jobs and achieve only fleeting security (Figs. 13.15 and 13.16).[32]

Two Contrasting Theories of Career Causation

If you ask a man or a woman what factors have been responsible for his or her success, the answer is usually a simple one. For example, business leaders say:

"Simply got into business I most enjoyed and went to it with all my energy and ability."

"Hard knocks, hard work, long hours, and constant plugging produced results."

"I'm just an average man, but I work at it harder than the average man."

"I was brought up in a small town where I learned that work was the normal lot of man, not a misfortune, as it is taught now."

"Every young man should choose the business in which he is intensely interested—in which he sees possibilities and in which he will be happy—and then stick to this one thing until he gets there. Keep his daily exercise in the outdoors—have plenty of fun and try to save half of his earnings for future investment."

"Everybody else being equal, I believe that friendship is very important to getting ahead."

"Enthroned within the consciousness of every man who accomplishes much in service to civilization there is a SUPER-PERSONALITY who silently drives, who chides, who commands, but who rarely commends. This personality shapes the destiny of the individual. A man's wife may supplement and give greater power to such influence."[33]

[32] Cf. Lipset and Bendix, *op. cit.*, p. 153; Joseph R. Gusfield, "Occupational Roles and Forms of Enterprise," *American Journal of Sociology*, May, 1961, pp. 571–580.

[33] F. W. Taussig and C. S. Joslyn, *American Business Leaders*, Macmillan, 1932, pp. 299–301.

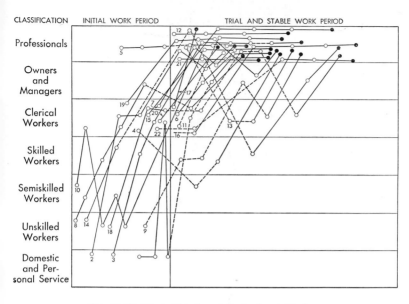

FIG. 13.10. Work Histories of Professional Workers.

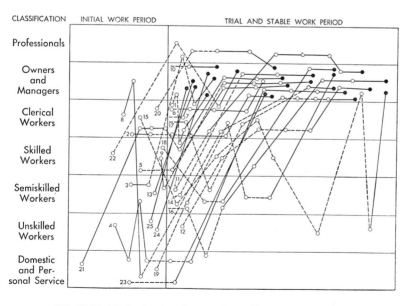

FIG. 13.11. Work Histories of Proprietors, Managers, and Officials.

579

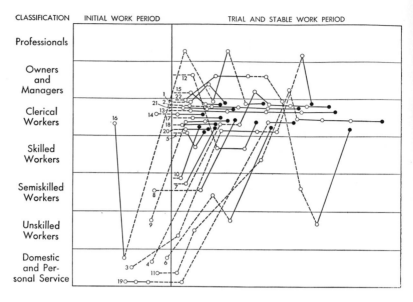

FIG. 13.12. Work Histories of Clerical Workers.

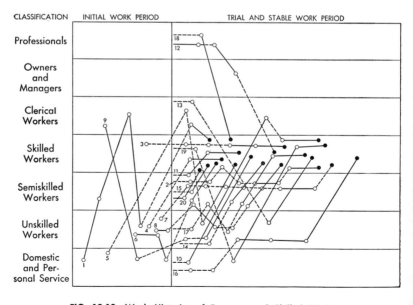

FIG. 13.13. Work Histories of Foremen and Skilled Workers.

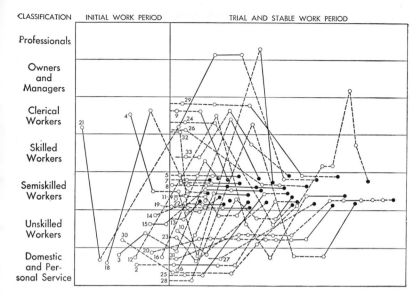

FiG. 13.14. Work Histories of Semiskilled Workers.

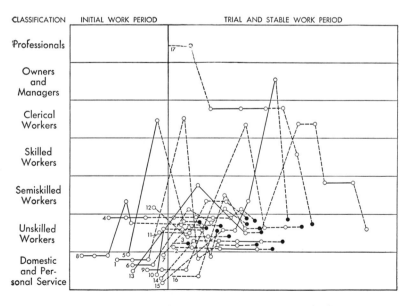

FIG. 13.15. Work Histories of Unskilled Workers.

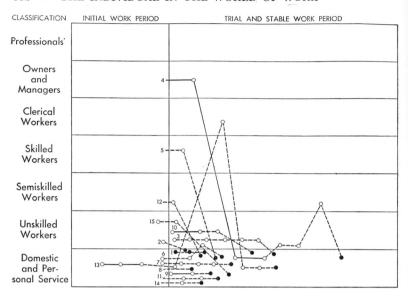

FIG. 13.16. Work Histories of Domestic and Personal Service Workers.

These beliefs represent the conviction that personal motivation and hard work explain the career pattern and that occupational success can be attained regardless of social background. This kind of thinking might be called the *individual* causation theory of career patterns. In contrast, the network of interrelated social factors that have been demonstrated to be associated with occupational levels might become the basis of a *social* causation theory of career patterns. Such a theory would impute the origin and development of a career to those social factors that have been identified. Relationships can be demonstrated between occupational level of a worker and (1) the father's occupation, (2) the historical circumstances, (3) the father's income and education, (4) financial aid and influential contacts, (5) social and economic conditions.[34] An accurate weighing of the facts will demonstrate that the social background of the worker is a base of opportunities and limitations. As opportunities are enlarged the *possibilities*

[34] Cf. Lipset and Bendix, *op. cit.;* W. Lloyd Warner and James Abegglen, *Big Business Leaders in America,* Harper, 1955.

of occupational mobility are increased. Personal motivation and native ability are necessary to an enlarging career pattern. However, there is good evidence that the social backgrounds of workers are the crucial determiners in the *number* who are able to come into various occupational levels. The reservoir of human ability among all socioeconomic levels is greater than is generally assumed. The discounting of ability goes on because observers are unable to visualize the possible growth of millions of workers who if placed within the kind of social settings which have been shown to be correlated with the upper occupational classifications would acquire new outlooks, motivations, and work skills. Some interesting evidence to substantiate this position comes from Arthur Kornhauser's Chicago Attitude Study.[35] He asked the following questions of his Chicago sample:

Do you feel that your children or those of your friends and neighbors have as much opportunity as they should have?
Do you like the kind of work you do?
Do you feel that your pay or salary is fair?
Would you say you are treated well by the people you work for?
Do you feel that there is any danger of losing your job?
Do you feel that you have as much opportunity to enjoy life as you should have?
Do you feel that you have a good chance to get ahead in life and become fairly well off?

The principal findings by income and typical occupational groups are summarized in Table 13.3. It is apparent that attitudinal responses to the above questions are correlated positively with income and occupation. A high correlation is indicated by the rather steep gradient from highest to lowest groups. Kornhauser's conclusion is that "the figures tend to support the hypothesis presented earlier that the differences among socioeconomic classes are largely differences in contentment, life satisfaction, and personal adjustment."

An Equilibrium Theory to Account for Career Causation

Forces making for the location of workers at various occupational levels have been identified and described. *Social back-*

[35] Arthur Kornhauser, "Analysis of Class Structure of Contemporary American Society—Psychological Bases of Class Divisions," in G. W. Hartmann and T. Newcomb, *Industrial Conflict,* Dryden, 1939, pp. 242–243.

TABLE 13.3 Comparisons of Groups on Personal Satisfaction Questions; Percent Satisfied vs. Dissatisfied on Following Questions

	Children's Opportunity	Kind of Work Done	Pay	Treatment by Employer	Job Security	Opportunity to Enjoy Life	Chance to Get Ahead
Income Levels							
A (over $5000)	83	95	90	96	89	82	96
B ($2000–5000)	60	91	69	90	80	69	78
C ($1000–2000)	46	81	53	86	72	55	69
D (under $1000)	39	67	34	77	49	36	43
Occupational Groups							
Major business executives	91	99	94	99	91	85	98
Engineers (professional)	72	95	70	93	84	71	92
Minor business executives and small owners	65	91	72	90	89	63	80
Office workers	49	74	55	92	82	63	87
Skilled manual workers	49	85	53	82	67	52	55
Unskilled and semiskilled	44	71	47	82	64	48	61

ground, native ability, historical circumstance, and acquired personality traits are the influences determining a given career pattern. These forces may be considered as intertwined and pulling upon each worker with different intensities at various times in his career. By the time a man or woman reaches 35 or 40 years of age the forces often become equilibrated, and what the occupational history is from 35 years to 60 years is a fair index of whatever stability the worker will experience.

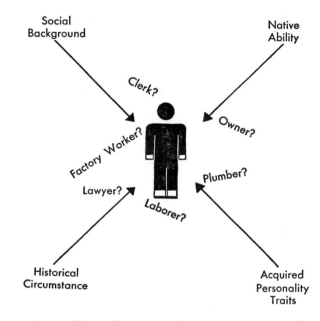

FIG. 13.17. Equilibrium of Four Forces That Determine Occupational Level.

Figure 13.17 shows the resolution of forces that bring about stability in a career pattern. How these forces work themselves out for contemporary American workers will be described.

PORTRAYAL OF CAREER PATTERNS

If occupational histories of a large number of workers in all occupational levels are analyzed, definite tendencies can be discerned. These tendencies reflect varying degrees of struggle for occupational stability and security. When the Ohio survey was made by the writers, the work histories were analyzed for the modal patterns. The professional, proprietary-managerial, clerical, and skilled workers have already been described as those having relatively high occupational security. The semiskilled, unskilled, and domestic and personal service workers are known to have relatively low occupational security as we have defined it. In Figs. 13.18 and 13.19 modal career patterns of the major occupational groups are shown divided by their degrees of occupational security. These histories show the trial and stable jobs held in each group. We have tried to suggest how the histories in each level may be affected by differences in such related variables as (1) the modal education of the fathers, (2) the occupation of the fathers, (3) the years of education attained by their sons and daughters.

The Occupational Pyramid

It would be useful if all the research data including our own from the above could be brought together so that a rather complete picture of a typical worker in each occupational grouping might be presented. Unfortunately studies to date have not been sufficiently numerous to make a full portrayal for the United States labor force. Those reported include the work of Davidson and Anderson, Miller and Form, W. S. Woytinsky, Lipset and Bendix, Gladys Palmer, A. J. Jaffe and R. O. Carleton, Reiss and the United States Census researchers, especially that of Alba M. Edwards.[36] These writers do not give all the information that is desired but the social background of the labor force can now be drawn in outline. All agree that the socioeconomic levels of workers form a rough pyramid composed of the unskilled workers at the base and ranging through levels of semiskilled, skilled, and clerical, farmers, proprietors, managers, and officials, and professional persons. These groupings can be seen to be the

---

[36] Studies not cited previously are W. S. Woytinsky, *Labor in the United States,* Social Science Research Council, 1958; Dewey Anderson and Percy E. Davidson, *Ballots and the Democratic Class Struggle,* Stanford, 1943; Gladys Palmer, *Labor Mobility in Six Cities,* Social Science Research Council, 1954; A. J. Jaffe and R. O. Carleton, *Occupational Mobility in the United States, 1930–1960,* Columbia, 1954; Albert J. Reiss Jr., *et al., Occupations and Social Structure,* Free Press, 1961.

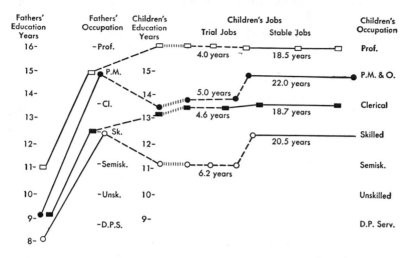

FIG. 13.18. Career Patterns for High-Security Occupational Levels.

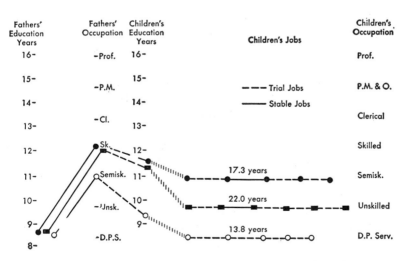

FIG. 13.19. Career Patterns for Low-Security Occupational Levels.

result of institutional forces, many of which have been described. The description of the average characteristics drawn from the sources indicated provides a set of summarizing sketches.[37] Specific occupational studies also offer confirming evidence.

Professional workers

The typical professional worker is a male, probably a teacher, lawyer, physician, or clergyman. He is born into an upper-middle- or upper-class family. His father is a business proprietor or manager who has received an above average education. He encourages the son to plan on going to college, which he does with the financial aid of his parents. The son enrolls in a professional curriculum and begins his specialized training. He may engage in part-time work for pay during college days, but upon completion of his professional schooling he moves directly into his professional career without floundering. During his first four years out of college he moves twice as he seeks a "good" firm or a "good" location for his professional practice. He finds what he wants for a permanent location and settles down in an urban community. At about twenty-five or twenty-six years of age he marries a college graduate about twenty-three years of age who comes from an upper-middle- or upper-class family. He receives an income which permits him to live above the comfort level. However, he limits the size of his family. He buys his home and lives in the better, more modern residential area in the community. The rise and fall of business activity usually curtails his income but seldom forces him to move from his job or to another community. He is, in fact, one of the most stable workers, occupationally, of any group in the community. He has high prestige and is widely sought as a leader in community organizations. He takes pride in the fact that his child is getting every educational and social opportunity that is available to the home or the community. His child is healthy and likes all kinds of outdoor sports. His boy or girl looks forward to college, makes a good record, and graduates

[37] Data on size of family secured from *Recent Social Trends in the United States*, McGraw-Hill, 1934, pp. 685–686; data on age at marriage from Joseph K. Folsom, *The Family and Democratic Society*, Wiley, 1943, pp. 129–131; data on educational expectation from W. Lloyd Warner, Robert J. Havighurst, and Martin B. Loeb, *Who Shall Be Educated?* Harper, 1947, pp. 58–72. See also Jaffe and Carleton, *op. cit.*

as he did. He watches his boy get established in a profession (or his girl marry a "good" professional man). He comes to know with finality, as he always really knew, that ability, hard work, and careful managing are responsible for individual success. He and his son usually vote Republican. Toward the end of his life, he looks back on a long career and a healthy life, satisfied that his contribution to society was substantial and that the future is safe in the hands of men like his son.[38]

Proprietors, managers, or officials

The second group is composed of merchants, business managers, farm owners and managers, manufacturers, and government officials. There is such a wide range that it is a difficult group to typify. Yet certain characteristics can be singled out as defining the "businessman." The typical businessman is a manager with all or some ownership interests in the business with which he is associated. He comes from a home where his father was either a farmer or a business proprietor. The ownership or management of property has always characterized the occupational setting. Generally, his home is rated as an upper-middle- or upper-class home in the community. His father has an education above the average (some high school) but regrets that he did not get more. He encourages the son to plan on either a professional or a business career. His son usually decides on the business career and he completes a college education. He makes his start in business and begins moving around to find better opportunities. Within five years he has moved to three different jobs but finally secures a "good" position as a minor executive. During this trial work period, he marries a college-trained woman who is from an upper-middle- or upper-class home. They limit their family to two or three children. He buys his home and lives in the best residential area of the city. His parents sometimes help him by loans or gifts to get started right. He joins clubs limited to higher-status groups and takes an active part in community life. His children are encouraged to participate in carefully selected groups

[38] A. M. Carr-Saunders, *The Professions,* Clarendon Press, 1933; A. J. Reiss, Jr., "Occupational Mobility of Professional Workers," *American Sociological Review,* December, 1955, pp. 693–700; Logan Wilson, *The Academic Man, A Study in the Sociology of the Profession,* Oxford University Press, 1942; Roy Lewis and Angus Maude, *Professional People in England,* Harvard, 1953.

in the neighborhood, in the schools, in the church, and in the summer camp. As he becomes a proprietor, his father helps him to get started with a business of his own by using family connections at the bank. He takes pride in the fact that the businessmen run the community. He is usually a confident man, but so many things seem to affect business that he is subject to fears. Depressions make it very difficult for the businessman, and the high rate of mortality in some businesses puts proprietorship in a precarious position. However, the above average proprietor has a high community standing, property assets, insurance policies, and savings which enable him to weather most economic disturbances. All in all he can count on more years of stable work life than can any other group of workers.

After his children are married and placed in the business class of some community, he can approach later maturity with general satisfaction that he has played an active part in managing his business, his home, and his community. He is convinced that there is plenty of opportunity for anyone to do what he has done, but it takes ability and hard work. He and members of his family vote Republican. They help support the Episcopalian or Presbyterian Church. They believe that any wealth they may have accumulated is a just reward for the work they have done. As grandparents they look with pride and anticipation to the day when their estate will be passed on to their children and their grandchildren. They have learned that money is important.[39]

Clerical and kindred workers

The typical clerk is a male who is a salesman, bookkeeper, or store clerk. He comes from a lower-middle-class home. His father had some high school education and was employed as a skilled or clerical worker. He encourages his son or daughter to plan on finishing high school and to secure some college or business training. His youngster does enroll in college and at considerable sacrifice to the parents is able to get a year or two of college training. For his first full-time job the son is able to secure a clerical posi-

[39] Cf. Delbert C. Miller, "The Seattle Business Leader," *Pacific Northwest Business*, February, 1956, pp. 5–12; Warner and Abegglen, *op. cit.;* R. Bendix, *Higher Civil Servants in American Society*, University of Colorado Press, 1948; Nigel Walker, *Morale in the Civil Service, A Study of the Desk Worker,* Aldine, 1959.

tion. He changes jobs twice within the first five years, hoping to get a better-paying job. He is proud to be a member of the white-collar group. At twenty-three or twenty-four he marries a clerk from an office in town—a young woman of twenty-one from a lower-middle-class family. He receives a lower income than his father but has higher status. He lives at a minimum comfort scale of living and feels that one child is all they can afford to raise. He finds that it is very difficult to manage their budget since their needs for clothing run high. He never seems to get ahead although his work is very stable. They rent their home in a middle-class section and are looking forward to buying a house in the future. He knows there is better money in the factory, but he prefers the associations he has in the office or the freedom he has on the road. He is trying to see that his child gets a chance to go right to the top and not remain a clerk all his life. He sees to it that his child understands the importance of education and plans to get a college education. He tells his daughter that it is important to get her education if she wants to marry well.

After his child is raised and educated he continues to plug away on his job. He is satisfied that the education which he gave his boy or daughter will give him or her a better opportunity than he had.[40] Sometimes he votes Republican; sometimes Democratic.

Skilled workers

The typical skilled artisan comes from the home of a skilled or farmer father. He is a machinist, a carpenter, a foreman, or a painter. His background is usually identified as lower middle. His father finished the eighth grade and worked as an apprentice in a machine shop until he became a skilled machinist. He encouraged his son to get a good education but is proud when the son shows interest in skilled work. He does not force him to finish high school. He arranges with a friend who is a foreman in another department at the plant to get the boy started so that he can learn the machinist's trade. The boy starts at semiskilled jobs and is moved about on various jobs to build his skills. At the end of six or seven years he is promoted to a skilled job, where he remains most of his working life. At twenty-two years of age he marries a girl from a foreman's family. They have two children.

[40] Francis Donovan, *The Saleslady*, University of Chicago Press, 1929.

They feel that they are quite fortunate. They have a steady job which pays well and they are respected in their neighorhood. They have started to buy their home, a substantial house in a good working-class neighborhood.

They encourage their children to make the most of their educational opportunities. At home the children hear a good deal about the problems of labor and the importance of strong organization to protect the skilled worker against hard times. The children learn that skilled workers are the aristocracy of labor, an abler, better-organized group of workers who play a strong part in the political elections and mostly vote Democrat. After the children are married and the boy is established in a good trade, the skilled worker continues to take pride in the achievements which his skill makes possible. Under his hands new construction and new machinery are built. In war he likes to hear himself called a soldier of production. He feels that as long as he has a strong union back of him he has a security that he needs.[41]

Semiskilled workers

The number of semiskilled workers has grown with the mechanization of industry. A typical semiskilled worker is a male who operates a semiautomatic machine tool, drives a truck, or is an apprentice tradesman. He begins his working career on the farm or on the manual labor level and remains there all the rest of his life. He comes from a lower-middle-class home. His father was a farmer or manual worker with average education, but the children did not like school too well and dropped out before finishing high school. The boy got his first job as a truck driver. He got tired of that after one year and went into the factory as a drill press operator. At twenty years of age he married a girl who lived in his neighborhood. They have had a rather difficult life. They have never had an income which permitted them to accumulate savings. They have three children and there has been more than an average amount of sickness. The doctor bills

[41] R. C. Stone, "Factory Organizations and Vertical Mobility," *American Sociological Review,* February, 1953, pp. 28–35; Richard R. Myers, "Interpersonal Relations in the Building Industry," *Applied Anthropolgy,* Spring, 1946, pp. 1–7.

have always kept them nearly broke. They rent their house. They have thought of buying but their income is so uncertain they are afraid to undertake it. A layoff or unemployment can come any time.

They try to give their children the best they can but there are a lot of things the family simply cannot afford. They live in an old house and drive a second-hand automobile. Their children associate with some rowdies in the neighborhood but there is not very much they can do about it. They breathe a sigh of relief as well as regret as their children marry and start out on their own. Release from the financial burden of the children comes just in time because there is talk of giving men past fifty their quit slips. The semiskilled worker sees a strong union as his only hope of security. He votes Democratic because that party, he believes, gives labor more support. He says there is little hope for decent wages and working conditions unless labor sticks together and fights for its rights.[42] He is worried about automation.

Unskilled workers

The unskilled workers, forming an extensive labor force, include factory and farm laborers, domestic and personal service workers. The women predominate in domestic service but males are in the overwhelming majority in other types of unskilled labor. The typical unskilled worker comes from the home of skilled and semiskilled workers. His father received an eighth-grade education and became an apprentice on a semiskilled job. The son completes grammar school and receives a year of high school. He starts to work at fifteen years of age as an un-skilled laborer. When he reaches about twenty years of age he marries a girl eighteen years old. They go to live in a rented house in the poorest residential section of the city. They have three children but their income is not sufficient to support them at the American standard of living. They have a great deal of sickness and are often in debt. They are not able to do much for the children except to keep them fed and clothed and get them

[42] Cf. W. F. Cottrell, *The Railroader*, Stanford, 1948; Charles R. Walker and Robert Guest, *The Man on the Assembly Line*, Harvard, 1952; J. S. Ellsworth, *Factory Folkways*, Yale, 1952; Eli Chinoy, *Automobile Workers and the American Dream*, Doubleday, 1955.

to school. The children work at odd jobs whenever they can find anything to do. The father and mother will both work when the children can be left alone. Neither can find a job which they can hold for long. When layoffs and unemployment come the family draws on unemployment insurance as long as it can. When they have exhausted their insurance they go on relief. They cannot seem to get ahead financially. A good home or a substantial savings account is out of their reach. They feel that they are doing well if they keep their health and get along without going into debt. They believe something has to be done in this country to help the little fellow more.[43] They vote Democratic, if they vote.

The Occupational Chain

A chain of cause-and-effect relationships is suggested by the stratified conditions that have been described. The social and economic status of the family, associated particularly with the occupation, education, and income of the chief breadwinner, exerts a strong and decisive effect upon the habits and attitudes and subsequent life patterns of its members. The links in the chain of cause and effect appear as follows:

1. The first job, obtained by and through the help of friends or relatives, dependent largely on the background, place of residence, occupation, and connections of the father.
2. Discovery of a "regular" occupation and the attainment of an occupational level at approximately that of the father, which somehow fixes the type of employment followed throughout the working life though not the specific jobs obtained.
3. The range of income associated with the employment secured on the occupational level attained.
4. The scale of living for self and family permitted by the occupational income received.
5. The place of residence and type of living permitted or encouraged by the occupation followed and the income received.
6. The consequent status or degree of prestige accorded by society to workers in this occupational level and living on this particular plane of well-being.
7. The degree of social and political influence wielded by the worker and his family.

[43] William F. Whyte, *Human Relations in the Restaurant Industry,* McGraw-Hill, 1948; F. Zweig, *The British Worker,* Penguin, 1952; K. Archibald, *Wartime Shipyard,* University of California Press, 1947.

8. The reflex effect of this status on the worker and his family, resulting in family attitude and conduct.
9. The consequent degree of health and personal and cultural attainments of the family, and their influence on the children.
10. As the cycle is renewed in the oncoming generation, the incentives, schooling, occupational training, and personal equipment of the children for competition in the industrial world and for the consumption of goods and services.[44]

When this cycle is broken, increased formal education is the usual elevator of social mobility.

THE SOCIAL BACKGROUND OF THE STABLE WORK PERIOD

Walter Pitkin has made a national slogan with his book *Life Begins at Forty*. Though a significant section of life is still to be lived after forty years of age, there is more reason to believe that the main outline of a person's life is fairly well drawn by forty or earlier. Indeed, if one is talking about occupational life, the probability of entering a given occupational level can be predicted for a worker with some degree of accuracy as soon as the father's occupation, income, and education are known. Even the first part-time jobs of the initial work period show low but significant relationships with the regular occupation the worker will come to pursue. These relationships derive from uniformities that grow out of social background and do not take into account personality traits, native ability, and historical circumstance. It takes some time for all of these influences to be tested out in the career of the worker. How long does it take? What stabilizing forces surround him as he grows in age and work experience?

By the time a man or woman is thirty or thirty-five years of age it is expected that the trial work period is about over and that the regular occupation has been entered. People say, "He should be pretty well set by now." This does not mean as he enters the stable work period that no further horizontal or vertical mobility will occur. Rather it implies a slowing down, a growing gravitation, a fixity within a given occupation and a given work plant. It was for this reason that in seeking an index of occupational

[44] Anderson and Davidson, *Ballots and the Democratic Class Struggle, op. cit.*, pp. 88–89.

stability and security we defined trial jobs as those held less than three years, whereas stable jobs were called those on which the worker spent three years or more. In Figs. 13.18 and 13.19 the trial jobs and the stable jobs of the modal career patterns of workers in the Ohio sample were shown. Professionals, proprietors, managers, clerical, and skilled workers were shown to have trial work periods of from 4.0 years to 6.2 years and then for each of them a long stable work period. For the semiskilled and unskilled laborer, the career pattern is characterized by a sequence of many trial jobs interspersed with an average of one stable job. For domestic service workers occupational stability does not usually occur at all. These patterns, it must be remembered, represent the typical job sequences for workers active now in the various occupational groups and not those who have completed their careers. Although occupational stability is not associated with all occupational levels or individual workers in equal measure, nonetheless certain stabilizing forces come to surround most workers and press them toward more stable career patterns.

Forces Stabilizing Careers

1. Realization or rationalization of the trial period goal

During the trial period the worker has been looking for a job he likes—that is to say, a job which fits his interests, his ideas about good working conditions, and his wishes for recognition and security. As he changes jobs he usually comes closer to "what he wants." This ordinarily means that he has gotten started in the occupation he wishes to pursue and has found an acceptable company or work plant in which to work. It does not necessarily mean that ambition is now satisfied. Far from it. New needs give rise to new goals. Strivings for more prestige, more money, or more authority may serve as a driving motivation quickening the pace of life rather than diminishing it. But what is important in understanding the significance of the stable work perod is the fact that the goals of the trial period do come to complete or partial fulfillment, and when this happens the rather frenzied mobility of the trial period is dampened.

Not all reach the goal they had earlier nourished in imagination and hope. But many of these persons defend their failure to attain the higher ranks and accept a more limited goal. Some accept their achievements with tolerance, others defend their egos by rationalization and substitution, and still others relieve their frustrated feelings by projection of the blame upon other persons. Whatever the reaction, it is apparent that many make their peace (on their own reservations) with the work position they have attained. The reason is that other pressures have come to act upon them. Among these job seniority looms large.

2. Seniority

As a worker acquires seniority, he stores up advantages over his fellow workers. Sometimes these advantages are formally written out in provisions for increases in wage or salary, or security against layoffs and dismissal. At other times they pile up as expectations in the minds of the worker's associates and in the mind of his employer. The prestige of experience displays itself in promotions, assignments to the better machines or offices, and other special privileges of many different kinds. Seniority becomes a kind of *insurance* against the risks of economic fluctuations which create unemployment in the work force. Moreover, as a worker increases his seniority within a given work position, routines often build habits which incapacitate him for further occupational movement. He becomes stamped in the habits of his work and finds his technical and emotional adaptability lessened. He "just wouldn't be happy doing anything else." If he does leave he may face the necessity of starting over in some other work plant in new duties without seniority. He may find himself engaged in competition with ambitious workers who are making their bids to attain higher work positions including his own. If you talk with him, he will tell you that "you think twice" before embarking on such hazardous occupational voyages.

3. Age

Age has a prestige which exhibits itself differently in various occupational pursuits. Young men may have unusual opportunities in a rapidly changing field of activity such as physics, aeronautics, and sociology. New enterprises—plastics, television, and prefabricated housing—may open new channels for young men and women. However, the upper levels of administration are not usually open to young men and women. Even the concept of "young" is redefined for administrative posts. A man of forty may well be described in such connection as "young." Advancing age can carry with it increasing prestige. As long as both younger and older men feel more confidence in the latter, it can be expected that older men will command respect and prestige that cannot be easily matched by younger men. Moreover, it is not uncommon to see older men and women accorded special rights and privileges. "You just don't talk to an older man like you do to a young fellow." Respect for age still survives in the culture in spite of the modern challenges of equal pay and deference for equal work. Therefore, age is a badge of experience and maturity gives certain advantages in many occupational pursuits. These advantages tend to stabilize career patterns of workers. Indeed, age acts also in a negative way to halt occupational movement. Conservatism often increases with age and is a psychological block which may diminish the willingness of a worker to change to a different work position and to assume new habits and risks.

4. Income

With advancing age and seniority income usually increases. Since the most common index of success in America is the pay envelope, the culminating rewards of ability, seniority, age, and experience are supposedly measurable in the dollars and cents returned. In classical economic theory the worker earns what he produces. The pay check, it is assumed, reflects, therefore, the contribution of the worker to the company. From it he can ascertain his relative worth to his employer. He is pleased to find that he is usually considered more valuable and rewarded with a larger wage or salary as he builds up service. Income advancement often provides a sense of career progress in the stable period comparable to the occupational movements of the trial work period.

5. Marriage and family

Financial burdens as well as financial rewards hold the worker in a more fixed position. As marriage and children add to the demands upon the family income, it is no longer possible to risk long periods of looking around for a new job or to assume the expenses of moving the family and furniture to a new locality. Many workers say it doesn't pay in the long run to move even though the new job would pay more.

It is also true that the financial burden of marriage and children can sometimes be bargaining assets which open new occupational opportunities and increase income. That is, the employer may feel that marriage and children make the worker "more stable." He is more strongly motivated and takes the "rough going" better. Moreover, there is less chance of his seeking amorous adventures that will complicate his business life.

When all of these assets are capitalized there remains still another appeal that can often be translated into increased income, the appeal to what Willard Waller called the pathos of marriage and parenthood. Implicit in the mores of monogomy is the belief that it is a good thing to marry and have children. The struggles which such responsibilities entail evoke a sympathetic, pitying, approving reaction. One who does such a good thing as marrying and rearing children deserves certain privileges. From then on, he is entitled to trade upon the pathos of the marriage relation in applying for a job, asking for a raise, or seeking promotion.

Thus marriage and children can be both reward and burden. In either instance the effect is to cause the worker to remain on the job and to diminish the possibility of moving either from his job or from his community.

6. Home ownership

Most homeowners share their pleasure or burden, as the case may be, with their banker, who holds the mortgage. To put it bluntly, they are in debt, and usualy this debt runs into thousands of dollars. Each month for ten, fifteen, or twenty-five years a payment must be made to the bank. In paying for his house, the worker is usualy buying the most expensive consumer good he will ever purchase. This good cannot be taken with him if he wishes to move. He is therefore faced with the necessity of selling his house if he wishes to accept a job in another locality. The risk of loss sometimes is a large consideration. The employer and the worker both recognize that home ownership tends to "tie you down." The employer knows he can count upon his home-owning workers to think twice before leaving their jobs for others, especially in the out-of-town market. Some will be deterred by the financial difficulties and losses that may be encountered. Others will remain because of their pride in their houses. Therefore, the answer to the question "Does he own his home?" gives aditional evidence of the probable stability of the worker on the job and in the community.

7. Friendship ties

We have spoken of financial rewards and burdens, of incentives and deterrents that keep workers stable on a job. Equally strong are the emotional bonds which the worker has forged with his society. His friendships represent a part of himself. First they are actively shared, then stored in the personality as memories. People often tell the worker that friendships are the most important possessions of life. Some of these friendships are in the plant and some are in the community. His wife and children share equally in certain of his friendships and in addition have circles of their own. Cutting each one of these friendship bonds to live and work in another community requires family surgery of a painful nature. When people say, "They won't leave Toledo because all of their friends live here," they are speaking about a major resistance to mobility.

8. Institutional ties

Related to friendship ties are connections with institutions and organizations. The children must be taken from their "good" school. The family is agreed that they have never been happier in any church than their community church. The Masonic lodge to which the father belongs is the best in the state. The mother has held all the chairs in the local Eastern Star. And so it goes. These ties lash the family to the community and it is only with difficulty that they may be broken.

9. Identification with work plant and community

The strongest emotional weld occurs when all of the emotional ties result in identity of the worker and his family with the work plant and the community. This merger of self with society is indicated when the worker speaks of "my company," "our city," "my club," or "my church." References to these organizations in conversations or in the newspaper are matters for emotional response. Praiseworthy references fill the person with pride; critical references evoke defensive reactions. Even the climate in the region, although insufferable, may be elaborately rationalized in order to impart a tolerable character to it!

All of these stabilizing forces operate either in totality or in part. Their action explains the decline in occupational and residential mobility which is associated with the years of work life that have been called the stable work period. However, the career patterns of many workers show that those forces are matched in intensity by disruptive forces. The latter break career patterns into insecure and unstable modes of work life, especially among semiskilled and unskilled workers.

Forces Disrupting Careers

1. Cyclical and seasonal unemployment

The greatest menace to stable career patterns is cyclical and seasonal unemployment. The depressed economic market hits semiskilled and unskilled workers hardest. These are the expendables. In contrast to the employment of executives, and specialists who are carried as overhead costs, the lower occupational levels are at the mercy of the sales chart and the profit margins of their employer. Full records on unemployment are not available, but such estimates as have been made confirm the opinion that unemployment never disappears and rarely falls much below 5 percent of the labor forces.[45] This would include workers out of work for short periods when changing jobs, and workers forced into longer periods of unemployment by seasonal and depressed market conditions. It would also include another form of unemployment which often has a very disruptive effect on the worker: technological unemployment.

2. Technological unemployment

Technological unemployment not only removes the man from his job but also forces him to change his job. A new machine or process can eliminate the need for skills which a worker has built

[45] J. Frederic Dewhurst and associates, *America's Needs and Resources,* Twentieth Century Fund, 1947, p. 550; cf. with current rates in *Monthly Labor Review.*

up in the course of a lifetime. Unless he can learn new skills he may discover that he has become unwanted. Machine methods of coal mining and cotton picking are but two examples of the technological apparatus disturbing and threatening to disturb the work of millions of workers. Automation of industrial and service processes is crowding out old skills and displacing both manual and white-collar workers at a rapid rate.

3. Sickness and physical disability

Sickness and accident are two additional perils to career patterns. Sickness can sap vitality and destroy initiative. Accidents can bring total or partial disability. These misfortunes may curtail the possibilities for a white-collar worker. A manual worker may be so incapacitated as to be unable to return to work. Unable to stand, unable to lift, or unable to keep up with his machine, he may have to shift to quite different work—if such work is available.

4. Divorce

When the family is broken by divorce, the social and institutional ties of the worker are changed. Some of his former friends may blame him for his part in disrupting the marriage. In consequence, he may try to avoid them and even some of his associates. He may feel young and fancy-free again and desirous of building a new life for himself. In such a mood, the worker may wish to change his occupation or his community or perhaps both. He is potentially an unstable worker; at best, a less stable worker.

5. Chance risks of life

There are such risks of life as fire, theft, flood, tornado, implication in crime, war, business failure, and death of friends and relatives that can markedly change the social world of the individual. These risks must always be reckoned with in analyzing certain career patterns. They shake up the personal habits and attitudes of the worker and change his established ways of living. The fact of risk gives the lie to the belief that all men and women are free to choose and can guide their lives on whatever course they may wish. Many careers seem to have followed sets of changing pressures which have caused them to move more like bobbing corks than like well-directed vessels.

THE STABLE WORK LIFE IN PERSPECTIVE

The stable work period can be understood now as a social and cultural experience. Some social forces tend to anchor the individual to a given job and to a given work organization; others act like crosscurrents to jeopardize occupational stability and security. All workers as they enter into middle-work life are exposed to these forces and counterforces. Some emerge with lifelong histories of stability and security; others are caught in the disruptive forces and have work histories that reveal high occupational and residential mobility. Yet whatever may be the history of a given career, there is a common set of cultural expectations and experiences which mark off the stable work period.

The retired period breaks active work life in a gradual or abrupt manner. In either case the retired worker must now learn to play new roles. He may find himself an independent proprietor of a small house in which he and his wife live, a provider of a home for his children or a dependent of his children, or a ward of the state. In any case he can look back on a long life filled with many experiences. A central core of those experiences has been built up of innumerable strands of work relationships and areas of life influenced by his work. He can remember his father at his work, particularly *how* his father worked and what he thought about work. He can recall his school days and the chores he had about the home. He remembers his first part-time jobs and how much money he was paid on some of them. The early years of struggle on his first full-time jobs come back to him as memories of successes and failures in the midst of marriage and parenthood. The middle years in good times and bad times stand out as rewards in the forms of a house, grandchildren, a promotion, a new car—or perhaps they appear as painful memories of deprivation and unemployment. The retirement years can be seen as burdens and joys. Work and leisure have blended together. A lifetime of work is concluded.[46]

[46] E. A. Friedmann, R. J. Havighurst, *et al., The Meaning of Work and Retirement,* University of Chicago Press, 1954.

SELECTED BIBLIOGRAPHY

Anderson, Dewey, and Percy E. Davidson, *Ballots and the Democratic Class Struggle,* Stanford, 1943.

Friedmann, E. A., R. J. Havighurst, *et al., The Meaning of Work and Retirement,* University of Chicago Press, 1954.

Ginzberg, Eli, *et al., Occupational Choice,* Columbia, 1951.

Goldsen, Rose K., Morris Rosenberg, Robin M. Williams, Jr., and Edward A. Suchman, *What College Students Think,* Van Nostrand, 1960.

Gusfield, Joseph R., "Occupational Roles and Forms of Enterprise," *American Journal of Sociology,* May, 1961, pp. 571–580.

Havemann, Ernest, and Patricia Salter West, *They Went to College,* Harcourt, Brace, 1952.

Hiller, E. T., *Social Relations and Structures,* Harper, 1947, chap. 23, "Child Status," and chap. 24, "Youth and Adolescence."

Hollingshead, A. B., *Elmtown's Youth,* Wiley, 1949, especially chap. 11, "Jobs and Ideas of Jobs," and chap. 14, "Toil and Trouble."

Lipset, Seymour Martin, and Reinhard Bendix, *Social Mobility in Industrial Society,* University of California Press, 1959.

McClelland, David C., *et al. Talent and Society,* Van Nostrand, 1958.

Nosow, Sigmund, and William H. Form (eds.), *Man, Work, and Society,* Basic Books, 1962. A comprehensive compilation of recent research on occupations.

Reiss, Albert J., "Occupational Mobility of Professional Workers," *American Sociological Review,* December, 1955, pp. 693–700.

Rosenberg, Morris, *Occupations and Values,* Free Press, 1957.

Super, Donald E., *The Psychology of Careers,* Harper, 1957.

Warner, W. Lloyd, Robert J. Havighurst, and Martin B. Loeb, *Who Shall Be Educated?* Harper, 1947.

Wilensky, Harold, "Work, Careers and Social Integration," *International Social Science Journal,* Fall, 1960, pp. 555–558.

CHAPTER 14

Personality
and
Organization

THE WILL TO WORK IN INDUSTRIAL SOCIETY

Production of every good and every service rests upon human will and purpose. The industrial revolution profoundly affected the work and status relationships of almost all workers. Some changes accompanying the industrial organization of society are apparent in the emergence of large corporations, the growth of great cities, and the modern ways of living which automobiles, radios, and movies have brought about. But the emergence of a national and international market for goods has had many implications which are not so immediately discerned. In earlier centuries duties were owed to a small local community which was mainly self-supporting and engaged in production for use rather than for surpluses to be placed on a market for sale. The religious view of work which predominated considered that a man was "called" to his vocation. The idea was held that each man, in performing his task well, fulfilled an earthly stewardship before God. Each person could thus feel that he not only contributed to his own and others' well-being and security but also gained in personal worth. Out of this belief grew the further idea that every approved calling had *equal* worth in the eyes of men and of God. In such a society men carried a sense of moral worth and of economic justice.

With the industrial revolution came the large market. Workers left the land to enter the factory, store, and mine. Work became more and more regarded as a source of gains—as a commodity to be purchased by an employer when sales were brisk and to be removed when the market was bad. Karl Polanyi points out in *The Great Transformation:*

> As the development of the factory system had been organized as part of a process of buying and selling, therefore labor, land, and money had to be transformed into commodities in order to keep production going. . . . Of the three, one stands out: labor is the technical term used for human beings, in so far as they are not employers but employed; it follows that henceforth the organization of labor would change concurrently with the organization of the market system. But as the organization of labor is only another word for the forms of life of the common people this means that the development of the market system would be accompanied by a change in the organization of society itself. All along the line, human society had become an accessory of the economic system.[1]

Gradually the ethical norms were weakened. Work was stripped of its public and moral significance. Workers reacted to their new status by repudiating the idea of moral obligation to the employer or to the public. They came to feel that work was performed because of economic necessity, not because of a sense of participation in a joint project.

As manual work became regarded as "inferior" work and subject to large insecurities, it was shunned by all who could avoid it. Parents urged their children to seek education in order to get "good" jobs promising high security and status—i.e., white-collar jobs, especially the well-regarded professional and technical jobs. To escape the insecurities of manual labor the mass yearning became one of getting into the big money, acquiring large savings, or owning a business. This brief picture of changing work and status relationships brings us to our own time.

The Meaning of Work

All monetary work plants and in addition our schools, families, and churches are faced in the twentieth century with perplexing problems of motivation and morale. What is the meaning and purpose of life and work, people ask, and none of the answers seem fully satisfying. In recognition of human needs, many sincere attempts have been made by farsighted industrial and labor

[1] Karl Polanyi, *The Great Transformation,* Holt, 1944, p. 75.

leaders to establish more meaningful work relations. Greater economic security has been achieved. The emerging of new ethical concepts can be discerned. However, there is evidence that work is regarded almost as a punishment by many in the labor force. It is pertinent, therefore, to turn our attention to the understanding of man's attempt to find meaning in work.

Interviews with employees in different socioeconomic levels reveal the wide range of positive and negative values of work. Table 14.1 shows these values as expressed.

TABLE 14.1   Positive and Negative Values of Work

Positive	Negative
1. Provides good living	Pay is inadequate
2. Fills the day comfortably	Dull, boring: or exhausting, dangerous
3. a. Brings self-respect	Reduces self-respect
b. Brings prestige, recognition from others	Low status: no prestige
4. Provides association with nice people; friendship	Forces association with people one does not like
5. a. Provides interesting experiences; purposeful activity	Uninteresting
b. Intrinsic enjoyment: self-expression, creativity	Distasteful
c. Permits service to others	No opportunity for service

Source: Table 28, p. 182, reprinted from *The Meaning of Work and Retirement* by Eugene A. Friedmann and Robert J. Havighurst, *et al.,* by permission of the University of Chicago Press. Copyright 1954 by The University of Chicago.

Research has also revealed certain similarities and differences in the meaning of work in various occupations. A comparative study of unskilled and semiskilled steelworkers, coal miners, skilled craftsmen, department store salesmen, and physicians (see Table 14.2) showed that

1. The workers of lower skill and socioeconomic status are more likely than the higher-status group to see their work as having no other meaning than that of earning money.

2. The five occupational groups all value association with people at their work about equally as a positive meaning of work.

TABLE 14.2 Comparison of the Five Occupational Groups (Unskilled and Semi-skilled Steelworkers, Coal Miners, Skilled Craftsmen, Department Store Salesmen, and Physicians) on the Meanings of Work.

Meaning	Steelworkers (unskilled and semiskilled) Percent	Coal Miners Percent	Skilled Craftsmen Percent		Sales People Percent	Physicians Percent
			20–64	Over 65		
1. No meaning other than money	28	18	10	11	0	0
2. Routine	28	19	*	15	21	15
3. a. Self-respect			30		12	7
b. Prestige, respect of others	16(3a,b)	18(3a,b)	15	24(3a,b)	11	13
4. Association	15	19	18	20	20	19
5. a,b, and c. Purposeful activity, self-expression, new experiences	13	11	28	30	26	15
d. Service to others	*	16†	*	*	10	32
Number of people responding	128	153	242	208	74	39

* Not covered in the questionnaire or interview.

† Work has given me a chance to be useful.

Source: Table 26, p. 173, reprinted from *The Meaning of Work and Retirement* by Eugene A. Friedmann and Robert J. Havighurst, *et al.*, by permission of The University of Chicago Press. Copyright 1954 by The University of Chicago.

3. Work as a routine which makes the time pass is recognized about equally by all five groups.

4. In various degrees all groups discover self-respect and secure respect or recognition from others by means of their work.

5. Physicians show a high awareness of the "service to others" meaning in their work.

6. Work is important to all five groups as a source of interesting, purposeful activity but skilled craft and white-collar groups stressed the extra-financial meanings of work to a much greater extent than did the workers in heavy industry. These social-psychological meanings of work are mentioned with increasing frequency as we ascend the occupational and skill ladders.

Some comments of workers in various occupations may illustrate the differences between workers.[2]

STEELWORKER A: I would not know what to do with myself if I did not work. I still feel strong, not like when I was young, though. When I was young, I was as strong as a horse. I liked hard work then. Sometimes I even worked a double shift, to earn more money.

STEELWORKER B. There was nothing I liked about the job—only the money. I couldn't think of anything else I could go into where I could earn as much money—it was good pay. Once I started, I couldn't quit or I'd have had to start over some place else at the bottom.

COAL MINER A: Outside of the money I get, my work doesn't mean anything—nothing! . . . I haven't seen a day I enjoyed my work.

COAL MINER B: A fellow may quit the mines, but when they whistle he goes back. I've had a lot better jobs, but I've always liked to work in the mines. I can't explain it, except I like being with the gang; I never could just sit around much.

WOMAN SALES CLERK: You like to occupy your mind. In other words, I like to get out in the public, I like to hear things—what do you hear when you're home? You hear nothing. And I don't like that. I like to get out and hear something different.

SKILLED CRAFTSMAN: This is a job which gives you respect for yourself. You get recognition from your fellows and your family and in the community. I would choose this work if I were to live my life again.

DR. M: There is something wonderful about having people depend upon you, have trust in you. . . . It is very important for the doctor to get the feeling that the patient needs and trusts him. When this confidence is had, the field of medicine is a nice profession to grow old in because one mellows with time.

These statements express differences between occupations but differences in work meanings will vary between the sexes, as can be seen in Chapter 16. Age and marital status also are important values in influencing different definitions of the meaning of work.

PERSON VS. ORGANIZATION

The organization of any group entails common restraints on the members. But the members are not identical and their needs vary. Individuality and conformity are opposite forces, and all persons

[2] Reprinted from *The Meaning of Work and Retirement* by Eugene A. Friedmann and Robert J. Havighurst, *et al.*, by permission of The University of Chicago Press. Copyright 1954 by The University of Chicago. Quotations appear pp. 27, 29, 69, 71, 110, 117, and 159, respectively.

experience organizational demands as disagreeable some of the time; others seem never to be content with their lot. By original nature, man seeks freedom from pain and restraint, but civilization implies a large amount of dependence and conformity. Philosophy is filled with man's search for ways to achieve independence in a society of constraint. The behavior of adolescents is often an index of the intensity of the conflict between these antagonistic forces. What is common to societal behavior is repeated in any formal organization. Formal organizations try to induce the person to accept a formal function and to discharge it according to methods and ends chosen by the organization. The ideal employee is one who fits into his description both cooperatively and productively.

The Meaning of Cooperation

Cooperation refers to joint efforts expended by two or more persons engaged in attaining a common goal. Appraising the role of a person in every situation in which other individuals are interacting with him requires a twofold consideration. The first involves an individual's *powers* in the situation and the second is concerned with his *determination* or volition within the limits set by his powers.

Chester Barnard has explained that

> In the millions of interactions that daily take place between men, these appraisals are not separate in any observable way in most cases. Nevertheless, they are so discriminated and separately expressed in numerous instances. The expressions of the first appraisal will be the answers to such questions as these: "Who is he?" "What kind of man is he?" "What can he do?" The second appraisal is expressed in answer to such questions as: "What does he want? What is he trying to do? What will he do?"
>
> These appraisals implicit in human relations affect the behavior of persons in two ways in matters of purposeful conduct. What actually may be done by one person to establish satisfactory relationships with another person may be approached either by the attempt to *narrow the limitations* of the second person's choice, or to *expand the opportunities* of his choice.[3]

These alternatives suggest that behavior with reference to other persons may take the form of regarding such persons either as

[3] Chester I. Barnard, *The Functions of an Executive,* Harvard, 1947, p. 39.

objects to be *manipulated* by changing the factors affecting them or as *subjects* to be *satisfied*.

The perspective in which people are viewed influences their action. In the first case, factors external to the person may be applied in the belief that they will be effective in securing desired goals. The earlier belief that improved working conditions or financial incentives would automatically raise production and morale is an instance of this thoughtway. When persons are viewed as *subjects* to be *satisfied*, attention must be turned to the feelings and attitudes of individuals. It is *within* rather than from *without* the person that results are sought.

Barnard has made it clear that an understanding and operation of cooperative relationships within an organization must of necessity involve both of these views of persons. An organization must become both *effective* and *efficient*. It must both attain ends and satisfy personal desires. It is *effective* if it accomplishes its specifically desired ends; it is *efficient* if it satisfies the motives of those participating in the accomplishment of those ends.

Leadership and Cooperation

It is possible for an organization to be effective but not efficient, or efficient but not effective. The function of leadership is precisely to weld these two aims together. On this point Barnard says,

> For the continued existence of an organization either *effectiveness* or *efficiency* is necessary; and the longer the life, the more necessary both are. The vitality of organizations lies in the willingness of individuals to contribute forces to the cooperative system. This willingness requires the belief that the purpose can be carried out, a faith that diminishes to the vanishing point as it appears that it is not in fact in process of being attained. Hence, when effectiveness ceases, willingness to contribute disappears. The continuance of willingness also depends upon the satisfactions that are secured by individual contributors in the process of carrying out the purpose. If the satisfactions do not exceed the sacrifices required, willingness disappears, and the condition is one of organization inefficiency. If the satisfactions exceed the sacrifices, willingness persists, and the condition is one of efficiency of organization.[4]

The problem of securing cooperative effort can be seen as a de-

[4] *Ibid.*, p. 82.

mand to build a specific cooperative system both *effectively* and *efficiently*. To secure efficiency, organizations depend upon the motives of individuals and the inducements that satisfy them. To secure effectiveness, organizations must depend upon goals and the demands made to achieve them. These two requirements often furnish a setting of opposed facts and of opposed thought and emotions of human beings. It becomes the function of executive leadership to reconcile the conflicting interests and ideals which determine finally the efficiency and effectiveness of an organization.

THE FUSION OF PERSON TO ORGANIZATION

If the organization is to accomplish its purpose, every person in it must be molded to some degree into the image of the organization. Bakke has suggested that the process by which this fusion is attempted be labeled the *formal socializing process.*[5]

The organization has a position to which have been delegated certain formal tasks or functions. An applicant takes a battery of tests and is screened by interviewers. If found to have the appropriate skills and aptitudes, he is selected. His induction can be formally planned with movies, lectures, and individual counseling. He finds himself meeting personnel specialists, the public relations officials, a line manager, a supervisor, and his fellow workers. He is told that this is all done to fit him into the organization as a perfectly coordinated and highly motivated employee. He is now expected to accept the position assigned and to function as defined. As he works he will be continually reminded of his organizational duty.

At the same time that the formal organization is trying to make an agent out of the individual for the accomplishment of organizational purposes, the individual is trying to mold the organization for the accomplishment of his personal aims and to realize his conception of himself. He may bargain for changes in the job, for special conditions, and personal favors. When he gets on the job he will emphasize the functions he likes to perform and will minimize those he does not like. He will form a conception of the

---

[5] E. Wight Bakke, *The Fusion Process,* Yale University Labor and Management Center, 1953, p. 17.

personal behavior or conduct which he expects of himself and a conception of the *standing* which is appropriate for him as a person to occupy. The process by which the person tries to impose his image on the formal organization has been called the *personalizing process.*[6]

In this process, he tries to make use of the resources of the organization in order to realize himself, to have other people occupy the reciprocal standings to those he desires for himself, and to behave in accordance with those standings. This is but to say that no one can play a role without reciprocal role relationships. No one can be a teacher unless there are persons willing to be students; no one can be a boss unless there are those willing to be subordinates. The worker may wish to be recognized as a popu-

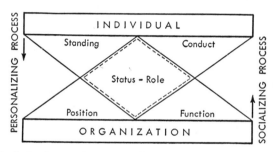

FIG. 14.1. The Fusion Process. (From E. Wight Bakke, *The Fusion Process,* Yale University Labor and Management Center, 1953, p. 20.)

lar person, a skillful craftsman, and a good bowler. But others must grant him these roles by their acceptance and recognition of him.

The formal socializing process and the personalizing process go on simultaneously. The operation of the organization on the individual and of the individual on the organization actually merges or fuses the two. Bakke calls this the *fusion process.*[7] Figure 14.1 shows the interpenetration of these two processes. The person creates a status as he applies his personal standing to the formal position. He also exhibits a role as he applies his conception of conduct appropriate to the function. The status and role are products of the fusion process. The process is endless and, while it tends toward equilibrium, it may be disturbed by any changes in the individual or in the organization.

Basic Growth Needs

Argyris claims there is a lack of congruency between the needs of individuals and the demands of the formal organization.[8] He assumes that human beings in our culture tend to develop

a. from a state of passivity as infants to a state of increasing activity as adults.
b. from a state of dependence upon others as infants to a state of relative independence as adults.
c. from being capable of behaving only in a few ways as an infant to being capable of behaving in many different ways as an adult.
d. from having erratic, casual, shallow, quickly dropped interests as an infant to having deeper interests as an adult.
e. from having a short time perspective as an infant to a much longer time perspective as an adult.
f. from being in a subordinate position in the family and society as an infant to aspiring to occupy an equal and/or superordinate position relative to their peers.
g. from a lack of awareness of self as an infant to an awareness of and control over self as an adult.[9]

Work situations cause many workers to participate under coercion, to be dependent, subordinate, submissive, and to use only a few of their most superficial abilities. This type of behavior may be observed on the assembly line where workers specifically rated in the following order the disliked characteristics of their jobs: mechanical pacing, repetitiveness, minimum skill. The mental demands of a majority of automobile assembly jobs are for surface attention; the work does not absorb mental faculties to any depth.[10]

Adaptive Activities of Frustrated Employees

These conditions in any work situation tend to be frustrating and to make the individual experience tension, psychological

[6] *Ibid.,* p. 18.
[7] *Ibid.,* p. 20.
[8] Chris Argyris, *Personality and Organization,* Harper, 1957, pp. 76–122.
[9] Chris Argyris, "Understanding Human Behavior in Organizations," in Mason Haire (ed.), *Modern Organization Theory,* Wiley, 1959, pp. 118–119.
[10] Charles R. Walker and Robert H. Guest, *The Man on the Assembly Line,* Harvard, 1952, p. 65.

failure, and short-time perspectives. Individuals will adapt to such conditions by one or more of the following activities:

1. Leave the situation (absenteeism and turnover).
2. Climb the organizational ladder.
3. Become defensive (daydreaming, aggression, grievances, regressions, projection, feelings of low sense of social worth).
4. Become apathetic, disinterested, non-ego involved in the organization and its formal goals.
5. Create informal groups to sanction the defense reaction in 3 and 4.
6. Formalize the informal groups in forms such as trade unions.
7. Deemphasize the importance of self growth and emphasize the importance of money and other material rewards.
8. Accept the above ways of behavior as being proper for their life outside the organization.[11]

Argyris believes that three major sets of variables associated with the formal organization structure are responsible for this adaptive behavior. The first set embraces the intense task specialization, the chain and unity of command, and the concept of limited span of control, all of which dominate formal organizations. Directive leadership of a close, authoritarian nature is the second factor, and managerial controls (budgets, incentive systems, quality control, motion and time studies) form the third. The degree of dependence, subordination, etc., that these three variables cause tends to increase as one goes down the chain of command and as the organization takes on the characteristics of mass production.[12]

Comparative Satisfactions and Dissatisfactions of Managers, Employees, and Union Officers

These impacts can be clearly seen in a study which sought to find the nature of job satisfaction among managers, employees, and union officers associated with the Southern New England Telephone Company and the Connecticut Union of Telephone Workers.[13] A uniform interview schedule was used in securing replies on similar questions. The qualities of the job (one object of the investigation) included use of abilities, respect for job, teamwork, fairness, steadiness, scope of freedom, fatigue, and job

[11] Argyris, in *Modern Organization Theory*, pp. 119–120.
[12] *Ibid.*, p. 119.
[13] E. Wight Bakke, *Bonds of Organization*, Harper, 1950.

instructions. Table 14.3 shows the order of satisfaction of these qualities by all management, all employees, and all union officers.

TABLE 14.3 Order of Job Satisfactions by Proportions Expressing Satisfactions with Selected Qualities of Their Jobs

Order	All Management	All Employees	All Union Officers
1 most satisfied	Use of abilities	Fatigue	Use of abilities
2	Respect for job	Steadiness	Steadiness
3	Job instruction	Scope of freedom	Scope of freedom
4	Fairness	Job instruction	Fatigue
5	Steadiness	Respect for job	Fairness
6	Scope of freedom	Fairness	Job instruction
7	Teamwork	Teamwork	Teamwork
8 least satisfied	Fatigue	Use of abilities	Respect for job

SOURCE: E. Wight Bakke, *Bonds of Organization*, Harper, 1950, p. 40.

The inversion of many satisfactions between the managers and the employees is striking. Use of abilities, respect for job, and fairness are rated as satisfactory most frequently among management and least frequently among employees. Union officers find use of abilities as satisfactory as management.

The Maslow Theory of Motivation

A. H. Maslow has presented a theory of motivation which explains these data fairly well. His fundamental postulate is that human needs arrange themselves in hierarchies of prepotency.[14] As soon as one need is satisfied, another appears in its place. Man continually seeks to gratify some need. At the lowest level, but most important when they are thwarted, are the physiological needs. A person who is lacking food, safety, love, and esteem would most probably hunger for food more strongly than for anything else. Physiological needs include water, rest, exercise, various sensory pleasures (tastes, smells, tickling, stroking, sexual gratification), and protection against the elements.

A satisfied need is not a motivator of behavior. Once physiological needs are gratified other "higher" needs emerge and domi-

[14] A. H. Maslow, "A Preface to Motivation Theory," *Psychosomatic Medicine*, 1943, vol. 5, p. 85.

nate the organism. And when these needs in turn are satisfied, new and still "higher" needs emerge. The second level of needs includes the safety needs: protection againt danger, threat, and deprivation. The infant will react as if endangered by loud noises, a flashing light, rough handling, or if disturbed or dropped suddenly. The adult exhibits the same behavior when he feels insecure in his job, unable to pay his bills, or fearful of a retirement for which he has no savings. Social security is the mass answer to the widespread need for protection against economic threats.

When man's physiological needs are satisfied and he is no longer fearful about his physical welfare, his social needs become dominant. Love, affection, and belongingness become a new center of attention. He will hunger for affectionate relations with people and will want to win acceptance in the groups he considers important. Mayo's research indicated how this factor emerges in work behavior, influencing absenteeism, turnover, and productivity. Management policies have often denied this need with the consequence that informal work groups and unions have filled a motivational vacuum. On the other hand, some managements have recognized that this need is an important one and have encouraged its fulfillment through picnics, dinners, sports activities, sponsoring of hobbies, and birthday celebrations. Supervisors have been trained in "human relations," personnel departments have instituted induction training, and managers have cultivated the art of "contact."

All people in our society have a need or desire for a stable, firmly based, high evaluation of themselves, for self-esteem and for the esteem of others. Esteem needs become increasingly important as the physiological, safety, and social needs are fulfilled. They may be classified into two sets: those that relate to one's self-esteem and those that relate to one's reputation. Self-esteem leads to feelings of self-confidence, worth, strength, adequacy, and the capability of being useful and necessary in the world. Related to one's reputation are the needs for status, recognition, and appreciation.

Unlike the lower needs, these needs are rarely satisfied. Once they have become important to the individual they provide an indefinite basis for motivational drive.

At the top of the hierarchy is the need for self-actualization: the desire to become everything that one is capable of becoming. Karen Horney called this the road to glory and she saw each person as holding a conception not only of his real self but also of an ideal self which he wishes to realize. Always a tension exists between the two. The person motivated to achieve an ideal self will find his wants insatiable.

Maslow regarded these five sets of needs as in a hierarchy but not in an all-or-none relationship to one another. Rather, he saw most persons as exhibiting decreasing percentages of satisfaction upon the hierarchical ladder of needs. For example, a person might be 95 percent satisfied in his physiological needs, 70 percent in his safety needs, 60 percent in his social needs, 10 percent in his self-esteem needs, and 5 percent in his self-actualization needs. Maslow asserts that the person who feels thwarted in any one of his basic needs is as surely "sick" as one who has been deprived of necessary vitamins and minerals. Reaction to deprivation may take many forms ranging from aggressive hostility to apathy and elicit the many different behaviors that Argyris has listed.

If we look at industrial situations in our "affluent" society we find that increasing numbers of workers at all levels of the labor force are achieving high satisfaction of their physiological and safety needs. Deprivation is occurring in the social, esteem, and self-actualization needs. Since satisfied needs are not motivators, management supplies fringe benefits in wages, overtime pay, shift differentials, vacations, health and medical benefits, retirement plans, and stock- or profit-sharing plans. All are destined to failure. As a matter of fact, most of these rewards can be satisfying *only when the worker leaves the job.* On-the-job performance is defined as an endurance or a price to be paid for various kinds of satisfaction away from the job.[15]

The observations made by Argyris and Maslow about the frustrations experienced by individuals in formal organizations are valid, but it may be that the logic of explanation is faulty. Certainly it is possible to explain their observations largely in social contexts. Thus we may observe that mass dissatisfaction in formal

[15] Douglas McGregor, *The Human Side of Enterprise,* McGraw-Hill, 1960, p. 40.

organizations is a function of the type of socialization, aspiration, and job experience. Clearly, Americans reared with the ideology of occupational mobility, job satisfaction, and personal recognition, when confronted with a job situation of routine work, limited mobility opportunity, and high control of work environment, will experience frustration and anxiety. Similarly persons reared not to expect mobility, job satisfaction, and recognition may not experience equal frustration. In either case, however, it is apparent that formal organization does not provide the chance for the creative growth of which workers of various backgrounds are capable.

Two Dimensions of Job Satisfaction

Herzberg and his associates have discovered two dimensions in job satisfaction. One set of factors accounts for satisfaction and a different set of factors is associated with dissatisfaction. In interviews satisfied workers stressed achievement, recognition, the work itself, responsibility, and advancement. Dissatisfied workers complained about company policy and administration, supervision, salary, interpersonal relations, and working conditions.[16] Note that those respondents who reported feeling happy with their jobs most frequently described factors reflecting success in the performance of their work and pointing to the possibility of professional growth. Conversely, when feelings of unhappiness were reported, they were not associated with the job itself but with conditions surrounding the doing of the job. Poor working conditions and bad company policies and administration will lead to job dissatisfaction. Good company policies, good administration, good supervision, and good working conditions will not lead to positive job attitudes. Herzberg and his associates liken these latter factors to hygiene or maintenance. Hygiene operates to establish a healthy environment, no more. All the motivating factors—recognition, achievement, advancement, responsibility, and work itself—lead to positive job attitudes because they fulfill esteem and self-actualization needs. The fewer the opportunities for the "motivators" to appear, the greater must be the hygiene offered in order to make the work tolerable. A man who finds his

[16] Frederick Herzberg, Bernard Mausner, and Barbara Snyderman, *The Motivation to Work,* Wiley, 1959, p. 81.

job challenging may tolerate bad hygiene. But good hygiene alone cannot be expected to pay motivational dividends. Many managers who have been expecting this result from salary and fringe benefits are mistaken in their assessment of motivation.[17]

McGregor has summarized the following conclusions about human motivation which he suggests as the base for restructuring organizational policy:

1. The expenditure of physical and mental effort in work is as natural as play or rest.
2. Man will exercise self-direction and self-control in the service of objectives to which he is committed.
3. Commitment to objectives is a function of the rewards associated with their achievement.
4. The average human being learns, under proper conditions, not only to accept but to seek responsibility.
5. The capacity to exercise a relatively high degre of imagination, ingenuity, and creativity in the solution of organizational problems is widely, not narrowly distributed in the population.
6. Under the conditions of modern industrial life, the intellectual potentialities of the average human being are only partially utilized.[18]

If this is the way the individual faces the organization, how does the organization face the individual?

THE NATURE OF ORGANIZATION

Individuals must be welded together to form effective organizations, for they express a wide range of differences in today's highly differentiated society. Common purpose and sentiment are not easily developed. Bakke has caught and explained this point with good humor:

What makes a team out of a crowd of individuals? Here they are in a plant or in a union. They've come from all sorts of social, political, religious, and economic backgrounds. They've been brought up in different ways. Some are polite, considerate and respectful; others are swashbuckling, bigoted pirates, born a hundred and thirty years too late. Some are skilled, competent chaps who know what to do and how to do it; others are fumbling fellows with ten thumbs on their hands and solid bone for brain. Some of them are natural cooperators; others

[17] *Ibid.*, p. 116.
[18] McGregor, *op. cit.*, pp. 47–48.

make the sparks fly whenever they come within sight of another person. The job is to take this bunch of varied individuals and weld them into a team.[19]

The team, when formed, is a group of persons who share common purposes and symbols. Individual effort and will are subordinated to group effort and will. A code of behavior develops and the group begins to exercise discipline over its own members. Elton Mayo, who became so conscious of the importance of the group in his later studies, describes the way work groups come to support formal organization:

As a team begins to form, it takes over the task of maintaining communication with all its members. The need for administration is not done away with, but it can be less concerned with problems of achieving the intimate discipline necessary to promote the objectives of the organization—regular attendance, for instance. This function the team takes over for itself; and it is a function that, if management alone is concerned with it, leads almost inextricably to an ever complicating web of complaints, the settlement of one of which serves only to provoke the expression of another. Thus teams and administration, the relation among workers and their relations to their supervisors, support each other when there is a balance in administration among technical, operational, and human considerations; where there is no balance, the result is discord and inefficiency.[20]

THE ADMINISTRATOR'S PROBLEM

The administrator who recognizes the importance of work teams must try somehow to make his entire department function as a unified group. This task requires a high degree of social skill, and administrators who possess it are scarce. Those who do have it find that the conditions of modern industry make it most difficult to build work groups. Layoffs, voluntary and involuntary terminations, transfers, and promotions move workers about with such rapidity that bonds of human sentiment often do not have a chance to form or are constantly being broken.

The administrator must learn to build work teams in this kind of setting. How shall he go about it?

[19] E. W. Bakke, "Teamwork in Industry," *Scientific Monthly*, March, 1948, p. 214.

[20] Elton Mayo and G. F. F. Lombard, *Teamwork and Labor Turnover in the Aircraft Industry of Southern California*, Harvard, 1944, p. 2.

E. W. Bakke has examined the bonds of organization which provide cohesion between members of a work group and has shown the kind of inadequacies which break down teamwork.[21]

FIVE BONDS OF ORGANIZATION

The bonds which hold individuals together are the same for a factory, an army, a football squad, or a union They are (1) job specifications and requirements, (2) the communication system, (3) the status system, (4) the system of rewards and punishments, (5) the organizational charter. Each of these bonds will be illustrated by references to efforts which throw light on the organization of teamwork.

1. Job Specifications

The first requirement of teamwork is that each worker shall understand clearly what his job is and how it relates to the jobs of the rest of the team. Increasingly, companies have made job analyses and organization charts to show exactly what each worker is responsible for and what authority has been delegated to him.

Job specifications may be unwritten, but they must be understood by all members of a work team. The manager especially must know what the requirements of his workers are if he is to understand the effect of his actions upon their work. Labor relations are improved when managers realize the responsibilities and pressures under which labor leaders must work. Union leaders, in turn, are probably more successful when they have a clear idea of the manager's position.

In general, managers and union leaders have given close attention to job specifications, but it is not uncommon to find workers in all levels of an organization who are uncertain of their responsibilities or their authority. In the last ten years the leadman position has been causing much difficulty in the factory. The leadman ordinarily serves a small group in the capacities of instructor, setup man, and worker. He is often made responsible for orders and productivity while at the same time being denied the authority of a supervisor to issue orders or command discipline.

[21] Bakke, "Teamwork in Industry," *op. cit.*, pp. 214–219. Cf. with his formulation in *Modern Organization Theory*, Mason Haire (ed.), Wiley, 1959, pp. 68–73.

The lead man complains that his responsibilities are not matched by an equivalent measure of authority and that this causes him great difficulty. His role, he feels, is imperfectly defined. Management replies that since he may join a union he cannot be trusted too far with the authority of a supervisor.

This contradiction of function and authority appears also at other levels of organization since informal, unwritten responsibilities often operate in place of formally designated specifications. For example, when a "weak" man holds a responsible position by virtue of "pull" or seniority or some other reason besides merit, many of his responsibilities are simply taken over informally by others. The same thing can happen to a capable but timid worker when an aggressive fellow worker or manager seizes responsibility and authority not formally assigned him.[22] Bakke has listed four other major inadequacies: (a) The specifications neglect to define how a particular job is related to other jobs. (b) They fail to leave an area of freedom for the initiative and inventiveness of the worker. (c) The job specifications are not matched by the actual or potential abilities of the job holder. (d) Changes are made so frequently and perhaps arbitrarily that workers do not know what they are expected to do or how their jobs are related to those with whom they work.[23]

2. The Communication System

A method of commmunication is the second essential for good teamwork. Information must constantly flow to workers explaining what is to be done, how it must be done, and why it must be done. Information must also flow up the line as recommendations and suggestions. An organization which has teamwork understands where it is going and why it moves in a given direction. No company is so big that it can afford to let its workers be cut off from information vital to the technical or social needs of the organization. Alexander Heron calls on management to develop an *aggressive willingness* to *share* with employees important facts about their organization, its progress and its plans. Yet inade-

---

[22] Hugh Estes, "Some Considerations in Designing an Organization Structure," in Mason Haire (ed.), *Organizational Theory in Industrial Practice,* Wiley, 1962, pp. 13–27.

[23] E. W. Bakke, *op. cit.,* p. 219.

quacies in the communication system of industry are very common, for difficulties grow apace in larger units. Some of these inadequacies are as follows:

a. The communication system, which was otherwise satisfactory, simply was not used to carry downward the kinds of information needed and desired. Workers want to know about their company as a totality. They want to know how the company fits within the larger social and economic structure and how it is prepared to meet changing conditions.

b. The communication system did not function to bring information up the line. The day-by-day reactions of workers, their suggestions, recommendations, and grievances, provide top management with a valuable tool for improving the *efficiency* and *effectiveness* of their organization. Everyone wants a chance to have his say. A channel must be open, and interested leaders must be available to hear and listen if teamwork is to be more than an empty word.

c. The communication line was not short and direct enough to carry information in either direction so that it came out as it was started. Distortion is common on long communication lines and misunderstandings may result.

d. Persons communicating information either lacked authority or had their position so poorly defined in the eyes of those who received the information that the messages were treated with a lack of confidence and sometimes mistrust.

e. The communications were so designed that they did not appear to be sincere. As a result they were often regarded as management excuses or efforts to conceal the underlying facts which workers wanted to know.

Efforts to improve the communication system through supervisory conferences

Increasing attention is being given to communication inadequacies. Many companies are redefining supervisory training as supervisory conferences. Figure 14.2 shows the kind of two-way channel recommended to one large industrial company in order to open the largest possible flow of two-way information in the shortest possible time. The machinery suggested was based on regular and continuous conferences, with foremen, supervisors,

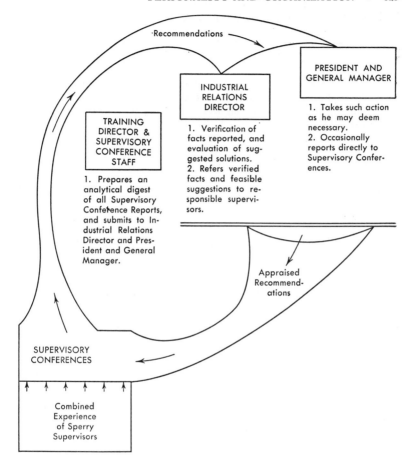

Recommendations

PRESIDENT AND GENERAL MANAGER

1. Takes such action as he may deem necessary.
2. Occasionally reports directly to Supervisory Conferences.

INDUSTRIAL RELATIONS DIRECTOR

1. Verification of facts reported, and evaluation of suggested solutions.
2. Refers verified facts and feasible suggestions to responsible supervisors.

TRAINING DIRECTOR & SUPERVISORY CONFERENCE STAFF

1. Prepares an analytical digest of all Supervisory Conference Reports, and submits to Industrial Relations Director and President and General Manager.

Appraised Recommendations

SUPERVISORY CONFERENCES

Combined Experience of Sperry Supervisors

FIG. 14.2. Supervisory Conferences as a Two-Way Channel for the Development of Policy and Procedures.

and executives meeting in small groups of fifteen to twenty persons.

The writers of the report said,

As our Company grows, and as organizational distances increase, both vertically and horizontally, there is greater need to help the supervisor feel that he still counts, and that the "boss is still interested in him and what he hopes he can contribute to the company." *There is no more effective way to do this than through the frank exchange of ideas gathered in conference, pooled in conclusions, and hammered into recommendations.*

The channel for the development of policies and procedures becomes a two way channel only when there is recognition by management so that supervisors feel their recommendations have been received, appraised, and considered for action. That recognition is best when it comes from the highest responsible official. It would seem desirable in our Company for the Industrial Relations Director to prepare reports which can be read or sent to the Supervisory Conference Groups at frequent intervals preferably once every month. An occasional letter from the General Manager or President would do much to convince supervisors of management's sincere interest.[24]

Efforts to improve the communication system by reduction of the levels of authority

The International Business Machines Corporation at Endicott, New York, has pioneered in reducing levels of authority and thus reducing the length of the communication line. Between 1940 and 1947 the company doubled in size and was faced with all the inevitable difficulties of an expanding industry. In 1940 there were seven levels of authority in the plant for those working in the main manufacturing departments. These were the executive's assistant, superintendent, assistant superintendent, department supervisor, foreman, assistant, and operator.

By 1947 the number of levels was cut to four by dropping the assistant foreman and by making the superintendent the plant head in charge of all manufacturing. This reduction still fell short of the company's policy of seeking to establish but three levels in the factory. The company policy is to support a structure composed of what it calls *management, manager,* and *man.*

These changes have increased the number of men acting as foreman or manager and have reduced section by section the number of workers supervised. Greater responsibility for human relations was given the foreman. As far as possible he was to manage all the affairs of his own particular section. He would be selected not only for his technical and supervisory ability but also for his qualifications as a human relations manager.

Richardson and Walker, who have appraised these changes in

[24] R. L. Witham, James H. Russell, and Delbert C. Miller, *Report on the Supervisory Conference Plan,* Sperry Gyroscope Company, 1942, pp. 45–46.

organization, say, "These adjustments had the effect of increasing, or at least retaining, the frequency and improving the quality of contacts characteristic of the smaller scale operations, and of simplifying the complicated method of dealing with dissatisfied employees. The marked increase in plant productivity plus the testimony of supervisory personnel suggests that human relations in the company had, during the same period, not only continued satisfactory but had improved."[25]

3. The Status System

A third requirement of good teamwork is a status system functioning in such a way that the worker's sense of justice is not violated. A status system of some kind is bound to arise. The formal structure of an organization with its organization chart places people in positions carrying authority over and obligations to others. Sometimes the actual organization of status is widely divergent from the organization chart as workers informally compare and evaluate one another. For teamwork, the informal status system should be consistent with the formal status system. The University of Washington uses a procedure of "jury rating" to determine promotions of faculty members. A jury of five colleagues from the faculty submit their personal rating of a faculty candidate following a standardized scale. On the basis of their ratings and other considerations promotion is either granted or denied. This procedure rests on the recognized importance of keeping the formal status structure consistent with the informal status system.

Violations of this principle cause teamwork difficulties. Some of the inadequacies which Bakke finds common to organizations include (a) a confused structure of authority causing workers to be uncertain to whom they must look for guidance and formal approval; (b) an autocratic structure which denies any real sense of importance to all except those at the very top; (c) a violation of merit in the selection of persons relative to the performance expected within a given position.

[25] F. L. W. Richardson, Jr., and Charles R. Walker, *Human Relations in an Expanding Company,* Yale University Labor and Management Center, 1948, p. 31.

4. The System of Rewards and Punishments

Teamwork requires satisfactions of attainment. Rewards range from simple praise—"Good work, Joe"—to monetary rewards and honorific titles. Punishments range from the ignoring of a worker to definite denial of advancement in status or money.

The system of rewards and punishments is one of the most important instruments of policy in determining good human relations within a work group. If it is to be effective, it must operate so as to be consistent with the view held by the people who are rewarded or punished. The failure of managers to consider such a view results in many defects in the system. Some of these are as follows:

a. The system is not understood by all concerned; misunderstanding arises between worker and manager.
b. The system of distribution is without plan, and rewards and punishments are distributed arbitrarily.
c. Equal pay is not distributed for equal work; such maldistribution violates workers' sense of justice.
d. The system rewards in such a way as to induce conflict by rivalry among individual workers rather than to encourage cooperation in groups. Wage systems which reward individual achievement instead of team accomplishments have this result.
e. The system emphasizes economic reward at the expense of the workers' desire for social respect and self-respect.

5. The Organizational Charter

Bakke uses the concept of the organizational charter to refer to the picture that members of the team have of the organization as a whole. The concept is similar to Durkheim's notion of "collective representations." It is the image which appears in the minds of a group as they reflect on the purposes, achievements, traditions, and symbols of the group. It is the picture that workers have who say, "I work for Boeing Aircraft Company" or "I am a member of the United Auto Workers of America."

Workers may have extremely different views of a business organization. One employee reports, "It's a big outfit. They are out to make money and they don't care how they do it. They don't care how the men feel; they only care about money. You're just a number to them. They number the stock, and they number you." Another employee in the same organization says, "I would say the company is doing everything possible for the men. The company looked out for me first rate. I cut my hand. They took care of me and gave me a light job. After all, they are running a business. It's the work that's rough, but it is a good company."

A major symptom of lack of identification with the organizational charter would be evidences of wide variations among participants in their perceptions of the central function and the distinguishing features of the organization. The activities of the organization must be legitimate in the eyes of participants. If they are not, then employee morale is weakened in varying degrees.

These five bonds of organization, (1) job specifications, (2) communication system, (3) status system, (4) system of rewards and punishments, and (5) organizational charter, are among the basic requirements for a stable social structure in the work plant. When implemented by well-conceived management policy and procedure, group formation may be strengthened. This much is known, but many unsolved problems still stand between existing knowledge and practical attainment of the optimum human organization.

An old question keeps repeating itself: Can satisfying social relationships be created in the organization for all employees?

Glenn Gilman of the Lockheed Corporation answers in the negative. He says that modern production with its mechanization, automation, and mass production techniques have "made it practically impossible for the greater share of our wage earners to experience major life satisfactions, acquire a significant status position, or attain anything that could be called functionally based security through the work they perform for a living."[26] He points out that our value system has urged us to set the attainment of a high status position through work as a goal, to aspire toward security based on excellence in some occupation, and to seek our major life satisfactions in our work. This value system was anchored to a young and expanding society whose most

[26] Glenn Gilman, in Haire, *Organizational Theory in Industrial Practice,* p. 130.

serious problems were those of production. But today technical and economic progress has mastered, for the time being at least, the problems of production. Distribution and consumption have become the critical areas. The former value system is not fully applicable to a new automated age. Yet individuals are still encouraged to seek the values which are denied by the technical and economic realities of life. Failing to fulfill their social wants, they blame their failure on the organization rather than on the sociocultural orientation that leads them to look for security, satisfaction, and status where they are in short supply. Lewis E. Lloyd of Dow Chemical concurs in this general appraisal. He concedes that Maslow's hierarchy of needs is a valid statement of worker motivation but concludes that "commercial organizations are designed to minister primarily to the first two levels of needs—physiological and security needs. Social clubs, hobby clubs, scientific or learned societies, and churches are organizations whose objective is to minister to the other levels of needs."[27] He hastens to add that "management can, and indeed must, stimulate as many of these [higher level] motives for each employee as possible in order to increase the unit's efficiency of working together."

The latter statement is almost universally accepted by both management and social scientists. There is no question also that many industrial situations are environments in which it is difficult to satisfy higher-level needs. If work is to be satisfying, the formal organization structure must be changed so that employees experience more activity than passivity and greater relative independence than dependence, use more than their surface abilities, have a longer time perspective, and are involved in decision-making. Four changes in the formal organization hold promise of satisfying higher-level needs. These are job enlargement, job rotation, employee-centered leadership, and employee participation in the plant community.

FOUR CHANGES IN THE FORMAL ORGANIZATION

Job Enlargement

Job enlargement is the increase of the number of tasks performed by the employee in his work. It is simply the recombining of two or more separate jobs into one. This means lengthened

[27] *Ibid.*, p. 47.

time cycles, so that psychological and social variables are taken into account in the content of individual jobs. Job enlargement reverses the concept of scientific management which sought efficiency by laying out jobs in space so fractionated that only one operation was required of the worker. It gives the employee a greater opportunity to use more of his important abilities. Schwab,[28] Katz and Kahn,[29] Hoppock,[30] and Super[31] state that one of the most frequent agreements found in research is that employee satisfaction increases as work becomes more complex and skilled. Even small changes may make an important difference in employee satisfaction. Walker and Guest report results of job enlargement on auto assembly lines.

> To one unfamiliar with assembly line work experience, the difference between a job with five operations and a job with ten, or between a job taking two minutes to perform and a job taking four might seem a matter far too trivial to concern any one. Our data have shown that this is not true. Management has a vital interest in such matters: the proper assignment of time cycles throughout an assembly plant will make an important difference in the efficiency of the plant. As for the worker, one of the most striking findings of the study is the psychological importance of even minute changes in his immediate job experience. The point may be given an oversimplified summary by saying: other things being equal, the difference between a satisfied and a dissatisfied worker may rest on whether he has a five-operation or a ten-operation job.[32]

Worthy, reporting studies that have been conducted at Sears, Roebuck and Company over a twelve-year period, concludes that job enlargement has been found to be effective in increasing morale. These studies have involved over 100,000 employees in several hundred different company units.[33]

Bibby reports a number of interesting examples of job enlargement at International Business Machines Corporation. One

[28] Robert E. Schwab, "Motivation and Human Relations Principles," *American Management Association*, 1953, pp. 30–39.

[29] Daniel Katz and Robert Kahn, "Some Recent Findings in Human Relations Research in Industry," in G. E. Swanson, T. M. Newcomb, and E. L. Hartley (eds.), *Readings in Social Psychology*, (rev. ed.), Holt, 1952, pp. 650–655.

[30] Robert Hoppock, *Job Satisfaction*, Harper, 1935.

[31] D. Super, "Occupational Level and Job Satisfaction," *Journal of Applied Psychology*, 1939, vol. 23, pp. 547–564.

[32] Walker and Guest, *op. cit.*, p. 152.

[33] James C. Worthy, "Factors Influencing Employee Morale," in S. D. Hoslett (ed.), *Human Factors in Management*, Harper, 1951.

example involves the assembly of the frame for an electric type-writer.

Prior to our job enlargement program, a typical sub-assembler might have had the job of simply fastening some parts to a typewriter frame. On down the line the parts would be aligned by a higher paid final assembly man and later on the operation would be checked for accuracy by a process inspector. In the new program, this same typical assembler now aligns as well as fits his parts and checks the accuracy of his align-ment. He is now completely responsible for all of the operations along his two yard stretch of the assembly line. To do this, he has had to learn how to read a blue print showing the electrical wiring and other me-chanical insides of the typewriter frame. At the same time he has be-come a more skilled assembler and he has a job which has become more varied and interesting.[34]

Bibby concludes that job enlargement resulted in marked improvement in morale, an increase in productivity, and a de-crease in apathy, disinterest, and goldbricking.

Job Rotation

Job rotation refers to movement of the worker among different jobs. Rotation holds the promise of adding even more possibilities for growth and new experience. Walker and Guest found that the utility man in an automobile assembly plant has a work experi-ence unlike that of any of the workers about him. He is a relief worker who is competent to take over any job in his section for a longer or shorter interval. His job demanded rotation. The job satisfaction of the utility man was high, and none of these workers complained of mechanical pacing or repetitiveness. They attrib-uted their greater than average job satisfaction to their constant rotation among jobs. They felt they had many advantages in their job, such as absence of monotony, getting to meet and talk with different workers, getting an idea of the whole line, and taking pride in knowing all of the jobs.

The average worker could undoubtedly have these same ad-vantages in any work situation where the gains would outweigh the losses. There are questions for both employees and managers

[34] Danse L. Bibby, "An Enlargement of the Job for the Worker," *Proceedings* of the 17th Conference, Texas Personnel and Management Associa-tion, University of Texas, October, 1955, pp. 29–31.

to consider. Will the employee be willing to move among a family of jobs or will he resist giving up a good job and learning many new ones? Can managers afford to take the risk of moving workers, with possibilities of lost production due to training time, spoilage, and resistance to the new assignment?

It has been found that most workers will accept rotation if management guarantees to the work group or to any single individual a return to stationary assignments if desired. Moreover, management finds that rotation more than pays for itself (unless it is altogether impractical because of technical demands) if the total costing is carefully evaluated. All innovations affecting people must weigh costs of reduced turnover and absenteeism, reduced spoilage and accidents, as well as production levels. Job rotation introduces a higher level of skill into the total labor force and provides management with a skilled reserve for all kinds of contingencies.

No one knows how much job enlargement and job rotation could do for the growth of skills and productivity in work because these techniques have been only sparingly used. More experimentation is probably going on currently at middle management levels than at any other parts of the work organization. Many companies put their college trainees through a series of rotating assignments in various divisions of their companies and prepare them for administrative positions. Their own middle managers are often moved laterally in the organization in a planned series of job assignments in order to prepare them for major posts. Figure 14.3 shows how one organization keeps its records on its managers for transfer purposes. The military organizations have probably done more with job rotation than any other large-scale organization. The contingencies of war as well as the complex pattern of a world-wide administrative complex enjoin the risks of job rotation. If the wall of fear and of inertia could be broken in other organizations the two techniques of job enlargement and job rotation might go far toward removing boredom and monotony from work behavior.

What more can employees require? Job enlargement and job rotation offer opportunities to grow in technical skill, but mature individuals want a work environment in which they have greater

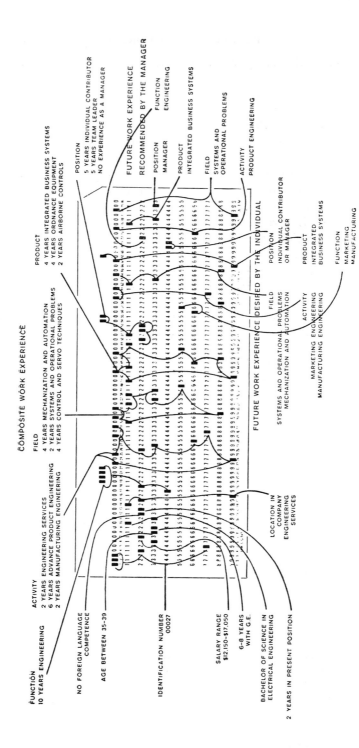

FIG. 14.3. IBM Card Lists Qualifications of Man Set to Transfer. (From *Life*, February 3, 1958.)

control, where they can make decisions affecting their immediate work environment. The capacity to become self-responsible is cultivated by an employee-centered supervisor.

Employee-Centered Supervisor

The employee-centered supervisor is one who increases the subordinates' control over their work environment, decreases their feelings of dependence upon the leader, and enlarges their time perspective. White and Lippitt write that a democratic leader

1. Permits all members to discuss policy formation. He encourages the group to make necessary decisions.
2. Permits discussion on future as well as present activity. Does not try to keep members "in the dark" about future plans.
3. Permits members to define their own job situation as much as possible. For example, the defining of the way to accomplish the tasks and the divisions of the tasks is left up to the group.
4. Focuses on obtaining "objective" facts on "human problems." Tries to base any necessary "praise" or "discipline" upon these objective facts and not upon his personal needs.[35]

Carefully documented with research findings from the Michigan Survey Research Center is Likert's conclusion that supervisors with the best records of performance focus their primary attention on the human aspects of their subordinates' problems and on endeavoring to build effective work groups with high performance goals.[36] The following are the words of a manager of a high-producing division.

One way in which we accomplish a high level of production is by letting people do the job the way they want to so long as they accomplish the objectives. I believe in letting them take time out from the monotony. Make them feel that they are something special, not just the run-of-the-mill. As a matter of fact, I tell them if you feel that the job is getting you down get away from it for a few minutes. . . . If you keep employees from getting hounded, they are apt to put out the necessary effort to get the work done in the required time.

I never make any decisions myself. Oh, I guess I've made about two since I've been here. If people know their jobs I believe in letting them make decisions. I believe in delegating decision making. Of course, if there is anything that affects the whole division, then the two assistant

[35] Ralph White and Ronald Lippitt, "Leader Behavior and Member Reaction in Three 'Social Climates,'" in D. Cartwright and Alvin Zander, *Group Dynamics,* Harper, 1953, p. 487.
[36] Rensis Likert, *New Patterns of Management,* McGraw-Hill, 1961, p. 7.

managers, the three section heads, and sometimes the assistant section heads come in here and we discuss it. I don't believe in saying that this is the way it is going to be. After all, once supervision and management are in agreement there won't be any trouble selling the staff the idea.

My job is dealing with human beings rather than with the work. It doesn't matter if I have anything to do with the work or not. The chances are that people will do a better job if you are really taking an interest in them. Knowing the names is important and it helps a lot, but it's not enough. You really have to know each individual well, know what his problems are. Most of the time I discuss matters with employees at their desks rather than in the office. Sometimes I sit on a wastepaper basket or lean on the files. It's all very informal. People don't seem to like to come into the office to talk.[37]

This self-description of an employee-centered leader must not be considered a formula. In many places persons in positions of responsibility must also assume roles where they have to be production centered, superior centered, and organization centered. Kahn and Katz conclude that a balance is required in the use of different leadership patterns. A "soft" leader who abdicates his formal organizational responsibility can have an adverse effect on both productivity and morale. They report "a moderate amount of emphasis on productivity is required to avoid both low production and low morale. But beyond a certain point, higher productivity by means of pressure appears to be obtainable only at the expense of morale.[38]

Employee Participation in the Plant Community

Employee participation may range from recreational activities supported by the organization to responsibilities as a union steward or as a member of a labor-management committee of the organization. Some organizations sponsor almost every recreational, hobby, and educational activity that can be framed. The traditional pattern has been to make this an off-work activity. However, a few companies are beginning to sponsor bowling on company time. One company pays for the employee's time if he plays in the championship softball contest. The pattern of paying university tuition for employees seeking college credits and degrees has been in evidence for years in some organizations. Many

[37] *Ibid.*, p. 8.
[38] Robert L. Kahn and Daniel Katz, "Leadership Practices in Relation to Productivity and Morale," in Cartwright and Zander, *op. cit.*

company-sponsored training programs take place on company time. In addition to these efforts to introduce variety and growth in the employees off work time, organizations frequently offer employees more on-the-job responsibilities by involving them in decision-making. Committee assignments for fact-finding, advisory, or decision-making purposes can increase an employee's identification with and growth as a citizen in his own organization. He can grow in leadership ability. The union offers a ladder of opportunity for those who have organizing and administrative skills. Profit sharing—the Scanlon plan, for example—offers the employee a share in the profits according to productivity of his work and the suggestions he can make for improving the efficiency of his job and of others.

Future Trends

All of the many possibilities for growth suggest that boredom and monotony might conceivably be banished from work and life. But social change has complicated matters. Mechanization and automation are threatening to reduce work to a secondary interest. Leisure is becoming man's preoccupation. There is a steady pressure to lower the hours of the work week. W. H. Ferry sees the United States caught on the horn of plenty: "As consumers, Americans are joyously sopping up affluence, quarter after quarter sending private debt for consumer goods to record levels, and inventing new categories of services. But the lesson of abundance is even here ambiguous; for while there is enough to go around, all are not sharing."[39]

Some 30,000,000 Americans are living below the poverty line and around 5,000,000 people are out of jobs. The labor force is growing at the rate of 1,250,000 annually, and technological progress permits the discharge of another 1,250,000. Fifty thousand new jobs have to be provided weekly. Ferry believes that the technology has created a technologically displaced class which he calls the "liberated margin."[40] The members of this group will be freed permanently from traditional work because of technological imperatives. He sees this group made up of persons from most

[39] W. H. Ferry, "Caught on the Horn of Plenty," *Bulletin*, Center for the Study of Democratic Institutions, Santa Barbara, Calif., January, 1962, p. 2.
[40] *Ibid.*, p. 3.

segments of the labor force. Skilled and semiskilled have joined the unskilled. White-collar workers are joining the group as automation reaches the office. Computers may send middle managers into the group in another decade. This permanent leisure group will be coupled with those employed workers who already have considerable leisure.

If these facts are proved accurate, then the meaning of work *within* work organizations and *outside* of work organizations may be markedly redefined. Creative growth may be increasingly possible only outside of traditional industry. If the work week is substantially shortened, "traditional work" may no longer be regarded as a central value, and industry may turn its attention to activities for its employees outside of its shops and offices. Already some supervisors are urging their employees to seek satisfying activities outside of work rather than finding their central satisfaction in work. If off-work time is to dominate man's life, who shall fill it with activity? The work organization, the union, the private welfare agency, the city, the state, or the federal government? Human welfare may become the biggest business in the United States, and the ancient problem of the role of the individual in a society may become more strange and wondrous than man has ever dreamed of. Humanity, with its politics and pastimes and poetry and conversation, will then occupy the central place in the culture of leisure.[41]

SELECTED BIBLIOGRAPHY

Argyris, Chris, *Personality and Organization,* Harper, 1957.
Bakke, E. Wight, *The Fusion Process,* Yale University Labor and Management Center, 1953, and *Bonds of Organization,* Harper, 1950. Bakke's most recent revision of the bonds of organization is in Mason Haire (ed.), *Modern Organization Theory,* Wiley, 1959.
Barnard, Chester I., *The Function of an Executive,* Harvard, 1947.
Friedmann, Georges, *The Anatomy of Work: Labor, Leisure, and the Implications of Automation,* Free Press, 1961.
Grazia, Sebastian de, *Of Time, Work, and Leisure,* Twentieth Century Fund, 1962.

[41] The most complete analysis of leisure and its implications for the future is found in Sebastian de Grazia, *Of Time, Work, and Leisure,* Twentieth Century Fund, 1962.

McGregor, Douglas, *The Human Side of Enterprise*, McGraw-Hill, 1960.

Riesman, David, *The Lonely Crowd*, Yale, 1950.

Stogdill, Ralph M., *Individual Behavior and Group Achievement*, Oxford University Press, 1959.

Whyte, William H., Jr., *The Organization Man*, Simon and Schuster, 1956.

Worthy, James C., "Organizational Structure and Employee Morale," *American Sociological Review*, April, 1950, pp. 169–179.

PART IV · Major Problems of Applied Industrial and Organizational Sociology

Applied research in industrial and organizational sociology has been centered around the organizational processes that produce morale, teamwork, and productivity. Administrators everywhere are seeking ways to motivate and commit employees to organizational goals. Their concern has resulted in a search for new leadership philosophies and practices, for new ways to organize formal structure, and for reward and penalty systems in accord with cultural requirements of a mature society. The impact of mechanization and specialization has brought into organizational life a considerable amount of alienation from work. The employee often does not feel he has a vital function to perform. He does not know where he fits or why. This feeling of anomie or purposelessness may be reinforced in the organization because of influences brought from the urban and cultural environment which molds his daily life. The larger society may also rob the individual of the primary group identifications which give a sense of acceptance and purpose. How to compensate for all these forces presents a challenge of high magnitude. Leaders are asking what they can do within a work organization to bring meaning and motivation to the work tasks. Three areas of study have proved to be the most fruitful for investigation: (1) search for a theory of motivation and an appropriate philosophy of leadership; (2) search for leadership practices and morale-building techniques that will improve employee satisfaction and productivity; (3) search for principles of decision-making and governing of subordinates that are consistent with the needs of both the employee and the organization.

CHAPTER 15

The Evolution
of
Managerial Philosophies

Leadership behavior in a work organization is almost solely derived from an image of the employees for whom the leader assumes responsibility. Management practices are, in turn, products of tradition, social science research, and general cultural values. However, leaders are prone to say that "what you do in directing employees depends on the type of employee you get."

The types of workers have been changing rapidly. It was pointed out in Chapter 3 that in 1870 over one-half of the labor force was engaged in agriculture and in 1960 only one-tenth was so occupied. American workers in 1880 were largely unorganized except for those in a few of the skilled crafts. Workers were dependent on the swings of the business cycle for their economic security; the safeguards of social security, a Federal Reserve system, a defense budget, and a public works program were nonexistent. As for education, the average worker was fortunate to be able to read, write, and do sums. The employer seldom asked for more than that. The great need for labor was predominantly in the unskilled and semiskilled occupations. What was most important was that the worker be capable of sustained work for six days a week and for ten to eleven hours a day. The best industrial laborers were likely to be the eager immigrants who came to the United States from a score of foreign countries. Labor meant brawn adaptable to hard work. Even today the concept of labor carries with it the image of a blue-collar man although

America in the 1960s has more white-collar than blue-collar labor.

Economists talked about labor as a commodity subject to competitive market conditions like land, raw material, and capital. They said that from an economic point of view labor was bought like any other good. Of course, the worker had his rights in a free society. He could offer his services to any employer he wished when he wished and refuse employment when it was his desire. This right, it was claimed, matched the right of the employer to hire and fire. The equation of these rights was regarded as balanced, and the worker was expected to be grateful to the more shrewd employer who had risked his capital to make a job for him. Moreover, the worker was expected to submit to the will of the employer in all matters affecting work. If he found conditions unbearable, he was free to go elsewhere. This was his right and his protection. The economist said that each man worked for his own self-interest and could be counted on to protect himself.

This was the historic setting at the beginning of the twentieth century. The image of the worker was characteristically that of a blue-collar man who was dirty, sweaty, uneducated, and weighted with the burdens of a large family. This man was not to be studied (for what was there to study?) but to be used in the growing industrialization of modern society. The classical economists assured us that as productivity rose, the standard of living would automatically rise, that all the laws of competition guaranteed this result whether men were good or bad. Income and work were products of impersonal forces, all under the sway of natural laws. The future was bright, and no matter what one's present station, progress was a national promise. America was emerging as a world power. Yankee ingenuity was showing what could be done with industrial resources. The economy of large-scale production was already demonstrated. It was in many ways the best of all possible worlds. At any rate, the economy was not to be tampered with, or the natural laws of competition would be upset and the propensity of capitalists to take risks, which were necessary for an expanding economy, would be blunted. Such was the temper of the times. There was no place for industrial sociology in this climate of ideas.

WHY DO WORKERS WORK?

Perhaps the first step toward a science of industrial sociology was taken when serious thought was given to the question, Why do workers work? This deceptively simple question keeps repeating itself, and the answers continue to show variety and change, as the student may find out for himself by asking it of many different persons. Here is a sample of respondents' opinions:

A SUPERVISOR: Necessity drives men to work. Men are inherently lazy, and you couldn't get them to do a lick of work unless they were forced to.

A TIME AND MOTION ENGINEER: Money is what they want and the only thing that will coax more work from the worker. The worker must see a clear-cut gain for himself, or he won't work any harder than he has to. A piecework incentive plan is the surest way to increase work effort and production.

A PSYCHOLOGIST: Men want satisfying jobs. You must discover each worker's interests and abilities, then assign him work that enables him to do what he likes and is competent to do.

A PLANT SUPERINTENDENT: Take it from me. The carrot and stick theory is the answer. A lot of things are important to workers, such as wages, seniority, health and pension plans, a good boss, and a feeling that they are getting a fair shake in the company. I can tell you one thing. They always want more of almost any benefit you can name. The union sees to that. Things are different when there is unemployment. Then you can make discipline work, and you don't have so much gimme.

A LABOR LEADER: Men work for their home and their families. They need more money to keep up with the rising prices of almost everything. They want their fair share of the production and they want security. That's why they support their union.

AN INDUSTRIAL SOCIOLOGIST: Workers want more than anything else to be considered an important part of a work group and of a work organization. They want a role that is challenging to their sense of purpose as adult workers and citizens.

The origins of these different opinions may be traced over three historical stages. Each arose in connection with the social structure of the time. Many of the ideas remain as residues of an earlier period. Table 15.1 shows how these ideas are related to three dominant images of workers spanning the first half of the twentieth century. From each image a dominating leadership philosophy arose and became an established part of the organizational behavior of work. A discussion of each stage follows.

TABLE 15.1 Orientations Toward the Worker

1900 View of the Worker as a Biological Machine (Survival)	1920 View of the Worker as an Individual Personality (Recessive)	1940 View of the Worker as a Group Member (Dominant)
Imported from "scientific management" or industrial engineering	Imported from industrial psychology	Imported from industrial sociology
Major characteristic:		
Importance of organizing and stimulating the energy of people and converting it into useful work	Importance of individual differences Importance of relating man to the job	Importance of group life and relating man to group Worker is a member of work group, of union, of community, and of the nation
Motivation of worker:		
Economic Man	Psychological Man	Social Man
Man acts rationally and advances his own interest Pay is principal incentive Workers will cooperate with management if you can show them financial advantages	Man acts to secure certain individual needs Special interest in his job, advancement, individual recognition	Man desires certain shared social associations like security, feeling of belonging, and recognition No motive is stronger than the desire for human association
Expressed in such personnel practices as:		

Time and motion study
Work simplification
Body energy and injury
Incentive systems—piece rate
Environmental Conditions
  Light   Physical
  Heat   health and
  Color   accident
  Music   prevention
  Noise Study of
  Food   fatigue and
    reverie
	Employee selection and placement
	Safety programs—accident proneness
	Improvement of job satisfaction: "Every person is an individual"
	Merit rating
	Performance appraisal
	Job specifications
		Group participation in decision-making
		Employee recreation and educational programs
		Supervisory and management training in human relations
		Public or community relations (importance of company image in community)
		Labor relations
		Group incentives

Department:		
Industrial Engineering	Personnel	Employee and Community Relations
Academic base:		
Engineering	Psychology	Sociology

IMAGE OF WORKER AS A BIOLOGICAL MACHINE
(a survival of 1900–1920)

The pre-industrial era commonly considered the worker a gross energy source. The muscles of men and animals moved the simple tools and conveyances of the world throughout man's history. Enslaved peoples proved an especially tractable supply of energy. When the steam engine brought a vast new source of inanimate energy, and new machine tools were designed to utilize it for work, workers became adjuncts in the new factory system. It was inevitable that someone would soon conceive of men as "human machines" to be adapted to the production process. A veteran in industrial relations wrote: "The worker was looked upon as just part of the machinery which kept the company operating, and he was treated like that. If he were injured or totally incapacited, even in line of duty, he was cast aside and replaced like a broken piece of equipment."[1]

In a very real sense, workers are inferior capital equipment for they are subject to fatigue, may fail in performance, and put up a stubborn resistance to job changes and speedup. Every engineer who has ever realized the frailty of human workers has been encouraged to replace these "parts" of the productive process with more efficient, inanimate mechanisms. Today production, control, and computing machines have progressively replaced the "human machine" at numerous points and have required transfer of men to other, less-mechanized functions required by a modern service society.

Frederick W. Taylor—Father of Scientific Management

Frederick W. Taylor was the first to implement the image of the worker as an organic machine capable of being more efficiently adapted to production. He brought an engineering mind and viewpoint to personnel and industrial management.

Born in Philadelphia in 1856 of well-to-do parents, Frederick Taylor received an excellent education in Philadelphia and in France and Germany as well as at Exeter Academy, where he stood at the head of his class. He suffered from overwork, and his

---

[1] Cy Ching, *Review and Reflection, A Half Century of Labor Relations,* Forbes, 1956, pp. 5–6.

doctor advised that he give up temporarily his plans to go on to Harvard for the study of law. Instead, he embarked on an unusual course—he became an apprentice patternmaker and machinist in a Philadelphia firm at the age of nineteen. In 1878 he took a job as a laborer at the Midvale Steel Company and in six years progressed through the positions of gang boss, assistant foreman, and foreman in the machine shop, then through master mechanic, chief draftsman, and to chief engineer of the plant. On his own, he took engineering courses at the Stevens Institute of Technology, and in 1893 he received his degree in mechanical engineering.[2]

This background was especially fortunate, for business enterprise was expanding in size and scope, and industrial production was becoming increasingly complex. The mechanical engineer was emerging as a key figure in the industrial structure because he could meet the needs of machine production. The American Society of Mechanical Engineers was founded in 1880, became the parent organization of "management engineering," and was to foster most of the later management societies. In 1912, for example, the Society for the Promotion of the Science of Management was formed and later rechristened the Taylor Society. It was a forerunner of the present Society for the Advancement of Management.[3] To this day, the management philosophy of many firms may be traced directly to the "engineering mind set."

Frederick Taylor, more than any other man, codified "scientific management." He won a reputation of international renown by putting himself squarely on the side of management when he was appointed gang boss over a group of lathe hands at twenty-three years of age. He estimated that production was only one-third of what could be normally expected. When a new man was taken on, he was talked to by the old hands. "Here," they would say, "you don't do any more than three pieces this morning. At noon we will let you in on the game." Taylor set himself to break this game. He used "every expedient" to speed up the workers. He cut

---

[2] The details of Taylor's life are described by his only biographer, Frank B. Copley, in *Frederick W. Taylor: The Father of Scientific Management,* Harper, 1923.

[3] Milton J. Nadworny, "The Society for the Promotion of the Science of Management," *Explorations in Entrepreneurial History,* May, 1953, pp. 224–247.

piece rates, fired "stubborn workers," and hired green hands.[4] He set out to determine a "fair day's work" and began experiments on worker fatigue, methods of shoveling, ball-bearing inspection, pig iron handling, and metal cutting. Accurate time study became the foundation of scientific management.[5] Note the following example.

The first illustration is that of handling pig iron and this work is chosen because it is typical of perhaps the crudest and most elementary form of labor which is performed by man. This work is done by men with no other implements than their hands. The pig iron handler stoops down, picks up a pig weighing about 92 pounds, walks a few feet or yards and then drops it on the ground or upon a pile. This work is so crude and elementary in its nature that the writer firmly believes that it would be possible to train an intelligent gorilla so as to become a more efficient pig iron handler than any man can be.

We found that this gang were loading on the average about $12\frac{1}{2}$ long tons per man per day. We were surprised to find, after studying the matter, that a first-class pig iron handler ought to handle between 47 and 48 long tons per day, instead of $12\frac{1}{2}$ tons. This task seemed to us so very large that we were obliged to go over our work several times before we were absolutely sure that we were right. . . .

Our first step was the scientific selection of the workmen. In dealing with workmen under this type of management, it is an inflexible rule to talk and deal with only one man at a time, since each workman has his own special abilities and limitations, and since we are not dealing with men in masses, but are trying to develop each individual man to his highest state of efficiency and prosperity. Our first step was to find the proper workman to begin with. We therefore carefully watched and studied these 75 men for three or four days, at the end of which time we had picked out four men who appeared to be physically able to handle pig iron at the rate of 47 tons per day. A careful study was then made of each of these men. We looked up their history as far back as practicable and thorough inquiries were made as to the character, habits, and ambition of each of them. Finally we selected one from among the four as the most likely man to start with. . . . This man we shall call Schmidt.

The task before us then narrowed itself down to getting Schmidt to handle 47 tons of pig iron per day and making him glad to do it. This was done as follows. Schmidt was called out from among the gang of pig iron handlers and talked to somewhat in this way:

"Schmidt, are you a high-priced man?"

"Vell, I don't know vat you mean." (Conversation on this point lasts several minutes.)

"Well, if you are a high-priced man, you will do exactly as this man

[4] Copley, *op. cit.*, p. 31.
[5] Frederick W. Taylor, *Shop Management,* Harper, 1911, p. 65.

tells you tomorrow, from morning until night. When he tells you to pick up a pig and walk, you pick it up and walk, and when he tells you to sit down and rest, you sit down. You do that right straight through the day. And what's more, no back talk. Now a high-priced man does just what he's told to do and no back talk. Do you understand that?"

Schmidt started to work, and all day long, and at regular intervals, was told by the man who stood over him with a watch, "Now pick up a pig and walk. Now sit down and rest. Now walk, now rest. . . ." He worked when he was told to work, and rested when he was told to rest, and at half past five in the afternoon had his 47½ tons loaded on the car. And he practically never failed to work at this pace and do the task that was set him during the three years the writer was at Bethlehem.[6]

Basic Principles of Time and Motion Study

In this example, the principles of time and motion study may be observed. Such study is designed to reduce operations to their simplest components and to find the number of time units required for each motion.

First, find, say, ten or eighteen men (preferably in as many separate establishments and different parts of the country) who are especially skillful in doing the particular work to be analyzed.

Second, study the exact series of elementary operations or motions which each of these men uses in doing the work which is being investigated, as well as the implements each man uses.

Third, study with a stop watch the time required to make each of these elementary movements and then select the quickest way of doing each element of the work.

Fourth, eliminate all false movement, slow movements, and useless movements.

Fifth, after doing away with all unnecessary movements, collect into one series the quickest and best movements as well as the best implements.

The best method is now introduced as the standard to be taught first to the teachers and by them to every workman. For the workmen, cooperation meant "to do what they are told to do promptly and without asking questions or making suggestions."[7] The "cooperative" role of the management was therefore an

[6] Quoted from F. W. Taylor, *The Principles of Scientific Management,* Harper, 1911, pp. 40–47.

[7] Frederick W. Taylor, "Why Manufacturers Dislike College Students," *Proceedings of the Society for the Promotion of Engineering Education,"* 1909, vol. 17, p. 87.

active one, while that of the worker was of the passive kind—merely to obey the scientific management "laws." A typical statement of such a law is embodied in a time study of one industrial operation as shown in Fig. 15.1.

Application of Incentive Payments

Taylor never doubted that workers would accept the new methods when they learned that they could make more money. He appears to have accepted the economic-man concept without reservation. This concept holds that man acts rationally to advance his own interest. Pay is the principal incentive.

Schmidt, the worker in the pig iron incident, was described thus: "A penny looks about the size of a cart wheel to him." At the offer of a wage increase from $1.15 to $1.85 per day, Schmidt hesitated, and Taylor exclaimed, "Oh, you're aggravating me. Of course you want $1.85 per day—everyone wants it."

Taylor proposed a "differential piece rate," which embodied two distinct rates of pay based on a combination of rewards and punishments. A high piece rate was paid to workmen who completed given assignments in the time allotted for them. A low rate was paid in case of failure—a return so small that the "slothful" could earn "scarcely a day's pay"; they were forced either to work at a faster pace or to quit. Therefore, in time, the work force would be composed solely of "high-grade" men.[8]

Workmen generally greeted scientific management with open opposition. In fact so bitter became the relations between the foreman Taylor and his workmen that he once wrote:

I was a young man in years, but I give you my word I was a great deal older than I am now, what with the worry, meanness, and contemptibleness of the whole damn thing. It is a horrid life for any man to live, not to be able to look any workman in the face all day long without seeing hostility there, and feeling that every man around is your virtual enemy. These men were a nice lot of fellows, and many of them were my friends outside the works. This life was a miserable one, and I made up my mind to either get out of the business entirely and go into some other line of work, or to find some remedy for this unbearable condition![9]

[8] Frederick W. Taylor, "A Piece Rate Rate System, Being a Step Toward Partial Solution of the Labor Problem," *A.S.M.E. Transactions*, 1895, vol. 16, pp. 856–883.

[9] Testimony of Taylor in 1912 before a special committee of the House of Representatives.

OPERATION OBSERVATION SHEET

THE ▬▬▬▬ COMPANY

"H-" Former Method   DATE 8-28-43

#2577

PART NO. 64857	PART NAME Point & Support
OPERATION NO 0531	OPERATION NAME Spotweld point to support
BASE RATE 82 + 10%	OTHER PART NO.'S USING THIS OPERATION
CLOCK NO —	WORKER'S NAME E. J. Bohinsky

MODEL NO —   MACHINE NAME Spotwelder   MACH. NO. —

TEMP. RATE ✓   PERM. RATE ✓

DEPT. NO. 2300   DEPT. NAME Machine Room

DESCRIPTION	UNITS 1	2	3	4	5	6	7	8	9	10	TOTAL MACH.	HAND	OCC. FACT.	LEVEL FACT.	ALL TI
1- Place point on bottom electrode of Spotwelder with L.H.												074	¹/₁	115	.0
2- Place cap on top of the point (Elemental Breakdown average of 10 pcs.)												054	¹/₁	115	.0
3- Step on lever with R.F. and spotweld, then remove, inspect and place in tray in front of machine												073	¹/₁	115	.0
Total average for breakdown												201			.2	
Production study (avg 10 pcs) Each												210	¹/₁	115	2.
" " (." , ") "												213	¹/₁	115	2
" " (" , ") "												189	¹/₁	115	2
Clean points average 1 time to 7 pieces (Each Cleaning)												118	¹/₁	115	1
Allowances allowed in study																
Salvage 7 pcs - (Re spotweld)																
Sand off points everytime there is a scrap												1931				1
												4				
Total pieces on Study = 40																

TIME STARTED	TIME STOPPED	ELAPSED TIME	PIECES PRODUCED				TOTAL	233	2

(C) ALLOWED TIME PER PIECE		268 MIN.	(E) STANDARD TIME PER PIECE 292
TOOL ALLOW. PER DAY (MIN.) In study		MIN.	(F) STANDARD HRS. PER 100 PIECES (EX1-67) 488
HANDLING ALLOW. PER DAY (MIN.) 10 00		MIN.	(G) STANDARD PRODUCTION PER HOUR 100/F 205
PERSONAL ALLOW. PER DAY (MIN.) 30 00		MIN.	COST PER 100 PCS. = (FXB.R.) = .488 × .902 = $.44
MISC. PER DAY (MIN.)		MIN.	STD. COST =
" " " (MIN)		MIN.	TIME TAKEN BY W. E. Hudec DATE 8/28/43 CALCULATED BY W. E. Hudec DA 8/2
TOTAL		40 00 ÷440= 9.1 %	024 MIN. FOREMAN'S APPROVAL E. M. DATE DATE EFFECTIVE
		TOTAL	292 MIN.

5M-9-45   — OVER —

FIG. 15.1. An Operation Observation Sheet.

Still Taylor believed that he would win acceptance. He wrote, "Workmen . . . are in time reconciled to time study when they appreciate that the ultimate outcome of it means higher wages for themselves."[10]

Taylor disliked and distrusted organized labor, and there was no complete acceptance in industry of scientific management until organized labor felt secure in its position. Labor's guiding acceptance of scientific management was set forth in the American Federation of Labor in 1930 on the proviso that the contract include union recognition, and participation of workers in research to determine the "best" way (which, in practice, usually meant the employment of stopwatch and motion studies).[11]

Union Reaction to Time and Motion Studies

In spite of its formal position as stated above, organized labor has never completely accepted time-study methods. The United Automobile Workers union asked its members: "Whose time does the stop watch keep?"

Whose time does the stop watch keep?

The worker, through his Union steward or committeemen, gives the answer: The stop watch keeps employer time. Not Eastern Standard, not Daylight Saving. The stop watch keeps management time.

It ticks off the needs and interests of the boss, not of the fellow who has to do the work out in the shop. . . .

It sprang to life out of the gap between the killing pace imposed by an unchallenged foreman and the levels of work that free men could accept and still stay human.

UAW believes in technological progress. A resolution of the 1949 Convention put it this way: "The UAW–CIO fully recognizes and supports the idea that the standard of living of the people can be raised only by reducing unit costs and making available more goods.

"However, we insist that reductions in the unit cost of production must be made possible by improved technology and production processes and in efficient engineering and management and not by placing unfair work loads on workers."

The 1951 Convention had this to say on the subject: "Many employers resort to so-called scientific methods. . . . Management experts seek to intimidate workers by the use of the stop watch, the slide rule, calibrated

[10] Letter from Taylor to Sanford Thompson, January 17, 1910, in Taylor Collection.

[11] Geoffrey Brown, "The New Trade Unionism," *Federationist*, May, 1930, pp. 542, 543.

motion picture films, elaborate standard data systems and various other devices, all calculated to increase the work pace. . . ."

The Union says bluntly:

1. Time study is strictly a management device. It is used solely because management has a general distrust of a worker's willingness to work.
2. Time study is a technique which was designed solely with management's interests in mind and it is used to achieve the following objectives:
   a. To raise the level of workers effort.
   b. To recapture all of the benefits of job improvement.[12]

Labor's opposition has probably had the effect of reducing enthusiasm for wage incentive plans, both individual and group, among workers and management. The AFL–CIO Collective Bargaining Report of 1960 states that the use of wage incentive plans is declining and that the substitution of hourly wage structure has shown that productivity did not drop. Based on U.S. Labor Department surveys, it is estimated that only one-fourth of production workers are at present under a wage incentive plan. In nonmanufacturing fields, AFL–CIO experts estimate that fewer than 10 percent of workers are under an incentive system, even considering commissions on sales as a form of incentives. The overall experience has been that incentive programs have generally fallen short of meeting either management's objective of increasing production or the worker's goal of higher pay. Another factor tending to reduce the use of incentives is the advance in technology, in which the pace of production is set largely by the capacity of the machine. Where output depends on machines rather than on worker effort there is little chance to apply wage incentives to workers.[13]

Evaluation of Scientific Management

"Scientific management" has come to mean management based on the systematic study of work relations in contrast to reliance on intuition and hunch. Alfred Sloan, Jr., who served as president of General Motors, once said, "There are two ways of running any kind of business. They are the 'hunch' method and the scien-

---

[12] "Time Study Is Spinach," *Ammunition,* United Auto Workers, August, 1956, pp. 9–10.

[13] "Wage Incentive Programs Losing Ground in Industry," *AFL–CIO News,* December 10, 1960, p. 3.

tific way. By temperament and education, I have always followed the latter. It has paid me big returns and it will for others. . . . I instituted a system that provided scientific means of administration and control whereby the corporation would be able to project itself as much as possible into the future so as to discount changing trends and influences and also to be prepared at all times to alter its course promptly and effectively if the necessity arose."[14]

Taylor initiated the idea that systematic analysis of work and management processes was a fruitful endeavor. Although labor has often opposed parts of this movement, the education of workers in management processes has been greatly expedited. Labor has learned about time study, work simplification, job evaluation, incentive systems, merit rating, and numerous other management methods. Joint consultation has been facilitated.

Meanwhile many personnel practices have been instituted around the idea of increasing the efficiency of the worker as a biological machine. Both biological and physical principles have been explored. Note in Table 15.1 the personnel practices, including the time and motion study and work simplification. If time and motion study is anathema, work simplification may be accepted. See the reference to the study of body energy and injury, from which industrial physiology has arisen. Food, health, and accident treatment and prevention are major concerns of most work organizations.[15] Interest in environmental conditions has resulted in various programs, including applications of plant design to light, heat, color, music, and noise. A great deal of research has been done on fatigue and reverie, and the almost universal rest period has its origin in scientific study. Yet, having said all this, the view of the worker as a biological machine is regarded as a survival stage. The economic concept of man has been exploded. The isolation of biological man is now regarded as an abstraction not appropriate to reality. The view of the worker as a biological machine has left a heritage which remains important because the significance of environment has been high-

[14] Quoted from Ernest Dale, *The Great Organizers,* McGraw-Hill, 1960, pp. 89 and 102.

[15] Milton J. Nadworny, *Scientific Management and the Unions, 1900–1932,* Harvard, 1955.

lighted. The work environment has physical features which may be supportive for either biological or socially symbolic reasons. It may represent a necessary but not sufficient reason for the morale, motivation, and productivity of workers. But this was not known in 1900. It was not clearly seen until a man named Mayo demonstrated it in research. Meanwhile a new great idea was taking root. The view of the worker as an *individual personality* emerged strongly about 1920 to command the stage.

VIEW OF WORKER AS AN INDIVIDUAL PERSONALITY
(a recessive view of 1920–1940)

Psychology became a scientific discipline when Wilhelm Wundt opened his Leipzig laboratory in 1879 and began to explore the responses of his subjects to controlled stimuli. Before Wundt, most psychologists had depended on introspection to gain insight into the nature of man. By understanding themselves, they believed they could understand others. Wundt, in contrast, recorded the responses of his subjects and from his quantitative averages constructed a "psychological man." Darwin's *Origin of Species,* published in 1859, had described the great tendency toward variation in the species. But it was not until twenty years later that Sir Francis Galton grasped the psychological implications of evolution. In the same year that Wundt opened his laboratory, Galton called for a study of individual differences.

Importance of Individual Differences

James McKeen Cattell, an American trained by Wundt and Galton, became convinced of the importance of the Darwinian approach and turned his full attention to individual differences. Using Wundt's measuring techniques he looked for the differences between persons instead of the similarities, as Wundt had taught. To his old teacher Cattell became a scholarly heretic. But in 1896 Cattell published his study of the abilities and capacities of students at Columbia University, where he was teaching. The psychology of individual differences was recognized and came to dominate twentieth-century psychology.

The search for universals, however, went on. The notion that men are dominated by conscious and rational decision was challenged for the first time by three powerful minds. Marx, Darwin, and Freud all emphasized the nonrational character of man and society. On this ground the instinct theory arose. William McDougall argued that man was born with processes which always led to particular actions or at least the impulse to such actions. For ten years instinct theory dominated psychological and social thought.[16] This theory seemed like a thrilling breakthrough promising to unlock the mysteries of human behavior. Only the search for the fundamental instincts destroyed the dream. For the search brought forth endless lists of these so-called instincts, and upon careful examination man was seen, not as a bundle of innate impulses, but as having a highly plastic and malleable nature. Yet a psychology of advertising began on the ground built by instinct theory. Walter Dill Scott at Northwestern published a theory of advertising in 1902.

Scientific management under Frederick W. Taylor was preparing the way for industrial psychology. Managers were beginning to accept the idea that the study of workers would pay off in dollars and cents. One manufacturer in 1916 said, "My success would be enormous if only a way could be found to select workers who were half as good as my machines."[17]

This vision was elaborated many years later by an industrial psychologist who yearningly said, "The ideal employment method is undoubtedly an immense machine which would receive applicants of all kinds at one end, automatically sort, interview, and record them, and finally turn them out at the other end nicely labelled with the job to which they are to go."[18]

The Rise of Industrial Psychology

Hugo Munsterberg, a former pupil of Wundt, became the first to think actively about the psychological problems of industry. In 1910 he asked several hundred executives what psychological traits they believed to be necessary in their employees. In 1912 as a professor at Harvard he prepared an English translation of

[16] Gardner Murphy, *Historical Introduction to Modern Psychology*, Harcourt, Brace, 1949, pp. 403–405.

[17] William F. Kemble, "Testing the Fitness of Your Employees," *Industrial Management*, November, 1916, p. 149.

[18] Henry C. Link, *Employment Psychology*, Macmillan, 1919, pp. 184–185.

his German lectures given in 1910–1911 at the University of Berlin. These were published under the title *Psychology and Industrial Efficiency*. Munsterberg described the psychology of industry as a new science which is "to intermediate between the modern laboratory psychology and the problems of economics. . . . Professional psychologists must do the actual work but the representatives of practical life are much better able to indicate the point at which the psychological levers ought to be applied."[19]

He advised psychologists to withdraw when they found themselves in the midst of industrial conflict. Psychologists should perfect their techniques and should cultivate complete scientific detachment. The psychologist, he said, "has no right to decide which effect is good and which effect is bad."[20]

Goals of Industrial Psychology

The industrial psychologists set their course as academic technicians who would help businessmen secure more productive efficiency from their workers—bring workers more job satisfaction. They joined and enlarged the scientific management movement, seeking to devise tests to select the best man for a given job, to find out whether he was working at full efficiency, to discover the extent of job satisfaction, and to rate workers for merit increases and promotions. They tried to discover causes of fatigue and boredom. They came to share the interests of industrial engineers in the psychological effects of temperature, lighting, noise, and humidity. Of all these interests, none proved more durable than the search for valid tests. World War I was the psychologists' finest hour. Army intelligence tests were eventually given to 1,727,000 men, and masses of men were assigned to specific jobs on their test results. Industrial psychologists emerged from the war with new confidence. "The most tangible instrument they had developed was the psychological test and on the success of this tool industrial psychologists were to stake their future."[21]

The history of testing may be summarized as one of slow

[19] Hugo Munsterberg, *Psychology and Industrial Efficiency*, Houghton, Mifflin, 1913, pp. 3–7.
[20] Hugo Munsterberg, *Business Psychology*, La Salle Extension University, 1915, p. 182.
[21] Loren Baritz, *The Servants of Power*, Weslyan University Press, 1960, p. 57.

acceptance, followed by business disillusionment. A later phase shows emphasis on better-designed instruments with attention to the validating of results. Management's acceptance of testing for certain specific skills is now well known. However, labor has maintained a posture of suspicion and cynicism. Many workers have seen these devices as instruments in the hands of employers who might now more easily manipulate them. Even executives may now be asked to take personality tests as requisites for promotion, and a lively controversy is raging whether business enterprise has a right to invade personal privacy in this manner.[22]

The Demise of Psychological Man

Psychological man emerges as an isolated man whose intelligence, ability, skills, and temperament are believed to be predictive of his work behavior. He is no longer the rational man, as "economic man" was, but he is still very much the biological machine reacting to the stimulations of the environment. In this period, reward and penalty systems still reflect simplified versions of the carrot-and-stick philosophy. Many managers were led to believe that financial incentives were the proper carrot. Sanctions are no longer so effective as they once were. The main problem facing industry today is how to apply sanctions in a situation where jobs are open to choice and dismissal merely means getting another job. It is apparent only two threats are available: (1) the fear of unemployment, (2) government legislation against indiscipline and organized labor resistance. After the tests have been given and the assignments of workers made so carefully on the basis of proper placement of job interests, the modern factory manager is often genuinely perplexed at the apparent lack of discipline, lack of interest, and perhaps even sabotage which appear to surround him. "The only way he can think of to stimulate workers to work harder is more money and in recent times, more 'welfare.' "[23] Could it be that the worker whose job had been relieved of much social significance and meaning to him had finally begun to accept it at the value placed upon it by the factory owner?

[22] See Douglas McGregor, *The Human Side of Enterprise*, McGraw-Hill, 1960, p. 13.

[23] J. A. C. Brown, *The Social Psychology of Industry*, Penguin, 1954, p. 37.

This situation called for new ideas. Morale and motivational theory was not yet adequate to the industrialized world of work. But another newcomer was coming forward. In a factory on the outskirts of Chicago, sociology was to enter industry.

VIEW OF WORKER AS A GROUP MEMBER
(a dominant view of 1940–1960)

The roots of industrial sociology may be traced in the United States to the early interest of sociologists in social problems, including the "labor problem."[24] There was a lively interest in the economic institution, and sociology was often linked with economics in a combined sociology and economic department. Sociologists began to explore occupations and communities with research methods. But there was one glaring omission. No one had studied a work group experimentally. Then came Elton Mayo and his Harvard associates to demonstrate the significance of social organization in work settings. This is best demonstrated in later studies which Mayo directed, including the bank wiring room study in the Western Electric Company, the study of absenteeism in the east coast metal plants, and finally the study of teamwork and labor turnover in the west coast aircraft companies.

The Bank Wiring Observation Room

Search for informal group structure

The final phase of the research program in the Hawthorne plant consisted of a detailed study of a shop situation from a sociological point of view. This study is significant in recording the changing thoughtways of the research group. Earlier an experimental study of five girls assemblying telephone relays in a test room had shown the importance of feelings and attitudes. T. N. Whitehead was discovering underneath his voluminous statistical compilations that it was the social organization among the test room operators which caused the differences in productivity. All the weather changes in Chicago, all the changes

[24] R. M. MacIver, "Labor in the Changing World," in E. T. Hiller, *The Strike,* University of Chicago Press, 1928.

in temperature and humidity, all the variations in rest pauses, hours of sleep, and diet did not explain as much as the social relationships formed in the test room. Likewise, the interviewers who talked with 21,000 workers found it impossible to catch the more subtle and spontaneous aspects of the employees' social organization. They recognized that "there was every indication that more intensive studies of small groups would have to be made before an adequate understanding of the social situation in which employees functioned could be obtained."[25] The bank wiring observation room study was projected to achieve this objective.

The interviewing staff discovered early in 1931 that social groups in shop departments were capable of exercising very strong control over the work behavior of their individual members. Interviewers were assigned to departments in the belief that concentrated interviewing might maximize the therapeutic values. Their reports showed that there were problems of employee interrelations and group organization which had escaped them before this time. Chief among these was restriction of output. The evidence obtained suggested that the wage incentive systems under which some of the groups worked had been rendered ineffectual by group pressure for controlled output.

The bank wiring observation room study then was planned to obtain more exact information about social groups within the company. It was conducted with a group of fourteen male operators who were working as they were accustomed to work, under standard shop conditions. The investigators spent the period of six and one-half months between November, 1931, and May, 1932, observing the work situation before them.

THE METHOD OF STUDY

The investigators were quite aware that the bank wiring observation room was to impose new problems of research method. Direct observation of the work group had not seemed to be of central importance in the test room although the test room observer did keep a record of important events.

In the interviewing program the interviewers had worked only with statements of how the employees said they acted. They

[25] F. J. Roethlisberger and W. J. Dickson, *Management and the Worker,* Harvard, 1939, p. 376.

had no means of relating these statements to what actually happened. What was now needed was a means of observing and recording overt behavior as well as verbal behavior. This demand led to an innovation in method which distinguished the bank wiring room study from all the others, namely, supplementing the interviewing method with carefully controlled methods of direct observation. In planning their experimental design the researchers were fortunate in having the counsel of William Lloyd Warner, at that time Assistant Professor of Social Anthropology at Harvard University and now Professor at Michigan State University. The general methodological concepts employed were chiefly derived from Mr. Warner. The responsibility for their detailed application rests with the investigators, who made a number of initial decisions. They decided to

1. Concentrate on one small group engaged in one type of work rather than to spread their efforts over a number of groups with dissimilar jobs.
2. Place the group to be studied in a separate room in order for the observer to keep adequate records without interfering with production in the shop.
3. Make base period studies before supervisors or workers knew anything about the study in order to assess the effect of placing the group in a separate room.
4. Say nothing in selecting the group to be studied which might alter their status in any way, either in explaining the study to them or in removing them from the department.
5. Make no records which might tend to make the workers apprehensive or consciously aware that they were being studied.

The investigating work was divided between an observer and an interviewer in the belief that the type of material to be gathered was quite different and that both types of material could not be gathered equally well by one person.

THE OBSERVER'S TASK

The observer was stationed in the group as a disinterested spectator; he was to establish friendly relations with everyone in the group. The observer was given certain general rules to guide him in playing an objective role.

1. He should not give orders or answer any questions which necessitated the assumption of authority.
2. He should not enter voluntarily into any argument. If forced to do so, he should be as noncommittal as possible.
3. He should not force himself into a conversation or appear to be either anxious to overhear what was going on or overinterested in the group's behavior.
4. He should never violate confidences or give any information to supervisors, whatever their rank.
5. He should not by his manner of speech or behavior set himself off from the group.

While playing a friendly but detached role it was the observer's job to secure a record of significant events in the behavior of the workers. But what is a significant event? Observation, if it is to be scientific, must be guided by a working hypothesis which enables the researcher to select relevant events from a welter of irrelevancies. The investigators agreed upon certain hypotheses. These were as follows:

1. There is a difference between the way the formal and technical organization is supposed to operate and the way it actually operates.
2. A strong informal organization of workers will be found.
3. The informal organization fulfills functions both for the people participating in it and for the larger structure of which the group is a part.

With these hypotheses as guides to observation the observer was instructed to look for and record the following:

1. Every item which indicated a similarity or difference between the actual situation and the way it was supposed to be recorded.
2. Evidences of any informal organization which the employees in their face-to-face relations consciously or unconsciously found, such as:
   a. Recurrent verbal utterances or overt acts indicative of the relations between two or more people.
   b. Manifestations of the kind and extent of a person's participation in the immediate group situation.

    c. Evidences of the existence of a group solidarity.

    d. Evidences, if group solidarity existed, of the occupational groups to which it extended and how it was expressed.

3. Evidences of the functions which the informal organization fulfilled in the lives of the workers.

Needless to say, the observer was aware of the necessity of avoiding personal judgments. His task was to ask such questions as, "Why does he act this way? What do his actions indicate his position in the group to be? How do his actions affect the interpersonal relations of others in the group?"

THE INTERVIEWER'S TASK

The interviewer was to remain outside the group. Although he was to keep in daily touch with the observer, he was not to enter the bank wiring observation room. This stipulation was made in the belief that the workers would feel more like telling the interviewer about themselves, their work, and occurrences in the observation room. The interviews were held by appointment and conducted in privacy.

The interviewer was to secure a maximum of insight into the attitudes, thoughts, and feelings of the workers. He was to discover the personal situation of each worker, which is to say, his personal values and the way they were related to personal history, family situation, and social life outside the plant.

SELECTING THE DEPARTMENT TO BE STUDIED

It was determined that the department to be selected should contain jobs fulfilling the following requirements:

1. Operators engaged in the same task.
2. Output for each operator capable of being exactly determined.
3. One unit of output completed in relatively short time, not more than a minute.
4. Work pace of operator determined by his own effort and not controlled by a machine or conveyor.
5. Assurance of reasonable continuance of employment of those selected.

6. Work group to be removed from the department without inconvenience.
7. Removal to a separate room not to require the installation of bulky or costly equipment.
8. Male operators to be experienced at their work.

The department best fitting these requirements was one engaged in the assembly of large electrical switches. One operation performed in the department, that of connector and selector bank wiring, was particularly suitable, and the men performing this operation were chosen for the study.

Three groups of workers—wiremen, soldermen, and inspectors —were necessary to perform the task of selector and connector bank wiring. Each of these groups performed a specific task and collaborated with the other two in completion of each unit of equipment. The work rate of one workman in any one of these groups was related to the rates of the two other workmen.

THE COMPOSITION OF THE BANK WIRING OBSERVATION GROUP

Some of the more important facts relating to the composition of the bank wiring group are shown in Table 15.2. All operators

TABLE 15.2 Composition of the Bank Wiring Observation Room

Operator	Age	Birthplace	Nationality	Marital Status	Education	Service Yrs.,	Mos.
Wireman 1	22	U.S.A.	Polish	S	7 G.S.	2	2
Wireman 2	25	U.S.A.	German	S	2 H.S.	5	5
Wireman 3	26	U.S.A.	American	M	8 G.S.	2	5
Wireman 4	20	U.S.A.	Irish	S	2 H.S.	3	7
Wireman 5	24	U.S.A.	Bohemian	M	4 H.S.	2	8
Wireman 6	21	U.S.A.	Polish	S	2 H.S.	3	1
Wireman 7	22	U.S.A.	Bohemian	M	8 G.S.	3	2
Wireman 8	22	U.S.A.	German	S	4 H.S.	3	8
Wireman 9	21	U.S.A.	American	S	8 G.S.	2	10
Solderman 1	21	U.S.A.	German	S	8 G.S.	5	4
Solderman 2	26	Yugoslavia	Bohemian	S	6 G.S.	9	8
Solderman 4	20	U.S.A.	Bohemian	S	8 G.S.	8	0
Inspector 1	23	U.S.A.	American	S	4 H.S	3	0
Inspector 3	40	Turkey	American	M	3 Col.	7	0

except one ranged from twenty to twenty-six years of age. Half of them had an eighth-grade education or less. Most of them were single men, but all fourteen, except one, had some person in their families dependent upon them.

Observation in the bank wiring room

The work of the bank wiring group took place in an observation room approximately 40 feet long and 20 feet wide and located about 200 feet from the regular department. The observer's desk was placed at the rear of the room. When he was seated, he faced a side wall and could not look directly at the group without turning to one side. It was believed that this position would minimize any feeling the operators might have of being watched.

Such considerations are not without importance, as the first weeks soon revealed. During the first week the men were under considerable strain. They behaved quite differently from the way they worked in the department. The observer was regarded with distrust. It was not until the end of the third week that the observer was on fairly good terms with everyone and was included in freely expressed conversations. The observer mingled and talked. He listened to complaints and occasionally asked for suggestions, but each time explained that he could do nothing to correct the conditions complained about. The interviewer discovered that all of the workers had misinterpreted the purpose of the study and he was able to help dispel the fears and uncertainties.

As the group settled down in their normal pattern of work, the observer and the interviewer kept gathering records. Records were made of output for each man at noon and at night. The quality rating of the work of each wireman for each day was recorded. The observer kept a daily record of significant happenings in the observation room, of conversations, and of his own impressions. Interviews were held with each man before the study began and two or more times during the study itself. Each person was given a thorough physical examination, which showed that all the men were in good health and had no interfering physical disabilities. Mental and dexterity tests were administered by a psychologist.

Significance of the bank wiring room experiment

The full account of the informal organization of the bank wiring workers can be found only in *Management and the Worker*. In Chapters 20–25 the informal organization of workers is discussed and many observations from this experiment are reported. At this point only a few significant conclusions will be drawn.

1. It was discovered very early that each individual in the group was restricting output in spite of the fact that the group piecework incentive plan in operation provided for a larger wage return the greater the number of units completed.

2. The working group as a whole actually determined the output of individual workers by reference to a standard predetermined but never clearly stated, that represented the group conception of a fair day's work.

3. The group output standard is only one of many social norms defined by the informal organization of the workers. Workers formed themselves into strong social groups with appropriate customs, duties, routines, even rituals. Strong social controls were constituted to command conformity to the group definitions and expectations.

4. In the contest between a management expectation and the group standards, the informal organization of the workers is most likely to prevail in determining conduct.

5. The power of the group controls is attested to by the fact that no relation was found between individual scores on dexterity or output or between intelligence test scores and output. The lowest man in output, for example, ranked first in intelligence.

Studies of Absenteeism in the East Coast Metalworking Shops

From records to supervisory relationships

During the war years, 1941–1945, absenteeism increased and leaders in government, labor, and industry became seriously concerned about its effects on war production. The concern was not without substance. When absenteeism reached the 10 percent level, as it did in some plants, it meant that many more workers were needed to carry the productive load. A company of 35,000 workers would require 3500 more employees to maintain a production schedule based on the original labor force. This situation was expensive not only in money but in manpower. The alleged reasons for the increased number of absences were many— the difficulties of transportation, the strain of long workdays, the special family and health problems of women workers, and so on. Some observers claimed that much of the absence was willful and caused by "more money in the workers' pockets than they had ever had in their lives." There was no doubt that many workers were taking a long week end, for absence on Saturday and Monday reached weekly peaks. What was the cause of absenteeism? How could it be remedied?

The industrial research staff at Harvard was asked by a government agency to investigate absenteeism in three metalworking companies located in the same industrial district of a small east coast industrial city.[26]

The first step the researchers took was to examine the official statistics of the three companies. The records were not immediately of great help since absence had been recorded in man-hours of work lost. The amount of total absence was shown for the company and for the departments but the total did not reveal to *whom* the absences were charged. In addition, the records of reasons for absence were unreliable. However, attendance data were available for each worker and this permitted an immediate attack on the problem. A significant decision was made. The investigators determined to discard the man-hour tables as being useless for purposes of analysis and to construct a simple index of regular attendance. The index was constructed by deciding to count any absence of a number of consecutive days as *one* absence. The reason for this decision was based on the fact that the greatest single reason for absence in the United States is sickness or injury. The real difficulty in the present situation was to distinguish between real sickness and alleged sickness. There was no way to do this quickly and accurately. But the counting of consecutive absences as one absence would have the effect of mini-

[26] The detailed account of the research is by John B. Fox and Jerome F. Scott, *Absenteeism: Management's Problem*, Harvard Business Research Studies, No. 29, 1943.

mizing successive days of absence and maximizing frequency of absences. The underlying assumption was that the successive days of absence probably represented a high proportion of real illness or injury, and the frequent absences probably represented a high proportion of willful absences. For example, two male workers were absent for twenty-two days in 1942. One was out for twenty-two successive days with appendicitis and was not otherwise absent; the other was absent eleven times for two days, mostly over the week end. The first was scored for one absence, the other for eleven absences. This device now made possible a meaningful interpretation of the group attendance pattern.

The records of men who had been continuously employed throughout 1942 were set aside in one group. In mid-1943 the majority of these men were still with the company. They were called the veterans. As a group their attendance record was good in all three companies. Many workers were not absent at all and most workers not more than a few times. However, there was striking variation between individuals and between some departments. The bulk of the absences could be charged to a small minority of persons whose records showed high frequencies. When the casting shops of the three companies were compared, significant variations were observed. The differences in attendance patterns can be seen in Fig. 15.2.

This figure shows that company A has experienced a steadily rising rate of absences which tops all of the other shops; in company B absenteeism rose steadily; in company C absenteeism rose until the July-September quarter of 1942 and thereafter began to fall. This is an observation of considerable interest—a genuine clue. What is the cause of the better record in the casting shop of company C?

Mayo says, "Whether we looked at the records of the whole casting shop or of the more regular attendants in it—in either event it was borne in upon us that some difference of method and of internal organization must be, at least in part, responsible for the remarkable difference. Was it possible, simply and directly, to detect this difference?"[27]

[27] E. Mayo, *The Social Problems of an Industrial Civilization,* Harvard, 1945, p. 100.

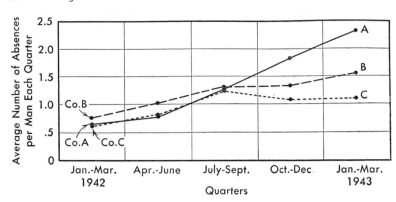

FIG. 15.2. Absences of Veterans by Quarters, January, 1942, Through March, 1943: Casting Shops of Companies A, B, and C. (From Elton Mayo, *The Social Problems of an Industrial Civilization*, Harvard, 1945, p. 96.)

The Mayo of 1943 is no longer the man of 1933 who sought reasons for absenteeism and turnover by looking for explanations in terms of monotony and pessimistic reverie of the individual. On the contrary, Mayo says the "answer to the question, which had become clear and specific, was not far to seek." Three findings are used to interpret the cause of lower absence in company C:

1. Foremen in company C had been trained to handle human situations. The company had supported a training program for twenty years which instructed supervisors not only in the technical details of their job but also in human relationships on the job.

2. The delegation of routine technical responsibilities to certain qualified technical assistants gave the foremen the time required for the responsibilities involved in team leadership. This improved communication from above down. In addition, payment of the three shifts for their twenty-four-hour output on a furnace built up a team spirit. No shift tended to slack off as the end of its period of work approached. "Teamwork and no buck passing" became a meaningful slogan.

3. Foremen and individual workers on the shift arranged every week which day off each worker should have. Unlawful failure of one worker to appear caused an upset in the whole arrangement.

As a consequence the workers put pressure on the individual of a severity that management could not have exercised.

Teamwork and Labor Turnover in the Aircraft Industry of Southern California[28]

Significance of the work team

Late in 1943 Mayo and certain members of his staff were asked to study the problem of labor turnover in the aircraft industry in southern California. The social setting was full of dynamic changes. The small airplane plants had grown to large industries in a few years. The drafting of workers into the army was a constant drain on the labor force for the industry and necessitated a constant induction of new workers. These new workers migrated into California by the thousands. Officers of the Los Angeles War Manpower Commission estimated that every month during 1943 approximately 25,000 people moved into southern California and between 12,000 and 14,000 moved out. In this social setting it is not surprising to learn that labor turnover in the industry was running between 70 and 80 percent. Mayo refused to believe that this unsettlement was in itself a sufficient explantion of the turnover. It is a large tribute to the acumen of this superb research man that he looked for prime determinants of work behavior within the *social organization* of a specific work situation. He was particularly emphatic in pointing out that no remedies external to a specific work situation can change a fundamental defect of organization within it. The reference here is to the application of rest periods, music, vitamin pills, free life insurance, steam baths, pretty entertainers, war heroes, dance pavilions, or other bread-and-circus measures which avoid the essential problems arising in face-to-face association in work groups. In place of these palliatives, if, in Mayo's view, an organization is to achieve its material and economic purpose it must secure the spontaneous cooperation of its workers. Three types of problems are continuously posed for management study: (1) the application of science and technical skill to a material product,

[28] Elton Mayo and George F. F. Lombard, *Teamwork and Labor Turnover in the Aircraft Industry of Southern California*, Harvard Business Research Studies, No. 32, 1944.

(2) the systemization of operations, and (3) the organization of sustained cooperation.

The labor turnover problem in the aircraft industry seemed to prove the validity of this theme just as all the other experiments had. It showed that management had done an excellent job of applying scientific-engineering knowledge and organizing operations, but the organization of teamwork had received scant attention.

The researchers soon realized that it would be necessary to ignore the larger groups—departments or shifts—and to center attention upon smaller groups of persons actually in daily intimate working association with each other. Seventy-one such groups were identified; among them were good and bad groups from the standpoint of attendance. They ranged from 100 percent regularity to no regularity at all.

One of the groups with excellent attendance came under observation. Its members had a reputation for "working like beavers." Their foreman said their efficiency ran 25 percent above that of the average of the plant. The group itself was thought by others to be somewhat clannish; members of it quite definitely thought of themselves as a group and in some degree different from other workers in the plant.

The teamwork which had obviously developed there could be definitely traced to key persons. The foreman of the department rarely visited this work group; his senior assistant visited it once daily. The work was actually in charge of a "leadman," a college man with considerable experience in steel mills. He did not have supervisory rank and in many ways was just another worker with the extra job of taking care of minor hour-to-hour interruptions in the operations of the group. Nonetheless, this leadman, with the support of the senior assistant foreman, placed the importance of group solidarity above other considerations. He functioned in three important ways to strengthen job relations.

First, he introduced new employees, always first getting acquainted with a new man as a person and then trying to get him congenial work associates. After a few days he would take the new employee to the assembly line and show him where the part he made was installed in the completed machine. He always listened to complaints and when he could not settle them would discuss them with the senior assistant foreman.

Second, he served as a troubleshooter, anticipating emergencies and shortages. When troubles arose he worked hard to get materials for his department.

Third, he became a buffer against and an effective link with the plant, the "outside world." The leadman handled inspectors, efficiency men, and the like; requests for raises went through him to the foreman.

This leadman made his chief self-imposed task that of securing for the individual worker an effective and happy relationship with his fellow workers and his work. The result was a well-knit human group superior in morale and efficiency to the disunited collections of workers scattered in so many other departments.

The problem of absenteeism, turnover, low morale, and poor efficiency reduces to the question of how groups may be solidified and collaboration increased in the large as well as the small work plant. The problem, as the famed sociologist Charles H. Cooley would say, is how to build primary group life. Mayo's theory is that the building and extension of group solidarity may be observed in three recognizable units: the "natural" group, the "family" group, and the "organized" group, all of which were identified among those having high attendance records.

THE "NATURAL" GROUP

The "natural" group is a very small group varying from two to three to six or seven workers (see Fig. 15.3). Twelve such groups were identified having almost perfect attendance records. The small group is apparently conducive to the development of intimacy and cohesiveness and stands as the strongest evidence that human beings are normal products of social interaction and should be expected unless interferences occur. However, unless there is a deliberate effort made to nourish and support such associations, numerous interferences may distort the social process or never give it a chance to develop.

THE "FAMILY" GROUP

The "family" group is merely an arbitrary name given to a larger group with a central core of regulars (see Fig. 15.4). This

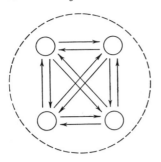

FIG. 15.3. A "Natural" Group. (After Mayo.)

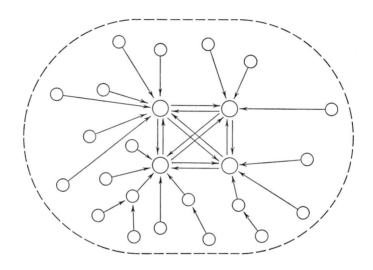

FIG. 15.4. A "Family" Group. (After Mayo.)

core of regulars may if they have prestige determine the standards for the group. "Family" groups contain from eight to thirty
members. It is estimated that a minimal period necessary for the
formation of a work team of this size may be from six months to a
year of continuous association. This assumes no explicit organization of human needs by management. Skilled management, by
establishing a favorable organizational "climate," can shorten the
time necessary for the formation of such a group. Under conditions of emergency or unusual stress even large teams may form
almost overnight.

The "organized" group might extend over the entire plant and include persons of widely different backgrounds (see Fig. 15.5). It envisages a community organization in which all or most individuals are members and participants of well-knit "natural" groups, with all of these groups linked together in common purpose. It requires that an administration with experience, intelligence, and skill *deliberately* set itself the task of creating group integrity of association. And above all, the planning for a work plant community requires new knowledge. Sociologists will be expected to supply an ever greater volume of basic and applied knowledge to the problem of group formation and collaboration. Industry, government, and community organizations are equally concerned with the formation of effective groups. The basic questions are: How can the formation of groups be stimulated? What conditions make for the growth of solidarity? How are leaders of teams found and trained? How can the purposes of a large organization be transmitted and effectively introduced into component groups in such a way that the entire organization actually strives

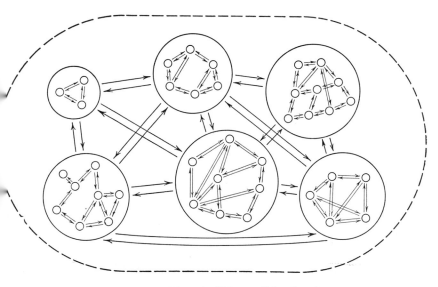

FIG. 15.5. An "Organized" Group. (After Mayo.)

for similar ends? To seek answers to these questions a growing body of researchers is studying group processes under such assorted titles as "group dynamics," "sociometry," "group discussion," and "group work."

Social changes and work teams

Vital as group processes are, still another large consideration intrudes. This is the impact of social changes upon the internal structure of industry. Mayo wrote in 1945 that he

had not fully realized in 1932 . . . how profoundly the social structure of civilization has been shaken by scientific, engineering, and industrial development. This radical change—the passage from an established to an adaptive social order—has brought into being a host of new and unanticipated problems for management and for the individual worker. The management problem appears at its acutest in the work of the supervisor. No longer does the supervisor work with a team of persons that he has known for many years or perhaps a lifetime; he is a leader of a group of individuals that forms and disappears almost as he watches it.[29]

In the southern California aircraft companies loans and transfers of workers caused by technical demands of production were constantly ripping work teams apart. On top of these internal changes, labor turnover continued to disrupt group formation with a vengeance.

These problems, which have diminished since the war, still exist with such intensity that they pose the severest obstacle to group formation and solidarity. The separation rate in manufacturing industries has long averaged about 50 percent for the year. It becomes difficult for the small "natural" group to form under these conditions; "family" groups do not have a chance to form without a central core of regulars; and the "organized" group which means a real work plant community is well-nigh impossible unless the plant is small.

A Sociological Orientation to Work Relations

A sociological orientation to work relations has emerged from these experiments to guide accumulated research knowledge. This

[29] Mayo, *op. cit.*, p. 75.

orientation is characterized by the following generalizations, which have been verified by the experimental findings:

Generalization	Drawn From
1. Work is a group activity.	All Harvard industrial research studies.
2. The social world of the adult is primarily patterned about work activity.	Textile mill; relay assembly test room.
3. The need for recognition, security, and sense of belonging is more important in determining worker's morale and productivity than the physical conditions under which he works.	Relay assembly test room.
4. A complaint is not necessarily an objective recital of facts; it is commonly a *symptom* manifesting disturbance of an individual's status position	Interviewing program.
5. The worker is a person whose attitudes and effectiveness are conditioned by social demands from both outside and inside the work plant.	Relay assembly test room; bank wiring observation room.
6. Informal groups within the work plant exercise strong social controls over the work habits and attitudes of the individual worker.	Bank wiring observation room; metalworking companies.
7. The first-line supervisor is the single most important factor in determining the morale and productivity of a work group.	Metalworking companies; Southern California aircraft companies.
8. The change from an established to an adaptive society tends continually to disrupt the social organization of a work plant and industry generally.	Southern California aircraft companies.
9. Group collaboration does not occur by accident; it must be planned for and developed. If group collaboration is achieved, the work relations within a work plant may reach a cohesion which resists the disrupting effects of adaptive society.	Southern California aircraft companies.

These principles form the core of the Mayo heritage. Social scientists have amassed a vast store of useful knowledge about the processes of group life. Although the record of research which has been chronicled in this chapter is an enduring monument to Mayo's achievement, these researches are not without shortcomings.

Critics and Criticism of the Hawthorne Research

So many critics have appeared and so much has been said about the Hawthorne research that a book on criticisms of the Mayo school was published by Henry A. Landsberger in 1958.[30] He notes that these criticisms have not been directed in the main at the empirical studies but at those books which are expressions of the school's ideologies, chief among them Mayo's *Human Problems of an Industrial Civilization, Social Problems of an Industrial Civilization,* and *Political Problems of an Industrial Civilization;* Whitehead's *Leadership in a Free Society;* and Roethlisberger's *Management and Morale.*

The first and most basic criticism takes issue with the group's view of modern society as one in a condition of *anomie,* i.e., made up of morally confused, isolated individuals surrounded by a society disorganized and full of conflict. As a solution to the problems of modern society the Mayo group is said to propose the reclaiming of individual and society through industrial organizations so managed that there is spontaneous collaboration for a common purpose. Three further criticisms assert that the Mayo group (1) projects an image of the worker which reflects both the acceptance of management's goals and its view of workers, coupled with a willingness to manipulate workers for management's end; (2) fails to pay attention to methods of accommodating industrial conflict such as collective bargaining; (3) fails to take unions into account.

Hawthorne revisited—twenty years later

Landsberger has concluded that many of the criticisms which have been leveled against Mayo do not apply to the actual report of the empirical research as found in Roethlisberger and Dickson's *Management and the Worker.* His review established that "the authors could not be accused of (1) being biased in management's favor; (2) that they did not regard workers as spurred on

[30] Henry A. Landsberger, *Hawthorne Revisited,* Cornell, 1958. Leading critics have included Michael Argyle, Reinhard Bendix, Herbert Blumer, John T. Dunlop, Ellis Freeman, Georges Friedmann, Mary Gibson, C. W. M. Hart, Clark Kerr, John B. Knox, W. A. Kowisto, Robert S. Lynd, C. W. Mills, Wilbert E. Moore, E. V. Schneider, Louis Schneider, Harold L. Sheppard, R. C. Sorenson, R. C. Stone, and Ordway Tead. (See Landsberger, *op. cit.,* pp. 28–29, for extensive bibliography of critical reviews.)

by irrational motives; (3) that they did not regard the factory as a suitable replacement for a vanished primitive society; and (4) that they did not regard the formation of groups as being caused by any instinct, but rather saw it as a reaction of workers to threats by management."[31] He concludes that the authors through a series of admitted trial and errors finally defined the core of their research problem as being that of exploring what, in the work situation, determined the attitudes of those within it.

The Variables of Work Relations

This relating of social structure to personality put the study of work relations solidly within a sociological framework. Moreover, as the research progressed, each problem led Mayo and his associates through the entire matrix of influencing variables within a social system.[32] This matrix is shown as Fig. 15.6, based on a

	Person[1]	Group[2]	Organi- zation[3]	Com- munity[4]	Society[5]	Culture Area [6]
Person[1]						
Group[2]						
Organization[3]						
Community[4]						
Society[5]						
Culture Area [6]						

FIG. 15.6. Matrix of Influencing Variables Within the Boundaries of Any Social System.

selection of six variables proposed as embracing any complete social system. The variables are the person, group, organization, community, society, and culture area. The matrix represents the underlying assumption of interaction between these six variables.

[31] *Ibid.*, p. 113.

[32] The idea for a depiction of an all-embracing taxonomy in matrix form was suggested by Robert Merton at the annual meeting of the American Sociology Society in New York City, August, 1960.

Thirty-six boxes or cells are shown. Each calls for a measurable datum, for each represents the quantum of influence that results from the impact of values as collectivities interact upon each other and upon the persons influenced within a given social situation. The complexity of such a scheme is so great that the interpretation of social behavior is usually made by treating the independent character of each variable as a constant or by selecting a narrow segment of the field variables considered most important to interpret the social behavior of a person or collectivity.

Mayo and his associates focused most of their research on personal and group relations. It is interesting to note that the stimulating effect of the Hawthorne studies was most immediately and most powerfully felt in the area of first-level supervision. The large amount of effort that has gone into research and training in supervision in industry in the last twenty years can probably be attributed more to the Hawthorne studies than to any other single influence emanating from the academic world.[33]

The Mayo research became a very important stimulant of the renaissance in small-group research, which was joined by such fresh new ideas as Kurt Lewin's field theory of group dynamics, J. L. Moreno's sociometry of interpersonal relations, and later E. Chapple, C. Arensberg, and Robert Bales' studies of face-to-face interaction in small groups. The impetus for the study of leadership can be seen in William F. Whyte's *Human Relations in the Restaurant Industry,* in the Michigan studies of industrial situations, in civilian and military agencies, in the Ohio State leadership studies, and in so many others that the list is too long to include here.

If Mayo and his associates had given us no other heritage this would have been sufficient. But Mayo was not concerned with the full matrix of the social system. He and his associates did not engage in a single research problem which embraced testable hypotheses beyond the person-to-group or group-to-group chain of interaction. Mayo knew that variables such as organization, community, and society were intruding—some he observed and some he simply theorized about. It was his interpretative writing that brought so much criticism down upon his head. Perhaps

[33] Landsberger, *op. cit.,* p. 101.

his greatest weakness, i.e., leaping ahead of his facts, was also a great endowment. His critics awakened the entire research community to the need of extending research into many unexplored areas, such as the role of union organization, the relation of work groups to the larger organization, the nature of bureaucracy, the conflict and accommodation processes in work organizations, the place of financial reward and nonfinancial motives in different occupations and with different types of workers, the influence of technology and technical factors in the work place, industry-labor-community relations including community power structures, the role of a modern capitalist society in introducing stratification and mobility into the community and into the work plant, the impact of alternate economic and social systems on work relations, and the role of cultural values on work and social life generally. These interests have been extended into every kind of formal organization.

Mayo and his associates posed the problems and pointed the way. Since World War II a mighty host of researchers have added new knowledge. All have been influenced by Mayo and Roethlisberger.

Changes in Orientation to Work Relations

The impact of the large-scale industrial experiments at the Western Electric Company caused Elton Mayo and his staff to alter their entire axis of thought, from the proposition that all social problems are individual to the proposition that all individual problems are essentially social. In July, 1925, after many years as a psychologist in industry, Mayo stated his thinking in positive terms. He wrote in *Harper's Magazine,* "When we talk of social problems, we are apt to forget that every social problem is ultimately individual. . . ."[34] By 1945 Mayo was writing, "In industry and in other human situations the administrator is dealing with well-knit human groups and not with a horde of individuals. . . . Man's desire to be continuously associated in work with his fellows is a strong, if not the strongest, human characteristic."[35]

[34] See "The Fruitful Errors of Elton Mayo," *Fortune,* November, 1946, p. 238.

[35] Mayo, *op. cit.,* p. 110.

While this transition in thinking was taking place, other changes were occurring in the political and economic order—changes which increasingly focused attention upon group relations, For example, while the framework of labor relations was set in the earlier pattern of individual bargaining, the individual worker remained the principal unit of attention. The growth of collective bargaining, with the passage of the National Industrial Labor Relations Act in 1935, emphasized the pressing need for knowledge of intergroup relations. This situation helped to stimulate the growth of interest in the application of sociology to industry and labor. Since then, industrial sociology has been seeking to develop a conceptual framework and a body of knowledge which will be helpful to students of labor and management.

Social Man as the Dominant Image

The image of social man dominates as the key concept. This man is viewed as one who seeks affiliation and identity with groups and associations of many kinds: family, neighborhood, work, recreational groups, church, political party, union or occupational association, and national interest groups. Kurt Lewin once wrote, "The group to which a person belongs is the ground on which he stands. His relation to this group and his status in it are the most important factors for his feeling of security or insecurity. No wonder that the group the person is a part of, and the culture in which he lives, determines to a very high degree his behavior and character."[36] The work group is seen as one of the most important group affiliations since it is through this group that the man pursues his occupation. Occupation is the major factor in providing his income, his status, his power, and the life chances for himself and his family.

This view of the worker has created the employee society. The status line between manual and nonmanual worker is rapidly disappearing because the education and pay levels of manual workers may now equal or excel those of the white-collar clerical staff in many work organizations. In most, the differential in education is small; the differential in pay, nonexistent. Differences in dress and working conditions between the two groups are often indistinguishable. Personnel programs are commonly

[36] Kurt Lewin, *Resolving Social Conflict*, Harper, 1948, p. 82.

directed toward all employees from the president to the employee of lowest status. They include employee recreational and educational programs and they may include group incentive plans. Supervisory and management training programs are based on the objective which specifies the creation of stronger ties between the employee and the managers as well as more cohesive work groups that build morale and teamwork. Emphasis on group participation in decision-making may be a personal policy even if this means only letting the employee know what is going on and allowing him to have his say on some matters that affect him. The public relations department has changed its name to community relations and is seriously concerned with how to build a better business climate through community participation. In fact, employee and community relations are becoming a combined responsibility because of the recognition that employees are the best source of good public relations and that good community relations are an important factor in building morale in employee relations. A vice-president of employee and community relations who views employees as group members draws no rigid lines between the motivations and needs of any group of employees. He sees the basic differences between people as differences in degree, not in kind. He knows that what goes on inside the work organization has an important bearing on what happens outside the organization in the community. A sociological approach is appropriate to his task because he must relate the work place to the local community and the larger society. He must seek ways to help employees find meaning for their lives in work and in citizenship because he believes that in that way they become more productive and more useful employees.

The Massive Shift in Leadership Philosophies

The first half of the twentieth century has witnessed a revolution in the leadership orientations of managers. Douglas McGregor has summarized this change by setting forth the contrasting assumptions of the polar types. Theory X is a statement of an earlier set of beliefs:

1. The average human being has an inherent dislike of work and will avoid it if he can.
2. Because of this human characteristic of dislike of work, most peo-

ple must be coerced, controlled, directed, threatened with punishment to get them to put forth adequate effort toward the achievement of organizational objectives.

3. The average human being prefers to be directed, wishes to avoid responsibility, has relatively little ambition, wants security above all.

Theory Y is a statement of an emergent set of beliefs:

1. The expenditure of physical and mental effort in work is as natural as play or rest.
2. External control and the threat of punishment are not the only means for bringing about effort toward organizational objectives. Man will exercise self-direction and self-control in the service of objectives to which he is committed.
3. Commitment to objectives is a function of the rewards associated with their achievement.
4. The average human being learns, under proper conditions, not only to accept but to seek responsibility.
5. The capacity to exercise a relatively high degree of imagination, ingenuity, and creativity in the solutions of organizational problems is widely, not narrowly, distributed in the population.
6. Under the conditions of modern industrial life, the intellectual potentialities of the average human being are only partially utilized.[37]

These two sets of beliefs stand in marked disagreement and have almost revolutionary repercussions for administrative behavior. Most managers feel that they personally stand somewhere between the two poles and that they are often forced by various conditions to oscillate back and forth. The most important factor seems to be the social environment which surrounds their work. If their superior is supportive of theory Y they move in this direction. If he believes in theory X he pulls the behavior of all subordinates toward that view. Cultural lags in managerial philosophies are as real as cultural lags in technology.

WORKER AS A SOCIOPOLITICAL MAN
(an emergent view of the 1960s)

Even while some nineteenth-century views of the worker still remain, the view of the employee as a sociopolitical man is al-

[37] Douglas McGregor, *The Human Side of Enterprise*, McGraw-Hill, 1960, pp. 33–34, 47–48.

ready over the horizon. It promises to be as revolutionary as any that preceded it. It may be outlined as follows:

1960—

VIEW OF THE WORKER AS A SOCIOPOLITICAL MAN (EMERGENT)

Imported from political sociology

Major characteristic:

Importance of group participation in decisions affecting the worker or work group.

Motivation of employee:

Political man desires an active part in decisions which affect him at work and in the community.

Expressed in such personnel practices as:

Staff meetings; joint consultation machinery.
Union as a communication and bargaining channel.
Cooperative ownership or management practices.
Community political participation programs.

Department:

Citizenship and political affairs.

Academic base:

Sociology and political science.

In this view the employee is working a short work week of, let us say, thirty hours. His work group becomes less important as his family and community groups become more important. His education includes some college. His higher standard of living and his greater education combine to encourage greater aspiration for participation in all matters that concern him. He will demand an opportunity to have his say in the work organzation and in his community; sociopolitical man wishes to play an active part in decisions which affect him at work and in the community. Personnel practices will include widespread use of staff meetings, joint consultation, collective bargaining, cooperative ownership, or cooperative management. Political or civic education will be defined as the greatest obligation of the school, mass communication, and industry. In industry the Department of Citizenship and Political Affairs should emerge.[38] Such services will require the combined knowledge of specialists in industrial and in political sociology.

The social pressures forcing this development can be foreseen as the continuing Communist threat, the automation of industry, and the emergence of a leisured, well-educated, high-income population. Industrial sociology under these conditions will increase its emphasis on industry-community relations as citizenship in the plant and citizenship in the community are seen as mutual goals in the enlarging experience of a person struggling to make a free society work.

SELECTED BIBLIOGRAPHY

Baritz, Loren, *The Servants of Power,* Wesleyan University Press, 1960.

Brown, J. A. C., *The Social Psychology of Industry,* Penguin, 1954.

Ching, Cy, *Review and Reflection, A Half Century of Labor Relations,* Forbes, 1956.

Copley, Frank B., *Frederick W. Taylor: The Father of Scientific Management,* Harper, 1923.

"Deep Therapy on the Assembly Line," *Ammunition,* the magazine of the United Auto Workers, April, 1949, pp. 47–51.

Knox, John, *The Sociology of Industrial Relations,* Random House, 1956.

Landsberger, Henry A., *Hawthorne Revisited,* Cornell, 1958.

Mayo, Elton, *The Social Problems of an Industrial Civilization,* Harvard, 1945.

McGregor, Douglas, *The Human Side of Enterprise,* McGraw-Hill, 1960.

Mills, C. Wright, "The Contribution of Sociology to Studies of Industrial Relations," *Proceedings of the Industrial Relations Research Association,* December, 1948, pp. 199–222.

Nadworny, Milton J., *Scientific Management and the Unions, 1900–1932,* Harvard, 1955.

Taylor, Frederick W., *The Principles of Scientific Management,* Harper, 1911.

---

[38] Ford Motor Company has a fully developed training program, and many companies have been developing political education programs.

CHAPTER 16

Leadership, Morale, and Productivity

Out of the Mayo heritage came a lively interest in the study of leadership, employee morale, and productivity throughout the United States. Mayo was constantly seeking means to secure sustained collaboration. He was equally determined to find ways by which human resources could be made more productive. These two goals are of major importance to managers everywhere. Labor leaders are also concerned with the means toward these goals. The European Productivity Agency, which the United States has provided with financial and consultative support, has given stimulus to the study of these goals in Europe. Industrial sociologists, industrial social psychologists, and business researchers are drawn into the study of morale and productivity because of their own interest and also because of contracts and grants which have been forthcoming from industry, government agencies, and foundations to study these factors.

The History of Measurement

Mayo showed that leadership was a major influencing factor of morale and/or productivity in almost all of his studies, especially those in a Philadelphia textile mill, in the Western Electric relay assembly room, and in the east coast metal plants and the west coast airplane industry discussed in Chapter 15. Kurt Lewin, at about the same time, in his classic experiment with boys' clubs was demonstrating the significance of laissez-faire, autocratic, and democratic leadership on the behavior of group members. Lewin pointed out the greater active participation and judgment exercised by the members of democratic groups. Traditionally work organizations had relied heavily on autocratic styles, and Lewin's work was a challenge. Interest in leadership as an independent variable reached a new high as psychologists, sociologists, and researchers in business approached the study of leadership from all directions. Role playing, group dynamics, personality testing, interactional process analysis, interactional chronograph analysis, skimmer charts, sociometry, profile analysis, projective techniques like the Thematic Apperception tests, and depth interviewing—these and many other methods of personality exploration were born. They are now so extensively used that a critical ethical question has arisen as to the propriety of an organization's using leadership data gathered by personality tests like the Minnesota Multiphasic test as a basis for promotion decisions.

Contributions from Ohio State, Michigan, and Chicago

Three research centers have especially concentrated large amounts of research energy on the three variables: leadership, morale, and productivity. The Ohio State Personnel Board, under Carroll Shartle's direction, instituted a ten-year program in the Study of Leadership in 1945.[1] Science Research Associates of Chicago, advised by the late L. C. Thurstone, and its university companion, the Industrial Relations Research Center, began to make a multiplicity of morale surveys in a variety of industrial situations and to derive comparative data for types and size of industry.[2] The Michigan Survey Research Center set out a long-range program in 1947 to obtain measures of performance which could be related to measures of motivation and morale. Impressionistic accounts of attitude and morale, as in the Hawthorne studies, were replaced with measures of the employees' psychological responses. Effects of supervisory practices were not judged on the basis of what management assumed the results to be. Independently derived measures were employed in testing relationships between factors.

In many research designs productivity was taken as the dependent variable, supervisory practice as the independent vari-

<hr>

[1] C. L. Shartle, *Executive Performance and Leadership*, Prentice-Hall, 1956.
[2] David G. Moore and Robert K. Burns, "How Good Is Your Morale?" *Factory*, February, 1956, pp. 130–136.

able, and morale as the intervening variable. The chain of causation would be drawn as follows:

Leadership Practices (Independent variable)	$\longrightarrow$	Individual and Group Morale (Intervening variable)	$\longrightarrow$	Productivity of Employee Members (Dependent variable)

The groups which were compared were equated in all the technological factors which could affect productivity. A great variety of organizations have been subsequently studied, including the home office of an insurance company, maintenance-of-way sections on a railroad, an electric utility, an automotive manufacturer, a tractor company, an appliance manufacturer, and two agencies of the federal government.[3] The research designs aim at repetition of the same design in a number of varying situations. A single study is suggestive rather than conclusive, and the findings from a single situation are not generalizable. The promise of genuine progress may be realized in a set of common findings for a wide variety of institutional settings. Moreover, field experiments are designed in such a way as to make new or more rigorous tests of original findings.[4] In this chapter the search for independent measures of each variable will be described, and some of the findings revealed by studies of the relationship between leadership, morale, and productivity will be reported.

LEADERSHIP

Search for Traits

The early history of leadership research is largely a search for "traits," i.e., relatively stable aptitudes and capacities of the person. The background of "leadership trait" research is similar to that of "instinct" research. The list of traits reported as necessary for leaders became longer and longer.[5] Consensus among researchers was lacking. Validation often rested on circular rea-

---

[3] Robert L. Kahn and Daniel Katz, "Leadership Practices in Relation to Productivity and Morale," in D. Cartwright and A Zander (eds.), *Group Dynamics*, Harper, 1953, p. 613.

[4] Human Relations Program of Survey Research Center, Institute of Social Research, University of Michigan, 1950.

[5] C. Bird, *Social Psychology*, Appleton-Century, 1940; also A. W. Gouldner (ed.), *Studies in Leadership*, Harper, 1950.

soning—i.e., certain behavior was inferred as due to the "trait" and the "trait" was said to cause the observed behavior. Meanwhile, no one could actually locate the source of the "trait." It was simply assumed to be present. Moreover, many traits were found to be highly unstable. Finally the whole structure of trait research fell into general disfavor and remains so today.

Leadership Viewed in Social Context

Investigators have generally come to the conclusion that certain minimal abilities may be required of all leaders but that these will also be widely distributed among the nonleaders. Furthermore, the traits of the leader which seem to be necessary and effective in one group or situation may be quite different from those of another leader in a different setting.

The search now is for leadership behavior or practices which can be related to certain observed consequences in group behavior under stated conditions. There is a recognition that leadership behavior is role behavior and that it has considerable fluidity. Necessarily, leadership behavior depends on the indiivdual, the followers, and the conditions. Among the variables which may affect a leader's role in a work organization are the following:

1. The way in which superiors, subordinates, and colleagues are performing their jobs.
2. The individual's qualifications including his experience and competence which change over time.
3. The individual's personal interests.
4. The individual's conception of his role as a leader.
5. The constantly changing requirements of the external situation such as economic conditons, political circumstances, competitive conditions and many other variables which affect the nature of the job.[6]

The definition of leadership is made more difficult by the concept of leadership role behavior. Chester Barnard once said, "I have never observed any leader who was able to state adequately or intelligibly why he was able to be a leader, nor any statement of followers that acceptably expressed why they followed."[7] But the field must be staked out for research. Leadership may be con-

---

[6] Douglas McGregor, *The Human Side of Enterprise,* McGraw-Hill, 1960, pp. 80–81.

[7] Chester I. Barnard, *Organization and Management,* Harvard, 1948, p. 39. President John F. Kennedy has tried to sum up his understanding of leader-

sidered as the process or acts of influencing the activities of an organized group in its efforts toward goal setting and goal achievement. It appears that the minimal social conditions which permit the existence of leadership include a group of two or more persons, a common task or goal-oriented activities, and differentiation of responsibility among the members.[8]

The Measurement of Leadership Behavior

Many efforts to measure leadership behavior have been made by the Ohio State Personnel Research group.[9] Fleishman has concentrated on the measurement of leadership in industry. The Leader Behavior Description started with over 1800 items and was reduced to 150 items by "expert judges" in obtaining consensus of proper classification (see Table 16.1). Subsequent factor analyses of the items showed that two independent factors were present. The major factors were defined as "Consideration" and "Initiating Structure," and these accounted for more than 80 percent of the common variance among the 150 items.[10] "Initiating Structure" describes behavior by which a leader organizes and defines the relationship between himself and the work group. He tends to define the role which he expects each member of the group to assume, and endeavors to establish well-defined patterns of organization, channels of communication, and ways of getting jobs done. "Consideration" describes behavior indicative of friendship, mutual trust, respect, and warmth in the relationship of the leader to his group. On results obtained from a test of 122 foremen the two factors were shown to be quite independent of each other ($r = -.02$).

After preliminary tests and an item analysis, a forty-eight-item revised Supervisory Behavior Description was prepared (Table 16.1). The revised questionnaire was administered to a sample of

---

ship. He says, "Whether a man is burdened by power or enjoys power; whether he is trapped by responsibility or made free by it; whether he is moved by other people and other forces or moves them—this is the essence of leadership." See Theodore H. White, *The Making of the President,* Atheneum, 1960.

[8] Ralph M. Stogdill, "Leadership, Membership, and Organization," in Cartwright and Zander, *op. cit.,* p. 41.

[9] Ralph M. Stogdill and Alvin E. Coons (eds), *Leader Behavior: Its Description and Measurement,* Ohio State University Bureau of Business Research, 1957.

[10] *Ibid.,* p. 104.

TABLE 16.1 Items Selected for the Revised Form of the Supervisory Behavior Description[a]

Item Number	Item

Consideration: Revised Key

1. He refuses to give in when people disagree with him.
2. He does personal favors for the foremen under him.
3. He expresses appreciation when one of us does a good job.
4. He is easy to understand.
5. He demands more than we can do.
6. He helps his foremen with their personal problems.
7. He criticizes his foremen in front of others.
8. He stands up for his foremen even though it makes him unpopular.
9. He insists that everything be done his way.
10. He sees that a foreman is rewarded for a job well done.
11. He rejects suggestions for changes.
12. He changes the duties of people under him without first talking it over with them.
13. He treats people under him without considering their feelings.
14. He tries to keep the foremen under him in good standing with those in higher authority.
15. He resists changes in ways of doing things.
16. He "rides" the foreman who makes a mistake.
17. He refuses to explain his actions.
18. He acts without consulting his foreman first.
19. He stresses the importance of high morale among those under him.
20. He backs up his foremen in their actions.
21. He is slow to accept new ideas.
22. He treats all his foremen as his equal.
23. He criticizes a specific act rather than a particular individual.
24. He is willing to make changes.
25. He makes those under him feel at ease when talking with him.
26. He is friendly and can be easily approached.
27. He puts suggestions that are made by foremen under him into operation.
28. He gets the approval of his foremen on important matters before going ahead.

Initiating Structure: Revised Key

1. He encourages overtime work.
2. He tries out his new ideas.
3. He rules with an iron hand.
4. He criticizes poor work.
5. He talks about how much should be done.
6. He encourages slow-working foremen to greater effort.
7. He waits for his foremen to push new ideas before he does.
8. He assigns people under him to particular tasks.
9. He asks for sacrifices from his foremen for the good of the entire department.
10. He insists that his foremen follow standard ways of doing things in every detail.
11. He sees to it that people under him are working up to their limits.
12. He offers new approaches to problems.
13. He insists that he be informed on decisions made by foremen under him.
14. He lets others do their work the way they think best.
15. He stresses being ahead of competing work groups.
16. He "needles" foremen under him for greater effort.
17. He decides in detail what shall be done and how it shall be done.
18. He emphasizes meeting of deadlines.
19. He asks foremen who have slow groups to get more out of their groups.
20. He emphasizes the quantity of work.

[a] Supervisor rates immediate superior by answering the statements with Always, Often, Occasionally, Seldom, or Never. *From:* R. M. Stogdill and A. E. Coons, *Leader Behavior: Its Description and Measurement,* Bur. Business Res., Ohio State Univer., p. 109, 1957; by permission.

122 foremen in one of the Harvester Company's motor truck manufacturing plants. Each subject was asked to ascribe the behavior of his own immediate supervisor in the plant. Split-half reliabilities give an $r = .92$ on consideration items and an $r = .68$ on Initiating Structure. These values indicate a definite consistency in the ratings for the scale items.

To make tests of validity (how well the scale measures what it purports to measure), correlations were obtained between descriptions of foreman behavior and independent indices of accident rates, absenteeism, grievances, and turnover among the foreman's own work groups. Correlations were also obtained between foreman behavior descriptions and ratings of foreman proficiency by management. Table 16.2 summarizes these results

TABLE 16.2. Summary of Test-Retest Reliability Coefficients Obtained with the Supervisory Behavior Description from Various Samples

Criterion	Department	Dimension	
		Consideration	Initiating Structure
		r	r
Proficiency ratings by	Production foremen	$-.31^b$	$.47^b$
foremen's supervisor	Nonproduction foremen	.28	$-.19$
Absenteeism by foremen's work group	Production foremen	$-.49^b$	$.27^a$
	Nonproduction foremen	.38	.06
Accidents by foremen's work group	Production foremen	$-.06$	.15
	Nonproduction foremen	$-.42^a$	.18
Formal grievances by foremen's work group	Production foremen	$-.07$	$.45^b$
	Nonproduction foremen	.15	.23
Turnover in foremen's work group	Production foremen	.13	.06
	Nonproduction foremen	.04	$.51^a$

$N = 72$ production departments and 23 nonproduction departments.
[a] Significant at .05 level of confidence.
[b] Significant at .01 level of confidence.

as they were developed for the Consideration dimension and the Initiating Structure dimension. It shows that the two dimensions of leadership behavior have different effects in production and nonproduction departments. A leader with a high score on Initiation tends to secure a high proficiency rating from his immediate supervisor in a production department, but high initiation tends to be of little help, if any, in a nonproduction department. Just the reverse is true for a high consideration score. It brings a low rating in production departments but tends toward a high rating in nonproduction departments. It has been said that in the higher reaches of organizational structure bosses seldom give orders to anyone. In the white-collar world, commands become requests and suggestions.

Other differences can be seen in the incidence of absenteeism, accidents, and turnover. A high initiation score is associated with high absenteeism and formal grievances in production departments. But in nonproduction departments high labor turnover is the most pronounced charcteristic associated with initiation. This finding suggests that white-collar workers will not accept the "driving" supervisor, and perhaps also they are in a position to be more mobile.

This study reveals how difficult it is to make wide-ranging generalizations about leadership behavior. Leadership is always a relationship between a leader and followers.

Leadership Styles

Hemphill reports that his study of leadership discloses a large variation among individual leaders in how they do their jobs. Interpretation of factor analysis reveals three major leadership styles: (1) A leader may stress being a socially acceptable individual in his interactions with other group members. (2) A leader may stress "getting the job done"; he emphasizes group production and concern with achieving objectives. (3) A leader may stress getting members of a group or organization to work together; the leader's job is to act as a group catalyst. These styles are not viewed as mutually exclusive. A leader may employ all of them to the same degree or he may use one at the expense of the others.[11]

These findings are similar to those emerging from the Michigan Institute of Social Research. They have reported that, "there

[11] John K. Hemphill and Alvin E. Coons, "Description of the Leader Behavior Questionnaire," in *ibid.*, p. 37.

is a distinct syndrome of behavior characteristics which can be called an employee-oriented supervisor. This supervisor gives major attention to creating employee motivation. In contrast, production-oriented supervisors stress production planning and achievement."

Other findings from the Institute show that

1. Supervisors may be distinguished by the closeness with which they supervise or the degree to which they delegate authority. The better supervisors delegated authority to others more than the poorer supervisors.

2. There is a "linking pin" function which greatly determines supervisory behavior. Briefly, this function refers to the relationship which reaches from the leader downward to his subordinates and upward to the superior. If a supervisor had above-average influence or power with his own bosses and followed procedures which are generally good supervisory behavior, his subordinates tended to react favorably. However, if supervisors who were below average in the amount of influence they had with their superiors practiced these same desirable supervisory procedures, they usually failed to obtain a favorable reaction and often obtained an adverse reaction. These findings have been interpreted as showing that the supervisor, to function effectively, must have sufficient influence with his own superiors to be able to affect the superiors' decisions when required.[12]

3. The supervisors of the more effective groups had work groups which had developed greater cohesiveness among members of the group than was evident in those groups which were doing a less effective job.

Both the Ohio State and the Michigan research groups agree that the supervisor's emphasis on either employee- or production-centered practices derives from the behavior of his own boss. A supervisor tends to behave as his boss does or at least to behave so as to please the boss. Proficiency ratings given by the boss are based on the superior's conception of what good leadership requires in a given situation. It is also known that workers prefer

[12] Rensis Likert, *New Patterns of Management*, McGraw-Hill, 1961, pp. 5–25. Cf. Delbert C. Miller and Nahum Medalia, "Human Relations Leadership and the Association of Morale and Efficiency in Work Groups: A Controlled Study with Small Military Units," *Social Forces*, May, 1955, pp. 348–352.

the supervisor who emphasizes consideration. In view of these facts, obviously every organization must make a policy decision as to the kind of leaders it wishes to recruit and to develop. Only then does the selection of leaders become a meaningful task.

Selection of Leaders

Research shows that effective leaders are persons who are able to achieve results in specific social situations. In the final selection, applicants should be tested in situations similar to the ones in which they will be expected to work. It is in the light of this hypothesis that the sociodramatic and interactional techniques of selection take on significance.

Selection by Sociodramatic Performance Tests

The sociodramatic performance test involves *activity by an individual or group in a social situation of simulated reality.* The test is usually given before an audience of observers and participants who provide the necessary social environment. An individual is presented with a task to be performed or a role to be played in a problem situation. Performance ratings and sociometric ratings of the performance of the person tested by the other participants are often included.

Sociodramatic methods have been used in the American and British armies, and the Office of Strategic Services during World War II developed an assessment program in which many role-playing tests were used for diagnostic purposes.[13]

The role-playing tests have been derived from J. L. Moreno's "Psychodrama," which, although originally developed as a therapeutic procedure for psychiatric purposes, has more recently been shown to have excellent diagnostic value in sizing up a man's tendencies to take a dominant or subordinate role in a social situation, as well as his tact, resourcefulness, forcefulness, ability to take criticism, and other important personal and social characteristics. A dramatic illustration of a role test as used by the OSS is reported as follows: The applicant was told that he had just

[13] A description of the work of the Office of Strategic Services Assessment School may be found in "A Good Man Is Hard to Find," *Fortune*, March, 1946, pp. 92–95, 217, 218, 220, 223. See also Henry A. Murray and Donald W. MacKinnon, "Assessment of O.S.S. Personnel," *Journal of Consulting Psychology*, March–April, 1946, pp. 76–80.

been caught in the secret files of a government department without authorization. He was given ten minutes to think of a good way to explain and justify his behavior. He was then subjected to a grilling cross-examination under a blinding eye-level spotlight to break his defensive story and observe his behavior when told that he had failed.[14]

Less spectacular but equally penetrating were the many other improvisations, in which one man was asked to play a role with another man in a dramatic situation usually involving conflict between them. The group was instructed as follows:

> Everyone at times finds himself in new and unfamiliar situations in which he has to exercise his ingenuity and resourcefulness. This evening we are going to place each of you in problem situations involving another man in order to discover how you can manage yourself. Two of you will be placed together to take these roles and you will be given certain facts. I want you to work out these situations in the most effective way you can. However, we do not want you to "act" in the ordinary sense of the word, but we want you to be yourself and to behave as you yourself would behave in a similar situation in actual life. . . . We want to find out how you yourself as you are now tend to meet certain situations.[15]

With these instructions, an improvised role situation which had been hand tailored to fit the individuals was enacted. First one member of the team was assigned a role, and then a role was assigned to the man whom he was to play opposite. It was customary to place one man in his home or office to receive the second man as his guest. In every case each man was given a motive for the meeting.

TYPES OF ROLE-PLAYING IMPROVISATIONS

The role-playing episodes were planned in order to test out the reaction of candidates along lines about which the interviewer of a candidate felt some uncertainty. The 111 improvisation situations used in OSS fall into seven types.

Type A. Personal criticism (one man is criticized for some fault or misdemeanor by the other)

[14] Reported by Joseph W. Eaton, "Experiments in Testing for Leadership," *American Journal of Sociology*, May, 1947, p. 531.

[15] Percival M. Symonds, "Role Playing as a Diagnostic Procedure in the Selection of Leaders," *Sociatry*, March, 1947, p. 43.

Briefing: (a) Person being criticized might be sent out and his critic told the nature of the charges against him and possibly how the interests of the critic were being adversely affected. (b) Critic might be sent out and the person being criticized told of some countercharge he might make.

Test variables: Criticized person tested for reaction to failure, reaction to attack, resourcefulness, tendency to give excuses, persuasiveness, diplomacy, ability to counterattack. Critic tested for tact, tolerance, ability to discipline a subordinate, forcefulness, resourcefulness, tendency to be severe, sympathy.

Type B. Interpersonal conflict of aims, goals, ideals

Example: Partnership dissolution

Briefing: One or both men might be sent out. Each man might be told the point of view and motives which he is to hold (to retain or break up their partnership) and the reasons for holding it (criticism of the other person, for his own advantage or disadvantage of the other).

Test variables: Both persons tested for tact, social relations, forcefulness, resourcefulness, integrity, and ability to control temper.

Type C. Situations involving moral issues

Example: Stealing

Briefing: Man who was at fault is sent out; the other man accuses the first.

Test variables: Accuser tested for his tact, forcefulness, and tendency to be severe. The person against whom the charge was made tested for his reaction to attack, resourcefulness, tendency to give excuses.

Type D. Interview

Example: Prospective business manager

Briefing: Interviewee is always sent out and the interviewer told what he is to find out—that he is to determine fitness of the prospective employee.

Test variables: Interviewer tested for resourcefulness in questioning, reporting ability, ability to judge and to make a decision. Person being questioned tested for his social relations, resourcefulness, and ability to sell himself.

Type E. Rejection

Example: Position which goes to another man

Briefing: The rejected man is sent out and the other man told the nature and basis of the rejection.

Test variables: Rejected person tested for ability to accept rejection, persuasive powers, assertiveness, and resourcefulness. Person doing rejecting tested for tact, diplomacy, social relations, and forcefulness.

Type F. Intrapersonal conflict and decision

Example: Conflict of loyalties—whether to be loyal to employer or union

Briefing: Man not in conflict is sent out and man with the conflict kept in and told the nature of the conflict.

Test variables: Man in conflict tested for his resourcefulness, ability to make a decision, and assertiveness. Other person tested for persuasiveness and resourcefulness.

Type G. Authority-subordination

Example: Disagreeable order must be issued and enforced.

Briefing: Man in subordinate role is sent out. Man in authority is told about role he is to play.

Test variables: Person in authority tested for resourcefulness, firmness, social relations. Person in subordinate role tested for his ability to take orders, to play the subordinate role, and to report.

Each skit was allowed five minutes. When the skit was finished, observers and participants were urged to describe the behavior of the two participants and to compare it with their ordinary behavior. Diagnostic and therapeutic purposes may be served in this way at the same time.[16]

These sociodramatic performance tests indicate the wide scope of situational possibilities which may be constructed for test purposes. In England the War Office Selection Boards have used this kind of test for making personality assessments of officers or officer candidates, to determine their suitability for various officer roles in the army. One example is a test of physical courage. Applicants were asked to climb a big oak tree. At a height of fifteen or twenty feet they had to jump from one of the branches two or three feet in the air to catch a suspended rope on which they could slide down. In addition to the tests of courage, many tests of leadership ability were constructed.

The United States Army ground forces also used sociodramatic tests. Every soldier in basic training was given the infantry infiltration test. He had to crawl a distance of several hundred yards through mud, wire entanglements, and ditches. Machine-gun bullets were fired a few inches above the crouching soldiers. Explosive charges were set off in close proximity. Highly realistic battle conditions were created. Soldiers who failed the test were considered unsatisfactory for combat units.

Sociometric ratings—"buddy ratings"—were solicited from each student in the officer candidate course about all other students in his training company. The United States Marine Corps made a study of 185 second lieutenants who had been in combat. It was found that success in OCS as measured by paper-pencil tests, such

[16] All of these improvisations are more fully described in *ibid.*, pp. 45–50.

as Personal Inventory Sheet, General Classification and Mechanical Aptitude Test grades, and final composite numerical OCS grades, was not significantly related to success in combat as measured by the combat efficiency report of the commanding officers. However, a tetrachoric correlation of .42 was found between reports of senior combat officers and the buddy rating scores. A research report states, "The evidence thus far presented points strongly to the conclusion that the men themselves are more capable of picking their own leaders than are their instructors and training officers."[17]

TWO POTENTIAL USES FOR SOCIODRAMATIC
PERFORMANCE TESTS IN INDUSTRY

These tests have two different functions which enhance their usefulness. It is possible to use them not only for selection purposes but also for the training of employees and supervisors. Bavelas gives an example which illustrates the double-barreled nature of sociodramatic performance testing:

1. Select and send out of the meeting room two or three of the applicants or trainees for the foremanship.

2. Describe to the judges (or trainees) the situation which will be played out. It might be a situation in which a foreman has decided to have a talk with one of his men regarding excessive absenteeism. The details might be: (a) The man has been employed for a year and a half and is a better-than-average worker; (b) up to three months ago his attendance had been very good; (c) a month ago he received a routine warning slip on his absenteeism, but the absenteeism continued; (d) the foreman has decided to do something about it; (e) the man's absenteeism is due to some very personal difficulties, and he would rather lose his job than talk about them to the foreman.

3. Select a member of the group to play the role of the worker. The examiner (or trainer) may play this role.

4. Call in one of the applicants (or trainees). Have him take his place at the desk and explain the problem to him. (It is usually important in a problem like this one to say nothing of the worker's resistance to revealing the reason for his absenteeism. Let the foreman applicant [or trainee] discover it for himself as he would in a real life situation.) Make sure he understands the setting and then start the action—"The

[17] "Validation of Officer Selection Tests by Means of Combat Proficiency Ratings," Progress Report No. 1, Medical Field Research Laboratory, Camp Lejeune, N.C., p. 10.

problem is clear? Very well. You are in your office and you have asked Jack to come in. Here he is. He walks in and says, 'Did you want to see me?' "

5. The role taking begins. The foreman may try to discover the underlying cause or accept rationalizations from the worker. He may threaten when the worker refuses to tell him his real reasons for absence. He may fire him. He may say it doesn't matter. He may be completely blocked. Whatever the pattern of interaction, the role taking ends either by the man going back to his imagined place of work or by a signal from the examiner (or trainer).[18]

This role-playing situation has not been standardized, so it is simply a raw test. Yet it can be clearly seen that this kind of problem situation offers excellent possibilities not only of selecting qualified people but of training persons so that they may achieve qualified levels of performance. The training of supervisory personnel in supervisory relations is particularly important where supervisors have come to their positions on the sole basis of technical competence or seniority. For them sociodramatic performance tests become training standards. In this discussion the central problem is improved selection and placement. In the following chapter the emphasis is turned to training and group morale. This sequence is a logical one. For it is important to first build an organization with qualified personnel.

STANDARDIZING THE SOCIODRAMATIC PERFORMANCE TEST

The data on hand give promise that sociodramatic tests combined with sociometric ratings can be developed to locate with increasing accuracy those persons most likely to succeed or fail as workers or leaders in a specified group. The application of these techniques to industry constitutes a research frontier that challenges industrial sociology. The guiding principles which must direct such research are now fairly well established. Joseph Eaton presents the following principles:

1. Criterion.—No research should be started without a clear definition of the criterion against which the test can be validated. . . .
2. Test Items.—The skill to be tested should be analyzed into as many components as possible. Sociodramatic tests should be constructed in such a manner that they contain measures of each component. They

[18] Alex Bavelas, "Role Playing and Management Training," *Sociatry*, June, 1947, pp. 183–191.

should involve the application of specific and typical technical, muscular, and social skills. They should be conducted in a social situation of simulated reality, with trained assistants and observer-raters.

3. Simplicity.—The tests must be kept as simple as possible to facilitate uniform and easy administration.
4. Scoring.—Each component of the test should be studied to discover the different alternative responses possible in the testing situation. Each response should be evaluated with respect to its significance and, if possible, be expressed in a numerical weight. This would improve the reliability of the judgments of those who score the tests.
5. Sociometry.—Sociometric ratings by all participants should be made use of.
6. Interpretation.—The final test results should be expressed in rough gradations, such as deciles or quartiles of the total test population or in sigmas of the mean if the distribution is normal.[19]

There are very few sociodramatic performance tests ready for industrial application that have been constructed according to these guiding principles.[20] However, such development should be rapid in the near future.

The task of locating personnel that will perform efficiently, happily, and continuously in their work positions is not an easy one. The search for better selection instruments must continue. Another promising attempt at improving the selection of supervisory personnel is the interactional chronograph invented by Eliot D. Chapple and Gordon Donald, Jr.

Selection of supervisory leadership by the interactional chronograph

The interactional chronograph method is designed to evaluate personality and temperament by measuring the promptness, frequency, and duration of the spoken reactions of persons in contact with one another. It is an objective method since it is based

[19] Eaton, op. cit., pp. 534–535. Professor Eaton served during World War II as a member of the Personnel Research Section, Adjutant General's Office, United States Army.

[20] For a major report on the research direction of future work see Urie Bronfenbrenner and Theodore M. Newcomb, "Improvisations—An Application of Psychodrama in Personality Diagnosis," Sociatry, March, 1948, pp. 367–382. Also useful is the section on improvisations reported by the staff of the Office of Strategic Services in Assessment of Men, Holt, 1948, pp. 168–176. (Reprinted in Sociatry, April–August, 1948, pp. 27–36.)

solely on observations of actual behavior of individuals. It examines the *time* element in interpersonal relations and yields a record which can be read by anyone. Chapple and Donald describe the development of their method as follows:

. . . We developed a simple recording instrument. Essentially, it consisted of a moving tape, driven at a uniform speed, upon which lines were drawn continuously when keys were pressed down. When an individual started to act, say in initiating a contact, the observer would depress the key assigned to that person. When he stopped acting, his key would be released and the line would end. The blank space between the lines provided a measure of his inactivity. The same procedure was used for each person under observation. Once we started to use this recording instrument, we found that we were obtaining far more information about the relationships among the individuals observed than we could get in continuous observation with stop watch and notebook.

PERSONALITY TRAITS REVEALED BY VERBAL BEHAVIOR

We soon found that conversational contacts provided a convenient and easily controllable medium in which to take our personality measurements. This does not necessarily mean that the individual who speaks longest, soonest, or most often has the best—or for that matter the worst—personality for any specific purpose or job. It only means that men in contact with one another reveal, by the way they respond and react to each other, certain personality traits like initiative, resourcefulness, and social adaptability; that the relative degree to which they possess such traits affects in one way or another the time—and the timing—of their conversational (or other) contacts; and that we had developed a device to measure and record that time element.[21]

With the interactional chronograph the researchers found that every individual had a characteristic pattern which remained constant regardless of the person with whom he interacted, and this pattern was not affected by any attempts on the part of the subject to conceal or distort his natural interaction pattern.

After early experiments Chapple and Donald began to consider what specific personal behavior, as revealed by chronograph measurements, might be appropriate for specific purposes or jobs.

[21] Eliot D. Chapple and Gordon Donald, Jr., "A Method for Evaluating Supervisory Personnel," *Harvard Business Review*, Winter, 1946, pp. 200–201; cf. E. D. Chapple, "The Standard Experimental (Stress) Interview as Used in Interactional Chronograph Investigations," *Human Organization*, 1953, vol. 12, No. 2.

INTERACTIONAL CHRONOGRAPH CURVES

Six curves were derived from the records. These were:

1. Activity curve—measures preponderance of the individual's activity to his inactivity.
2. Speed curve—measures the length of time between his starting one action and starting the next.
3. Subject's adjustment curve—measures the preponderance of his interruptions against his failures to respond.
4. Interviewer's adjustment curve—measures the interviewer's interruptions of the subject against the subject's failure to respond.
5. Initiative-dominance curve—records relative frequency of the subject's initiative and dominations relative to the other person's.
6. Free give-and-take—measures the frequency of the occasions when he is able to adjust without interrupting or failing to respond in consecutive exchanges.

EVIDENCE FOR VALIDITY OF MEASUREMENTS

These curves, drawn from a standardized experimental interview, proved to be of sufficient weight in the requirements for success as an executive to serve as an index of overall supervisory capacity. In one of a number of tests, the interaction measurements of the foremen, superintendents, and general operating executives of an industrial company actually showed as potentially top-caliber supervisory personnel 92 percent of the men whom the company had already rated highest on the basis of their records and other criteria, and none of those rated lowest. This means that if the interactional chronograph had been used before the men were placed in their present positions, it would have foretold the kind of record they would make with a high degree of accuracy.

A NEW POSSIBILITY OF RELATING THE WORKER TO PERSONALITIES OF WORK GROUP MEMBERS

One of the possibilities of the interactional chronograph is the attack it permits on the problem of worker placement. This method embraces not only fitting the right man to the right job but also fitting him to the right group. The researchers point out that

All too frequently job placement ignores these two factors: (1) the differences in initiative, in drive, in speed, in adaptability, in emotional stability which a given job imposes on the person who fills it and (2) the added impact of the other people with whom the individual comes into contact—people who have their own personalities which modify the structure of the job itself. A common example is the subordinate placed in a position where considerable initiative should be exerted and yet reporting to a chief who feels it necessary to initiate all the contacts himself. If the subordinate has a good deal of drive and dominance, he and his chief will soon be at loggerheads, and the resultant effects on the organizational structure will be such as to warp it considerably from its original design.[22]

A summary of selection methods designed to appraise leadership

Two methods of analyzing leadership performance have been presented: (1) sociodramatic performance tests and (2) the interactional chronograph method for appraising supervisory personnel. The newer approaches are seen to be efforts to secure measurements of leadership role behavior within a social situation of simulated reality. The major difficulty in perfecting these newer instruments is found in the troublesome problem of standardization. When each response can be evaluated in respect to its significance and expressed as a numerical weight, new sociodramatic performance scales and interactional scales will be available. These promise to increase the accuracy of the predictions regarding work behavior which may be expected from a given worker in a given work position.

MORALE

The Problem of Definition

Morale is an intriguing variable because it is well known that people will respond according to their general emotional state of readiness. Morale appears both as an individual and as a group phenomenon. Research often attempts to secure measurements

[22] *Ibid.*, p. 214.

of group morale by measuring the morale of individual members of the group. The concepts of "satisfaction," "motivation," and *"esprit de corps"* float around ambiguously within the scope of employee morale. Let us look at three definitions:

1. Morale is the sum of satisfactions which the individual (or group members) experiences because of his membership and involvement in an organization.
2. Morale is the state of motivational drives through which the individual (or group members) experiences confidence in his ability to achieve goals and to cope with future challenges.
3. Morale is the consensus or *esprit de corps* exhibited by a group in pursuit of group goals.

These definitions suggest that morale may range from a passive complacency to an eager desire for goal-directed activity.[23] The failure to sort out these different emotional states has made problems of reliability and validity of special difficulty. Many researchers have worked energetically to isolate the dimensions of morale and to measure them. The most comprehensive work has been conducted by the Industrial Relations Center at the University of Chicago. The SRA (Science Research Associates) Inventory was developed by the Center using a research team representing the fields of sociology, psychology, business, and economics.

The first step was to select factors that were significant to employees, and selection was based on the analysis of nondirective interviews conducted in many different industrial settings. Table 16.3 shows the factors organized in fourteen categories and the attitudes of over 500,000 people in industry. The sample is a fair cross section of American workers in all kinds of occupations and industries. The categories in the inventory range from the most materialistic elements in the work environment, such as pay, benefits, conditions of work, to the interpersonal relations in the organization and to the intangible, nonfinancial incentives and individual satisfactions.

The next step was to construct items to represent the categories to be included in the inventory. Item analysis was used to select

[23] See Bernard M. Bass, *Leadership, Psychology, and Organizational Behavior,* Harper, 1960, pp. 46–47.

Category	Questions Asked	Percent of Favorable Answers
1. Job demands	Work pressure, fatigue, boredom, work load, hours of work	72
2. Working conditions	Annoyances, management's concern for conditions, equipment adequacy, safety measures, effect of these on efficiency	70
3. Pay	Adequacy, comparison with pay of others in the company and in other local companies, administration of pay system	44
4. Employee benefits	All benefits, comparison with benefits in other companies, knowledge of program, administration of benefits	74
5. Friendliness, cooperation of employees	Bossiness, friction	77
6. Supervisory-employee relations	Friendliness, fairness, treatment of suggestions, credit for good work, concern for welfare, follow-through on promises	71
7. Confidence in management	Belief in management's integrity and its concern for employee welfare, adequacy of personnel policies, friendliness	67
8. Technical competence of supervision	Administrative skill, knowledge of job, ability to train employees, decision-making, work organization	73
9. Effectiveness of administration	Competence of higher levels of management, efficiency of company operations, cooperation among departments	65
10. Adequacy of communication	Freedom to express opinion and suggest improvements, complaint handling, information about operations and plans	64
11. Status and recognition	Standing with the company, fair appraisal of work done, respect for judgment	71
12. Security of job and work relations	Security from arbitrary discharge and layoff, recognition of length of service, handling of job changes	59
13. Identification with the company	Pride in the company, interest in its future, sense of belonging and participation with the company	80
14. Chances for growth and advancement	Opportunities to use one's skills, to grow and develop on the job, to get ahead in the organization.	65

SOURCE: David G. Moore and Robert K. Burns, "How Good Is Your Morale?" *Factory*, February, 1956, pp. 130–136.

the present seventy-eight items in the SRA Employee Inventory. Questions are phrased as statements with which an employee could agree or disagree or on which he could be undecided. For example:

Agree   Undecided   Disagree

There's too much pressure in my job.
The people I work with get along well together.
My boss really tries to get our ideas about things.

The test-retest reliability for the inventory gives an r of .89. Inventories have been administered in such companies as United States Steel, Campbell Soup Company, Johnson & Johnson, New York Central Railroad, Sears, Roebuck and Company, Spiegel Incorporated, Continental Can Company, Incorporated, Weyerhaeuser Timber Company, and many others. Validity rests upon the good correspondence found to exist between the inventory results and the considered judgments of experienced observers. In consequence of the extensive application, comparative norms for industries are now available for the first time.

This type of inventory may become a diagnostic tool by which employee attitudes can be sorted out by particular factors in specific departments. Such an instrument is especially valuable in formulating recommendations to improve morale. The proper effort can be pinpointed.

One of the major findings of morale research is that attitudes held by employees are a reflection of factors determined mostly by their job or occupation, because the job itself determines what the employee is expected to do, the persons he works with, the kind of equipment and job skills required, the pay system, the physical surroundings, the kind of supervisors, etc. The pattern of attitudes expressed by employees in specific occupational groups is almost a direct reflection of the job itself. The SRA Inventory has described attitudes of three major occupational groups: production workers, first-line supervisors, and office employees. Figure 16.1 shows the morale profiles of these three groups based on national norms.

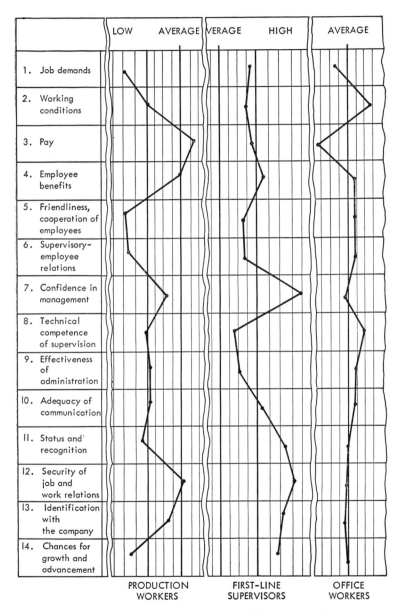

FIG. 16.1. Employee Attitude Profiles of Production Workers, First-Line Supervisors, and Office Workers.

Employee Attitudes of Three Major Occupational Groups

Production Workers

General morale of production workers is low to average. They take little satisfaction in their work as such. They are critical of the pressure and work load imposed on them. They complain of fatigue and boredom in their job. They see little opportunity for personal growth or advancement in their jobs.[24]

Office employees

Morale is just average for office employees. They are neither strongly negative nor strongly affirmative. Indeed, they tend to be indifferent—especially the women. Still, their morale is better than that of the typical factory employee. This difference seems to reflect the higher status of office work, the closeness of the office group to management, and the more attractive physical conditions in the typical office. Dissatisfactions arise because office employees feel overworked and underpaid. They experience fatigue and boredom growing out of the routine of many office jobs. Feelings about pay are perhaps the most crucial measure of dissatisfaction because it is in this area that office employees feel at greatest disadvantage compared with factory workers.[25]

First-line supervisors

Foremen and first-line supervisors are shown to have high morale and to be management oriented. As Fig. 16.1 shows, they express (see category 7) high confidence in management, identify with the company (category 13), and have hopes for growth and advancement (category 14). They feel secure in their jobs and have a definite feeling of status and recognition. Some supervisors react negatively to pay and working conditions. Morale among first-line supervisors suffers most when their status in the organization is threatened by the replacement of old-line supervisors by young college graduates or when production planning de-

[24] Moore and Burns, *op. cit.*

[25] *Ibid.;* Nancy Morse, *Satisfactions in the White Collar Job,* University of Michigan Institute for Social Research, 1953, pp. 86–93.

Morale According to
Age of Employees

Fig. 16.2

Morale According to
Length of Service of Employees

Fig. 16.3

Morale According to

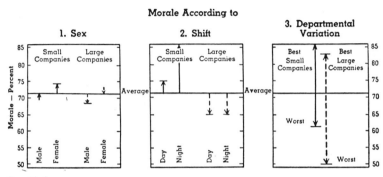

1. Sex
2. Shift
3. Departmental Variation

Fig. 16.4

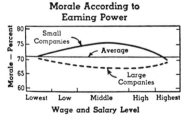

Morale According to
Earning Power

Fig. 16.5

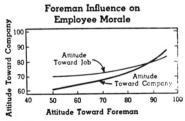

Foreman Influence on
Employee Morale

Fig. 16.6

FIG. 16.2. Morale According to Age of Employees.

FIG. 16.3. Morale According to Length of Service of Employees.

FIG. 16.4. Morale According to Sex, Shift, and Departmental Variation.

FIG. 16.5. Morale According to Earning Power.

FIG. 16.6. Foreman Influence on Employee Morale. (From Eugene J. Benge, "How to Learn What Workers Think of Job and Boss," *Factory Management and Maintenance,* May, 1944, p. 104.)

partments are introduced into the organization for the first time.[26]

Important Morale Relationships

Other important relationships that have been discovered in morale surveys are reported by E. J. Benge. Some of his findings are shown in the following figures. Note that the figures show the relation of morale to age (Fig. 16.2, to length of service of employees (Fig. 16.3), to sex, shift, and departmental variation (Fig. 16.4), to earning power (Fig. 16.5), and to attitudes toward foreman or supervision (Fig. 16.6).

Benge draws these conclusions:

1. In small companies, morale rises with age; in large companies, it falls from age 20 to age 24, then rises with increasing years.
2. In large and small plants, morale falls off with each year of service until the eighth, then rises to a high point after the twentieth year.
3. The morale of employees in small companies is appreciably better than in large companies.
4. In both small and large companies, the morale of women surpasses that of men.
5. In small companies, the morale of the night shift markedly exceeds that of the day shift. In large companies, there is no difference as to morale between day and night shifts.
6. The morale variation from the best department to the worst is greater in big companies than in small.
7. In small plants, the middle bracket earners have better morale than the high and low earners; in large plants they have lower morale.
8. When the attitude of employees toward their foreman is good, they are likely to have good attitudes toward their jobs and even better attitudes toward their company. The converse is true; when employees feel dissatisfied about their foreman, they are likely to have poor attitudes toward their jobs and even worse attitudes toward their company.[27]

We know now that morale is a global concept and contains many factors. The Michigan Survey Research Institute has identified five major dimensions of employee morale for intensive research:

[26] Moore and Burns, *op. cit.* Yuzuk reports that "the most important single correlate of morale is labor grade or level of skill." See Ronald P. Yuzuk, *The Assessment of Employee Morale,* Ohio State Bureau of Business Research, 1961, p. 39.

[27] Eugene J. Benge, "How to Learn What Workers Think of Job and Boss," *Factory Management and Maintenance,* May, 1944, p. 104.

1. Intrinsic job satisfaction.
2. Involvement in the immediate work group.
3. Identification with the company.
4. Interpersonal relations with supervisor.
5. Satisfactions from work status and income transmitted into community function and status.

A repeated observation is that satisfaction is significantly related to good interpersonal relations among employees and the desire to stay in the company.[28]

Morale-Building Techniques

Two techniques of building better interpersonal relations are of special interest to industrial sociologists: (1) feedback of morale surveys to provide for the improvement of organizational morale and (2) building group morale by sociometric placement.

Feedback of morale survey results

The management of the Detroit Edison Company in Michigan has made serious efforts to change policy and supervisory attitudes in conformance with sociological principles.[29] This company is a major electric utility with about 10,000 employees. In 1948 an attitude survey was conducted among all employees of the company, white collar and manual, nonsupervisory and supervisory, staff and line. The questionnaires covered a variety of topics: the job itself, supervisory practices, relations with others in the organization, satisfaction with company policies and practices, and so forth. The results of this survey were distributed widely in the company, and a series of discussion meetings was held to obtain broad participation in the interpretation of the information and the development of ideas for dealing with some of the problems raised or emphasized by the data.

The meetings began at the top level of the company and were carried down through the supervisory levels wherever interest

[28] Morse, *op. cit.;* Delbert C. Miller and Nahum Z. Medalia, "Efficiency, Leadership, and Morale in Small Military Organizations," *Sociological Review,* July, 1955, pp. 93–107.

[29] See the Detroit Edison Feedback Programme by Stanley E. Seashore, in Rensis Likert and Samuel P. Hayes, Jr. (eds.), *Some Applications of Behavioural Research,* UNESCO, 1957, pp. 103–112.

was shown. A discussion group consisted, in most cases, of a supervisor and his immediate staff of eight to ten people. The survey results were presented so that a comparison could be made between nonsupervisory employees as a whole and nonsupervisory employees in the part of the organization of immediate concern to the group. No individual or work group was identified in the data. Interpretations, ideas, and recommendations arising from the meetings were transmitted back to the line organization for action.

Many supervisors reported that this was their first serious attempt to discuss problems of human relations with their subordinates and superiors. There was widespread and systematic participation in a program for self-appraisal and joint decisions on matters of importance to the company.

In 1950 a second survey of attitudes was conducted in certain parts of the company. The data used in feedback included a comparison of the 1948 and 1950 results in order to detect changes in employee attitudes and in the attitudes of supervisors on certain issues. The chief executive of the accounting department held a number of individual meetings with his department heads in order to examine the survey results and to work out a plan for similar discussions at other levels of the organization. Some department heads were encouraged to go ahead with feedback meetings within their own units. The purpose was to make the feedback more intensive than it had been after the 1948 survey and to carry the process down through all levels of the organization, including nonsupervisory ones.

In many departments the data were first presented by the department head, and then employees met in small groups to discuss the material and formulate what they considered to be the chief problems raised by the survey results. The meeting concluded with a report from each group to the department head and a brief discussion of the questions raised. One of the objectives of the management was to develop habits of free interchange between the supervisor and his subordinates.

A third survey of attitudes was conducted in 1952 within the accounting department to evaluate the survey feedback process. The amount of favorable change in morale between 1950 and

1952 was found to be roughly in proportion to the amount of time and energy given to the feedback process. The chief changes were shown in the following areas: interest in one's job, feeling that one's work is important; feeling that one's supervisor is considerate, likable, reasonable, and not officious; and belief that one's supervisor tends to handle complaints in a constructive way.[30]

Building group morale by sociometric placement

The problem of social placement can be denied and the traditional practice of filling a job in terms of technical skills and personality traits can be continued. But it should be recognized that such practice ignores interpersonal relations and assumes that collaboration will take place without any further consideration. In ever greater numbers, management executives are saying "We dare not leave the development of human relations to chance." The charts of interpersonal feelings of the work groups will make it possible to guide the induction and assimilation of the worker into a work group with a minimum of difficulty. The line supervisor as well as the personnel director may come to employ such charts with increasing frequency. The contributions of sociometry to social placement deserve our careful attention.

THE MEANING OF SOCIOMETRIC PLACEMENT

Sociometry is the study of interpersonal feelings or relationships. For a long time management and labor alike have given lip service to an intangible factor called employees' feelings toward each other. Sociometry recognizes that all work groups have a dynamic structure of feelings which lies under all of the formal and informal groupings. This underlying structure penetrates and encompasses the surface structure of groups. Neither can be separated from the other; in reciprocal relationship each exerts pressure and influence upon the other with the result that every sphere of human action is affected.

The network of interpersonal feelings is exposed by the use of sociometry tests, which reveal the spontaneous feelings and

[30] Floyd Mann, "Changing Superior-Subordinate Relations," *Journal of Social Issues,* Spring, 1951, pp. 56–63.

choices that workers make. The spontaneous feelings within a person are shown by free choice. Feelings are divided into three classes: (1) attraction (like), (2) repulsion (dislike), and (3) indifference (neutral feeling).

Such a test is commonly set up as a group preference schedule with the names of all work group members listed. Each worker in the group then indicates how he feels about working with the various members of his group by marking Like, Dislike, or Indifferent.

A spontaneous choice test gives more information on whom the worker most likes to be associated with in work assignments. Ordinarily each person is asked to choose workers he would prefer to work with. (The test commonly seeks three or five choices from each worker.)

These choices can then be shown as sociograms or charts, which display in graphic form the interpersonal feelings of workers making up work groups. J. L. Moreno was a pioneer in the study of measurement of interpersonal feelings of participants in work groups. Figure 16.7 is one of his sociograms of a work group in a steam laundry. It is made up of seven workers and one forewoman. Stella, DB, and Philamina, LR, the feeders, reject each other. Myrtle, WL, rejects the feeder opposite her, Philamina. Lillian, FR, and Rosalie, CV, the two folders, attract each other. Lillian and Rosalie reject Myrtle. Esther, GM, the shaker, is attracted to Rosalie and rejects Hilda, GR. Esther, Stella, Hilda, and Lillian reject the forewoman, but only Stella is rejected by her. Philamina, Myrtle, and Rosalie are attracted to the forewoman. The sociogram reveals considerable rejection of the forewoman and some other crucial internal relationships of rejection.

This work group demands reconstruction. Some transfers will make it more effective. To this end DB and WL are assigned to another work group. Their replacement by newcomers RS and CE changes the psychological structure so that the new sociogram appears as in Fig. 16.8. The two feeders, RS (new member) and Philamina, LR, attract each other. The two catchers, CE (new member) and Hilda, GR, attract each other. The two folders, Lillian, FR, and Rosalie, CV, attract each other. The two catchers

STEAM LAUNDRY
Structure of Work Group Before Reconstruction

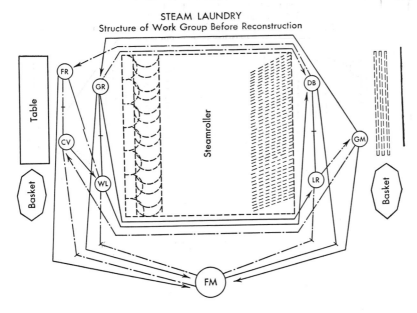

FIG. 16.7. Sociogram of a Work Group Before Reconstruction. (From J. S. Moreno, *Who Shall Survive? A New Approach to the Problem of Human Interrelations,* Nervous and Mental Disease Publishing Company, 1934, p. 318.)

are attracted to the two feeders opposite them. All the workers except Esther, GM, are attracted to the forewoman.[31]

THE RELATION OF SOCIOMETRIC CHOICES TO COOPERATION

Since this early application of sociometry to a work group a number of additional studies have been reported.[32] Maria Rogers in her review concludes that "all of the studies of work situations made by sociometrists have revealed that liking, or attraction, between members of a group results in heightened cooperation; that repulsions between workers cause frictions on the job, lowered morale, and limited productivity. In this context, the supervisor or immediate administrator must be considered a member of a group, for 'leadership' is a function of interpersonal relations,

[31] J. L. Moreno, *Who Shall Survive?* Nervous and Mental Disease Publishing Company, 1934, pp. 318, 319.

STEAM LAUNDRY
Structure of the Same Work Group After Reconstruction

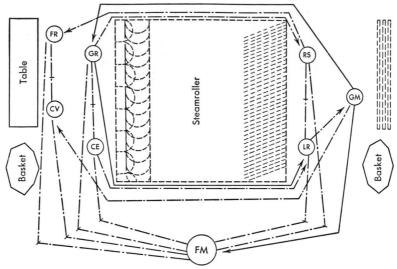

FIG. 16.8. Sociogram of a Work Group After Reconstruction (From Moreno.)

dependent on the give-and-take between the members of a group. It is relative to the group process."[33]

These findings thus stress the importance of selection by sociometric choice. A study by Leslie D. Zeleny has demonstrated that opportunities for cadets to express spontaneous choices and rejections with respect to flying partners provided a better basis for the selection of compatible flying teams than the method of random selection in use.[34] A "flight" of forty-eight cadet pilot observers in an advanced Army Air Forces flying school was studied. Since a cadet actually placed his life in the hands of his partner when the latter flew the aircraft, there was ample motive to make positive and negative choices of members in one's element and

[32] For a review and bibliography see Maria Rogers, "Problems of Human Relations Within Industry," *Sociometry*, November, 1946, pp. 350–371. Especially useful is the suggestive work of John H. Jacobs, "The Application of Sociometry to Industry," *Sociometry*, May, 1945, pp. 181–198.

[33] Rogers, *op. cit.*, p. 364.

[34] Leslie D. Zeleny, "Selection of Compatible Flying Partners," *American Journal of Sociology*, March, 1947, pp. 424–431.

flight. Each cadet was permitted to express his feelings on a sociometric test about flying with each of the cadets in his flight and
to make choices.[35] His sociometric test contained the following
instructions.

1. If you would like to fly with a particular cadet in a flying team,
encircle "Yes" after his name. If you would like not to fly with a particular cadet in a flying team encircle "No" after his name. If you do not
know how you feel about flying with a cadet encircle "I" for "indifferent." Remember, your choices may determine with whom you will fly
the next few weeks.

2. Examine the name of each cadet after which "Yes" has been encircled; place a "1" to the upper right of the "Yes" following the names
of the five cadets who are your *First Five Choices* as persons with whom
to fly. (Do this now. Then read on.)

3. Examine the name of each cadet after which a "No" or "I" has
been encircled; place an "L" to the upper right of the "No" or "I" following the names of five cadets who are your *Last Five Choices* in your
flight as persons with whom to fly.

Each cadet was free to choose or reject as many persons as he
wished in his flight of forty-eight cadets. His responses were of
necessity based on limited acquaintance since the flight had been
in the advanced school only a short time. However, at the very
beginning of instruction it was customary for members of a flight
to be listed in alphabetical order, divided into "elements" of five
to seven cadets each, and assigned to a flight instructor. Teams
were taken in pairs from the elements. This random method often
created flying teams of a relatively low degree of compatibility,
and the results can be seen in Fig. 16.9, which shows the pattern
of choices and rejections for thirty-one of the forty-eight cadets
actually tested. This figure shows the reaction of each cadet to
every other cadet and, especially important, the reactions within
each *instructional element*. The verbal responses have been translated into mathematical symbols, as follows: Yes^1 (yes, a first,
second, third, fourth, or fifth choice) $= +1.0$; Yes (no special
choice) $= +0.5$; No $= -0.5$; I (indifferent) $= 0.0$; $I^L =$ indifferent
and with some rejection $= -0.5$; No $= -0.5$; No^L (no, a first,
second, third, fourth, or fifth rejection) $= -1.0$. The degree of
compatibility or morale among the cadets in each instructional
element has been computed. This index is defined as the average

[35] *Ibid.*

CHOICES EXPRESSED BY CADET NO............

FLYING CADETS	1	2	3	4	5	6	7	8	9	10	11	12	13	14	15	16	17	18	19	20	21	22	23	24	25	26	27	28	29	30	31
1		0	0	.5	.5	0	1	.5	1	0	0	0	0	.5	0	0	0	0	0	.5	-.5	1	.5	.5	0	.5	0	0	0	.5	.5
2	-1	0	-1	.5	0	1	0	0	.5	-.5	0	0	0	.5	0	0	0	.5	1	-1	0	1	1	1	0	0	0	0	-1	-1	-.5
3		-1	0	-.5	0	-1	0	0	.5	-.5	.5	0	-.5	0	0	-.5	0	0	-1	0	-.5	.5	-.5	-1	0	0	0	0	-1	-.5	0
4	0	0	1		0	1	0	.5	0	-.5	0	0	0	-.5	0	-.5	0	0	.5	0	-.5	0	-.5	-.5	0	0	0	0	0	-.5	0
5	-1	1	1	.5	.5	1	.5	0	1	0	-.5	0	0	0	0	-.5	0	0	-.5	-1	-.5	.5	-.5	-.5	-.5	0	0	0	0	-.5	-.5
6	-1	-1	1	.5		0	.5	0	.5	0	-.5	1	-1	0	0	-.5	0	0	-.5	0	.5	.5	.5	1	0	0	0	1	0	0	-.5
7	-1	0	0	-.5	0	0		0	.5	0	0	0	0	0	0	0	0	0	0	0	0	.5	-.5	-.5	0	0	-.5	0	-.5	-.5	0
8	-1	0	0	.5	0	-1	-1	1	.5	0	0	1	0	0	.5	0	0	0	0	0	0	-.5	1	1	0	0	0	0	0	-.5	-.5
9	0	0	1	0	1	.5	.5	1		.5	0	1	0	1	-1	0	0	0	0	.5	0	1	.5	-.5	-1	-1	0	0	0	-.5	0
10	0	1	0	0	0	.5	0	1	.5		-1	-1	0	0	0	0	0	0	0	.5	0	.5	.5	-.5	1	-1	0	0	0	-.5	0
11	0	0	0	0	0	0	0	0	.5	-1		-1	1	0	0	0	0	0	0	0	0	.5	-.5	1	0	0	0	0	0	-.5	.5
12	0	0	0	0	0	0	0	0	.5	-.5	1		-1	0	0	0	0	0	0	0	-.5	.5	-.5	-.5	0	0	0	0	0	0	.5
13	0	0	1	0	0	0	0	1	1	0	1	1		0	0	0	0	0	.5	0	1	.5	1	1	0	.5	0	0	1	0	.5
14	0	0	0	0	0	0	0	0	.5	.5	.5	1	0		1	1	.5	1	1	0	-.5	1	.5	-.5	0	1	1	0	0	0	.5
15	0	0	0	0	0	0	.5	0	.5	.5	0	0	0	1		0	.5	0	0	0	-.5	.5	-.5	-.5	.5	.5	0	0	0	0	0
16	0	0	0	0	0	0	.5	0	0	0	0	0	1	-1	.5		1	0	-.5	.5	1	.5	1	.5	0	0	0	0	0	0	.5
17	0	0	0	0	0	0	0	0	.5	0	1	0	1	1	1	1		0	1	.5	-.5	1	1	-.5	1	0	0	0	0	0	.5
18	0	0	0	0	0	0	0	0	.5	0	1	0	0	.5	1	0	0		1	0	0	-.5	-.5	-.5	1	.5	0	0	0	0	.5
19	0	0	0	0	0	0	0	0	.5	0	1	1	1	0	1	0	1	1		0	-.5	1	1	1	1	1	0	0	0	0	.5

ELEMENT I (columns 1–7) · ELEMENT II (columns 8–13) · ELEMENT III (columns 14–19)

MORALE INDEX +.25 · MORALE INDEX +.50

CHOICES "RECEIVED" BY

FIG. 16.9. Pattern of Choices and Rejections of Flying Partners. (Adapted from Leslie D. Zeleny, "Selection of Compatible Flying Partners," American Journal of Sociology, March, 1947, p. 425.)

FLYING TEAMS SOCIOLOGICALLY GROUPED

ELEMENT I	ELEMENT II	ELEMENT III	ELEMENT IV	ELEMENT V
1-7	8-9	14-15	20-22	26-27
2-6	10-13	16-17	21-23	29-30
4-5	11-12	18-19	24-25	31-?
3-				

MORALE INDEX +.60

MORALE INDEX +.40

MORALE INDEX +.18

ELEMENT IV

ELEMENT V

of the units of intensity of the interpersonal choices and rejections in a group $(\bar{I})$ plus or minus the average deviation of the intensities from $\bar{I}$ (D).

$$C \text{ (compatibility index)} = \bar{I} \pm D.$$

When I equals the intensity of choices or rejections and N equals the number of persons in the group, then

$$C = \bar{I} \pm D, \text{ where } \bar{I} = \frac{\Sigma I}{N(N-1)} \text{ and } D = \frac{\Sigma(\bar{I} \sim I)}{N(N-1)}$$

Using this formula, five instructional elements show the following index numbers:[36] Element I = +.25; Element II = +.50; Element III = +.60; Element IV = +.40; Element V = +.18.

Element III has the highest morale or compatibility. However, this is not very high since an index number of almost +1.00 is possible. The random method of alphabetical selection carried out by administrative decision obviously does not bring high sociometric scores. *Much better compatibility could be attained by selection through sociometric choice.*[37] It was possible to select the most compatible teams within the elements. These have been indicated at the bottom of Fig. 16.9. In actual practice a number of these recommended teams were used by flying instructors with satisfactory results.

This study explains the technique by which industry could match workers with groups in such a way as to maximize the efficiency and morale of both worker and group. If such a method

---

[36] Consider the compatibility of a flying team composed of the first two members of Element I; that is, selected at random, as was the practice. No. 1's response to No. 2 was one of rejection (−1), and the response of No. 2 to No. 1 was one of indifference (0). The compatibility index would be computed as follows:

$$\bar{I} = \frac{\Sigma I}{N(N-1)} = \frac{-1+0}{2(2-1)} = \frac{-1}{2} = -.5 \text{ unit}$$

$$D = \bar{d} = \frac{\Sigma d}{n}$$

where d represents the deviation of any one attitude from the mean of all the attitudes. The sign of the intensities is considered only in the relation of the distance of $\bar{I}$ from I.

$$= \frac{\Sigma(\bar{I} \sim I)}{N(N-1)} = \frac{.5+.5}{2(2-1)} = \frac{1}{2} = .5 \text{ unit}$$

$C = \bar{I} \pm D = -.5 \pm .5$ where the −.5 represents the average intensity of the interpersonal reactions and $D \pm .5$ represents the average deviation.

[37] For example, cadet No. 1 and cadet No. 7 have a compatibility index of 1.00.

seems at first startling and impractical to the reader it may be well to reflect upon the alternative. A continuation of selection and placement which is guided only by the technical skill of the worker and the location of equipment or office space denies the importance of social factors. Such a denial proceeds in the face of a growing research consensus. Perhaps Mayo put this consensus most convincingly when he wrote, "The fact that the United States has developed a successful series of tests for technical skills does not provide any extenuation for psychology. Within its narrow limits, this is useful and, indeed, excellent. But the general effect is to focus attention on technical problems and blind us to the importance of the problems of human cooperation—social skill. This blindness has unquestionably contributed to the advent of calamity."[38]

PRODUCTIVITY OR EFFICIENCY

The search for social factors related to productivity or efficiency of organizations is compelling because it is frequently alleged that human resources are utilized with less efficiency than any other resources employed in producing goods or services. The administrator wants to know how he can achieve greater productivity. The research scientist may accept this as a dependent variable either because he seeks to make himself useful to the administrator or because he is trying to relate social factors to "hard" variables. The numbers of students trained, the numbers of services rendered, or the numbers of products manufactured are specific units. Machines can often count these results with an impersonal reliability and validity that is unchallenged.

The Measurement of Productivity or Efficiency

The measures of productivity are best prescribed by the engineer or administrator.[39] It may be necessary in some instances to assist him in developing a standardized system of identifying and counting each unit of output.[40] This is often the case in work

[38] Elton Mayo, *The Social Problems of an Industrial Civilization*, Harvard, 1945, p. 20.
[39] Bass, *op. cit.*, pp. 39–59.
[40] Hiram S. Davis, "The Meaning and Measurement of Productivity," *Industrial Productivity*, Industrial Relations Research Association, December, 1951, pp. 1–13.

organizations like government agencies, schools, and offices in which *services* are the main outcomes. Other criteria often employed to measure performance include absences, turnover, accidents, grievances, requests for transfer, strikes, scrap loss, etc.

Four Combinations of Morale and Efficiency

We know now from research study that four combinations of efficiency and morale occur in various work groups and work organizations.[41] These combinations are:

A. High Efficiency High Morale	C. High Efficiency Low Morale
B. Low Efficiency High Morale	D. Low Efficiency Low Morale

The sociological problem is to determine what factors and processes are operating to produce these combinations. The research literature reveals a growing knowledge of the social dynamics in work groups.

Combination A (High Efficiency-High Morale) may occur because

1. Group goals are satisfied (such as pride in work groups, group recognition, etc.) which contribute to high productivity.
2. Individual goals are satisfied (such as freedom on the job, good wage rate, intrinsic job interest, etc.) so that high motivation is achieved. The resulting high individual morale contributes directly to high productivity.
3. Supervisor is able to motivate employees to higher performance standards by his human relations approach.
4. High productivity produces high morale and high morale reinforces high productivity.[42]

---

[41] Louis Schneider and Sverre Lysgard, "Deficiency and Conflict in Industrial Sociology," *American Journal of Economics and Sociology*, October, 1952, pp. 49–62. See also research analysis of Nancy C. Morse, *op. cit.*

[42] Daniel Katz and Herbert Hyman reported a circular causal relation between morale and production in their study of five shipyards during World War II. See "Morale in War Industries," in Guy E. Swanson, T. Newcomb and E. Hartley (eds.), *Readings in Social Psychology*, Holt, 1947, pp. 437–447.

Combination B (Low Efficiency-High Morale) may occur because

1. Worker goals other than those contributing to high productivity are satisfied (for example, desire for good working conditions, pleasant fellow workers, etc.).
2. The level of individual application is determined informally by the workers, who set the work group norms. This is the factor operating in restriction of output.[43]
3. Supervisor's lack of technical and administrative skills reduces efficiency of a high-morale group.
4. Workers' lack of adequate skill or training may result in low efficiency but high morale.

Combination C (High Efficiency-Low Morale) may occur because

1. Supervisor can increase productivity through his skill or through his planning ability rather than through ability to motivate his men.
2. Supervisory and organization practices may stimulate high productivity through the use of fear of penalty or punishment (loss of pay, loss of job).[44]
3. Equipment or process has a built-in productivity such as the fast-moving belt-line assembly in which speed of production is determined by the pace set by the machinery and not the workers.

Combination D (Low Efficiency-Low Morale) may occur because of the absence of any factors stated under combination A.

These factors suggest that the relationship between morale and productivity is a complex one and research bears out this conclusion.

The Relationship of Leadership, Morale, and Productivity

In Elton Mayo's pioneering studies in industry, efficiency, leadership, and morale were reported as directly related in a positive

[43] Solomon Barkin, "Discussion," in *Proceedings of the Industrial Relations Research Association,* Madison, Wisconsin, 1952, p. 38.

[44] W. J. Goode and I. Fowler, "Incentive Factors in a Low Morale Plant," *American Sociological Review,* October, 1949, pp. 618–624.

manner.[45] Numerous studies have been conducted since World War II to investigate this relationship in civilian work groups. The studies are characterized by use of attitude scales or indices for the measurement of leadership and morale. A summary of findings shows the following:

1. No consistent relationship between morale and efficiency of work groups has been shown. While a positive association has often appeared in research study, the coexistence of low morale and high productivity does occur; high morale and low productivity is also found but somewhat less frequently.[46]

2. A positive relationship between employee-oriented leadership practices and morale has been repeatedly shown.[47]

3. A positive relationship between certain leadership practices and productivity has been demonstrated in a number of studies. It is reported that higher-producing supervisors assume more of the functions associated with leadership, such as planning the work and spending more time on actual supervision, but practice general, not close, supervision of employees. High-producing supervisors more often secured good communication with employees.[48]

4. A democratic leadership style along with membership par-

[45] Mayo, *op. cit.*

[46] These findings are based on a summary of research reported by Robert L. Kahn and Daniel Katz on work conducted by the Survey Research Center. Their studies centered on the home office of an insurance company, maintenance-of-way section gangs on a railroad, an electric utility, an automotive manufacturer, a tractor company, an appliance manufacturer, and two agencies of the federal government. See Kahn and Katz, *op. cit.*, pp. 625 ff; cf. Morse, *op. cit.*, p. 165.

A finding of negative correlation between job satisfaction and perceived productivity is reported by University of California researchers in the work of two divisions in a naval research laboratory. See Irving R. Weschler, Murray Kahane, and Robert Tannenbaum, "Job Satisfaction, Productivity and Morale: A Case Study," Reprint No. 23, Institute of Industrial Relations, University of California, Los Angeles, 1952, p. 7; Goode and Fowler also confirm the existence of high productivity and low morale in a Detroit electroplating plant—*op. cit.*

[47] The human relations-minded or employee-oriented supervisor, in contrast to the production-oriented or institution-oriented supervisor, is associated with the satisfaction of the employee with the job, supervisor, and company. See Kahn and Katz, *op. cit.*, p. 165. Also Weschler *et al.*, *op. cit.*, pp. 11–12.

[48] Kahn and Katz, *op. cit.*, pp. 613–623.

ticipation may improve organizational morale and effectiveness.[49] (Wilensky claims the evidence is inconclusive and that insufficient data have been reported on type of union, structure and character of local labor markets, product markets, and class identification and mobility aspirations. He urges caution in interpretation and application.)[50]

5. Group cohesiveness or pride in work group has been identified as a major determinant of productivity in industrial and military situations.[51]

To summarize: The three social variables which have shown the most consistent relationship to productivity are the degree of identification of work group members with the larger organization and its goals, the supervisory leadership style, and the degree of diffusion of authority in the organization. How these variables

[49] H. H. Carey, "Consultative Supervision and Management," *Personnel*, March, 1942, pp. 286–295; L. Bradford and R. Lippitt, "Building a Democratic Work Group," *Personnel*, November, 1945, pp. 142–152; J. C. Worthy, "Factors Influencing Employee Morale," *Harvard Business Review*, January, 1950, pp. 61–73; Katz and Kahn, in Swanson, Newcomb, and Hartley, *op. cit.*, especially pp. 663–664, and in *Industrial Productivity*, Industrial Relations Research Association, December, 1951, pp. 168–171; Daniel Katz, in Arthur Kornhauser, Robert Dubin, and Arthur M. Ross (eds.), *Industrial Conflict*, McGraw-Hill, 1954, pp. 100–106; Coch and J. R. P. French, Jr., "Overcoming Resistance to Change," in Swanson, Newcomb, and Hartley, *op. cit.*, pp. 474–491; Morse, *op. cit.*; D. Katz, N. Maccoby, and N. C. Morse, *Productivity, Supervision and Morale in an Office Situation*, Part I, Survey Research Center, University of Michigan, December, 1950; N. C. Morse, E. Reimer, and A. Tannenbaum, "Change in Control Processes in Social Organization: A Field Experiment," symposium presented at American Psychological Association meetings, New York, September, 1954; R. C. Davis, "Factors Related to Scientific Research Performance," in *Interpersonal Factors in Research*, Part I, Survey Research Center, University of Michigan, October, 1954, chap. 1; D. G. Marquis *et al.*, "A Socio-Psychological Study of the Decision-Making Conference," pp. 55–67, in Guetzkow (ed.), *Groups, Leadership and Men*, Carnegie Press, 1951; J. Levine and J. Butler, "Lecture vs. Group Decision in Changing Behavior," *Journal of Applied Psychology*, February, 1952, pp. 29–33; W. Scott, *Industrial Leadership and Consultation: A Study of Human Relations in Three Merseyside Firms*, University Press of Liverpool, 1952; A. Bavelas' research reported by K. Lewin, "Frontiers in Group Dynamics," *Human Relations*, June, 1947, pp. 5–41.

[50] Harold L. Wilensky, "Human Relations in the Work Place: An Appraisal of Some Recent Research," *Research in Industrial Human Relations*, Harper, 1957, pp. 33–34.

[51] Kahn and Katz, *op. cit.*, pp. 624–626.

interact to produce different levels of productivity is not clearly known.

Four Divergent Propositions

There seem to be four divergent propositions as to the cause of high efficiency.[52]

1. Employees produce more if they have group goals which require high production for their satisfaction. Generally this is the case, however, only when the group goals are induced under conditions of job security.

2. Employees produce more if they are happy with their working conditions. This is the commonest notion but it has not been well explored. Obviously, physical comforts alone will not increase production. The critical element identified in most studies is the supervisor and the relations he builds with his workers.

3. Employees will produce if they are rewarded for doing so and dismissed for not doing so, even though they may be generally unhappy about their work. This notion underlies the assumption that unemployment or the threat of unemployment is conducive to more productive work. Incentive pay systems are often based on this assumption—that monetary reward or penalty is the main determinant of productivity.

4. Employees will produce more if they are given more productive equipment or processes irrespective of their morale. This is the assumption behind much industrial engineering including time and motion study. The level of wages may be an important accompanying factor.

The firmest conclusion which now emerges is that efficiency and morale are positively related only when the leader is able to bring the individual and group goals of employees into close conformance with efficiency goals of the organization. It appears that this

[52] Cf. A. Zaleznik, C. R. Christensen, and F. J.. Roethlisberger, *The Motivation, Productivity, and Satisfaction of Workers*, Harvard, 1958, especially chap. II, "Theories of Worker Motivation," pp. 34–76. See also Arthur H. Brayfield and Walter H. Crockett, "Employee Attitudes and Employee Performance," *Psychological Bulletin*, September, 1955, pp. 396–424; and Ralph M. Stogdill, *Individual Behavior and Group Achievement*, Oxford University Press, 1959. The last two sources contain extensive bibliographic review of the research literature.

synthesis between cooperation and organization may pose varying difficulties for the leader, depending upon many personal and organizational conditions under which he attempts to lead. The recruiting of personnel, their selection, training, placement, and payment may be completely or partially outside his control. Operational policies may be set by higher levels of management. These factors may intrude and make his leadership ineffective in securing morale and efficiency no matter how human-relations minded he may be seen to be.[53] Many fruitful opportunities for studying these major variables now exist. To gain more insight into the correlates of productivity it will be necessary to explore the conditions under which the group is strongly motivated toward goal achievement. What role does leadership play? What role does incentive, financial and nonfinancial, play? What happens when more productive equipment is added?

New Discoveries of Relationships Under Specified Conditions

An almost untapped area is the differential effect of particular kinds of organization structure upon the attitudes and performances of employees with different motives, aspirations, and expectations. James C. Worthy has studied the reactions of more than 100,000 Sears, Roebuck and Company employees to alternate forms of organization. He reports that flatter, less complex structures, with a maximum of administrative decentralization, increase both supervisory and employee potentials for self expression.[54]

The relationship between leadership performance and employee attitudes is now being more clearly revealed. The Survey Research Center has reported a study of supervisors rated from low to immediately promotable by a panel of superiors who judged them on their ability to get high productivity and quality from their groups. It was found that more employees of the supervisors rated promotable said these things about their supervisor:

He is good at handling people.
He is a man with whom employees feel free to discuss important things about their job.

[53] Miller and Medalia, "Efficiency, Leadership, and Morale in Small Military Organizations," *Sociological Review,* July, 1955, pp. 93–107.
[54] James C. Worthy, "Organizational Structure and Employee Morale," *American Sociological Review,* April, 1950, pp. 169–179.

He is also one with whom employees feel free to discuss personal problems.

He goes to bat for them.

He pulls for both the company and the men.

He lets employees know where they stand.

He lets his employees work pretty much on their own instead of supervising them closely.

He holds group meetings where problems can be discussed.

He is a leader of men, likeable, and reasonable—not bossy, quick to criticize, a driver, or unnecessarily strict.

He gives recognition for good work done.

He gives employees recognition by training them for better jobs.

In turn the linking-pin function is in evidence as the supervisors evaluated high by their employees say:

His superior lets him participate in decision making.

His superior lets him know what he thinks of his work.

His superior frequently asks him for his opinion.[55]

These employee-oriented behavior patterns must not be interpreted as a mandate for "soft" leadership. The study reported earlier in this chapter by Fleishman of the Ohio State Personnel Board showed that no overall generalization was warranted. The Michigan Survey Research Center concurs. If a leader abdicates his interest in and responsibility for production it has an adverse effect on both productivity and morale. "A moderate amount of emphasis on production is required to avoid both low production and low morale. But, beyond a certain point, higher productivity by means of pressure appears to be obtainable only at the expense of morale."[56] (See Fig. 16.10.)

The Prediction of Productivity and Satisfaction

Zaleznik, Christensen, and Roethlisberger have presented the first study attempting to *predict* the productivity and satisfaction of workers. They find that group membership (the degree of acceptance an individual has in a group) and group identification (the degree to which the individual identifies with the group) are the most important independent variables for predicting productivity and satisfaction. Four external system factors are identified

[55] Floyd Mann and James Dent, *Appraisals of Supervisors and Attitudes of Their Employees in an Electric Power Company*, Survey Research Center, University of Michigan.

[56] Seashore, *op. cit.*

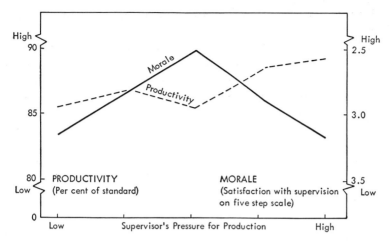

FIG. 16.10. The Relation of Productivity and Morale to Supervisor's Pressure for Production (Reprinted by permission of the publishers from *Some Applications of Behavioural Research,* edited by **Rensis Likert** and **Samuel Hayes,** UNESCO, Paris, 1957.)

as forming the variables for predicting group membership and group identification: status, status congruence, in-group value, and social conditioning and past group membership. Status is defined as a position score assigned to pay, age, seniority, education, ethnicity, and sex. Status congruence refers to the degree to which a member's total social status realizes consistency among the status factors that define his total status; an index was constructed to show the degree of alignment among these status factors. The in-group value refers to the extent that the individual is acceptable to the group. Social conditioning involves the individual's expectations of group behavior as it affects identification and acceptance. The following diagram summarizes the prediction problem:

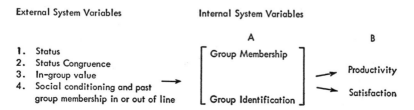

This is a system of interrelationships beginning with the four external factors forming group membership and the group identification. The double-headed arrow connecting group membership and group identification denotes the notion that, as an individual identifies with a group, there is a greater likelihood that he will realize membership and regularity. Also, the greater the degree of acceptance an individual has in a group, the greater his degree of positive identification. The diagram also shows double-headed arrows between internal system variables A and B. These arrows are intended to show the mutual dependence of group membership and identification with productivity and satisfaction. Over time, a worker's productivity and satisfaction are likely to affect his group membership through the degree of conformity represented in productivity and the attitudes toward the group implict in the concept of satisfaction.[57]

Further clarification of the determinants of productivity and morale under specified conditions must await additional research. This is a goal sufficient to keep the the next generation of social scientists and administrators busily engaged.

SELECTED BIBLIOGRAPHY

Barton, Allen, *Organizational Measurement,* College Entrance Examination Board, 1961.

Bass, Bernard M., *Leadership, Psychology, and Organizational Behavior,* Harper, 1960.

Brayfield, A. H., and W. H. Crockett, "Employee Attitudes and Employee Performance," *Psychological Bulletin,* September, 1955, pp. 396–424.

Dubin, Robert, George Homans, Floyd Mann, and Delbert C. Miller, *Leadership and Productivity,* Chandler, in press.

Form, William H., and James A. Geschwender, "Social Reference Basis of Job Satisfaction," *American Sociological Review,* April, 1962, pp. 228–237.

Kahn, Robert L., and Daniel Katz, "Leadership Practices in Relation to Productivity and Morale," in D. Cartwright and A. Zander (eds.), *Group Dynamics,* Harper, 1953.

Likert, Rensis, *New Patterns of Management,* McGraw-Hill, 1961.

Mann, Floyd C., and L. Richard Hoffman, *Automation and the Worker,* Holt, 1960.

[57] Zaleznik *et al., op. cit.,* pp. 382–383.

Miller, Delbert C., and Nahum Z. Medalia, "Efficiency, Leadership, and Morale in Small Military Organizations," *Sociological Review*, July, 1955, pp. 93–107.

Miller, Delbert C., and Nahum Z. Medalia, "Human Relations Leadership and the Association of Morale and Efficiency in Work Groups: A Controlled Study with Small Military Units," *Social Forces*, May, 1955, pp. 348–352.

Miller, Delbert C., *Handbook of Research Design and Social Measurement*, McKay, in press. (Contains scales of leadership and morale).

Morse, Nancy, *Satisfactions in the White Collar Job*, University of Michigan Institute for Social Research, 1953.

Seashore, S. E., *Group Cohesiveness in the Industrial Work Group*, University of Michigan Institute for Social Research, 1954.

Shartle, Carroll L., *Effective Performance Leadership*, Prentice-Hall, 1956.

Stogdill, Ralph M., *Individual Behavior and Group Achievement*, Oxford University Press, 1959.

Stogdill, Ralph M. (ed.), *Leader Behavior: Its Description and Measurement*, Ohio State Bureau of Business Research, 1957.

Tannenbaum, Robert, Irving R. Weschler, and Fred Massarik, *Leadership and Organization*, McGraw-Hill, 1961.

Viteles, Morris S., *Motivation and Morale in Industry*, Norton, 1953.

Westerlund, Gunnar, *Group Leadership*, A Field Experiment, Nordisk Rotogravyr, Stockholm, 1952.

Yuzuk, Ronald P., *The Assessment of Employee Morale*, Ohio State Bureau of Business Research, 1961.

Zaleznik, A., C. R. Christensen, and F. J. Roethlisberger, *The Motivation, Productivity, and Satisfaction of Workers*, Harvard, 1958.

CHAPTER 17

The Governing
of
the Work Organization

Three questions of an applied nature represent large challenges to the industrial and organizational sociologist who is interested in those group processes which deal with decision-making. They are questions which the managers of any work organization also ask, for they represent persistent problems of administration. These questions are: How does a manager decide what to do when he is confronted with two conflicting expectations or demands upon him? How shall a manager govern his immediate subordinates? How shall an administrator govern an enterprise?

These three problems have similarities. Each requires the decision-maker to predict the consequences of his decisions and to weigh their effects upon goals he is trying to achieve. Invariably, all of the problems make some kind of demand upon the moral and ethical values of the manager, whether he is aware of it or not. Each problem involves a role system, i.e., a pattern of role relationships between other employees and managers. Actions taken within role systems send repercussions throughout the entire system, involving many others. The questions that have been posed apply to groups as small as three and as large as 100,000 employees. Such decision-making requires the most careful projections and evaluations. In this chapter, theoretical guides and research findings will be marshaled to indicate how the social scientist may provide useful knowledge to the practitioner who must make important decisions.

MANAGERIAL DECISION-MAKING

The decision-making process involves a rational and intelligent calculation of (1) a set of alternative actions, (2) an array of outcomes for each action, (3) probabilities associated with the outcomes, and (4) values resulting from each outcome. When these data are available, a course of action is selected through the application of a decision criterion. The decision criterion refers to a generalized action principle utilized by the decision-maker, who chooses a partcular mode of action from his own hierarchy of values to fit the expected outcomes in order to make a specific choice. To summarize: the key elements in decision-making are possible actions, outcomes, probabilities, values, and a decision criterion.[1] It is not difficult to find these elements when a manager has made a decision. The researcher simply asks him to recite the data he had and the calculations he made in coming to the decision. What is difficult is to predict what decision an administrator will make. All kinds of problems present themselves: Will the decision-maker act in a rational manner? Does he foresee all of the alternative actions? Has he carefully calculated the outcomes of each possible action? Does he know the probabilities associated with each outcome? Does he understand what values he will secure from each outcome? What is his own personal value set? How stable are his own values? Will he be consistent or yield under pressure to expedient action?

These questions indicate the immense complexity of decision-making. There is cause to wonder whether anyone should attempt to predict how any person might act in a situation involving many alternative actions. Not even the miraculous computer can assemble data which are absent. These dilemmas of decision-making are so real that Chester Barnard, who spent a lifetime making administrative decisions, once said that he believed only about 50 percent of his decisions were the best that could have been made.

The opportunity to improve the decisions of an administrator constitutes the research attraction to a researcher. Can he demonstrate how decisions are made? Can he show the consequences to

[1] Irwin Bross, *Design for Decision*, Macmillan, 1953, p. 28.

the administrator? Can he prevent mistakes of judgment which injure morale and productivity of employees?[2]

The researcher rushes in where angels fear to tread. It is his job to take risks on knowledge and explore on the rim of the unknown. As he creeps out on the shaky foundation of the known, he grasps a theory, resorts to simplifying assumptions, and then follows hypotheses he thinks will be fruitful.

The Theory of Conflict Resolution

Neal Gross and associates present a theory of role conflict resolution which they have validated with data drawn from Massachusetts school superintendents.[3] A typical role conflict with which a school superintendent may be faced is encountered when he makes salary recommendations for his teachers. The teachers and the PTA are likely to press him very strongly to raise the salary levels, but such action may be just as strongly opposed by the taxpayers' association and the town finance committee, who complain that the community cannot support higher tax levels. It is not surprising, therefore, to find that the superintendent's decision on salary recommendations, as well as on other matters, must be made in a climate of incompatible expectations.

Briefly, the theory states that the incumbent of a position chooses one of four different actions when confronted with two conflicting role expectations: conformity to expectation A, conformity to expectation B, compromise, or avoidance. Thus, in the role conflict dealing with salary recommendations, the superintendent may make a strong recommendation for the salary expectations of the teachers, or may recommend no increase, or may compromise by recommending a slight increase, or may avoid by delaying or even refusing to make a recommendation.

It is hypothesized that three factors account for the incumbent's choice: *legitimacy, sanctions,* and *personal orientation. Legitimacy* refers to whether or not the incumbent believes that the individual or group making the claim had a right to expect him to conform to the expectations. *Sanctions* refer to penalties perceived as a consequence of following either of the conflicting role

---

[2] Chester I. Barnard, *The Functions of an Executive,* Harvard, 1945.

[3] Neal Gross, Ward S. Mason, and Alexander W. McEachern, *Explorations in Role Analysis,* John Wiley and Sons, 1958, pp. 281–318.

expectations. The respondent was asked to indicate how those pressing him to conform to expectation A and to expectation B would react if he did not do what each expected of him.

Some persons react differently to the moral aspects of a situation as well as to the varying pressures that either promise to reward him or threaten to penalize him. Thus, the third factor in the theory is the orientation of the incumbent as he brings his own values to bear upon a decision. *Personal orientation* refers to three possible evaluations of legitimacy and sanctions which the incumbent may make. The morally oriented person places more weight on legitimacy than upon sanctions. The expediently oriented person places more weight on sanctions than upon legitimacy. The moral-expedient person weighs both dimensions relatively equally.[4] Correspondingly, Gross constructed three models, each with sixteen predicted actions, to represent the behavior of position incumbents of these three orientations when faced with a situation involving two conflicting role expectations.[5] The predictions of behavior, then, were based on an assessment of legitimacy and sanctions for each conflict situation according to a moral, moral-expedient, or expedient orientation.

Significance of Managerial Decision-Making

The prospect of testing this theory of conflict resolution was especially inviting since it appeared that Gross and his associates had developed the theory far enough to make it fruitful when applied to other populations. Certainly, a model explaining conflict resolution verified by empirical evidence could aid significantly in the understanding of administrative decision-making. Role conflict situations are ubiquitous in all work organizations. Two examples from industry will illustrate the nature of these conflicts.

Jim Underhill, a training director, is caught in the pull between two powerful officers in his company. The personnel manager expects him to install a foreman training program which stresses "human relations" methods of supervision. The plant manager, who came up through the ranks, is thoroughly opposed to what he calls the "charm school" approach. Jim can't get the

[4] *Ibid.*, pp. 289–293.
[5] *Ibid.*, pp. 285–288.

program going and his boss is disappointed with him. Jim doesn't know what to do or think; he is caught in the middle of opposing views.

John Rainboldt, a plant manager, had received general, but specific, instructions from the home office that no overtime of any type would be approved during the current period. This order conflicts with his sales manager's belief that temporary conditions require work on a holiday to meet a critical deadline. Harry doesn't want to appear unable to make a decision; yet he really feels the squeeze of these conflicting demands.

Here is an example of role conflict faced by a business agent of a local union:

Strauss and Sayles (*The Local Union*) describe the case of a business agent confronted by a group of clerks who demand that he file a grievance for full pay for a day when they had been sent home early because of insufficient work. Another group of clerks in the same local union argues against filing this grievance. This group feels that the first group of clerks doesn't deserve full pay —it was the second group that worked all day.

In spite of its pervasiveness in all types of organizations, including business firms, little exploration has been made of role conflict. Thus, much remains to be learned about its resolution, its influence upon the organization, and its impact upon the individual. It is known, however, that such phenomena at different levels have all sorts of costs to the organization, from higher pay scales, turnover, and absenteeism to ulcers and coronary pathology in executives.

Causes of Conflict

During a recent study, D. C. Miller and Fremont A. Shull, Jr., found the following two major causes of conflict in organizations:

1. Departmental suboptimization. Managers focus upon and emphasize the needs of their departments at the expense of an optimal attainment of overall company objectives. Example: Seven managers ask for a 40–50 percent increase in their department budget. They claim they absolutely need it to accomplish their work load.

2. Multiple group loyalties. The manager's loyalties are split

among groups with whom he identifies, such as family, community, church, company, and profession. Example: A family-oriented executive with two children in the local high school is given a promotion and asked to move in the middle of the school year.

Miller and Shull attempted to predict the outcome of such conflicts. They set forth the hypothesis that the behavior of position incumbents when confronted with role conflicts can be predicted with a high degree of accuracy if the incumbent's perceptions of legitimacy and sanctions are given. Two groups of business managers, one group of training directors, and one group of labor leaders were studied—115 decision-makers in all. The hypothesis presents two major factors: legitimacy and possible penalty. Accordingly, the authors first asked about the legitimacy of the opposing claims; i.e., was each a legitimate and proper request? They asked the managers: "Do you think it is right and reasonable for A to expect you to follow his demand?" and "Now, do you think it is right and reasonable for B to expect you to follow his (opposing) claim?"

Secondly, the researchers examined the perception of the decision-maker as he evaluated the *penalties* that might result from these opposing pulls. Initially, the manager incurs the displeasure of those who feel offended because their ideas or demands were not accepted. Then this *displeasure* becomes really effective if the decision-maker *fails* in implementing his choice of one of the suggested courses of action. Thus the question was asked: "What penalties do you anticipate will result if you do not follow the wishes of B, but do what A wants and then *fail to produce good results?*" and "What do you anticipate will happen to you if you fail to produce a successful program under the conditions that you go ahead with B's wishes?"

The major task is to match the *evaluations* of the legitimacy of each request and the anticipated penalties of failure with the *action* that the decision-maker would choose. There are really two types of sanction involved from which the man-in-the-middle would withdraw: (1) those penalties which others can impose for thwart and for failure of goal accomplishment, and (2) the internal (psychological) pain for violating one's own sense of rightness. Where these two sanctions reinforce each other, as the judgments do in the following example, the answer is fairly clear cut. To review the incident above:

A training director was instructed to prepare a supervisory training program and administer it according to best known practices. (He believes that these instructions call for a *compulsory program on company time.*) The general plant superintendent, now operating under a heavy production schedule, insists that the training program be *voluntary and off company time.*

To this incident, some respondents said that (1) the president's (A's) expectation was right and reasonable, (2) the superintendent's (B's) desires were unreasonable and improper, (3) penalties for failing to produce a good program under the president's expectations would be slight, (4) penalties for failing while following the superintendent's wishes, on the other hand, would be high.

All of these forces operate so that the man-in-the-middle would follow the president's expectations. It is helpful to see this in diagrammatic form. Shull and Miller offer a "tree" in Fig. 17.1 showing the courses of action that they predicted for different evaluations of a conflict situation. These predicted actions assume that the decision-maker weighs *both penalty and legitimacy.* Although only 16 of the 100 possible evaluations that they studied are presented here, this tree illustrates a general array of the problem situations. Given the evaluations described above, the reader can follow the tree: The president's (A's) expectations were right and reasonable (*Yes* in Column I) but should the decision-maker fail in producing a good program, the penalties would be *slight* (located in Column III). At the same time, the superintendent's (B's) demands were unreasonable (*No* in Column II) and the penalties would be *high* for failure while following the superintendent's wishes (located in Column IV).

For these evaluations, the authors predicted that the man-in-the-middle would follow the president's (A's) wishes. Miller and Shull predicted correctly 71 percent of the actions taken. Allowing for chance probability, the result proved statistically significant (1 percent level).[6] It is highly unlikely that such a result

[6] Delbert C. Miller and Fremont A. Shull, Jr., "The Prediction of Administrative Role Conflict Resolutions," *Administrative Science Quarterly,* September, 1962, pp. 143–160.

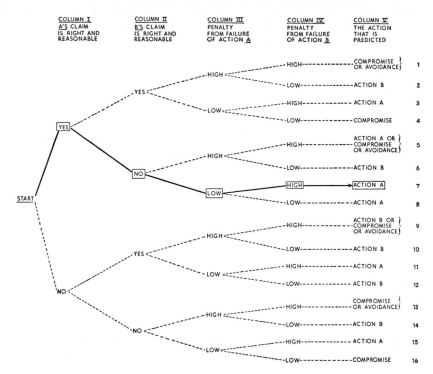

FIG. 17.1. Predicted Decision Tree for the Man-in-the-Middle. (From Fremont Shull and André Delbecq, *Selected Readings in Management,* Irwin, 1962, p. 311. By permission of the publisher.)

could have been obtained by chance. Gross and his associates report 83 percent correct predictions for their "legitimacy sanction" model.[7] Results such as these hold promise that the process of decision-making may be better understood and perhaps more accurately predicted.

Two applied outcomes hold fruitful possibilities. One of these is the construction of social-psychological job descriptions.

Construction of Social-Psychological Job Descriptions

Mason Haire says, "In the area of social perception . . . we have barely opened the field of role perception in hierarchical

[7] Gross *et al., op. cit.,* p. 309.

structures. We have virtually nothing of what has been called 'psychological job descriptions.' That is, descriptions of the aspects of the job which, besides simple duties, makes demands on the person—the fact, for example, that a waitress is caught between the customer's demands and the kitchen's inflexibility."[8] Haire's concept of psychological job descriptions suggests that the theory of role conflict resolution, if applied to a series of selected conflict situations, could produce more meaningful definitions of position stresses and strains facing a business or labor leader. Such knowledge could be coupled with an analysis of the social structure encompassing the position in the organization. The resulting social-psychological job description could constitute a useful advance in job placement and training.

Improvement of Executive Decision-Making

Moreover, it is entirely possible that the social science consultant could help an administrator "work through" a role conflict situation focusing upon the pressures of legitimacy and sanctions and thus provide training of major value. Such an approach would be reality based, involving role taking at one of its most critical junctures in decision-making. The social science consultant would try to improve the administrator's ability to assess the consequences of his action in advance and to give him a measure of his decision-making proficiency by comparing actual consequences occurring in a conflict situation with his previous assessment of them. This kind of training takes place in a situation demanding high social insight and awareness on the part of the administrator. He would learn to imaginatively project the social consequences of his alternate courses of action before making his decision. And, after implementing the decision, he would obtain and assess the feedback of those affected. Thus, the process of executive development might become a continuous evaluation of the behavior of all those persons within his sphere of influence. As the administrator narrowed the gap between predicted and actual consequences, the success of training could be evaluated.

If these two outcomes of the research can be secured, *viz.,* the building of social-psychological job descriptions and the improve-

---

[8] Robert Dahl, Mason Haire, and Paul F. Lazarsfeld, *Social Science Research in Business,* Columbia, 1959, p. 91.

ment of executive training, we will have witnessed the special accomplishment of translating social science research into applied practice. It may now be possible to parallel in social science the modern developments in the physical and biological sciences, where, increasingly, discoveries are being rushed into rapid technical utilization.

THE GOVERNING OF SUBORDINATES

When a person is given a work position carrying responsibility for the work activities of others, he is placed in a focal spot within a clearly integrated role system. Subordinates will immediately look to the new manager for indications of the behavior he expects from them. From the moment of the new managerial assignment, the employees will seek to assess their future, first in security, status, and freedom of action, and then in prospects for promotion, merit increases, and interesting assignments. Many of their waking hours at work and away from work will be preoccupied with their standing in the eyes of the boss and his wife. Unless there is great animosity between them, they will invariably become somewhat like the manager as the years go by. From him they will derive their area of responsibility and freedom of action and acquire attitudes about the "higher-ups" and the work organization generally. The manager, in turn, will establish how he wants to work with his subordinates and how much he wants to involve them in decision-making about matters which affect them and the department in which they work. His image of the ideal employee will infuse his philosophy of leadership. He may see his employees as variously defined in Chapter 15—as biological machines, individual personalities, group members, or political beings. Wilensky suggests that two images of the ideal employee are prevalent. The first is

the happy, contented, but autonomous, decision making, participating worker. He goes about his work with a cheerful willingness to comply with managerial directives, and where management considers it appropriate he participates in decisions, usually of minor importance (but sometimes of major importance). . . . The second image sees him as happy, contented, but typically docile. He, too, goes about his work with a cheerful willingness to comply with managerial directives. Sometimes, but not too frequenlty, he exercises limited initiative in the pursuit of managerial aims. He has ambition, but it is ambition with limited goals, compatible with management's requirements that there be discipline, regularity, and somebody to do the less interesting work.[9]

Whatever the manager's image of his subordinates, it will profoundly influence his practices. Perhaps the most significant of these practices will be his use or disuse of committees or group meetings.

Four Patterns of Superior-Subordinate Relations

Committees or group meetings serve various functions. They may be used by the manager to impart information (or ascertain it), to secure advice, or to elicit a decision from the subordinates. Therefore, the manager can elect any one of four main options in his relations with his subordinates. He can (1) operate without any committee or group meetings, (2) use committees and group meetings for informational purposes only, (3) use committees for advisory assistance, or (4) use committees for group decision-making. The manager sets into motion quite different expectations by his choice.

The industrial sociologist has a challenging applied problem to solve here. If the major options open to the manager for the governing of his subordinates are arrayed on an authority continuum, they would look as shown in Fig. 17.2.

This continuum shows the options in a sequence in which the manager is sharing an increased amount of his delegated authority with his subordinates in order to achieve a more cooperative organizational structure. In spite of the "defects" of the democratic process, democracy has a remarkable capacity to develop leadership and independent action in persons as well as loyalty in the group. Let us examine the strengths and weakness of each option.

No committees or group meetings

Many managers frankly regard committee meetings as a flat waste of time. They believe nothing is accomplished either in securing assent or in building morale. For the imparting of information they suggest the memo or company newspaper as the

[9] Harold Wilensky, "Human Relations in the Work Place," in *Research in Industrial Human Relations,* Harper, 1957, p. 39.

No Committees or Group Meetings	Committees for Informational Communication	Advisory Committees	Decision- Making Committee		
			Majority Vote with Managerial Veto Power	Principle of Una- nimity	Majority Vote— No Veto Power
0	1	2	3	4	5

FIG. 17.2. Group Decision-Making by Degree to Which Manager Shares His Authority.

fastest medium. Generally, they prefer to deal with persons on an individual basis in their office or at the subordinate's place of work. Many would agree with Ralph Cordiner, who as president of General Electric saw no use in holding meetings to dodge responsibility or to make committee-like motions when the decision was going to be reached by one man later on. He defined in writing the exact degree of authority and accountability of each executive. He said, "We have no committees to make decisions that individuals should make. We have no committees with power."[10] The American Telephone and Telegraph Company has no standing committees beyond its monthly board meeting. The parent company operates on the principle that everyone knows what ought to be done—a principle that encourages informal consultation.[11]

These practices are followed because it is believed that they are efficient and accomplish the goals of the enterprise. Yet many shortcomings may exist in attaining coordinated and cooperative performance. The subordinates may be confined too narrowly to their specialized area and may not be able to coordinate activities with the highest efficiency. Mistakes may be made because group communication is inadequate. Since cooperative activity comes to rest on authority as the principal motive force, morale may be weakened by a failure to develop a sense of common enterprise. Leadership training for a more responsible post may be stunted

[10] Herrymon Maurer, "Management by Committee," *Fortune*, April, 1953, p. 192.
[11] *Ibid.,* p. 147.

for lack of opportunity to participate more completely in the total process.

Committees and group meetings for informational purposes only

Many managers say they could not get along without committees and group meetings. Some use them to impart information to their group of key subordinates, conveying job information and coordinating the work of the latter. Many see this as a straight-down-the-line communication channel. Others use the committee to gather substantial amounts of information and feedback for the technical and social goals they stress. This up-the-line function signifies a willingness of the leader to listen and to be governed by the information brought to him. There are values to be gained by these practices: better coordination, fast communication, and perhaps a limited sense of participation on the part of subordinates. The employee wants to know what is going on especially if it may affect him.

On the other hand, the employee may feel a disdain for meetings that go no further in enlisting his support than to hear what he may contribute to an informational gathering. He may feel his facts are desired but not his ideas. He may find that all the boss really wants from him are good reports, so he filters the information to provide the respected coloration. He may find that the meetings provide little more than an arena in which all of his immediate rivals for advancement jockey for status and recognition. He learns that the really important decisions occur in the privacy of the boss's office.

Committees for advisory assistance

Managers who place prime importance on committees for advisory assistance convey a specific role conception to their subordinates. They indicate that they want and need advice on some problems and they want to find out what ideas and what group consensus exist. They make it clear that the final decision will be that of the manager himself. The values of such a practice reside in building a more cooperative atmosphere and acquiring better performance when the decision is made. Moreover, as groups of subordinates engage in exercising their judgment, they secure a broader managerial experience. Some managers report a reduction in the number of grievances and more peaceful managerial-subordinate relations. This pattern of advisory meetings is used widely in Swift and Company, Continental Oil Company, and many others. Leonard McCollum, president of Continental, reserves for himself the final say in the management-advisory committee and has reserved the same right for the chairman of every other committee in the company. Responsibility for decisions, he emphasizes, must be carried by individuals—along with suitable rewards for carrying it.

Liabilities for this method of using committees include their time-consuming character. They can seldom be held to a schedule. Split votes introduce latent conflicts which can open wide at any time. Perhaps above all, there is the feeling that, since the superior will decide, the opinions of the subordinates do not really count for much. At the worst, the committee becomes a battlefield in which each subordinate vies with the others to influence the boss. Clique warfare may break out. Reason may not turn out to be sweet.

Committees for group decision-making

The DuPont Company has governed itself since 1921 with an executive committee. Today the committee is composed of eight vice-presidents and the president of the company. The president has only one vote; he can be and at times is overruled.[12]

In American Can, which is comparably group minded, the president has the right of veto in his executive committee but has never used it. Former Board Chairman Frank Abrams of Standard Oil Company of New Jersey says "one must submerge one's own ideas into those of the group. Above all one must work toward unanimity."[13] The Society of Friends has long used methods of reaching agreement without resorting to votes. Quakers have run their religious society for three hundred years by committee. They emphasize the will to unanimity as the responsibility of every member of its meetings and its committees. The system works because Quakers are united in a body of common conviction. It also works in many companies, in the Joint

[12] *Ibid.*, p. 191.
[13] *Ibid.*

Chiefs of Staff, and in many voluntary organizations in which the members are united in a common concern.

Exponents of the decision-making committee claim that it is the only method of using committees that can bring both a high sense of personal commitment and also serve as a primary source of executive training. Each person becomes a decision-maker; each is given greater authority and responsibility and with it an insight into the managerial process. Managers often testify that better decisions emerge from the group than they would have made had the decisions been theirs alone.

Difficulties with the Democratic Method

But the decision-making committee option is admittedly fraught with dangers. It is time consuming, to say the least. It encourages patterns of democratic governing among subordinates who are not aware of the fundamental dilemmas of the democratic process. Four "defects" of democracy are discussed by Chester Barnard. He points out (1) the opposition between partial consent and complete performance, (2) the discrepancy between abstract decision and concrete action, (3) time lags, and (4) political conflict.[14]

1. The dilemma of consent and conformance

The democratic method is one of decision by partial consent, whereas cooperative action rests upon substantially complete conformance. Thus, the democratic process involves a conflict of principle. Unless unanimity is achieved, the committee meeting ends with many persons requested to do what they may have strongly urged was unwise. To expect their enthusiastic conformance is unrealistic. Barnard sees in this dilemma a fundamental conflict of principle: cooperation means approximate unanimity of will; the democratic process means decision by division.[15]

2. The dilemma of the abstract and the concrete

The second dilemma emerges because the democratic process is one for determining consent or dissent to intellectual abstrac-

---

[14] Chester I. Barnard, *Organization and Management,* Harvard, 1949, p. 31.
[15] *Ibid.*

tions while conformance rests on concrete acts. Men often agree to do what in fact is beyond their capacities. They accept proposals in the abstract but avoid carrying them out because they seem either undesirable or painful when the concrete act is upon them. Often they fall to quarreling over the concrete details when they have previously expressed acceptance of the abstract proposal. A common method of avoiding such conflicts is for the participants to disregard the decision. "Hence, there is a persistent tendency for the democratic process to create illegality and thus destroy itself."[16]

3. The dilemma of the time lag

Time lag is inherent in the democratic process. It arises out of the difficulty of securing assent between the need for action and decision and between decision and corresponding action. The need for making important decisions often arises suddenly and requires almost immediate attention. There is often not time even to assemble the committee; in other cases there is the question of whether the group can arrive at a quick decision. The democratic process of decision-making is almost always long. The fears of each member must be allayed and alternate plans adopted. It is a commonplace that many members seem to give verbal assent only to have their fears reassert themselves. Delay upon delay can ensue before a decision is reached. Then comes the problem of arriving at a consensus about implementing the decision. Faced with such a committee history, a manager feels compelled to act. In order to get prompt answers, techniques for circumventing the democratic process are often necessary.

4. The dilemma of political conflict

The democratic discussion of a proposal may disorganize by inciting political conflict. The discussion opens up a variety of proposed actions and reasons. It brings into sharp focus the rewards and penalties which may accrue to each person if the decision goes one way or another. Reasons are given for desired ends. It is not that men disagree as to what should or should not be done, but that they disagree as to reasons. "It may be true that

[16] *Ibid.,* p. 34.

differences of philosophy are even more important sources of discord than differences of material interest."[17]

The manager will be loath to submit proposals to group decision if he finds that the democratic process seriously disorganizes group relations and makes a mockery of group consent.

These and other dilemmas confront the manager who weighs the advantages and disadvantages of the democratic process.[18] Almost no research has been conducted in work organizations themselves on the social processes in committee activity as a decision-making tool. However, considerable knowledge about small problem-solving groups in laboratory settings is being built up and will provide considerable assistance to a manager or supervisor.

LEADERSHIP BEHAVIOR: PROBLEM-SOLVING GROUPS

One of the approaches to the observation of leadership behavior is sociometric analysis of the interpersonal relations and of the communication networks that make a group an organic entity. One such study will illustrate the approach to the understanding of leadership role and group cohesion.

Figure 17.3 illustrates a sociogram or chart of a work group of eighteen student workers who were asked, "With what persons would you most prefer to work?" Each worker was asked privately to name five persons in order of his choice. It can be seen that the most important constellations are grouped around workers 2, 5, 13, and 16. These workers we have called sociometric leaders.[19] The remaining workers were grouped around the sociometric leaders so that four working groups were formed. Each worker was placed in such a way as to maximize his likelihood of being in contact with the persons to whom he was most attracted.

---

[17] *Ibid.,* p. 37.

[18] A very real dilemma is whether the manager should share private information of great bearing on a decision when it may jeopardize the reputation of a person or the competitive position of the organization were it to be communicated outside the group.

[19] This study was conducted by D. C. Miller, James Reilly, and Virginia Hertzler, "Leadership in Small Work Groups," *Proceedings of the Pacific Sociological Society, Research Studies of the State College of Washington,* April, 1950.

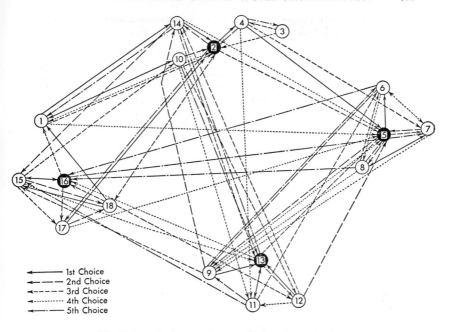

FIG. 17.3. A Sociogram Composed of Eighteen Workers.

Figure 17.4 shows the four groups as they were constituted in January when they began to work together.

Each group was asked to elect a leader and to begin work on projects assigned to them. The elected leader is shown in each of the four groups. It should be noted that in only two of the four groups did the sociometric leader win election. This distinction is important. It demonstrates that the person whose qualities of personality are most pleasing to others may not have in the eyes of those same people the leadership quality which they seek in the active direction of a group.

Another distinction is to be noted. The observation of these groups in active work demonstrated that the elected leader was not always the "natural" leader. We have called a worker a "natural" leader of a group when he provided the initiative and energy which moved the group forward. The natural leader could be relatively easily identified by the observers who watched the group activities. In two work groups natural leaders were not

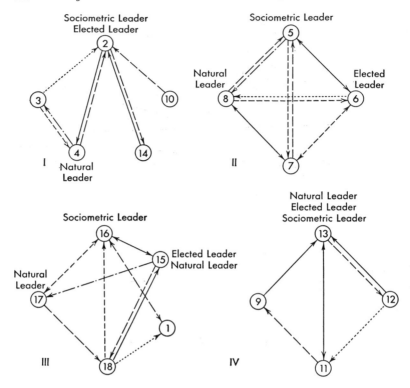

FIG. 17.4. Four Working Groups in Sociometric Arrangement, in January.

elected to leadership. In three work groups natural leaders were
not able to achieve the position of sociometric leader. This diver-
gence seems to indicate that many persons of high ability, initiative, and dominance may be neither especially liked nor able
to achieve popular election as a leader. It was our hypothesis that
a leader who could secure his position simultaneously as the sociometric, elected, and natural leader would be able to build the
greatest amount of cohesion. To test this hypothesis we made
especially careful observations of group IV, where worker 13 was
the sociometric, elected, and natural leader. His group was a
well-organized, cooperative, interested group. Number 13 showed
by far the greatest initiative and dominance of any person in the
group. His interaction score was the highest and he spoke longer

at a time and interrupted more freely than any other member of the group.[20] At times the observers felt that he repeated himself unnecessarily and in some cases showed little discretion in speaking. Number 9 seemed inclined to hurry the group on but the other members seemed well satisfied.

To learn more about the nature of the interpersonal relations and the role of the leader a second measurement of sociometric choice was planned, to be given to the entire class three months after the initial formation of the four working groups. Since the eighteen members participated together three times a week in the classroom as well as within the small working groups, there was ample opportunity for all of them to know one another. However, at the end of March the sociometric pattern demanded only minor readjustments in the working groups. These changes can be seen in Fig. 17.5, which shows groups I, II, III, IV as they were reconstituted to maximize attractions. The correlation between the first and second sociometric choice tests was r = .704, indicating a fairly high degree of stability. The question of how persons could be regrouped to insure higher compatibility revealed that only three moves would be necessary. Number 10 was moved from group I to group IV, number 9 was moved from group IV to group II, and number 1 was moved from group III to group IV.

This second measurement revealed more clearly what had been happening between January and March in group III. Here, number 15, a woman, was obviously winning sociometric leadership in addition to her achievements as an elected and natural leader. Group III consisted of five members, all women. Number 15 was the determined "natural" leader and the elected leader. In addition, by March she had emerged as the sociometric leader. Number 15 might be characterized by her attempt to please all members of the group, to ask their opinions on nearly all moves. She opened the meetings, organized the material, and kept the records, but always asked for the opinion and decision of the group on all important issues. Number 17 was also a "natural" leader in the group but she achieved a slightly lower choice status in the small group and a much lower rating from the total classroom population. In contrast, number 15 by March had secured the

---

[20] The qualities compare with those that E. D. Chapple has identified in leaders with the use of his interactional chronograph. See Chapter 16.

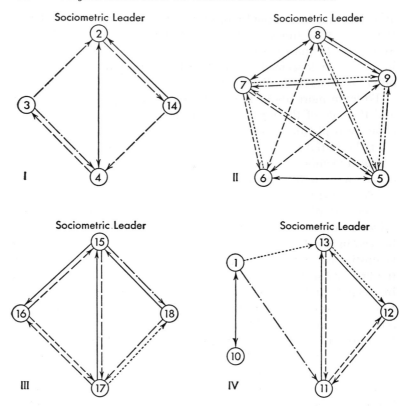

FIG. 17.5. Four Working Groups in Sociometric Arrangement, Two Months Later.

highest choice status in her working group and more choices than any other member on the total class preference test. Therefore, of these two natural leaders (15 and 17) in the same group, 15 has won leadership on her natural ability as well as ability to gain acceptance. It is apparent that her more democratic manner and discretion in speaking are most satisfactory to this closely knit group.

Thus, groups III and IV tend to validate the research hypothesis, but group II as strongly contradicts it. Group II consisted of members 5, 6, 7, 8, all men (see Fig. 17.4). Three different types of leadership were offered this group by three different persons.

The sociometric leader is number 5, the elected leader, number 6, and the natural leader, number 8. There is no evidence that this separation of leadership was incompatible with group harmony. On the contrary, this group emerged in March as the most cohesive as measured by sociometric choice. More choices were given to members inside the work group than were given by any other group to its own members.

Roles of Group Members in Problem-Solving Groups

Leadership is shared activity regardless of the titles distributed to persons in a group. In problem-solving groups members can be divided into those who exercise group task roles, group building and maintenance roles, and individual roles. The group task roles are taken by those participants who contribute a unit act that facilitates and coordinates group effort in the definition and solution of a common problem. The group building and maintenance roles are taken by those who contribute a unit act designed to strengthen, regulate, or perpetuate the group as a group. Individual roles are taken when participants contribute unit acts which simply satisfy an "individual" need without relevance either to the group task or to the functioning of the group as a whole.[21] Researchers now observe groups in action and record every unit act. They have discovered that the interplay of group task and maintenance roles is necessary for group problem solving. Persons who contribute group task acts are often disliked but their absence can diminish the effectiveness of a group. Likewise, group maintenance roles are essential for group stability and consensus when conflict must be resolved and an action decided upon. Leaders who understand and facilitate good human relations in their groups are more successful. There is more group- and task-oriented activity, rather than person-centered activity, when members also know and can apply human relations principles. Group dynamics has been developed so that groups now have the opportunity of studying their own interactional patterns as they seek to solve problems. Many organizational leaders are

[21] Kenneth D. Benne and Paul Sheets, "Functional Roles of Group Members," *Journal of Social Issues,* 1948, vol. 4, pp. 41–49; cf. Robert F. Bales, *Interaction Process Analysis,* Addison-Wesley, 1950.

now taking group sensitivity and group dynamics training in preparation for more effective conference leadership.[22]

Experiments are now needed with the workings of the committee itself in the ongoing organization. The background and training of subordinates required for committee decision-making are unknown except for the observation that long managerial experience, common stakes in the organization, and stable work relations are conducive to efficient decision-making processes. Little is known about dealing with the dilemmas of the democratic process. These problems are of the highest importance if democracy is to be extended to work organizations.

The Participation Hypothesis

The participation hypothesis offers the most fruitful starting point. The hypothesis states: If it is desired to bring about a change in the behavior of an organization and to get effective acceptance, it is necessary to secure the active participation of those persons who will be affected by the change.[23] This hypothesis may hold best in a democratic as opposed to an autocratic society.

Some "principles" that might be tested empirically include the following:

1. A group of subordinates should be involved in the sharing of managerial decision-making to the extent that they have the capacity and experience appropriate to the problems they are given.
2. Policy committees should be restricted to matters of major policy. They should not be given administrative or supervisory responsibility.
3. Any subject should be explored thoroughly ahead of time by

[22] Ronald Lippitt, *Training and Community Relations*, Harper, 1949, describes some of the work of the Laboratory for Group Dynamics Training which is operated each summer by the National Educational Association and the University of Michigan at Gould Academy, Bethel, Maine. The University of California at Los Angeles is also active in this area. See Robert Tannenbaum, Irving R. Weschler, and Fred Massarik, *Leadership and Organization*, McGraw-Hill, 1961, chaps. 9–14; George M. Beal, Joe M. Bohlen, and J. N. Raudabaugh, *Leadership and Dynamic Group Action*, Iowa State University Press, 1962.

[23] Cf. R. Likert, *New Patterns of Management*, McGraw-Hill, 1961, p. 163.

the committee's staff, and results should be in the hands of the members before the committee sits.

GOVERNANCE OF THE ENTERPRISE

Every work organization must discharge in various ways three diverse functions. It is an *economic* institution providing goods or services by collective organization of men and materials. It is a *governmental* institution controlling the access to the productive organization and distributing authority and responsibility to all those who come under its control. It is also a *social* institution providing social status or function in the work organization and to a great extent in the local community as well.[24]

It is as a governmental institution that a work organization exhibits a gap in research and theory. We have thought of government as a matter for cities, states, and nations. But the study of organizational politics and government has been limited. Recently, government bureaucracies have been compared to other large-scale organizations in industry, education, and religion. This comparative analysis has thrown some light on governmental process, but a host of questions remain for the student of work organizations.

Unsolved Questions of Government in Work Organizations

What is the jurisdiction of a work organization over its members?

What corresponds to the executive, legislative, and judicial branches of a work organization?

Does due process of law apply in a corporate body? Where can one secure a fair trial?

Does an employee have freedom of speech, freedom to publish and to invent?

Does an employee have a right to a share in the profits he has helped to create?

What pension rights does he have if he leaves the company?

Does an employee have a right to be represented on the board of directors?

[24] Peter F. Drucker, *The New Society,* Harper, 1950, pp. 44–50.

What does the actual distribution of authority in an organization look like when compared with its formal blueprint?

How are principles of centralization and decentralization of authority applied?

What are the sanctions actually utilized by strategically placed decision-makers?

The work organization has a community life of its own. Every study of employees reveals that they place the fulfillment of their status and function before and above even the satisfaction of their economic demands. The need for a responsible self-government in the work community is constantly indicated by the studies of social scientists. The central finding is that the employee needs and demands the actual experience of responsible participation in his own job and in those affairs of the plant that concern him directly. The most marked expression is found in the establishment of unions, whereby the employee can command a voice in the settlement of grievances and the negotiating of wants. Joint consultation of management and employee representatives is another such expression.

Joint Consultation

Joint consultation may be explained as a formal organization of employee and management representatives who exchange information and advice and in some cases make decisions on matters of common concern. The traditional prerogatives of management and union are recognized. In fact joint consultation differs from union organization by providing elected representation of all sections of personnel in the organization, whether organized or not. Trade unions are usually urged to cooperate and present candidates. The plant or works council aims at being an instrument of and for the well-being of the entire organization. Works councils in the Netherlands set up permanent committees to study various matters. Thus many people can be teamed up in the work of the council.[25]

Indeed, joint consultation between employer and employee has been made mandatory by national law for many work organiza-

---

[25] N. D. Relieveld, "Improvements of Human Relations by Works Councils," *Human Relations in Industry*, European Productivity Agency, Project No. 312, Paris, 1956.

tions in West Germany (1951; 1952), the Netherlands (1950), Belgium (1948), and France (1945; 1950).[26] In Switzerland, Sweden, Italy, Austria, Great Britain, and the United States autonomous agreements of the parties guide the developments of joint consultation without the intervention of the state. In the United States joint consultation reached its peak in World War II when labor-management committees were formed to speed production. Since that time, most committees have been allowed to die as unions insisted on their role as the major representative of the worker. In Great Britain there was great enthusiasm for joint consultation after the Second World War. It was speedily found to be inadequate as a solution to perplexing industrial problems because "it frequently failed either to evoke any noticeable response from employees in general or to lead to any concrete results in terms of productive efficiency."[27] However, research shows mixed results, and enough is known to conclude that the formal and informal organizations of any work organization must be in harmony for communication to be effective in establishing better relations or achieving goals. Mere provision for the machinery of joint consultation is useless unless there are individuals available who are prepared to trust each other, who desire to meet together to discuss matters of mutual interest, and who have the necessary social and psychological attributes to enable them to do so. The problem is one of basic organization, and selection and training of staff, rather than one of administrative techniques.[28]

A study of joint consultation bodies in Sweden has revealed that such bodies tend to lapse into information agencies in which management's information giving dominates. The employee reaction is often apathetic. The researchers found that these employees were engaged in highly specialized work that required little knowledge of organizational structure. Moreover, their physical contact outside of their department was limited, and they had neither technical knowledge nor knowledge of the organizational structure of the company. Moreover, they rarely

---

[26] Dr. Otto Neuloh, "Decision Making Process and Human Relations in Industry," in *ibid.*

[27] W. H. Scott, *Industrial Democracy*, University Press, Liverpool, 1955.

[28] T. S. Simey, "Problems of Communication in Modern Industry," in *Human Relations in Industry, op. cit.*, p. 19.

had contact with those supervisors who did have knowledge of the organizational structure.[29]

Drucker has acknowledged these obstacles and has called for measures to overcome them. They "require for their overcoming concrete, radical and major changes, in the policies, the organization, the practices, and even in the philosophy of the enterprises."[30] He argues that no part of the productive resources of industry operate at a lower efficiency than the human resources and that the management of men should be the first and foremost concern of operating managements. Unless each employee at all levels sees his work in relation to the whole organization and to the society and is convinced that his own operation, however small, is vital to the success of the whole, the potentialities of the economic performance of that employee are not tapped. Society has a right to demand the individual's responsible participation as a citizen, both in work and in nonwork activities.[31] The great sociologist William G. Sumner would have said this is no more than the strain for consistency among the mores in a democratic society. Responsible citizens are responsible workmen and the dignity of man extends into work life. The social pressure is a pressure for assimilation of democratic values.

> Executives have it within their power to frustrate the creative energies of most of the men under their direction or to help them to fulfill their capacities. . . .
>
> It was the moral imperative of Immanuel Kant, the German philosopher, that every man must be treated as an end in himself. . . . Is there any way that this moral idea can be made consistent with the idea of a corporation in which work is done through men? I can think of only one way and it is an imperfect one. This is to attempt to design each man's job in such a way that he fully comprehends it, that he sees it as a job worthy of him as a man, that he does it of his own choice, and that he is permitted to take the responsibility for his acts and to develop the moral fiber that comes from accepting the consequences of his decisions.[32]

The road to responsible industrial citizenship may be a long one and may require many adjustments. The transition is already

---

[29] Edmund Dahlstrom, "Internal Communication," in *ibid.*, p. 23.

[30] Drucker, *op. cit.*, p. 167.

[31] *Ibid.*, p. 162.

[32] Charles A. Nelson, "The Liberal Arts in Management," *Harvard Business Review*, May-June. 1958, pp. 91–99.

under way and certain steps can be foreseen. If research knowledge can be marshaled, the movement might be fraught with fewer hazards.[33]

The Establishment of a Work Community Government

The first step in establishing a government in the work community is to determine the jurisdiction of that government and its relation to the union and to management as parties with traditional prerogatives. It has been suggested that six major categories of function can be identified.[34]

1. Transportation, safety, recreation and health matters. These are clearly employee matters primarily and have little bearing on economic performance. The following are examples: transportation to and from work, parking, cafeteria, hobbies or sports, parties, educational activities, vacation schedules, shift assignments, and safety rules and equipment.

2. Matters in which management has strong interest in basic policy but little concern with detailed administration. Examples include profit-sharing funds, security benefits, guaranteed income, and seniority rights.

3. Problems of personnel management requiring joint responsibility. Examples are placement and assignment of jobs, training, absenteeism and turnover, organizational discipline and rules, and transfer of workers.

4. Problems requiring joint negotiation and compromise. Examples are promotion within the ranks, wage differentials, job evaluation, time and motion study, standards of output, incentive pay, and cuts in the work force.

5. Problems of technological change. Communication of job changes to the work community is management's function. Questions of transfer and retraining become vital factors in establishing psychological security of employees. These are matters for the work community to have a joint say about.

6. Problems of promoting greater productivity. The securing of greater productivity is the measure by which the individual employee achieves a higher standard of living. Efforts to secure

[33] The student who wants to read the best study now available is urged to see Elliott Jacques, *The Changing Culture of a Factory*, Dryden, 1952.

[34] Drucker, *op. cit.*, pp. 283–286.

increases in production have usually failed unless reasonable job security has been attained and an equity in wage differentials has been established. These are matters of the highest importance to employees and are urgent to management as well.

Jurisdictional definition and procedural matters are bound to be the source of much conflict. The steps to a co-determination of authority may now seem a ladder to the stars, but some organizations are already functioning in this way. The West German National Law of Co-Determination sets a pattern of joint consultation as a national goal for mining, steel, and the iron industry.

Figure 17.6 is a suggested hierarchy of authority relations which moves from a traditional, authoritarian relationship (shown at the lower end of the figure) through progressively more democratic stages called Legalistic, Employee-Oriented, Democratic Decision-Making, and finally to Co-Determinate Management. Each stage makes new demands on the education, experience, and responsible capacity of both management and employees.

If a wider extension of democratic practices does continue to take place within work organizations, research problems of a sociopolitical character will be of increasing importance as employees' education, skills, and aspirations increase. Elliott Jacques, reporting on the two-year record of the Glacier Metal Company of England in establishing joint consultation, said that the "beliefs that caused the most arguments were those based on ultimate values associated with principles of democratic living."[35] Likert has reported on the basis of the extensive research of the Michigan Survey Research Center: High-producing managers are using the principle of supportive relationship; i.e., "The leadership and other processes of the organization must be such as to ensure a maximum probability that in all interactions and all relationships with the organization each member will in the light of his background, values, and expectations, view the experience as supportive and one which builds and maintains his sense of personal worth and importance."[36]

The application of this principle is not easy for an organization that has operated with an authoritative or legalistic pattern. Likert estimates that a shift to a more democratic process of man-

[35] Jacques, op. cit., p. 317.
[36] Likert, op. cit., p. 103.

Management		Employees
	Co-Determinate Management	
Offers full opportunity to participate in ownership and management		Participate fully in stock purchase and in cooperative management
Offers employee representation on board of directors	11	Accept; employee representative reports back to employees
Prepares and distributes complete financial and social audit	10	Read and ask questions of management in councils of joint consultation
	Democratic Decision-Making	
Asks for joint consultation on major matters such as guaranteed annual income, job evaluation, technological changes	9	Discussion on basis of union approval and equal representation of employees and management
Asks for joint consultation on minor matters such as physical facilities, cafeteria, safety	8	Discuss minor matters by department or by division or in an organization-wide council
	Employee-Oriented	
Asks regularly for advice on important matters affecting employees	7	Give or withhold advice
Asks regularly for information	6	Give or withhold information
	Legalistic	
Negotiates with individual and union	5	Bargain individually and collectively in a union of their own election
Accepts requests and adjusts grievances under an agreed plan acceptable to employees	4	Make requests and submit grievances
	Authoritarian	
Gives information	3	Listen and act as expected
Gives advice	2	Accept advice as given
Gives orders	1	Respond to orders as given
Wage contract is offered		Wage contract is accepted

FIG. 17.6. Steps to Co-Determination of Authority.

agement may take ten years or more in a large corporation. He cautions that haste is self-defeating because of the anxieties or stresses that such changes may create. However, he predicts that the decisions an organization makes today with regard to the extent it uses social science research and experimentally tests new theories, principles, and practices will exert a major influence on the character and effectiveness of its management system a decade hence.[37]

SELECTED BIBLIOGRAPHY

Banks, J. A., *Industrial Participation Theory and Practice: A Case Study*, Liverpool University Press, 1963.

Barnard, Chester I., *Organization and Management*, Harvard, 1949.

Blum, Fred H., *Toward a Democratic Work Process*, Harper, 1953.

Coch, L., and J. R. P. French, "Overcoming Resistance to Change," *Human Relations*, August, 1948, pp. 512–513.

Davis, Keith, "Management by Participation," *Management Review*, February, 1947, pp. 69–79.

Drucker, Peter F., *The New Society*, Harper, 1950.

European Productivity Agency, *Human Relations in Industry*, Project No. 312, Paris, 1956.

Gross, Neal, Ward S. Mason, and Alexander W. McEachern, *Explorations in Role Analysis: Studies of the School Superintendency Role*, Wiley, 1958.

Jacques, Elliott, *The Changing Culture of a Factory*, Dryden, 1952.

Likert, Rensis, *New Patterns of Management*, McGraw-Hill, 1961, chap. 14, "A Comparative View of Organization," pp. 222–236.

McMurry, Robert N., "The Case for Benevolent Autocracy," *Harvard Business Review*, January–February, 1958, pp. 82–90.

Mason, Edward S. (ed.), *The Corporation in Modern Society*, Harvard, 1960.

Maurer, Herrymon, *Great Enterprise*, Macmillan, 1955.

Scott, W. H., *Industrial Leadership and Joint Consultation: A Study of Human Relations in Three Merseyside Firms*, Liverpool University Press, 1952.

Scott, W. H., *Joint Consultation in a Liverpool Manufacturing Firm: A Case Study in Human Relations in Industry*, Liverpool University Press, 1950.

[37] *Ibid.*, p. 248.

PART V · Industry, Community, and Society

Industry, community, and society are in a state of interdependence. In this part we shall examine the interrelations between industry and labor, and other institutions of the community. The strike reflects a crisis in industrial relations; often, as its repercussions spread, it mirrors power conflicts in all community institutions. The day-to-day life of a community is generally placid, but all the many forces of change erupt occasionally in community-wide issues. The issue may be the question of building a new school, raising taxes, annexing new areas contiguous to the city, or undertaking renewal of a residential or a commercial area. These matters may cause a mass stirring of the public, and labor and industry are often major antagonists in the contests. Other community decisions are made more quietly in such power centers as the Chamber of Commerce, the central labor council, the school board, the city council, the mayor's office, the city planning commission, the social welfare board, and the council of churches.

Chapter 18 describes how business and labor interact with government, education, welfare, religion, and family. The final chapter is a note on the future of industrial society with some projections of things to come.

Industry-Community
Relations

INTRODUCTION

In Chapter 4 industry was conceived principally in terms of economic endeavors or services. We shall now study industry as composed of specific work organizations of managers, employees, and their associations. Although the impact of the economy on the community is pervasive, the latter is not a passive agent of the economy. Industry and community, like all segments of society, are interdependent. While this is not always a simple and direct causal relationship, it is nonetheless always present for several reasons. First, other institutions have ends and norms which differ from those of industry. Second, since industry is dependent on other institutions for various services, it must adapt to demands made on it. Third, man responds not only to economic needs but also to the needs of his family, church, school, social class, and other associations. Fourth, and probably most important, economic organizations are aware of the impact of the community on their well-being and they organize to control it. In the process they find themselves objects of control.

In this section we shall examine both the interrelations between industry and community agencies and the attempts of each to control the other. First we shall examine community impact on an industrial relations problem—the strike. Then we shall demonstrate how industry must adapt to cultural factors in its daily operations. Finally we shall see how management and the union attempt to influence institutional behavior and the institutional responses to these attempts.

The network of organizational relations which labor and

management have in a typical urban community is very complex. Figure 18.1 presents an idealized picture of some of the ties commonly found. Although omitting references to pet projects as well as the degree and direction of influence wielded by various groups, the diagram suggests two important conclusions. First, individual business firms have direct access to many community agencies, while labor unions seem to have access largely through their own

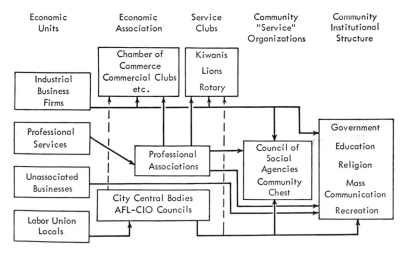

FIG. 18.1. Idealized Relations of Economic Organizations in the Community. Dotted lines represent occasional ties.

central bodies. Second, business seems to sponsor a larger number of community-oriented associations.

While it may appear that labor should have more community influence because it has a more integrated organizational structure, this apparent advantage is often counteracted by labor's necessity to obtain membership approval prior to action. Business groups, on the other hand, can approach important community agencies even when they do not agree on community goals. More important, such organizations as the Chamber of Commerce and service clubs have access to influential and sometimes powerful professional associations. The association between businessmen and professional people is more direct and frequent since they often meet together under the auspices of the Chamber of Commerce, the service clubs, and community agencies. Labor unions are sometimes represented in these business-dominated agencies, but such representation gives management still another opportunity to influence them. Thus the public gets the impression that business is speaking for the entire community. The main arenas of common participation for management, unions, and professional groups are social welfare agencies, government, and education. In some instances the professionals may constitute a mediating group between management and labor.

THE COMMUNITY AND THE STRIKE

Management and unions want the public to be sympathetic to their point of view. If either party can get "public support" for its position, the other party becomes defined as the "minority" which is attempting to impose its will on the community. In a society which responds to democratic slogans, the "minority" label tends to weaken bargaining positions.[1]

As Hiller and Chamberlain have indicated, most urban residents are inclined to be indifferent toward most strikes.[2] Since they are usually not informed about the issues at stake, or, if informed, have no interest in them, they are, properly speaking, a "mass" which can be activated into becoming a public under given circumstances.

Most labor and management officials are persistent publics in industrial disputes. Other associations (such as political parties and voters' leagues) and workers in some occupations (such as lawyers, government officials, certain professionals, and community leaders) quickly become aroused when labor and management issues are not settled quickly. Unorganized labor and the mass of the citizens need to be stimulated by newspapers and pressure groups to become concerned. This does not mean that the citizen is completely unaware of or unconcerned with problems in labor-management relations. He generally assumes that labor and management are operating within certain socially pre-

[1] See the extensive discussion of community publics below.
[2] E. T. Hiller, *The Strike*, University of Chicago Press, 1928, Part VII; Neil W. Chamberlain, *Social Responsibility and Strikes*, Harper, 1953.

scribed norms. When made aware of a dispute he tends to evaluate it in terms of the norms which he believes should apply. He has his own ideas about what kinds of employers and unions are found in the community, and when disputes arise he appraises the parties in terms of their general reputations.

Community attitudes toward property, business, and labor are important factors which may influence industrial relations. After examining a large number of public opinion polls, Neil W. Chamberlain concluded, "Of all aspects of the union-management relationship, strikes are the only issue which has been designated not only as a major problem of that relationship itself, but as a major national problem."[3] He further observed that substantial majorities of the citizens favor rigorous control of strikes during wartime and under emergency conditions in peacetime. Large minorities would outlaw all peacetime strikes, while majorities would subject all peacetime strikes to restraints, especially in "essential" industries. In addition, there is a majority sentiment opposed to sympathetic, jurisdictional, and general strikes, and strikes in the civil service.[4] The public tends to condemn, not the bargaining issue which is involved, but the strike itself. This opposition derives from the feeling that the public's "rights" are being unnecessarily disregarded by the management and/or the union.

Strike Impact on the Community

Why is there such strong rejection of the strike and the lockout on the part of the public or community? Two general answers may be suggested. The first is that strikes and lockouts are perceived as negatively affecting the community or the public in concrete and material ways. That is, the consequences of strikes are seen as extending beyond the partisans and violating community rights. Put differently, large sectors of the community feel that labor and management should have a sense of responsibility toward the community of which they are a part, and exercise restraint.

The second answer is that strikes violate the norms of labor-management relations. Since strikes or lockouts always have an

[3] Chamberlain, *op. cit.*, p. 65.
[4] *Ibid.*, pp. 65–66.

overcast of violence, their existence amounts to a failure of community procedures to settle internal differences. Moreover, strikes or lockouts constitute a threat to the ongoing pattern of relations not only between management and labor but between industry as an institution and the rest of the community. Labor and business officials may protest that strikes or lockouts are the traditional weapons used to resolve issues, and they may point to statistics proving that violence is rare and real losses to the community are exaggerated. Nonetheless, there remains among the large unorganized middle-status groups of the community the belief that strikes represent a moral breakdown of community norms which should be avoided.

Family pressures

Family members are usually the first to hear of the breakdown of industrial relations, and they are first to be affected. Both labor and management feel pressure from family members to get disputes settled. To be sure, the economic pressures of a strike are felt more keenly by working-class families. The food budget is restricted, the kinds of food purchased change, unpaid bills pile up, credit is difficult to obtain, and satisfaction of children's wants is postponed. As the plane of living is depressed, the wife pressures the husband to go back to work. Union officials are aware of this pressure and try to acquaint wives both before and during disputes with the ideals of the labor union movement, the specific issues in a dispute, techniques of stretching the budget, and so on. Management of course is also aware of the limited financial resources of working-class families and the pressure which wives exert on their husband to end strikes. "Back-to-work" movements commonly associated with prolonged strikes are often initiated by employers.

Businessmen are not exempt from family pressures during industrial disputes. Their wives, who participate in various community activities, become aware that other local groups are not always sympathetic with employer objectives. During prolonged strikes other businesses may suffer; newspaper advertisements decrease, retail and wholesale sales drop, and doctor bills are not paid. Sensing the urgency of the situation, wives press their husbands to settle the mess. "The nature of the sanctions involved scarcely requires any specification. The employee (or employer) who loses the support of his wife, who is subjected to reproachful glances, to continued nagging, or—even worse—the silent treatment, is being subjected to penalties which are real indeed and pressures which are sometimes difficult to resist."[5]

Unorganized public pressure

Can the unorganized public exert influence on industrial relations? Do management and labor officials believe that the public can influence the outcome of industrial disputes? We are not aware of public opinion polls which have gathered systematic evidence on this point. However, the experiences of many labor and business leaders[6] suggest that public opinion can, under certain circumstances, affect conduct in industrial disputes, for several reasons.

In the first place, many business and labor officials believe in public opinion. Businessmen who have spent many years in building a favorable community image of their industry are convinced that the good labor they recruit, brand loyalty, and consumer loyalty are the result of their efforts. Likewise, many labor leaders feel that the reputation of a responsible union which looks after the economic interests of workers and the welfare of the community is worth building. The fact that both groups have nurtured good community relations is evidence that they believe in the power of public opinion, and that they will act on this belief during industrial conflict. Second, experience has shown many labor and management officials that public opinion can stimulate the formation of crisis agencies which, once organized, are often difficult to control. Such a threat may be sufficient to induce officials to act "before it is too late." As a matter of fact, mediation officials often use the threat of public exposure to force parties to resolve their differences. Third, businessmen and labor officials have had experience in either introducing publics into industrial relations disputes or attempting to forestall "public intervention."

Several conditions almost invariably provoke public clamor to do something about industrial disputes. The use or threat of vio-

[5] *Ibid.*, p. 154.
[6] See the collection of such opinions in *ibid.*, pp. 113–136.

lence commonly elicits strong protests. Violence immediately results in newspaper publicity, as well as police and governmental
investigation. Violations of standards of decency and morality
likewise provoke public indignation. Two other conditions stimulate public demand for intervention: interruption of vital consumer services, such as milk delivery, electricity, gas, and public
transportation; and a threat to the economic survival of the
community, such as the loss of an industry.

Clearly the threat of undesirable public opinion may be more
effective than the resultant intervention. When labor and management practice restraint for fear of bad publicity, they do not
fear the publicity but its possible repercussions. To be sure, the
public has no sanctions which it can directly apply on the con-
testing parties. It is the threat of sanctions, the threat that adverse
public opinion might stimulate the formation of agencies which
could exert sanction, which makes the contestants concerned
about bad publicity. Moreover, an aroused public may stimulate
already existent groups to act.

The newspaper

The newspaper is the first agency other than the family which
acts in critical industrial disputes. Since publicity is usually a
precondition of intervention by local agencies, newspapers are
indirectly responsible for the application of sanctions. Rarely is
the newspaper an active intervening party. At most, it provokes
other parties, such as government, trade associations, and labor
officials, to act in a certain direction by fostering the necessary
climate of opinion. Many observers exaggerate the power of the
press to help the business side of an industrial dispute by pointing
to its promanagement and antilabor bias. It would be more realistic to examine the conditions under which the city newspaper
takes a given position in an industrial dispute.

If newspapers were not subjected to some restraints, they would
openly favor management in most disputes. After all, newspaper-
men are recruited from business segments of the community and
have close business and social ties with local business interests.[7]
It would be strange for them not to be loyal to business when

[7] For a depiction of antilabor newspapers, see Harold L. Ickes, *America's
House of Lords*, Harcourt, Brace, 1939.

circumstances permit. Thus, prior to and soon after the enactment of the National Labor Relations Act, which gave unions legal recognition and the right to organize, newspapers were often openly antilabor. However, as unions gained strength, newspapers were unable to maintain this position. Journalistic ethics to present news objectively were now buttressed by other organizations which demanded the same thing. Organized labor had begun to represent a large body of readers who "justified" the advertising rates of the papers. Alienation of these readers could reduce advertising revenues. Retail businessmen, who supply most of the advertising revenues, became more sympathetic with the workers who might be on strike. Since retailers wanted customers with high steady wages they now began to redefine their position toward unions and strikes.

Newspapers are therefore beginning to take a reconciliation position during strikes. Generally their editorials reveal a stronger promanagement bias than their news columns. The "slant" of the news usually continues to favor management, but union news is also reported. At best, the paper serves as a platform for the opposing parties. Since industrial disputes, in a sense, put publishers in an awkward position, they try to exert pressure on both parties to come to terms. Publishers persistently point to the needless loss of income to both sides and the "senselessness" of prolonged struggles. Not infrequently they urge arbitration or mediation.

Certain conditions modify this general description. They are the use of violence, prolonged suffering among nonparticipants, uncompromising positions, unwillingness to negotiate, and a violation of property rights. In such cases, the papers take a stand for the public, condemning one or both sides, urging compromise, or advocating the use of arbitration machinery. Soon after the settlement, almost irrespective of the history or relations, both sides are congratulated and charged to carry on with statesmanlike methods.

The mayor's office

In cities with strong unions, the office of the mayor is expected to function in a more or less neutral manner during industrial disputes. Although the mayor does not have an official role in strikes, he may be pressured to assume certain functions. He may anticipate public reaction and exert the influence of his office at will, or he may wait until there is clamor for "something to be done." In either event he usually takes pains to appear neutral or to condemn both parties for ignoring the welfare of the total community.

In cases where public health, welfare, or safety is threatened, the mayor cannot refrain from becoming involved in industrial relations. When public utilities, food deliveries, and pay rolls are severed the public demands action. Since the mayor is an elected officer, he cannot openly appear to be antilabor because he may be defeated in the subsequent election. Since the prosperity of the city is built on pay rolls, he cannot appear antibusiness. Moreover, it is difficult for him to maintain a posture of neutrality in a situation where each side is quick to misinterpret his behavior.

The primary sanction available to the mayor is his ability to focus adverse public opinion on either management or the union.[8] Chamberlain suggests four main types of actions available to the mayor and other public officials. The first is persuasion, not because the mayor is well versed in the technique, but because he represents authority. If persuasion does not work, he can threaten to issue a public statement identifying the responsible party or parties. This may be followed by an active campaign to mobilize public opinion against the recalcitrant disputants.[9] The line of pressure is diagramed below.

Affected public
↓
Government official
↓
Affected public
↓
Parties to the strike

During the strike police action may be taken, court injuctions

[8] The following section is based on Chamberlain, *op. cit.*, pp. 176–180.

[9] The actions of the mayor in an industrial relations crisis, the pressures on him, and the sanctions at his disposal are well documented in the case of a strike of the Independent Association of Employees against the Duquesne Light Company in Pittsburgh, 1946. See Chamberlain, *op. cit.*

may be pressed, discriminatory legislation may be passed, past legal violations may be publicized, and other devices may be used to exert pressure. Punitive action is also possible after strike settlement, especially against management. Municipal contracts may be awarded to other companies; building, fire, and other inspectors may become overly conscientious while examining business premises; licenses may be revoked.

Local courts

The position of local courts is also critical during a strike. They may be called upon to protect the rights of labor or of property, as the case may be. Students of law recognize that courts have been and are affected in their decisions by current opinion. Historically, the courts have tended to buttress the most powerful groups in the community. As changes in the relations between groups in the community and nation have occurred, courts have been inclined to make decisions in accord with the new power alignment.[10] Whether or not the court will grant an injunction in a strike depends upon the historical pressures put on it. This does not mean that judges are subject to pressure in all daily decisions, but it does mean that they are selected by those in power on an assumption that they will perform according to certain expectations. The political party and those who control it influence executive selection of judges. They also screen judicial candidates who run for election.

Church intervention

Generally speaking, church leaders in the United States hesitate to become directly involved in an industrial dispute. Churchmen tend to preach the doctrine of responsibility and stewardship but do not themselves enter a dispute unless invited by one or both parties.[11] To be sure, some churchmen manifest a strong interest

[10] Charles A. Beard, *Economic Interpretation of the Constitution,* Macmillan, 1923.

[11] See, for example, Liston Pope, *Millhands and Preachers,* Yale, 1942, p. 173. "Most ministers in the country deny that the proper role of religious institutions in relation to the social and economic order is indifference. On the other hand, they assert that the church as an institution must not become embroiled in economic and political affairs, but must save the world through 'changed individuals' and the extension of the church."

in labor relations and others have dedicated their lives to the improvement of labor-management relations. However, the institutional pattern is to avoid involvement or to become involved under restricted conditions.[12] This is understandable because the church has a relatively poor arsenal of sanctions to apply to disputing parties.

Clerical sympathies usually follow those of their congregations. Thus, the clergy in management-dominated congregations tend to be promanagement, and the clergy of working-class churches tend to be prolabor. When long strikes and widespread suffering occur some clergymen are constrained to ask the parties to settle their differences, which appeal is likely to be most effective when all parties belong to the same religious faith. If the mayor or someone else selects a citizens' committee to intervene in a dispute, clergymen who represent the main faiths will be among those appointed.

Clergymen become involved in industrial disputes under two conditions. First, they intervene when they feel a vital religious or moral issue is at stake. Catholic priests have urged workers to abandon unions dominated by Communist leaders, or to settle with employers when instigated to fight by Communists. Second, intervention may occur when the labor-management division in the community is paralleled by a religious cleavage. Each antagonist may get the active support of his clergy. The more frequent situation is one in which union officials ask the clergy to persuade managers to show compassion for suffering workers and give in to their demands. When faced with the prospects of a long strike and possible adverse publicity, both labor and management groups may organize "citizens' committees" in which the clergy are represented. Their purpose is to legitimize their actions by associating them with religious symbols.

Education

Educators become involved in industrial relations in much the same way as the clergy. They are supposed to be either neutral or at least not opposed to the existing economic order. Since most of

[12] *Ibid.,* p. 163. "Ministers in the country have seldom inveighed against any practice of the mills. Dozens of interviews with clergymen of all denominations elicited only three specific criticisms of economic policies."

them teach in publicly supported institutions, they are vulnerable to pressures which outside interests can bring to bear on school systems. Therefore, they generally avoid conflict.

Under certain conditions, however, educators may be sought to serve on citizens' committees to represent the public in industrial disputes. They may be asked to moderate or arbitrate conflicts in the capacity of neutral experts in industrial relations. In such cases their obligations tend to be narrowly defined and not concerned with major policy goals. This stricture places them in an anachronistic position because, unlike the clergy, educators often have extensive contacts with and knowledge about business and labor. In some situations they are the only people who have complete and impartial knowledge of the total system of industrial relations. However, knowledge does not always result in power, and this seems to be the case for educators.[13] Some recognition is provided by the appointment of a tripartite committee of the public, employer, and union in the 1959–1961 contract between Kaiser Steel and the United Steel Workers of America. This committee seeks proposals for the long-run solution of labor-management problems. The public members include Dr. George W. Taylor, Dr. David L. Cole, and Dr. John Dunlop, all university professors.

Organized Community Pressure

It is very difficult to organize "the community" directly to exert pressure on contestants in an industrial relations dispute. Most communities do not have the suitable organizational facilities to intervene. Usually associations which serve other purposes can more readily "intrude themselves" into the dispute. The frequent intervenors are governmental bureaus, other labor and management groups, and other local commissions and boards. Since these agencies are sometimes resisted because they are partisan or ineffective, on rare occasions attempts are made to organize a representative community body *de nouveau*. In such cases teachers, lawyers, clergymen, housewives, and governmental, labor, and business officials are given representation with no group having numerical dominance. Speaking for "the community," this body

[13] C. Wright Mills, "The Powerless People: The Role of the Intellectual in Society," *Politics*, April, 1944.

attempts to exert "mass public censure" on the parties, defines them as minorities which are obstructing the general welfare, and urges them to accept whatever actions they deem appropriate.

Contestants Organize the Community

Understandably, contestants to an industrial relations dispute suspect citizens' committees. Organized labor especially has found that many committees have turned out to be management devices to break a strike and get employees back to work.

The Mohawk Valley formula, which is now illegal, represented a well-worked-out technique to challenge union control over the workers. It worked successfully many times before and soon after the passage of the National Labor Relations Act. The Johnstown Citizens' Committee, which was formed during the Bethlehem Steel strike in 1937, and the Flint Alliance, created during the Chevrolet sit-down strike in 1937, are representative types.[14] Such citizens' committees are illegal because they are financed by management to break a union of the workers' own choosing. Since it is sometimes difficult to identify the source of financial support for such "citizens' committees" and since there are loopholes in the present law, it is still possible for labor and management groups to organize pseudo citizen groups. These groups cannot easily crush a union, but they may be successful in affecting strike tactics and strategy.

CULTURAL INFLUENCES ON INDUSTRIAL BEHAVIOR

The modern industrial city is a complex of subcultural groups. Different class, racial, ethnic, economic, and religious groups have distinctive values, sentiments, organizations, and behavior patterns. These groups must interact with each other, especially in the factories, market place, and other economic establishments. As the modern industrial system grows and expands into new areas, segregated groups are often brought into contact with each other. Residential areas that have long guarded their racial or

---

[14] See Keith Sward, "The Johnstown Strike of 1937," in George W. Hartman and Theodore Newcomb (eds.), *Industrial Conflict*, Cordon, 1939, pp. 93–95, and Dwight W. Chapman, "Industrial Conflict in Detroit," in *ibid.*, pp. 63–67.

ethnic identity are invaded. Conflicts and accommodation between invaders and invaded invariably occur. At the same time
as the industrial system expands, it becomes more diversified and
segregates people, reducing their common sentiments. Thus various groups evolve systems of stereotypes and prejudices against
each other, even as they attempt to find ways of living together.

Managers have sometimes behaved ruthlessly in the face of
cultural heterogeneity. Dominated by an ideology of productivity,
they have tried to sweep away impediments to rational work
organization.[15] Such a position ignores the cultural values of
workers and inevitably leads to frustration if not open conflict.
Management must adjust its practices to the social and cultural
realities of communities in which it operates.

A Colonial Situation

Perhaps the most illuminating example of changes forced upon
management may be found where industrial enterprises were
built in technologically underdeveloped areas. Extractive industries, for example, often need an abundance of local unskilled
laborers. Inexperienced managers at first tried to behave much as
they did at home. They introduced an individual wage system
(itself an innovation of considerable magnitude), economic incentives for production, and threats of layoff and wage reduction.
Of course, these practices were not successful. The reluctant
workers were neither attracted by the wages nor threatened by
unemployment. Countless difficulties arose in the recruitment,
direction, and retention of workers.

Hughes points out, "The natives themselves are often not
accustomed to individual wage work, at least as a continued and
sole means of getting a living. They may have worked only as
members of communities, their tasks and rewards determined by
their places in a social system. . . . The economic incentives do
not bring in a labor supply. Industry departs from its mother-
country practice of encouraging free movement of labor, and uses
the police power instead."[16] Native labor, though forced into

[15] See Clark Kerr et al., *Industrialism and Industrial Man,* Harvard, 1960,
chap. 2, "The Logic of Industrialism."

[16] Everett C. Hughes, "Queries Concerning Industry and Society Growing
Out of Study of Ethnic Relations in Industry," *American Sociological Review,*
April, 1949, p. 215.

industry, is not given the opportunity to climb in it. Executive, technical, and skilled workers are usually nonnative. These monopolistic job practices reinforce racial and ethnic prejudices. Although such practices are continued only with tremendous economic and social costs, they nevertheless persist. Further, the more the natives embrace the ideology of the industrial system, the more anachronistic it appears to them. As ethnic self-awareness increases, independence movements begin which lead to economic expropriation and related phenomena.[17]

A similar situation has existed, though in less extreme form, in the isolated communities of the United States. When New England industries moved into the southern Appalachian rural areas, they brought with them managers and technicians whose behavior toward the local population was not unlike that of industrial imperialists. The managers attempted to control the lives of the workers, prohibited labor unions, provided a minimum of local services, discouraged local recruitment of managers, and let the community founder during economically depressed periods.

On the other hand, some industries have made easy accommodations to new cultural situations. In some southern regions resentment against Yankee employers has not been great, partly because the local customs and traditions of the feudal plantation system, with its paternalistic responsibility and profitable control, were merely adapted to the industrial system. "Housing and village communities, Sunday schools and night classes, commissaries, sanitary regulations, child labor, working mothers, employment of whole families, physical and social isolation . . . were direct inheritances from the older order."[18] Manufacturers continued the old social order within a new technological setting and did not interfere with the local religious, political, and racial mores.

This feudal industrial pattern was in fact so well knit that labor leaders had to adjust to it. The use of folk and religious songs in union meetings, identifying owners as Yankees, belittling the "dangers" of Negro competition, appealing to the traditional

[17] Wilbert Moore, "Primitives and Peasants in Industry," *Social Research,* March, 1948, pp. 71–72.

[18] Harriet Herring, "The Outside Employer in the Southern Industrial Pattern," *Social Forces,* October, 1939, pp. 115–116.

individualism of the natives was one of the techniques that organizers had to use.

The Effect of Community Organization on Daily Plant Operations

Technical operations within plants may be bottlenecked because of failure to take into account the social and cultural organizations in the community. For example, changes in operations which alter the flow of work will sometimes disturb the established web of relationships. Arensberg reported a case in which management had inaugurated an incentive scheme in the cutting room. The resulting disturbances led to a strike by the paper machine crew. Management was mystified as to why men in an unrelated department would walk out over an affair which concerned another department. Actually, the workers in these departments were tied together in a system of kinship, age patterns, and occupational prestige. "The company engineers . . . had reversed the customary pattern of authority by setting the juniors and inferiors to hurrying up their seniors and superiors. The machine room men had struck against the disturbance of their community."[19]

The influence of cultural variation on plant operations may be seen by comparing identical plants in two different communities.[20] In Algonac and Holland, Michigan, there is a company which manufactures cabin cruisers. The original plant is located in Algonac, a town of 2000 people located in the vacation-metropolitan hinterland of Detroit. Upper-middle-class suburban residents constituted the majority of the population. They wanted to keep Algonac a residential community and discourage industries from settling there. The nearby labor force is culturally heterogeneous, being made up of Indians, French Canadians, native and foreign born who have traditional antagonisms toward each other.

Apart from a small nucleus of older native workers, the majority of the employees were recent arrivals from other sections of the country. During the winter a number of Great Lakes sailors

[19] Conrad Arensberg, "Industry and the Community," *American Journal of Sociology*, July, 1942, p. 6.

[20] This section is based on a report by Willis D. Richardson, student at Michigan State University.

were employed, and their place was taken in summer by local schoolteachers. Despite the pressure of a strong union in the plant, very few values and sentiments bound these groups and management together. The general work atmosphere was full of bickering and tension. Management had to deal continuously with strikes, high turnover, drinking, and absenteeism.

In order to escape some of these problems, especially the spread of unionism, the corporation purchased a plant in Holland, Michigan. Holland is a neat, clean city of 14,000 people. Its inhabitants are deeply religious Dutch descendants who take their callings seriously. When the corporation moved to Holland it sent a skeleton crew to build an organization similar to that in Algonac. The crew encountered several unexpected difficulties. The religious Dutch would not work on Sunday and the Seventh-Day Adventists would not work on Saturday. The imported Algonac foremen could not get obedience or cooperation when they swore at the workers. The Irish foremen were irritated at "the stubborn Dutch," and the Dutch didn't like the blasphemous Irishmen. Not until local people became foremen did the sources of friction disappear.

Other changes in plant operations were necessary. At ten o'clock in the morning workers stopped their machines for "coffee." This pattern was so strong that it was soon institutionalized. When the workers also asked that the plant start operating earlier so they could spend more time at home with their families, the starting time was changed. Although a union obtained recognition shortly before World War II, it remained weak because many workers refused to join it on religious grounds. These brief descriptions indicate how the official everyday activities of management and union executives are affected by the cultural diversities of communities.

The Problem of Race and Ethnic Differences

Ethnic and racial groups in industrial communities represent subcultures. Puerto Ricans and Mexicans are the newest of these in the United States. Managers find themselves changing their routines, and minority groups slowly accept some of the values of management. During the early part of this transitional period the intermediary or "go-between" makes his appearance. Although the go-between may not be the informal leader or a foreman, he is always someone who understands the cultures of both groups. He interprets the aims and motives of each group to the other and finds a path which is suitable to both.

Labor union leaders found very early that it was best not to try to change the behavior of immigrant workers. They were allowed to conduct union business in their native tongues. Union officers demanded that employers recognize the rights of workers to observe their special religious and other holidays.

During World War II a group of American Indians was employed in one of the navy yards. When the foreman complained that they were a sullen, unmanageable, and soldiering crew, a counselor was sent to investigate conditions. She located the chief in the group, found that he had had supervisory experience, and urged that he be given the job of the foreman.

"The Indians went to work with a will. The supervisor wisely ignored complaints that the Indians were loafers because they took their accustomed siestas, dozing in the shade. The work was done in unexpected ways, but results were, by highest production standards, excellent. Through utilization of established group leadership . . . the productivity of the group was released. . . . It seemed simpler to alter the procedures than to change the habits of the workers."[21]

It is through such a process that ethnic job structures emerge in the plant. Chapters 11 and 12 analyze the economic and status problems which emerge from these structures.

INTERINSTITUTIONAL RELATIONS

Government, Labor, and Business

The influence that local government has on industry's behavior should not be underestimated. During a crisis, such as a strike, municipal officers can ignore the issue, join either side, or attempt a conciliation. Whatever its course, government purports to speak and act for the "public"—that is, the mass of citizens who are not parties to the dispute. When government acts it invariably affects the relative positions of management and labor. We have men-

[21] Esther Boorman Strong, "Individual Adjustment in Industrial Society," *American Sociological Review*, June, 1949, p. 341.

tioned the role of government in industrial relations in a preceding section and in Chapter 10 on industrial relations. Other areas of government-industry relations will be examined here.

The municipality can influence the economic position of business directly through its tax policy. Obviously, taxes are a cost of production and may be varied by political means. The attitude of local government may range from the one extreme, of subsidy, to the other, of punitive taxation. The kind of tax decision depends upon the power relations between business, labor, and government, and on the attitudes that community leaders have toward these groups.

It is not an accident when business fails to carry its share of local taxes, or is made to pay more than its share. Homeowners and other citizens often pay disproportionately high taxes when they cannot control the tax machinery. This situation is found when large industries move to fringe areas of the city. There they escape paying taxes for schools, roads, and transit systems which the workers must have. At the same time, they make demands for local governmental services all out of proportion to the taxes they pay.

When business pays exorbitantly high taxes, the reasons for the antagonistic attitude of local government must be located. A discriminatory tax policy arises when business has lost not only local control of party machinery and municipal offices but the loyalty of the citizens as well.

This was the case in the Gogebic and Mesabi Iron Range communities in the upper peninsula of Michigan and Minnesota.[22] In these towns the surface rights belong to the public and the underground rights to iron-mining companies. The Range towns, although they contain only one major industry, are independent and not company towns. Since 1921 they have lacked nothing in the way of ordinary public facilities and utilities. Not infrequently over 90 percent of all funds to pay for these facilities come from taxation on mining properties. Wakefield, Michigan (4000 population), has an elaborate, well-lighted boulevard, modern schools, and other major facilities. Like other towns it has taxed the mines while they were running full blast. No surplus

[22] Paul H. Landis, *Three Iron Mining Communities*, Edwards, 1938, p. 112 ff.

money was allowed to accumulate in the city treasury, so that the companies would have no justification to ask for tax reduction.

Many people believe that every cent possible should be collected from the companies while they are still operating and that the town should retain a share of the wealth which, once removed, will never return. Although the town governments try to collect all taxes possible, they overlook violations of the mining codes.

Local government affects industrial operations in many other areas. Some have ordinances dealing with noise, smoke, building codes, zoning, parking, licensing, employment, transportation, utilities, health, and so on. Whether ordinances are passed and how they are enforced depends on the amount of influence business and labor have on the local governmental control structures. Sympathetic people must be elected to office, and regulative and service bureaus must be staffed with neutral or favorable employees. This procedure, in turn, is facilitated by control of the local party machinery and the operation of an effective party organization. Since the party needs money to function well, making contributions to it and controlling its central (policy) committee are crucial to control of the entire governmental apparatus.

Business has traditionally dominated local politics and government in the United States. Studies of many cities—Atlanta, Seattle, El Paso, Lansing, Pittsburgh, Denver, Newburyport, Rockford, Battle Creek, and Philadelphia, among others—document business control of the wide range of governmental offices and services.[23] Warner and Lunt have demonstrated in Yankee City a general phenomenon: the higher the governmental office, the greater the tendency for higher-status groups to occupy it.[24] The control of party machines has also belonged to those who contributed most to their operations. Studies of financial donations show that their primary source of control has been business. Apart from such formal control devices, the participation of business in local gov-

[23] These studies are reviewed in William H. Form and Delbert C. Miller, *Industry, Labor, and Community,* Harper, 1960, chaps. 15 and 16.

[24] W. Lloyd Warner and Paul S. Lunt, *The Social Life of the Modern Community,* Yale, 1941, p. 370.

ernment has been so traditional as to lead many to believe that to contest this control was to fight legitimate custom.

Organized labor has never accepted this pattern of control and has demanded that government respond more to the needs of the workingman. The dominant philosophy of the American Federation of Labor from its inception in 1887 was to avoid labor's identification with a single political party. Nonpartisan political action was based on the use of pressure-group and lobbying techniques. Individual candidates and political groups were supported when they indicated favorable disposition to labor's goals.

After 1940 unions changed their tactics. Although not irrevocably tied to one major party and its candidates, they now primarily support the Democratic party. However, they have not necessarily become part of the Democratic party machine. They have created their own political organization to get union members and their sympathizers concerned with politics from the local precinct to the national level. Far from refraining from political action directly, the present strategy is to become fully involved in party politics as part of the "full involvement" program in community affairs. Like management, labor is interested in electing officers, affecting legislation, influencing party machines, and providing financial support to the machines.

In a study of voting behavior in Steelport McKee has shown conclusively the importance of labor's participation in party activities.[25] Before 1937, local government was controlled almost exclusively by the Republican party, which represented the older, Protestant, Anglo-Saxon, higher socioeconomic segments of the community. Although a minority, they had more political power than the newer arrivals from central and southern Europe, who were predominately Catholic. The unions set about to weld this heterogeneous body of workers into a solidary political organization to wield influence in local affairs. Prior to 1945, Democratic candidates occasionally were elected to city offices. After this date, with the support of the unions, the party won a majority of the elective offices and all the administrative positions.

[25] See James B. McKee, "Status and Power in the Industrial Community," *American Journal of Sociology*, January, 1953, pp. 364–370.

Calkins' study of four communities in Ohio, Illinois, and Michigan revealed similar trends.[26]

A note of caution is necessary here. Political activity is not automatically translated into political control. McKee found that businessmen in Steelport were not greatly worried about the rise of labor representation in government. In a crucial issue involving increases in taxes business decisively defeated the proposal. Party control is only one facet of control of the community power structure. Labor does win certain objectives occasionally, such as a fair-employment bill, better city services for poorer areas of town, unions in government, increased expenditures for recreation, city-subsidized housing, and a voice in administration of local government. However, in most small and middle-sized cities, labor does not take an oppositional posture toward business in governmental affairs. In fact, one of labor's continuing weaknesses has been an inability to develop a coherent program of community objectives.

Education

In some ways the educational system of the local community may be considered an extension of its governmental political system and its power structure. Public taxes are used to support education, the board of education is publicly elected, and the operation of the school system is exposed to public scrutiny. Although theoretically the schools are supposed to be politically neutral and free from political party control, they are in fact part of the broader political order simply because different groups in the community associate different values with the school system.

Major value orientations

MAJOR VALUE ORIENTATIONS OF BUSINESS

Business wants (1) to have efficient educational administration with low tax rates (generally, business wants schools to be financed by sales and excise taxes with a maximum of state support; when property is taxed, it seeks lower rates for business property; it strongly opposes federal aid to education); (2) to have teachers

[26] Fay Calkins, *The CIO and the Democratic Party,* University of Chicago Press, 1952.

endorse actively the American free enterprise system and convey facts relative to the contribution of business to the community and nation; (3) to provide academic education of the highest quality for its children in order to prepare them for business, professional, and white-collar careers; (4) to secure suitable vocational training for future manual and clerical workers; (5) to get youth trained to be law-abiding, industrious, and well mannered.

MAJOR VALUE ORIENTATIONS OF EDUCATION

Education wants (1) to have higher salaries for its teachers and administrators; (2) to have plant equipment adequate to the goals of a professional program; (3) to develop the pupil as a person who shall participate as fully as his talents permit in a future vocation, in citizenship, family life, and leisure pursuits. (The public school program has two facets: the fundamental education required of all pupils, and the special program for developing skills and talents which permit each person to grow into a definite personality. The educational institution is concerned especially with the core curriculum through which the individual may acquire a common tradition and a common language.) Education also wants (4) freedom to teach and behave according to professional standards; and (5) access to industries, labor unions, and other community resources available for teaching purposes.

Each of these value orientations—of business or education—is exhibited in various kinds of behavior as officials play roles consistent with the structural pattern of this organizational complex in the local community.

Pattern of control

The ends of business, labor, and education are similar in some areas and divergent in others. Understandably, the relations among these groups vary according to the issue at hand. In general, whoever controls the board of education will control the educational system. W. W. Charters, Jr., located sixty-two studies which investigated the occupational backgrounds of board members in a wide variety of school districts.[27] His findings support an earlier finding that over three-quarters of city school boards are

[27] W. W. Charters, Jr., "Social Class Analysis and the Control of Public Education," *Harvard Educational Review*, Fall, 1953, pp. 270 ff.

composed of business and professional people. The assumption has been made that people with these backgrounds are conservative and will protect the interests of the propertied groups in the community. Research bearing on this question is scanty, but it suggests that board members are more liberal in their educational outlook than corresponding groups in the community.

While this may be true, people from comparatively privileged economic groups may fail to represent the experience and needs of all elements in the community. Dr. Floyd W. Reeves has said,

> There are certain very important things in our social, economic, and political life that we hardly touch upon in our public schools—such things as the organization of labor unions and consumer cooperatives. I know of only one state in the United States that has any systematic program of instruction in the cooperative movement; and I don't know of any state that has systematic instruction with reference to the organization of the workers of this nation.[28]

Since World War II labor has undertaken just this type of instruction, especially in industrial states where it is strongly represented. Compared to earlier eras it has increased its representation somewhat but its influence has probably not risen proportionately. Where possible they put pressure on local school systems to abstain from antilabor teaching. In several states labor-backed Democratic candidates have been elected to the boards of trustees of universities. These universities have inaugurated Institutes to study labor-management relations and have had courses in labor economics, labor law, grievance procedures, labor history, and other areas, taught by college professors in local communities and even in union halls. The institutes have had to be on their guard against attacks from the business community that they are prolabor and stimulating "class warfare." Labor-backed majorities of university boards have not always been able to prevent pressure groups from hamstringing operations of institutes interested in organized labor. Thus, in 1949, representatives of large corporations attacked courses being taught by university personnel in Michigan to labor unions as "Marxist." This situation eventually led to the abolition of the Workers Educational

[28] "What Should We Teach Our Youth Now?" University of Chicago Roundtable Broadcast.

Service.[29] In 1962, a university institute in the same state was attacked as presenting an "unbalanced" program in favor of labor, despite the presence of a strong College of Business on campus. The legislature then passed a bill forbidding the university to use state funds to support the institute.[30] As in the case of city councils, a majority of members in local school boards cannot guarantee control. Power is a broader phenomenon than a representative majority.

In local communities both business and labor are also interested in school apprenticeship programs, adult education courses, and business-industry-education day. These can be areas of cooperation or conflict. The joint apprenticeship program committee of the city school system supervises job training and part-time schooling of those planning to enter the trades. Management and the union typically have equal representation on such committees. However, industry is usually in a dominant position because it can reject candidates for the program and because foremen are usually responsible to the committee for progress reports of candidates. In strongly organized trades, the full cooperation of the unions is needed for the program to function well. Although conflict is possible in this area, it happens only occasionally.

Although the board of education has control over adult education course offerings, usually adult education is administered without much interference by the superintendent. Whether he permits courses to be offered which have limited or great appeal to the unions depends on his relations with them. It is possible in a business-dominated community to have an adult education program which is highly sensitive to the needs of organized labor. Generally the courses must avoid controversial problems.

After World War II some educators and businessmen urged closer relations. Teachers expanded their field trips to get children to observe factories and businesses in operation. The new plan was to lay a day aside for teachers to visit work plants and listen to needs of local industry, and for businessmen to visit the schools to learn more about educational needs and operations. These business-industry-education days were attacked by some labor

[29] *Michigan CIO News,* February 9, 1949.
[30] Lansing *State Journal,* July 20, 1962.

leaders as being either propagandistic or partial. They felt that labor's point of view and labor's contribution to the local economy needed to be equally stressed. In general, labor and management have not succeeded in cooperation in such programs. Where labor has instituted a labor-education day, it has generally failed to obtain widespread support.

Influencing the educational system

The greater influence which business has over the local school reflects its greater integration into the school's functions and its greater interest in its operations. In almost every locality business enterprises donate medals to students for highest achievement in science, scholarship, or citizenship. Scholarships are sometimes given to students to continue their education. Unions have begun to give a growing number of scholarships.

Business also releases a flow of "educational materials" to schools. The National Association of Manufacturers, for example, distributes pamphlets, slides, charts, and films for use in schools. These materials not only give technical information about industrial operations and job opportunities but endeavor to instill favorable attitudes toward business, the free enterprise system, and work. As sentinels of democracy the local businessmen oversee the educational program to assure the loyalty of teachers, the Americanism of the textbooks, and the conduct of students.

Business leaders also are concerned when schools do not prepare students well in basic skills needed to make a living. They do not want the taxpayers' money to be spent on nonuseful frills. This attitude sometimes spills over into campaigns against ineffective teaching exemplified in the "Why Johnny can't read" movement. A dated but representative illustration of business pressure on the Detroit school system is revealed in the following news item:

SCHOOLS FAILING, EMPLOYER'S CHARGE

Detroit schools are grinding out another "lost generation." Ignorant of the three R's children are "sloughed off" upon a business world which rejects many of them as "unacceptable" and "unemployable."

Employment managers told the Free Press that up to 40 per cent of the boys and girls leave school without mastering simple arithmetic.

One personnel executive said their handwriting is atrocious. Their statements were made as the school board prepared to ask a record-breaking 1949–50 budget of $73,000,000. Three new board members will be elected this spring. . . .

Employers charge that youngsters are turned out with a "poor work attitude," lacking in responsibility toward the job and the employer. . . .

Blame for this is placed on the modern method of education in which emphasis is placed on stimulating the child's imagination, his wish to learn, power of analysis and sense of inquiry. . . .

"Children have flitted through school like a game," said one personnel expert. "School is work like any job. Pupils should be taught that they must produce. . . ."

More than one-third of Detroit public school students take the college preparatory course. They graduate with a smattering of cultural knowledge but no "saleable" training.[31]

Industry wants the public, wherever possible, to assume the expense of training future workers for specific skills. Commercial, vocational, and business courses are constantly being added to the curriculum from grade school through college. Education assumes more and more the burden of how to sell insurance, care for golf courses, test cloth, make cheese, and write business letters. Increased educational expenses may be taken from various sources: property tax, sales tax, income tax, state or federal funds. Generally business is not in favor of increasing property taxes and is pushing for a "wider" population to share in the expense of education.

The general point here is that control of a system must go beyond representation on control structures. Business is effective not only because it has representation on school boards but because it has educational objectives, it oversees educational operations, and it tries to influence educational changes. Other groups, such as labor, must do likewise if they intend to be effective. So far they have been timid and unimaginative.

Welfare

Private charity was the main pattern of welfare in early industrial cities. If a company felt any obligation toward its employees or local inhabitants, it might dispense private relief in the form of Christmas baskets or help to the handicapped, indigents, or unemployed. Money might be contributed to favored welfare

[31] Detroit *Free Press*, February 2, 1949.

organizations—settlement houses, sanatoria, or medical clinics. These private philanthropies have tended to disappear although some corporations still continue their support.

One reason for the decrease in private philanthropy is that smaller companies found themselves unable to dispense welfare on a large enough scale to enhance their status in the growing community. Their individual contributions were lost in the maze of welfare effort. To meet this situation service organizations grew, such as Kiwanis, Lions, and Rotary. Many small businessmen together might sponsor a welfare project which could not be supported by individual companies. Thus in one community a service club builds a swimming pool, in another it maintains a speech clinic for children, in another it provides eyeglasses for poor children, and so on. Whatever the project, these clubs feel that by helping the community they improve the status of business.

After World War I private businesses and business associations were urged by social welfare workers to pool their contributions with those of other organizations. Social workers pointed out that there was a lack of coordination between needs and resources available to different social agencies. Some services had more money than they needed and others did not have enough. They urged all businesses, unions, and other organizations to aid them in raising money, but insisted that professional social workers be permitted to evaluate community needs and disburse the funds. At first there was resistance because business felt that its contributions would remain anonymous and they would lose control of local philanthropy. When business found techniques to maintain publicity and control of private philanthropy it backed the Community Chest and the Council of Social Agencies—the financial and control agencies of local welfare.

Labor unions have also had a continuing interest in welfare. This was a natural expression of the philosophy of mutual aid which underlies labor organization. However, apart from insurance schemes and sporadic giving, organized labor was not a part of the community welfare structure. To be sure, workers were pressured to contribute to the Community Chest by their employers from the inception of the Chest movement. When organized labor became strong in the late thirties, it insisted that it participate in collection efforts and in control of local welfare. During World War II, in a spirit of national unity, labor took part in many local welfare efforts and inaugurated many of its own. After the war, it decided not only to maintain earlier contributions but to expand them. Through the local AFL–CIO councils, labor announced its intention to have proportionate control over collections and to have representation and a voice in every agency receiving support from community collected funds.

Strategic structures

The important formal structures through which control is exerted are the Councils of Social Agencies, the Community Chests, or the United Funds, the boards of directors of these coordinating agencies and their constituent agencies, and the boards of directors of agencies outside the councils. In addition, there are the crucial finance committees of all these agencies and the professional staffs. Important control centers are found in the community which are not recognized as a part of the welfare complex. They will be analyzed later. The task here is to document the interlocking character of the welfare complex and to demonstrate its domination by a management-representational coalition.

Figure 18.2 portrays the interlocking character of the Council of Social Agencies, the Community Chest, and some tangent welfare agencies. For the uninitiated, it should be pointed out that the Council is an organization created to coordinate welfare activities, while the Chest is an agency to coordinate fund raising. Individual welfare agencies determine and execute their own policies. Although they may have some independent sources of income, they are largely dependent on the Chest and its strategic budget and distribution committee for much of their operating funds. The interdependency of these structures can be noted by the broken lines in Fig. 18.2, which indicate how each segment may affect the operations of the other through an interlocking nomination system. Thus, the board of directors of the Chest is nominated from the campaign committee and delegates of the agencies themselves. Labor union members, businessmen, professionals, and "society" women are found in many places in this complex structure. The full-time professional staff members of

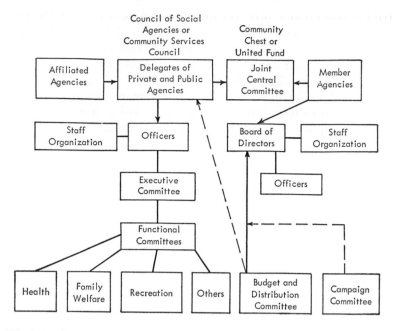

FIG. 18.2. The Interinstitutional Welfare Complex. Dotted lines represent privilege of nomination. (Adapted from John R. Seeley *et al., Community Chest, A Case Study of Philanthropy,* University of Toronto Press, 1957, p. 92.)

the Council and Chest are dependent on the cooperation and financial support of these diversified groups. The occupational background and financial resources of the sponsoring groups provide some clues to the controls which can be exerted.

Seeley, Form, and others have made detailed studies of the occupational compositions of the Community Chest boards, boards of the Council of Social Agencies, and individual welfare boards.[32] They found that business and professional groups had dominant representation on all boards, but that the collection agencies were more representative than the controlling structures.

Seeley, Schulze, and Mills and Ullmer report that the highest-

---

[32] John R. Seeley *et al., Community Chest, A Case Study in Philanthropy,* University of Toronto Press, 1957; William H. Form, "The Place of Organized Labor in Community Power Structure," *Labor and Industrial Relations Review,* July, 1959, pp. 526–539.

status people have withdrawn from Community Chest activities.[33] However, Wilensky, Fowler, and our studies have shown that where locally owned industries represent a sizable proportion of total industry high-status people still participate in welfare activities. Thus in Lansing, Michigan, no person holding a secondary position in business has ever headed a Chest drive unless his boss had first done so. The top union leaders are also represented in the Chest organization, and top local influentials head all important financial drives in the city.

Financial dependencies

The success of the campaign, the adequacy of services, and even the tenure of the professional staffs are dependent on an adequate flow of contributions. The latter are primarily small individual donations of employees, large personal gifts, and contributions from corporations and foundations. Although there is no unilinear correlation between size of contribution and control of welfare, a general relationship exists. In Indianapolis, Seeley and others found that business firms and foundations provided from two-fifths to three-fifths of the funds for the Red Cross, Community Chest, and hospital drives, while employees and private individuals supplied the remainder.[34] Thus, the dependency on large impersonal donors is readily apparent. Of course, many individuals who make large gifts are known to the welfare administrator. Not infrequently, he has in his possession a confidential list of those donors whom he may call upon from time to time for supplementary financial or policy-making assistance. These people, known as the "Club 200" or a similar designation, constitute a roster of the top influentials in the community. Since many small donors are labor union members, union officials are frequently made cochairmen of the labor-industry section of the fund drive. In some industrial centers the unions may be responsible for collecting one-half of the total funds. Therefore, agencies and their professional staffs cannot afford to antagonize labor officials, who are increasingly demanding a voice in welfare policy-

[33] Seeley, *op. cit.;* Robert O. Schulze, "Economic Dominants in Community Power Structure," *American Sociological Review,* February, 1958; C. W. Mills and M. J. Ullmer, "Small Business and Civic Welfare," U.S. Senate, 79th Congress, 2nd Session, Document 135, GPO, 1946.

[34] Seeley, *op. cit.,* p. 205

making and administration. A labor participation committee is usually found in the Chest organization of large cities. Made up of representatives of management, unions, and the public, this committee is a source of both power and potential conflict within the organization.

Budget control

The central point of control in the private welfare agency structure is the budget committee of the Community Chest. The job of this committee is to determine the budgets of the individual agencies and the total budget of the annual Chest drives. If partisan or other interests are to be served, they must get the committee to approve of larger expenditures. In order to understand the pressures on the committee, it is necessary to describe briefly the interlocking structures of social welfare as they impinge on the budget committee.

The Community Chest and the Community Services Council have separate boards of directors, but they work together on the fund campaign and budget committees.[35] The same people can and often do sit on both boards. There is, in addition, a joint central committee of seventeen members to coordinate the work of the Chest and the Council. These are the only paid persons on the staffs. The Chest board contains thirty-seven members; one-half of them are elected for three-year overlapping terms at the victory dinner which concludes the annual campaign. All contributors may mail in their ballots or cast them at the victory dinners. The overwhelming and consistent result of these elections is to give at least one-half of the vacancies to the local business community. The other half of the vacancies are one-year terms and go to six appointed representatives from organized labor, so that the latter is assured some voice. Three are named by the Council, and the others represent the surrounding townships. The board itself can name one member "to assure representation."

The budget committee of 152 members includes the boards of directors of the Chest and Council. It also contains representatives from the agencies, who must be approved by the Chest

[35] This is the case in one metropolitan community. Variations exist in other cities.

board, representatives from organizations in "all walks of life," and staff members of the Chest. Thus, all segments of the welfare complex focus on this committee. The budget committee meets three times a year. In the spring, the individual agencies report on their expenditures and budget conditions. In midsummer, the agencies present their budget requests to the committee, which divides into six panels, each panel reviewing four agencies. Requests are carefully considered in terms of the agencies' load requirements, forecasts of needs, past performance, and related considerations. Finally, the panel and committee set budgets for the following year. The total of all the approved budgets comprises the goal of the Chest campaign held in the autumn. In December, after the campaign, the actual fund allocation is made.

Obviously, the crucial meetings are before the panels, which contain thirty members. If the panel is "balanced" in its representation and if the system works as designed, all agencies should receive budgets which represent the community norms. Typically, businessmen who do not have pet agencies try to keep budgets down, while welfare workers, union members, and others may respond to the "needs" of particular agencies. The economy-need dilemma must be resolved, and it usually follows the pattern of the previous year.

Some observers believe that, in many communities, the complex structure of budget fixing is a façade and that the actual budget decisions are made by the executive secretaries of the Chest and Council. One ex-secretary reported that he would call in his staff and they would hold buzz sessions, in which the work of each agency was evaluated according to professional standards, as were the pressures being exerted by influential people and groups for particular agencies. The staff would then decide on the budget for each agency. Key people on each panel were then given "background information" needed to make decisions. Together with staff people, they "helped the panel" to arrive at decisions previously made in secret.

Needless to say, this procedure does not automatically reduce conflict among parties. It may merely shift the arena of issue resolution to behind the scenes. The chief problems of the panels are to respond to the agencies' definitions of a "fair share" of the Chest funds, or to get a new agency into the Council. Labor and business sometimes take opposing views on the importance of rehabilitation of old people, the proportion of the budget to be given to recreational agencies during periods of economic recession, the size of the drive, how much religious welfare groups should receive, and related matters.

The power to make policy decisions within the financial limits set rests allegedly in the hands of the lay boards of the individual agencies, the Chest, and the Council. Usually the boards and the professional administrator get along. As Wilensky and LeBeaux indicate, lay boards are not concerned with mundane administration but with "big decisions," such as housing, preservation of private medical vested interests, and so on.[36] Typically, board members attend less than half of the meetings and remain relatively uninformed on the agency's operations. The administrator therefore has to give them background information; i.e., he tells them how to vote. In the process the administrator may obtain control and actually make the big decisions. After discovery, he may be fired, and the cycle of neglect, power shift, and crisis may be repeated.

Generally, policy conflicts within the board are minimal because the main battles on financial resources and partisan board representation have been settled earlier. Unions can increase their influence only by increasing the flow of funds in desired directions or increasing their representation on boards. A stable pattern seems to have emerged today. The unions have a representative on all important boards, but he is usually relatively inexperienced and must follow the lead of business representatives. Unless labor works out a distinctive welfare philosophy and program, the present system will endure.

Religion

Business and religion

The influence of the church on industry and labor is of increasing interest to the sociologist. The role played by this institution

[36] Harold L. Wilensky and Charles N. LeBeaux, *Industrial Society and Social Welfare*, Russell Sage, 1958; Irvin Fowler, "Local Industrial Structures, Economic Power and Community Welfare," *Social Problems*, Summer, 1958.

in economic affairs is important because it is the only one that relates itself to powers above those of mortal men. Positions taken by clergymen are difficult to ignore because they presumably speak the word of God. Moreover, they are supposed to provide men with a code of conduct which will guide them in everyday affairs.

Historically, churchmen have generally ignored local economic problems or have dealt with them on an abstract theological level. As the Lynds observed, "The gap between religion's verbalizing and Middletown life has become so wide that the entire institution of religion has tended to be put on the defensive. . . . It is timid in jeopardizing its foothold in the culture by espousing unpopular causes."[37] In the past churchmen have sanctioned if not underwritten prevailing business sentiments—hard work, the rights of property, duty, individualism, loyalty, and the inevitability of suffering. Moreover, many churches have large business investments which they want to have protected. Notwithstanding the variety of sophistication among religious appeals, most churches have not criticized specifically and directly vested groups, some of which they eventually depend on for survival. The result has been a general support of the status quo.

This conservative position is rather strange in the face of religious heterogeneity. Liston Pope has shown that the churches are more or less stratified according to the socioeconomic status of their members.[38] The Episcopal, Congregational, and Presbyterian denominations, for example, appeal most to business, professional, and white-collar groups, while the Catholic Church has support from middle- and lower-status groups, and the Baptists, Jehovah's Witnesses, and similar fundamental denominations appeal more to lower-status groups. One might expect churches having congregations from lower socioeconomic status to support working-class organizations and movements. Two major factors have inhibited this development. First, fundamentalistic and ritualistic churches feel that salvation is more important than

[37] R. S. Lynd and H. M. Lynd, *Middletown in Transition,* Harcourt, Brace, 1937, p. 311.

[38] Liston Pope, "Religion in the Class Structure," *Annals,* March, 1948, pp. 84–91.

economic and political affairs. Second, large segments of lower economic categories, perhaps majorities, have remained un-churched. They have neither influenced nor been influenced by formal religious groups.

After World War I the situation changed slowly. Since 1930 a small vocal minority of religious leaders have urged churches to play a more direct and vigorous role in local affairs. Supporters of the Social Gospel movement during the depression insisted that the church could not ignore the demoralizing effects of poverty and industrial strife.[39] They urged churches to take an active interest in labor-management relations. The Presbyterian Fellowship for Social Action, the Methodist Federation for Social Service, and the Unitarian Fellowship for Social Justice are just a few of the religious associations studying critical local social problems.

Clergymen began to study social problems and labor-management problems in their seminary training. Students preparing for the ministry began to practice in the city slums. Some obtained fellowships to learn the problems of organized labor. The Catholic Church developed a vocal prolabor wing to work with labor unions and problems of the workingman. It established institutes of industrial relations in universities and even an Association of Catholic Trade Unionists. The latter is a lay body of active unionists who are dedicated to insuring adherence to Christian values in established trade unions. These exploratory efforts remained feeble as long as labor was feeble. With the legal recognition of labor unions, their increasing strength, and their social acceptability, the liaison between churches and unions has become stronger. In this sense the church has been clearly an *adaptive* institution, asserting itself as far as the wider society permitted it to do so. Labor itself established agencies to encourage contact and cooperation with religious bodies.

At the same time businessmen became more interested in the relevance of religion to their daily activities. Six general areas may be singled out as areas of business concern with the church and religion. The first is an extension of the traditional position

[39] See Milton Yinger, *Religion, Society and the Individual,* Macmillan, 1951, p. 275.

of helping the church economically. Today, businessmen do more than give churches financial support. Either as official board members or as unofficial economic consultants they are asked to give economic advice and direction. Churches have become so large and complex—in building operations, personnel, and sponsored activities—that they need business management beyond that which amateurs can provide. As business managers of church activities businessmen may be expected to have more than ordinary policy influence. Second, businessmen have felt the need for individual religious direction in their daily business lives. They have inaugurated regular breakfast meetings with clergymen to discuss ethical dimensions of business decisions, telephone prayer service to gain inspiration when needed, and related innovations. Third, on the group level they have fostered meetings, symposia, and panels to arrive at codes of ethical business practices and fair labor-management relations. Fourth, business associations have seen religion as buttressing the American way of life. Consequently they have launched publicity campaigns to get people to "attend the church of your choice regularly." Fifth, in the attempt to regularize business-religion contacts they have inaugurated clergy-business days so that each can learn more about the problems faced by the other. Last, there has been some attempt to bring the clergy in on the bargaining process itself. Mr. George Romney asked clergymen to sit in on pre-bargaining meetings with business to help them wrestle with ethical problems of bargaining. Businessmen have also accepted, if not urged, the clergy's help in mediating bitter disputes with the unions, especially during prolonged strikes.

Labor property and the church

The position which organized labor has taken toward the church and the clergy in the community has changed with the change in the status of the unions. Between the two wars, when unions were weak, the church was attacked as being part of the business community, as being insensitive to the needs of the workingman, and as abandoning its doctrine of help to the poor and downtrodden. Jerome Davis documented the social control of the church by businessmen, the failure of nerve on the part of the clergy to speak out on the abuses they saw in the community, and the support the clergy gave business during periods of industrial strife.[40]

As labor grew stronger it increased its ties with churches and the clergy and became less critical of them. Today there is an elaborate network of contacts from central to community labor organizations. The AFL–CIO has a Religious Relations Department which encourages local unions to develop contacts with churches in their communities. These contacts vary in scope and purpose. In many communities unions have initiated labor-clergy days, wherein both groups meet, have dinner, and discuss local problems. The unions try to get local clergymen to publicly commit themselves to programs of interest to labor: for example, a fair-employment-practices law, adequate housing for low-income workers, adequate facilities for migrant workers, an increase in recreational budgets, support for a Community Chest project such as an old age drop-in center, and so on. Support for such projects may incur the hostility of other local interests.

Local unionists are also concerned with the support of their national union programs involving the clergy. In 1957 the UAW established a public review board of independent citizens to which the members might appeal their grievances against the union and which could censure an unfair union's conduct.[41] The board also polices the ethical practices codes of the AFL–CIO and its internationals. This board is made up of clergymen of the three dominant faiths, two judges, two professors, and a lawyer.

The good will and support of the clergy are also sought during prolonged strikes and other crises. In such instances the clergy are urged to pressure management to have compassion for the economic suffering of workers, not as union members but as human beings who have familial obligations. The unions have also sought and obtained the support of the clergy to speak against so-called "right to work" laws.

Only rarely does the church enter a labor dispute directly. However, the Catholic Church especially has been concerned

[40] Jerome Davis, *Capitalism and Its Culture,* Farrar and Rinehart, 1941, chap. 19.
[41] See Jack Stieber, *U.A.W. Review Board: Examination and Evaluation,* Michigan State University, School of Labor and Industrial Relations, Reprint 35, 1960.

about communist influence in unions or communist-dominated unions in the United States. For example, the Church entered the certification dispute between the CIO and the allegedly communist-dominated Mine and Mill union in El Paso. It was unsuccessful here despite the fact that most workers were nominal Catholics. The clergy have sometimes sought union aid to pass laws involving the closing of stores on Sunday, betting, and related matters. Generally speaking, however, the church has maintained its position of being at best an ethical monitor of local economic affairs.

The Family

While the impact of industrialism on family structure is well known, we do not have systematic knowledge of how specific family forms are related to specific industrial situations in the contemporary city. Although the family has adapted in general to economic change, under certain circumstances industry must accommodate to particular family patterns. For example, highly seasonal enterprises need many workers during some seasons and very few in other periods. Marginal industries need a labor supply during lush years but will release workers in normal or depressed periods. Some industries need large numbers of women and children as workers, whereas others demand only men.

Such industries can operate successfully only where family systems are characterized by great flexibility—where families can readily shift from one form of subsistence to another. Arensberg maintains that the location of the plastic industry in New England towns rested on the presence of such a family system. The immigrant family in New England showed remarkable solidarity despite the fact that some of its members were farmers and others were factory workers. When factory employment was high, sons, daughters, and wives became wage workers; when employment became scarce, the family shifted greater energy to farming.[42] Needless to say, such marginal-seasonal industries cannot survive where wives will not accept factory work or where children leave home early and set up separate households.

The rubber industry of Akron, which needed a flexible labor supply, was aided by the mobility of "hillbilly" families from

[42] Arensberg, *op. cit.*, p. 5.

West Virginia which moved in and out, depending on the needs of the industry. Zimmerman has documented the helplessness of people in stranded industrial towns whose family structure did not permit them to shift from urban to rural employment. Neither would these families supply labor to marginal industries when stable employment was available.[43]

In other ways the family affects industrial and union operations because all workers have family roles which must be articulated to their economic roles. There is a daily pattern of relationships revolving around the home. Every day people rise from a night's sleep to prepare themselves for work or leisure. Out of 168 hours in a week the average worker will spend 56 in sleep, 40 in work, and 72 in miscellaneous activities—including the journey to and from work, eating, making love, participating in organizational activities, watching television, and so on. Increasing purchasing power and the decline in work hours permit the worker to spend more time in leisure and recreation. However, there still is room for conflict as he seeks to accommodate to changes in the work plant, union, home, and community. Disruptions of family life and routines may result from changes in shift, layoff, and strike, while disruptions in industry may result from marital conflict, illness, pressures for higher income, and so on.

Values of business, labor, and the family

Even without disruptive changes, problems in articulating family and industry arise out of the different values which the family, business, and union hold. Divergent value systems call for different ends and a struggle to achieve them.

Family life itself is of concern to business because a well-adjusted family member tends to be regular and punctual in attendance, his conduct is marked by sobriety and morality on the job, and he usually is better satisfied in his job and becomes a good teamworker. Moreover, a company wants people who are good representatives of the firm in the community. They give the company a good name, which is a prime asset in attracting the better worker. For these reasons business generally seeks to im-

---

[43] Carle C. Zimmerman and Merle E. Frampton, *Family and Society,* Van Nostrand, 1935, chap. 17, "Subsistence Adjustment in a Stranded Industrial Town."

prove working conditions, but it is, of course, limited at any particular time by the productivity of the plant and competitive conditions in the market.

Labor organizations approve a family system which produces loyal union members and leaders for the union. They know that this support is most assured when there is a continuity from father to son. The father is the family historian who can describe the early struggles of labor and what it was like "before the union came." Family approval and support of the union member is very important in strengthening his various roles as a member who attends union meetings regularly, who assumes leadership and responsibility for union business, and who is willing, when necessary, to sacrifice by contributing money and support to a strike or other union activities.

None of these roles may be easy. When the union local is a considerable distance from the plant, a man tired from a day of manual work may find it hard to attend union meetings. Assuming leadership is even more burdensome. A strike is still more demanding and involves the family more intimately. It may require a material sacrifice, a risk of status, and a risk of bodily injury. In a long strike it is not uncommon for a man to lose his car, his furniture, and even his home. The union needs full family support during a crisis of this nature; women's auxiliaries are being given increasing attention by the AFL–CIO. Last, a labor organization also has a reputation at stake in the community. It wants members to support the union's community endeavors and maintain the status of union representatives in local organizations.

Most families seek (1) stable employment for the chief breadwinner. To marry a "good man" often means to marry a man who is a steady income producer. (2) Pay is important, too, because this establishes the level of living for all family members. Working hours of the breadwinners generally set the schedule of such family activities as eating, sleeping, and leisure. (3) Good working hours are sought so a schedule of family activities can be worked out to the satisfaction of all members. Families like to have (4) the working members doing work and belonging to firms (and unions) which they feel are approved by their relatives and friends.

Pattern of control

There are seven areas of management-union struggle for control which affect the economic well-being and the style of life of the family. They are (1) hiring and firing, (2) economic payment, (3) work scheduling, (4) seniority rights, (5) leisure, (6) health and welfare, and (7) education. Traditionally, management has had sole control over hiring, firing, wages, and work scheduling. It still has dominant control today, but the unions are attempting to limit this power or to circumscribe its execution. Labor's primary successes have been in obtaining seniority rights, limiting firing, and increasing wages. It is also pressuring business to supply more health and welfare services, better retirement plans, recreational facilities, and so on. At the same time, unions are themselves promoting health, welfare, and recreational services. No longer do they permit management the monopoly of educating the workers' families on the contribution which business is making for their welfare. Many union publications are dedicated to capturing the interest and loyalty not only of the worker but of his family.

Customary relationships

The home is a social center, a dormitory, a restaurant, a school, a church, a playground, a laundry, a repair shop, and many other things. In some ways it resembles a work plant; it has services to perform, a group of workers with specific tasks, an authority structure, and so on. Perhaps its most important function is to socialize children with the values necessary for effective performance as worker and as citizen. Chapter 13 examines the social origins of traditional work values which are inculcated in the child, and some of the changes in these values. In general, industry relies upon the home training and attitudes appropriate to a productive worker, while the union expects training appropriate to producing a loyal union member.

The home and industry interpenetrate also on an ecological level. Not much research has been done on the relevance of plant location to the social life of workers.[44] Obviously industries differ

[44] Leo F. Schnore, "The Separation of Home and Work and the Spatial Pattern," *Social Forces*, March, 1952, pp. 271–282.

in their occupational composition. Some draw primarily from one occupational level, in which case all workers may live near the plant. Inevitably the industry will have an impact on the physical as well as social character of the neighborhood. When industries employ workers who represent the labor force more adequately, they draw them from all major residential areas of the city.

The pattern of industrial ecology has consequences for the job travel path and social mixing.[45] When the job travel path of the worker is short, he spends more time at home and sees the plant as an extension of his neighborhood relations. When it is long, plant, neighborhood, and family relations tend to become segmented. For the manual worker the location of the union hall adds another dimension to locational activities. The movement of either home, industry, or union hall throws a large network of human relations out of equilibrium. The plant which draws workers from all over the city must expose many to a job travel path that runs through different types of neighborhoods because occupational groups tend to be residentially segregated. The consequences of a diversified as opposed to a uniform exposure of the journey to work have not been explored. Those who travel a diversified path have a more complete view of city life, and this view may affect their behavior and sentiments.

While it is clear that the residential location of the worker is fixed by his occupation and income, other consequences are not well known. The occupation of the breadwinner sets the social class position of all his family members. Other things follow: the type and amount of organizational activities, the amount and type of education, the style of consumption, the amount and type of illness, the degree of family stability, the political outlook, and related items flow from occupational status. Obviously a significant change in occupation will result in a chain of changes in the aforementioned items. For this reason, personnel departments are increasingly viewing the employee with a wider lens. They try to make the job more attractive to the worker, they institute family nights to inform other family members about the company, and they offer counseling and other company services to the entire

[45] See K. Liepman, *Journey to Work*, Oxford University Press, 1947.

family and not just the employee. Unions have made parallel moves.

Conflict relations

Several points of issue may arise as the family responds to changes initiated by management or the union. The most important of these is the subordination of family life to management decisions involving layoff, transfer of personnel to other departments or cities, overtime work, shift changes, and bankruptcy. Such activities may force the wife to go to work, sever kinship and social ties, change family routines, lower the standard of living, and bring related disruptions. American society does not provide many cushions to ease the shocks which industrial changes force on the family. The closing down of a plant not only affects the lives of its former employees; it may affect others who depend indirectly on the survival of the industry. The multiplier effect cuts both ways—industry creates added jobs when it grows, and it subtracts extra jobs when it shrinks.

The effect of the removal of an industry is rehearsed during a strike. Not only are the family plane of living reduced, the wife and children forced to find extra income, the social relationship with others altered, the status of the family altered, but other business and other organizations are affected. The grocer waits for his money, church collections go down, taxes are unpaid, and relatives are asked to lend money, ad infinitum.

Some types of conflict do not have such serious consequences, but they are a source of family tension nonetheless. Included here are contest for worker loyalty by management and the union. Occasionally both sponsor athletic contests, leisure programs, insurance schemes, holiday celebrations, and related programs. If ideological differences and industrial relations conflicts are present, they spill over into these other activities.

CONCLUSIONS

The interinstitutional relations between industry and its community institutions are now drawn. Obviously, industry interacts with more than one institution at a time. Sometimes industry can dominate the flow of community decisions, and sometimes it is dominated. In general, the most other institutions can do is to blunt or modify industrial demands and influences. In an industrial society the economic sector initiates changes and the remaining sectors adapt.

SELECTED BIBLIOGRAPHY

Calkins, Fay, *The CIO and the Democratic Party*, University of Chicago Press, 1952.

Chamberlain, Neil W., *Social Responsibility and Strikes*, Harper, 1953.

Form, William H., and Delbert C. Miller, *Industry, Labor, and Community*, Harper, 1960.

Landis, Paul H., *Three Iron Mining Communities*, Edwards, 1938.

Lynd, Robert S., and Helen M. Lynd, *Middletown in Transition*, Harcourt, Brace, 1937.

Pope, Liston, *Millhands and Preachers*, Yale, 1942.

Seeley, John R., *et al.*, *Community Chest, A Case Study in Philanthropy*, University of Toronto Press, 1957.

Warner, W. L., and J. O. Low, *The Social System of the Modern Factory*, Yale, 1941.

Wilensky, Harold L., and Charles N. LeBeaux, *Industrial Society and Social Welfare*, Russell Sage, 1958.

CHAPTER 19

The Future
of
Industrial Society

THE IMPACT OF INDUSTRY UPON SOCIETY

Western civilization has developed around a machine technology, a market economy, and an industrial society. The industrial mode of production has given rise to an economic organization which influences all parts of society. Industrialism, as a configuration of technology, economy, and business values, emerges as one of the most widely spread culture systems in human history. No modern social institution has escaped its influence; the school, the church, the home, and recreational institutions are built upon the values arising from it. Industrial society refers to more than machines and markets; it refers to men and institutions locked in the network of relationships dominated by economic mores and folkways.[1]

Industrial society is dynamic. Hardly is a pattern set before another emerges. Our purpose here is to identify the kinds of changes which are inherent in the present industrial system. Clearly, we are entering another era marked by changes as dramatic and as massive as the industrial revolution itself. To understand what may be ahead, we shall examine briefly some of the basic changes occurring in the economy, changes in the type, amount, and meaning of work, and changes in other institutions as they accommodate to economic changes. Finally, we shall look at institutional relations in American society in the past and

[1] Thorstein Veblen has demonstrated this thesis brilliantly in *The Theory of Business Enterprise,* Scribner, 1927, and *The Theory of the Leisure Class,* Macmillan, 1924.

present, and speculate on what can appear in the year 2000.

It is now apparent that the era of manufacturing—the era of factory domination over the economy and society—is ended. It is ended not only in the sense that the majority of urban workers are not engaged in manufacturing but in the sense that the ethos of manufacturing is disappearing. This is what is meant by the second industrial revolution. No longer is the objective of production to break down jobs into smaller individual components with special machines designed to do special tasks. On the contrary, the important characteristic of automation is integration of manufacturing functions by developing multipurpose machines run by electronic brains.

The consequences of integrating jobs by automatic means are manifold. Not only is production increased many times, releasing workers to engage in nonmanufacturing tasks, but the type of workers needed is changed. Untrained workers are industrial scrap who become underemployed or fitfully employed. Even workers with highly developed skills may become displaced or find their skills not functional to the new industrial order. An anachronism develops as one center of manufacturing becomes depressed while another suffers from a lack of highly trained workers.

New institutions must obviously be created to avoid the persistent dislocations experienced during the Great Depression. Unskilled and semiskilled workers must go back to school, and even skilled workers, technicians, professionals, and managers find their training is soon outmoded by the new demands of a complex technology. They too must reenter educational institutions to learn of the new contributions made by the rapidly changing natural, physical, and social sciences. Communities must undertake, with or without governmental assistance, orderly economic development of their industries, their manpower, and their local institutions. Let us examine specific changes occurring at work.

FUNDAMENTAL CHANGES IN WORK

Work is changing its meaning in fundamental ways for people living in a consumption-oriented economy. One man-hour of work today produces what it took three man-hours to produce sixty years ago. Robert Lynd pointed out that industrialization gives each nation three options: It may increase the standard of living by increased production; it may have more babies; or it may have more leisure.[2] Most Western societies have taken their increments in all three ways, although they have chosen less leisure and fewer babies because of the dominant desire for a higher standard of living. A considerable increase in leisure is now possible. The time has come when work need no longer be a necessity for the whole of adult life. Life expectancy has been extended so that a rather substantial period of time is assured after retirement. Life expectancy at age sixty-five for all persons is estimated at fourteen years.[3] Earlier retirement is a social trend almost certain to be accentuated by the increasing application of automation. The work week is destined to decline. Figure 19.1 shows the normal extrapolation of the curve of declining hours of work per week. The four- and three-day work week is a distinct possibility within this century. Longer vacations are being written into labor-management contracts. Kenneth Galbraith has said that automation gives us three choices: to shorten the work week, to cut the labor force (longer school preparation or earlier retirement), or to work less on the job.[4]

The advance of science has for many years been undermining the structure and value of both property and work. Property is no longer the primary social divider in society. Many forces are blurring the line between owner, manager, and worker. The corporation has stimulated absentee ownership. Increasing public investment has brought the same result. Stock purchase plans, pension trust funds, and mutual investment schedules have put property ownership on a very broad base. High employee income has raised more and more workers into middle income brackets. The shift in occupational needs has put white-collar employees in the majority. High progressive income taxes have depressed managerial incomes. One result of all these changes is that everyone has a boss and everyone, even the board of directors, has to account to others. This has made employees out of almost all who

[2] Robert S. Lynd, *Knowledge for What?* Princeton, 1939, p. 89.

[3] *Current Population Reports: Population Estimates,* U.S. Bureau of the Census, Series P-25, No. 93, April 26, 1954.

[4] John Kenneth Galbraith, *The Affluent Society,* Houghton Mifflin, 1958.

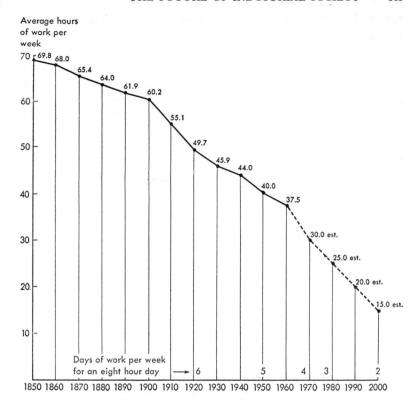

Average hours of work per week

FIG. 19.1. Average Hours of Work per Week from 1850 to 1960 with Estimated Projections from 1960 to 2000. (After J. Frederic Dewhurst, *America's Needs and Resources,* Twentieth Century Fund, 1955, p. 40; United States Bureau of the Census, *Population Reports,* Labor Force Series P-50, Nos. 59, 67, 72, 85, and 89.

work.[5] Modern society has been called variously the Employee Society, the Affluent Society, and the Leisure Society. In this society W. H. Whyte sees a new Organization Man being formed in the constraints of large-scale organization. This man is said to be losing independence and individuality and is becoming increasingly group centered. David Riesman agrees that this is the social character of the new employee and says he is becoming an "other-directed" person whose behavior tends to adapt itself

[5] William H. Whyte, Jr., *The Organization Man,* Simon and Schuster, 1956.

superficially to each of the many groups in which the person moves.[6]

Changes in the meaning of work, the amount of work done, the type of occupational structure, variety of leisure activities—these must inevitably force changes in organizations built to respond to earlier social realities. Thus, the managers of industry must interest themselves in broad social and political policies which were earlier the concern largely of government officials. Labor unions must accommodate to the new occupational and industrial changes. Not only must they organize clerical, service, technical, and professional employees, but they need to address themselves to the question of whether economic collective bargaining will be their primary function in the future. Similar confrontations face leaders of governmental, educational, welfare, and other institutions.

Changes in institutional functions and loyalties do not occur smoothly and evenly throughout the society. Inevitably, old and new institutional and value systems create vast contradictions which are not easily resolved. Five such contradictions current in American society will be described.

FIVE CONTRADICTIONS
IN MODERN LIFE
INTRODUCED BY INDUSTRIALISM

Cultural contradictions in modern society, as truly as pressure groups, splinter the social structure and divide men's minds. They make it increasingly difficult for the citizen to make up his mind what he should think, what he should want, and what he should do.

1. Work vs. Leisure as a Central Purpose of Life

We believe that man's purpose in life is to demonstrate his worth through work. Man should save and build for himself, his family, and his future.

But we are told that we should live well and accept the promise of ever greater leisure and prosperity. Work occupies fewer hours and years in the life of everyone. What work there is grows less like work every year. The virtues of hard work and profit are rooted in scarcity. They have no relevance in an affluent society.

[6] David Riesman, *et al., The Lonely Crowd,* Yale, 1950.

The pains of transition from a production-oriented to a consumption-oriented economy are injecting some unusual value conflicts in work societies. Eric Larabee suggests that most employees are being paid today in both "affluent money" and "scarcity money." The affluent money is given in recognition of the worker's role as a consumer. The worker is told that he has a duty to buy and consume, for unless he does the great mass production machinery will slow down and unemployment will increase. He is not supposed to ask whether he needs a good or can make do with what he has. He is to live up his income. He should buy much (and often), using any one of some thirty or more credit cards and other installment credit opportunities available to him. Executives are also issued ample expense accounts and told to use them. ("It all comes off of income tax.") Workers are told not to worry about scrap. ("Everything is on a cost-plus basis.") Saving before buying is regarded as passé (indeed, declassé). Frugality has become synonymous with boorishness and miserliness.

Still, "scarcity money" is also legal tender, and its value becomes accentuated in hard times. This is the dollar which is earned when the employer calls for added effort and sacrifice. It is the dollar paid when everyone is asked to help cut costs. Savings are encouraged, especially of United States savings bonds, to help in the fight against inflation. Old guilt feelings are aroused by charges that workers are not doing a fair day's work for a fair day's pay. Everyone is urged to cut down on installment buying when prices rise, and when the response is poor the government orders all down payments increased. No one is expected to be against automation for that is necessary for a higher standard of living and leisure. Yet it is said that more leisure will corrupt the national character.

It has been suggested that we must discover and apply the principle of *equivalance of work and play*.[7] In our economy of abundance, many of the values of play could be achieved through work and of work through play. Play has the unique value of activity free from outer compulsion—something only rarely found in work. The promise of work is to combine freedom from com-

---

[7] Gerard Piel, "Consumers of Abundance," Center for the Study of Democratic Institutions, Santa Barbara, Calif., 1961, p. 9; Sebastian de Grazia, *Of Time, Work, and Leisure*, Twentieth Century Fund, 1962, pp. 381–437.

pulsion with the satisfactions formerly found only in play. If a richer life can also be created in this new freedom, work may take on entirely new meanings and the work organization may become as much a social organization as an economic one.

These superimposed scarcity and abundance patterns introduce ambiguity in work behavior and social behavior generally. Within and without work organizations irregular behavior results, much to the perplexity of employers and employees alike. Neither are quite certain to which pattern they owe allegiance. These massive cultural tides affect motivation, leadership, management practices, collective bargaining, and the formal organization of work itself.

To the contradiction of scarcity and abundance in the same culture must be added other value conflicts that social change has created.

2. Democratic Ideals vs. Concentration of Economic Power

We believe in the democratic ideal of political equality—that each man is the equal of any other man in human right and human dignity. We believe that there should be equality between a man's political power and his economic power.

But we are faced with a concentration of economic power and we believe that private individuals can run a business better than the government can. We believe, furthermore, that concentration of economic power in the hands of government men would be more dangerous to a free society than leaving such power in the hands of businessmen.

The American republic was founded on the edge of a vast wilderness. Land was free to those who had the courage and initiative to go forth and claim it. Ownership and management of a farm was bought by hard work and persistence. This easy entry into ownership encouraged widespread ownership of property and satisfied the economic ideal. We still believe that every worker should have the chance to go into business for himself. The image of a society of small manufacturers, merchants, free farmers, and artisans continues to keep alive the Jeffersonian ideal. In the America of 1820–1830, sixteen out of every twenty Americans owned their independent means of making a livelihood in the form of small property, mostly free farms. Most Americans could say, "What I work I own and what I own I work." One hundred years later an almost exactly opposite condition prevailed. Seventeen out of every twenty Americans were propertyless, and dependent for a livelihood upon the property owned by a small minority. This transference of ownership constitutes a revolutionary change in the entire fabric of society. Most men no longer "make a living"; they "earn a living." The corporation has replaced and is replacing the small businessman all along the business, agricultural, and industrial front. In this shift from a base of widespread ownership to a base of corporate business the relation between political power and econimic power is drastically changed. Concentration of economic power has always been regarded as a threat to democratic institutions. We know that large-scale enterprise is here to stay. The private operation of such enterprise has been a mixed blessing. Higher levels of living have been accompanied by distribution problems causing widespread suffering. To transfer ownership to the government would not be a restoration of the Jeffersonian ideal. It would mean that government men would control the same corporate property which businessmen had controlled before. Our tradition has been one in which a free people have feared their government more than they have feared their businessmen. We have believed that businessmen were held in check by competition and the democratic processes, but that government men were eager to seize power and able to establish a coercion that would quickly destroy a free society. As the industrial and corporate growth has moved on, the question of business ownership vs. government ownership or regulation has become the major political question of the century. Americans are caught in a dilemma. Democratic ideals are threatened by the concentration of economic power, but the harnessing of such power by government threatens to strangle them. Moreover, we are badly prepared as a body of citizens to think our way clearly through this contradiction. Our psychology is provincial and our society is cosmopolitan. And here lies still another cause of cultural confusion.

3. Provincial Folkways vs. Cosmopolitan Society

We believe that the only way any man gets ahead is through hard work; we believe that competition determines price and quality and that big business has the same problems as little business except that big business has more and bigger problems; we believe that anyone can understand what business and the nation are faced with by focusing attention upon the problems in the local community.

But society is now a vast world-wide network of interdependent forces which largely determines what local business conditions are and what local problems are. The initial generation of a change in conditions usually originates in a center or centers far removed from the local community. The forces generated tend to be different in kind and in magnitude from those arising in the local community.

Walter Lippmann in his analysis of public opinion differentiated between the "seen" world and the "unseen" world in which each person lives.[8] The "seen" world refers to the narrow and immediate pathway over which the daily course of personal life is run. The mental horizon tends to be limited to this "seen" world. Yet it is in the "unseen" world that the vast majority of influences over living are generated. The "unseen" world refers, of course, to the world-wide network of events which come into the local community and act silently upon it.

Men forget that for thousands of generations living has been going on in small communities where the personal relations of face-to-face contact have existed. Individual acts were judged in the arena of public opinion, and the important values of life were determined in the concrete terms of the local event. In such a world, provincial thoughtways and folkways were largely insulated against outside forces.

Then, with the coming of industrialism, modern communication and transportation began to spread a multitude of new ideas and new ways of living. The strands of economic life began to draw all local communities into one interdependent economy. F. Stuart Chapin has found a cause for the many economic contradictions which have made it so difficult for the average person to understand the nature of the economic process. He says that throughout the whole of our economic life "there runs the principle of individual decisions and acts, each made independently of all the rest and arrived at on the basis of provincial habit systems trying to operate in a world network of communication."[9]

Some of these provincial habit systems in popular economic thinking may be identified. They gain significance as contrasted

[8] Walter Lippmann, *Public Opinion,* Harcourt, Brace, 1922.
[9] F. Stuart Chapin, *Contemporary American Institutions*, Harper, 1935, p. 5.

with the cosmopolitan thoughtways demanded by the modern economic structure. Let us take, for example, the conception of work. Stuart Chase likes to describe how his grandfather plowed the rocky New England fields for long hours each day. *Hard work* meant manual labor mixed with sweat. In contrast, modern life with its many white-collar tasks demands much sedentary or semi-sedentary activity. *Hard work* may come to mean concentration plus monotony. Grandfather snorts that the younger generaton has forgotten how to work; the modern urban dweller replies that "it's so peaceful in the country" and that the old-timers never knew what nervous strain meant.

In his view of *business* it is not surprising that the average man carries a psychology of small business. The stores and services on Main Street represent *business* to the bulk of Middletown's citizens. When the local merchant complains of *competition,* he speaks mostly of the prices and quality of products which the chain stores and other local stores are placing on the local market. In contrast, large corporate industry has practically discarded price competition and competes on quality, styling, or advertising of the product. Property in the nineteenth century meant land and buildings—i.e., real estate. Today the richest man in town may have his entire property locked up in a small box labeled "Stocks and Bonds." *Law* once meant that the local mores against crime had been written down, a far cry from the proliferation of economic and social regulations which municipal, county, state, national, and international agencies have pressed into legal form.

It is this contradiction between the thoughtways of provincial living and the imperatives of cosmopolitan society that causes much of the problem we call social change. Each small locality has been opened up to the drive and play of great forces generated in the large urban centers of society. These forces spread outward and act upon the local community. Provincial habit systems respond, and a myriad of individual acts and decisions take place. Almost immediately, their reverberations move back upon the urban centers. Chapin has likened this process to an alternating current which moves back and forth linking large and small communities of the nation into an endless chain.[10] In this process, contradictions between provincial and cosmopolitan habit systems

[10] *Ibid.,* p. 7.

are compounded and their consequences spread over the entire society. The irrationalities of a society which matches efforts to increase production with efforts to restrict production can be understood as a clash of habits as well as a clash of economic structures.

4. Cooperation vs. Isolation

We are drawn ever closer together. Modern technology, the threat of war, the promise of abundance all force men to recognize that this is "one world." *We believe* that men must cooperate or perish.

But society is divided into large interest groups, into classes, into regions, into racial and ethnic divisions. In the city, particularly, the person becomes dwarfed by large organizations and the impersonality of social contact. He tends to become isolated in the midst of frenzied attempts to get him to join and participate in organizations.

Industrialism has set loose twin forces of opposition.[11] These are cooperation and isolation. Human relations have become both organized and atomized, and this contradiction has strengthened and weakened social structure simultaneously. We can observe that society is in an unceasing process of organization and disorganization.

Modern economic organization requires a very high degree of cooperative activity. The need for cooperative activity becomes particularly clear if our industrial society is compared with a peasant society. In the peasant society almost everybody works at the production of the same things. The subsistence economy of such a society consists of numerous and almost identical units all engaged on the same tasks. Moreover, the contacts are very slight as the individual peasant plows, sows, and reaps his harvest without any outside cooperation. In contrast, each producer in an industrial society turns out a different product, but he does it, not alone, but in close association with many others. The producers of automobiles, steel, glass, cement, and cloth must somehow get along with one another in order to insure that the right proportions of goods are produced. As John Strachey has said, "Men cannot live by tin cans alone." Thousands of different goods and services are needed to keep our economy in operation. Without a proportionate flow of goods, the whole economy would

[11] Cf. Paul Meadows, "Human Relations in Industrial Civilization," *Technology Review*, April, 1947, pp. 341–348.

come to a halt or be destroyed. Legend has it that "for want of a nail, a shoe was lost; for want of a shoe, a horse was lost; for want of a horse, a king was lost; for want of a king, a kingdom was lost."

Much of the tremendous quantity of cooperative relationship in our society is bought as men are tied by salaries and wages into large-scale organizations. In the place of group in-feeling based on custom and sentiment all too often there is only the impersonality of a contractual relationship mediated by a specialized skill or money income.

We have shown how the city with its large population masses is a product of the industrial economy. The transformation of community life into urban patterns has brought a fragmentation which isolates the individual while at the same time placing him in a fast-moving stream of human contacts. The mobility of the urban dweller tends to rip out his community ties (if he lives within a community long enough to develop them). The size of the city makes it difficult for him to see and know people who wish to lead the political and social agencies. He is more likely to read about them or hear about them if he has developed an interest in them. Social stratification builds status walls that make access to some persons all but impossible. Entire strata of people live their lives beyond the daily horizon of other dwellers. In such a society the individual comes to realize that he counts for little unless he is organized within a group. When he is organized in a group he may find that group ends distort individual purpose and morality. In this contradiction, cooperation and isolation are both real and far apart.

5. Sympathy vs. Aggressiveness

Modern man is lonely. He seeks companionship, affection, love. *He says* that his religion calls all men his brothers.

But everywhere men compete aggressively and sometimes ruthlessly with one another for money, status, mates, and power. The pattern of competition is encouraged in the school, in work organizations, in the church, and in the home. The child is taught as was the father that the future belongs to those who have drive and who are willing to push themselves.

The loneliness of modern man is brought about by a convergence of many different forces. Science has shattered much of the comforting religious belief he once held. J. H. Randall has written:

It swept man out of his proud position as the central figure and end of the universe, and made him a tiny speck on a third-rate planet revolving about a tenth-rate sun drifting in an endless cosmic ocean. . . . Purposes gave way to mathematics, human will and foresight to immutable and inflexible mechanical order. Throughout the whole vast windy stretches of infinity, in stone and plant and animal, nowhere a being who felt and suffered, loved and feared and hoped, who thought and knew. Man was alone, quite alone, in a vast and complex cosmic machine. Gone were the angelic hosts, gone the devils and their pranks, gone the daily miracles of supernatural intervention, gone even was man's imploring cry of prayer.[12]

Modern man has had to rediscover what he could believe in to give purpose to living. The threats of war and depression beating down daily on his personal security have driven him to find some "ways to relax nerves" and capture an elusive "peace of mind." The loosely knit ties of kinship and community life tend to sterilize emotional life and focus it upon the small family. A man or woman who fails to establish himself within a family is left with poor emotional substitutes in the large city. Casual, exploitative relationships of dalliance replace the interwoven ties of marriage. Spectator amustments provide vicarious enjoyments which stimulate but seldom feed and satisfy man's basic biological and social needs. The poet Wystan Hugh Auden in his book *The Age of Anxiety* expresses the anxious frustrations of modern life through a shipping clerk named Malin:

> But the new barbarian is no uncouth
> Desert-dweller; he does not emerge
> From fir forests: factories bred him;
> Corporate companies, college towns
> Mothered his mind, and many journals
> Backed his beliefs. He was born here. The
> Bravura of revolvers in vogue now
> And the cult of death are quite at home
> Inside the city.[13]

Men in the midst of modern life have sought more purposeful

[12] John H. Randall, *The Making of the Modern Mind*, Houghton Mifflin, 1926, pp. 226–227.

[13] Reprinted by permission of Random House, Inc. Copyright 1947 by W. H. Auden.

ways to live with one another. Generous impulse is still alive in the conduct of human affairs, but opposed against the desire for sympathetic identification with persons and groups are respectable patterns of aggressiveness and some times ruthlessness. Veblen has pointed out that wherever the institution of private property is found, the economic process is marked by a struggle between men for the possession of goods. Such a struggle carries far beyond the subsistence level of living, for the motive that lies at the root of ownership is emulation. The possession of wealth confers honor and brings the holder satisfaction or dissatisfaction as he compares himself with others.[14] Veblen said that pecuniary emulation through invidious comparison becomes the basis of esteem. Thus, property or wealth in some amount becomes necessary in order to have any reputable standing in the community. There is no limit to the property desired, for the process of invidious comparison is dynamic. A person desires as much wealth as those have with whom he classes himself. When this is gained he desires more. "The invidious comparison can never become so favorable to the individual making it that he would not gladly rate himself still higher relatively to his competitors in the struggle for pecuniary reputability."[15]

In our society material accumulation is roughly equated with honor. The pattern of aggressive behavior is approved for career climbing. It is "one against all" and "may the best man win." If this aggressive pattern must ride down human sentiment in order to gain material advantage, then sentiment must go. "Business is business," after all. So it follows that even as sympathy and the desire for human response are ground down in business contacts, the need for a more satisfying emotional life remains.

As the five major contradictions are surveyed, it becomes apparent that social and psychological problems have been stirred up in the train of influences which have accompanied the industrial way of life. Industry is intimately tied to the most subtle nuances of daily living. We are drawn to reflect upon the future. Will industry continue to dominate institutional life? Will cultural

---

[14] This notion is thoroughly analyzed in Chapter 11, "Income, Class, and Social Structure."

[15] Veblen, *The Theory of the Leisure Class,* Macmillan, 1924, pp. 31–32.

patterns assume more consistent and less contradictory forms? We do not know the answers to these questions but we can follow some trend lines and make some speculations.

THE FUTURE RELATIONSHIP OF INDUSTRY AND SOCIETY

Sociologists are wary of long-range forecasting. The forces which move through modern society are fluid, and manifold possibilities of social change present themselves. However, there are ways to discern the future which surpass idle speculation. When the social scientist wishes to discover probable social developments in the proximate future, he begins by selecting those prime factors which seem to be most instrumental in causing current changes in the social segment he is examining. He isolates and measures the trend of such factors over a period of time in order that the rate of change may be carefully determined. He must then make an estimate of what such a conjunction of the prime factors will bring in the way of new social changes.

Among the prime factors acting on American society are (1) the advances of technology applied to manufacturing, transportation, and communication; (2) rapid population expansion; (3) equalization of regional patterns of industrialization; (4) the increasing urbanization of society; (5) the increase and extension of formal education; (6) the ideological conflict of state socialism, democratic socialism, and democratic capitalism.

Our purpose is not to develop an appraisal of these forces but to direct attention to them as we make a brief examination of the changes in American institutions.

Power Structuring of American Institutions in 1900

American institutions may be viewed in relation to their power structuring. Such a view reveals their relatively uneven influence over American life. If we turn to the beginning of the twentieth century we find an institutional power structure in which business institutions dominate. Figure 19.2 is a heuristic diagram which purports to suggest the relative ranking of institutions in terms of their power and influence on American life. In this figure the prominent position of business dwarfs the remaining

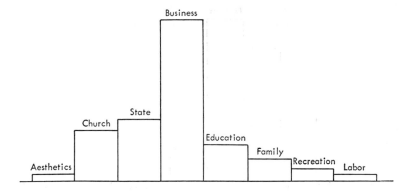

FIG. 19.2. A Suggested Ranking of American Institutions by Power and Influence in 1900.

institutions which lie about its base. In 1900 private business was relatively free from political regulation. Businessmen made the important decisions affecting the economy and the society. They became the established social leaders and set the values in most American communities. The school, state, church, recreational and aesthetic institutions were largely controlled by boards of businessmen or lived by their philanthropy. The family was drawn ever more tightly into the orbit of the business institutions as economic self-sufficiency was replaced with an economic dependence upon those who owned factories, offices, and stores.

Institutional Structure in 1960–1965

Between 1960 and 1965 a change in the relation of American institutions could be observed. Figure 19.3 shows the prominent rise of the political state into a new level of power. The state so increased its power during the sixty-five year interval after 1900 that it now threatens to rival the long-established dominance of business institutions. Government men (who are very often former businessmen) began to make the more important decisions regarding the overall direction of the economy. Federal government appropriations calling for an expenditure of $80 billion give government men a large organization with great national powers and responsibilities. The military organization, by reason of the world power struggle, has grown to a huge peacetime

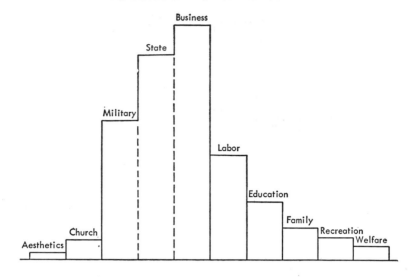

FIG. 19.3. The Power Structuring of American Institutions in 1960–1965.

establishment. The threat of an atomic war gives the military organization an enhanced authority and prestige. Labor organizations have grown rapidly in power. Their active participation in supporting political candidates and parties has revealed a growing capacity to influence elections and governmental policy.

Education has risen slightly in power as the state increasingly recruits its staff from among teachers and college graduates. Business also is seeking more scientific and technical personnel from the universities. Such institutions as the family, church, and aesthetic institutions seem to have remained at their previous level or to have suffered slight declines. Recreational institutions, led by the movie, radio, and television industries, have come to occupy a larger place of influence, and welfare institutions under state support are obviously growing. The overall picture reveals the power dominance of business and political institutions. The largest question confronting institutional life is the kind of relationship which should be or will be established between the political state and business institutions. Russia with state socialism, Spain with state capitalism, England with democratic socialism, and America with democratic capitalism are the major political-economic amalgams that are present in the world today. The United States with its democratic capitalism is confronted in the world scene with a powerful Russian state which represents state socialism. The external power struggle between these great states is affecting the organization of society even as internal forces act upon the development of political and economic institutions in each nation. The commitments of the emerging nations in Asia and Africa are also at stake.

Many writers have regarded the society of 1960–1970 as in a state of transition. The search for a stable society must go on, and great forces only partly understood and still less controlled will grind away until a new stability is achieved. This particular transition stage in human history is different from all others. For the first time technological advance has accomplished the miracle of abundance. Men no longer need to starve. The machine on the farm and in the factory can produce a tremendous quantity of food and living commodities so that Americans and, in time, all peoples can live in comfort and security. A Utopia of abundance has a material base that will pass an inventory in terms of machines, men, and materials. Against the promise of this material Utopia looms the threat of war and internal strife. Both are real and both are possible. H. G. Wells said many years ago that the world is caught in a race between education and catastrophe.

Two Contrasting Structures for 2000 A.D.

In 2000 A.D. two possible forms of institutional structuring may be envisioned. Figures 19.4 and 19.5 attempt to show these possibilities. The structuring of these two hypothetical societies is a study in contrast. Figure 19.4 represents a society in which economic and military security is threatened. As a result, the military, political, and economic institutions have lost their separate identity and are now merged in one all-powerful state. All other institutions defer in complete subservience to the state. Labor organizations have been abolished by state edict.

Figure 19.5 pictures a completely different society—one in which the economic struggle has almost ceased and armed warfare has been abolished. Men have turned to a struggle for status and prestige in educational, civic, and welfare institutions. Leisure-

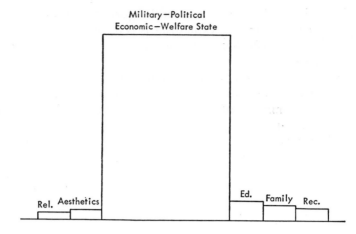

FIG. 19.4. A Possible Power Structuring of American Institutions in 2000 A.D.— Option A.

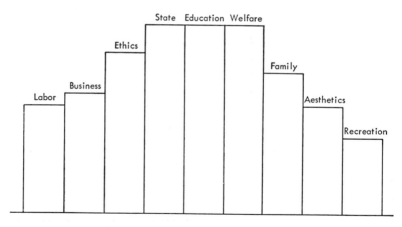

FIG. 19.5. A Possible Power Structuring of American Institutions in 2000 A.D.— Option B.

time activity predominates, and status must be won in the institutions which enrich human living. The family and aesthetic institutions have secured a position of much greater importance, while economic institutions have declined in importance. Automatic machinery has cut labor demands in the manufacture and distribution of goods so drastically that very little time or skill is required to service the economic needs of society. Labor organizations have changed their primary function as economic bargaining institutions and have become mainly educational and recreational agencies. The political state has assumed a function of interrelating the ethical obligations of the person to society in conjunction with his educational and recreational growth. The governmental, educational, and recreational institutions share this large responsibility.

It must be admitted that human imagination in the 1960s is strained by these two contrasts in the structuring of institutions. The revolutionary changes suggested by Fig. 19.5 may seem beyond belief. The writers hasten to disclaim any great concern with their success in forecasting hypothetical societies. What is most important is the fact of social change in institutional structuring. To grasp the significance of a changing relationship between institutions is to open the mind to new interpretations of current life and to pose new possibilities in the future. The relationship between industry and society has changed, is changing, and will continue to change. The student of industrial sociology never forgets that all of his observations and interpretations of industry take place within a changing society. If he shuts his eyes to the larger context, he loses perspective as researcher, teacher, or citizen. The interrelationship between industry and society is not the ending but the beginning of industrial sociology.

SELECTED BIBLIOGRAPHY

Dahl, Robert A., Peter Drucker, and Delbert C. Miller, in W. D'Antonio and H. Ehrlich (eds.), *Power and Democracy in America,* University of Notre Dame Press, 1961.

Form, William H., and Delbert C. Miller, *Industry, Labor and Community,* Harper, 1960.

Galbraith, John Kenneth, *The Affluent Society,* Houghton Mifflin, 1958.

Grazia, Sebastian de, *Of Time, Work, and Leisure,* Twentieth Century Fund, 1962.

Kaplan, Max, *Leisure in America: A Social Inquiry,* Wiley, 1960.

Mannheim, Karl, *Man and Society in an Age of Reconstruction,* Kegan Paul, Trench, Trubner and Company, 1942.

Nisbet, Robert A., *Community and Power*, Oxford University Press, 1962.

Polanyi, Karl, *The Great Transformation*, Holt, 1944.

Riesman, David, *et al.*, *The Lonely Crowd*, Yale, 1950.

Schermerhorn, Richard A., *Society and Power*, Random House, 1961.

Veblen, Thorstein, *The Theory of the Leisure Class*, Macmillan, 1924.

Whyte, William H., Jr., *The Organization Man*, Simon and Schuster, 1956.

APPENDIXES

APPENDIX **A**

Outline for the Organizational Analysis and Reconstruction of Social Structure in the Work Organization

FIELD OBSERVATION: DIRECT OBSERVATION OF A SELECTED WORK PLANT (TO ACCOMPANY SELECTED CHAPTERS)

Select a work plant to observe as you study this text. In making your choice it will be important to consider whether you will have convenient access to the work plant and the workers you wish to observe. It would be helpful to choose a work plant which is easily available from your home or your campus. A work plant is simply a place where people work, whether such work commands pay or not. Therefore, your choice may be a store, a warehouse, a factory, a fraternity, a home, a dormitory, a church, a construction site, a restaurant, a school, or any other place where work is performed. It may be well to select a work plant in which you are now working or one in which you have worked, but it is acceptable to choose one in which you have never had any previous contacts as long as you can find a vantage point for observation. The workers should not know they are being observed, for such realization may affect their behavior. Either select a small work plant (under 100 workers) or narrow the range of your observations to no more than 100 workers. A useful approximation would be to consider no more of a work area than can be accurately seen within a full circle of your vantage point or points. A vantage point from which your observations may seem casual and unobtrusive is greatly to be desired.

When you have selected a work plant, describe (1) the type of work plant and (2) your personal experience and present relationship to the plant.

PART I: ANALYSIS

Describe the social structure of the work plant by analysis of the type parts shown below in the left-hand column. Watch for tension and adjustment points that may be present. The most frequently occurring tensions are indicated in the right-hand column. Record the nature of such tensions as may be associated with the appropriate structural part. Avoid any discussion of suggested changes since it is important to restrict examination to analysis of the entire structure before planning a program of organizational reconstruction. Part II will provide a suggested outline for reconstruction after analysis is completed. This is especially developed for graduate student training.

Elements of Work Plant Structure	*Common Tension and Adjustment Points*
I. Industry-Community Relationships (Chapter 4)	
1. Brief history of community	1.1 Discrepancies between community standards and plant standards
a. "Reputation" of the community	
2. Brief history of company with the community	2.1 Hostility of community directed toward the work plant
a. "Reputation" of the company	a. Hostility directed against the workers or groups of workers (charges of "undesirables," "striking at expense of community prosperity," etc.)
b. "Reputation" of the union	b. Hostility directed against the owners or managers (charges of "labor haters," "monopolists," discriminate against workers, dump factory wastes in rivers, etc.)
3. Social contacts of workers in the community	3.1 Hostility of work plant directed against the community
	a. Hostility of workers toward the community (charges of "unfriendly," discriminates in housing, credit, schooling of children, etc.)

Elements of Work Plant Structure	*Common Tension and Adjustment Points*
	b. Hostility of owners or managers toward community (charges of "lack of understanding," "unsympathetic," discrimination in taxation, access to facilities, and harmful governmental regulations, etc.)
4. Status of workers in community	4.1 Discrepancies between role and status achieved in plant as compared with the community (*Ex.:* Low status in work plant in contrast to higher status in community organizations may induce dissatisfaction)

II. Culture Content of Work Plant

  1. Material culture
    Invoice culture traits[a]
    Identify culture complexes and core traits[b]

2. Physical and social atmosphere[c]	2.1 Dissatisfaction with physical conditions and services, particularly differential facilities for different groups of workers and supervisors
3. Jargon and argot[d]	3.1 Bewilderment and frustration from failure to understand or to communicate
4. Folkways, mores, rules[e]	4.1 Discrepancies between mores and rules
5. Social myths about work	5.1 Disillusionment about equity in pay advancements, etc.
6. Public values and ideals[f]	6.1 Discrepancies between ideals and actions
7. Style of life induced[g]	7.1 Conflict in different styles of life: supervisory vs. workers, conflict in work plants between workers who hold puritan values of hard work and those who hold "group norms" of work and think bosses are no better than they are

Elements of Work Plant Structure	Common Tension and Adjustment Points

III. Grouping and Contacts

1. Make a rough floor plan of the work plant showing arrangement of workers at their *work stations;* show *work* routes

   1.1 Inadequate definition of work routes and work stations

   1.2 Differences in the estimated time to arrive at the work station and to leave the work station, in reporting to work, in rest periods, in other allowed time, in cleaning up and leaving work

2. Describe size and number of separate work **groups**

   2.1 Discrepancies between the work group desired by the worker and the actual work group in which he has been placed
     a. Physical and social isolation from other workers
     b. Conflicting values or attitudes produced by heterogeneous work groups

   2.2 Differences in the estimated number of individuals deemed necessary for the project as judged by workers, or as judged by superiors

3. Identify the kind of interaction
Primary[h]
Quasi-primary[i]
Secondary[j]

   3.1 Improper social placement, i.e., placement on job either demanding social skills not possessed by the worker or not calling for the social skill for which the worker desires expression

   3.2 Differences in the judgments of supervisors and of workers as to effect of social interaction on worker efficiency

4. Describe the workers: list age, sex, and background; indicate where they live and some of the characteristics of their *paths to and from work*

   4.1 Strains produced in getting to and from work because of poor roads, traffic congestion, length of time in travel, etc.

5. If customer contacts, describe

   5.1 Tension over ritual and etiquette of superordinate-subordinate relationship induced in seller-buyer contacts

Elements of Work Plant Structure	Common Tension and Adjustment Points

IV. The Organization of Management and Work (Chapter 5)

1. Describe the chain of command showing line and staff
   a. Examine "span of control," i.e., number of subordinate executives or supervisors reporting to a single individual

1.1 Inadequate definition of the chain of command causing confusion in the authority and responsibility relationship

1.2 Span of control is too great to give direction needed; span of control is too short to develop self-reliance and initiative in the supervision leadership

2. Describe the segmentation of the structure
   Time
   Space
   Divisional, subdivisional, and departmental
   Breaks between supervisory levels
   Breaks between line and staff

2.1 Certain segments claim that they are not being used or that their functions have been usurped by other segments

2.2 Blockage of action by superior officials or coordinate officials in other segments

2.3 Blockage of action caused by difficult job conditions, lack of parts, inadequate tools, complicated procedures, etc.

2.4 Differences in the estimates of quantity or quality of work that was expected by supervisors and/or workers on successive shifts

2.5 Tensions over values, hours of work of different work groups such as office, shop, etc.

V. Communication (Chapter 5)

1. Communication structure down the line
   a. Order-issuing procedures and contacts of supervisors and employees
      Use of bulletin boards
      Use of public-address system
      Use of newspaper
      Use of conferences
   b. Effects and defects of

1.1 Lack of adequate channels for communication down the line

1.2 Failure of structure to deliver information to supervisors and employees
   a. Inadequate definition of responsibility for delivering communication

1.3 Dissatisfaction with slowness or manner of communication from the top or any other position in the chain of command

Elements of Work Plant Structure	*Common Tension and Adjustment Points*
communication	1.4 Misinterpretation of the meaning of communication induces tension
Down the line	
Blockage	
Distortion	
2. Communication structure up the line	2.1 Lack of adequate channels for communication up the line
a. Procedures	2.2 Social distance maintained by supervisors who block access
Access to supervisors	
Grievance procedure	2.3 Dissatisfaction with grievance procedure
Suggestion box	
Personnel department	2.4 Ideological resistances to criticisms and reports
Channel	
b. Effects and defects of communication	
Up the line	
Filtered information	
Short-circuiting	
Deliberate blockage	
3. Coordinate status or peer communication; describe:	3.1 Fragmentary or distorted horizontal communication causes misinterpretation
Work flow contacts	
Rest period contacts	
Lunch group contacts	
Transportation contacts	
Dormitory contacts	
4. Oblique communication, describe:	4.1 Inability to achieve confidence and rapport
Contacts with staff and service	4.2 Secret sharing induces jealousy and charges of favoritism
Operation of grapevine (overt medium)	
Secret Sharing (covert medium)	

VI. Work Flow (Chapter 5)

1. Diagram the main stream of work flow	1.1 Defects in the technological arrangement of the work plant, restricting movement of workers, inducing strained body posture, etc.
2. Diagram the tributaries of work flow	2.1 Lack of supplies, equipment, transportation, storage, etc.
	2.2 Limited labor force available to do varying jobs which must be done; tensions arising in

Elements of Work Plant Structure	*Common Tension and Adjustment Points*
	the ensuing competition among departments for more workers
3. Mark the points where action originates and chart the line or lines of pressure	3.1 Excessive demands placed on any part of the main flow of work
	3.2 Pressure applied by various tributaries on each other to get the various jobs done in order that any particular tributary may go ahead
4. Describe the manner in which pressure is transferred or absorbed	4.1 Pressure transferred from person to person by delegating jobs to others, trying to speed up the work pace of others, projection of blame to others, etc.
	4.2 Pressure absorbed by working faster, crying, joking, laughing, rationalizing, etc.
5. Describe human relations problems and tensions induced	5.1 Frictions between work positions under greatest pressure
	5.2 Fears due to dangers of inadequate safety devices, toxic substances, dangerous materials, etc.
	5.3 Conflicting definitions of performance standards a. Sense of unjust work load
	5.4 Inadequate job performance inducing greater burdens on work associates
VII. Work Positions and Work Roles of Managers (Chapter 6)	
1. List the work positions and analyze the work roles which are observed a. Patterns of routine behavior b. Exceptional behavior	1.1 Differential judgments of desirable standards in managerial performance a. Differences in formulating or executing policies b. Discrepancies alleged between managerial ability and authority
	1.2 Conflicts over qualifications desired in the selection, assign-

Elements of Work Plant Structure	*Common Tension and Adjustment Points*
	ment, and promotion of supervisory leaders, specialists, and workers
	1.3 Ambiguity and inconsistency in managerial roles exhibited by one or more managers
2. Examine the manner in which workers with authority exercise their power or influence over their work associates	2.1 Authoritarian, arbitrary, and/or unreasonable exercise of authority
3. Indicate any real or potential cleavages and conflicts	3.1 Promotional and status conflict between managers and supervisors
a. In the line	3.2 Staff influence contested or ignored by line officers
b. In the staff	
c. Between line and staff	
4. Describe the informal organization of managers	4.1 Exclusion of some managers from informal group because of personality, social background, or other considerations
a. Talk patterns	
Who talks	
Amount of talk	
b. Sociometric patterns	4.2 Demands that managers affiliate with social clubs or otherwise maintain a standard of living beyond economic means
Cliques	
Lunch associations	
Recreation associations	
Club and lodge associations	4.3 The conflict or ostracism of one or more of the wives of the supervisors by the other wives
Clique of managers' wives	

VIII. Behavior of Work Groups (Chapter 7)

1. Kinds of technical, sociotechnical, and social behavior in which the worker engages	1.1 Discrepancy between managerial-supervisory goals based on cost and efficiency and worker goals and satisfactions
	a. Refusal of workers on the job to conform to technical, sociotechnical, and social behavior expectations of the managers
2. Talk patterns	2.1 Discrepancy between group standards and individual patterns
Who talks	
Amount of talk	

Elements of Work Plant Structure	*Common Tension and Adjustment Points*
Content of talk Interest subjects Avoidance subjects Patterns of ideas and sentiments	a. Worker talks too much, especially ego-centered talk b. Worker introduces topics not the concern of the group c. Workers refuses to participate in lunch group, adhere to group standards of work, group standards of behavior toward supervisors, etc. d. Group refuses participation to worker
3. Sociometric patterns Cliques Car pools Lunch associations Recreation associations Interpersonal relations and feelings Reciprocal behavior patterns such as job trading, helping one another, etc.	3.1 Clique antagonisms 3.2 Work position isolates worker shunting informal group participation
4. Initiation, ceremonies, and rituals a. Naming b. Hazing	4.1 Changes in rituals resisted
5. Work play such as gambling, horseplay, practical joking, singing, joking relationships, etc.	5.1 Suppression of these activities resisted
6. Conflicts such as fighting, "politicking," and sabotage	6.1 Individual rivalries contesting for popularity, prestige, or power in the work group
7. Informal group code a. Social controls to enforce the code	7.1 Violations of the informal group code; "rate buster," "chiseler," "stealer"
8. Race and ethnic relations	
9. Cooperative and conflict behavior evidenced between formal and informal organization	9.1 Conceptions of: a. Fair day's work b. Just wage c. Safe or desirable tools, equipment, etc.

IX. Union Local (Chapters 8 and 9)

Elements of Work Plant Structure	*Common Tension and Adjustment Points*

1. Chain of command
  a. Line
  b. Staff
	1.1 Inadequate definition of responsibility and authority
	  a. Overlapping of responsibilities and authority
	  b. Inadequate delegation of responsibility

2. Segmentation of the structure	2.1 Certain segments claim they are not being used or that their functions have been usurped by other segments

3. Work positions and work roles
  a. Patterns of routine behavior
  b. Exceptional behavior
	3.1 Differential judgments of desirable standards in leader performance
	  a. Differences in formulating or executing policies
	  b. Discrepancies alleged between managerial ability and authority

4. Exercise of power and influence	4.1 Authoritarian or autocratic control and behavior of union leaders, steward over union members
	  a. Worker-steward resentment
	  b. Union leader-steward resentment

5. Cleavage and conflicts	5.1 Group cleavages
	  a. Between line and staff
	  b. Between full-time leaders and part-time leaders and workers
	  c. Between college-trained leaders and rank-and-file leaders
	  d. Between those with ideological and those with pragmatic conceptions of trade unions
	  e. Between local leaders and international representatives

6. Relations with union members	6.1 Members display hostile or halfhearted attitudes toward the union and participation in it

Elements of Work Plant Structure	*Common Tension and Adjustment Points*
7. Relations with management	7.1 Union is not recognized by management as socially desirable or necessary

X. Power and Industrial Conflict (Chapter 10)

1. The political structure of management	1.1 Cleavages with formal supervisory structure
2. The political structure of labor	2.1 Union factionalism
3. Major conflicts between union and management	3.1 Major differences in interest, worker rights, management prerogatives, etc.
	3.2 Conflicting values and role expectations of union leaders and managers in contact with one another. a. In grievance bargaining b. In collective bargaining
	3.3 Lack of communication channels between management and the union
4. Tactics and weapons each structure uses	4.1 Conflicts over strategy and tactics such as work stoppage, use of press and radio, etc.
5. Types of union-management cooperation	
6. The play of external forces Public opinion Government Community pressure Newspapers	6.1 Bias and partiality of external groups

XI. Income, Class and Social Structure (Chapter 11)

1. The salary and wage structure	1.1 Discrepancies between worker's expected standard of living and his economic return
	1.2 A wage incentive system which sets worker against worker in violation of group standards
2. Material evidence of differences in class position	

Elements of Work Plant Structure	*Common Tension and Adjustment Points*

3. Prevailing mores regarding pay	3.1 Lack of relationship between skill and responsibility on job required and wage return
	  a. Within wage structure of plant
	  b. In comparisons of wage structures of other plants
	3.2 Violation of merit in administration of wage system

4. Problems of gross or felt inequality
  a. By individual workers
  b. By groups of workers
	4.1 Discrepancies between individual's subjective evaluation of his effort and the recognition received in pay
	4.2 Differentials in living facilities provided
	4.3 Misunderstanding or lack of information of wage system

5. Way pressure is exterted to relieve gross or felt inequalities
  a. By individual workers
  b. By groups of workers
	5.1 Threats, fawning, organizing, striking, slowdown, sabotage, stealing

XII. Status and Prestige in Work Organization (Chapter 12)
  1. Status hierarchy
	1.1 Discrepancies between formal status and informal status
	  a. Seniority vs. ability
	  b. Position or pay vs. ability or function

2. Status symbols	2.1 Discrepancy between status position and the status symbols awarded or assumed by the worker
3. Rights and limitations surrounding various status positions	3.1 Inadequate or ambiguous definition of status rights and limitations resulting in tension over use of particular tools, rooms, seating arrangements, etc.
4. Status problems and grievances	4.1 Violations between status position and the status rights and privileges assumed 4.2 The exploitation by particular individuals of their status,

Elements of Work Plant Structure	*Common Tension and Adjustment Points*
	such as burdening lower-status persons with disagreeable jobs, preferential treatment of those with higher status
5. Relationships and adjustments demanded by the status structure	

XIII. Bonds of Organization (Chapter 13)
   1. Job specifications
   2. Communication system
   3. Status system
   4. Reward and punishment system
   5. Organizational charter

PART II: RECONSTRUCTION

Carefully review the tension and adjustment points that have been identified in the analysis.

Prepare a suggested program of organizational reconstruction designed to eliminate or reduce tension to a minimum. Review adjustments required in each of the twelve elements of the work plant structure.

The procedure suggested is illustrated.

1. Describe tension or adjustment point
   a. The nature and context in which tension is located
   b. The origin and history of the tension
   c. Pragmatic or ideological resistance to adjustment (may be impossible to proceed farther)
2. Suggested change for remedy
   a. Nature of change
   b. Resources required
      Personnel
      Material
      Time
3. Social repercussions expected from change
   a. Probable
   b. Possible
4. Suggested procedure for introduction and monitoring of change
   a. Introduction of change
   b. Monitoring of change

5. Suggested research design to assess effects of proposed change
   a. Design
   b. Instruments of measurement

[a] A culture trait is the smallest functional unit of culture. It may be a unit of material culture such as a hammer, micrometer, uniform, blueprint, or stamping machine. It may be a unit of nonmaterial culture such as a folkway, *mos,* rule, or law.

[b] A culture complex is a combination of two or more culture traits that functions as a unit. Culture traits tend to function around core or central traits. A college classroom often revolves around the professor's lecture notes. Every other material trait tends to assume meaning as it clusters about this core trait. Therefore, the "lecture complex" includes blackboard, chalk, notebooks, pencils, chairs, desks, walls, windows, etc.

[c] The physical atmosphere refers to such qualities as noise, odor, color, heat, volume and intensity of activity. The social atmosphere refers to the culture traits and the patterns of activity which influence the worker's pace, his work outlook, his sentiments, and culturally prompted observable acts.

[d] Jargon refers to the technical or secret vocabulary of a science, art, trade, profession, or other special group. The aim is to identify the terms which constitute the language of the trade as you hear them and to record them with meanings if you can ascertain them. Argot refers to the conventionalized slang of the group. College students speak of taking "soc," "econ," and "P.E." courses. They make appointments with professors or go to their committee meetings during a "float." Every work group tends to adopt a slang. To be able to speak it identifies the worker as assimilated, i.e., one who understands the trade and one who may be quickly accepted. Failure to understand or to speak the jargon or the argot stamps the worker either as a "greenhorn" or as one who is inexperienced and not practical.

[e] Folkways are simply habits of action common to the members of the group. They have some degree of traditional sanction for their persistence. The greeting "good morning," the handshake, the eating of three meals a day, taking rest periods are familiar examples. Mores are folkways which come to be defined by the group as the "right" ways. Group members are more conscious of the mores and they are always in some degree emotional. The violation or threatened violation of the mores causes concern or resentment. The mores need not be written down. For example, college students may have different definitions of cheating but there is common agreement that the professor should not have "favorites" and give better grades to "apple polishers." That is not "right." Rules refer to explicitly prescribed standards of conduct, usually written, and often imposed upon a group without prior agreement of the members.

[f] The public values and ideals of the work plant refer to the rationalized purposes of the activity which are presented to outsiders to justify morally the service of the work plant. Examples of such public or service ideals are "Safe milk for your baby," "Boeing builds the finest bombers," "We build poise and confidence in your personality."

[g] Style of life refers to the particular mode of living which the work position tends to establish for a worker. It may be useful to describe the salient features of the daily routine for a typical member of the work group, starting when the worker rises and tracing through a full twenty-four-hour cycle.

It is important to describe the major habits, the attitudes, bearing, dress, and manner of the worker. A thorough description when you can get the data will include the way the work role affects the lives of family members, and contacts in the neighborhood and community as well as other members of the work group.

[h] *Primary group interaction* is characterized by (1) face-to-face association, (2) small numbers, (3) unspecialized purpose, (4) comparative intimacy, and (5) relative permanence.

[i] *Quasi-primary group interaction* is characterized by (1) face-to-face association and (2) small numbers but it is limited in some degree by special purpose and (3) tends to be more formal and less intimate.

[j] *Secondary group interaction* is characterized by (1) formal association, (2) large numbers, (3) specialized purpose, and (4) communication by such devices as telephone, letters, bulletins, etc.

Some Guidelines for
the Research Study of
Human Relations in Industry

FIVE TYPES OF RESEARCH STUDY

Five major types of research study are conducted by industrial sociologists as they seek to describe the social adjustments of workers or the
functioning of work groups. The industrial researcher, depending upon
the design of his project, may wish to

1. Interview employees on the street, in their homes, at the union hall,
   Chamber of Commerce building, or in some other community
   organization outside the work plant.
2. Analyze industrial records such as application cards, merit rating
   forms, absence and turnover files, counselor reports, production and
   spoilage records, etc.
3. Observe work behavior as it normally proceeds in a work group or
   department within a work plant.
4. Observe and interview employees in a work group or department
   within a work plant.
5. Arrange work behavior within the work plant so that it takes place
   under controlled conditions; introduce given social factors and
   ascertain the effect upon some dependent variable such as production or morale.

The five different types of research study have been arranged in an
order which indicates increasing difficulty of access to the kind of data
ordinarily desired by the industrial sociologist. Some of the most needed
studies fall within the first two types, which may not require any access
to the work plant itself. Studies based on interviews or records usually
inquire into some aspect of employee adjustment. Studies of 3, 4, and
5, which are based on observation and interviewing of workers, usually

make work group behavior the focus of attention. Some projects call for a combining of some or all of these five types.

The initiation of research on work group behavior within a work plant poses the problem of establishing a research relationship with industry. A discussion of this relationship is necessary because of the special difficulties involved.

ESTABLISHING A RESEARCH RELATIONSHIP WITH INDUSTRY

Burleigh Gardner and William F. Whyte have aptly said, "Factories are social organizations with walls around them." There is no access without permission of management and the union. Furthermore, both parties may be reluctant to permit an outsider to come in and view their problems. There is a widespread suspicion that a researcher may stir up discontent in the worker's mind while probing for causes and effects of industrial and union policies.

Research in industry requires, therefore, fulfillment of certain conditions:

(1) The researcher must be able to get into industry.

(2) He must be able to establish and maintain relationships within the organization to be studied.

(3) He must have tools for collecting the pertinent data without interfering with his relationships.

(4) For anything more than superficial studies, there must be a continuity of research relationships with a given organization.

(5) To permit such relationships to continue and to allow for the possibility of experimentation, management must understand the research and take an interest in its development.[1]

Gardner and Whyte emphasize that when an observer (especially if the observer is a student) seeks entry into industry, the way must be carefully paved for him. Management and union leaders must have confidence in the research sponsors. The building of confidence requires time. It cannot usually be accomplished by a persuasive talk but must grow out of a more informal sort of relationship maintained over a period of time.

When access and permission to initiate research have been granted, the researcher has a decision to make in designing his project. He must decide whether he shall make observations with or without introducing

[1] Burleigh Gardner and William F. Whyte, "Methods for the Study of Human Relations in Industry," *American Sociological Review*, October, 1946, p. 506. Errors that can be made easily by the industrial researcher are described by Robert K. Bain, "The Researcher's Role: A Case Study," *Human Organization*," Spring, 1950, pp. 23–28.

changes into the situation. It is much easier to get permission to make studies if changes in personnel and working conditions need not be made. But this condition limits the area of research. Facility to experiment opens new possibilities.

THE DEVELOPMENT OF RESEARCH

Gardner and Whyte describe the manner in which they have been working out research arrangements with industrial and business firms. Their program involves the following five steps:

1. We make an intensive study of the problem situation.

2. On the basis of that study, we map out a course of action for management, which, we think, will improve that situation.

3. We communicate these recommendations to management in a form such that they can be understood and acted upon. This must be done primarily through informal conversations with executives. Written memoranda may be submitted also, but they are distinctly supplemental to the direct person-to-person relationship.

4. Management takes action along the lines agreed upon.

5. We follow closely every step of management action and make an intensive study of the resulting developments. If events follow the course we have anticipated we are in a position to observe just how and why these results were obtained. If the results are substantially different, then we are in a position to study the factors that accounted for the discrepancies and gain knowledge out of our own failures.

It can be noted that the researchers make contact with a problem situation in the role of clinicians. After diagnosing the situation they work with management in such a way that management introduces the variables the researchers wish to study. When they have reached step 5 of their program an experimental design has been achieved and research is under way. This demand for the preparation of contact, the gaining of permission, and the designing of an experiment in a problem situation will not attract impatient researchers. Those who have believed that industry or a union could be treated like a laboratory which would gladly welcome the changes researchers wished to make will find themselves sadly disillusioned. Those who are willing to practice human relations can find alert managers and union leaders everywhere who are willing to assist capable researchers. To these administrators of experimental bent industrial sociology owes a growing debt. Together the administrator and researcher may be able to find basic knowledge about the formation and functioning of the work teams. Increasingly, both recognize that solutions to many problems of production and industrial organization await advances in the knowledge of group interaction.

The Institute of Social Research at the University of Michigan has been very successful in pursuing a research program that is aimed at basic hypothesis testing within highly diverse work organizations. The researchers adroitly combine basic theoretical interests with the practical concerns of the administrators in the research design.

Some excellent guidebooks now exist. These include R. N. Adams and J. J. Preiss (eds.), *Human Organization Research*, Dorsey, 1960, William F. Whyte, *Man and Organization*, Irwin, 1959, and D. C. Miller, *Handbook of Research Design and Social Measurement*, David McKay, in press.

Index of Names

[*References to footnotes are in italics.*]

Index of Subjects

Emory & Henry College   Kelly Library

3 1836 0000 8321 2